SEWING
The Complete Guide

Sewing machine on front cover courtesy of American Sewing, Tucson, Arizona.

TABLE OF CONTENTS

Published by HPBooks, a division of Price Stern Sloan, Inc.
360 North La Cienega Boulevard, Los Angeles, California 90048
ISBN: 0-89586-253-0
Library of Congress Catalog Card Number: 82-84457

Printed in U.S.A.

Hutchinson & Co. (Publishers) Ltd.

TABLE OF CONTENTS

Photography: Cover by Ray Manley Studios, Tucson, AZ

IMPORTANT SEWING TERMS

Before you begin, there are many things about sewing you need to know and understand. Knowing the following terms will help you select a fabric, choose a clothing style and be more familiar with methods and techniques before you sew. Read this section first, then refer to it for clarification as you go through the book.

Fashion Terms

A-Line—Dress or skirt resembling the outline of the letter *A*.
Accent—Color or design feature that draws attention to the finished garment.
Accessories—Items of apparel to complete an outfit, such as shoes, hats, scarves or belts.
All-Over Pattern—In fabric, a design without obvious direction, such as top or bottom.
Ascot—Broad neck scarf. Tied so one end extends beyond the other.
Asymmetric—Unbalanced. One side is different from the other in shape, color or design.
Avant-Garde—Ahead of the trend.
Bateau—Neckline following the curve of the collar bone.
Bell Sleeve—Full sleeve, flaring at the lower edge like a bell.
Bishop Sleeve—Full sleeve gathered by a band to fit closely at the wrist.
Blouson—Bloused effect created by gathering in fullness that is allowed to fall over a seam, such as a bodice over a skirt.
Bodice—The part of a garment above the waist.
Bolero—Close-fitting jacket that ends above the waist.
Border—To finish an edge with trim or self-fabric.
Boutique—Small, specialized store selling fashion garments and accessories.
Caftan—Long, flowing coatlike garment, often with bell sleeves.
Camisole—Close-fitting underbodice, sometimes attached to a skirt and worn with a jacket.
Cap Sleeve—Short sleeve that covers only the outside of the upper arm, tapering away to nothing on the lower edge of the armhole.
Cape—Bell-shape outer garment with no sleeves. It hangs from the shoulders and has a front opening.
Cardigan—Collarless sweater or jacket with front opening, often with pockets.
Chemise—Blouse cut like a man's shirt.
Chic—Original, stylish way of dressing.
Coat-Dress—Front-opening dress having the appearance of a coat.
Couture—Garment made by hand by a seamstress.
Couturier—Male fashion designer.
Couturière—Female fashion designer.
Cowl—Soft, draped neckline.
Cravat—Wide scarf tied with the ends tucked inside the front of the garment.
Crew—Round neckline that fits closely at midneck.
Culotte—Flared, pantlike garment, with the appearance of a skirt.
Decolléte—Bare neck and shoulders, with plunging neckline.
Dicky—Detachable shirt front.
Dirndl—Garment with a full, gathered skirt.
Dolman—Sleeve set in a deep armhole, such as a Japanese kimono.
Double-Breasted—Overlapped front opening with two rows of buttons or fastenings.
Edwardian—Styled after the fashions of the early 1900s, when Edward VII was King of England.
Empire Line—Styled after the fashions of the French empire period. Characterized by decolléte, a waistline close under the bust and a loose, straight skirt.
Ensemble or Outfit—Complete outfit. Usually describes a coat-and-dress combination.
Epaulet—Shoulder decoration of braid or cloth. Fastened by a button on the shoulder or head of the sleeve.
Epaulet Sleeve—Sleeve with a square-cut section extending to the neck in the form of a yoke.
Flap—Loose fabric section, attached to the garment along one edge.
Flare—Widening or spreading of fabric in a garment.
Fly—Lap of fabric used to conceal an opening.
Fully Fashioned—Shaping a flat-knit garment with stitches, unlike the shaping of circular knits by cutting and sewing seams.
Godet—Triangular piece of fabric inset in a garment to give fullness or decoration.
Gore—Tapered section of a garment that is wider at the bottom edge.
Halter—Band of fabric extending from one side of the bodice front, around the neck and back to the other side of the bodice front. Enables bodice to be backless.
Harem Pants—Pants with softly draped legs, gathered on a band at the ankle.
Haute Couture—"High fashion." The product of a fashion house or group of designers.
Jabot—Ruffle down the front of a bodice.
Jerkin—Short, sleeveless pullover or jacket.
Jewel—Simple, round neckline set at the base of the neck.
Jumper—Simple garment with a low-cut bodice.
Jumpsuit—Bodice and pants joined in one garment.
Keyhole—Round neckline with an opening cut in bodice front.
Kick Pleat—Pleat to ease a narrow skirt. Usually inverted, knife or box pleat. See Pleats, page 138.
Kilt—Short, pleated skirt.
Kimono—Loose, wide-sleeve robe fastened at the waist by a broad obi sash.
Lantern Sleeve—Bell sleeve with the lower part shaped to the wrist, resembling a lantern.
Lapel—Part that turns back, usually the front neckline fold.
Line—Style or outline given by the cut and construction of a garment.
Lingerie—Women's underclothing.
Lougette—Style of garment having a below-the-knee hem.
Macramé—Lace knotted in geometrical patterns.
Mandarin—Narrow standing collar, close fitting at the neck.
Mannequin—Dressmaker's dummy or dress form. Also the model who wears new clothes at fashion shows.
Maxi—Hem length falling between midcalf and ankle.
Micro—Hem length falling to upper thigh.
Middy—Slip-on blouse, usually with a sailor's collar.
Midi—Hem length falling to midcalf.
Mini—Hem length falling to midthigh.
Motif—Simple design used as decoration.

Negligee—Lightweight dressing gown worn over a nightgown.
Obi—Broad sash.
Overblouse—Loose blouse, not tucked in at the waist.
Overskirt—Decorative skirt worn over another garment.
Pants Suit—Jacket and pants outfit worn by women.
Peasant Sleeve—Full sleeve set in a dropped shoulder, gathered in a wrist band.
Peignoir—Woman's robe that matches a nightgown.
Peplum—Small flounce around the hips of a garment, usually as an extension of the bodice.
Peter Pan—Flat collar with round edges.
Pinafore—Sleeveless overdress, serving as an apron.
Plunge—Low-cut neckline, revealing the curve of the breasts.
Princess Line—Garment fitted with seams instead of darts.
Sash—Piece of fabric worn around the body as decoration over a garment.
Scalloped—Edge-cut or border-cut with semicircular shapes.
Scoop—Deep, U-shape neckline.
Semifitted—Conforming to the general shape of the body, without being closely fitted.
Shawl—Separate piece of fabric, often knitted, worn around the shoulders.
Sheath—Close-fitting dress with a straight skirt.
Shift—Loose-fitting casual dress.
Shirtwaist—Dress with a bodice buttoned like a shirt.
Silhouette—Outline or shape of a garment or figure.
Single-Breasted—Center-front closing with overlap for only one row of buttons.
Soutache—Narrow-braid trim.
Sportswear—Informal garments designed for leisure activities.
Stole—Long scarf of the same width worn around the shoulders.
Tab—Small loop or flap sewn only at one end.
Toile—Copy of an original garment design made in cotton fabric, such as muslin, sold by designers to companies for making a commercial line. May also be made for personal use.
Train—Extension on the back of a dress that trails along the ground, such as a train on a wedding dress.
Tunic—Simple dress worn over another garment.
Turtleneck—High, neck-hugging, turnover collar.
V-Neck—Simple, V-shape neckline.
Vent—Faced or lined slash inserted in a garment to allow greater ease of movement.
Vest—Short, close-fitting garment without sleeves, usually worn over another garment.
Wraparound—Garment that wraps around a person, such as a wraparound skirt. Allows a good overlap of fabric at the closure.

Fabric Names and Terms

Bolt—Length of fabric wound on a board or tube.
Brocade—Colorful Jacquard-weave fabric with the design over a satin background.
Chiffon—Soft, light, plain-woven fabric. Seems to float in the air when handled.
Circular Knits—Method of knitting that produces wide-width knit fabrics in a continuous tube. The tube is often slit open before sale. There is no selvage.
Colorfast—Fabric guaranteed not to lose color in wash or wear.
Corduroy—Cut-pile fabric with a ribbed surface and plain backing.
Crepe—Light-to-medium fabric, with a textured look.
Deep-Pile Fabric—See *Fur Fabric.*
Denim—Strong, twill-weave fabric, usually made of cotton. It is washable and available in colors, but traditionally is blue.
Felt—Non-woven fabric made by heating and pressing together a mass of loose fibers to form a sheet. Often thick, usually solid-color.
Flannel—Wool fabric of plain or twill weave with a soft, napped surface.
Fur Fabric—Fabric resembling fur made of synthetic fibers, usually acrylic or nylon.
Gabardine—Tightly woven fabric with an obvious twill weave.
Gingham—Plain-woven fabric. Usually yarn-dyed threads make a prominent check pattern on a white background.
Grosgrain—Fabric with a pronounced rib. Often ribbon.
Jacquard—Patterned fabric with a design coming through from the back of the fabric that appears on a plain background.
Lace—Fabric made of a network of threads drawn together to form decorative designs.
Lamé—Metallic threads in fabrics that give a glittery appearance.
Lawn—Light, woven cloth used frequently for blouses and handkerchiefs.
Nap, Pile—Soft, raised surface, often on wool fabrics.
Net—Mesh fabric of various weights.
Organdy—Plain-woven, light fabric with a crisp finish.
P.V.C.—Film of polyvinyl chloride bonded to woven or knit fabric. It is waterproof and long-wearing.
Pelt—Natural fur.
Piqué—Firmly woven fabric with horizontal ribs or cords.
Poplin—Plain-woven fabric with fine horizontal ribs.
Remnant—Odd length of fabric left at the end of a piece often sold at a discount.
Sailcloth—Strong, firmly woven cloth available in medium to heavy weights. Usually plain colors.
Satin—Fabric weave that produces a smooth, shiny surface on the fabric.
Seersucker—Woven fabric with a prominent, overall surface design. Easy to care for, it needs little ironing.
Selvage—Finished edges of a woven material. May have the manufacturer's name and fabric style name printed on it.
Sheer—Ultralight fabric that is transparent.
Slub—Coarse place in a yarn that produces a variation in the weave. Previously a yarn fault, it is now introduced by yarn manufacturers to achieve a required effect in fabrics. Traditionally seen in Shantung silk fabric.
Stretch Fabrics—Fabrics that stretch because they contain elastic fibers, such as *Lycra.* Ideal for ski pants, swimsuits and other garments that need to stretch. A smaller degree of stretch is achieved by including crimped polyester or nylon yarns. Stretch fabrics need special stitching techniques.
Taffeta—Plain-woven fabric with a crisp feel, often used to line garments.
Terrycloth—Absorbent towel fabric with closely woven loops on one or both sides.
Thread Count—The number of threads within a square inch of woven fabric, such as 24 warp, 24 weft.

Tricot—Light, single-knit jersey fabric.
Tweed—Woven-wool fabric with a rough surface and distinctive design. Usually heavy, long-wearing and practical.
Twill—Weave of cloth with a diagonal ribbing on the surface. See *Gabardine.*
Velvet—Fabric with a cut-pile surface. Traditionally made of silk or cotton, now available in man-made fibers. It is washable and crease-resistant. The pile on velvet may be crushed by careless handling.
Voile—Light, plain-woven fabric with an open weave, often used for blouses and shirts.
Warp Knits—Wide knit fabric. More stable than circular knit.
Warp—Threads running the length of a fabric.
Weft—Threads running across a fabric.

Sewing Terms

Applique—Method of decorating a garment by stitching a shaped piece of fabric on it.
Backing—To attach lining on the wrong-side of a garment.
Balance Marks—Points on a pattern where two sections of garment fit together. Marks are transferred to the fabric.
Basting—A way to join two pieces of fabric with loose, temporary stitches.
Bias Tape—Tape cut on the true cross grain, with edges folded over. It may also be cut as strips from fabric.
Bias—Edge or fold of material across the grain. *True cross* or *true bias* is at a 45° angle to the straight grain.
Binding—Strip enclosing an edge as finish or trim.
Blind Hem—Hem sewn invisibly with hand- or machine-stitches.
Bodkin—Blunt needle used to pull something through a casing.
Casing—Tunnel of fabric around a garment that encloses a drawstring or piece of elastic.
Clip—A cut in the seam allowance to allow ease on corners and curves.
Construction—Making or sewing a garment together.
Contrasting—Different color or texture—tone, color or texture do not match.
Cording—Filling a narrow fabric tube with cotton cord to use as decoration. See *Piping.*
Dart—Pointed, tapered fold of material to take fullness out of a garment.
Ease—To hold fullness without making pleats or gathers; the room allowed on a pattern for body movement.
Edge-Stitching—Machine-stitching placed close to a folded edge. Often used to finish open seams.
Enclosed Seams—Seams with raw edges concealed during the construction process, such as French or double-stitched seams.
Eyelet—Round hole in fabric to take a cord or thong. Finished with stitching or a circle of metal.
Face—Right-side of the fabric. The application of a fitted piece of fabric to finish an edge.
Fitting Line—Also called *seam line, pattern line* or *stitching line.* The line along which two pieces of a garment are sewn.
Fly—Lap of fabric that conceals an opening.
Gathering—Rows of stitches pulled to reduce width or control fullness in a garment area.
Grading—See *Layering.*
Grain—Direction in which thread runs in a fabric.
Gusset—Fabric piece inserted to ease strain in a garment.
Inset or Insert—Piece of shaped fabric inserted to aid fitting. Also used as decoration.
Interfacing—Fabric placed between the facing and garment to give shape, support, warmth or bulk.
Lap—Edge extending to cover another edge, such as a placket.
Layering or Grading—To trim two or more seam allowances to reduce bulk.
Layout—Chart that comes with a pattern showing ideal placement of pattern pieces on fabric.
Lining—Extra layer of fabric attached to the inside of a garment to make it hang better, to finish it and give it strength.
Marking—The transfer of construction marks from paper pattern to fabric.
Miter—To make a pointed, triangular or square shape on the end of a belt or the inside diagonal seam of a corner.
Motif—Single design used as decoration.
Mounting—Placing lining fabric on the wrong-side of the garment fabric and sewing both as one piece.
Nap or Pile—Raised, soft surface with fibers lying in one direction, such as natural fur.
Notch—Symbol on a pattern transferred to fabric to show matching points. Also the cutting of V-shapes from seam allowances.
Notions—Items needed for sewing, such as pins, needles, binding, buttons, fastenings.
Open Seam—Also called *flat* or *plain* seams. Joins two garment pieces with one row of machine-stitching. Seam allowances are pressed open and flat on the wrong-side.
Opening—Part of a garment that can be opened and closed for putting on and taking off.
Pin Basting—Pinning seams before stitching.
Piping—Strip of fabric, folded and added in a seam for emphasis and decoration.
Pivot—Leaving the machine needle in the work when reaching a corner, then turning the work around the needle after lifting the presser foot.
Placket—Garment opening closed by snaps, buttons or zipper.
Prefold—To fold and press a binding or garment section before attaching it to the garment.
Preshape—To steam fabric in a curved shape before stitching to the garment.
Preshrink—To shrink fabric or binding with steam pressing before making into a garment.
Puckering—Uneven folds or gathers, usually made by accident when the tension of the stitching is incorrect.
Raw Edge—Unfinished edge of a fabric.
Right-Side—Finished side of the garment.
Roll—To produce a soft, curved fold, usually on a collar.
Rouleau—Tube of fabric with the raw edges inside, used for fastenings or decoration. Sometimes used to finish an edge.
Saddle-Stitch—Even, running stitches for decorative effect, often made with contrasting thread.
Seam Allowance—Width of fabric between the seam line and raw edge. Most patterns allow for a 5/8-inch seam allowance.
Seam Binding—Same as binding.
Secure—To fasten a thread with a back-stitch or knot.
Self—Fabric the same as the rest of the garment.

Shank—Link between button and fabric formed by the threads holding the button to the garment or part of the button itself.
Shrink—To use steam or water to make the fabric contract for shaping a garment or to keep the garment shape from changing during later washing.
Slash—Controlled cut made in fabric during garment construction.
Slit—To cut fabric lengthwise. A long, narrow opening.
Stay-Stitching—Row of machine-stitching outside the seam allowance. Keeps the shape of an edge that might stretch during sewing.
Straight Grain—Following the straight threads across or along a piece of fabric, usually with the warp thread parallel to the selvage.
Tack—To join two pieces of fabric with loose, temporary stitches.
Tailor's Tack—Special tacking-stitch using double thread to transfer pattern markings to the fabric.
Tailoring—Special construction techniques using stitching and steam pressing to make a finished garment, such as a man's suit.
Taper—To sew or cut fabric to produce a narrowing effect.
Tension—Controlled pull or pressure on thread or fabric during construction. Also applies to correct tightness of machine stitches.
Thread Tracing—Sometimes called *trace-tacking.* Lines of running or tacking-stitches used to mark the position of the center front, buttonholes and other points. Both ends are left unsecured.
Top-Stitching—Line of stitching parallel to an edge or seam, sewn from the right-side. Often used as decoration.
Trim—To cut away excess fabric. Also decorative feature added to a garment.
Underlining—Term sometimes used for a lining mounted on the back of a garment before actual garment construction begins. See *Mounting.*
Welt—Strip of material stitched to an edge or seam, usually on a pocket top.
Wrong-Side—Side of the fabric on the inside of a garment.
Yardage—Length of fabric of a given width needed to make a garment.
Yoke—Fitted part of a garment, usually at the shoulders or hips, from which the garment hangs.
Zigzag—Stitch produced by swing-needle sewing machines, looking like a row of joined *Vs.* Used for finishing, decorating and sewing seams.

CONVERSION CHART

SEWING MEASUREMENTS
1/16 inch = 2mm
1/8 inch = 3mm
1/4 inch = 6mm
3/8 inch = 10mm
1/2 inch = 13mm
5/8 inch = 15mm
3/4 inch = 20mm
7/8 inch = 22mm
1 inch = 25mm or 2.5cm
1-1/4 inches = 3.2cm
1-1/2 inches = 3.8cm
1-3/4 inches = 4.5cm
2 inches = 5cm
4 inches = 10cm
5 inches = 13cm
6 inches = 15cm
7 inches = 18cm
8 inches = 20cm

FABRIC WIDTHS
36 inches = 90cm
42 inches = 105cm
45 inches = 113cm
48 inches = 120cm
54 inches = 135cm
56 inches = 140cm
60 inches = 150cm
68 inches = 170cm
72 inches = 180cm

FABRIC LENGTHS
1/8 yard = 10cm
1/4 yard = 20cm
3/8 yard = 30cm
1/2 yard = 40cm
5/8 yard = 50cm
3/4 yard = 60cm
7/8 yard = 80cm
1 yard = 90cm

ZIPPER LENGTHS
4 inches = 10cm
5 inches = 13cm
6 inches = 15cm
7 inches = 18cm
8 inches = 20cm
9 inches = 23cm
10 inches = 25cm
12 inches = 30cm
14 inches = 35cm
16 inches = 40cm
18 inches = 45cm
20 inches = 50cm
22 inches = 55cm
24 inches = 60cm
26 inches = 66cm
28 inches = 70cm
30 inches = 76cm

CLOTHING SIZES

WOMEN'S

Size	**10**	**12**	**14**	**16**	**18**
Bust					
inches	32	34	36	38	40
cm	80	85	90	95	100
Waist					
inches	22	24	26	28	30
cm	55	60	65	70	75
Hips					
inches	34	36	38	40	42
cm	85	90	95	100	105

MEN'S

Chest or Waist								
inches	30	32	34	36	38	40	42	44
cm	75	80	85	90	95	100	105	110
Inside Leg								
inches	29	30	31	32	33			
cm	73	75	78	80	83			
Collars								
inches	13	13-1/2	14	14-1/2	15	15-1/2	16	16-1/2
cm	33	34	35	36	38	39	40	41

CHILDREN'S

Height									
inches	36	38	40	42-1/2	45	47-1/2	50	52-1/2	55
cm	90	95	100	106	113	119	125	131	138
Approx. Age	2	3	4	5	6	7	8	9	10
Chest									
inches	21	21-1/2	22	23	24	25	26	27	28-1/2
cm	53	54	55	58	60	63	65	68	71

STITCHES

PER INCH		PER CM
8	=	3
10	=	4
13	=	5
15	=	6

Get Ready

FASHION AND YOU

Fashion may be less important than it used to be, but it is important to know about design elements. If you are interested in clothes, you can develop a style that suits your figure, personality and lifestyle. Even if you want to live in jeans, you should know how to choose a flattering style and suitable fabric.

Collecting the right clothes for you and your lifestyle is not easy. Often it must be done on a limited budget. When you make your own clothes, they cost less than when you buy them off the rack.

PLANNING NEW CLOTHES

Study pattern books, advertisements, magazines and fashion books. Find out what is new, and make notes of anything that appeals to you. Start a scrapbook, and add to it. Look at the style, color, fabric, accessories and trims of different clothes.

Check your wardrobe, and list clothes you want to keep. Dispose of clothes you do not want. Clean and repair garments that need it. Try on clothes to see how well they mix and match together. Make note of anything needed to complete a basic collection, suitable for your lifestyle.

List clothes you need in order of importance so you know what to make first. Decide whether you want a few expensive items or a lot of inexpensive things that do not last long. It is not worth spending a lot of time and effort making an intricate garment out of poor fabric.

A well-made classic dress or skirt can be worn many times with different accessories. Faddish clothes may be out-of-date before they are worn out.

FIGURE TYPE

Because people's figures vary a lot, you must know your figure type and faults. It will make it easier to choose suitable, flattering styles for you. See the section on *Choosing and Using a Pattern,* page 44, for details.

COLOR

Choose colors that go with your clothes and suit your personal coloring. Rules about not wearing blues and greens, or reds and pinks together no longer hold true. Try different colors to see if you are happy in them. Fashionable colors may date quickly and do nothing for your coloring or personality.

The different colors worn by some people can look exciting. Accessories in matching or contrasting colors can make a difference to an outfit. Color can draw attention away from figure faults. Relate makeup to the color of the clothes you wear. Alter makeup slightly for each outfit.

Colors can create optical illusions. Cool, dark colors make you look smaller. Warm, light colors make you look larger. Subtle, muted colors can be slimming. Bright, contrasting colors draw attention to the figure and make you look larger.

General Rules—These are general rules to follow. They do *not* always apply to everyone.

Redheads should avoid reds, pinks and oranges that clash with their hair color. Choose natural, gray, cream, camel, brown, black or white. Yellows, greens and blues are pretty for a contrast or for accessories.

Blondes should avoid some yellows and oranges but usually look good in pastel blues, greens and browns. Richer colors look good with dark blond or mousy hair.

Brunettes look good in most bright colors.

Elderly people with white hair look pretty in pastel shades. Sallow skins need warm colors without too much yellow. Pale skin needs colors strong enough to contrast with it. Dark skin looks attractive with most colors, although exotic color combinations can look out of place in the daytime.

Planning Color Schemes—There are three types of color schemes for an outfit or a collection of clothes. Always try color schemes by holding fabric combinations near your face. Look in a mirror to see if the colors suit you.

A *monochrome* color scheme uses shades of a single color or one color with black and white. A *contrasting* color scheme uses two or more different colors in varying strengths. A *toning* color scheme uses two or more similar colors.

STYLE LINES

Style lines of a garment can emphasize or conceal parts of your figure. Style lines are affected by changing fashions.

Vertical Lines—These add height and make a figure look slimmer. The princess style is a good example of vertical lines.

Horizontal Lines—They tend to add an appearance of width. Place these at flattering points of the figure.

Curved Seams—Also called *draping,* these create soft, flattering lines. Diagonal lines go from left to right when looking at a garment. Long diagonals take the eye down in a slimming line. Be careful about lines that appear in the weave or pattern.

Straight lines are usually severe and give a tailored or classic look. Curves and drapes appear graceful and feminine.

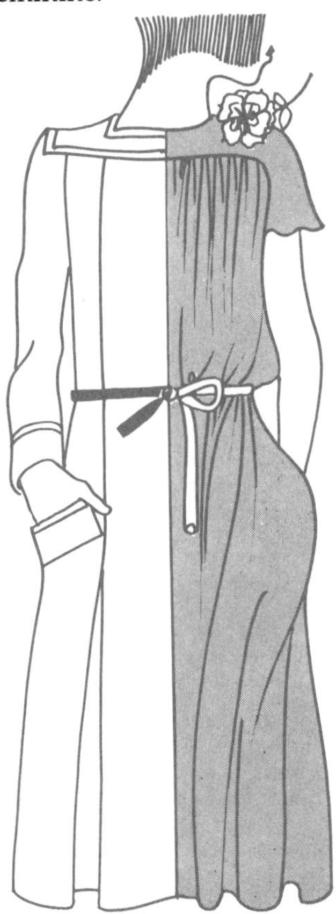

Basic Garment Silhouettes—There are four basic garment silhouettes.

Fitted garments fit the natural curves of the body and may show off the figure. Fitted garments must be well-cut and carefully fitted. This style may crease easily.

Semifitted garments are usually fitted over the bust with a slightly looser cut at waist and hips. This style is more flattering to an imperfect figure than a completely fitted garment.

Slightly fitted garments are easy to wear. They have room for movement and barely follow the body outline. They may be bias cut.

Loosely fitted garments are often fitted only on the shoulders. Fullness disguises the body outline from the bust down.

Most paper patterns allow ease in the cut, whatever the silhouette. Some close-fitting areas may be fashionable, such as empire bodices fitted under the bust or shirtwaists with snug waistlines.

BALANCE AND PROPORTION

A garment looks best when details are not concentrated in one area. Maintain balance by keeping an equal amount of eye appeal in two or more garment areas. Two halves may be identical so the garment has a symmetrical look. If one area has special emphasis, it may be balanced by having another point of interest elsewhere.

Proportion is important when relating areas of the garment to one another and to the figure. Take into account style lines, design details, fabric, pattern and figure type. The

scale and size of the fabric and garment must also suit the figure type. A full midiskirt may swamp a tiny, slim figure, while a miniskirt is unflattering on a tall, plump figure.

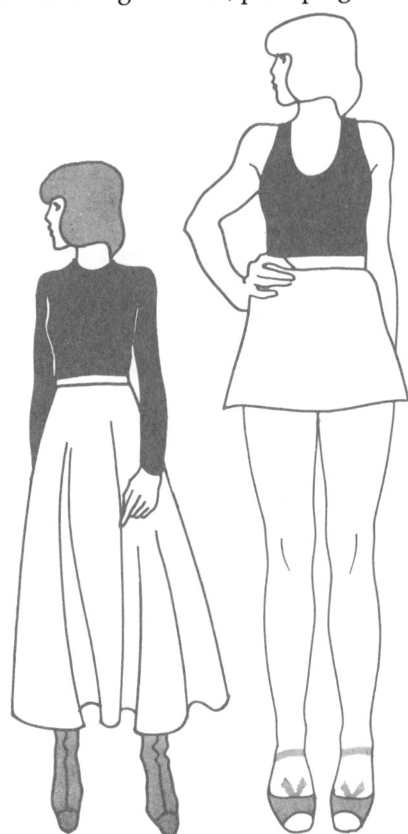

Pleasing proportions may be achieved by planning the garment areas in halves, thirds or quarters. For some figures, slightly uneven proportions may be more suitable. The overall look is important.

Try on ready-made garments to get an idea of what suits you best. Check the effect of shiny and dull fabrics, large and small prints, sheer and bulky fabrics, and various color combinations.

FABRIC TEXTURE

The texture of fabrics affects the final appearance of a garment. Fabric can be stiff or flowing, rough or smooth, shiny or dull, sheer or bulky. Soft, clinging fabrics reveal the figure, while a stiff fabric may conceal figure faults by creating a sleek outline.

Shiny or bulky materials make the figure appear larger. These fabrics may be useful for someone who is too thin. Someone who is heavy should avoid bulky or shiny fabrics, unless they are used as trim or accessories. Soft, clinging fabric, such as jersey, bias-cut silk, wool and crepes, make soft, feminine garments.

Soft, loosely woven fabrics, such as heavy wool, crepes and jerseys, make attractive flared clothes or clothes with unpressed pleats. Light evening fabrics can be draped closer to the body. Firmly woven wool, linen, cotton, silk and fine tweed make tailored clothes with a seamed or sculptured look.

PRINTS AND PATTERNS

Prints and patterns add beauty and interest to your wardrobe. Consider the style and function of the garment when using a print. Too many seams and other style details may break up the fabric design so it is not seen to best effect. Choose a pattern suited to the figure in size and color. Small patterns are pretty on tiny figures, while larger prints might be overpowering.

Vertical stripes make a figure look slimmer and taller. Horizontal stripes add width and reduce height. Bright colors or sharp contrasts make a figure appear larger.

The main color should be flattering. Use combinations of other colors in small areas, such as a printed pocket on a plain dress. Limit eye-catching designs to areas where they are complementary and do not draw attention to figure faults.

The curves and angles of fabric and garment design should be in harmony. Straight, boxy jackets look better in checks than paisleys. Curved bodice seams and collars may spoil a plaid or striped effect. Also consider the direction of the pattern and the body movements so they do not conflict.

FABRICS AND FIBERS

Fabrics

You may buy a fabric, then find it is unsuitable for a pattern. The information in this section will help you select a fabric suitable for the garment you want to make.

Most pattern envelopes give fabric suggestions. Follow them closely. Do not make a pattern in woven fabric if the pattern is designed for knit. Knit fabrics have built-in ease and stretch. Patterns recommended for knits often exclude construction details such as darts. If a woven fabric is used, the results will be disappointing.

Fabric should suit the person wearing it. Emphasize good figure points, and disguise bad points.

Tall, thin figures should not wear vertical stripes. If natural complexion is highly colored, do not wear multicolor prints. Short, plump

figures are not complimented by large designs, horizontal stripes or shiny fabrics.

Select fabric to blend with the colors and textures of other things in your wardrobe. A blouse can be made in a pattern and pants in a plain color, or a skirt can have a check design and the blouse be plain. The blouse can pick up one of the colors in the skirt. Color should be suitable for the occasions when the garment will be worn.

Do not choose a fabric with a busy design when making a garment with unusual lines, pin-tucking or other stitching detail. The design will detract from the finished effect, and many hours of handwork may be unnoticed.

Fabric should be an appropriate weave or knit for the item of clothing. Choose closely woven fabrics for tight-fitting garments. Full skirts, loose-fitting coats and short jackets can be made in loosely woven fabrics.

Fabrics should be washable or easily cleaned, depending on the amount of wear they will receive. Check washing and cleaning instructions when you buy fabric, so mistakes can be avoided.

When selecting fabrics to be worn together, avoid a muddled effect. If you want to mix fabrics, have one common factor, such as a common color or design. A variety of plain fabrics may be used together. Any patterned fabric that highlights one of the plain colors can be included.

Do not forget texture. Compare fabrics, and try to have a contrast in texture. If it is difficult to choose color schemes with balanced design and color, copy ideas from magazines and books. Try on ready-made garments to see which colors and designs suit you best.

CHECKLIST

Ask yourself the following questions when selecting a fabric:

1. Is it soft or stiff?
2. Will it drape?
3. Will it stretch and recover its shape?
4. Will it shrink?
5. Is it washable or must it be dry-cleaned?
6. Is it clingy?
7. Is it rough or scratchy?
8. Is it soil- and stain-resistant?
9. Will it be cool or warm?
10. Is it absorbent?
11. Is it colorfast?
12. How does it handle?
13. Will it need ironing?

Fabrics To Choose And Use

Fabrics Suitable For Beginning Sewers

COTTON

Width	36, 45, 54 inches
Uses	Dresses, shirts, nightwear, children's wear, blouses.
Advantages	Easily pressed and easy to handle. Gathers well and can be tucked. Useful for embroidery. Will not fray. Often reversible.
Disadvantages	None.
Laundering	Iron on either side while damp.

GINGHAM

Cotton, polyester

Width	36, 45, 54 inches
Uses	Overalls, housecoats, beachwear, children's wear.
Advantages	Easily pressed and easy to handle. Gathers well, so smocking can be used. Patterned on both sides.
Disadvantages	Does not pleat well.
Laundering	Wash in hot water. Can be starched for extra stiffness. Iron on either side while damp.

LAWN
Cotton, polyester
Width 36 inches
Uses Blouses, dresses, underwear.
Advantages Will not fray. Crisp but easy to work with. Easily pressed. Gathers well.
Disadvantages None.
Laundering Can be pulled in shape while wet. Can be starched.

PIQUÉ
Width 36, 45, 60 inches
Uses Skirts, shorts, jackets, dresses, blouses, collars, cuffs.
Advantages Will not fray. Maintains shape, wears well.
Disadvantages Too springy for gathering. Need to match ribs.
Laundering Starch to keep crispness. Iron on wrong-side while damp.

POPLIN
Width 36, 45, 60 inches
Uses Children's wear, shirts, vests.
Advantages Will not fray. Firm to handle. Gathers well. Easily pressed.
Disadvantages None.
Laundering Iron on either side with hot iron while damp.

SEERSUCKER
Cotton, polyester
Width 36, 45 inches
Uses Dresses, underwear, nightwear, blouses, children's wear.
Advantages Will not fray. Easy to handle. Little pressing needed except for seams. Gathers well. Hangs well.
Disadvantages Cannot be tucked or pleated. If pattern is large, be careful matching seams.
Laundering Iron lightly when dry.

Fabrics Suitable For Semiskilled Sewers

WOOL BOUCLE
Widths 54, 60 inches
Uses Suits, coats, dresses.
Advantages Will not crease. Lightweight. Drapes and hangs well.
Disadvantages Stitching difficult to keep straight if weave is heavy. Does not pleat easily.
Laundering Brush well. Dry-clean only.

CHINTZ
Width 45 inches
Uses Dresses, soft furnishings, housecoats.
Advantages Will not fray. Easily pressed. Hangs well in unpressed pleats.
Disadvantages Cannot be gathered if glaze is too high. Hard to handle.
Laundering Washes easily. Starch when glaze becomes impaired. Iron on right-side while damp.

COTTON SATIN
Width 36, 45 inches
Uses Skirts, blouses, dresses, shirts.
Advantages Strong. Will not fray. Hangs well. Often crease-resistant. Presses well. Tucks and gathers easily.
Disadvantages None.
Laundering Use hot water when washing. Iron on right-side while damp. Glazed surface helps repel dirt.

CREPE
Wool, acrylic
Width 36, 54, 60 inches
Uses Dresses, blouses.
Advantages Tucks, drapes, hangs well. Gathers well. Can be embroidered.
Disadvantages Springy.
Laundering Press either dry or slightly damp. Press on wrong-side with warm iron so glaze is avoided. Some crepes can only be dry-cleaned.

CREPE DE CHINE
Width 36 inches
Uses Blouses, lingerie.
Advantages Easy to handle. Does not fray badly. Usually reversible.
Disadvantages Ironed-in creases difficult to remove.
Laundering Washes and irons easily. Iron while damp.

DENIM
Widths 36, 48 inches
Uses Jeans, shirts, overalls, dresses.
Advantages Long wearing. Pleats well. Does not fray. Strong.
Disadvantages Does not gather easily.
Laundering May be boiled. Iron while damp. Normally colorfast. Shrinks when washed.

WOOL FLANNEL
Widths 45, 54 inches
Uses Suits, dresses, blouses, skirts.
Advantages Hangs well. Pleats. Does not fray. Suitable for tailored styles.
Disadvantages None.
Laundering Wash in warm, soapy water. Rinse well. Press on wrong-side.

WOOL GABARDINE

Width	45, 54 inches
Uses	Suits, jackets, coats, skirts.
Advantages	Good for tailored styles. Pleats well. Strong.
Disadvantages	None.
Laundering	Brush well. Dry-clean only.

LINEN

Widths	36, 45 inches
Uses	Suits, skirts, dresses.
Advantages	Pleats and hangs well. Easily pressed. Suitable for tailored clothes. Keeps shape.
Disadvantages	Creases and frays badly.
Laundering	Washes and presses well. Iron on wrong-side unless surface is glazed.

MUSLIN

Width	36, 45 inches
Uses	Blouses.
Advantages	Ideal for fine sewing. Can be tucked and frilled.
Disadvantages	Frays.
Laundering	Shrinks when washed.

ORGANDY

Widths	36, 45 inches
Uses	Children's dresses, blouses.
Advantages	Ideal for fine sewing. Can be tucked and rolled. Good for hand- or machine-embroidery.
Disadvantages	Springy. Does not gather easily. Frays a little. Transparent.
Laundering	Washes easily. Shrinks. Iron while damp. Can be starched to keep crispness.

SATEEN

Widths	36, 45 inches
Uses	Underskirts, lining for nylon, net or lace dresses.
Advantages	Other materials can be used over it without it clinging.
Disadvantages	Frays. Slips while being cut or sewn.
Laundering	Loses much of its body when washed. Can be stiffened with sizing.

LINGERIE SATIN
Polyester, rayon

Width	36 inches
Uses	Lingerie, nightwear, blouses.
Advantages	Can be gathered, embroidered and tucked. Hangs and drapes well.
Disadvantages	Frays easily.
Laundering	Most lingerie satins can be washed with warm soapy water. Iron on right-side while damp.

WOOL SERGE

Widths	54, 60 inches
Uses	Coats, jackets, suits, skirts.
Advantages	Holds pleats. Does not crease easily.
Disadvantages	None.
Laundering	Brush well. Dry-clean.

SILK

Widths	36, 45 inches
Uses	Suits, dresses, children's wear, lingerie, blouses, evening clothes.
Advantages	Pleats and gathers easily. Strong but soft. Ideal for fine sewing. Keeps shape. Hangs and drapes well.
Disadvantages	Frays badly.
Laundering	Presses easily. Iron when completely dry.

POLYESTER WOOL

Widths	54, 60 inches
Uses	Skirts, suits, coats, jackets, dresses.
Advantages	Holds pleats. Does not crease easily.
Disadvantages	Frays. Can be bulky to wear.
Laundering	Brush well. Dry-clean.

VOILE

Widths	36, 42 inches
Uses	Dresses, blouses.
Advantages	Good for fine sewing. Can be tucked or frilled.
Disadvantages	Frays. Seams must be strong and reinforced.
Laundering	Washes and irons easily. Needs to be stiffened. Iron while damp.

WORSTED WOOL

Widths	54, 60 inches
Uses	Skirts, coats, dresses, jackets, suits.
Advantages	Pleats well. Strong material, suitable for all tailored styles.
Disadvantages	Difficult to work on. Tends to be bulky. Highly flammable unless treated.
Laundering	Brush well. Dry-clean.

Fabrics Suitable For Skilled Sewers

CHIFFON

Width	36 inches
Uses	Blouses, evening wear, neckwear, nightdresses.
Advantages	Drapes, gathers and hangs well.
Disadvantages	Frays easily. Needs skilled handling.
Laundering	Wash in warm, soapy wash. Press with a warm iron.

GEORGETTE
Silk, nylon

Width	36 inches
Uses	Dresses, blouses, neckwear, lingerie.
Advantages	Gathers and drapes well. Does not fray easily.
Disadvantages	Seams and edges may stretch.
Laundering	Wash in warm, soapy water. Press with warm iron.

JERSEY
Silk, cotton, wool

Widths	42, 48, 54, 60 inches
Uses	Blouses, suits, dresses, skirts, coats, pants.
Advantages	Drapes and hangs well.
Disadvantages	Edges tend to stretch. Handle gently so material is not distorted. Sew with a stretch-stitch.
Laundering	May need to be dry-cleaned. Press along grain to maintain shape.

MOIRÉ
Tafetta, rayon

Width	36 inches
Uses	Evening dresses.
Advantages	Gathers, flares and hangs well. Maintains crispness.
Disadvantages	Frays badly. Shows water marks. Match pattern at seams.
Laundering	Dry-clean only.

NYLON

Widths	36, 48 inches
Uses	Dresses, children's wear, lingerie.
Advantages	Does not need much pressing. Fine but strong.
Disadvantages	Frays easily. Transparent.
Laundering	Washes easily. Use warm, soapy water. Dries quickly. Do not use hot iron.

TAFFETA

Width	36 inches
Uses	Blouses, petticoats, dresses.
Advantages	Can be dressy.
Disadvantages	Frays badly.
Laundering	Dry-clean. Press on wrong-side or fabric glazes.

VELVET
Silk, rayon, nylon, cotton

Widths	36, 45, 54, 60 inches
Uses	Jackets, dresses, evening wear.
Advantages	Hangs and drapes well.
Disadvantages	Can only be cut in one direction. Not easy to press. Pins mark the pile, so use fine needles.
Laundering	May need dry-cleaning. Corduroy velvet washes well. Press with iron on the wrong-side.

FABRIC WIDTHS AND LENGTHS

There are many different widths of fabric to choose from. The most common widths are 36 inches, 42 inches, 45 inches, 48 inches, 54 inches, 56 inches, 60 inches, 68 inches and 72 inches.

Fabric lengths are normally cut to the nearest 4 inches. You may have to decide whether to round the required fabric length up or down. The most common lengths are 1/8 yard, 1/4 yard, 3/8 yard, 1/2 yard, 5/8 yard, 3/4 yard, 7/8 yard and 1 yard.

Fibers

Fiber content of fabric may be natural, man-made or a combination of both. Fabrics are now produced from man-made fibers, as well as natural fibers. The way fibers are made into yarns, and yarns made into finished fabrics, affects the choice and use of fabrics. Knowledge of fibers will help you choose the right fabric for your garment.

Long strands or continuous filaments of fiber are twisted to make yarns. Silk and most man-made fibers are made into continuous filaments.

Shorter fibers are called *staple fibers.* These include natural and some man-made fibers. These fibers are combed, carded, stretched, twisted and spun into bulkier yarns.

To make bulky or stretchy textured yarns, filaments may be coiled, crimped or looped. Different types, thicknesses and colors of fibers may be combined to make complex yarns with slub or other special features.

NATURAL FIBERS

Cotton—The fluffy seed-pod, or *boll,* of the cotton plant contains cotton linters. Linters are cleaned, combed, carded and processed into thread.

Cotton is always popular and makes strong, absorbent, easily washed fabric that is comfortable to wear. Fabrics range from fine, smooth voile to thick toweling. Cotton is mothproof but may be affected by mildew in damp conditions. If stained by accident, most white cotton can be bleached.

If not pretreated, cotton may shrink when washed. A variety of finishes can be applied to these fabrics. Cotton can be blended with wool, polyester and other fibers.

Linen—The fibrous stalks of ripe flax plants are processed and spun into threads. Linen fabrics are stronger and longer-wearing than cottons. They are cool and absorbent to wear, but linen is more expensive than cotton. Bleach may be used on white linen, but bacteria or acid may cause rotting. Linen is mothproof. Special finishes may be applied to prevent shrinking and creasing. Blending with man-made fibers also achieves these effects.

Silk—Silkworms spin filaments for their cocoons, and these fibers can be spun into thread. Silk is expensive but makes beautiful fabric that is strong, warm, absorbent and springy. Unless labeled *washable,* silk must be dry-cleaned.

Wool—The hair and fur of animals is suitable for making fabrics. In addition to wool from sheep, luxury fibers are obtained from alpaca, goats, rabbits and llamas. Although not a strong fiber, wool makes elastic, warm, absorbent fabric in many weights. These weights range from light crepes to heavy tweeds. Wool is usually crease-resistant but is attacked by moths and bacteria. It is affected by strong bleaches. Except for wool labeled *machine washable* or *dry-clean only,* wool fabric may need special care. Hot water shrinks it, and an iron will scorch it if too hot.

MAN-MADE FIBERS

Acetate—Acetate is derived from cellulose, which is obtained from wood pulp or cotton linters. Wood pulp or cotton linters are put through a chemical process to form *cellulose acetate.* This is dissolved in a solvent to give a viscous liquid, which is then spun into acetate.

Acetate is silklike and drapes well. It is absorbent and cool to wear. Satins, taffetas, brocades, surahs, jersey and lining fabrics are often made from acetate. Acetate fabrics are not long-wearing.

Some trade names are *Celanese, Chromspun, Entron.*

Acrylic—Acrylics are made from *acrylonitrile,* derived from products of the oil industry. They are soft and warm, like wool, but do not stretch as much. Acrylics are long-wearing and mothproof. White acrylics may yellow with age. Knitwear is often made from acrylic.

Some trade names are *Acrilan, Creslan, Orlon, Zefran.*

Modacrylic—Modacrylic is made from chemicals from oil and coal processing. It is strong and long-wearing and used for furnishings, overalls and other tough jobs. Modacrylic is flame-retardant.

Some trade names are *Elura, Verel.*

Nylon—Nylon is made from products of the oil industry. It can be made in continuous filaments or short lengths that are made into staple yarn.

Nylon is often blended with wool or cotton, and the resulting fabric is strong. If used alone, nylon attracts dirt because of static electricity. Nylon does not stretch, shrink or absorb water. Low absorbency means it is clammy to wear. It is easily washed, and moth- and rot-resistant. White nylon may gray or yellow with age. Drip-dry and minimum-iron finishes are common. Nylon is used in hosiery, lingerie and shirts. Anti-static nylon is available when static buildup may be a problem.

Some trade names are *Antron, Enkalure, Qiana.*

Polyester—This fabric is made from products of the oil industry. It is strong and adds strength to wool or cotton. Polyester fibers may be crimped or bulked.

Polyester is usually warm to wear, with low absorbency and little stretch. Resistant to moths and rot, it may shrink when washed unless pretreated. White polyester stays whiter than other man-made fibers. Woven and knit polyester is washable and can be drip-dried.

Some trade names are *Dacron, Encron, Fortrel, Trevira, Ultron.*

Spandex—This is stretchy yarn used in hosiery, foundation garments and swimwear. It can be washed gently by hand or machine.

One trade name is *Lycra.*

Triacetate—It is made from the same source as acetate but by a slightly different process. Triacetate is stronger than acetate. It is crease-resistant, easy to care for and often blended with nylon.

Some trade names are *Arnel, Tricel.*

FABRIC CONSTRUCTION

The two most common ways of making yarn into fabric are *weaving* and *knitting.* There are also other ways to make fabric, such as *bonding* and *felting.*

Weaving—Two groups of yarns are put together at right angles in woven fabrics. *Warp* is the lengthwise set of threads that run parallel to the selvage. These are strong. In the simple weave, the crosswise, or *weft,* threads run over and under the warp threads.

There are many plain weave variations—rib, basket, twill, satin, pile, dobby, jacquard. Look at fabrics under a magnifying glass to see variations.

Knitting—A continuous yarn is knit into interlocking loops to form a stretchy, flexible fabric. Recent developments in knitting machines have led to a variety of weights and textures of knit fabrics.

A *wale* is a row of loops running lengthwise, like warp threads. A *course* is a crosswise row, like weft threads. *Denier* refers to weight and thickness. *Gage* is the number of stitches used.

Yarn can be *weft knit* into flat or tubular fabrics. A single continuous thread makes a course of loops that links with the previous and following rows.

When many yarns are used to produce lengthwise rows of loops, it is called *warp knit.* The rows of loops link with the ones on either side. Fabrics made this way are almost run-proof.

Bonding—Fibers can be bonded or stuck together without knitting or weaving. There is no grain or stretch. These fabrics are *not* self-lined or laminated, which means two layers of material are fused together.

Felting—This is an inexpensive, warm, non-woven fabric. It is made from wool or fur fibers joined together by heat, moisture, friction and pressure. Felt is made in many thicknesses and colors. It does not fray but is not durable enough for most clothes.

FINISHES

Many finishes have been developed to improve the appearance or performance of fabrics. Finishes are applied to fabric, not yarns.

Colorfast—Fabrics do not bleed or lose color during washing.
Crease-Resistant—Chemicals are used to make the yarn or fabric more springy.
Flameproof—This finish is applied to fabric to make it non-flammable. This means fabric will not burn. The law says sleepwear for children must be flame-resistant, but many chemical treatments wash out.
London Shrunk—Wool suiting is dampened and left to dry naturally before tailoring.
Luster—Resins and starches can be applied to cottons to make a crisp, shiny surface such as chintz.
Machine Washable—A finish is applied to fabric to make it washable. In addition to the usual fabrics, it is possible to wash some suede, leather and wools in a washing machine. Look for special labels and instructions.
Mercerizing—This process requires treating cottons under tension to make them strong and lustrous.
Permanent Press—Often called *durable press.* Fabrics resist creasing and stay in shape without ironing.
Preshrink—A manufacturing process to reduce the amount of shrinkage in home laundering.
Waterproofing—Silicone is used on the surface of rainwear to make it water repellent, waterproof or rain-resistant. For complete waterproofing—100% resistance to rain—fabric must be coated with plastic, rubber or wax. It should have reinforced seams.
Sizing or Dressing—Glue, clay or wax is added to fabric for body. It usually washes out.

COLORS AND PATTERNS

There are many ways of adding color and patterns to fabrics.
Dyeing—This is used to produce different effects. Man-made fibers may have color added to the filament liquid. Bundles of fiber yarns may be dipped in dye before processing or pieces of fabric may be piece-dyed.

Batik dyeing is used commercially for delicate designs. Wax is applied to the fabric in areas not to be dyed. The whole cloth is dipped in dye before wax is boiled off.

Tie-dyeing is also used commercially. Areas of fabric are gathered into tight bunches, and the whole piece is dipped in dye. This creates sunburst designs.

Printing—This prints color and design on a piece of fabric. *Screen printing* is a slow way of stenciling beautiful, complex patterns. In the less-expensive, faster process of *roller-printing,* designs are engraved on rollers, dipped in dye and rolled on the fabric.
Machine-Embroidery—This is used to decorate the surface of fabrics. It is combined with cutting or punching out fabric to make a lacy effect. On some fabrics, certain areas may be carefully dissolved to make a kind of lace. This is sometimes described as a *burned-out effect.*

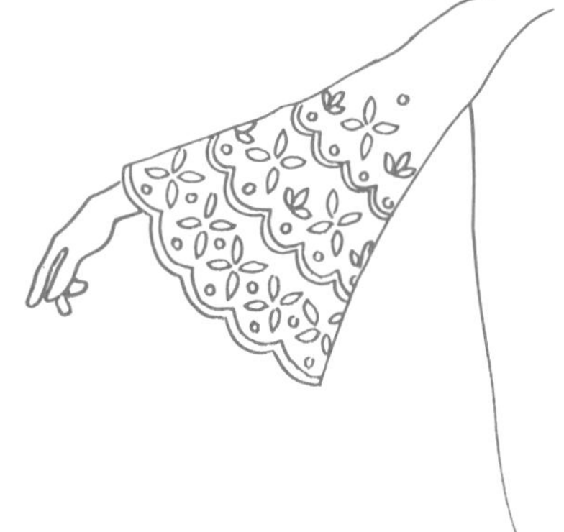

STRETCH FABRICS

Most fabrics stretch a little. Some yarns are made with built-in stretch. Stretchy yarns are made by tight-twisting or crimping yarn. Special extendible fibers may be used, or fibers may have a fine rubber core.

Knit fabrics made from these yarns stretch the most. Many fabrics stretch both ways and are used for sportswear. Warp-stretch or weft-stretch fabrics stretch in *one* direction only.

When choosing and using stretch fabrics, use patterns designed for stretch fabric, and follow pattern instructions carefully. Use a stretch-stitch for sewing, if possible. If lining is necessary, it should be a jersey fabric.

SELF-LINED FABRICS

These were once called *bonded fabrics.* Some original bonded fabrics were stiff and gave garments a blown-up appearance. Today, self-lining allows fabric to be manufactured for its appearance only. The fabric is easy to handle because of the self-lining process. Experienced seamstresses have tested self-lined fabrics and found many advantages.
Save Time, Money—You only cut one fabric and lining. Both are purchased for the price of fabric alone. The fabric resists fraying, which reduces the need for finishing edges. Making hand or machine buttonholes is easier.
Better Stitch Retention—The fabric moves more easily over the needleplate of the machine. Patterns and checks cannot twist out of shape because the fabric is stable. It retains a soft, fluid drape.

Keeps Shape—Garments made in self-lined fabrics keep their shape and retain their tailored look longer. Creasing and bagging are resisted through properties built into the fabric by the self-lining process.
Helps Beginners—A professional finish can be accomplished because the fabric is easy to handle. Many self-lined fabrics drape and handle easily, and it is hard to guess they are self-lined. Many sewers use extra lining to give an expensive, professional finish to the inside of the garment.

INFORMATION TAGS

Make an information tag for every garment you sew. Unless details are written down, you might forget vital care information for the fabric. Information tags can be hung together or attached to the hanger used for that garment.

Write down all useful information. Include fiber content, fabric construction, any special finishes, trim information, ironing instructions and any other pertinent data.

ESTIMATING FABRIC QUANTITIES

It may be useful to make a quick calculation of the amount of fabric needed for a garment. Estimating fabric quantities depends on the fabric width, but use the following approximate measures for 36-inch-wide fabric. Extra fabric is needed for stripes, checks and nap. If you are uncertain, do a pattern layout for the exact length required.
Dress—Measure the length from the nape of the neck to the desired hemline. Double this, and add 5-1/4 inches for seam allowances and hem. Short sleeves need an additional 18 inches, long sleeves 27 inches. A full skirt needs one extra waist-to-hem length.
Skirt—Measure from the waist to the desired hemline. Double this, and add 5-1/4 inches for finishing edges and hem.
Blouse—Measure from the nape of the neck to the waist. Double this, and add 13 inches for the tail. Add 18 inches for short sleeves, 27 inches for long sleeves.
Nightgown—Measure from the nape of the neck to the desired hemline, and double this. Add 5-1/4 inches for finishing edges and hem. Add 18 inches for short sleeves, 27 inches for long sleeves.
Housecoat—This is the same measurement as for a nightgown. Calculate three times the total length.
Pajamas—Measure from the nape of the neck to the jacket hemline. Measure pant length. Double the jacket length, and add 5-1/4 inches. Add this measurement to the doubled pant length, plus 5-1/4 inches and enough for sleeves as above.

TRIMS FOR DECORATION

There are many ways to make clothes interesting and original. Adding trims for decoration can transform a garment from plain to personal. A lifeless-looking fabric can be made more exciting by adding braid, ribbon, lace or appliqué. A remnant can be made pretty by using trim. Outdated garments can be updated with new, stylish trim.

Whatever trim you choose, it should complement the fabric and style of the garment. A heavy, embroidered braid on a richly textured evening dress loses its impact and looks tasteless. Creative use of trim on a plain dress can give the garment an exotic look.

Avoid fussy or frilly trim on casual or tailored clothes. Use simple braid or ribbon. Evening wear can carry elaborate trim, beading and feathers in the traditional manner or more unusual ways.

Use simple trim with elaborate fabrics and styles. Use elaborate trim with simple fabrics and styles. Look in upholstery departments for trims with unusual textures. Make your own if your sewing machine can do this.

SIMPLE RULES

Do not detract from the line of the garment by adding decorations in odd places. Use trim to emphasize the line and any unusual features without spoiling the balance of the style. Never add bright decoration at figure-fault points. It emphasizes them.

Decide before you cut out a garment when the decoration will be added. Some are added during construction, and some are added after.

Use trims of the same type of fabric as the garment, such as cotton trim on cotton fabric. Sew trim with the correct type of thread. When this is not possible, such as when cotton braid is applied to a man-made fabric, preshrink the braid before use. If you do not pay attention to these details, the garment may pucker after washing.

Test-stitch scraps of fabric and trim before sewing trim to the garment. If there are any problems, these can be dealt with without spoiling the garment.

SUITABLE TRIM

Hand-Embroidery—This is easily done on most fabrics. It often takes the form of a design embroidered on collar, cuffs or belt. It can also be used to decorate a complete section of the garment before it is cut out.

If large areas are embroidered, do it *before* cutting or sewing the garment section. Otherwise the garment will be overhandled and will look soiled, even before it is worn. Embroidery is easier to do on a small piece of fabric.

Iron or chalk the design on a piece of fabric slightly larger than the garment section. Mark the outline of the garment pattern piece on the fabric, and work the embroidery inside this outline.

Support the fabric and keep it smooth while embroidering. Tack a piece of fine muslin or organdy on the wrong-side of the area. Use a fine, non-woven interlining.

Backing fabric can be cut away on some fabrics after the embroidery is complete. On other fabrics, it is better to leave it and include it in the construction of the garment.

A chemical gauze can also be used. It pulls apart easily by gentle tearing. It may also be ironed off with a warm iron after embroidery is complete. It provides support while the work is being done.

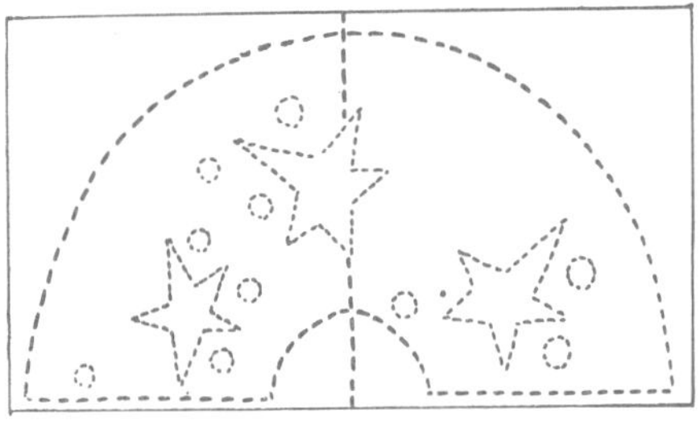

Small motifs may be embroidered after the garment is made. If fabric needs support, use a backing. On finished collars and cuffs, there is usually an interfacing and two layers of fabric. This is enough support.

Saddle-Stitching—This trim is used on tailored or casual sportswear. It is easy to do on a finished garment. Evenly spaced running-stitches, usually 1/4 to 3/8 inch long, are used to emphasize collar edges, pockets and other parts of the garment. A contrasting color is often used.

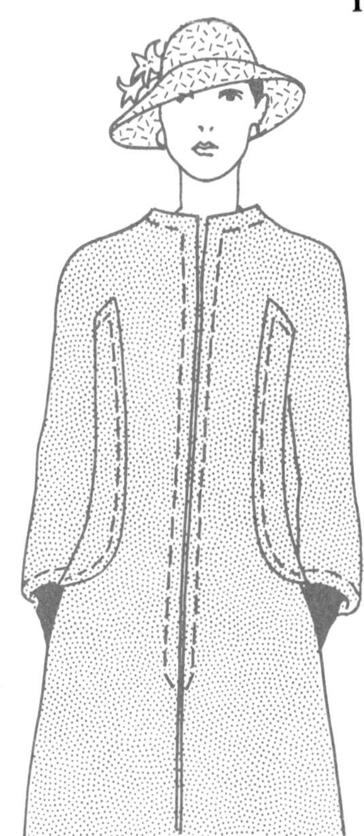

Decorative Tacks—Use these for strength and for decorating pockets and pleats.

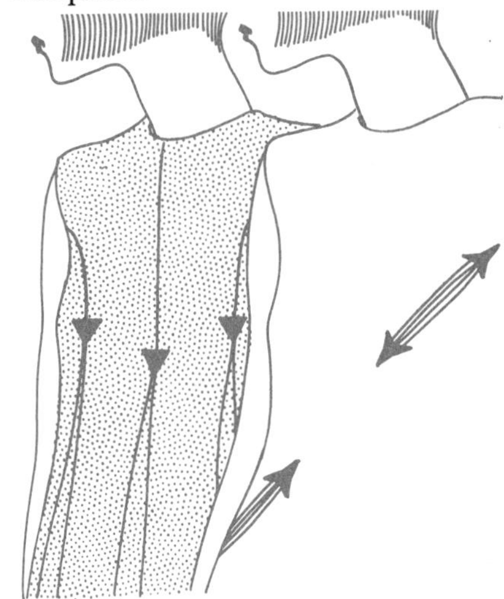

Machine-Embroidery—This is done the same way as hand-embroidery. A sewing machine makes a stitch with strong pull when it is set on embroidery-stitch. It may pinch the fabric into puckers unless it is well-supported, so use a backing. The top tension can be slackened to eliminate puckering, but this is not usually sufficient. Use non-woven interfacing, iron-on interfacing, organdy or a firm fabric of similar weight for backing.

Tack or pin backing to the wrong-side of the fabric to be embroidered. Trace tack or chalk guidelines for the design on the right-side of the fabric. When an elaborate design is required, draw it on tracing paper first. Put the paper in position on the fabric. Machine-stitch from the top to transfer the design in line-stitching to the fabric.

A variety of thread is available. For a bold effect, two threads may be threaded through the eye of the needle and used as one. If a heavy needle is selected, use a thread to give the effect of peasant embroidery.

Fine wool may be wound on a spool and used if the needle is big enough. Metallic thread can be beautiful on evening wear. Rows of automatic embroidery stitches may be grouped together to give a braided effect.

Experiment with machine-embroidery stitches. Some companies publish books of ideas, showing ways to group or mix embroidery stitches to give interesting effects.

Match the thread to the fabric. If this is not possible, preshrink yarn by winding it loosely by hand on a separate spool. Immerse it in soapy water for a minute or two, rinse and allow to dry. Rewind the thread on the original spool.

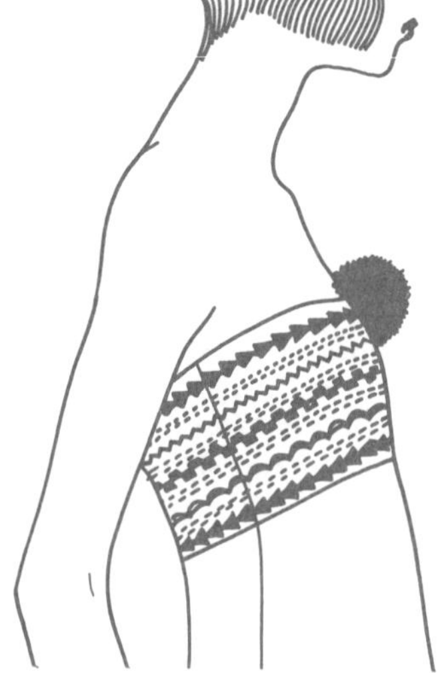

FREE EMBROIDERY

If you have an idea for a design, use the free-embroidery technique. The feed dog on the sewing machine is covered or dropped. Fabric is put in an embroidery hoop to hold it taut.

Remove the sewing foot. The machine is used without any type of foot. With many machines, there is a darning-embroidery foot that can be used. But this may block vision when making detailed designs.

On heavy fabrics, it may not be necessary to use an embroidery hoop. But results are usually better with one.

With machine-embroidery, the needle and thread make the design. This is done by moving the hoop back and forth, from side to side, or in circles or scrolls. If the work is not moved, the machine just stitches in one spot.

The foot take-up lever must be *down* before sewing. Without the foot, it is easy to forget to put it down. Leaving it up results in tangled thread.

The straight-stitch or zigzag-stitch machine may also be used for machine-embroidery. With practice, some lovely designs can be made. Move the hoop smoothly and slowly, and keep the machine running fairly fast.

TOP-STITCHING BY MACHINE

Top-stitching is a popular, simple way to decorate completed garments. It emphasizes the line or details of a garment. It is also used when making some pockets, collars and pleats to keep seams and edges in place.

Use thread in a matching or contrasting color on your sewing machine. Test the stitch length, pressure and tension on a scrap of fabric. Use the same number of layers as for the final garment stitching.

Top-stitching must be parallel to the edge. Use a guide, and stitch slowly and carefully. If necessary, chalk or thread trace the line before starting. Pivot the work at corners. Sew in the threads at the ends for a neat look. Top-stitching may be worked by hand, but it is slow and time consuming.

MONOGRAM

One way to personalize a garment is to use a monogram. It may be machine-embroidered or hand-embroidered in a satin stitch. Initials may be purchased ready-to-stitch or embroidered directly on the garment. Back the fabric area to give it support and to avoid distortion.

Iron-on transfers are available or you may design your own initials. Do this on tracing paper. Transfer the outline to the fabric with thread-traced lines or tailor's chalk. If the monogram is machine-stitched, use an embroidery hoop to hold fabric taut. Do not stretch it. Use a satin-stitch or another embroidery stitch. Refer to your sewing-machine handbook. Monograms may also be made using the appliqué method.

SMOCKING

This is a method of controlling and decorating full areas, such as yokes and cuffs. Extra fabric is needed to

create many close folds on which smocking stitches are worked. See the section on *Gathering and Shirring,* page 119.

Most smocking is done by hand in a combination of single stitches, such as cable or honeycomb. See the section on *Stitches and Threads,* page 67.

It is possible to simulate hand-smocking. Decorative machine-stitching is used on top of rows of shirring. Prepare the garment area as described in the section on *Gathering and Shirring,* page 119.

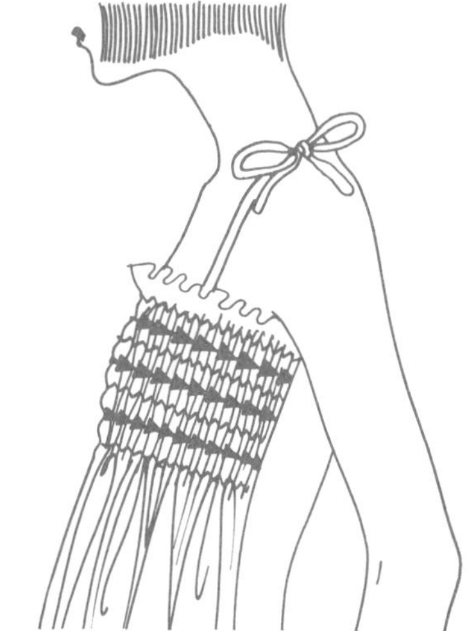

QUILTING

Complete garment sections or small areas of a garment may be quilted as a decoration, to add warmth, or both. There are several methods of quilting two or more layers of fabric. Fabric may also be purchased already quilted.

Quilt the fabric before you cut out garment pieces. The garment fabric, a padded inner layer and a backing fabric are sandwiched together and held with stitching.

Stitching may be straight rows, squares or diamonds. It may outline the fabric patterns and produce a raised, padded effect. Carefully pin and tack all layers together before sewing. With slippery fabric, all-over tacking at intervals may be needed.

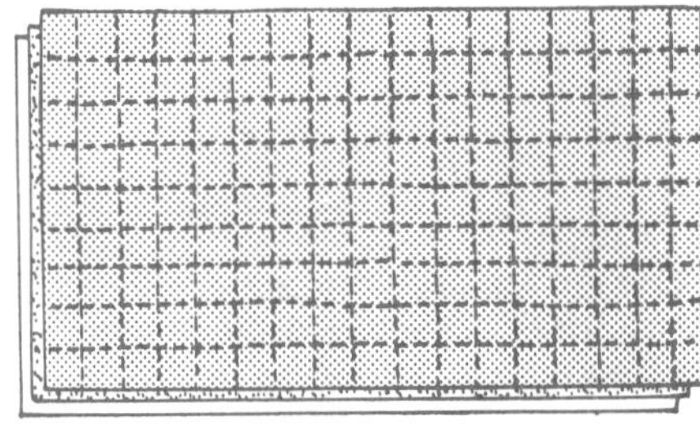

When machine-quilting in rows, use a quilting guide if it is supplied with the machine. This helps line up each row with the previous one and keeps lines parallel and equidistant. *Trapunto quilting* leaves the background unpadded so the design stands out.

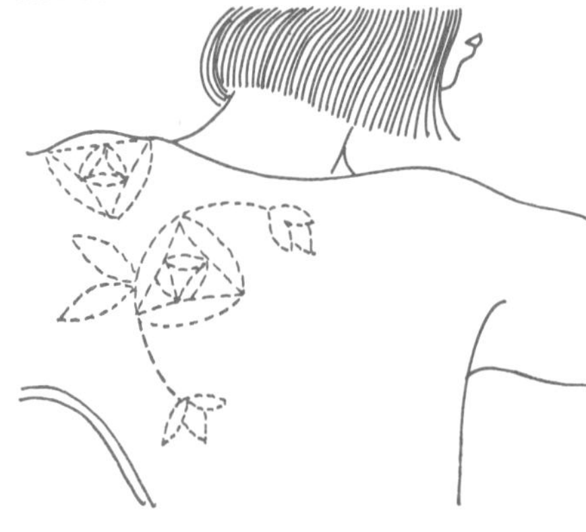

Create your own design or buy a special quilting transfer. Back the area to be quilted with a firm, soft fabric. Stitch the outline of the design with small running-stitches. This forms a pocket that needs padding. To pad it, thread thick strands of matching thread through a bodkin. These threads are passed back and forth through the backing fabric until the whole area is padded.

A slit can also be made in the backing. Padding is pushed through the slit and positioned in the pocket. The slit is sewn up, and the finished effect is similar to the pocket type.

Another way to quilt is to place the padding in position with backing under the area to be quilted. The padding is eased out so there is little bulk on the stitching lines.

APPLIQUÉ

When you appliqué, separate pieces of fabric are positioned on the top of fabric and stitched in place by hand or machine. Make appliqués from firm fabric that does not fray. Motifs can be purchased, but it is less expensive to make them. Ideas can be collected from many sources.

Patches can be appliquéd as decoration, or to strengthen or repair a garment. Use contrasting or patterned fabrics. See the section on *Repair of Clothes* for methods of attaching patches, page 77.

Appliqué by Hand—Draw or trace the design on a piece of fabric. Apply a piece of lightweight, iron-on interfacing to the wrong-side of the fabric. This prevents fraying and keeps the applique in shape. Sew a row of fine stitches around the outline before trimming the design to shape. Tack the motif in place, then blanket-stitch it in position with contrasting or matching thread.

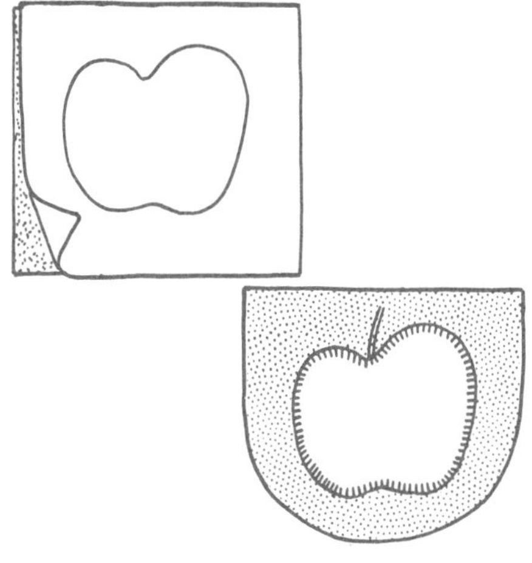

An alternative way to finish the edges is to turn raw edges to the wrong-side along the outline. Slip-stitch the motif in position. With this method, backing comes only as far as the stitching line. This makes turning easy.

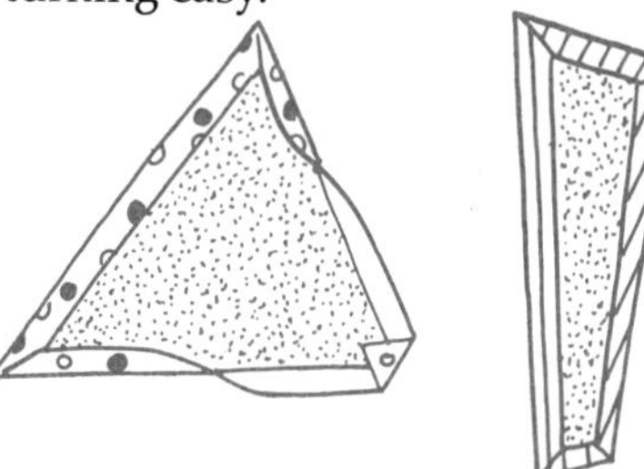

Appliqué by Machine—Draw your design on tracing paper. Leave a seam allowance. Pin the paper to the fabric, and machine-stitch around the outline. Pull the paper away. If the design requires only one layer of applied fabric, the procedure is simple. Position the fabric on the right-side, and pin or tack it in place. From the *wrong-side,* using the machine-traced outline, stitch the fabric in place using a straight-stitch.

On the right-side, cut away excess fabric outside the stitching line. Use a satin- or embroidery-stitch to stitch the outline from the right-side to enclose cut edges.

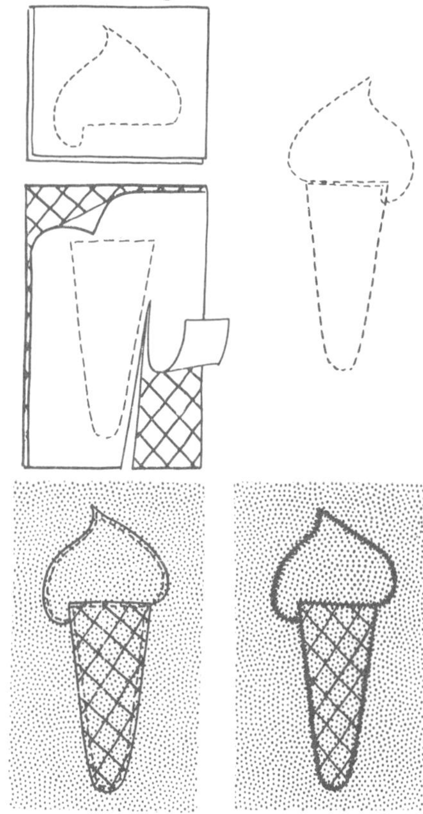

When applying more than one layer of fabric, apply them in the correct order. Smaller details in the design are added at the end.

Heat Bonded—You can purchase fusible interfacing to put between the appliqué and garment. When ironed, it fuses or bonds the appliqué to the garment. This helps eliminate fraying during cutting and sewing stages.

BRAID AND RIBBON

There are many braids and ribbons available. They are narrow, wide, flat, textured, plain and fancy.

Flat Ribbon Braid and Grosgrain—These may be stitched in place by hand or machine along both edges. Instead of stitching ribbon to a garment, use it to close an opening, as fringe, as a sash around the waist, for basket-weave sleeves, or for crosses or rosebuds on an outfit.

When applying braid, start and finish where ends do not show. Sew an end before sewing it on a garment. Tack the required length in place.

Bands of braid and ribbon may be inserted between two garment pieces during construction. Ribbon can also be used to lengthen a garment that is too short.

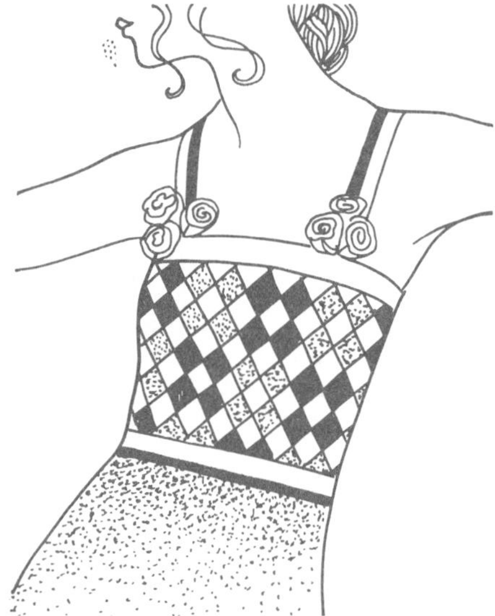

A wide braid or ribbon may need two rows of stitching close to the edges. Narrow ones may be stitched in place with one row of zigzag-stitches. Different embroidery stitches in matching or contrasting colors may also be used.

The decorative effect may be improved if more than one row or color of braid is used. When starting and finishing the sewing, overcast the braid ends. Turn them under 1/4 inch. Sew in place with tiny, hidden slip-stitches to finish.

Soutache Braid—This is narrow, bias-woven braid. It is often used to outline a round design or style line, or to create a peasant look.

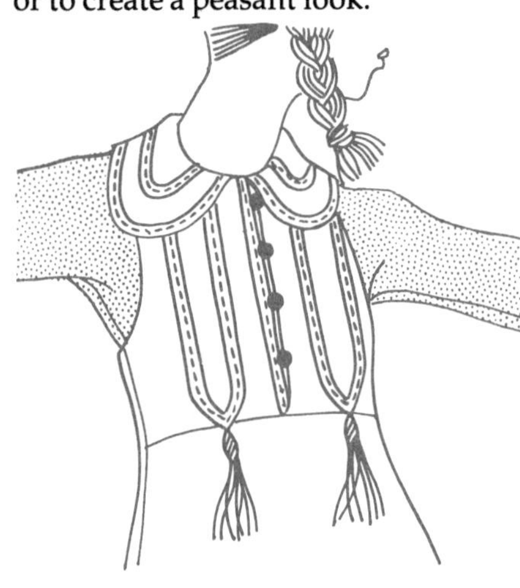

Stitch it in place with one row of stitching down the middle. Mark the design in chalk or thread tracing, and tack the braid in place. Slip-stitch or machine-stitch the braid on the garment. When machine-stitching, use a see-through embroidery foot.

Embroidered Braid—This is treated in the same way as plain ribbon. Choose braid to complement fabric color. Be selective when choosing patterned braid to go on a patterned fabric. If in doubt, don't use it.

Metallic Braid—This braid is attractive on evening clothes. Many effects can be created by combining metallic braid with ruffles, bows and machine-embroidery.

Rickrack—Rickrack is not expensive and is available in many colors and sizes. Use many rows together, or wind two pieces around one another to form one braid.

Rickrack is available in a mat finish for day wear or shining metallic for evening clothes. To apply it, stitch straight along the center or slip-stitch it in place along either edge. It may be necessary to catch down only the points.

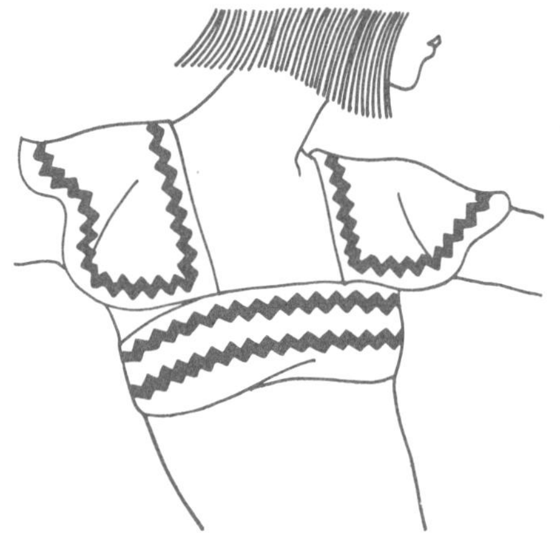

Rickrack may be inserted in seams or used under the edges of garment sections so only the points show. Match thread to the rickrack when only surface stitching is used.

Folded Braid—This is also called *military braid.* It is available in wool, rayon or man-made fibers. It is ideal for finishing raw edges on cuffs, collars and other edges. Folded braid may be pressed into curves for round edges. It is usually available only in plain, unpatterned colors.

BOWS AND TIES

A pretty bow can alter the character of a garment. Last year's fashions can be updated with the addition of a bow or tie. With bows and belts in different colors, one outfit can have many different looks.

Bows and ties can be made from many types of fabric—knit, woven, glittery or plain. Satin and grosgrain ribbon can be used for flat bows. Extra fabric may be used for bows and ties.

A plain shirt with a bow or tie at the neck can look smart. Attach the bow to a length of elastic—neckties may also be attached this way. It eliminates an extra layer of fabric around the neck.

Bows may be made from fabric on the straight or bias grain. Turn in all raw edges, and finish neatly. The bow should suit the garment.

Patterns are available for bows and ties in a variety of styles.

Tieing a Bow—To make a neat bow, tie a single knot in the usual way, keeping the two ends even in length. Make the first loop with the lower piece. Bring the other end down and around the first loop, making a knot. Hold the first loop in place. Make a second loop, and pull it through. Both loops can be pulled tight so the bow is even in size. The two loose ends are about even. Arrange the knot so it lies flat.

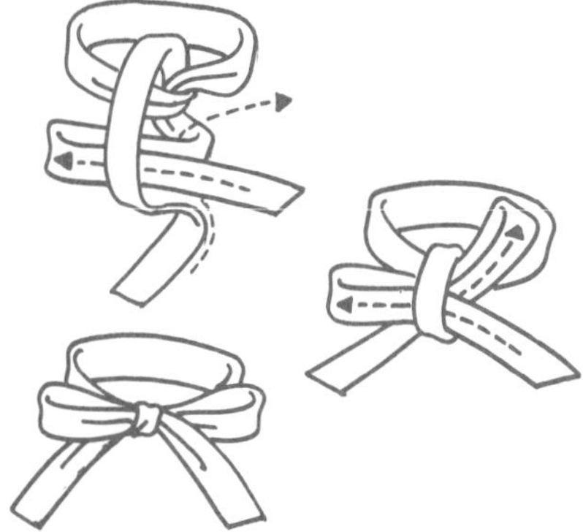

Making Tailored Bow—This bow is made and permanently sewn together, not retied each time the garment is worn. Use a finely woven ribbon, or sew a piece of the garment fabric in a flat tube. See the rouleau method in the section on *Fastenings*, page 114.

Cut a length of ribbon twice the required width of the finished bow. Fold it and stitch across about halfway from the fold. Flatten the loop so stitching lies on the center fold. Tack in place, and press lightly. Take a shorter piece of ribbon and fold it around the center of the bow. Stitch in place at the back.

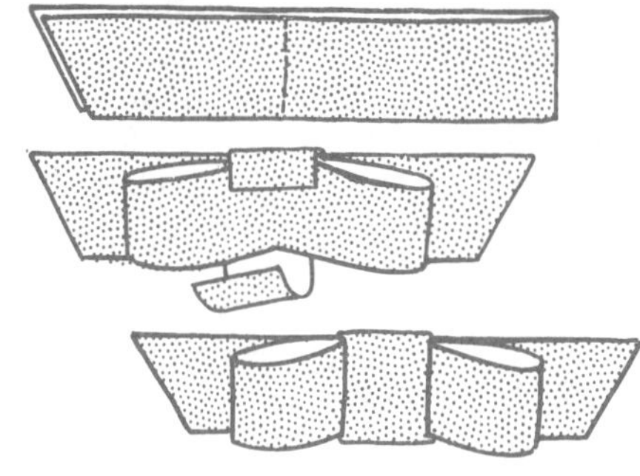

FRINGE, TASSELS, POMPONS

Purchased fringe and tassels can be more economical than handmade ones, especially if a large quantity is needed. Most lampshade fringing is reasonably priced. If used cleverly, it is not recognized for what it is on an article of clothing.

Add fringe to the edge of stoles or ponchos to give them a luxurious look for evening wear. Fringe often looks best in two or more rows.

To make fringe, wind a number of yarns around a length of heavy, folded paper the depth of the fringe required. Insert a piece of seam binding along one edge. When enough yarn has been wound, sew two or three rows of machine-stitching along one edge through yarn, tape and paper.

Perforations made by the needle allow the paper to be torn away after stitching. The loops that are left may be cut. Many paper sections must be joined to make a long length. This may be an expensive project, so be sure the style or color fringe you need is not available commercially.

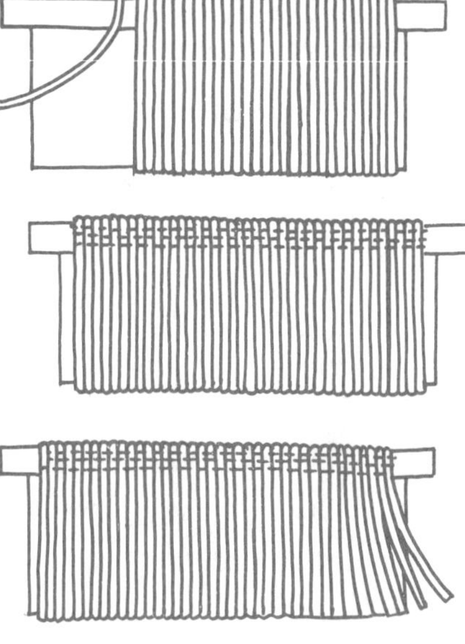

Self-Fringe—Most soft, thick fabrics can have threads pulled out to make a self-fringe. Try it on a scrap of fabric to see if the effect is attractive. Use a guide to straighten the edge to be fringed. Cut along the guide. Decide how deep the fringe needs to be, then pull out a cross thread on this line.

Machine-stitch with a narrow zigzag-stitch along this line. Lengthwise threads are secured in place. Pull out all crosswise threads below the stitching.

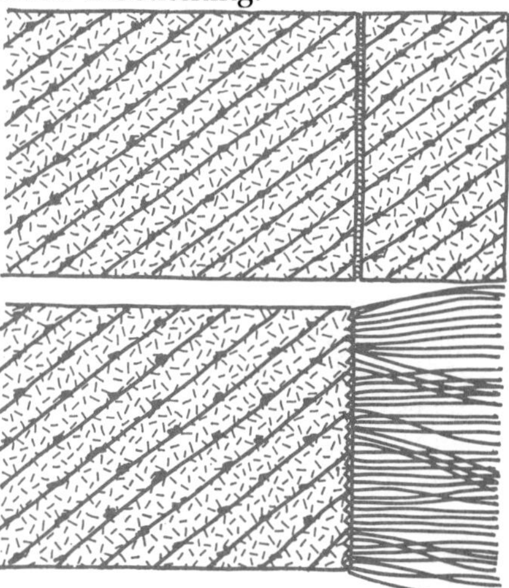

Fringe Made with Sewing Machine— The rug fork available with some sewing machines may also be used to make fringe. Yarn is wound around the fork, then stitched. Use a zipper foot to sew fringe directly on seam tape as each section is wound. After one section is stitched, the fork is carefully moved until it is almost out of the loops. The

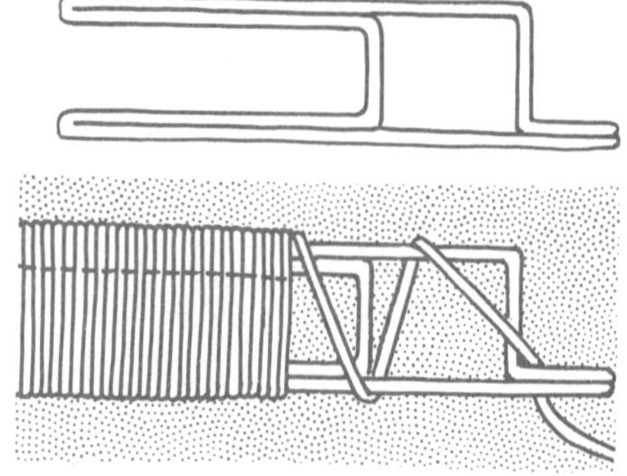

exposed part of the fork is rewound. Loops are stitched down. This is repeated until the required amount has been made. Fringe may be left as loops or cut.

Fringe may be applied under or over an edge, depending on the effect required. If it is applied under an edge, slip-stitch it in place on both edges of the supporting band. If surface application is required, hand- or machine-stitch it, using matching thread.

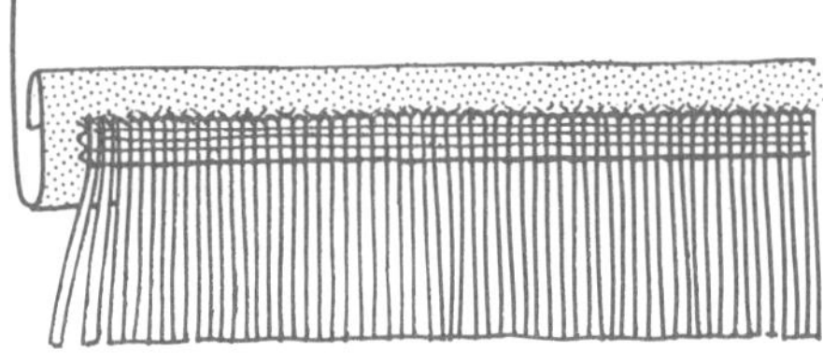

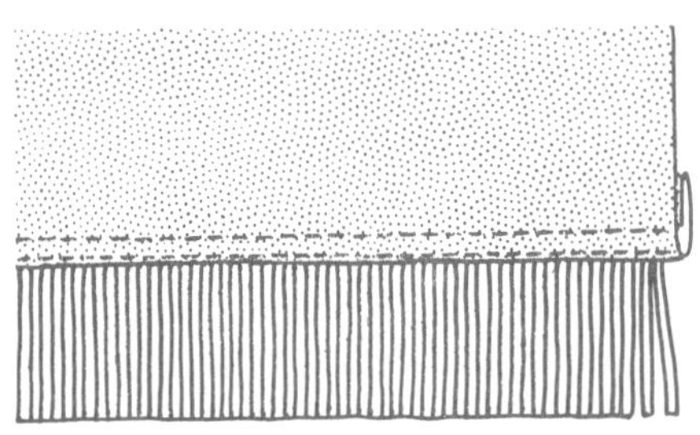

Tassels—Tassels may be purchased or made, and applied singly or in rows. To make tassels, cut a piece of cardboard the required width. Lay a double strand of the yarn across the top of the card. Wind yarn around the card until there is enough to make a tassel. Tie the double strand around the yarn, and remove the card. Tie another double thread around the yarn about 1/2 inch below the top. Cut the lower loops.

Pompons—Make pompons the same way as tassels but use more yarn. Or wind the yarn around two or three fingers, and tie yarn in the middle. Cut both ends.

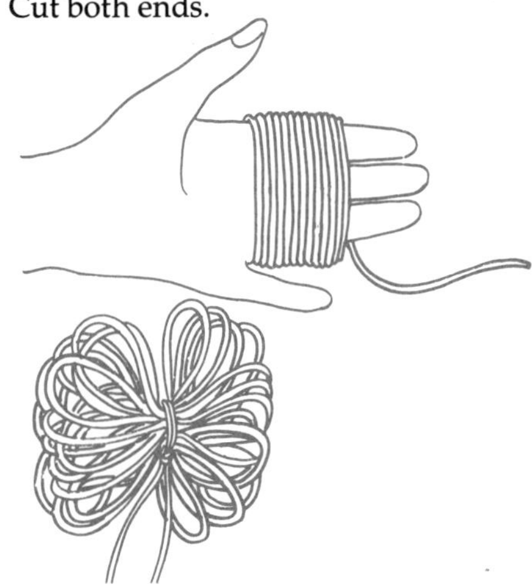

Large, fluffy pompons are often made of yarn and used to trim knit scarves and hats. Cut two thick cardboard circles the diameter of the pompon needed. Cut a smaller circle from the middle. If this circle is too large, a lot of yarn is needed, and the pompon becomes heavy.

With the two pieces together, wind yarn around the circle until the center hole is almost closed up. Thread the yarn through a bodkin, and keep winding. Cut strands at the outer edge, and gently push the two pieces of cardboard apart. Cut a new piece of doubled yarn or strong thread. Tie it tightly around all the threads at the center, between the two pieces of cardboard. Pull the cardboard away.

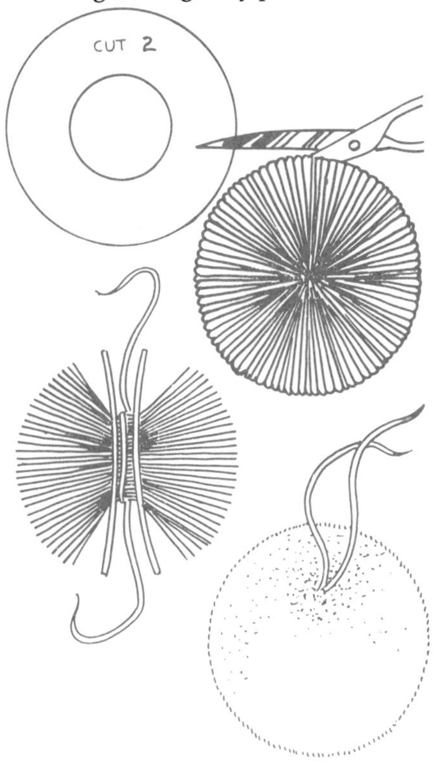

Leave a long end on this thread to sew on the pompon. Carefully arrange the cut ends to make a round, fluffy ball. Trim straggly ends.

FUR AND FEATHERS

Real or imitation fur trim can be purchased by the yard in many qualities and widths. If real fur is used, make it detachable because it cannot be dry-cleaned. Sew snaps to the lining of the trim and the garment where it needs securing. Fur collars and cuffs may be purchased ready-made, then slip-stitched in place.

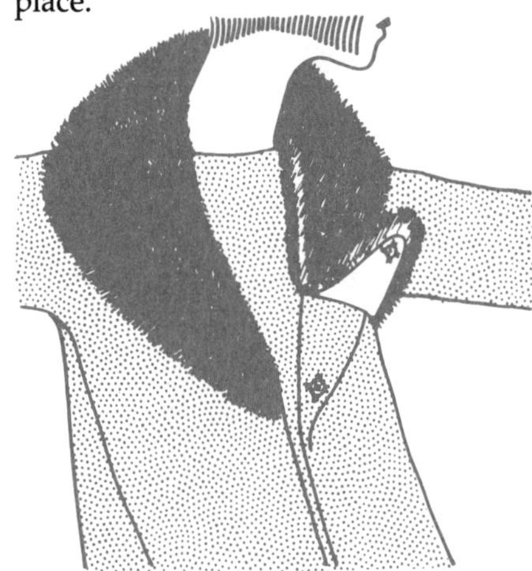

Down and feathers can be purchased by the yard or in strips. They are ready to be stitched to the garment. They need to be secured by the stem at intervals so feathers or down may be eased out to hide stitches. Feathers are available in many shades and make a plain garment look exotic.

LACE

Lace is available in many styles. It can be gathered, re-embroidered, pleated or as edging. Lace comes in many motifs. It is available in cotton or nylon, and in many colors. It can be combined with other trims, such as ribbon, for a pretty effect.

Fine lace is used on lingerie and baby clothes. Thick lace looks beautiful on special-occasion clothes. Lace may be used on collars, cuffs and hems, around pockets and inserted between seams. Joined-lace motifs may be purchased by the yard and cut in individual sections. Lace can be used according to the effect you want to achieve.

Decide whether lace should be applied by hand or machine. Most simple lace bands or edgings may be attached to the fabric using a narrow machine zigzag-stitch. If there is a transparent embroidery foot with your machine, use it to see where stitches fall.

Hem or roll the cut end of the lace. To join lace, use a plain seam. Trim edges to 1/8 inch and overcast. Or use a fine French seam if you cannot overcast on your machine. The best way to join lace is to lap the edges to be joined. Place them so there is no break in the design. If there is a pronounced motif in the overlap, cut around it and whip-stitch it to the underlayer.

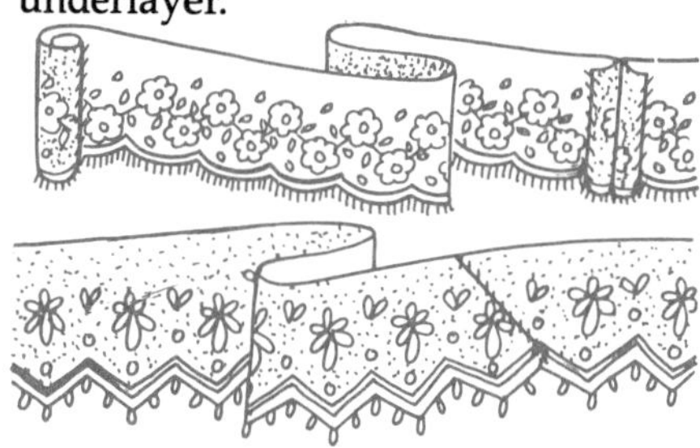

One motif will be double. On the sewing machine, use a narrow zigzag-stitch to sew the double lace together. Excess fabric may be cut away at the back.

If the edges of the lace band are straight, sew the band by machine. If edges are curved or scalloped, it is easier to hand-stitch lace in place. Stitches should be invisible and encase the edge of the lace.

Lace on blouses and dresses is popular. The lace is tacked in position and stitched by hand or machine, depending on whether the edges are straight or curved. If a zigzag-stitch is used, the fabric underneath is cut away along the

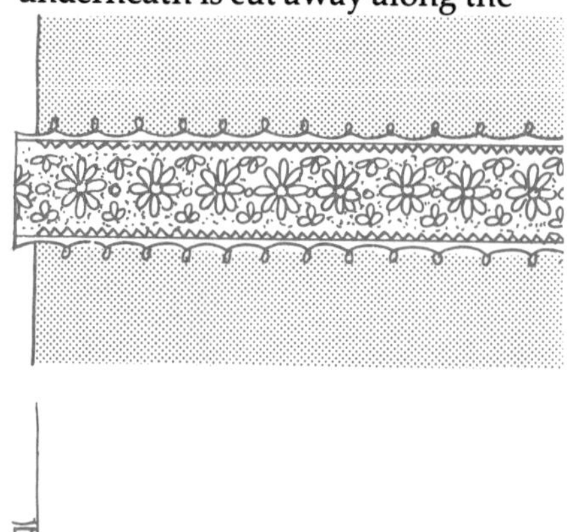

edge of the stitches. If a straight-stitch is used, cut fabric along the middle. Finish edges, and press up toward the garment fabric. When lace is applied to a corner, miter it on the inside edge, or gather it so it lies flat.

Lace may be purchased already gathered or pleated. This can also be done at home. On some lace, a thread may be drawn up along one edge. Lace can be gathered by machine, using the bottom thread to draw up the fullness, or with a gathering foot. To pleat, use the pleating attachment available with some sewing machines. Use enough lace when a gathered effect is required or the result may look skimpy. Use at least 2-1/2 times the required length.

LEATHER AND SUEDE

Real or imitation leather may be used to trim a garment with simple patches, bands, binding and thonging. Suede and real leather are available in beautiful colors—some are even washable. Real leather is available in squares and whole skins, but not by the yard.

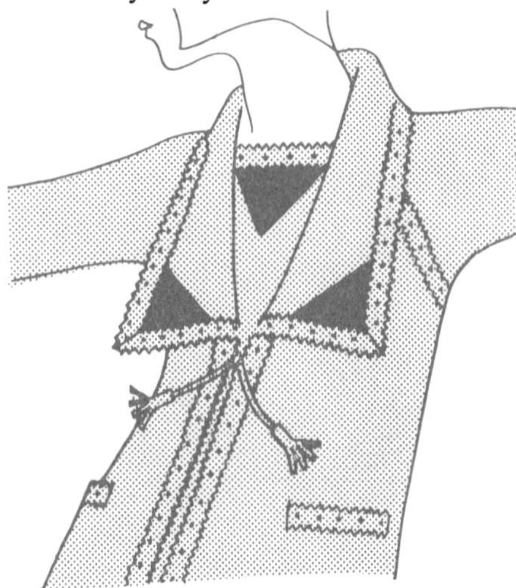

Choose a simple design for the trim. Appliqué it to the surface of the garment. Buy ready-made thonging or cut narrow strips and thread through eyelets in the garment.

PATCHWORK

Leftover fabric scraps can be sewn together in patchwork belts, pockets and other finishes to trim a plain garment. Choose a combination of colors and shapes for the best effect, and experiment before sewing.

FRILLS

There are many frilled and pleated trims available in many widths. Some frills are embroidered. Frilling is usually inserted in a band, which may be concealed under the edge of the fabric. It is sewn by machine or hand, using a slip-stitch, depending on the desired effect.

Nearly all fine fabrics may be frilled or pleated. For frilling, one side of the fabric strip may be gathered. The free edge can be hemmed or rolled. A jersey fabric may have a lettuce edge for an extra-full effect.

Finish the fabric strip on either side. Gathering or pleating can be done along the center line. The ruffle is stitched to the garment along the center gathering line. Use fabric on the straight or true bias. Cut the width of the frill required, plus finished edges. Frills may also be made with scalloped edges, or edges can be bound with a contrasting or matching binding.

An attractive edge may be made by using the scallop embroidery-stitch. This is found on some automatic machines. Fold the edge of the fabric under the stitch as you work it along the edge. By doing this, the edge is strong. It is not necessary to cut around scallops.

SEQUINS AND BEADS

Sequins and beads may be purchased loose, in packages, in strands or on motifs. Strands and motifs are probably the fastest and easiest to handle. Strands can be stitched in any design. Mark the design in chalk or trace tack it on the fabric. Strands are attached by taking small stitches at intervals over the thread between the beads or sequins. Curves and scroll designs are easy to attach this way.

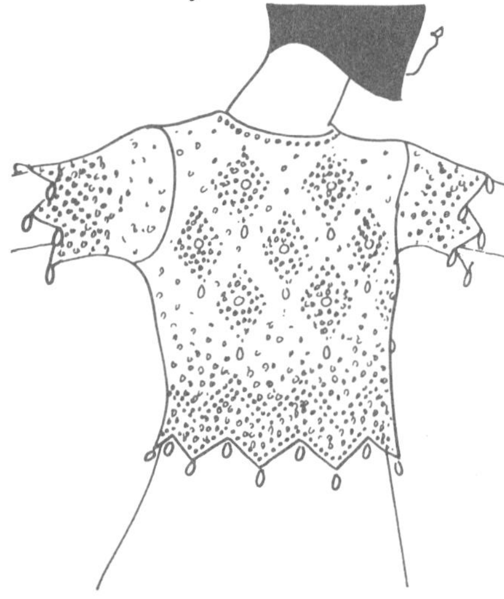

Individual sequins and beads may be used to highlight a fabric design, such as a flower center. They are attached by taking the thread through the fabric, through the hole in the bead or sequin, and back through the fabric. If closely spaced, the thread can be carried from bead to bead after securing each one. If wide apart, finish each bead or sequin individually.

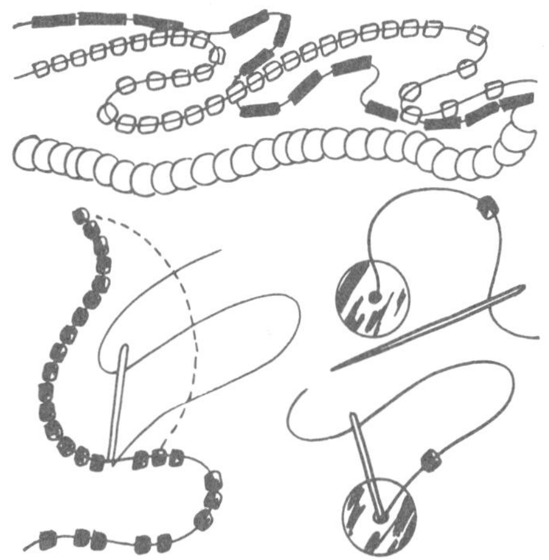

For an added effect, use beads and sequins together. Sew them with thread that matches the bead. Bring the thread up through the sequin, through the bead and back through the sequin to the wrong-side. Sequined or beaded motifs may also be slip-stitched in position.

EQUIPMENT FOR SEWING

Having and using the right equipment is important. An inexperienced sewer may try to make do, then find the finished results are disappointing.

The wide range of sewing aids available can be confusing. Begin with a basic set of good-quality equipment, and add to it. The cost of basic equipment is recovered when you make clothes instead of buying them.

A neat, well-stocked sewing box is important. A good set of supplies is economical because little is wasted.

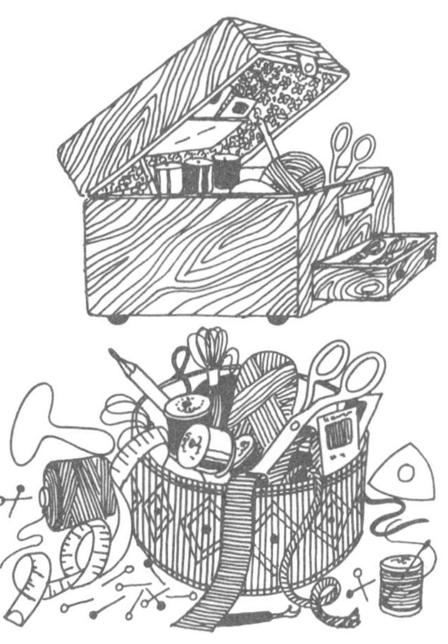

Consider where you will sew and how you will store equipment. Trying to make a garment in a cramped, messy corner is tiring, and results in poor-quality work. Not having a necessary tool when you need it can make sewing a chore, instead of a pleasure.

EQUIPMENT

SEWING AREA

Not many people have a special room for sewing. Even if it is possible, careful planning is *still* necessary because sewing can be messy. Work is often spread over a period of time. The living room is probably not the best place to sew.

For occasional mending tasks or embroidery, a small box of equipment to carry around is probably sufficient. But for someone who sews regularly, there are many things to consider when choosing and planning a suitable place.

Time and effort are saved if the project does not have to be unpacked and packed away each time you sew on it.

Good natural and artificial light is important. It is easy to make mistakes and tire your eyes in poor light. Avoid blocking the light during sewing. Use a close-work type of lamp for detailed work. When there is no source of daylight, use a high-intensity lamp or color-balanced fluorescent light.

Your cutting area should be large and flat. It may have to be the floor. Ideally, use a table at a comfortable working height. It is best to work from all four sides. Folding cutting boards marked with useful grid lines are available.

Keep a small dustpan, brush and large wastebasket in the work area.

Electrical outlets for the sewing machine, iron and lamp are necessary. You may have to use an extension cord if outlets are too far away. Keep cords safely out of the way. Do not overload an extension cord with too many appliances.

A table is needed for the sewing machine. It should be at a comfortable working height and in good light. Have enough space around the machine for fabric and tools.

A comfortable chair to support your back is necessary. Sewing can be tiring.

A place to hang unfinished garments is useful. Flat storage space is needed for fabrics and other pieces of work.

Adequate, suitable storage for sewing notions and equipment should be nearby. Have a small sewing box with a few essentials to carry around for fitting, mending, embroidering or other work.

An ironing board is necessary for pressing. If you have a full-length mirror in good light, it makes fitting easier. A three-section mirror is ideal.

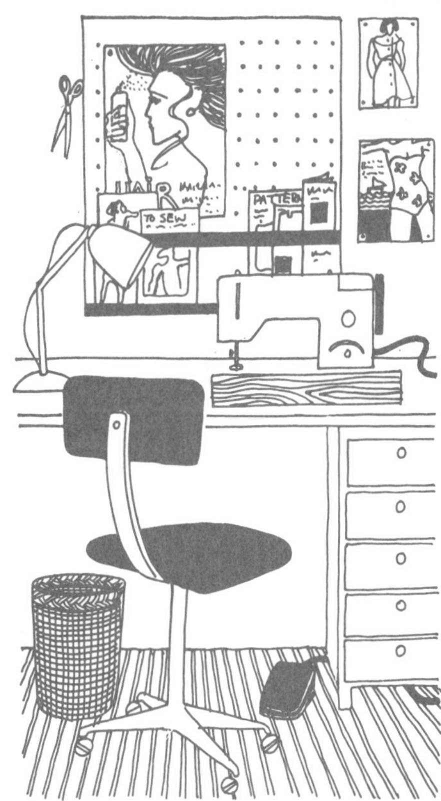

PLACES TO SEW

An alcove or large closet in a bedroom can be used as a sewing area. A corner of a room, hidden by a curtain or screen, may be converted to a sewing place. A fold-down table

can be stored in a cupboard. A large cabinet with suitable space is another way to keep your sewing area organized.

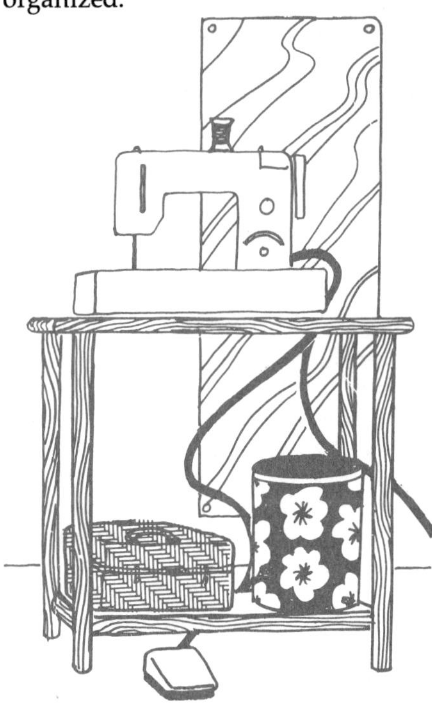

STORAGE

Fabrics, notions, patterns and books need storage. Plan where to put them before you buy anything. It is not always necessary to have special storage if drawer or shelf space is available. Strong, cardboard boxes are also good for keeping things neat.

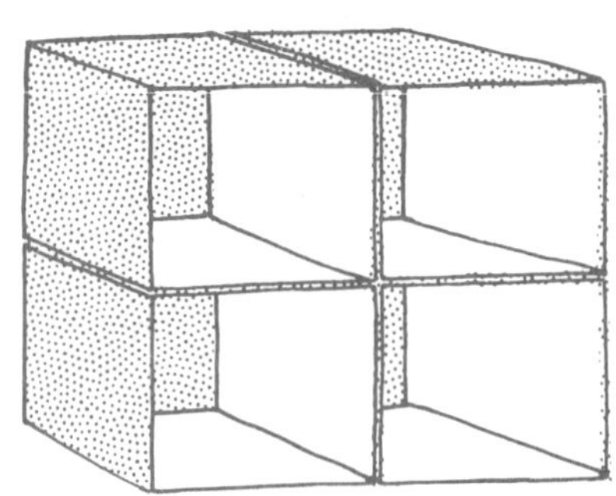

Consider each item needing storage, and try to use the correct storage method for it. Cup hooks, open shelves, pegboard, shallow and deep drawers, large envelopes, hanging rails and bags are a few of the ways you can store things. Secondhand filing cabinets can also be used for storage.

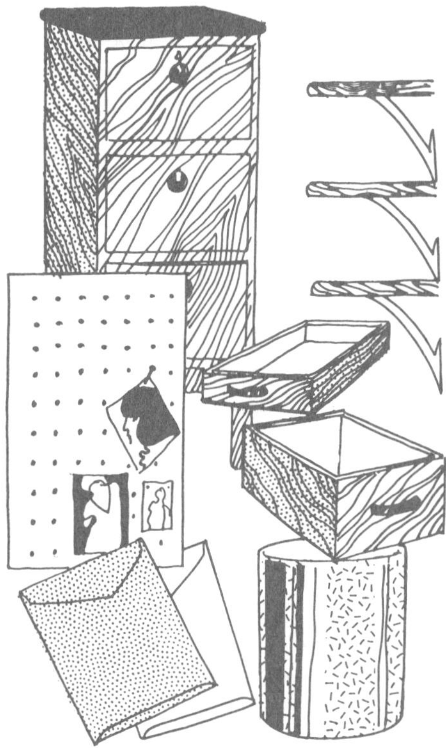

A good sewing box is useful but it can be expensive. A wicker basket or small cardboard box covered with pretty paper can work as well. Small boxes can be stacked to form open cubbyholes, and a cutlery tray helps keep equipment in order.

A sectioned, plastic box with transparent lid is another way to keep things in order. It is easy to see inside. Plastic boxes are available to hold spools of thread. A less-expensive alternative is a strip of wood with nails. Paint and label cigar boxes or coffee cans for storing small items.

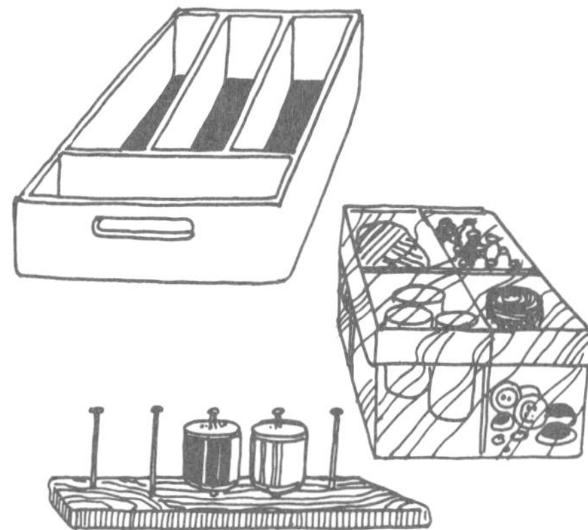

Equipment

It is not practical to list all the tools suitable for every seamstress. A suggested list is given below, and details of other sewing aids follow. Always buy the best quality you can afford. Your equipment will last if you take care of it.

Look before you buy, and try an item to be sure it is right for your needs. Keep it in good working order, ready for use. Be careful when considering buying new gadgets—you can be disappointed.

A first-aid kit is necessary for everyone who sews. When using seam rippers, pins, needles and scissors, you could have an accident. Bloodstains can ruin fabric if not dealt with immediately. It is wise to take care of yourself, too.

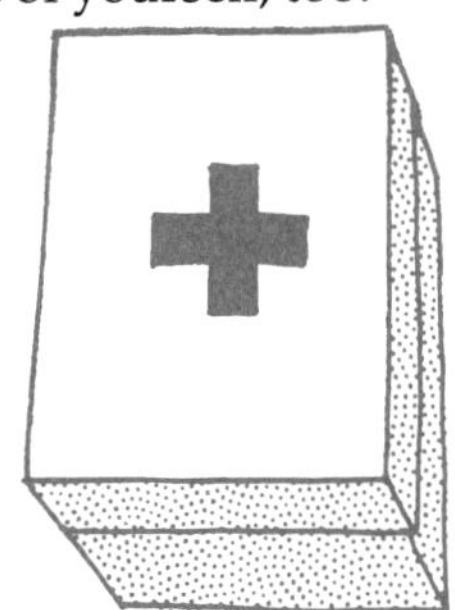

Below is a basic list of the equipment a seamstress needs. Read it over carefully before you buy anything.

1. **Sewing Machine**
2. **Pressing Equipment**
   Iron and ironing board
   Sleeve board
   Pressing cloth
   Tailor's ham
3. **Measuring and Marking Equipment**
   Tape measure
   Transparent ruler
   Yardstick
   Hem gage
   Tailor's chalk or pencil
   Pins and pincushion
4. **Cutting Equipment**
   Fabric-cutting scissors
   Paper-cutting scissors
   Embroidery scissors
   Seam ripper
5. **Needles and Threads**
   Needles for handwork
   Needles for sewing machine
   Needle case
   Needle threader
   Tacking thread
   Thread

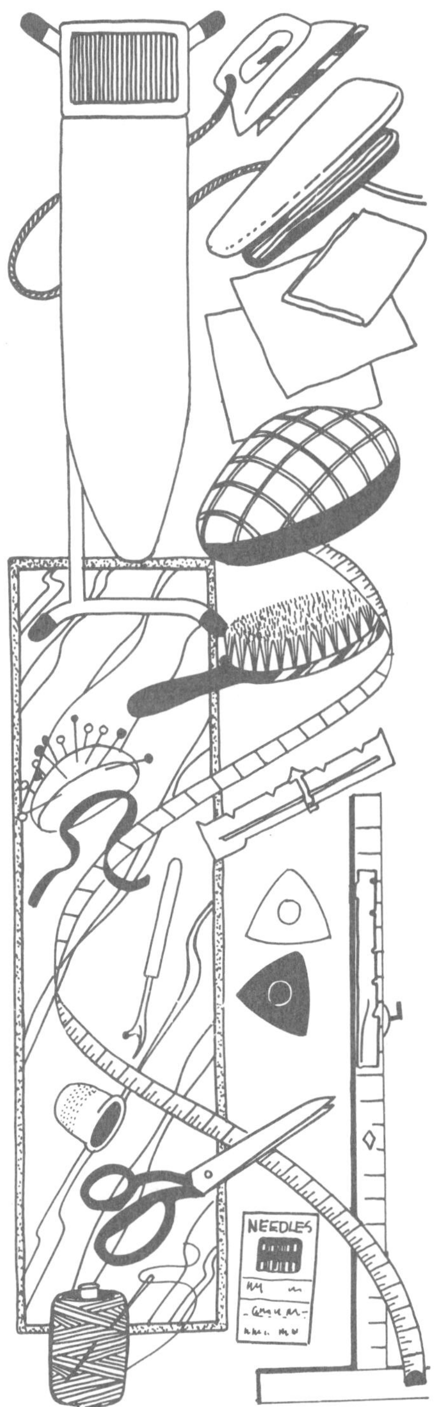

6. **Miscellaneous**
   Mirror
   Magnet
   Thimble
   Adhesive bandages

SEWING MACHINES

There are four types of sewing machines—straight-stitch, zigzag, automatic and superautomatic. A variety of attachments is available for most sewing machines.

Straight-Stitch Machine—This machine sews forward and backward and has limited use. Feed dogs may be covered or lowered for darning or free embroidery.

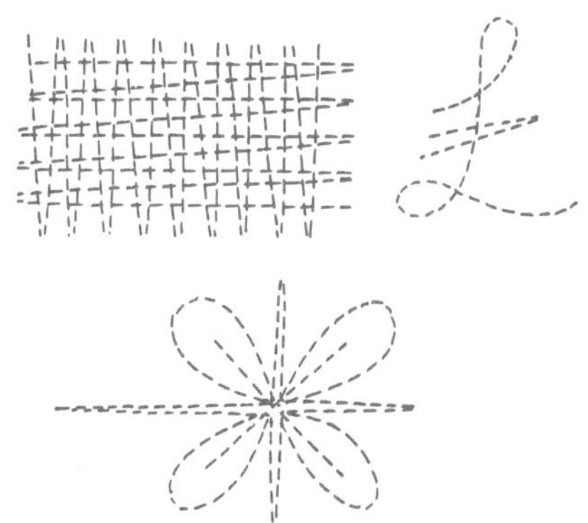

Zigzag Machine—The zigzag sewing machine has a needle that moves from left to right. A zigzag-stitch is useful for many sewing functions. It can produce simple decorative patterns when set on satin-stitch. This machine can sew buttonholes, attach buttons and overcast. It also sews simple stretch seams, and free embroidery is possible.

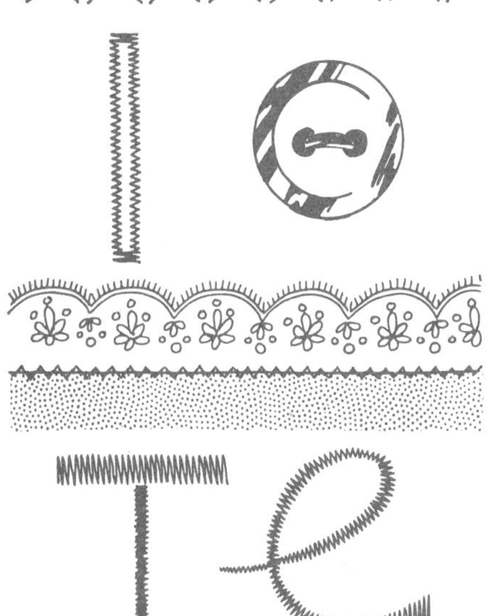

Automatic Machine—There are semiautomatic and automatic sewing machines. Semiautomatic machines have a small selection of practical stitches. The two most useful stitches are the straight- and zigzag-stitch. A step-stitch for mending and overcasting and a blind-hemstitch for jersey fabrics may be included. The machine may have two to four other stitches for finishing and stretch-sewing purposes.

Automatic models usually do the same things as semiautomatic models. They also have decorative stitch possibilities. Stitches can be changed quickly and easily on some machines because stitch patterns are built in the machine. Other machines have pattern disks. Free embroidery is often possible.

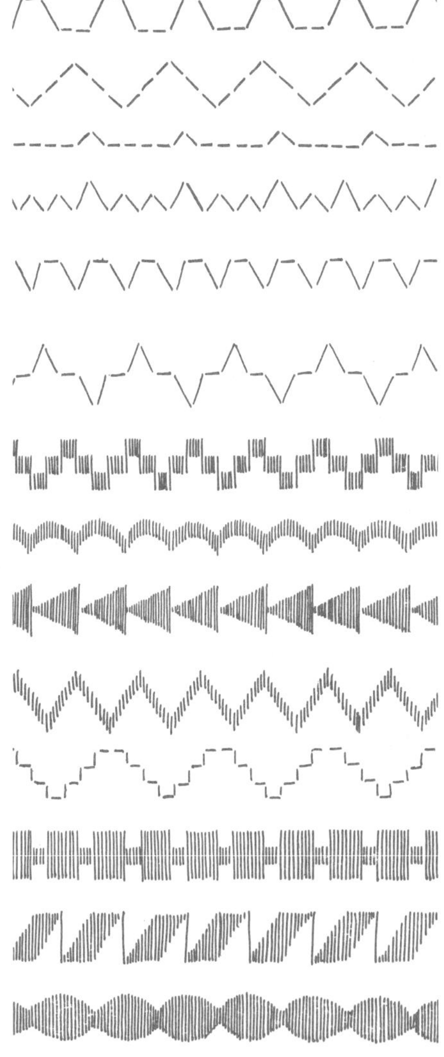

Superautomatic Machine—This machine does many different things. It can do everything other machines can do. It can also sew stitches similar to industrial machines.

Superautomatic machines help when sewing stretch fabrics. The action of the feed allows extendable stitches to be sewn that resemble hand back-stitches. The superautomatic machine can also do decorative work and free embroidery.

The most widely used, practical stretch-stitches are listed below.

Overlock-Type Stitch—This back-stitches the seam and overcasts at the same time.

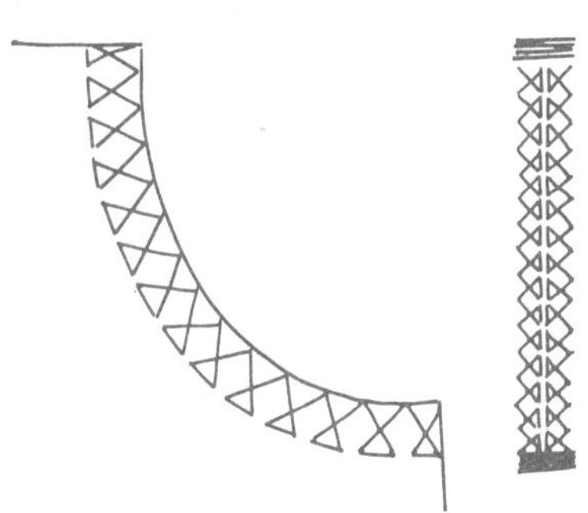

Elastic Triple Seam—Sews two stitches forward and one backward, or a similar sequence. Ideal for jersey or elastic fabric, underarm seams or where a lot of strain is placed on a seam.

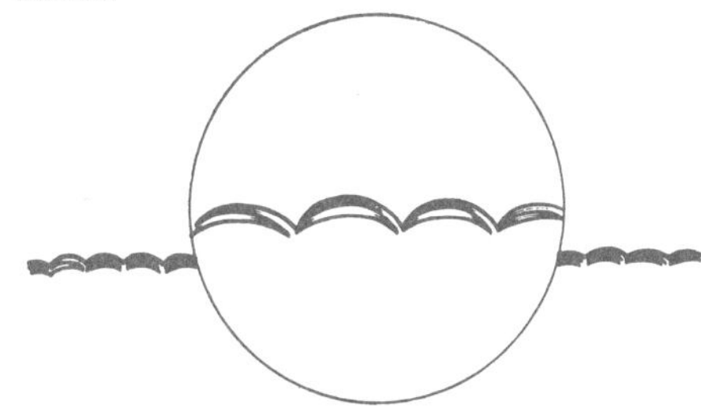

Super-Stretch, Overlock-Type Stitch—This is an extendable straight-stitch with slanting overcast. It is ideal for loosely knit fabrics, hand- or machine-knitting, or stretchy fabrics, such as stretch terrycloth. It allows you to sew swimwear and sweaters the same way as manufacturers do.

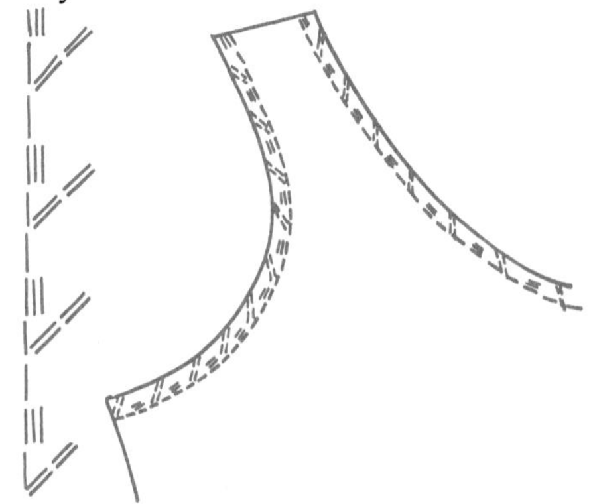

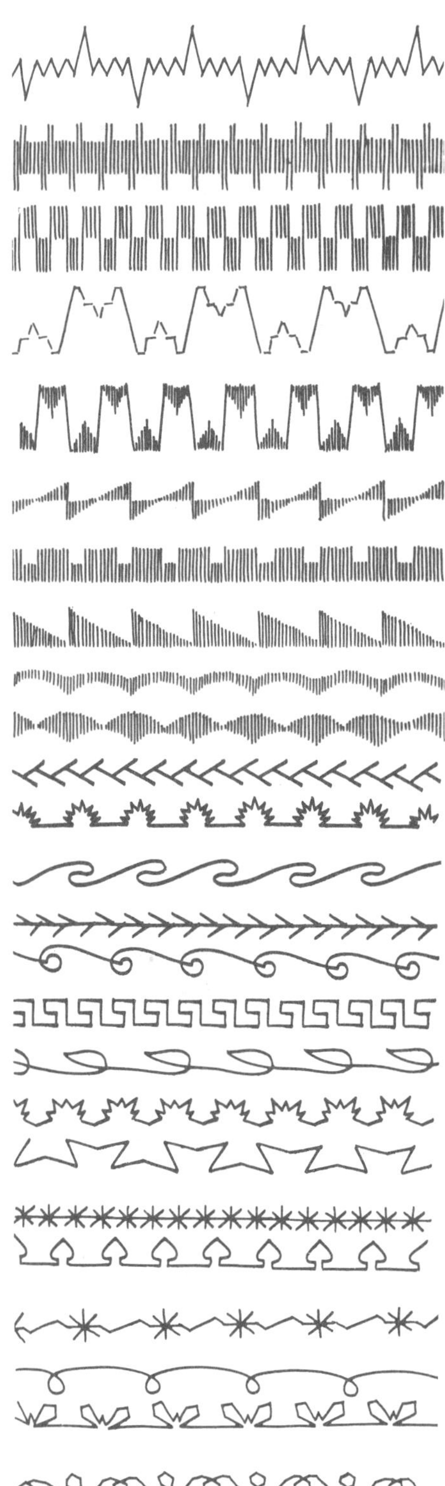

PRESSING EQUIPMENT

For good results, press as you sew.

Irons—Irons are available in many different types. Dry, steam and steam-and-spray irons are the ones you find most often. A non-stick, Teflon-coated sole plate is available on some irons.

Dry irons can be lightweight. They are easy to use on thin fabrics or with a damp cloth. Steam irons can be used without a pressing cloth.

Ironing Board—This is necessary for good pressing. It is possible to use a blanket on a table or bench, but it is difficult. Choose an adjustable ironing board that stands level. Pad the top. The removable cover should fit snuggly without wrinkles. Special covers prevent scorching.

Sleeve Board—This board is like a tiny ironing board. It is designed for pressing small, shaped areas, such as sleeves and necklines. A sleeve board should be padded, with a snugly fitting cover.

Pressing Cloth—This is necessary when pressing some fabrics. Use a square of muslin or soft cotton for most fabrics. A wool cloth, used with steam, prevents flattening of the surface of wool. Special pressing tissue is also available. Pressing with a cloth between iron and fabric keeps the garment's surface from becoming shiny. Brown paper can also be used, especially under folds, to prevent the edges of darts and pleats from showing through.

Tailor's Ham—A ham is a small, tightly stuffed cushion. It is used under curved areas, such as darts, during pressing. You can buy one, or make one out of cotton stuffed with kapok or sawdust. It should be a round oval, about 10 inches by 6 inches.

Clothes Brush—This is used to brush threads and lint from fabric and to raise the surface of fabric after pressing. Use the back of the brush to bang the edges of hems and tailored clothes, as directed in pattern instructions.

Full-Length Mirror—A mirror is helpful to check the appearance of garments during fitting. A three-part mirror, hinged so it folds out, is best.

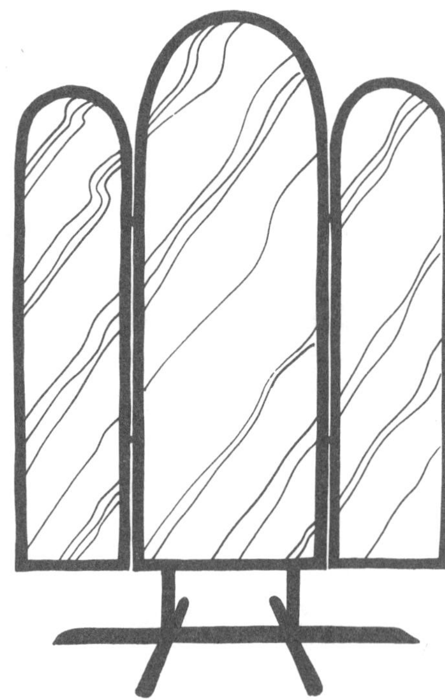

ADDITIONAL PRESSING EQUIPMENT

The following items are not necessary for pressing but are nice to have.

Sponges—Useful for many things, a clean sponge can be used to dampen fabrics during pressing.

Mist Sprayer—This is used to dampen fabric during pressing.

Coat Hangers—Hangers have many uses. Keep some in the sewing area for hanging partly made garments and to allow skirts to hang before turning up the hem.

Needleboard—A needleboard is not necessary for every sewer. It is a piece of strong canvas covered with fine wires, used for pressing pile fabrics, such as velvet. The fabric is placed with the pile *down* on the wires, so it cannot be flattened during pressing.

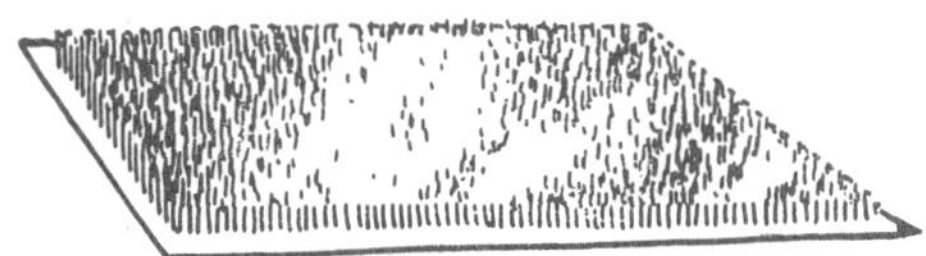

Seam Roll—A seam roll can be made at home. It is a long, firmly padded roll. It is used to press seams so ridges do not form on the right-side. Buy one, or pad a piece of broom handle and cover it tightly with cotton.

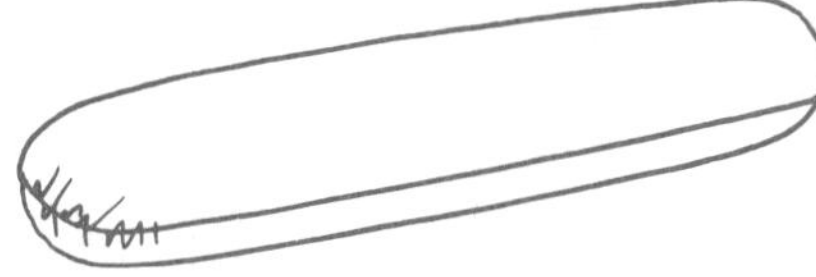

Press Mitt—Like a small tailor's ham, it is made to fit over the hand. Use it for hard-to-reach curves.

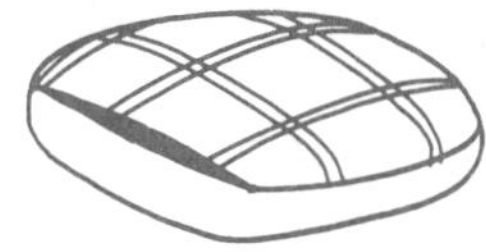

MEASURING AND MARKING EQUIPMENT

This equipment is necessary if you want a quality-finished garment.
Tape Measure—A good tape measure is necessary for many types of measuring. Choose one that will not stretch.
Ruler—A ruler is helpful for many small measuring tasks. A clear-plastic one with plain edges is the most useful.
Yardstick—It is used for checking the straight grain when laying out patterns on fabric. Also useful for marking hem lengths.
Hem Gage—It is used for measuring the depth of a hem so it can be turned and pressed. Buy a plastic gage or make one from cardboard.

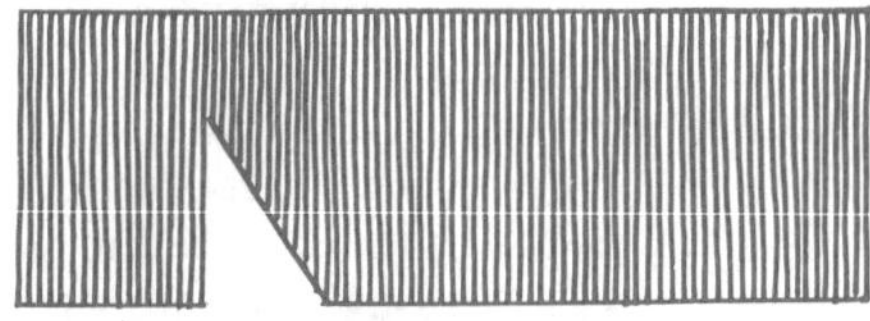

Sewing Gage—This is a special ruler with a sliding marker. It is used to measure buttonholes, pleats and other things. A *dressmaker's gage* has scalloped edges for measuring scallops.

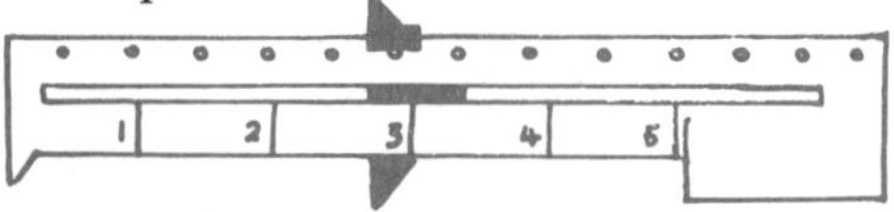

Pins—Pins are important in any sewing kit. Choose good-quality, stainless-steel pins. Keep them in a box lined with special paper to protect them from rust. *Never* use rusty pins. You can buy a pin dispenser, so pins pop up ready to use.

Pincushion—This holds pins. The most useful ones fit on a band around the wrist.

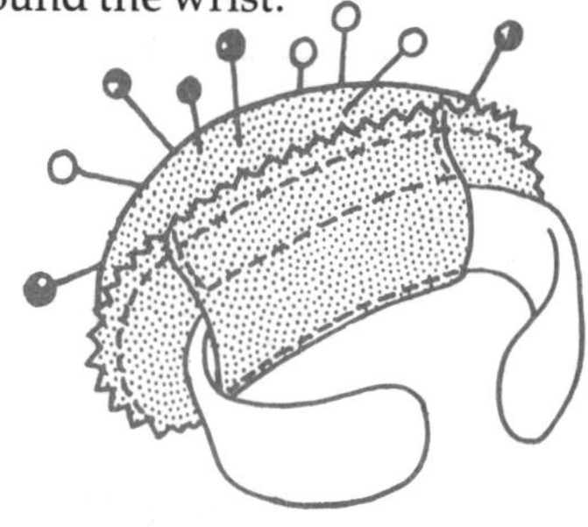

Magnet—A magnet is useful for picking up pins and needles from the floor or work area.

ADDITIONAL MEASURING AND MARKING EQUIPMENT

The following items are not necessary for measuring and marking but are useful.
T-Square—This has many uses, including checking the straight grain. A triangle or tailor's square may be preferred.

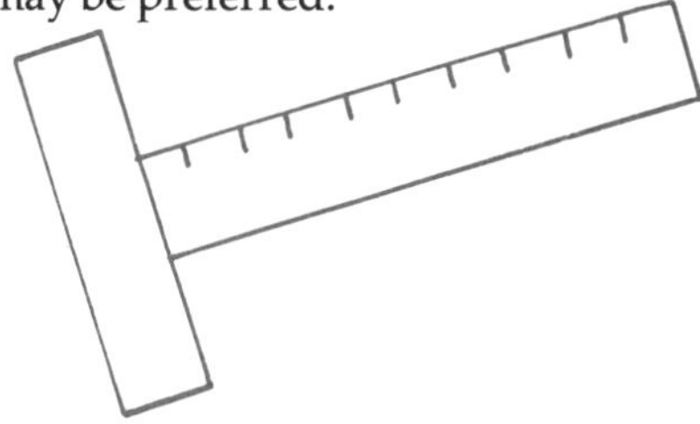

Tailor's Chalk or Chalk Pencil—These are available in several colors. They are used for putting pattern markings and alterations on fabric. The wax type may be difficult to remove. A small brush removes the French-chalk type. Sharpen chalk occasionally for accurate marking. Pencils give thin, precise lines. Have at least two colors for different markings.

Tracing Wheel—A tracing wheel is used with dressmaker's carbon paper to transfer pattern markings onto fabric.

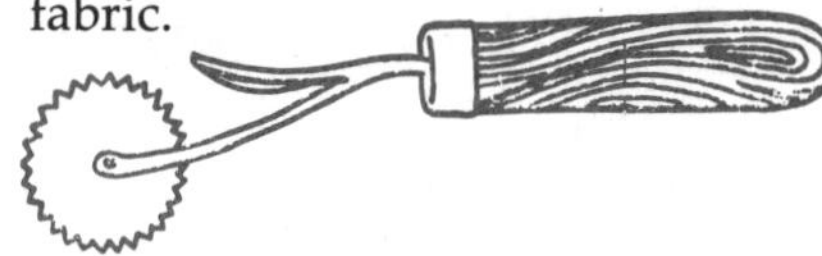

Dressmaker's Carbon Paper—This is special carbon paper to use with a tracing wheel. It is available in several colors.
Transparent Tape—Tape can be used instead of tacking. It is more expensive but faster than tacking.
Hem Marker—This puts a thin line of powdered chalk at the required hem length. Some markers use pins, or pins and chalk. This can be useful if there is no one to help pin up a hem.

CUTTING EQUIPMENT

Well-designed, sharp scissors are essential for accurate cutting. Choose forged-steel blades that bolt or screw together for long wear. Store them in a safe, dry place. Oil the screw occasionally.

Store scissors in a sheath to protect blade points. Always try sewing scissors before buying them, to make sure they are right for you. Have them sharpened regularly.

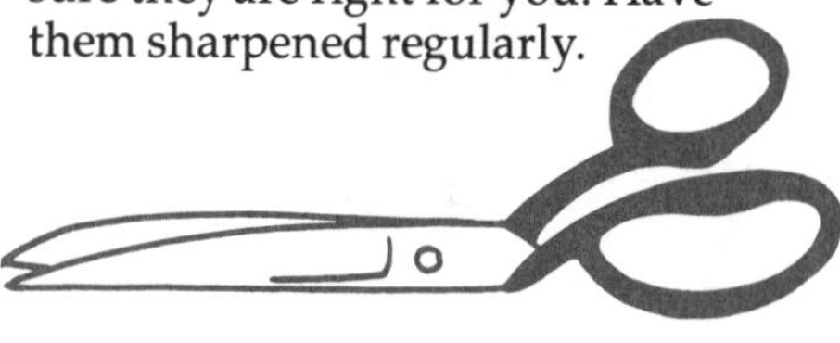

Cutting Shears—These are necessary for good sewing. Buy the *bent-handle type.* Bent-handle scissors have one blade that rests flat on the cutting surface. The handles of cutting shears are two different sizes to fit the thumb and fingers. Blades are usually 7 to 8 inches long. Left-handed shears can be bought in specialty stores.
Paper-Cutting Scissors—These scissors are different from cutting shears. Keep an old pair of scissors for cutting patterns and other paper. Do *not* use your cutting shears to cut paper.
Embroidery Scissors—These have fine, sharp points and are useful for trimming fine details, cutting buttonholes and other close work.
Seam Ripper—A seam ripper is an inexpensive aid for undoing seams.

ADDITIONAL CUTTING EQUIPMENT

The following items are not necessary for pressing but are useful.

Electric Scissors—These scissors run with electricity and are light and easy to use for cutting heavy fabrics.

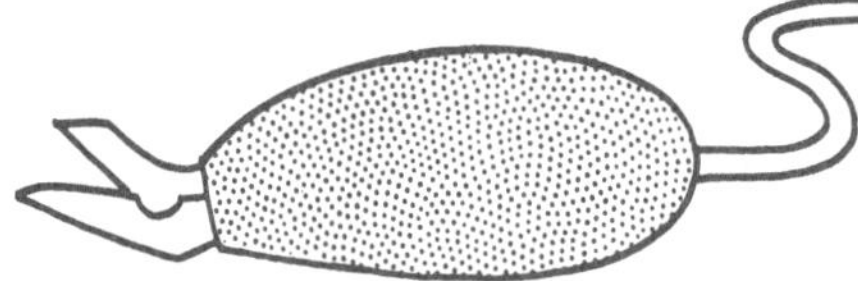

Pinking Shears—Overcasting is unnecessary with pinking shears. They have serrated blades to trim edges of non-fraying fabric. Use them carefully because they are difficult and expensive to sharpen.

Buttonhole Scissors—The screw on these scissors can be adjusted so only a cut of the required length can be made.

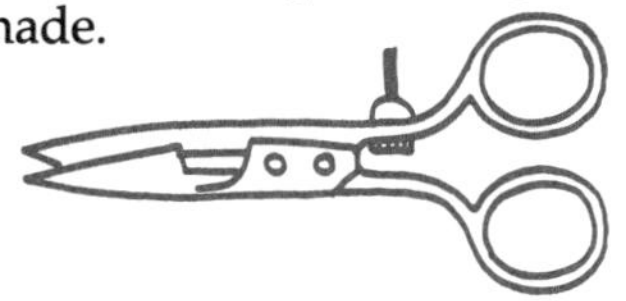

Jersey Scissors—These scissors have finely serrated edges for ease in cutting knit fabrics.

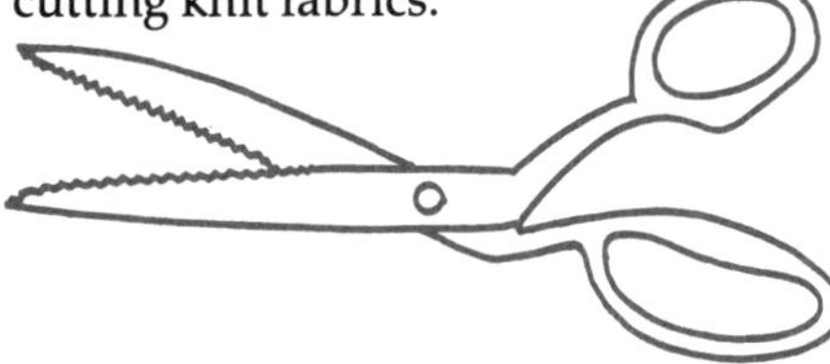

Scissor Gage—This gage has a sliding device that fits on one blade of the scissors. This makes it easy to cut long pieces of fabric to a required width.

Cutting Board—A cutting board is useful if you only have a small table. A board can be laid on top to support the full width of the fabric. It is usually marked with a grid and lines to indicate straight and true cross grains.

NEEDLES

These are an important part of your sewing equipment. Buy a selection of good-quality needles, and keep them in a needle case so they are available. Use needles suited to the fabric and thread. Personal preference should dictate your final choice.

Needles for Hand-Sewing—Needles come in many types and sizes, for many uses. They range in size from No. 1, for coarse work, to No. 10, for fine handwork.

- Sharp—Long, oval eye, all-purpose.
- Between—Shorter than sharp. Beveled edge for fine sewing on heavy fabric.
- Self-threading—Easily threaded because of the opening at the top.
- Darning—The long eye takes wool or thick thread.
- Milliner—Long, round eye, thin. Use for hand-shirring and basting.
- Crewel—Embroidery, long eye. Takes embroidery thread. Similar to the length of sharps.
- Beading—Straight, fine needle with a long eye. Can thread pearls and beads.
- Ball-point—Round point for use with knits.

Sewing-Machine Needles—These needles come in many sizes, for all weights of fabric. Ball-point machine needles can be used for elastic fabrics and knits because they have a round point. They do not pierce or damage fibers but push yarns aside.

Bodkin—This is a thick needle with a blunted end and a long eye. It is used for threading cord, ribbon and tape through lacing holes.

Needle Threader—This makes threading hand or machine needles quick and easy.

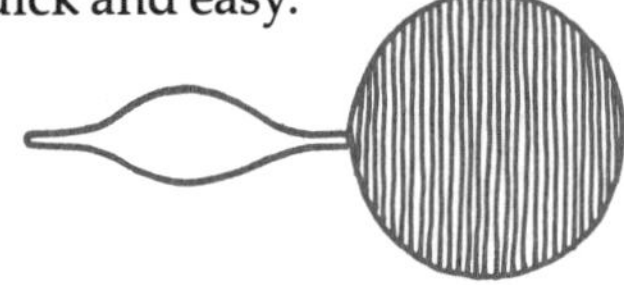

Thimble—A thimble should fit snugly on the middle finger of the sewing hand. It can be plastic or metal, plain or fancy.

THREAD

Thread is important when sewing. If you do not choose the correct thread, it can affect the garment you make. Also see the section on *Stitches and Threads,* page 67.

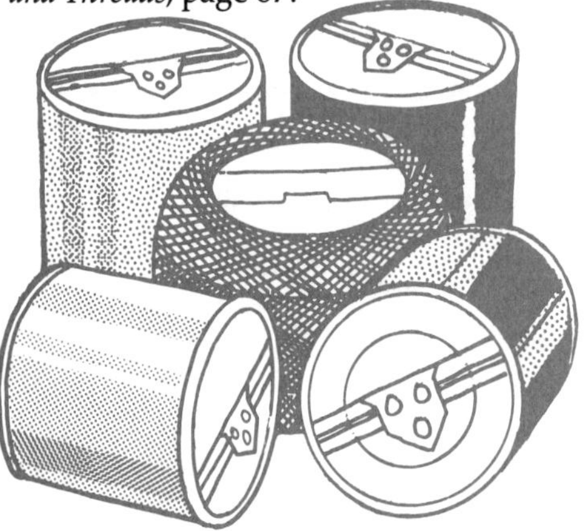

Tacking Thread—This is a special thread. It clings to the fabric, yet can be broken and pulled out easily. Use it in a color that contrasts with the fabric.

Sewing Thread—This thread is used to sew garment pieces together. Consider the type, weight and color of the fabric. Select the type and thickness of thread required, then the color. Use mercerized cotton thread for cotton and linen fabric, and silk thread for silk and wool fabric. Use nylon, polyester or cotton-covered polyester thread for man-made fabric.

MISCELLANEOUS EQUIPMENT

Below is a list of equipment you might want for specific tasks. Buy this equipment *only* if you need it. It is not necessary for everyone.

Awl or Stiletto—This tool has a round shaft and sharp, pointed end. It is mounted on a handle. It is used for making holes in embroidery, for eyelets and for pulling out tacking threads.

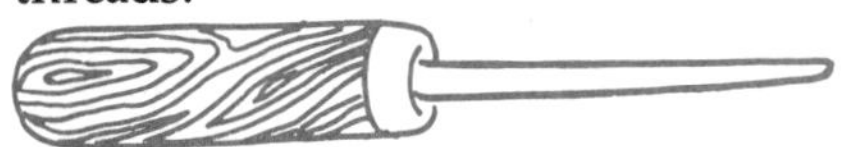

Beeswax—Beeswax is used to strengthen thread and reduce knotting.

Crochet Hooks—Hooks can be used for odd jobs, such as poking out corners of collars.

Dress Form—Also called a *dressmaker's dummy.* It is expensive and usually needed only by those who sew a lot for themselves. Choose one with as many adjustable measurements as possible. It should be on a sturdy base.

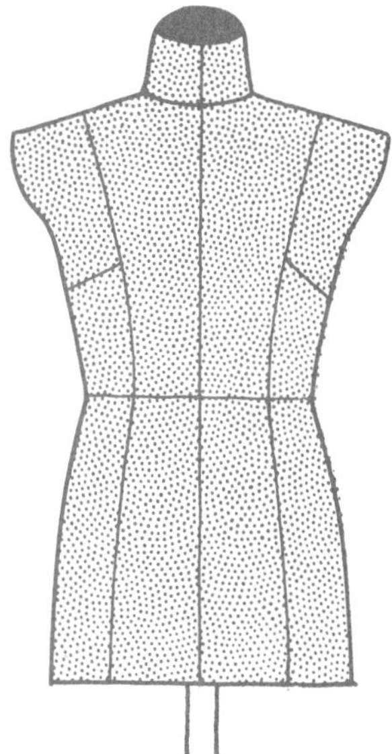

Embroidery Hoop, Frame—A hoop or frame can be used for hand- and some machine-embroidery. Two hoops fit tightly together to hold fabric taut. Ask for advice before using one.

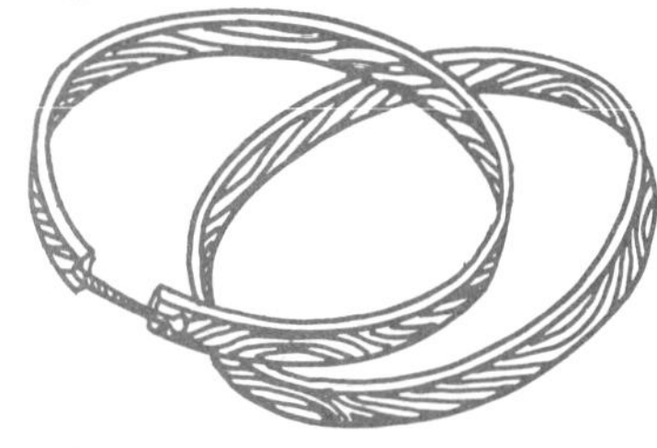

Mushroom—This tool is useful for darning knit fabrics.

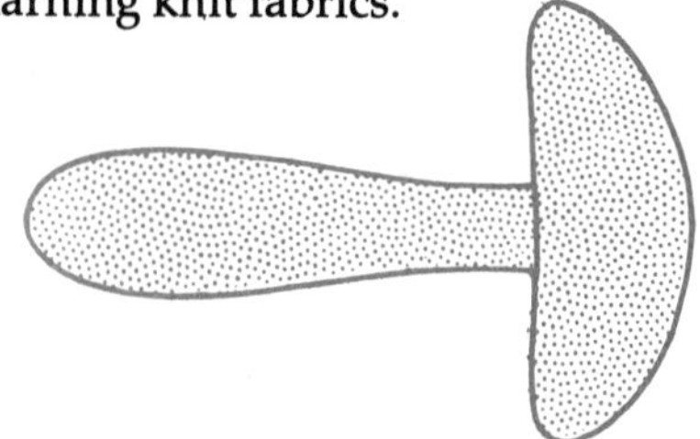

Pattern Paper—This paper comes in large sheets or rolls. It is flimsy graph paper used to make patterns.

Tissue Paper—Tissue is placed under a fabric while machine-sewing so fabric does not catch in the feed teeth.

Tweezers—These are good for pulling out tacking threads and machine-stitches.

USING YOUR SEWING MACHINE

We often blame equipment if something goes wrong. When things go wrong while using the sewing machine, the *user* is often to blame.

Always refer to your sewing-machine instruction book. Read it for a basic idea of possible stitching techniques when using your machine.

Sewing machines should run quietly and smoothly for maximum efficiency. If your machine is noisy and sluggish, something is wrong. A noisy machine usually indicates cleaning and oiling are necessary.

Clean first, then oil. This applies to *all* sewing machines. Most accessory kits include a cleaning or dust brush. Use this to remove dust, lint and fluff before oiling the machine. Use only the highest quality, fine machine oil. Refer to the instruction book for the location of oiling points.

Oil the machine *before* use, not after. Apply two small drops of oil to each oiling point. Follow the instructions in the book *exactly.* Careless oiling results in the machine becoming flooded with oil. This could spoil fabric you are sewing on.

After oiling, wipe the machine with a clean rag. Run it unthreaded for a minute or so on a piece of fabric.

When you constantly use your sewing machine, give it regular care and attention. If well cared for, repairs will seldom be necessary.

MACHINE-STITCHING

There are two separate threads operated by the sewing machine. The *thread controlled by the bobbin* runs underneath the cloth. The *thread controlled by the needle* stitches through the cloth from the top.

When machine-sewing, threads pass around each other and tighten to form a stitch. Even-running of the threads and the way they pull against each other is called the *tension.* To have perfect sewing, tension must be accurate. Controls can be adjusted to give correct tension. Read your machine handbook.

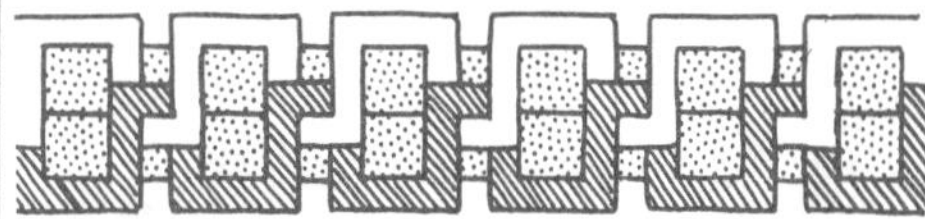

Correct tension

Top tension too tight or bottom tension too loose.

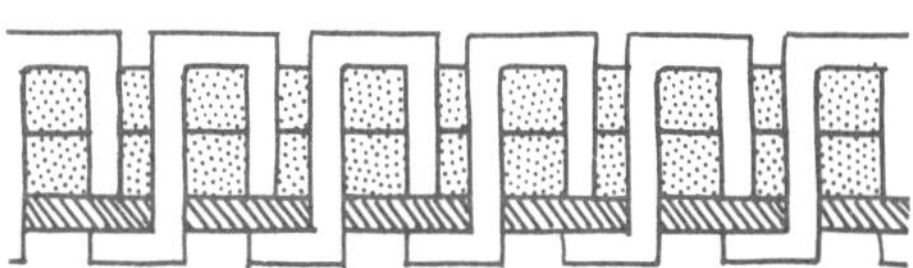

Bottom tension too tight or top tension too loose.

STITCH LENGTH

Various fabrics require different stitch lengths. The following information will help you select the correct stitch length for a particular fabric.

Machine-basting or tacking uses the longest stitch on the machine. This is usually for temporary stitching.

On thick, heavy fabrics, use long stitches. Short stitch lengths must be set for fine and lightweight fabrics.

Fullness can be eased in evenly by setting the length to approximately 8 stitches per inch. Place the index finger lightly on the fabric behind the sewing foot while sewing. This is sometimes called *ease plus.*

PROBLEMS USING SEWING MACHINE

As you sew, you may have some problems with your sewing machine. Before you call the serviceman, try the tips listed below.

Stitches of Uneven Length—Look for the following causes.

1. Stitch-size indicator incorrectly adjusted. Vibration may cause it to move.
2. Needle put in backward.
3. Incorrect pressure.
4. Feed dog adjusted incorrectly.
5. Feed dog clogged with lint or dirt.

Upper Thread Breaks—Look for the following causes.
1. Upper tension too tight.
2. Poor thread.
3. Incorrect threading.
4. Needle set too high or too low.
5. Needle bent or blunt.
6. Needle too fine for thread.
7. Needle put in backward.
8. Needle rubs against presser foot, needle plate or shuttle.
9. Sharp or rough place on shuttle or needle.

Lower Thread Breaks—Look for the following causes.
1. Lower tension too tight.
2. Poor thread.
3. Bobbin case incorrectly threaded.
4. Bobbin wound too loosely or too tightly.
5. Bobbin wound too full.
6. Bobbin wound unevenly.
7. Rough or sharp edges on bobbin.
8. Rough or sharp edges on lower tension spring.
9. Burr or rough edge on needle plate.
10. Dirt or accumulation of thread in bobbin case, preventing bobbin from turning freely.

Missed Stitches—Look for the following causes.
1. Needle blunt.
2. Thread too thick for the needle.
3. Needle threaded incorrectly.
4. Needle put in backward.
5. Needle set too low or high.
6. Wrong type of needle.
7. Wrong length of stitch.
8. Needle bent.
9. Needle too small for thread.
10. Needle too long or too short.
11. Oil on needle.

Seams Pucker—Look for the following causes.
1. Top and bottom threads different.
2. One or both tensions too tight.
3. Wrong sewing foot.
4. Incorrect thread.
5. Dull needle causing side puckers.

Stitches Looping Underneath—Look for the following causes.
1. Tension incorrect. Top tension too loose or bottom tension too tight, or both.
2. Lint or thread caught in tension disks.
3. Two weights of thread used.
4. Incorrect threading.
5. Thread caught under lower tension spring.

Stitches Looping on Top—Look for the following causes.
1. Incorrect threading.
2. Different weight of thread used on top and bottom.
3. Thread or lint caught in tension disks.
4. Incorrect tension. Bottom tension too loose, top tension too tight, or both.
5. Bobbin incorrectly threaded.
6. Thread caught under lower tension spring.

Broken Needle—Look for the following causes.
1. Needle too fine for type of fabric used.
2. Poor-quality thread that knots easily.
3. Needle incorrectly centered and hitting needle plate or sewing foot.
4. Upper tension too tight.
5. Fabric pulled when sewn so the needle bends and hits the foot or needle plate.
6. Needle bent, of poor quality, incorrectly inserted, backward or incorrect size.
7. Presser foot incorrectly attached.
8. Failure to lift needle before removing material.
9. Zigzag setting too wide when using twin needles.

Machine Not Running Properly—Look for the following causes.
1. Bobbin winder engaged.
2. If machine is belt driven, belt may have stretched.
3. Faulty plug.
4. Wrong oil used or machine may need cleaning or oiling.
5. Thread wound around wheel.
6. Tight bearings.

Tangled Thread at Beginning of Seam—Look for the following causes.
1. Bobbin thread wound in wrong direction.
2. Bobbin wound too full.
3. Underthread not drawn up.
4. Threads not pulled back under presser foot and held for first two or three stitches.
5. Improper oiling and cleaning of machine.

Machine Jammed—Look for the following causes.
1. Threads jamming bobbin case.
2. Threads wound around upper thread holder.

Staggered Stitches—Look for the following causes.
1. Too little pressure of presser foot.
2. Take-up spring missing.
3. Take-up spring incorrectly adjusted.

Material Not Feeding Correctly—Look for the following causes.
1. Stitch-length regulator turned too far, so feed is out of action.
2. Dirt around feed dog.
3. Feed dog incorrectly set.
4. Pressure incorrect.
5. Bent presser foot or feed dog.

Bobbin Winds Incorrectly—Look for the following causes.
1. Drive wheel on winder not bearing firmly enough on hand wheel or belt.
2. Rubber on bobbin-winder wheel loose, greasy or worn.
3. Thread guide on winder bent, making thread pile up on one side of bobbin.
4. Wheel that operates thread guide of winder badly set or not turning freely.

Hand Wheel Hard to Turn—Look for the following causes.
1. Thread or dirt in bearings.
2. Bearings rusted or jammed.
3. Bearings too tight.

Machine Runs Noisily—Look for the following causes.
1. Needs oil.
2. Lint in moving parts.
3. Loose bearings.
4. Loose shuttle in holder.
5. Loose bobbin case.

SEWING AIDS AND SEWING NOTIONS

SEWING AIDS

There are many sewing aids available today, so check them occasionally. Some are unnecessary, but most equipment is designed to make sewing easier, quicker or more efficient. Keep the sewing aids you use in your sewing box. Before using them, read instructions. Practice with each device before using it on important work.

Bodkin—This is a long, thick needle with a hook at one end. It is used for threading elastic, cord, tape and

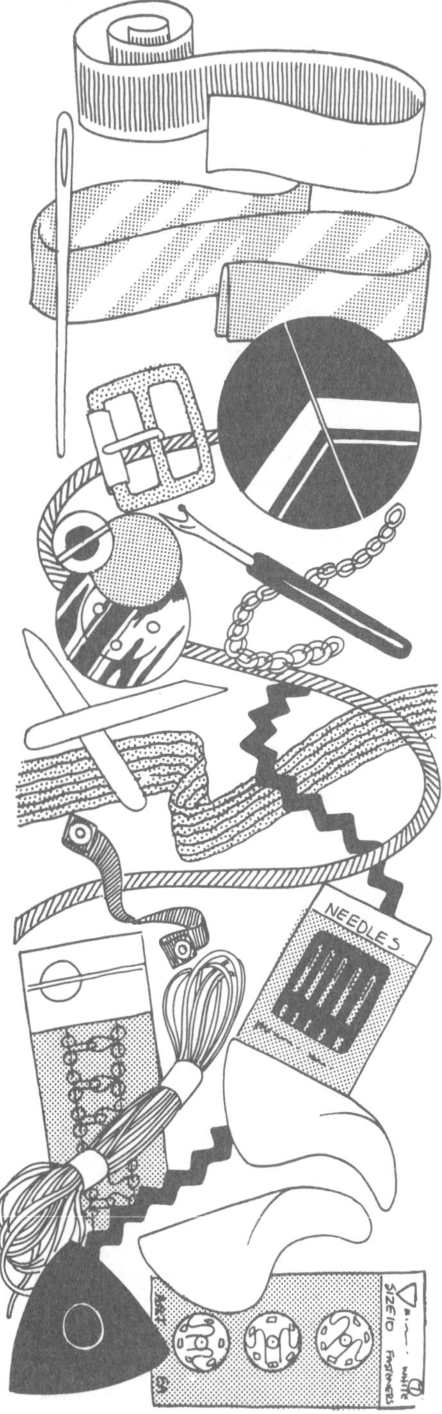

ribbons without snagging fabric. It can also be used to turn collars, belts and loops. One type can be threaded.
Beeswax Holder—This is a block of beeswax in a plastic holder. It helps prevent snarling and knotting when thread is pulled through it.
Bobbin Box—Make your own, or buy a clear plastic box to hold rows of machine bobbins or spools.
Bound-Buttonhole Maker—An accessory for a sewing machine. It makes easy, accurate preparation of bound buttonholes.
Coat Hangers—These are available in many shapes and sizes. When sewing, do not use wire hangers from the dry-cleaner.
Curved Square—This is a tailor's square with a curved edge for drawing accurate curves. It can be used for pockets, waistbands, hems and pattern alteration.
Dressmaker Kit—Kit transfers pattern markings by chalking both sides of the fabric.
Fashion Ruler—Rulers are available in transparent plastic with parallel slots for marking edges, buttonholes or bias strips.
Fix-a-Snag—This is a small latch hook with a plastic handle. It is used to pull snagged threads through to the wrong-side of knit fabrics.
Hem Marker—Used for level hemlines, it marks the required skirt length on a garment with a puff of chalk or pins. Some mark hemline and sewing line.
Invisible-Zipper Foot—Small metal foot that attaches to the sewing machine. It is used with adhesive tabs to attach invisible zippers.
Leather Punch—This is a scissors-type punch with a rotating head. It cuts holes of various sizes.
Magnetic Seam Guide—Small metal attachment for the sewing machine. Held in place by a powerful magnet, it is a guide for spacing tucks, pleats, seams, edge-stitching and top-stitching.
Marking Pencil—This pencil is used like an ordinary pencil or tailor's chalk. It transfers pattern markings and alteration lines and marks pleats. The brush on one end is used to remove marks after use. It is not suitable for all fabrics.
Needles—Anti-static and ball-point needles are used on knits and man-made fabrics to aid penetration between threads. This prevents snags and missed stitches. Self-threading needles are useful for people with poor eyesight. Color-coded machine needles are easy to identify.
Needle Threader—A fine-wire loop makes needle threading easy. It is good for children or people with poor eyesight.
Oil—Most sewing machines must be regularly lubricated. Non-stain, all-purpose oil is available for this.
Pins—Pin size is stated in sixteenths of an inch, according to length. A size 8 is 1/2 inch long (8/16). Size 16 is 1 inch long (16/16). Most people use size 17 (1-1/16 inch) pins for general use. Choose good-quality, rustproof pins for sewing. Dressmaker pins are used most often. Silk pins have fine points. They are good for fine sewing and delicate fabric. Plastic or glass-head pins contrast with the fabric.
Point Turner—A point turner is shaped for turning collars. Some have markings to use as a stitch guide to make collar points symmetrical. Some have a gage for sewing button shanks.
Seam Ripper—A small device used to remove stitches. Choose one with a protective ball on one point. A seam ripper is good for cutting buttonholes after stitching.
Sewing Gage—This small ruler has a sliding marker for measuring hems, seams, tucks, pleats, buttonholes, scallops.
Tailor Marker Chalk—Another method of transferring pattern markings to fabric. A pin is inserted in a chalk block, then put in the fabric. It leaves chalk marks on both pieces of fabric when the pin is withdrawn.
Tailor's Chalk Holder—Helpful with tailor's chalk, it keeps the chalk from crumbling in the sewing box. Look for one with a sharpener.
Tailor's Chalk Pencil—This holds sticks of tailor's chalk.
Tailor's Tacking Kit—A kit with a spool holder, needle holder, needle threader and special needles. It is faster than hand tailor tacking.
Thread Clipper—This flexible scissorlike tool clips thread.
Thread Lock—A plastic disk fits in the top of thread spools to keep the cut end of thread in place. It is useful for storing partly used spools of thread.
Tracing Wheel—This is a serrated, rotating wheel on a handle. Use it with dressmaker's carbon paper to transfer markings and designs to fabric. Use carbon paper that can be removed by washing or dry-cleaning.

Transparent Bobbin—Allows the color and amount of thread to be easily seen.

SEWING NOTIONS

Ban Rol—Flexible waistband elastic that does not roll over.

Beads, Sequins, Decorations—These are available in many materials, colors, shapes and sizes. They are an inexpensive way to decorate a garment.

Belt Stiffening—Special belt stiffening is available for stiffening and backing garment fabric to make a self-belt. It may be in kit form. Other stiffenings are also available to put in fabric to make belts.

Bias Tape—This bias-cut fabric strip is folded for binding edges, especially curved ones. It makes edges neat and adds strength. It is available prefolded in cotton or nylon, in several widths and many colors. Match color to fabric.

Blanket Binding—Wide, prefolded binding, often satin. It is used for edging and repairing blankets. It can be used to trim household linens, such as pillowcases.

Bra-Back Repair Kit—This replaces worn elastic and fastenings at the back of a still-usable bra.

Bra Cups—Use these in dresses, especially halter and sundresses. They are good for bathing-suit tops that need to be preshaped. They are available in many sizes.

Braid—Use this for decorating clothes and furnishings. Many colors, widths and types are available. Choose one that is appropriate for your fabric.

Buckles—These are for fastening belts and flaps. Choose the correct size and weight in the required color. Kits are available for covering buckle shapes with garment fabric. Finish them neatly for durability.

Buttons—Choose washable or dry-cleanable buttons in the correct size, weight and color. Take a piece of fabric when choosing buttons and match in daylight. Buy one or two extra buttons for a garment. Label and keep them separate. It may be more economical to buy buttons that are not prepackaged in groups.

Button Kit—This kit contains metal button molds in many shapes and sizes for covering with fabric.

Coat Chain—Short, lightweight chain made to sew in the neck of a coat or suit. Use it to hang the garment from a hook, if necessary. It is easier and stronger than sewing a loop.

Cotton Tape—Use for loops, strengthening seams and stay-stitching.

Decorative Patches, Motifs— These are fashionable for decorating garments. Buy them or make your own. They can also be used to disguise a hole or tear.

Dress Shields—Use these fabric shapes at underarms to prevent perspiration stains. They are useful for garments that cannot be washed.

Dressmaker's Paper—Pattern or graph paper used for drafting or altering patterns.

Dyes—These substances alter the color of fabric. Check type of dye and method to use. Not all fabrics can be dyed. You may need dye remover before some fabrics can be dyed. Some can be used for tie-dyeing. Paint-on dyes can be used with embroidery.

Elastic—Select the one for your purpose such as bra-back, braid, cord, flat, millinery, round, shirring, shoulder-strap, skirt-pant waist, suspender and waistband elastic.

Eyelet, Eyelet Punch—It may be necessary to make eyelets as decoration or as part of a fastening. A special eyelet punch is needed to put in eyelet rings. Rings are available in several sizes.

Fabric Paint—Paint is available in liquid, powder, crayon or pen. Apply color to the surface of fabric and garments. Be sure fabric and paint are compatible. Colors can usually be blended to produce a variety of tones. This technique can be combined with dyeing hand-embroidery.

Fringe—Many types and colors are available for trim. Fabric and trim must be compatible. You can make fringe by hand or machine.

Hooks and Eyes—These are available in many sizes. It is not appropriate to use one size and color for all your sewing. Bars are less obtrusive than eyes. Adjustable hooks and bars are available for waistbands. They can be adjusted by up to 1 inch while the garment is being worn.

Horsehair Braid—Used to stiffen hems of special garments.

Hosiery Mending Thread—Assorted colors for tights and hose are available.

Initials—Adhesive and sew-on types are available. Some iron-on embroidered initials have a backing that disappears when ironed on. They are attractive on blouses, shirts, bags, hats.

Jean Patches—These are iron-on patches for decorating or repairing denim jeans.

Kilt Pins—Used to close homemade kilts.

Labels—Use these with a special pen for marking names and sizes, especially on children's clothes. They can also add care details. Personalized labels are also available.

Lace—Lace is available for all types of trimming. Fabric and lace must be compatible.

Lead Weights—Small pieces of lead, sometimes a button-shape or chain. They weight curtain hems, pleats, dresses, wedding-dress trains and other things so they hang correctly.

Mending Tape—Iron-on tape is available in several colors for mending. Press it to the wrong-side of the garment.

Paris Binding—This firm binding is sometimes used as a decorative finish.

Patches—Leather and suede patches are available. They are used as decoration or for worn areas.

Piping Cord—This soft, cotton cord comes in various thicknesses. Preshrink it before use. It is used for piping buttonholes and seams in garments and soft furnishings. A special silky-finish cord is available for edging cushions.

Pajama Cord—Available as a replacement cord or for homemade pajamas.

Punch Snaps—This type of fastener is punched on the garment, not sewn. It is a fast, strong, fashionable method of fastening clothes and soft furnishings, including plastic and PVC. It can be used decoratively. Plain and fancy designs are available in several colors.

Repair Tape—Tape stops fraying when ironed to the wrong-side of fabric. A tear can be machine darned if necessary. Heavy-duty repair tape is useful for carpet binding and repairing plastics.

Get Set

BODY MEASUREMENTS

An accurate set of body measurements must be taken before you can choose a pattern or make a garment. *Pattern sizes* are usually based on measurements around the body, such as bust, waist or hip sizes. *Figure types* are based on back-neck-to-waist length and height, such as Misses, Women's and Junior Petite.

It is impossible to check *all* your measurements yourself, so ask a friend to help. If a friend is not available, ask a clerk in a fabric store for assistance. The more accurate the measurements, the better the finished garment will fit.

When measuring, wear suitable underwear and shoes. Measure snugly but not tightly. Use the following chart to record your measurements. Retake measurements frequently because your size may vary even if your weight does not change. Details of how to take measurements are also given.

Make the following lists for anyone you will be sewing for:
Date:
Height:
Bust:
Waist:
Hips:
Back-neck to waist:
Shoulder width:
Back width—armhole to armhole:
Shoulder length—right:
Shoulder length—left:
Front bodice—center front:
Front bodice—right:
Front bodice—left:
Side bodice—right:
Side bodice—left:
Chest—above bust:
Chest—on bust at front:
Chest—diaphragm:
Upper arm:
Shoulder to elbow:
Sleeve length:
Wrist:
Neck:
Center-neck to hem:
Waist to hem:

TAKING WOMEN'S AND GIRLS' MEASUREMENTS

These are measurements to take for women and girls.

Height—Stand on the floor in bare feet, with your back against the wall. Look straight ahead. Chalk a tiny mark on the wall level with the top of the head. Measure from the floor to this mark.

Bust—Have your helper stand behind you. Measure over the fullest part of the bust, with the tape slightly higher at the back.

Waist—Tie a piece of string around your natural waist. Measure the string without removing it. Leave the string there for other measurements.

Hips—Place the tape around the fullest part of figure. This is usually about 9 inches below the waist for Misses and Women's, or 7 inches below the waist for Miss Petite, Half-Size, Junior Petite and Young Junior/Teen.

Back-Neck to Waist—Find the bone that sticks out at the nape of the neck. Measure from this point down to the middle of the waistline.

BODY MEASUREMENTS

Shoulder Width—Clasp hands together at the front waistline. With arms slightly forward and raised, measure across the back from shoulder-point to shoulder-point.

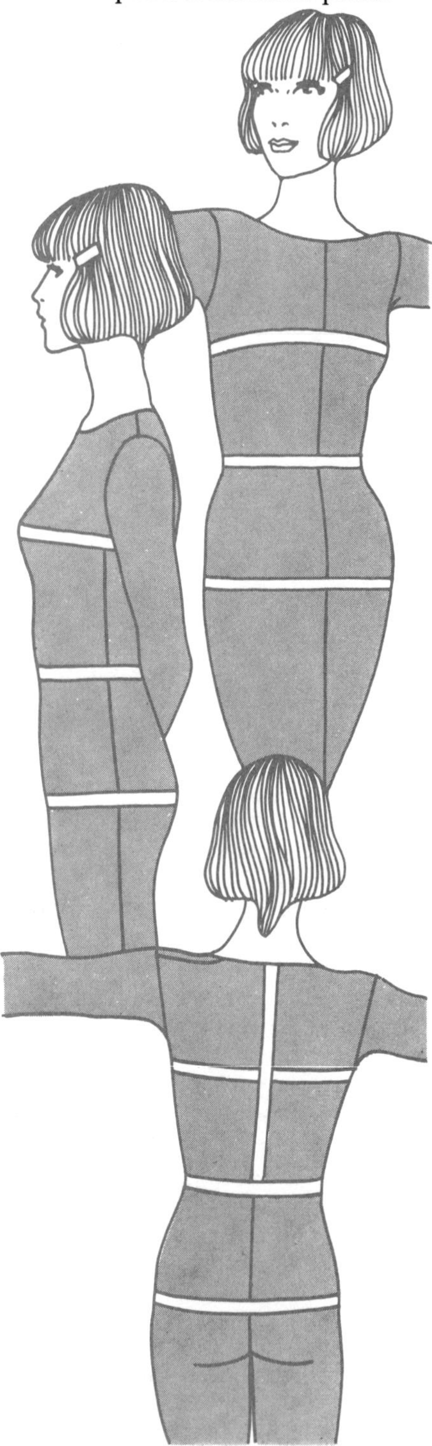

Back Width—Measure across the back at shoulder-blade level. Start and finish where the normal armhole seams lie.

Shoulder Length—Measure from the base of the neck to the point of the shoulder on each side. The two measurements may be slightly different.

Front Bodice—This center-front measurement is taken from the neckline straight down to the waistline. Also measure from shoulder seam placement to waistline on each side, over the bust.

Side Bodice—Stand up straight with hands resting on hips. Measure each side from 1 inch below the armpit down to the waistline. There may be a difference between the two sides.

Chest—This measurement is taken above the bust. Measure around at underarm level above the bust. On the bust at front, measure from underarm-seam to underarm-seam over the bust. If this measurement is 2 inches or more than the back width, the pattern may have to be altered to allow more room.

Diaphragm—Take this measurement around the rib cage, halfway between the waist and fullest part of the bust.

Shoulder to Elbow—Bend the arm, and measure from the point of the shoulder to the point of the elbow.

Sleeve Length—Bend the arm slightly. Measure from the point of the shoulder to wrist, over the bend. It is also useful to measure 1 inch from below the underarm seam to the wrist, with the arm straight.

Wrist—For long sleeves, measure around the wrist over the wrist bone.

Neck to Hem—Measure from the nape of the neck to the required hem level. Hold tape in at the waist.

Waist to Hem—For skirts, measure down to the required hem level.

MEASURING FOR WOMEN'S PANTS

Wear undergarments and shoes you will wear with the pants. Take the following measurements.

Waist to Crotch—This is an important measurement. Accuracy makes a difference in the final fit. Sit on a firm, flat seat, and take the measurement from the side waist to the seat. On the pattern piece, the waist-to-crotch measurement should be equal to your own measurement, plus 1/2 to 1 inch for ease. Extra is allowed to make it possible to sit, crouch and move easily. If the pattern does not conform to this measurement, adjust it.

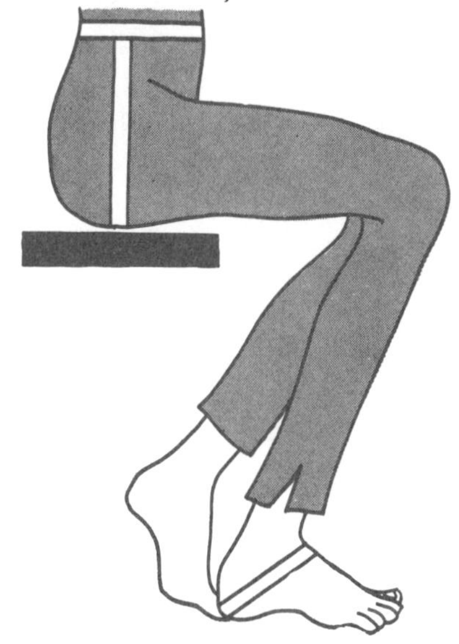

Waist—Use a piece of string tied around the waist to locate the natural waistline.

Upper Hip—Measure around the top

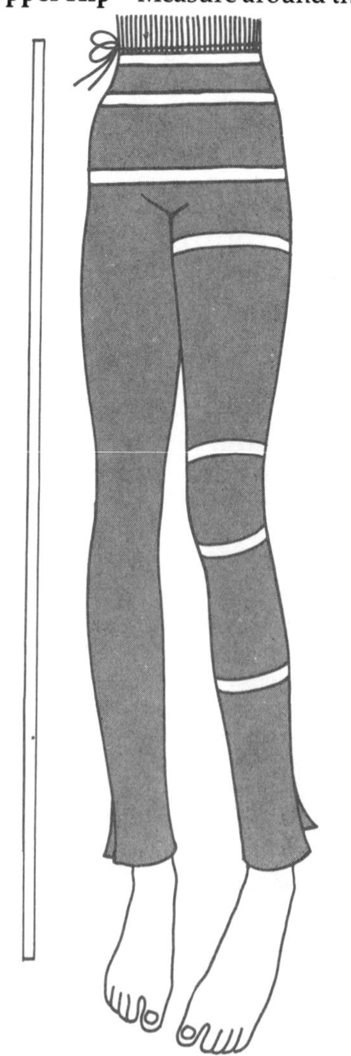

of hip bones, usually 3-1/4 to 4 inches below the waistline.
Seat—Measure around the fullest part of the hips. This may be about 9 inches below the waist, depending on the proportions of the figure.
Thighs—Measure around the largest part of the upper thigh, usually about 2 inches below the crotch.
Knees—Take measurements above the knee and below the knee.
Calf—Measure around fullest part of the calf.
Length—Measure the side, from the waist to floor, or the required length of pants.
Instep—Measure around the heel and over the instep.

TAKING MEN'S AND BOYS' MEASUREMENTS

A few basic measurements are essential for buying or making clothes for men and boys. When making closely fitted or tailored garments, take more detailed measurements. Shirts are usually made to fit by neck size. Some patterns also state chest size. Jackets and suits are sized by chest measurement. Pants are fitted to waist and inside leg measurement.
Basic Height—Measure without shoes, the same way as for a woman.
Neck—Measure around the fullest part of the neck, and add 1/2 inch for ease.
Chest—Measure around the fullest part of the chest under the arms.
Waist—Tie a string around the natural waistline, and measure here. Men may prefer to wear pants higher or lower than the natural waistline.
Seat or Hips—Place the tape around the fullest part of the hips.
Inside Leg—This measurement is taken over clothes. Measure from the crotch to the top of the shoes.
Shoulder—Measure from the base of the neck to the point of the shoulder at the top of the arm.
Center Front—Measure from the base of the neck down the front to the waist.
Back Width—Measure across the shoulder blades, from armhole to armhole.
Sleeve Length—With the arm slightly bent, measure from the point of the shoulder to the elbow, then from elbow to wrist bone.
Upper Arm—Measure around the biceps at the fullest part of the upper arm.

Wrist—Take measurements over the wrist bone.
Thigh—For closely fitted pants, measure around each thigh at the fullest part.

TAKING CHILDREN'S MEASUREMENTS

Children grow quickly, so measure them frequently. Always measure before making or buying clothes for them. No system for sizing-by-age has been devised, so choose by height and weight.

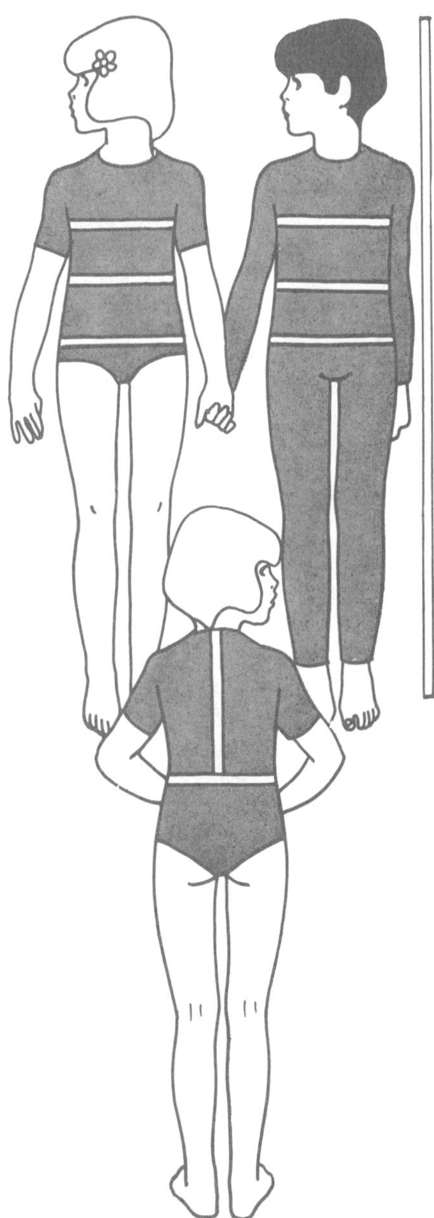

Babies—Use weight, age and height to choose a pattern. Little alteration is usually needed, unless the baby is unusually tall or chubby.
Toddlers—Allowance is usually made for diapers. Measure height, chest, waist and length from nape of neck to the required hem level.
Young Children—This is the same as for toddlers. Take hip measurements and inside-leg length for pants.

SIZES

Common sizes are used for pattern making. For women, the bust, waist and hip measurements may also be given in metric measurement. To take measurements in metric, measure the figure with a tape measure, and round up or down to the nearest centimeter.

WOMEN'S SIZES

SIZES	**8**	**10**	**12**	**14**	**16**
Bust					
inches	31-1/2	32-1/2	34	36	38
Waist					
inches	23	24	25-1/2	27	29
Hips					
inches	33-1/2	34-1/2	36	38	40

MEN'S SIZES

Chest						
inches	34	36	38	40	42	44
Waist						
inches	28	30	32	34	36	39
Collar						
inches	14	14-1/2	15	15-1/2	16	16-1/2

CHILDREN'S SIZES

Measurement is based on height and approximate age.

Size	**2**	**3**	**4**	**5**	**6**	**6X**
Height						
inches	34	37	40	43	46	48
Chest						
inches	21	22	23	24	25	25-1/2

PATTERN AND BODY MEASUREMENTS

Body measurements and fabric amounts may be given in American and metric units. Compare actual body measurements with those in the pattern book, and buy the nearest size. See the section below on *Choosing and Using a Pattern* for details.

CHOOSING AND USING A PATTERN

Choosing a pattern can be fun. Visit fabric stores, and look through pattern books to discover the latest fashions.

By studying pattern books, you know which ones to look at when you have a garment in mind. A pattern book may offer an interesting selection of blouses. Skirts in one book may appeal to you more than those in another book.

Pattern companies publish smaller versions of their pattern books at regular intervals. These include selections of up-to-date patterns. Many patterns are suitable for people learning to sew.

Keep a notebook and pencil at hand when looking at patterns. Tracing paper may come in handy if you want to remember an idea but cannot purchase the pattern at the time.

When pattern books are out-of-date, many stores give them away or sell them to regular customers for a small charge. Ask for one, and keep it as a reference. Or compile your own personal book of pattern ideas.

Be critical and honest about your figure, and try to learn what suits you. If you see a picture of a dress in a magazine or catalog, cut it out and paste it in your idea book. Divide the book into blouses, skirts, dresses, coats, jackets and other sections. If you make it a loose-leaf book, styles can be replaced as fashions change. When you want to make a new garment, you have a source of ideas to help you make a decision.

Each pattern company offers patterns for a wide variety of tastes, although fashion ideas vary. Intricate or exclusive patterns are usually more expensive than simple ones.

Patterns fall in certain figure categories. Figure types are grouped according to height and proportion. All figure types are based on two main measurements—height and back-neck-to-waist length. Choose a pattern to suit your figure type. Use the charts in the pattern catalogs for guidance. The descriptions *Young Junior-Teen, Junior Miss, Women's, Junior Petite* and *Half-Size* are used for grouping sizes and figure types in catalogs.

To find your figure type, stand in front of a mirror in your underwear. Compare yourself with the descriptions in the chart. Look at your body proportions, and check them against the description. Select the type nearest to your figure. Choose the correct pattern size. Take your body measurements, and compare them with the appropriate figure-type chart. See the previous section on *Body Measurements.*

Choose a dress, jacket or blouse pattern by your bust size. For skirts and pants, choose by waist measurement, unless hips are large in relation to your waist. In that case, choose a pattern by the hip size.

If your measurements fall between two sizes, choose the larger one if you are large-boned or like a loose fit. Choose the smaller one if your have a small frame or like a tight fit. Some patterns allow more ease for movement than others.

After determining the correct figure-type and size, choose an appropriate pattern. Look at each sketch you like. Assess how it would suit your figure. Check to see if it is marked as an "easy-to-sew" garment. If it comes from a couturier section, it may be more difficult to sew.

Some ideas for choosing patterns according to your figure are discussed on the next page.

FIGURE TRAIT
Flat chest.

Styles to Avoid—
Fitted bodices, wide necklines.

Styles to Choose—
Gathered and draped styles, so the bodice has added fullness.

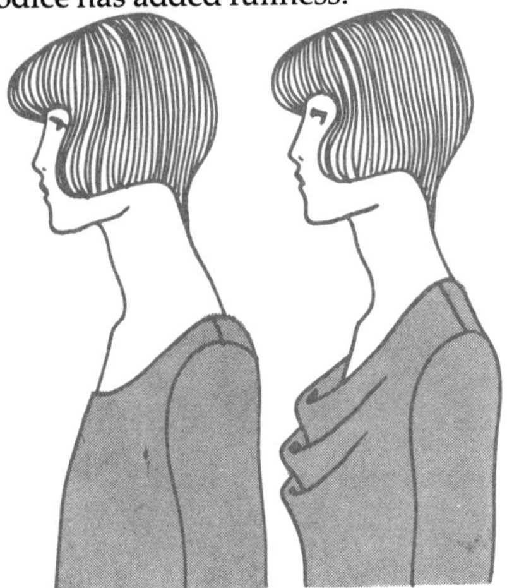

FIGURE TRAIT
Large bust.

Styles to Avoid—
High neckline, frills, draped and gathered bodices, full sleeves.

Styles to Choose—
Tailored top-bodice, fitted sleeves, skirt trims.

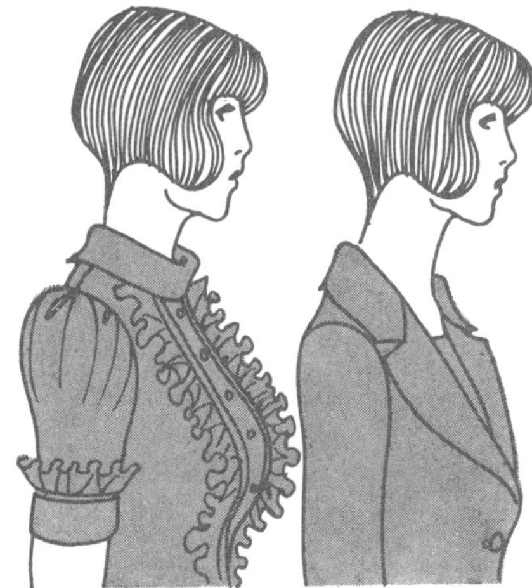

FIGURE TRAIT
Short neck.

Styles to Avoid—
Tie neck bands, high polo necks, mandarin necklines, wide shoulder lines.

Styles to Choose—
Plunging, long, square or V-shape necklines, with narrow shoulder lines.

FIGURE TRAIT
Plump, short figure.

Styles to Avoid—
Wide neck, full sleeves, gathered skirts, frills, horizontal stripes, wide belts.

Styles to Choose—
Fitted sleeves, gored skirts, princess lines.

FIGURE TRAIT
Thin, tall figure.

Styles to Avoid—
Straight skirts, fitted bodices, princess lines.

Styles to Choose—
Gathered or draped skirts with wide belts, neck trim.

FIGURE TRAIT
Thin or thick upper arms.

Styles to Avoid—
Sleeveless styles.

Styles to Choose—
Cap sleeves or 3/4-length sleeves.

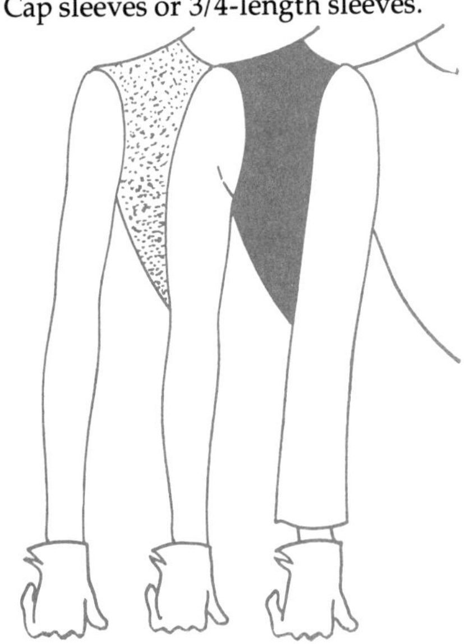

PATTERNS

FIGURE TRAIT
Large hips.

Styles to Avoid—
Fitted skirts, pockets at hips, narrow bodice.

Styles to Choose—
Shaped skirt from waist, gathers only if the waist is small.

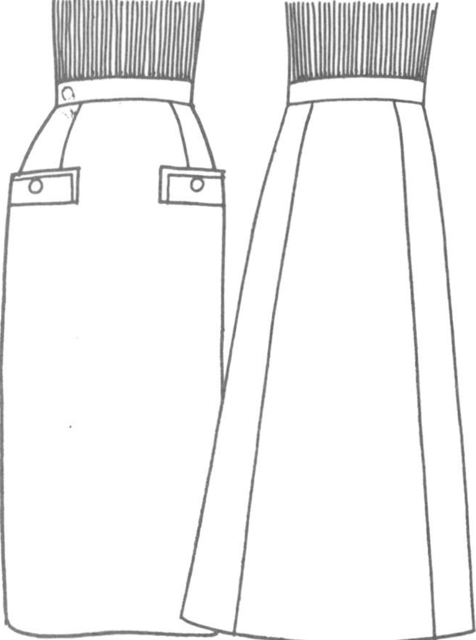

FIGURE TRAIT
Thin neck and shoulders.

Styles to Avoid—
Wide, boat-shape necklines.

Styles to Choose—
V-shape necklines, tie collars, mandarin standing collars.

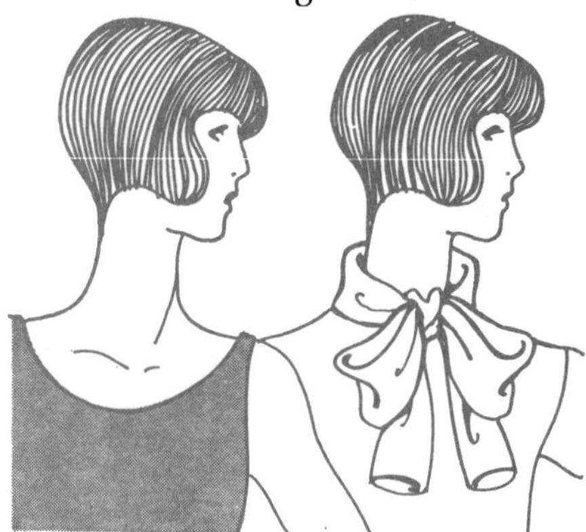

FIGURE TRAIT
Thick waist.

Styles to Avoid—
Cummerbund, wide belts, slim skirts.

Styles to Choose—
Narrow belts, tapered lines on bodice, gored skirts.

MAKING PATTERNS

After you have been sewing for a time, you will probably have a lot of patterns. Take care of them because they may be useful. You may find some patterns you really like and use often. You may have a sleeve or collar pattern that appeals to you. Make a copy of it in pelon or fabric, so it will last. Make a copy of any pattern you want to save—it saves money.

Any sewer can benefit from using a mock-up pattern known as a *fitting shell, standard pattern* or *toile.* A basic paper pattern is carefully adjusted to your personal measurements. It is cut out and tacked together in a fabric, such as muslin. This garment is carefully and accurately fitted on the figure. All new patterns can be compared with it before cutting and sewing, so mistakes are avoided.

Checking the fit of each pattern this way takes time but can be worthwhile. Any process or unusual detail can be tried in muslin before cutting fabric.

To make clothes fit, you can combine two patterns. Unless you are knowledgeable, combine only patterns of the same size from the same figure-type range. The structure of the garments should be similar. If you have any doubts, try the idea in muslin first.

PATTERN MARKINGS AND SYMBOLS

Pattern markings vary according to the manufacturer, but most markings are similar. Learn to recognize the following markings, which are standard.

Straight Grain—*Arrows.* These instruct you to place the pattern on the grain line.

Fold Line—*Bracketed grain line.* Place the pattern edge on the fabric fold on the grain.

Darts—*Two broken lines* for stitching. For simple darts, the solid line at the center is called the *fold line.*

Notches—*V-shape points* along the cutting line used for matching pieces.

Seam Allowance—*Broken lines* around the pattern area indicate the stitching line. The width of allowance can vary from area to area on the pattern. It is normally 5/8 inch wide. The hem allowance is usually written against the bottom cutting line.

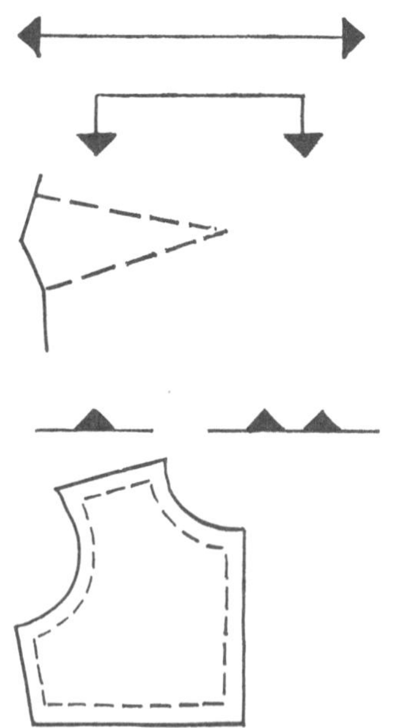

Arrows—These appear on seam lines. They show the direction to sew a seam to avoid distortion of fabric.

Dots, Squares and Triangles—Found in various places on the pattern for matching construction details.
Clip Lines—Usually a *small line with arrows* that indicate where to clip.
Gathering—A *broken line* between two points.
Pleats—Shown by *alternate broken and solid lines on an arrow.* They give the direction of pleats.
Buttonholes—These are indicated by a *solid line.*
Long, Solid Lines—These indicate center-fold lines.
Zipper Line—This shows the position of the zipper and its opening length.
Cutting Lines—The outline of the pattern along which you cut the pattern piece.
Adjustment Line—*Double line* showing where a pattern may be lengthened or shortened.

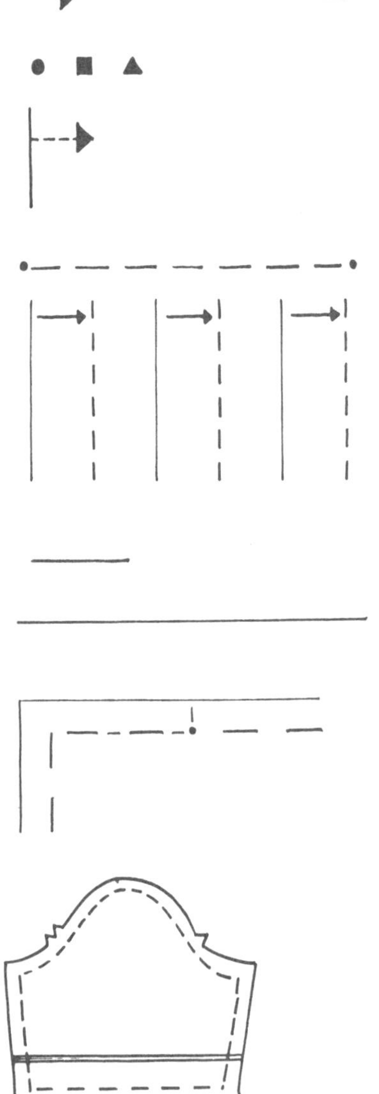

BACK OF PATTERN ENVELOPE

The back of the pattern envelope includes a lot of information. You will usually find:
1. Standard body measurements.
2. The number of pattern pieces.
3. Back views.
4. Identified pattern pieces.
5. Description of the garment.
6. Fabric-requirement charts, showing fabric widths and pattern sizes.
7. Requirements for interfacing, lining and trims, if any.
8. Amount of fabric required for different views.
9. Sewing notions.
10. Recommended fabric for pattern and fabrics not suitable.
11. Measurements for finished garment.
12. Information regarding choice of fabrics with pile, nap, stripes, checks or one-way design.

Consider accessories to be worn with the garment. Buy all the notions listed on the pattern. Match buttons or top-stitching thread to accessories. Buy a few extra buttons in case one is lost in wear.

INSIDE PATTERN ENVELOPE

Cutting and sewing instructions are given on a sheet included in the pattern. Layouts are shown, indicating various pattern sizes on different fabric widths. Circle or mark the diagram you will use, so you can refer to it quickly and easily. Sewing instructions are also found inside on information sheets, along with illustrated stages of garment construction.

PATTERN PREPARATION

Select pattern pieces for the view chosen. Put the pieces not required back in the envelope. Check pattern pieces with the back of the envelope.

Cut out the paper pattern pieces before laying them out. Leave a margin unless you are working on fine or heavy fabrics, then cut the margins away. Use the pattern edge as a cutting guide.

Iron the pattern pieces with a warm iron. Do not use steam because tissue shrinks.

Check your measurements with those shown for your size on the pattern envelope. Compare the pattern pieces with an adjusted personal pattern you have prepared. Transfer any alterations to the new pattern. Lay the personal pattern pieces on the new pattern and transfer fitting adjustments.

PATTERN ADJUSTMENT

Your figure measurements may correspond with those on the pattern you choose. If they do, you will need only slight adjustments to the pattern. Often only the length may need to be changed. Whenever adjustments are made to a pattern, try to change the original line and design of the garment *as little as possible.*

When a garment needs adjustment in an area close to a seam or by a dart, make the alteration at the fitting stage. Problems may occur where there are no seams or darts. Then a section of the pattern may need to be redrawn and fabric recut for the correct fit. When a pattern line is altered, redraw the altered section to preserve the original shape. Seams should have the same lines or curves as before alteration.

If measurements on the pattern do not correspond to yours, other adjustments are needed. Sometimes the bust, waist or hip measurements need to be changed. Your shoulders may slope or one hip bone may be higher than the other. Further adjustments are needed. Altering a pattern piece is quick and easy, once you learn how to make adjustments.

EQUIPMENT FOR PATTERN ADJUSTMENTS

Ruler—Use a transparent ruler with a variety of measurements for accuracy.
T-Square—It is used to check grain lines. A small transparent one is best.
Tissue Paper—Insert this between pattern pieces when they are altered. Use white tissue, and iron it smooth before using.
Soft-Lead Pencil—Use a pencil to redraw pattern lines.
Tape—Permanently fix adjustments in position with tape.
Pincushion—A bracelet-type that fits over the wrist is best.

Pins—Use these to position insertions or additions to the pattern width and length.
Tape Measure—A plastic tape measure with markings on one face is best.
Paper Scissors—Do not cut paper with your *fabric* shears. Paper blunts them quickly. Use special scissors for cutting paper.

SPECIAL POINTS

Press pattern pieces and tissue before you start. Alter adjoining pattern pieces when any adjustments are made. If you do not, pieces will differ in length. If the length of the front of the bodice is altered, make the back of the bodice the same length. If a dart is enlarged, make the seam on which it is placed equal in length.

When redrawing pattern lines, make them clear and bold. Use a thick lead pencil, not a felt-tip pen. Ink may spread and obscure other pattern markings.

Always keep the fold line and grain lines straight. Use the transparent ruler for this purpose.

When increasing or decreasing the size of pattern around your body, make the adjustment in the correct place. The adjustment must not be too high or too low.

When making circumference adjustments, each pattern piece represents a quarter of your body. A line across your figure at waist level and down the center front divides it into four sections. Each skirt or bodice pattern piece needs to be adjusted to 1/4 the total adjustment.

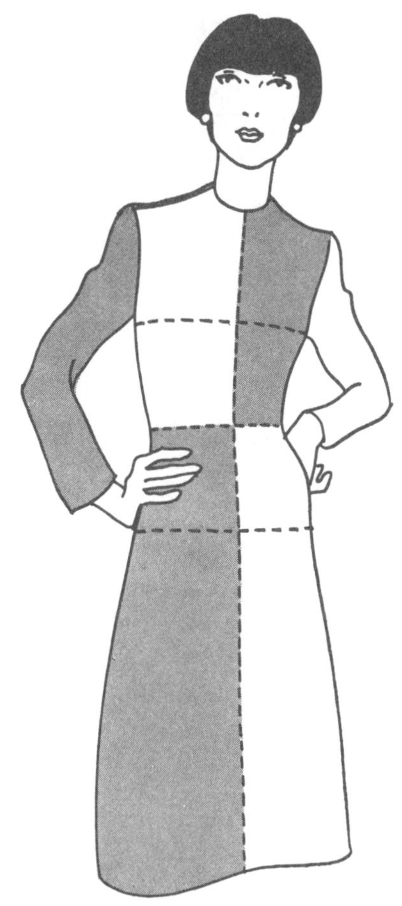

TO LENGTHEN

If the pattern is the correct size, add a piece on the hemline to lengthen it. On some patterns, other places for adjusting the length are marked. If not, follow the methods below.
Skirts and Pants—Note the straight-grain line. The adjustment line must be drawn at *right angles* to it. Draw a line across the pattern about 1/3 the distance between hips and hem levels. For pants, adjust the crotch length first.

Cut across the pattern on the marked line, and separate the two pieces. Cut a piece of paper 6 inches deep, slightly wider than the pattern piece. Lay the pieces the correct distance apart on the insert. Pin or tape in position. Cut away excess paper.

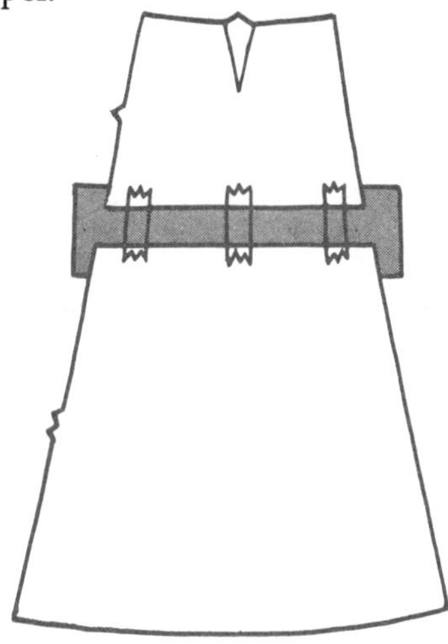

In new seam lines, draw cutting and dart lines to continue those on the pattern pieces. Repeat on the pattern pieces.
Crotch—The crotch of pants must fit well. Measure your crotch length, and compare it with the pattern length. Measure pattern pieces along the side seam line. Measure from the waist seam line to the bottom of the crotch seam allowance.

Insert a piece of paper, and cut the pattern pieces about 3-1/4 inches above the crotch. Straighten the crotch seam to the waistline if necessary.

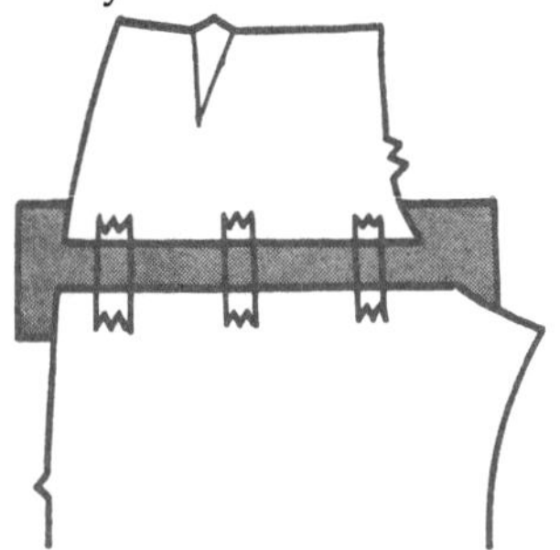

Bodice—Insert a strip of paper. Cut across the pattern between the bottom of the armhole and the waist.

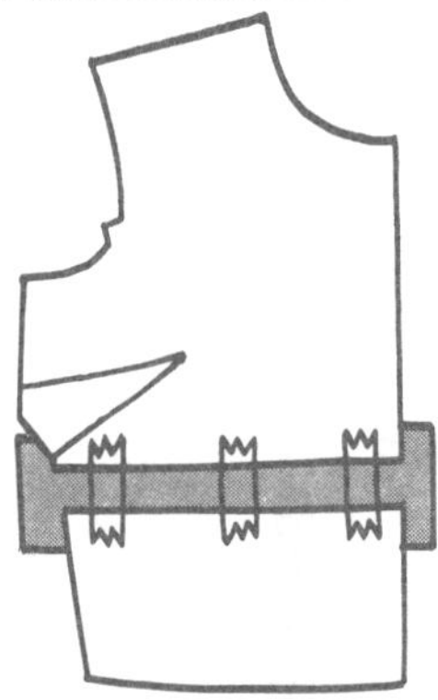

Sleeve—Measure your arm length, and compare it with the length of the sleeve pattern. Measure the pattern from the seam allowance at the center of the sleeve to the hemline.

Draw the adjustment line halfway between the top of the sleeve and the elbow. On long sleeves, draw another line halfway between the elbow and hemline. Cut the pattern, and insert paper to adjust the sleeve to the desired length.

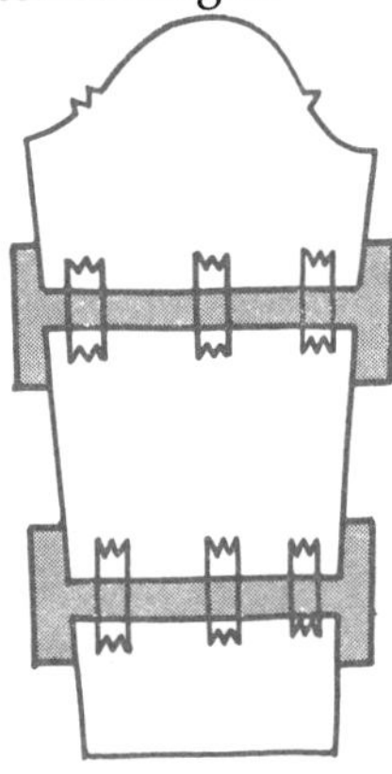

Waistline—A dress without a waist seam may be adjusted for length. Insert a strip of paper at the level of the waist. This is usually marked on the pattern. Check the total length of the pattern to make sure the hemline is in the correct place.

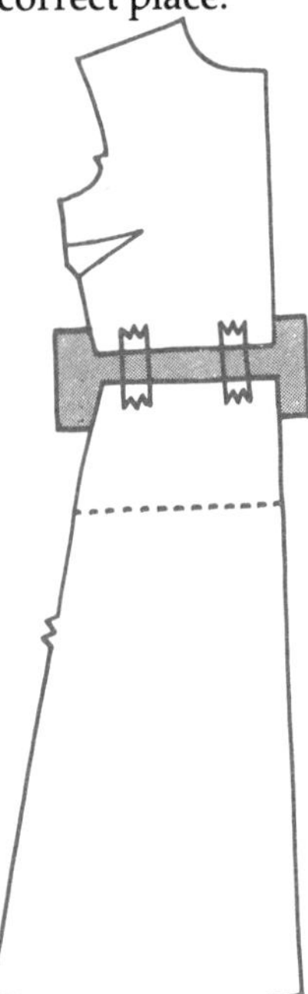

TO SHORTEN

See the section on lengthening opposite, for details on where to adjust pattern pieces. If there is no adjustment line on the pattern, draw it in. Draw another line above that, equal to the amount the pattern is to be shortened.

Fold the pattern so the lower line meets the upper one. Crease or iron a pleat in the pattern. Pin or tape the lines in place.

The seam line will be displaced and must be redrawn. Use a piece of paper as an extension. At the hemline, some of the original seam allowance may have to be trimmed off.

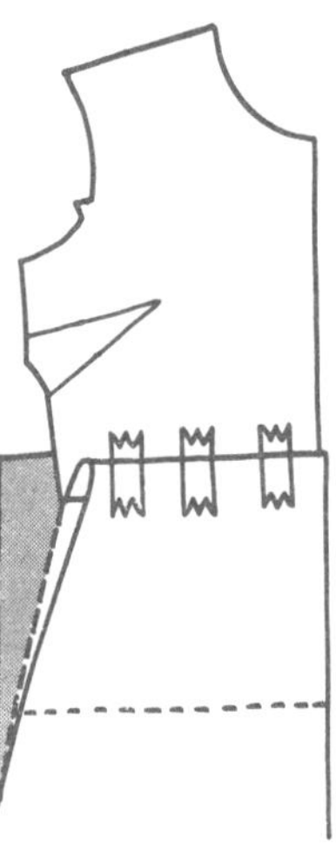

Skirts and Pants—Follow the previous instructions. Adjust the crotch length of the pants before shortening. If only a small adjustment is needed, cut off a little at the hemline. Follow the shape of the pattern pieces.

To raise the hip line, shorten along a line just above the pattern hip line. If this is not necessary, make the adjustment about midway between the knee and hemline. Pin a paper extension to the side of the pattern, and draw in a new seam line.

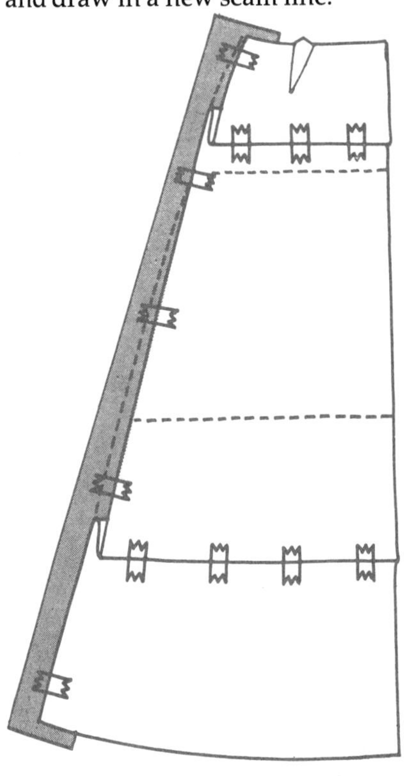

Crotch—Compare body and pattern measurements as described for lengthening. Make a fold on the adjustment line, and extend the pattern with a paper strip at the sides. Tape a new seam line in the original stitching line. Redraw the cutting line.

Bodice and Sleeves—Shorten the same places as described for lengthening, page 49. Follow the instructions for shortening at the beginning of the section.

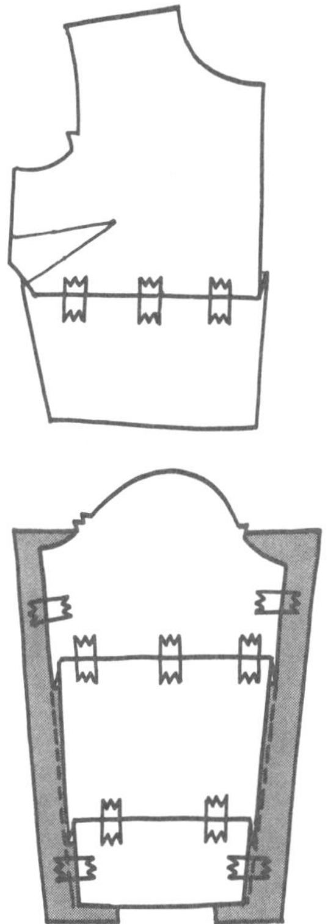

TO ENLARGE

If adjustments are up to 2 inches in width, add extra paper at the sides of the pattern pieces. When adding more than 2 inches, insert a whole strip of paper in the pattern piece. The methods for inserting paper are described below.

Up to 2 Inches—Place the edge of the pattern piece on a strip of paper about 4 inches wide. The paper should extend along the area to be adjusted. Measure the required amount from the seam line. For a four-piece garment, measure only 1/4 the total extra width needed on each side seam. Draw in a new tapered seam line and cutting line. Trim excess paper.

Over 2 Inches—Draw a line down the pattern pieces, parallel to the straight-grain line. On bodices, this new line is halfway between the neckline and the edge of the shoulder. On skirts, it is halfway between the side seam and center line. Cut and insert a strip of paper as described for lengthening a pattern. Relocate darts if necessary.

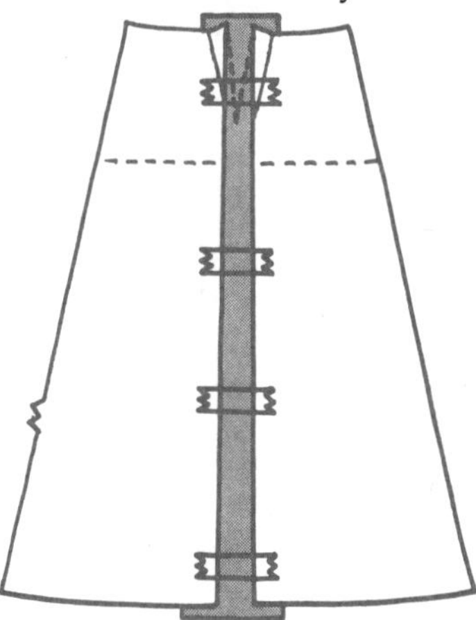

Skirts and Pants—Compare your waist and hip measurements with those on the pattern envelope. If up to 2 inches is needed on the whole pattern, follow the method described earlier.

Waistline—Add 1/4 the extra width needed to each side-waist pattern piece. Taper the new seam line to the hip line.

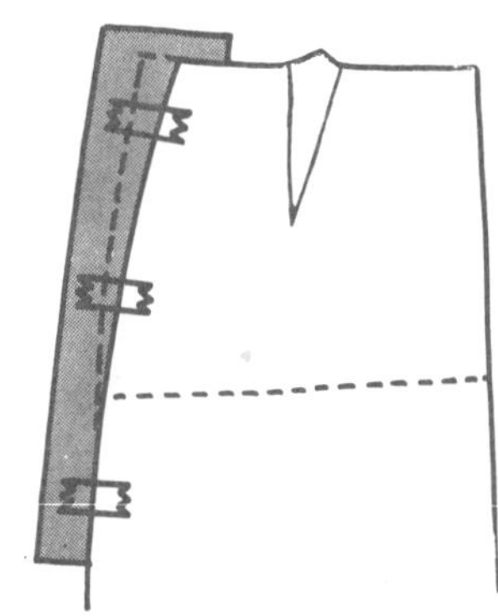

Hip Line—Add 1/4 the extra width needed to each side-hip of the pattern piece. Taper the new seam line from the waistline to the hip line and back to the seam line in the hem area.

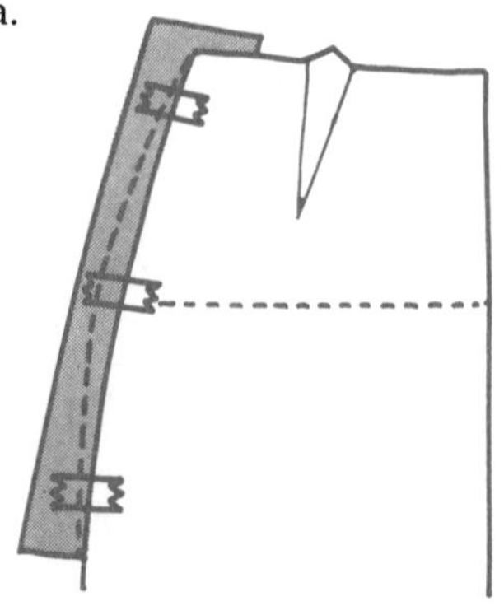

Bodice—Follow the methods given if extra width is needed all over. If using paper, insert only 1/4 or 1/2 the total. Make small adjustments at the bust and waist by extending seam lines in those areas.

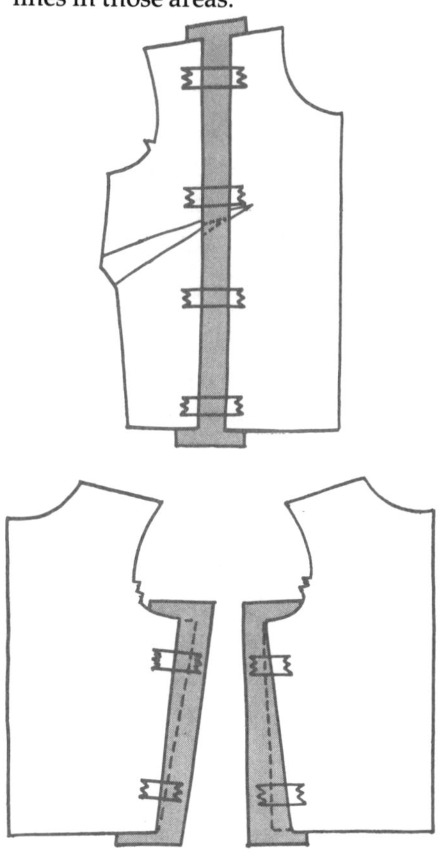

Sleeves—Follow the general methods given at left for inserting a strip of paper. If the sleeve is too small at the wrist, make a slash instead of cutting the pattern in two. Insert a shaped strip.

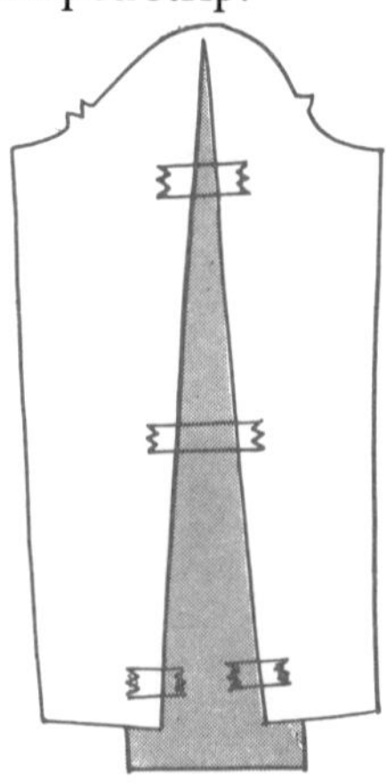

TO REDUCE

To reduce the width of a pattern piece, reverse the method given for enlarging. If up to 2 inches needs to be taken out, alter the sides of the pattern pieces. If more than 2 inches is removed, draw an adjustment line parallel to the straight-grain line. Pleat the pattern piece there.

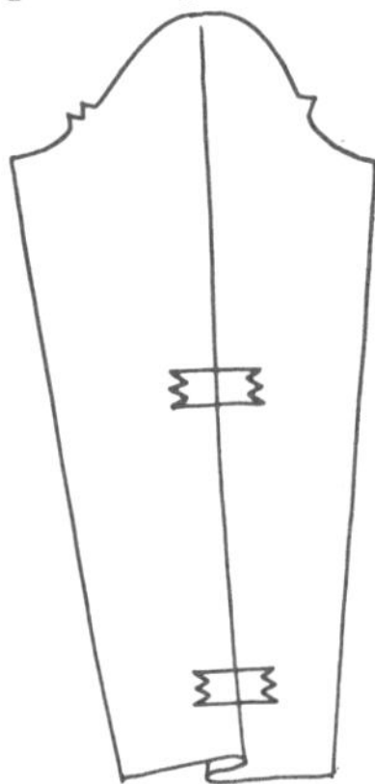

Skirt and Pants—Compare your waist and hip measurements with those on the pattern envelope. If a general reduction in width is needed, make a *vertical* pleat in the pattern. This is described in the section on shortening, page 49.

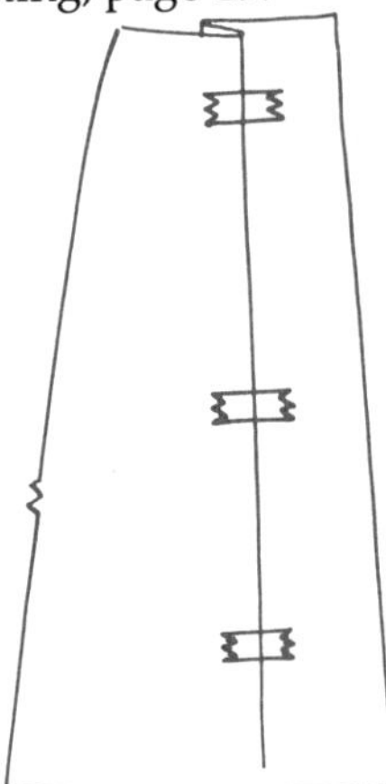

Waistline—Measure in from the original side seam line along the waistline. Mark 1/4 the amount to be reduced. Draw a new seam line. Taper from the new waistline mark to the original hip line. Follow the shape of the pattern piece.

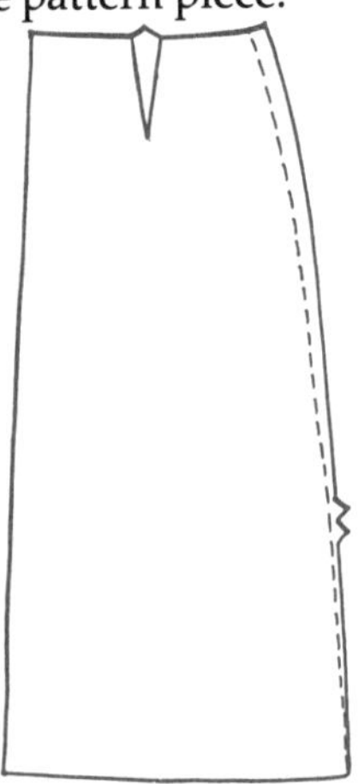

Hip Line—Make a new hip-line mark 1/4 of the amount to be reduced in from the original side seam line. Taper the new seam line from that point up to the waistline and down to the hem area.

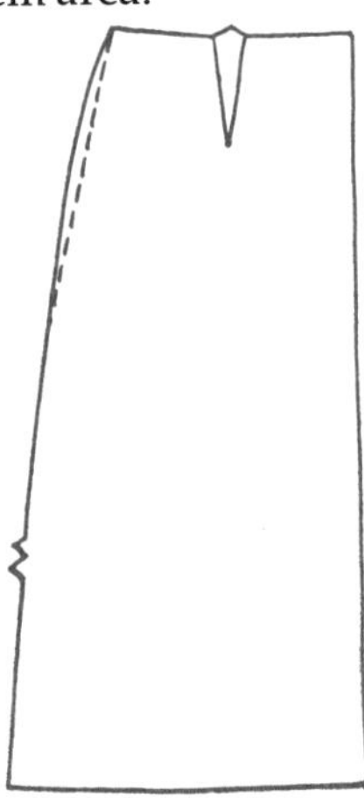

Bodice—To reduce the bodice all over, fold the pattern along the line for enlarging a bodice. To reduce only the bust or waist areas, mark a new seam line at the top or bottom of the underarm seam. Redraw the seam line.

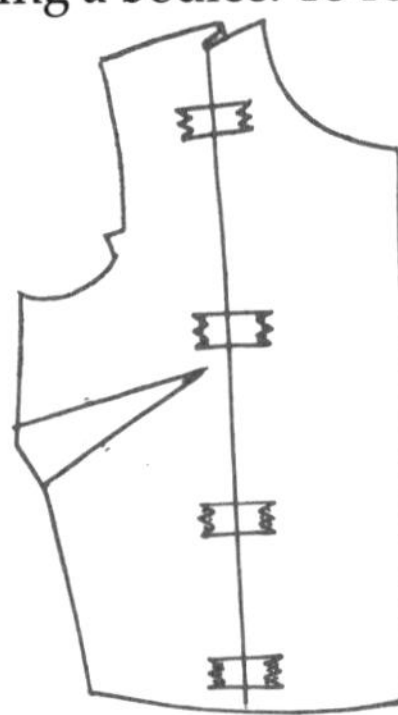

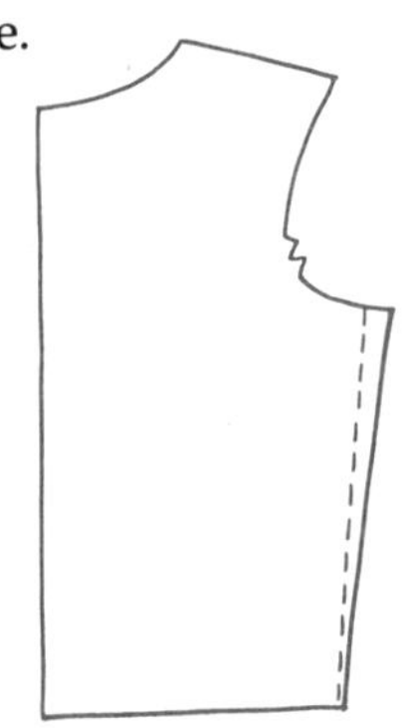

ADJUSTING PINNED PATTERN

Minor adjustments should be made *on* the figure. Do this with the paper pattern pieces. Pin the main paper pattern pieces together, and try them on. Do this carefully or the pattern may tear. Wear foundation garments and shoes you will wear with the garment. Stand in front of a mirror.

The pattern is only half a garment, so ask someone to help you with this fitting. It is difficult to fit yourself properly. A pinned pattern may also be tried on a personal dress form.

Check the shoulder, neck, bust and waistline of the bodice for a good fit. The waist and hip lines of skirts or pants should fit well, with ease for movement. If adjustments are slight, repin pieces. For larger adjustments, make a note of the alterations on the pattern or on a separate piece of paper.

ADJUST PAPER PATTERN FOR FAULTS

Specific figure faults must be adjusted on every pattern. Make the adjustments on the paper pattern *before* laying it out on the fabric.

Large Bust—Cut the pattern from the shoulder almost to the waist. Cut it from the center of the bustline almost to the underarm seam. Put paper under the slashes. Pin paper in place to add the extra amounts needed.

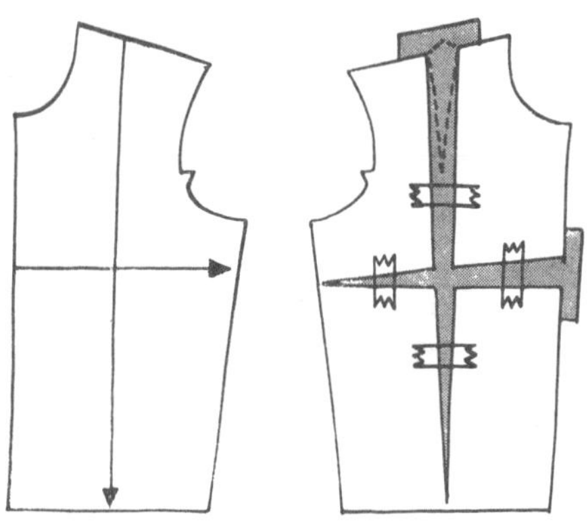

Small Bust—The pattern piece usually must be made narrower and shorter. Often you can shorten the pattern and make a larger bust dart.

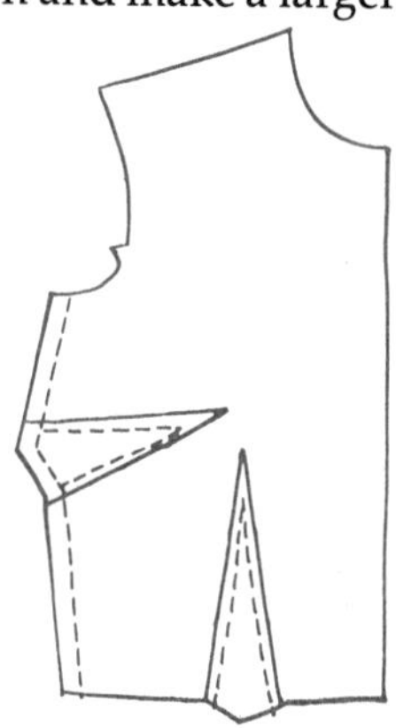

Low Bust—If the bust dart is too high, the bodice is tight and unflattering. Shorten the pattern slightly, then lower the point of the dart.

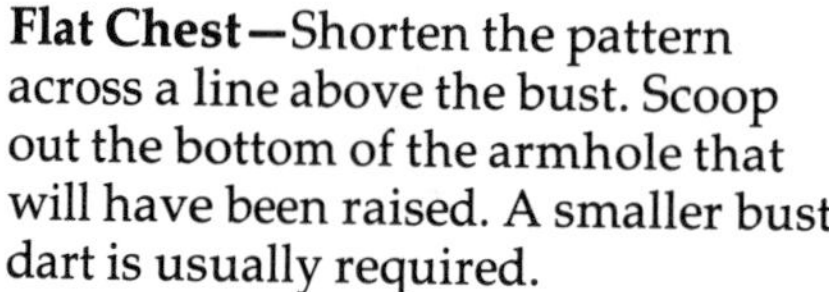

Flat Chest—Shorten the pattern across a line above the bust. Scoop out the bottom of the armhole that will have been raised. A smaller bust dart is usually required.

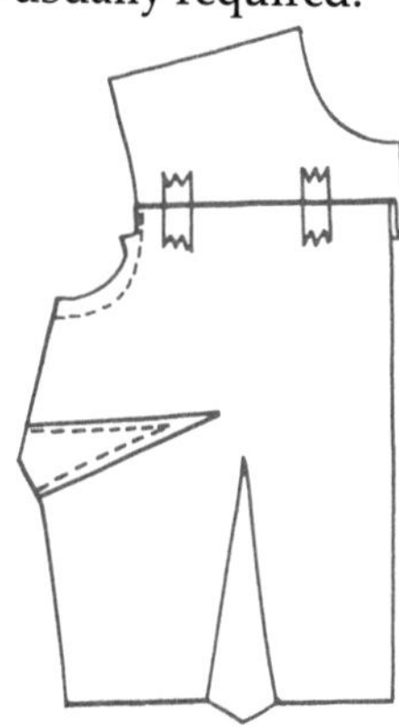

Narrow Chest—Pin a wedge-shape piece out of the center front from the neckline. Mark a new straight-grain line parallel with the new center front. Reduce the bust dart a little.

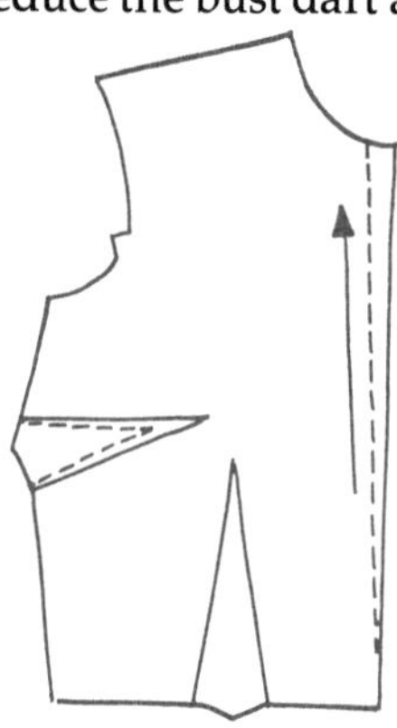

Round Shoulders—Split the back bodice across almost to the underarm seam. Open the pattern to the required size.

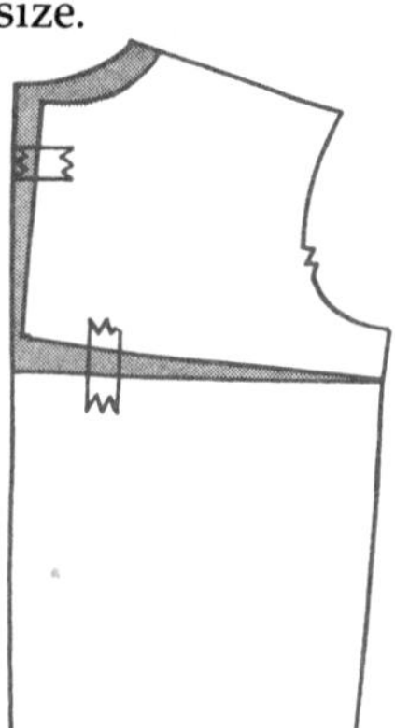

Broad Shoulders—Slash the back bodice from the shoulder seam almost to the waist. Insert a strip of paper.

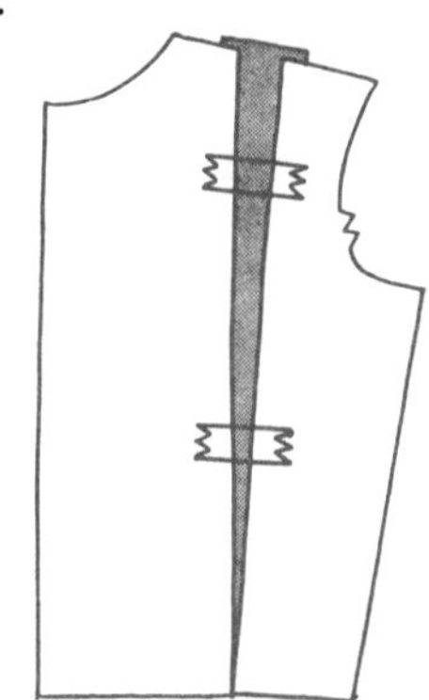

Narrow Shoulders—Fold or cut a diagonal line from halfway along the shoulder line to halfway down the armhole. Overlap the cut edges to reduce the width, and draw a new seam line.

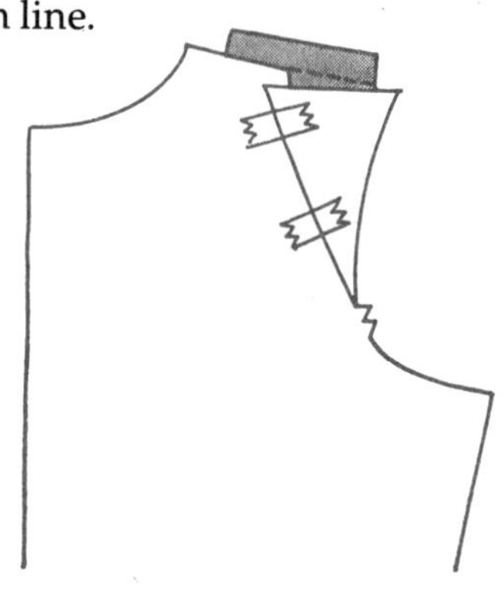

Square Shoulders—Extend the top of the armhole seam to raise the outer shoulder line. Raise the bottom of the armhole to match or it will be too loose.

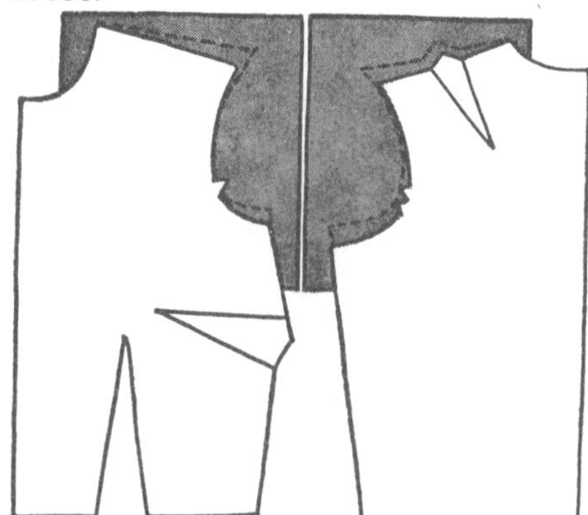

Sloping Shoulders—Start at the neckline. Slope the shoulder seam line down to the armhole. Lower the bottom of the armhole or it will be too tight.

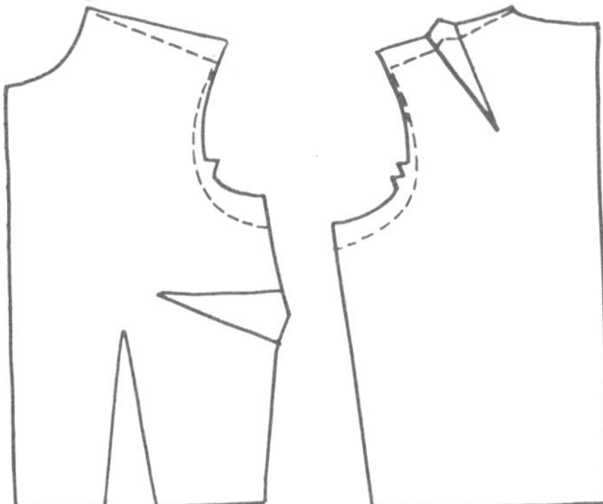

Prominent Hip Bones on Pants—Unpin the darts, and repin them to fit. Make them bigger and shorter. If necessary, make the waistline wider by extending it at the side seams.

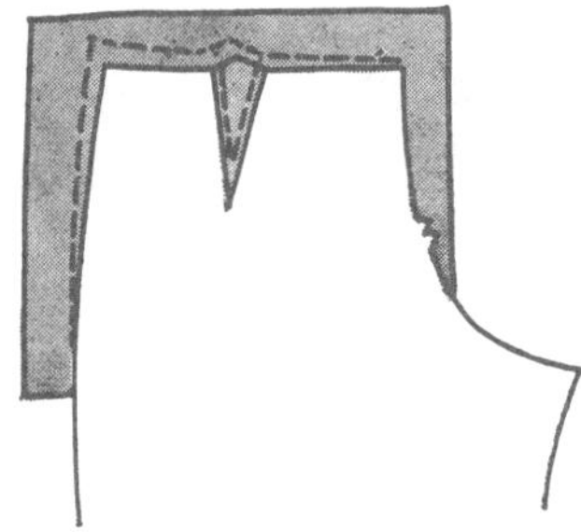

Thick Waist on Bodice—Slash from the waistline almost to the armhole. Open out, and insert a piece of paper.

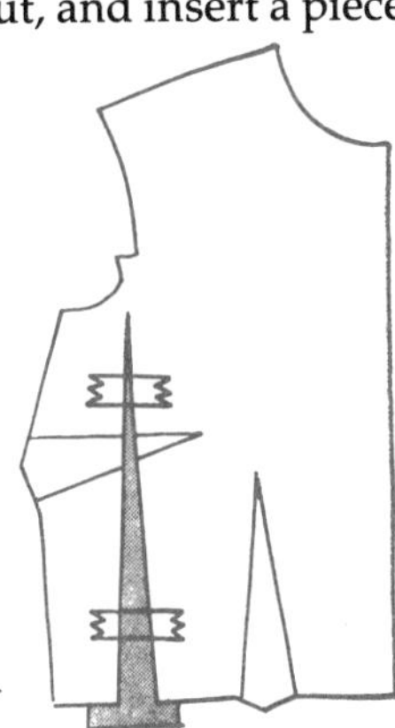

Thick Waist on Skirt—Slash from the waist almost to the hem, and insert a piece of paper.

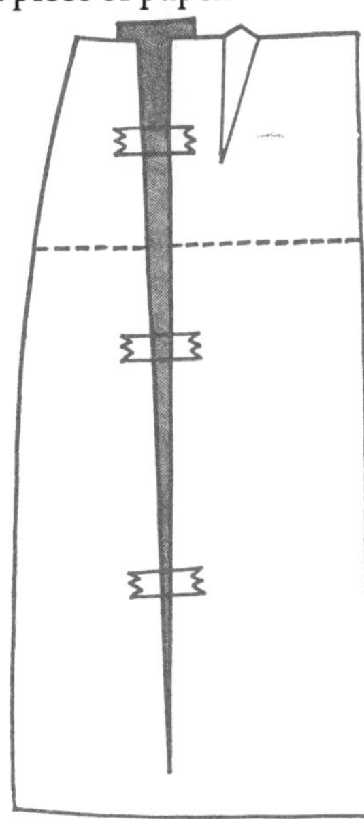

Large Seat on Skirt—Slash the skirt as shown, and insert paper to increase size. Enlarge bodice pieces to match at waist if necessary.

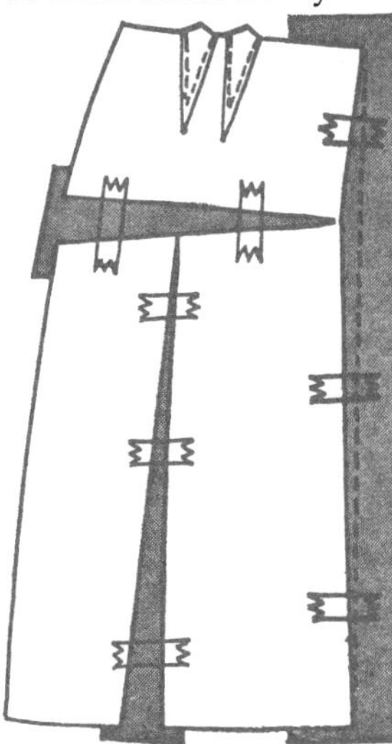

Large Seat on Pants—Unpin the darts. Let the back of the pattern fall in position without creasing or pulling. Add extra paper to the top of the back inner-leg seam, and repin darts. Add to waist side seams if the waistline is too tight.

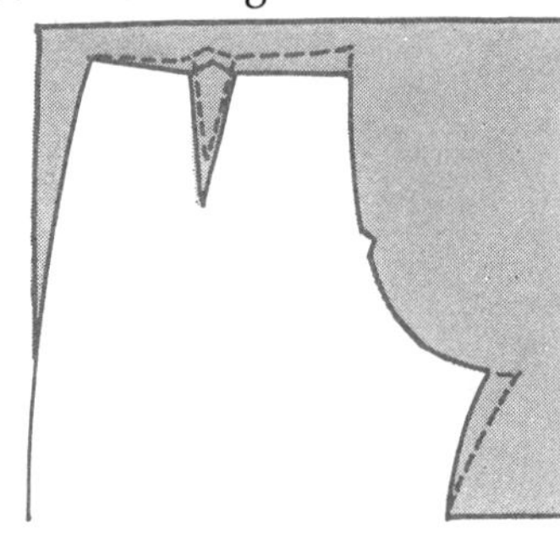

Flat Seat on Pants—Make folds across the top of the hips and down the legs to take out excess. Repin darts to fit. If waistline is still too large, take out excess at side seams.

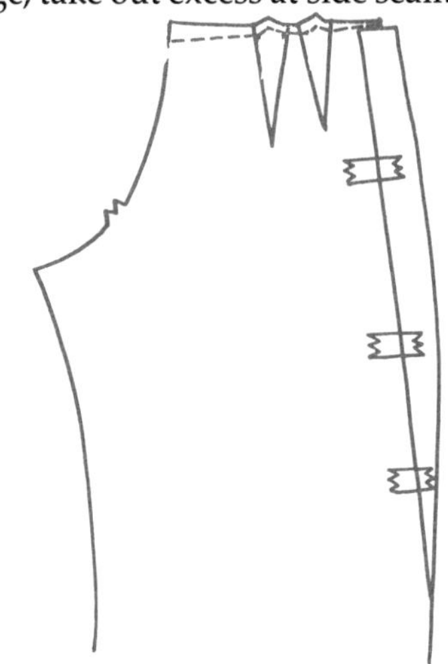

Hollow Back on Skirt—Ease the skirt above the hip line. Make a wide fold at the center back, finishing to almost nothing at the side seam. Draw a new center-back line.

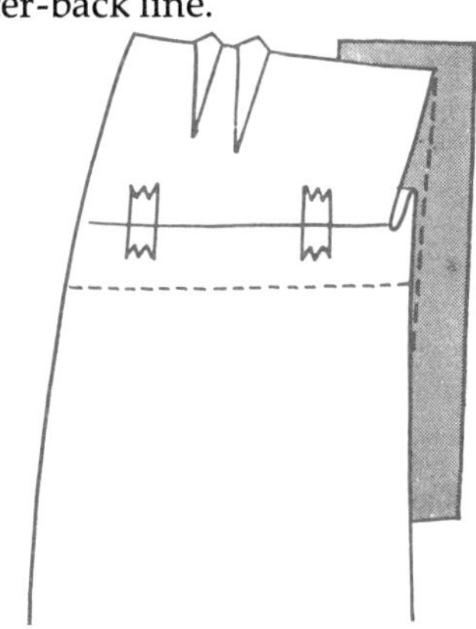

Large Stomach on Skirt—Make larger darts in the skirt front.

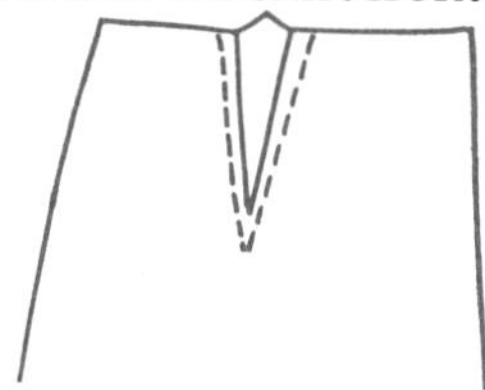

Large Stomach on Pants—Unpin the darts, and allow the front of the pattern to drop until the side seams lie flat. Add a piece of paper to the front inner leg seam. Repin waist darts to fit.

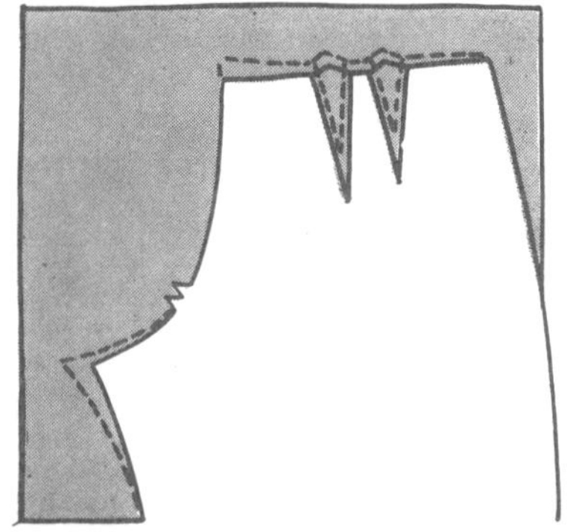

Flat Stomach on Skirt—Move the darts in the skirt front closer to the side seams.

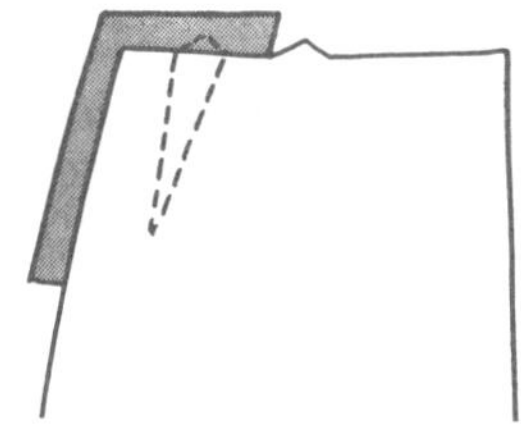

Plump Upper Arm on Short Sleeves—Insert a straight strip of paper down the center of the sleeve.
Plump Upper Arm on Long Sleeves—Slash as shown in diagram below. Lay pattern pieces on a sheet of plain paper, and pin or tape in place.

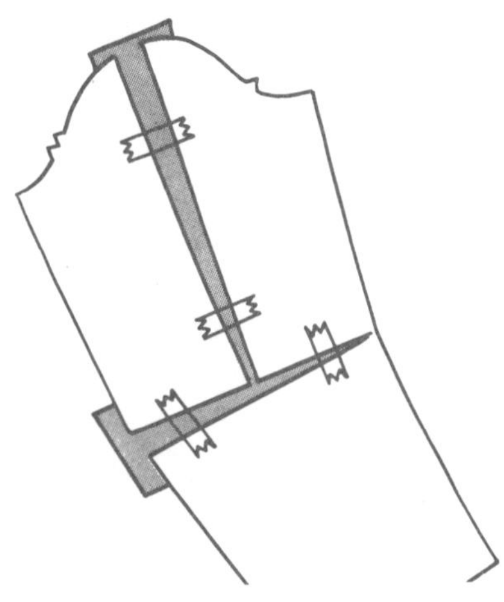

PREPARING FABRIC

Examine fabric before buying it. If it is flawed, a store may allow a price reduction or extra fabric to compensate for the flaw. Be sure you will be able to avoid the flaw when cutting out garment pieces. Some fabrics need to be prepared by pressing, shrinking or straightening. This allows the finished garment to fit and hang well.

Study the fabric to see if there is an up-and-down motif, one-way design, unusual stripe or nap. Fabric is usually rolled on a bolt or tube. Wide fabrics may be folded in half lengthwise.

All fabrics, except tubular-knit fabrics, have two finished edges called *selvages.* They are at each side of the bolt, or both at one side, if the fabric is folded.

When you get the fabric home, check for the right-side and wrong-side. Check the grain, and straighten the ends of fabric. Test for shrinkage. Shrink, straighten and press fabric *before* laying out pattern pieces.

If it is not obvious which is the right-side, look at the selvage. It may help. Selvages are usually rougher and more uneven on the wrong-side of the fabric. As long as all pattern pieces are cut on the same side, it does not matter with some fabrics which side is used.

Two sets of thread run at right angles to each other in the fabric. The thread running lengthwise is the *warp.* The thread running crosswise is the *weft.* These are also called *straight grains.* Sometimes after storage or handling, the warp and weft do not run at right angles to each other. Look at the cut length of fabric to see if it is crooked or if the grain is not straight.

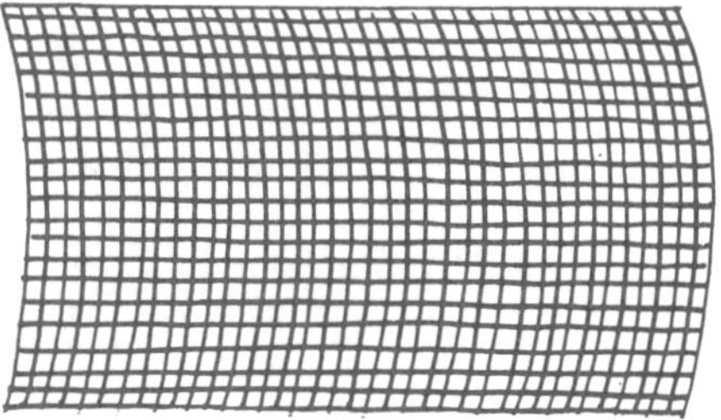

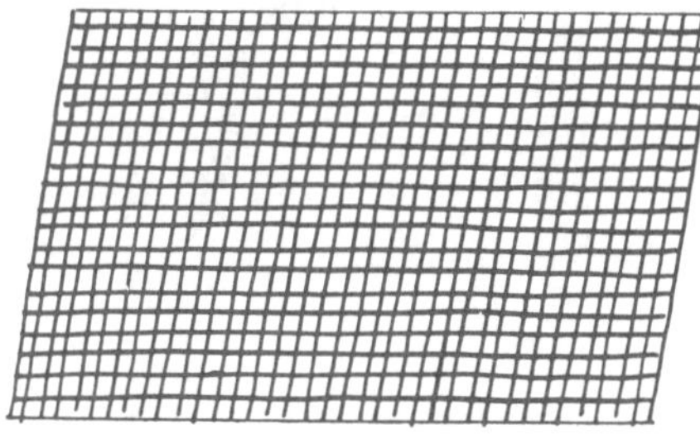

If both weft and warp are slanted, the material is *off grain.* Cut the garment from fabric with the two grains at right angles to one another. Garments cut *on the grain* maintain their shape and hang well. Those cut *off the grain* may be a failure. The true bias is a line at a 45° angle from the straight grain.

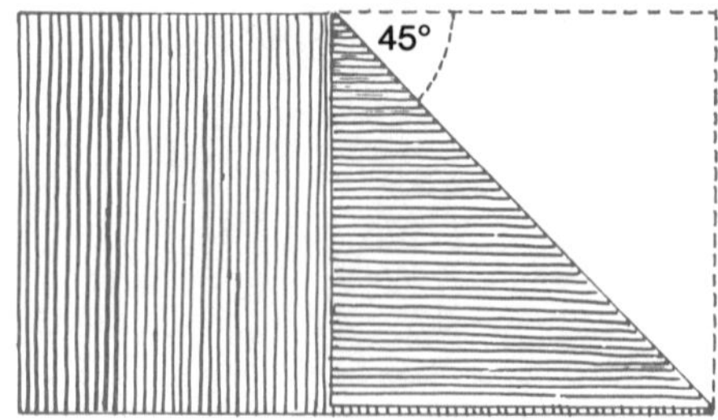

STRAIGHTENING WOVEN FABRIC

Method One—Cut into the selvage edge with scissors. Pick up one or more weft threads with a pin. Pull gently, slipping the material along the thread with the other hand. Cut along the space shown by the pulled thread. Cut as far as the space is visible. If the thread breaks, continue cutting along the line it has made until you can again pick up the end. Continue until the opposite selvage is reached.

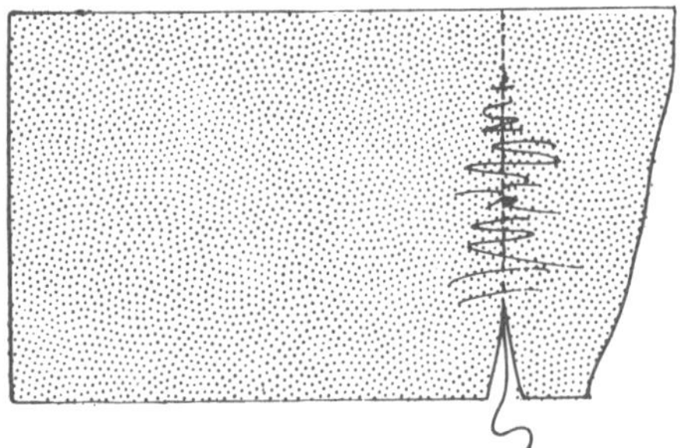

Method Two—Do this if the material is ribbed, checked or woven with a pattern. Use the *pattern* in the fabric as a guide for cutting from one selvage to the other.

Method Three—Check the material to see if it will tear. Snip one selvage with scissors about 1 inch from the cut end. Tear sharply to the opposite side, then cut the selvage. If the material tears easily, repeat the tearing process at the other end. Often ends of evenly woven cotton, synthetics and silk can be straightened by tearing. Do not tear linen fabrics on the crosswise threads.

Method Four—Cut napped or pile fabrics on a thread. Unravel threads on the weft edge until one thread can be pulled off the whole width of the material. Cut off fringe, and make the

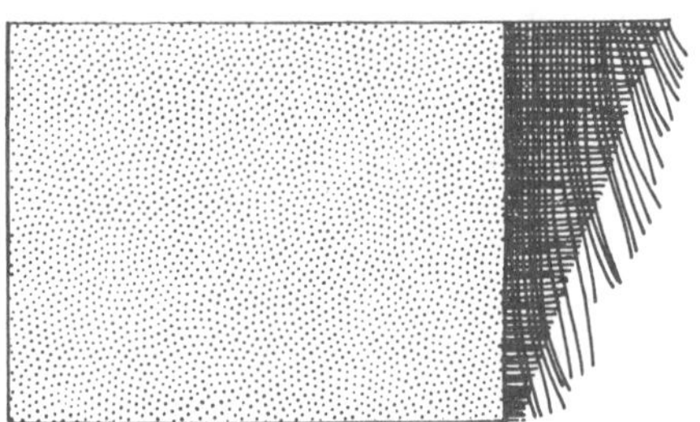

edge even. Fold the fabric in half lengthwise. Line ends up with a cutting board or a table corner. The crosswise edge should form a right angle with the selvages. This proves the material is on grain. If necessary, preshrink fabric before straightening the grain.

STRAIGHTENING KNIT FABRIC

Method One—For loosely knit jersey, pull one weft thread. Work across the width of fabric so the raw edge is separated from the main length of fabric.

Method Two—Carefully run a small tacking thread across the weft. Pick up the same horizontal thread, and cut along tacking. On some fabrics, run a line of machine-basting along this cut edge to prevent stretching.

SHRINKAGE

Always check for shrinkage. If you do not know how fabric will shrink, make a shrinkage test. Some fabrics can shrink as much as 3 inches to a yard. Wool, inexpensive cotton and rayons may also shrink.

Test for Shrinkage—Lay out the pattern pieces on the fabric. Find a small sample square to cut for a test. Do not cut a piece off a corner. You may have to buy an extra length to cut out a whole garment piece.

Cut a square from the fabric 1/4 yard by 1/4 yard (1/4-yard square). Make note of *exact* measurements. Soak the fabric square in hot water for about 15 minutes. Lift it out of the water. Remove excess water by blotting fabric gently with a thick towel. Allow the fabric to dry naturally. When completely dry, measure for shinkage. If shrinkage has occurred, follow the instructions below for preshrinking the fabric type.

You can also trace a carefully measured square of fabric. Press with a damp cloth, and allow the fabric to dry. Measure again. This test may also give an indication of color fastness.

Preshrinking and Pressing Fabrics

WOOL

If wool needs shrinking or straightening, use the following method.

Check for crosswise thread or weft ends. Fold material in half lengthwise, with right-sides together. The edges of warp ends and selvage ends should be even. Hand-tack the ends together.

Use a clean, absorbent cotton fabric. Old sheets are good for this task. There should be enough cloth to equal the length of the fabric. The cloth should be wider than the folded fabric being treated. Have cloth evenly damp, and remove excess moisture.

Place the fabric flat on a table, and put the damp cloth on top of it. Fold from one end toward the center, turning the lengths together in wide folds. Push down while folding, to push moisture through. Handle the opposite end the same way. Place the whole piece in a large plastic bag to evenly distribute moisture.

Let the wool fabric remain like this for two to four hours, depending on thickness. This allows the moisture to be thoroughly absorbed.

Unfold the fabric. Do not hang it up or it will stretch out of shape. Pull and smooth the fabric gently by hand to straighten the grain. When the top layer is almost dry to the touch, rearrange it so the underlayer shrinks and dries evenly. Pressing is usually unnecessary. If pressing is needed, use a steam iron on the *lengthwise* grain.

COTTON, LINEN AND WASHABLE FABRIC

Check crosswise thread and weft ends. Fold fabric in half lengthwise with right-sides together. Pin and tack selvages. Put crosswise ends together. Place pins near edges, parallel and a hand-span apart. Fold the length of fabric in accordian pleats. Make folds about the width of your hand.

Immerse the fabric in warm water until it is thoroughly wet. Check between the folds of the fabric for uniform wetness.

Lift fabric from the water. Remove excess water by wrapping the fabric in a towel. *Do not* wring the fabric out.

Lay the fabric on a flat surface covered with plastic. Do not hang it up, or the fabric will stretch and distort. Gently pull and smooth fabric to straighten the grain. It may be necessary to pull and smooth it while drying to keep the grain straight.

Press the fabric with a steam iron when it is completely dry. Press on the *lengthwise* grain.

Corduroy—Avoid crushing the pile when wet. You can do this by following this method. Fold the corduroy as described above, then soak it in water. Remove the fabric from the water. Gently press with your palms to get rid of excess moisture. *Do not* wring the fabric.

Place the corduroy in a dryer. This raises the pile, and pressing should be unnecessary. If corduroy must be dry-cleaned, do not wash or dry it.

MAN-MADE FABRIC

Acetate, triacetate, rayon, nylon, polyester, acrylic and other materials are man-made fabrics. These fabrics usually do not need to be shrunk. Read the care label to see if the material has been preshrunk or for information regarding its finish.

If shrinking is not necessary, follow the instructions for straightening the grain on woven fabrics. If shinking *is* needed, follow instructions for cotton and linen.

Off-grain materials labeled "preshrunk" can be straightened by pressing, unless they have a permanent finish. These finishes lock the material grain in place. Straighten and shrink fabrics blended with wool using the method for wool.

SILK FABRIC

No shrinking is necessary for fine silk fabric. To straighten off-grain silk fabric, press in shape with a steam iron.

TORN-EDGE FABRIC

Press raw edges of torn material to restore a smooth grain line. Flatten any rippling edges. Press ends, even if the rest of the material is on grain.

For material torn in both directions, press lengthwise and crosswise. Never deliberately tear a fabric along its length. This can stretch the weft and distort the weave. To maintain perfect grain, fold the material in half before pressing it.

JERSEY FABRIC

Most man-made jersey fabrics do not shrink. If they are washable, *test* them before cutting out the garment. If a self-lined fabric is off-grain, it cannot be straightened. Thoroughly examine fabric at the time of purchase.

If the test piece shrinks, follow instructions for shrinking cotton and linen at the first stages. Carefully remove fabric from the water, and support the fabric weight. Jersey fabrics hold more water than woven ones, so you may need help. Two pairs of hands are better than one. You can also put fabric on a large wire rack or in a draining bowl while in the water. Lift out the rack or bowl with fabric, and let it drain.

On a flat surface, carefully sandwich the fabric between layers of towels. Place the fabric and towels in a dryer, and dry for about 15 seconds.

Remove the fabric, and put it on a flat surface. Rearrange the fabric on plastic so it is smooth, straight and flat. Let it dry. Turn layers occasionally to help drying.

Pressing is usually unnecessary. If pressing is needed, use a cool iron. Work along the length of the fabric.

Wool Jersey—Almost all cotton jersey fabric is washable. Many washable wool jerseys are also available. When washing these fabrics, some weft shrinkage usually occurs. It is natural for jersey fabric to stretch during the washing process.

Shrink wool jersey the same way as wool. Use slightly wetter wrapping cloths. Lightly press wool jersey to shape, and straighten it along the length of the fabric. Use a dry pressing cloth and steam iron.

Cotton Jersey—Shrink cotton jersey the same way as cotton. Finish with a 15-second spin in the dryer.

Lightly press cotton jersey to shape, and straighten it along the length of the fabric. Use a dry pressing cloth and steam iron.

STRAIGHTEN GRAIN BY PRESSING

When fabric has been preshrunk and is slightly off-grain, it can usually be straightened by pressing with a steam iron. Do not handle wool this way.

Check the thread ends for regularity. Fold the fabric in half lengthwise, with right-sides together. Pull diagonally to straighten the ends.

Pin the crosswise or weft ends, then tack selvage edges together. Remove pins.

If the material is off-grain, diagonal wrinkles and puckers will appear when the doubled material is laid on a flat surface. The wrinkling gives an indication of how much the fabric is off-grain.

Dampen the underlayer of fabric with a wet cloth or sponge. When a steam iron is used, it provides enough dampness for the top layer of the fabric.

Move the iron along the lengthwise grain when pressing the fabric. If the fabric remains off-grain, press the iron along the weft or crosswise grain.

Avoid pressing the center fold of the material. The crease is difficult to remove.

FITTING AND ALTERATIONS

Fitting

Figure types vary from person to person, even though body measurements are similar. Accurate fitting of a garment must be made during construction. Correct fitting relies on accurately placing the pattern on the fabric grain line. Pay attention to cutting and transferring construction marks.

If inaccuracies occur before you cut the pattern out, a good fit is difficult during later stages. There is a relationship between each stage of garment construction. The accuracy of each process depends on attention to detail in previous stages. The final success of the garment depends on *all* these steps.

PREPARING TO FIT

If you have made adjustments to the pattern, the fitting stage should be easy. For a perfect fit, minor adjustments may be needed.

If clothes fit well, you feel comfortable and self-confident wearing them. Garments that fit well are more flattering than those that are lopsided, wrinkled or bulging in the wrong places.

Stitching—Complete all stay-stitching before assembling the garment. This prevents stretching bias edges that are not sewn.

Wear underclothes and shoes you will wear with the garment. These make a difference to the appearance of the fitted garment.

If shoulder pads are needed, pin them in place before fitting. If the garment is belted, make the belt first.

Stand in a relaxed manner while the garment is being fitted. Move around, sit down, bend, reach up and down. This aspect of fitting is often overlooked. A garment must allow room for body movement, and it must fit well.

Look as well-groomed while your garment is being fitted as you will when you wear it. The overall appearance helps you visualize how your finished garment will look.

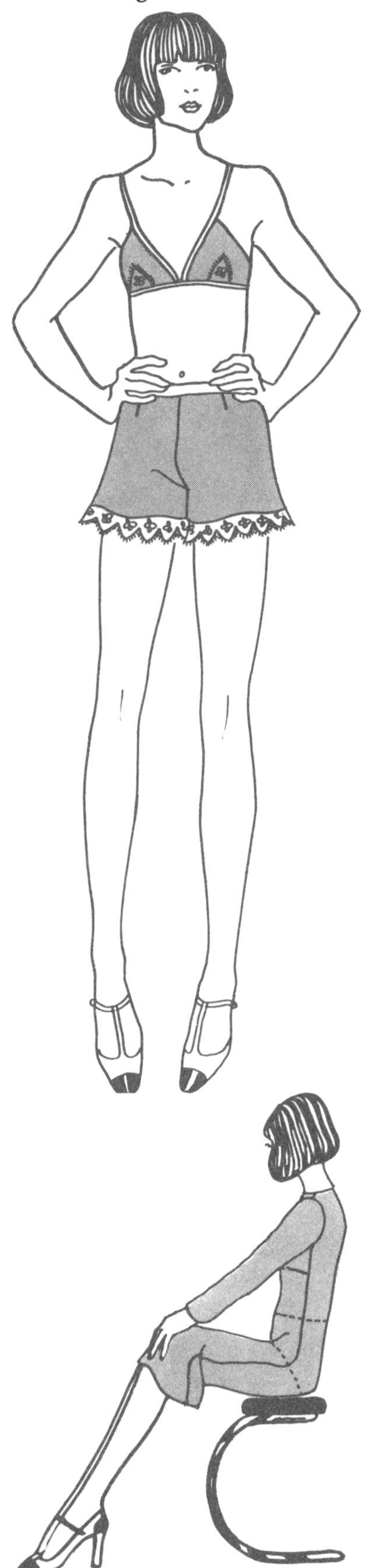

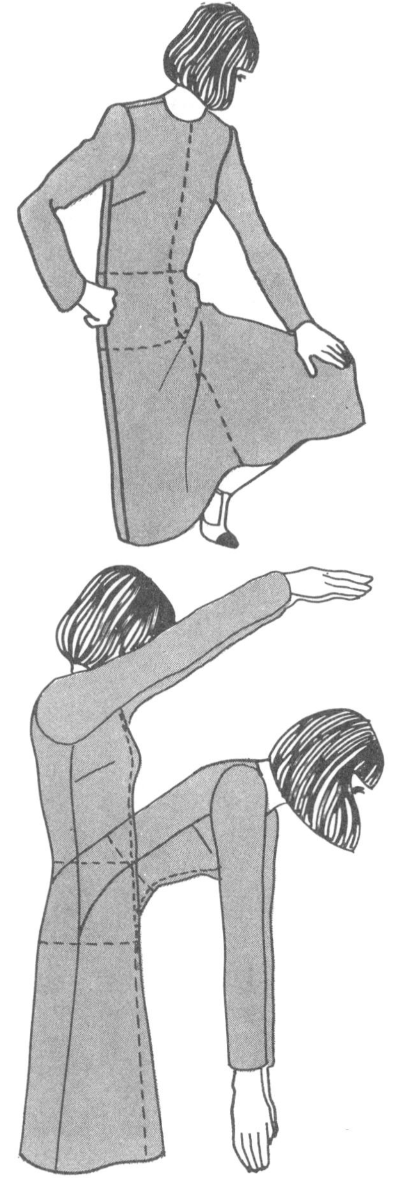

Fitting Hints—Trace-tack the front and center-back lines on garment pieces. Also tack suggested lines for attachment of pockets, cuffs and other surface details. Tack major parts of the garment together. Clip neckline and armholes to stay-stitching.

Mark the center-front and center-back line of your slip with trace-tacking. Pin the center-front and center-back line of the garment to these lines. This should help the garment hang straight at the fitting stage.

Place a 1-inch-wide ribbon around the waistline, and pin it. Pin the bodice and skirt to the ribbon. This locates the correct waistline and gives added support while fitting.

Overlap centers, seam lines and openings by pinning them horizontally. Increase or decrease width by taking in or letting out at the *seams* or *darts,* not at closure areas.

When wrinkles occur, *pat* the fabric in position. Relocate seams where wrinkles indicate they are needed. This may mean reducing one seam allowance and increasing another.

It may help with some fabrics to lightly press the fitting adjustments before finally sewing. This gives a better idea of the finished effect.

When pockets or flaps are used, position them with the final hemline in mind. Tack up the hemline on a skirt or jacket so you can check the proportions. These should be pleasing and flattering to your figure. Pockets may appear too large, too high or too low. They may even give unwanted emphasis to a large bust or broad hips.

Try on the garment in a well-lit room. Stand before a full-length mirror, with the garment turned right-side out.

Side seams and center seams should be perpendicular to the floor. They should meet exactly at the side or center. Make sure the waistline seam is located where the pattern indicates. Shoulder seams should be straight along the mid-line between the top of the shoulder and base of the neck. Clip the neckline to the stay-stitching for a smooth fit. The shoulder seam should end about 5/8 inch from the base of the neck.

Both sides of the garment must look the same. Pay attention to any figure irregularities. Do not rely on fitting only one side of the garment—fit *both* sides. One side of the body is often larger than the other.

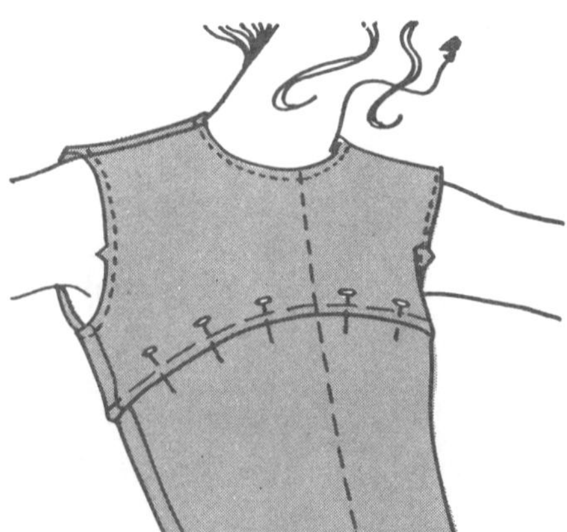

Bustline darts should end a little way from the fullest part of the bust. For comfort, the armhole seam line should be about 1 inch below the armpit at its lowest point.

Before fitting sleeves, remove the garment. Tack any changes on major seams, darts and facings. Try on the garment again with the sleeves tacked in the armholes. Check the fall of sleeves and position of ease or darts at the elbow. Make sure the sleeve joins the bodice at the point of the shoulder bone. The cap and body of the sleeve are placed as shown in the picture on the pattern envelope.

When garments are cut on the cross grain, let them hang for at least two days before marking the hemline. Atmospheric changes, as well as the weight of the fabric, may cause the fabric to droop. Nothing looks worse than a drooping hemline.

If lining is used, alter this at the same time. Finish seams step-by-step at each stage of construction.

Never pull or smooth fabric in place when fitting. It may distort the grain line and stretch the fabric. Always *pat* fabric in place.

A certain amount of ease is included in all patterns. This allows for line and movement. The amount of ease varies from pattern to pattern and seam to seam. Do not ignore this when fitting. If you do, the garment may look different from the way the designer intended.

Tack for Fitting—There are two ways to tack garment pieces together for fitting.

Normal tacking is along seam lines with right-sides together. The garment is tried on *right-side* out.

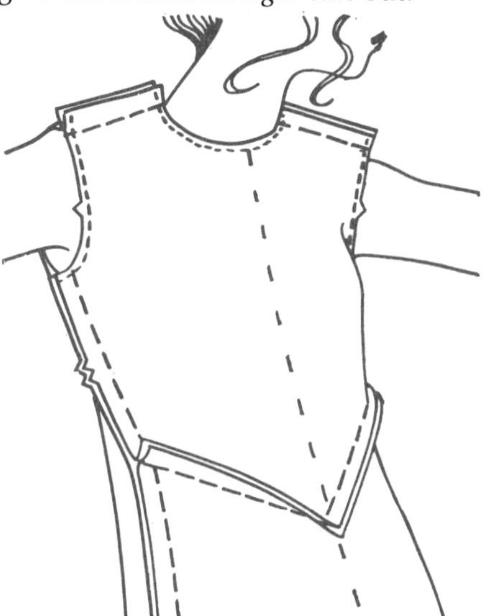

Use a long, thin needle and a long length of thread. Sew even basting stitches 3/8 to 1/2 inch on straight seams. Use slightly shorter stitches on curved seams and shoulders. Start with a knot, and finish with a few back-stitches that can be removed later. Pull out the thread with the knot. Keep the pieces flat so the garment does not look creased when fitted. Leave out sleeves and collar on the first fitting.

Surface tacking is used when seams are pinned and tacked flat on the right-side. This emphasizes design details and holds seams flat. Alterations can be accurately made while the garment is on the dress form or figure.

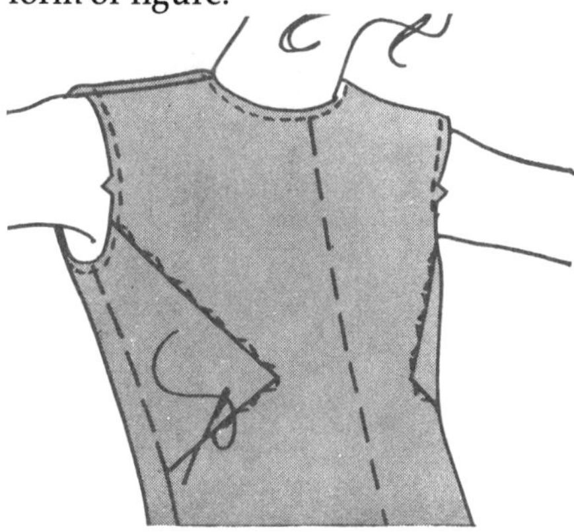

FIRST FITTING

Put the garment on, and spend time looking at it. Note whether it hangs well and if the grain of each piece is correct. Check to see if anything must be altered. Be sure waist and hiplines are horizontal and center lines vertical.

Experiment with design details. See if moving a pocket or using a different belt improves the appearance. Make fitting alterations. Mark the garment with pins on both sides so when it is taken apart it can be tacked on these lines.

Fitting Alterations—Check the back shoulder darts. If the back is loose or wrinkled, undo the shoulder seams. Raise or lower the back *only* at the

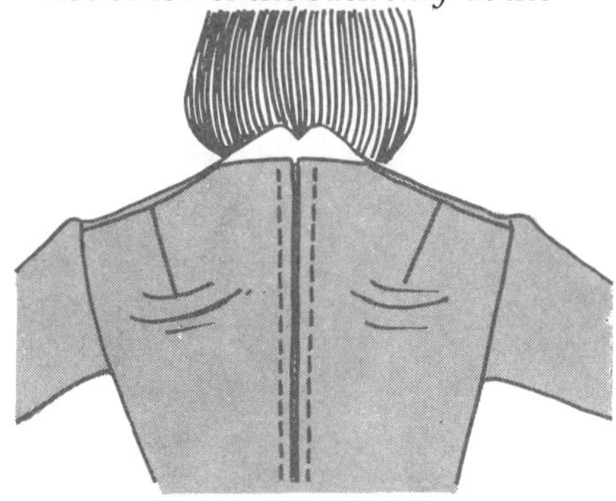

shoulder seams. If wrinkling is below the armhole, remove the entire back piece. Recut the neck, shoulders and armholes.

Check the center front line and the grain line across the bodice. Alter bust darts, side seams and the waist seam as necessary. If fabric drags from the bust to the sides of the waist, undo side seams. Lift the fabric into the bust darts from below, and repin side seams.

If bust darts are not pointing to the fullest part of the bust, undo the side seams and darts. Raise or lower the points of the darts.

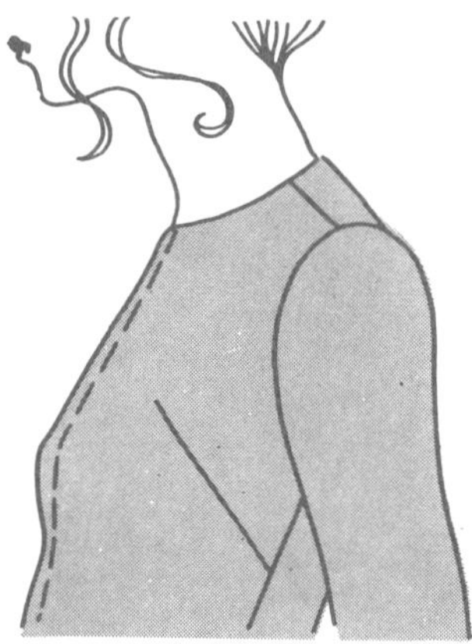

If the fabric bulges under the arm and drags at the armhole, undo the side seams and bust darts. Lower the darts a little at the side seams. Let out the side seams above the darts.

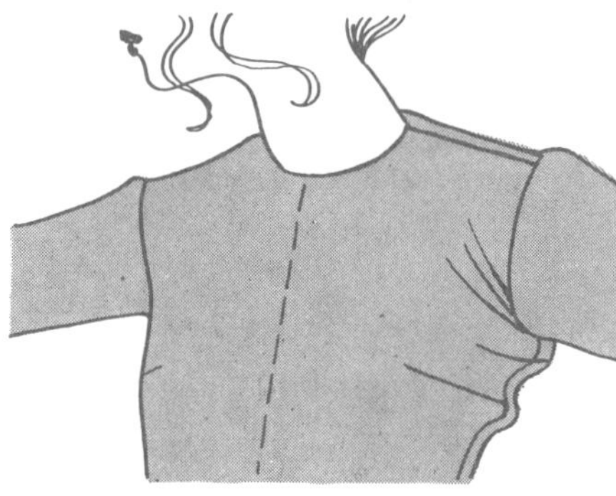

If the neckline gapes, undo the shoulder seams and raise them. If the

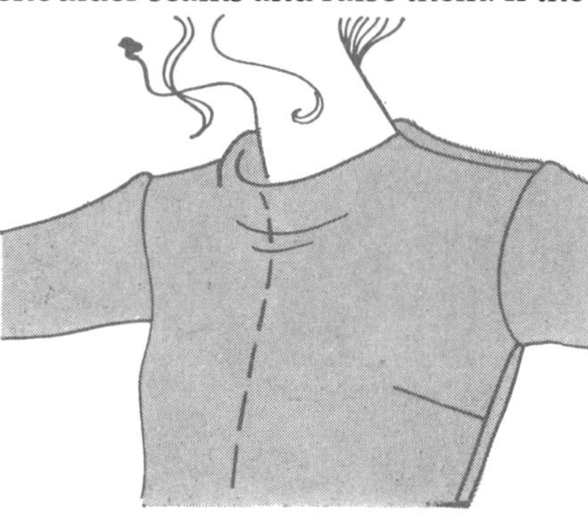

neckline is too tight or too high, snip into the seam allowance. Mark a new seam line with pins.

If armholes are too tight, alter them as for the neckline. Partly pin in one sleeve so the grain hangs straight. Make marks on the sleeve and armhole as a guide for tacking in sleeves for the second fitting.

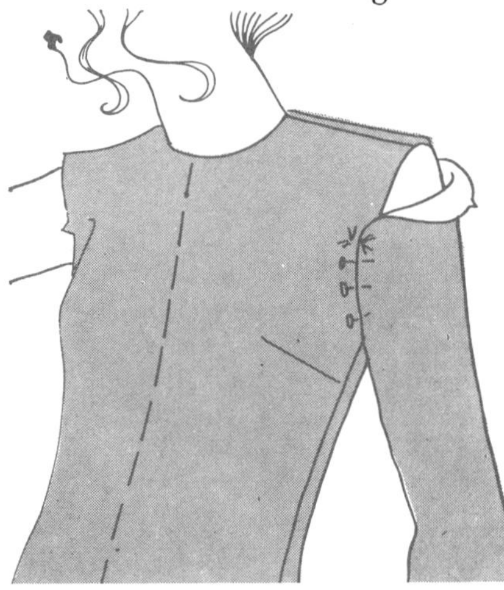

Check the front of the shoulders. If fabric pulls at the outer end of the seam lines, undo the shoulder seams. Let them out. If the shoulder seams

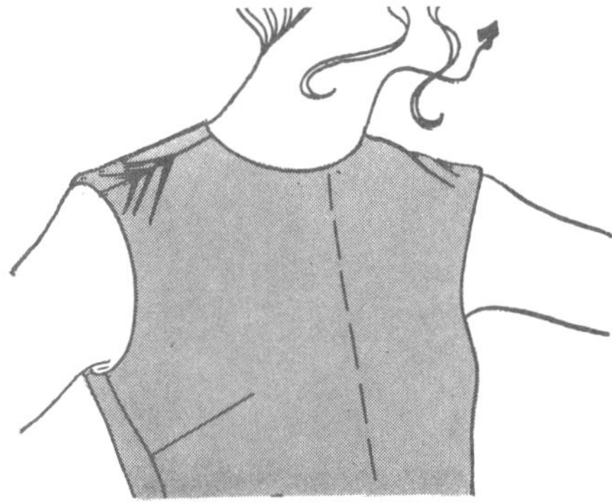

do not lie flat at the outer edge because of sloping shoulders, undo the seams. Put extra fabric in the seam.

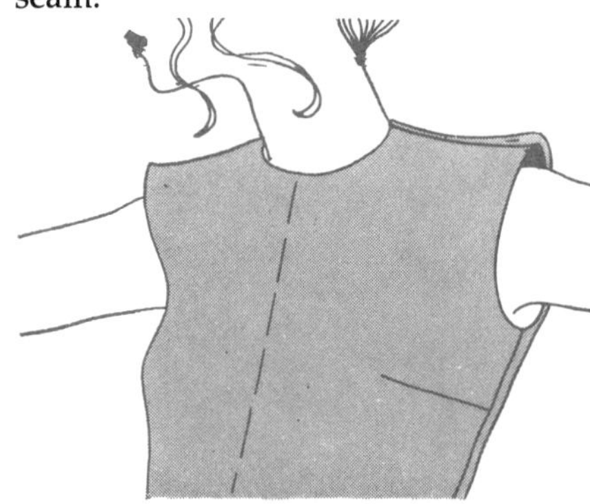

Look at darts, grain lines and side seams on the back of the skirt. If the skirt pulls in below the seat, repin the side seams to add extra width in back pieces. Repin waist darts for a smooth fit.

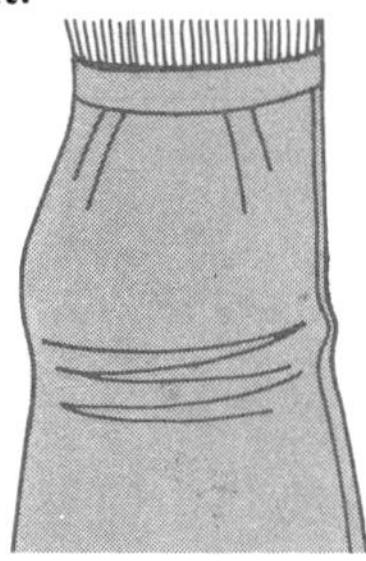

If the skirt pulls across the waist and hips, let out side seams. If there

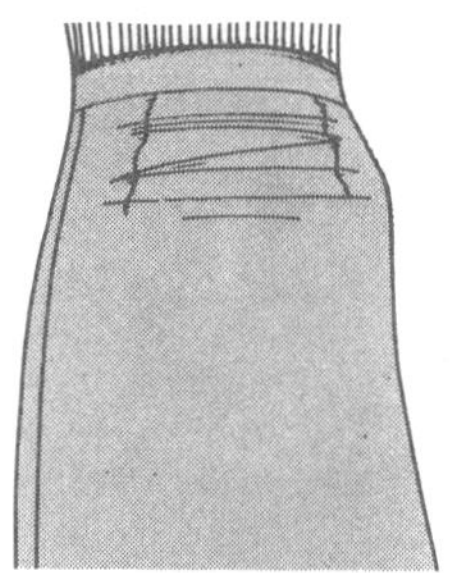

are creases below the waistline, hollow out the waist at the back. If

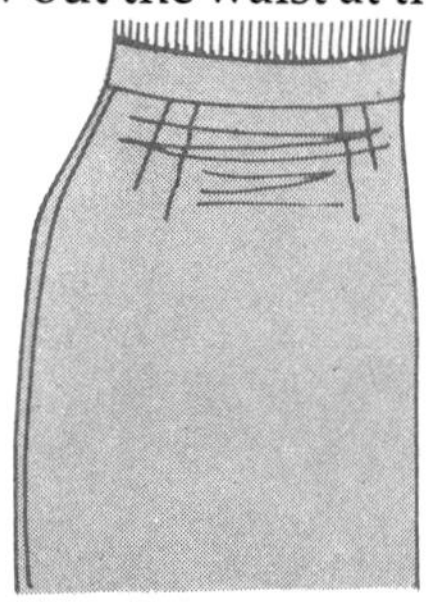

the skirt sticks out at the back hem, take in side seams on the back piece only.

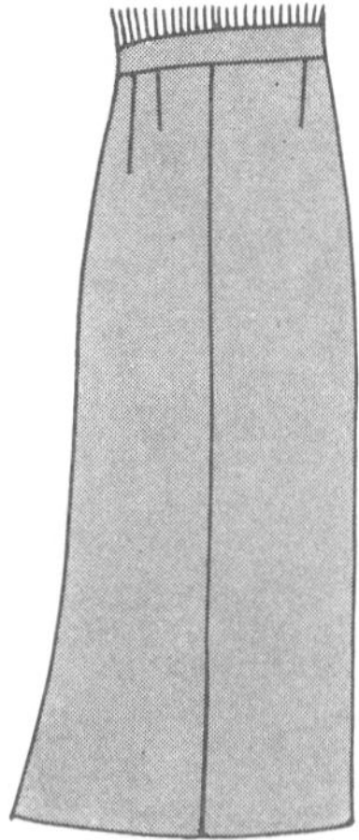

Alterations—Carefully take off the garment. Trace tack over the pins marking the areas to be altered. Use contrasting thread. Remove pins.

Remove thread while holding the garment together in the areas to be altered. Transfer new markings to the paper pattern for the next use. Make all required alterations, and tack the garment together again. Tack in the sleeves and collar.

SECOND FITTING

Try the garment on again to make sure the alterations have had the desired effect. If necessary, refit side seams.

Fit the sleeves. The inside seam should be in line with the thumb when the arm hangs naturally. The elbow dart must be at the right level. Grain lines must be vertical and horizontal, except when the garment is cut on the cross grain. If the sleeve is too wide, take it in from nothing at the armhole to the required width at the wrist. Reposition any wrist darts. Reverse this process for sleeves that are too tight.

If the sleeve cap has loose folds, alter the crown by pinning wider seam allowances. If the sleeve cap is too narrow and causes horizontal creases, let out the seams.

Be sure openings and fastenings are in the correct place. If there have been no alterations, mark the hemline.

Make all necessary alterations. Put the garment together for final fitting.

FINAL FITTING

Look at the garment critically and in detail. If it now fits perfectly, mark the hemline, and sew pieces together.

FITTING PANTS

Pants means bermuda shorts, jeans, culottes, shorts, gauchos and pants. Whatever the style or name, pants are a part of many women's wardrobes. At one time, pants were only worn by women for work, as part of a uniform or for sports. Today, they are popular and accepted as a part of any wardrobe. Pants are for everyday wear and glamorous evening wear.

Whatever the figure type, pants *can* be worn by a woman. Pants look smart and slimming if the correct style is chosen. Take a critical look at yourself from the front, side and back. Use a full-length mirror to help decide the most flattering style. Be realistic about figure imperfections, and choose pants to disguise these. It may mean the pants chosen will not be the latest fashion, but they will suit and flatter *you!*

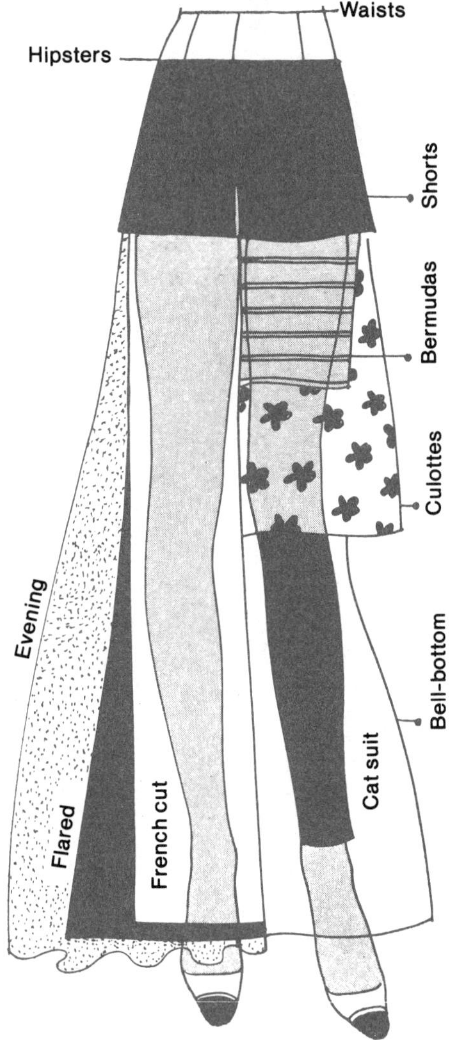

Fitting pants takes time and effort and must be done carefully. If the crotch is too low, pleat across the

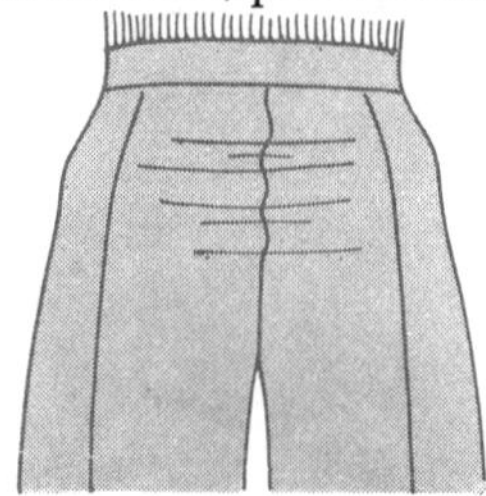

pattern below the waist. Repin the pattern on the fabric, and recut the waist area.

If the crotch is too tight, let out side seams. Lower the curve of the crotch.

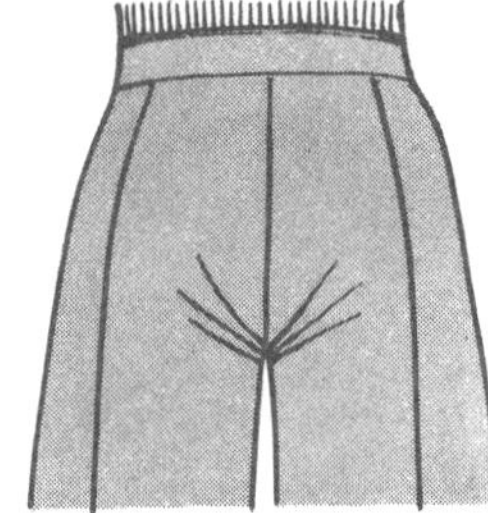

If waist or hips are too tight, let out the darts and side seams. If the width

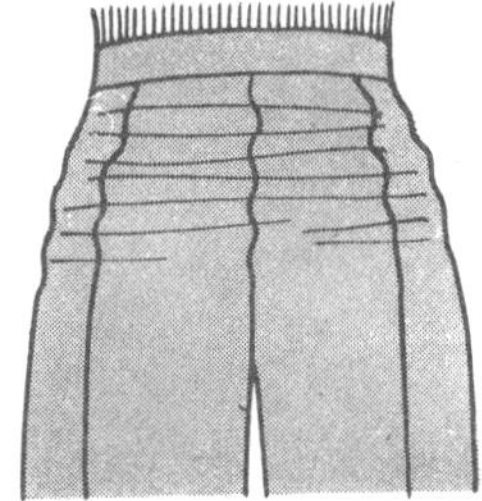

of the legs is not right, alter seams equally.

Even the slimmest girl does not look good in poorly cut, poorly fitting pants or in ones that do not suit her silhouette. If pants are too short, they look as if there was not enough fabric available. If they are too big, too wide-legged or too long, they add pounds to your appearance. This is the effect most people want to avoid. If you are underweight, a generous cut can help. But length, waist and hip fitting should be smooth.

Take note of any leg faults—thick thighs, large calves, thick ankles or large feet. These can be disguised by your choice of style. For fleshy knees, bermuda shorts are not good. A-line, knee-length culottes can flatter knees and make them look smaller in proportion.

Tall, hip-heavy girls can achieve a clean-cut, balanced look by wearing a long tunic with pants. A tunic disguises extra pounds and makes the wearer appear slimmer. A short, cropped jacket makes the leg line appear longer. Long tunics make short women look dumpy, rather than emphasizing a small, trim figure. If you are short and plump, wear a knee-length, A-line garment over pants. A matching color will avoid breaking the line.

Fitting Style and Size—The principles of making pants are similar to those of making a skirt. The same rules apply, whatever the style of pants. Pants may be slim-fitting or have full, wide legs. Seams run from the waist to the ankle.

The warp thread of the fabric runs down the center front and center back. Pants may be cut on the cross grain if the style is full and flaring, such as for evening wear. However, this is an exception to the general rule.

Pants are easy to make if you pay attention to measurements and fitting. Choose a pattern by the waist measurement, unless the hip measurement is much larger than what is listed on the pattern. Then choose the pattern by the hip size, and adjust the waist to fit. Choose a pattern that needs as few alterations as possible.

What to Wear Under Pants—Always wear flattering underwear with pants. Girdles that are too tight or dig into the thighs change the natural shape of the body. They cause unsightly bulges where they are least wanted. If foundation garments must be worn, they should be soft and pliable. They should not cause bulges at the hips or thighs. The best undergarments are pantyhose with briefs or a lightweight, long-legged panty girdle. Girls with fleshy hip and thigh areas should buy support hose. These give legs, hips and thighs support and firmness.

Tight-fitting bikini briefs under slim-fitting pants show through the fabric. They spoil the smooth, elegant line.

Making Standard Pattern—Adjust a basic pants pattern to suit your figure and fit you. Then make a permanent record of it on non-woven interfacing. Use your standard pattern to make necessary alterations to other patterns you choose. If you gain or lose weight, revise the standard measurements.

If you have a pair of ready-made pants that fit well, make a pattern from these. Use a seam ripper and a pair of fine-pointed scissors. Carefully open the seams until each piece is separate. Press each section carefully, and pin it on drafting paper. Place grain lines of the fabric along guidelines on the paper. Record darts and other markings. Pants that have had a lot of wear generally spread a little. The fabric may be about 1/8 inch larger in the places where there was strain. Reduce the size accordingly. The pattern can be permanently transferred to non-woven interfacing. Use paper first because it costs less than interfacing if you make a mistake.

Pant-Style Selection Chart

FIGURE FAULT
Heavy hips.

Styles to Avoid—
Hip-huggers, fitted thighs.

Styles to Use—
The French cut gives a long, straight line from hip to floor when seen from every angle.

FIGURE FAULT
Large seat.

Styles to Avoid—
Hip-huggers, fitted thighs.

Styles to Use—
Wear shorts with pleats or flare, or long pants as shown on page 62.

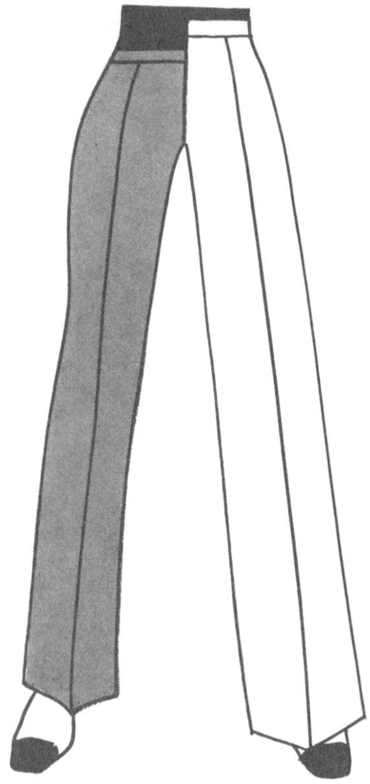

FIGURE FAULT
Heavy knees.

Styles to Avoid—
Bermudas shorts, fitted shorts, flares from below knee.

Styles to Use—
Wear pants that flare slightly from above the knee or from the calf down. Use the straight, French look and pleated or flared shorts.

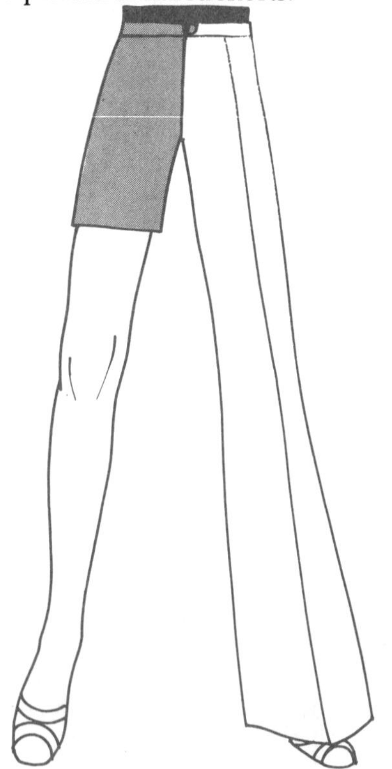

FIGURE FAULT
Thick thighs.

Styles to Avoid—
Styles that cling at the thigh.

Styles to Use—
A long straight look or with slight flare from midthigh down.

FIGURE FAULT
Large calves.

Styles to Avoid—
Tight pants that cling at the calves.

Styles to Use—
A long, straight look or with flare from midthigh or knee.

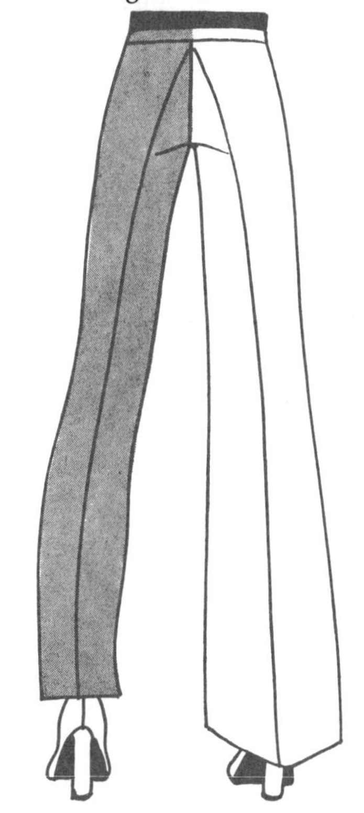

FIGURE FAULT
Thick ankles.

Styles to Avoid—
Pants that stop short of the ankle.

Styles to Use—
If a shorter look is required, gauchos are flattering. They stop at mid-calf but are wide, giving the ankle the illusion of being small.

FIGURE FAULT
Large feet.

Styles to Avoid—
Leg-clinging styles that are narrow at the ankle make medium or large feet look big.

Styles to Use—
Wide-bottom, mid-heel finish. Bottoms must be wide enough to expose only the toe of the shoes. Wear dark, plain, elegant shoes.

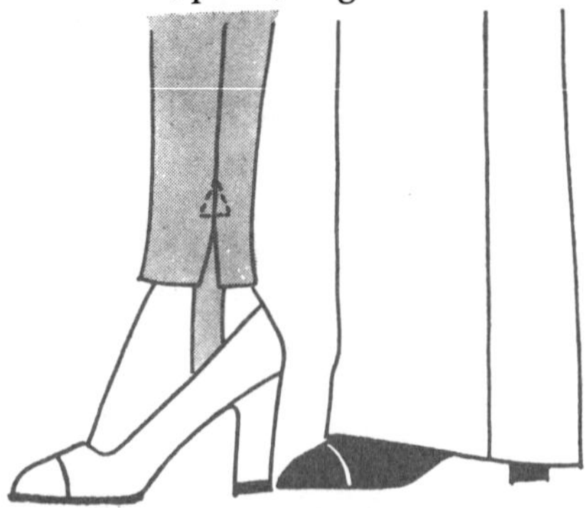

FIGURE FAULT
Bow legs, knock knees.

Styles to Avoid—
Tubular, tight-fitting or ankle-flared styles.

Styles to Use—
Wear the straight look or styles that flare from just above the knee. Culottes and full-legged styles also suitable. See illustration on page 63.

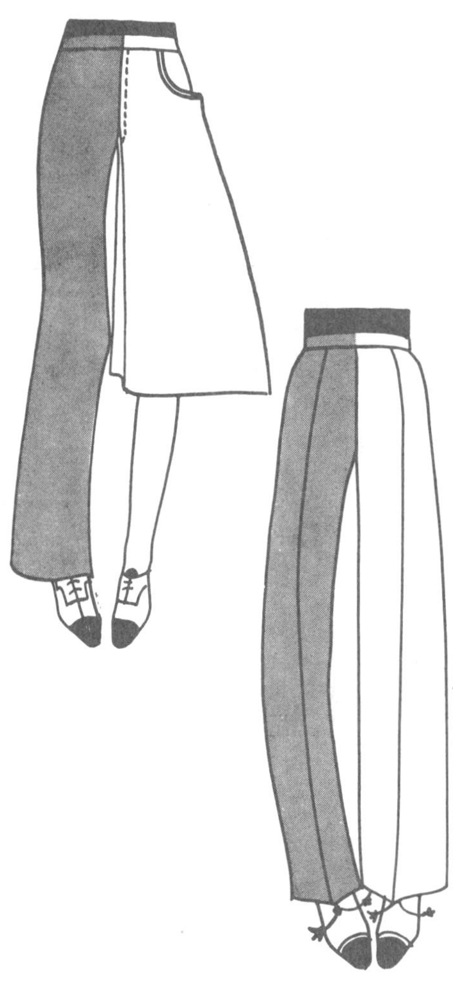

ALTERATIONS

ALTERING PURCHASED CLOTHES

If you like a garment that does not fit well, it may be possible to alter it. Decide if alterations are worthwhile.

It is almost impossible to make a tight garment fit well. Choose a garment that is larger, rather than smaller. Seams that have been let out may show stitch marks. Some fabrics, such as poplin, satin and gabardine, show alteration marks. Avoid altering them.

On many man-made fabrics, the crease left when a hem is let down cannot be removed. Waistlines can be difficult to alter. Do not move fastenings more than about 1/4 inch or the garment looks unbalanced. Follow the fitting instructions given earlier in this section.

Belts—It is easier to shorten a belt from the buckle end, leaving eyelets untouched. Remove the buckle. Cut off the required length of belt, and replace the buckle.

Waistbands—If the waist is too tight, remove the waistband. Replace it with a piece of shaped ribbon. Let out darts as needed. If the waist is too loose, remove the waistband and zipper. Take in darts and side seams to fit. Adjust the length of the waistband, and replace it.

Hip Line—Extra width can be gained by opening side seams almost to the waistband. Stitch side seams with tiny seam allowances.

Crease Across Skirts—When creases form below the waist at the back, pin up the surplus. Mark a new waistline. Remove the waistband, and refit the waistline. Adjust the hemline if it is affected by this.

Low Crotch on Pants—Let down leg hems and remove the waistband. Lift the pants by the waist until the crotch fits snugly. Refit darts and side seams, and mark a new waistline. Cut away surplus fabric, and replace the waistband. Apply false hems if needed.

Hems on Pants—Straight legs are no problem. Bell-bottoms may be taken up but not let down because they usually have faced hems. Remove the facing, shorten the legs, and put on new facings. Tapered pants can be let down but are more difficult to take up. Undo the side seams, and turn up the legs. Leave side seams unstitched in the hem so they lie flat.

Necklines—It is difficult to refit a loose neckline. A tight, round neck can be eased by removing facings and opening shoulder seams. Let out the seams, scoop out the neckline if necessary, then restitch seams. Replace facings.

Shoulders—Wide shoulders that slip down are unflattering. Lift the top of the sleeve into the armhole.

Armholes—Loose armholes can be fixed by opening the armhole seam under the arm. Take in the bodice side seams. Adjust the armhole facing to match, then replace it.

Hems—False hems may be used to lengthen a garment to its maximum length. Use a wide bias tape or crosswise strip, and apply it as a facing. To shorten a permanently pleated skirt, take it up from the waist. It cannot be lengthened. Coats can be lengthened with a false hem but this requires care and attention for a good result.

RECYCLING OLD CLOTHES

Clothes that are in good condition but out of style can be recycled. They can also be cut down for a child.

Consider using yard-sale or rummage-sale bargains for this purpose.

To restyle a garment, use a pattern, unless the alteration is simple. Consider making a vest from a jacket, a tunic or smock from a minidress, a jacket and skirt from a long dress, or a skirt from a dress.

Start with a clean garment. Open seams where necessary, and press them. Ripped seams may be hidden with top-stitching. Hide worn spots or stains with pockets, darts or trim.

Change the trim on a garment. Add decorative stitching, or change the collar or neckline. Shorten sleeves.

Take the garment apart, and discard worn or stained areas. Press each piece. If the wrong-side looks brighter and fresher, use that. Most fabrics are suitable for children's clothes but some designs are too large or sophisticated. Pockets and buttons are not usually suitable for use.

Choose a simple pattern or style. It should have the same number of garment pieces as the old one.

Make coats into jackets, skirts, coats, vests and pants. Dresses can be made into skirts, children's dresses, vests, pants, blouses or shorts. Knitwear can be made into jumpers and tank tops. Use small fabric pieces for toys.

PATTERN LAYOUT, CUTTING AND MARKING

Pattern Layout

All paper patterns include a suggested pattern-layout guide. This is found on the instruction sheet. Directions also include the length and width of fabric required.

Before purchasing fabric, check the layout. It is often possible to buy less fabric than the amount stated. Follow the layout for the *size* and *style* required. There are special layout instructions for one-way designs and pile or napped fabrics.

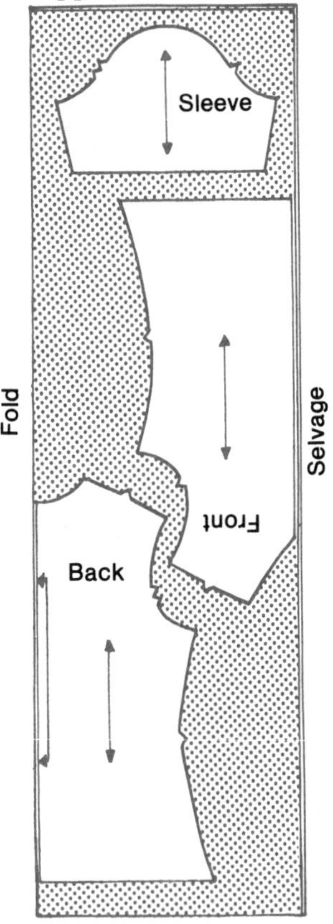

Look at the pattern pieces to see where straight-grain arrows are placed. Check for any pieces to be placed on the fold. See if other pieces are placed on single or double fabric.

Make all necessary pattern adjustments. Redraw seam lines and cutting lines. Use pattern pieces with the printed side up, unless the instuction sheet advises otherwise. If the fabric has a nap, pile or one-way design, see the following section.

Prepare and preshrink the fabric. See the section on *Preparing Fabric,* page 54. Place fabric on a large, flat surface. Use the floor if you have nowhere else. If the fabric is a double thickness, pin along the ends. Fold selvages to keep them in place.

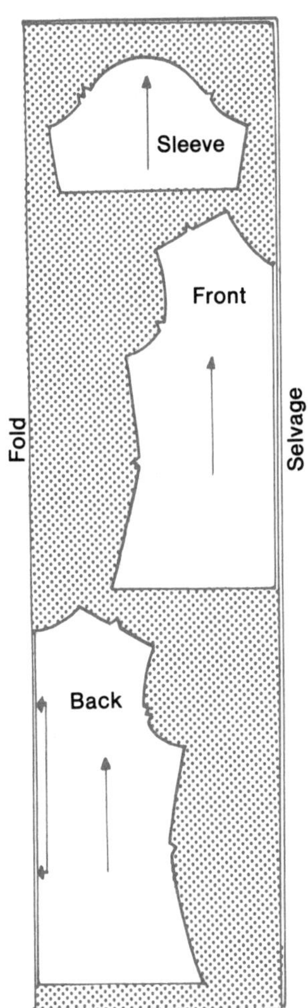

Lay pattern pieces on the fabric according to the layout. Place the large, main pieces first. Pin pattern pieces along fold lines and lengthwise grain lines. Keep the grain lines parallel with the fabric grain.

Make sure the grain line is parallel to the selvage of the fabric. Measure the distance from each end of the grain line to the selvage. The two measurements are the same if the piece is on the straight grain.

Do not try to squeeze in pattern pieces by laying them off the straight grain. The finished garment will not hang well. Do not overlap pieces so seam allowances are cut off. Do not place pieces over the selvages.

Be sure pattern pieces are correctly placed. You do not want two left sleeves or a bodice front on the wrong-side of the fabric.

Pin down all pieces. Place pins at right angles to the seam line about 1/4 inch from the cutting line. Pins should be about 3 inches apart.

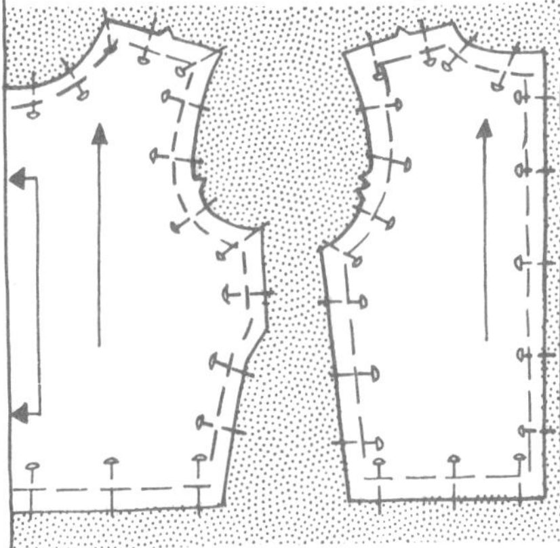

If a pattern piece extends beyond the folded edge of fabric, leave it in place until all pieces have been cut out. Then unfold the fabric, smooth the pattern piece, and pin it flat.

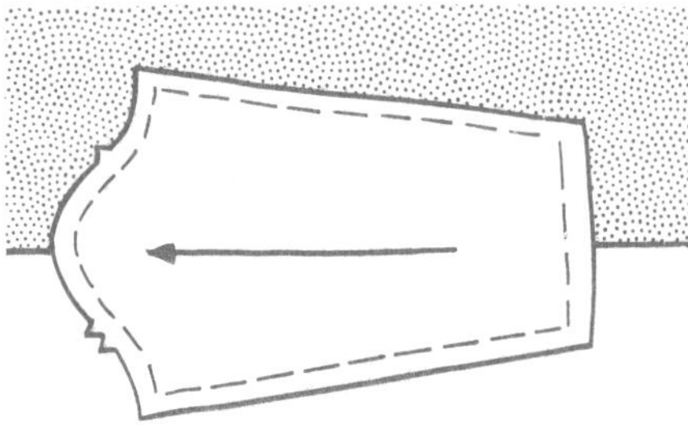

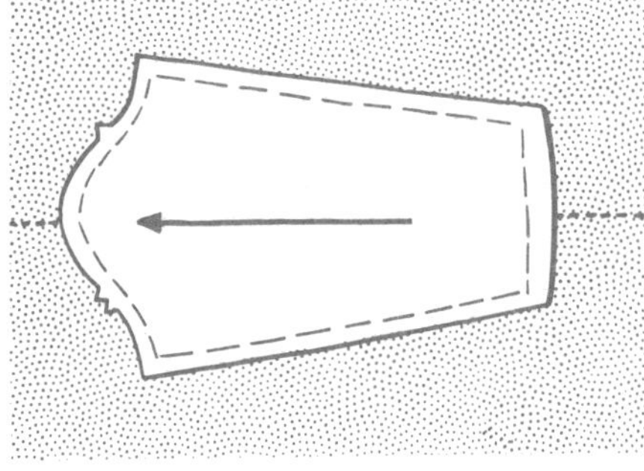

ONE-WAY FABRIC

The fabric may have a one-way print, an uneven check or plaid, or a nap or pile. The garment will not look right unless each section is cut in the same direction. More fabric is often needed. Pieces do not fit together as easily on the layout. Seam lines, not cutting lines, need to match when the garment is finished. This is important for fabric with a woven or surface design.

Consider the fabric surface in nap and pile fabrics. These feel rough when brushed one way and smooth when brushed the other way. Velvet has a nap. Some shiny or textured fabrics must also be cut out on one-way layouts. The surface may have a shaded effect in strong light.

EVEN CHECKS AND PLAIDS

Check to see if the pattern is marked "unsuitable for plaids." If you use a checked fabric, the garment design should be simple, with few pattern pieces. Extra fabric is usually needed for matching checks and plaids.

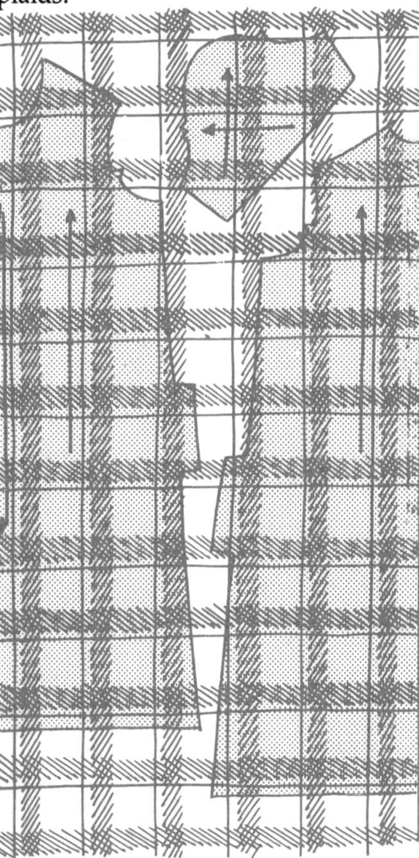

Look at the fabric to see if there are prominent design lines. Place these on the garment for the best effect. Lines must be continuous around the garment and from neck to hem. They should also match on bodice and skirt, or jacket and skirt. Use uneven plaids only if you are experienced.

Follow the *with-nap* layout. Place pieces so notches match at side seams and center-front lines. Start matching from the hem. Diagonal lines and curves, such as sleeve heads, are not always matched. Shaped seams stitch into chevrons, if correctly placed. Pay attention to details and symmetrical pieces, such as collars. Fashion details, such as pockets and cuffs, may be cut on the true cross grain.

STRIPES
Lay out stripe fabric the same as plaids and checks. Stripes need to match in one direction only. They run the same way in a garment, except for special fashion features.

PRINTS
If the fabric has a definite one-way design, use the fabric layout marked *with nap.* If large motifs are a feature of the fabric, experiment to see where to place them on the figure. Do not put large motifs on the bosom or buttocks! Balance motifs vertically and horizontally. Choose simple garments with few pattern pieces.

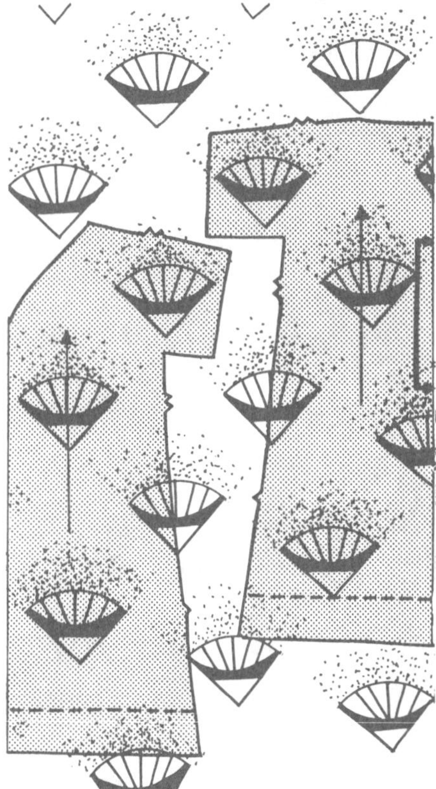

BORDER PRINTS
With this fabric, the printed border appears along a garment hem. Choose a straight style, and match the print at the side seams as accurately as possible.

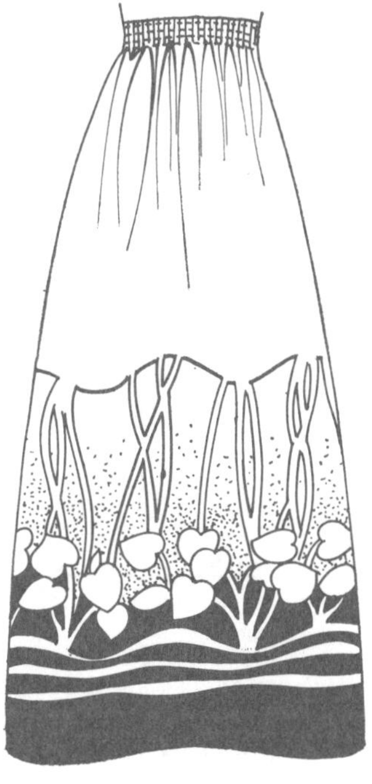

PATTERN LAYOUT
Layouts are provided to show the most convenient way to cut pattern pieces from fabric. If no printed layout is available, make a mock layout to calculate how much fabric is needed. Measure the width of the widest pattern piece. If it is not wider than 18 inches, the garment can be cut from 36-inch fabric. When some pieces are wider, lay the pattern on open 36-inch fabric, instead of folded lengthwise. Wider fabric may be necessary.

Use sheets of pinned-together pattern paper or newspaper for your mock layout. Look at other paper-pattern layouts for ideas.

Cutting Pattern

Use sharp fabric-cutting shears, preferably with bent handles. Do not use pinking shears because they are for finishing seams. Cut in a direction going *away* from yourself to avoid accidents.

Keep fabric as flat as possible. Place one hand flat on the piece while cutting. Do not lift the fabric up because it distorts the shape of the pattern.

Cut along straight edges with long, smooth strokes. Use the whole length of the blades. Use shorter, snipping movements around curved lines and pattern notches. Notches may be easier to cut using smaller scissors.

Cut along the cutting line, *not* the seam line. Cut the pattern notches outward, so they project beyond the edge. They can be matched more easily when putting seams together.

Be sure each pattern piece is used enough times. Some pieces should be cut out more than once. Cut the main pieces first, and pile them without folding. Do not remove pins.

When the pieces have been cut out, sort the fabric that is left. A large piece might be useful for another small garment or accessories. Put one piece in the pattern envelope for matching or patching later. Throw away small scraps. Save larger pieces for bound buttonholes, matching, testing and patchwork.

Pattern Markings

Pattern markings are important. When pieces have been cut out, transfer all necessary marks from the pattern to the fabric *before* removing the paper pattern, if possible.

Transfer construction symbols or marks from the pattern to the *wrong-side* of the garment sections. There are five basic methods of marking and transferring symbols from the pattern to the material.

TRACING
Put a piece of tracing paper, shiny side down, between the pattern and fabric. Place another piece of tracing paper, shiny side up, under the second layer of material. Pin the pattern in position.

Use a transparent ruler for straight lines. Run the tracing wheel over the pattern marking. Apply enough pressure to mark both layers of fabric. Remove the pattern.

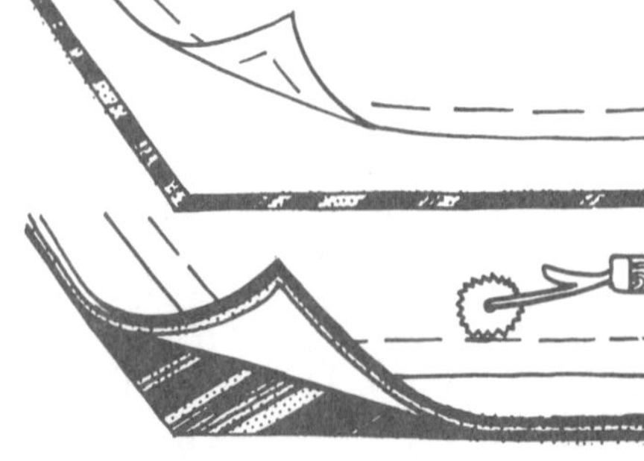

Use a slightly darker-color paper to make markings distinguishable on the material. The shiny side of the carbon paper is placed on the *wrong-side* of the fabric.

Mark notches with tailor's tacks in the normal way. Handle carbon paper carefully to prevent finger marks on fabric. When marking is complete, put carbon paper away so fabric does not get marked in the wrong places.

CHALK AND PINS

Lift the pattern edge to mark the position of notches. Beginning at the outside of the pattern, put pins through each of the marked dots on the pattern. Fold back pattern to the pins.

Use a transparent ruler and a sharp pencil. Mark the piece of material held by the pins on the wrong-side. Remove the pattern.

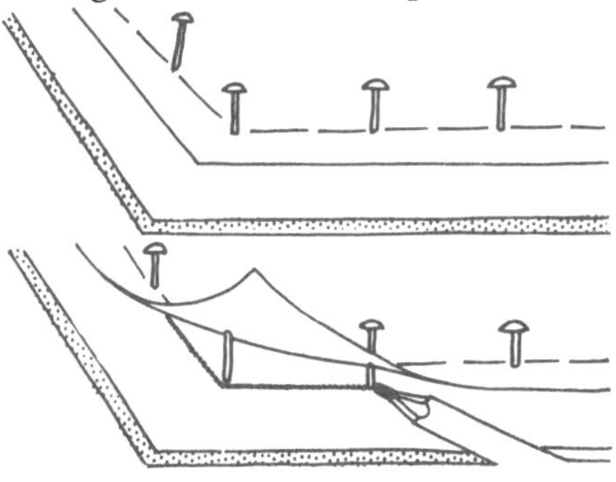

Work tailor's tacks because chalk marks rub off easily.

TAILOR'S TACKS

Use thread that contrasts with the fabric. Use one color for seam lines and another for darts, buttonholes and pleats.

Thread the needle with about a yard of thread. Place tacking stitches at dots and intervals along the marked lines. Use different colors for different symbols.

Put the needle through the pattern and the layers of fabric. Leave a length about 1 inch. Take another stitch over the first one, leaving a loop. Cut the thread leaving 1 inch at the end.

Continue tailor tacking on various pattern markings. Do not cut loops on individual tailor's tacks.

When tailor tacking is complete, gently remove the pattern so threads are not pulled out. Separate fabric layers a bit. Cut the threads between, leaving thread tufts on both layers.

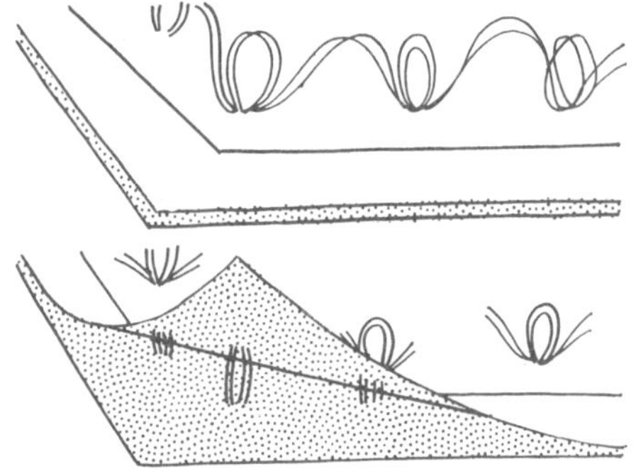

PENCIL MARKINGS

On light-color fabrics, some pattern markings can be transferred to the *wrong-side* with a No. 2B pencil. Push the pencil point through dots or dart lines. You can also cut out the dart from the paper and draw around it. Stick or pin the paper in place, ready for next time.

THREAD TRACING

Uneven tacking is used on single layers of fabric to mark grain lines, center-front and center-back lines. Use fine thread.

STITCHES AND THREADS

To be successful with stitching techniques, your choice of stitch, stitch length, pressure and needle must be correct. Use the correct thread for the fabric.

It is important to know why certain threads are used on some occasions and other threads used on other occasions. You should also know what type of needle to use for a particular project.

Stitches

HAND-STITCHING

Choose the right needle and thread. Always wear a thimble, especially when sewing firm fabrics. A thimble makes hand-sewing easier.

Practice different stitches until they appear neat and even. Work from right to left. Left-handed sewers find it easier to sew from left to right. Do not pull stitches too tight because it causes puckering. Begin and end with one or more back-stitches. For tacking, begin with a knot.

MACHINE-STITCHING

Choose the correct thread. Change the needle if necessary and prepare the machine. Practice stitching on a piece of garment fabric to get the stitch's proper length, pressure and tension.

TEMPORARY STITCHES

Tacking—This is also called *basting*. It is important because it can make the difference between a beautiful finish and a messy one. There are times when it is not necessary to tack, but not often.

Tacking is used to hold the garment together for fitting purposes. It holds hems, seams and darts in position ready for final stitching. It also marks construction details on the fabric. Tacking is used to identify certain parts of garment sections, such as center-front lines or hemlines. It can also position items to be added to the garment such as zippers, braid and pockets.

Even Tacking—Stitches are equal in length on both sides of the fabric. Work from right to left. Begin with knotted thread. You can also make a back-stitch to secure thread. Work a regular, large running-stitch along the area to be sewn.

When tacking a garment for fitting, sew a back-stitch evenly every 1/4 inch for strength. This makes it more difficult to pull the thread out later.

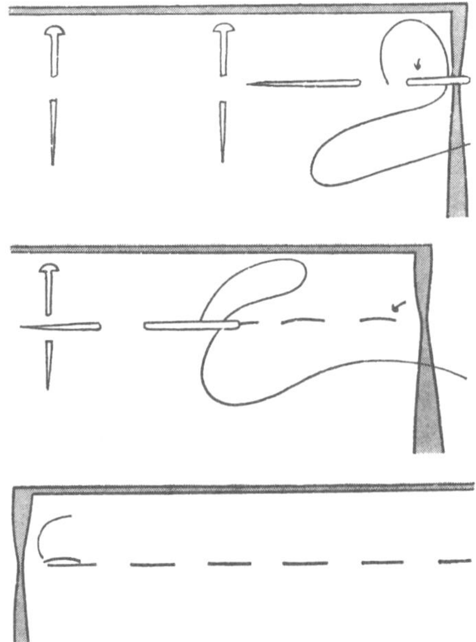

Long and Short Tacking—This type of tacking produces a long stitch on top and a short stitch underneath. It is used for hems, joining interfacings and linings to garments, and marking lines on fabric.

Diagonal Tacking—This is useful for holding together two or more layers of material. It keeps them from slipping out of position until final stitching is complete. The needle is pushed through all layers vertically, then drawn out. It is pushed in again, level with the top of the first stitch. The result is a set of diagonal lines running the length of the fabric. Short level stitches appear on the other side.

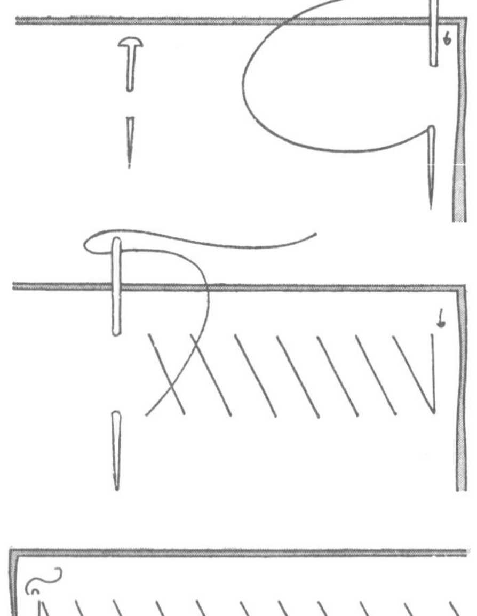

Tailor's Tacks—These transfer pattern markings to two pieces of fabric at the same time. They are only suitable for strong, firm cloth. After cutting, thread can easily slip from fine, smooth material.

Work single tailor's tacks or a series from right to left with unknotted, double thread. For single tacks, take a small stitch through the pattern and fabric layers. Leave a thread end 1 inch long. Take a second stitch over the first, leaving a long loop about 1 inch. Cut the thread.

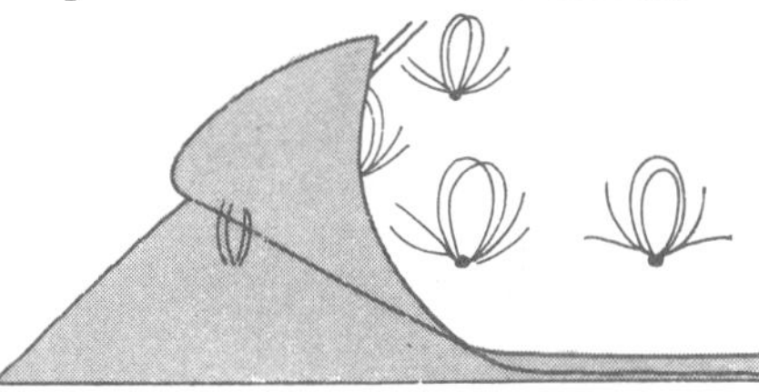

Do not cut through the loop. This keeps the tailor's tack from pulling out of the fabric and tearing the pattern. Remove the pattern, and pull fabric layers apart. Cut the threads.

For a series of tailor's tacks, take a small stitch through the fabric and pattern layers. Take a second stitch over the first, leaving a loop. Repeat this procedure until seams have been tacked together. Cut the thread, leaving a 1-inch end. Next, cut through the tops of the loops. Remove the pattern to keep from pulling threads out. Separate material layers. Cut the threads between, leaving thread tufts on both layers.

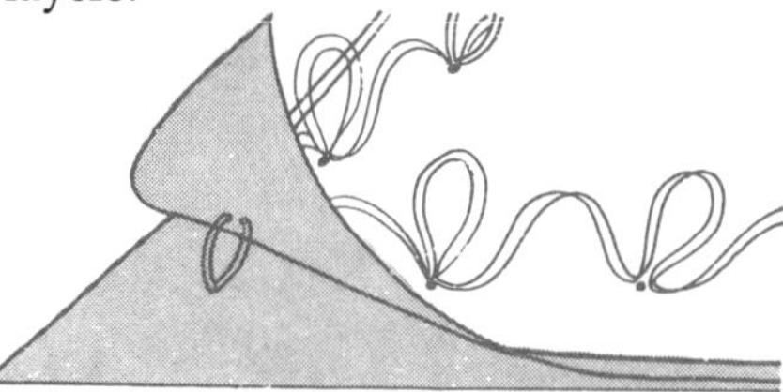

Trace-Tacking and Thread Tracing— Rows of uneven tacking mark grain lines, centers of garment sections, pocket positions and other details. Use a single thread. This may also be used to mark seam lines, instead of tailor's tacks.

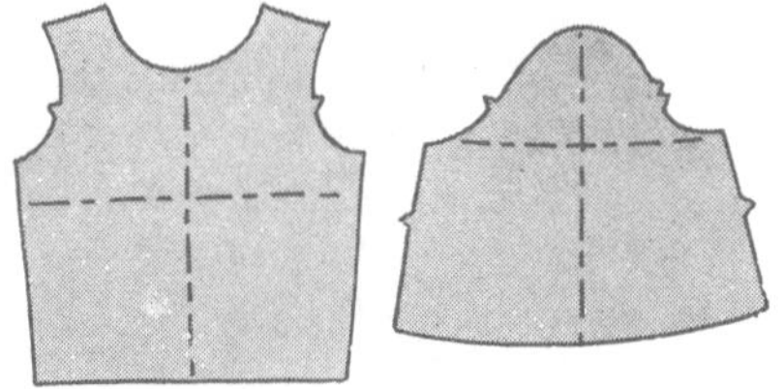

Machine-Tacking—Some machines sew a chain-stitch that can be pulled out. You can also use a loose top tension and the longest stitch. Use machine-tacking only on firm fabrics that will not be marked by the needle.

Slip-Basting—This is also called *slip-stitch.* It is the best method to use when matching stripe or check fabrics and for lapping curved seams. Seams are tacked together from the right-side so they are in place before permanent stitching. The edge of a hem can be held down invisibly by slip-stitching.

Start with the right-side of the fabric on top. Turn under one seam allowance. Position it over the other, which is kept flat. Place pins at right angles to the seam, and bring the needle through to right-side at the fold. Insert the needle along the fold, and bring it out about 1/2 inch to the left. Insert the needle below the fold underlayer, and make a stitch of the same length. Continue alternating stitches in the below-fold.

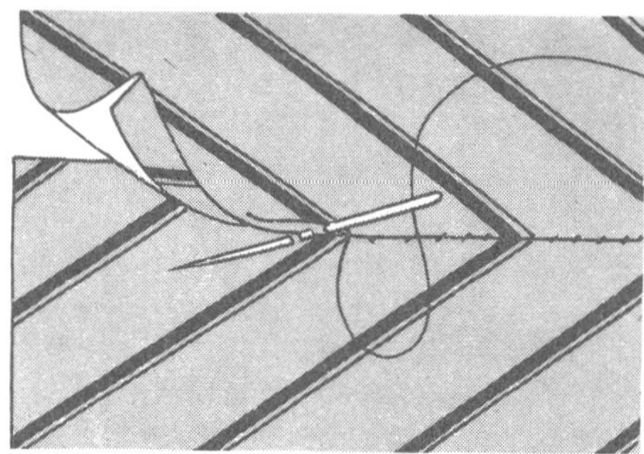

JOINING STITCHES

These stitches can join two or more separate pieces of material together. Thread must be compatible with the fabric.

Running-Stitch—This is a basic straight-stitch. It is used when there is not much strain, and for easing and gathering. For seams, make stitches 1/16 to 1/8 inch long. For easing or gathering, stitches are 1/8 to 1/4 inch long.

Push the needle tip in and out of the material. Make small, regular stitches, evenly spaced, in straight or curved lines as required. Use a long, fine needle. Push it in and out for about six stitches before pulling the thread out.

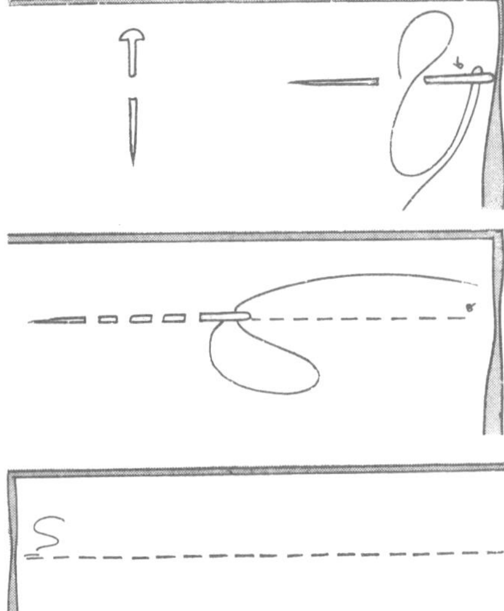

Back-Stitch—This is a strong hand-stitch that can be used in place of straight machine-stitching. The stitches look like machine stitches on one side, yet overlap on the other.

With right-sides together, attach the thread. Take one long running-stitch. Take a stitch back, and bring the needle out again a little way along the seam line. Repeat.

Many sewing machines back-stitch. The seam is elastic and strong. It is usually called a *triple seam.*

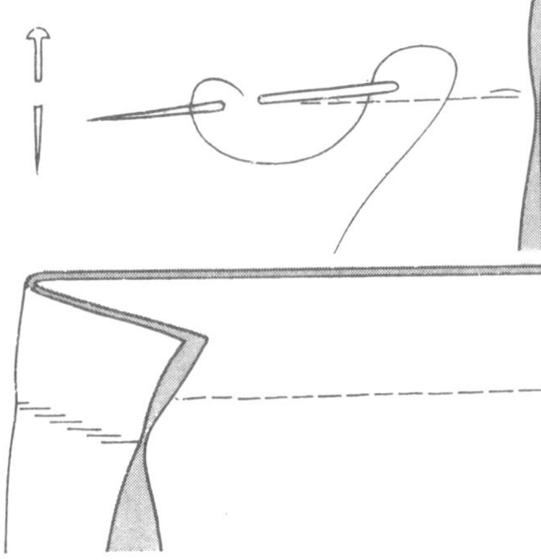

Half Back-Stitch—This can be used for hand-sewn seams. It is also useful for understitching facings to prevent edge seams from rolling to the right-side. The backward-stitch is only half the length of the last stitch. Otherwise, the method is the same as for back-stitch.

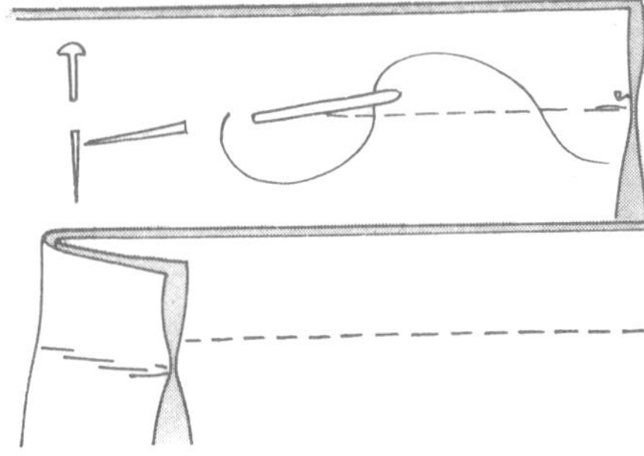

Stab-Stitch—This is also called *prick-stitch* or *hand-picking.* It is similar to the half back-stitch. The needle is only taken back over 2 to 3 threads each time. It is often used for inserting zippers by hand and for top-stitching collars and lapels.

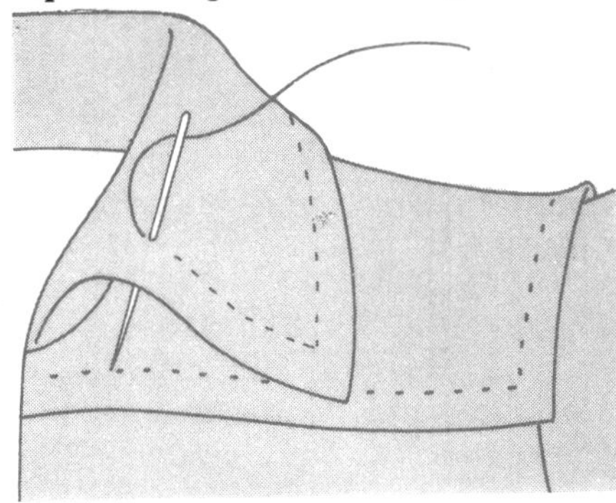

Oversewing—This can be used to join two finished edges or selvages. Move the needle from right to left, over the two edges. Also see *Overcasting,* page 71. If tiny stitches are used, it is called a *whip-stitch.* Oversewing may also be done with the needle slanting so tiny, straight stitches are formed.

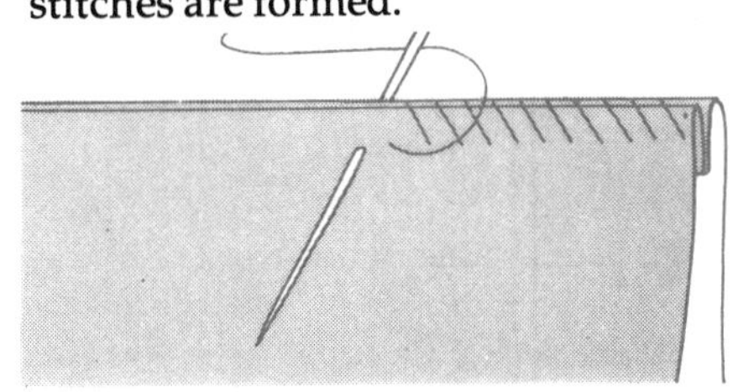

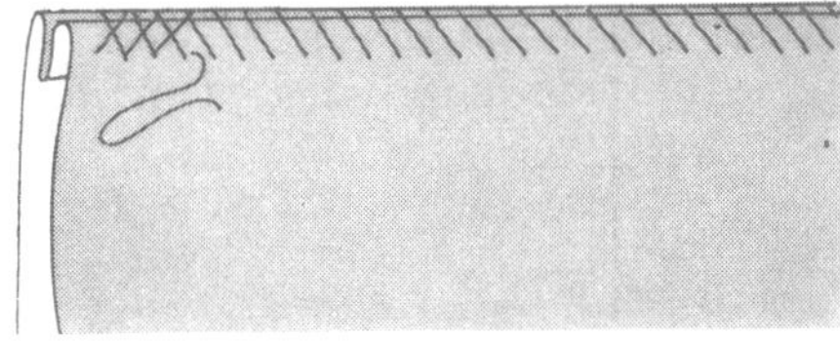

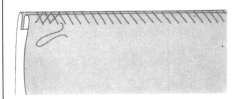

Pad-Stitch—This is a tailoring stitch. It is used to attach interfacing to the garment fabric, and mold it to shape. It is often used for undercollars and lapels.

Stitches are similar to diagonal tacks and worked from the wrong-side. Point the needle to the left. Take a stitch about 1/2 inch long through the interfacing. Pick up one or two fabric threads. Make another stitch about 1/2 inch below the first. On medium and thick fabrics, these stitches do not go through to the right-side. Continue making slightly curved rows until the interfacing is in place. Stitches on the right-side should not be seen.

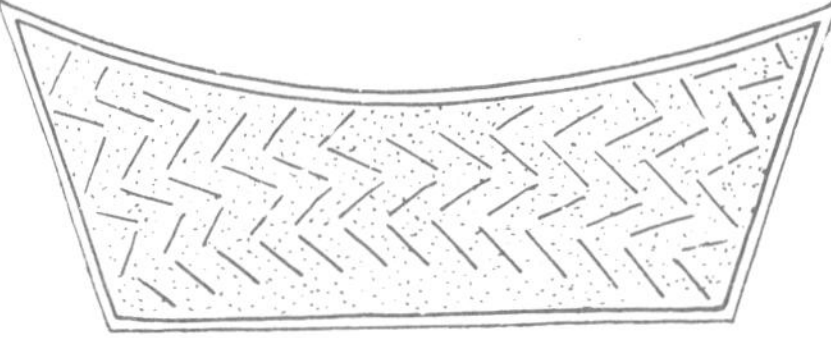

French and Swing Tacks—This stitch loosely holds two layers of fabric together. It is often used to join lining and garment or the edges of pleats. It is sometimes called a *bar tack;* see page 70.

Work one or two back-stitches to secure the thread. Make several long stitches about 1 inch to join the two pieces of fabric *loosely* together. Sew a buttonhole-stitch along the length of these threads. Finish off securely.

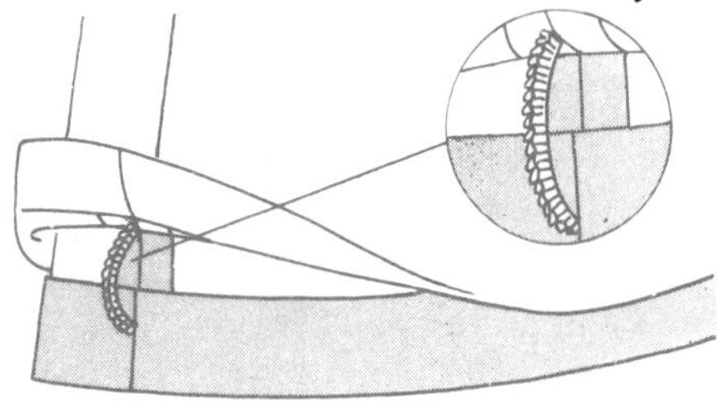

FINISHING AND DECORATIVE STITCHES

These stitches prevent raw edges from fraying, and add decoration to a garment.

Arrowhead Tacks—These are sewn at the top of pleats as decoration and reinforcement. They are usually made from embroidery thread in a matching or contrasting color.

Fasten the thread in the tack area. Bring the needle out at the base of the left angle. Stitch across to the opposite angle base. Put the needle through the baseline, to the right angle. Bring it out on the baseline within the stitch at the left angle.

Repeat this process. Stitches on the baseline should touch in the center. The stitches across the opposite point widen out from the angle points. Fasten off on the wrong-side.

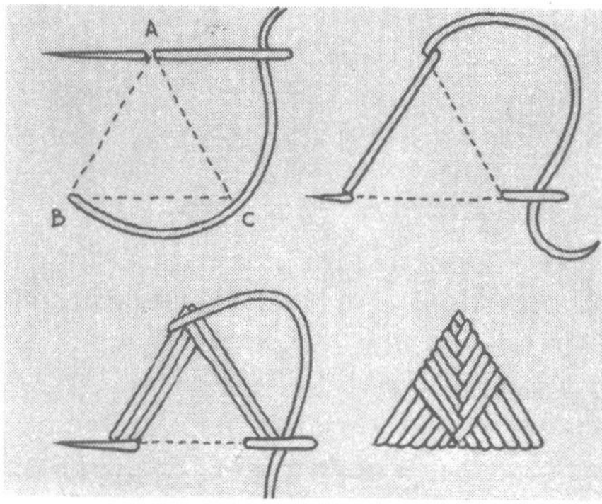

Bar Tacks—These are used to reinforce pleats. They are made at the end of buttonholes and slits. Work them on the surface of the fabric, usually on the right-side.

Using buttonhole twist, make several long stitches using the same two holes. Sew closely over these threads along the length, using the buttonhole-stitch.

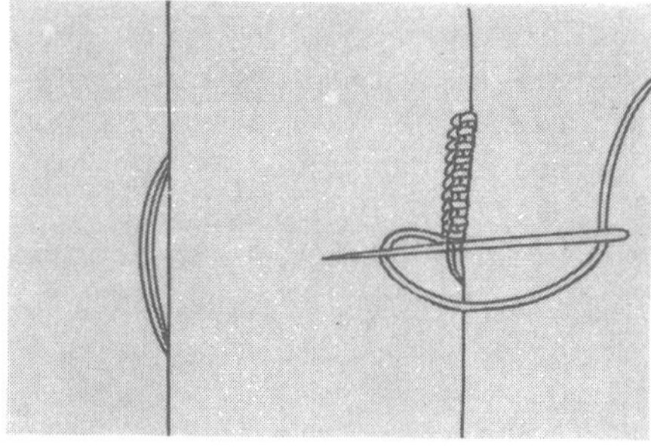

Blanket-Stitch—This is also called a *loop-stitch.* It is used to finish raw edges, especially on blankets. It is also used on seams and to strengthen thread loops and bar tacks. It may be used as a simple decorative stitch. It can be worked from right to left or left to right.

Attach thread with one or two back-stitches. Push the needle in behind the fabric and through the loop. Keep the fabric edge toward the worker. Repeat.

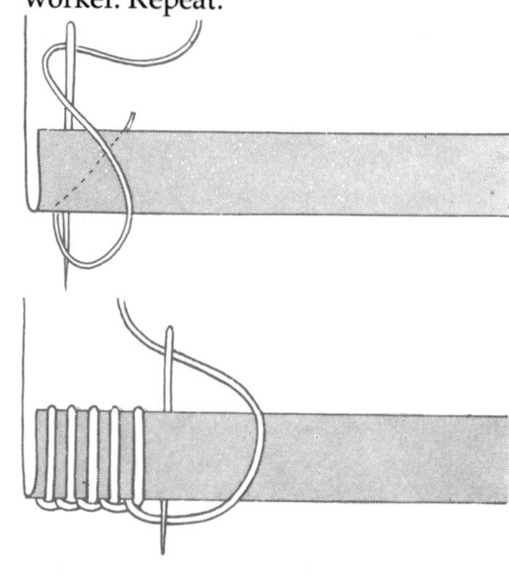

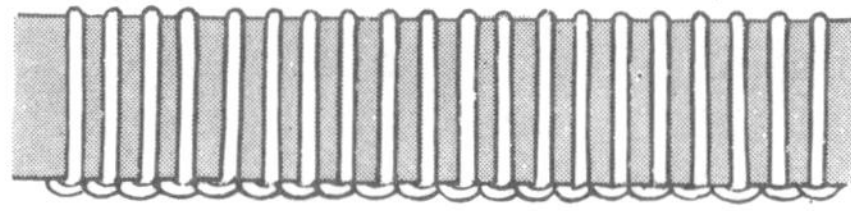

Blind Hemming—This is a way to sew hems and facings in place. The stitches are almost invisible on the right-side or wrong-side.

Finish the raw edge of the hem or facing. Roll it back about 1/4 inch, and attach thread securely. Sew a small stitch under one thread of the garment. Pick up one thread of the facing or hem a little farther along. Leave stitches fairly loose. This may also be done on some sewing machines.

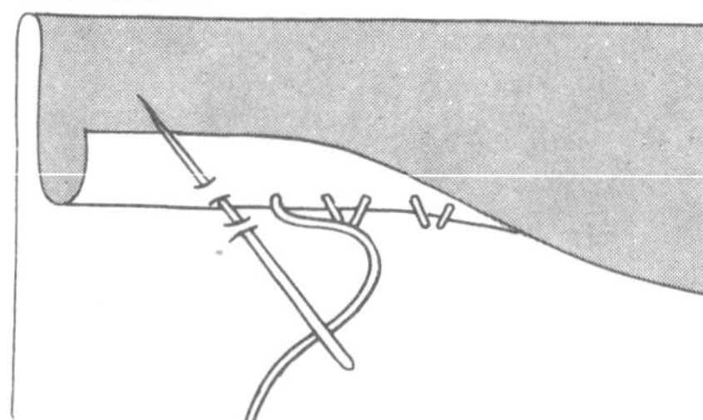

Buttonhole-Stitch—This is used to finish and strengthen raw edges, especially buttonholes. It is worked from left to right.

Attach thread with one or two back-stitches. Loop the thread behind the eye of the needle. With the needle behind the edge, push the needle point out over the loop of thread. Pull the needle through. Ease the thread up to form a knot on the edge. Stitches should be close enough to make a continuous row of knots along the edge.

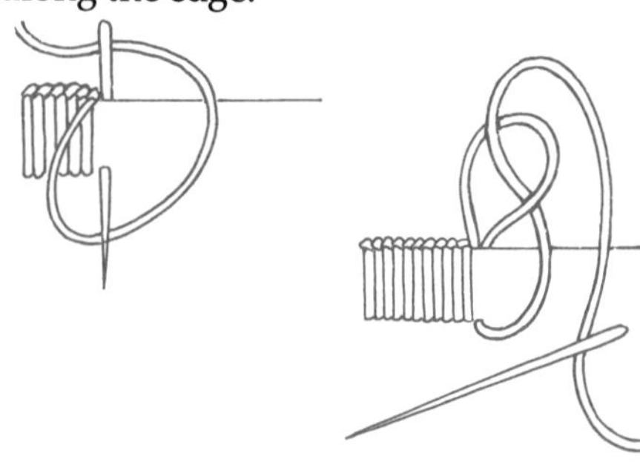

Chain-Stitch—This is a decorative hand-embroidery stitch. Insert the needle in the right-side of the material. Hold the thread down with your left thumb. Move the needle back to where the thread emerges. Bring out the needle and thread a short distance away. Bring the needle out over the loop.

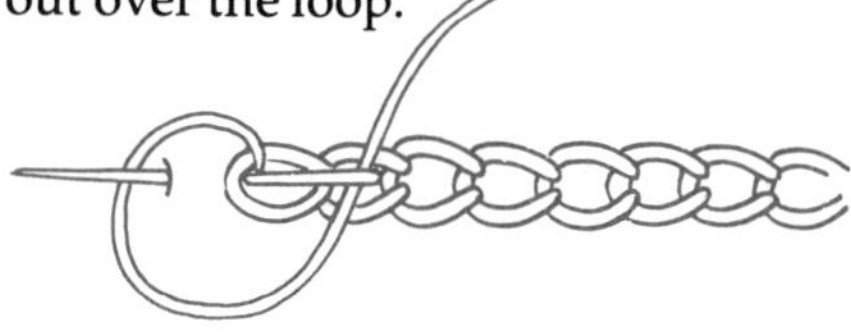

Coral-Knot-Stitch—This hand-embroidery stitch has two stitches crossing in the center. The crossing direction of all the stitches in a design must be the same, so it is even.

Move the needle from left to right. Keep the needle straight between two lines, making half the cross. Move from right to left to make the second half of the cross.

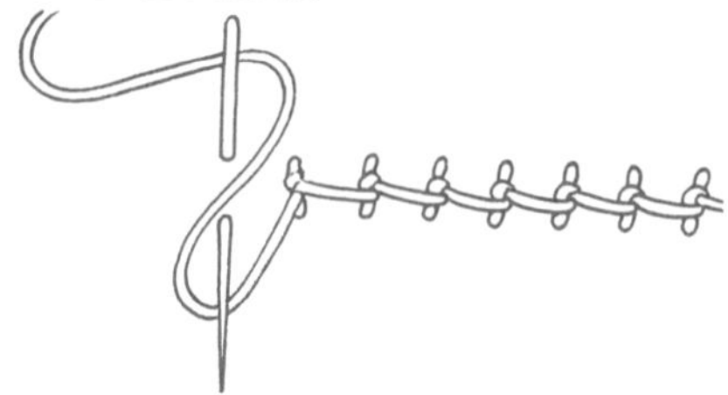

Crow's-Feet Tacks—These are similar to arrowhead tacks. Mark the triangle where the tack is to be sewn. Attach the thread with a back-stitch in the middle of the triangle. Make a stitch at each corner, inserting the needle through from right to left.

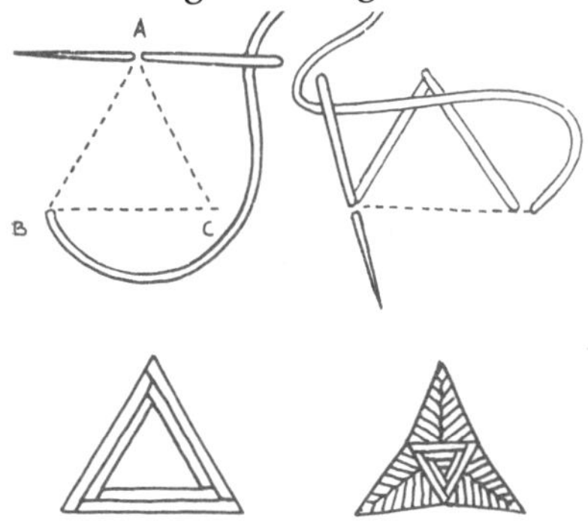

Each stitch widens across the angle, filling the area. Stitches must not overlap. Repeat the process until stitches meet each side of the angle. Fasten off on the wrong-side.

Feather-Stitch—This is another hand-embroidery stitch. Insert the needle to make a blanket-stitch, but slant the needle to the right. Put the thread to the left under the needle to make a blanket- or loop-stitch. It is slanted to the left. Repeat the process.

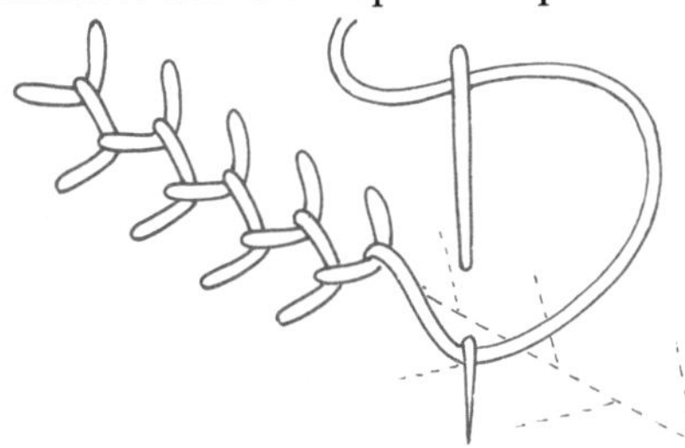

French Knots—This hand-embroidery stitch is often used to make the center of embroidered flowers. Mark dots where knots should be. Pick up one or two threads of fabric. Wind the embroidery thread around the needle two or three times. Hold the thread down with your thumb, and pull the needle through. Insert the needle in the material close to the starting point.

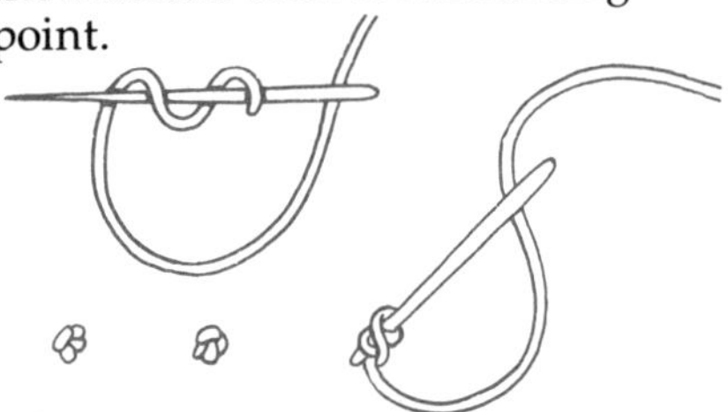

Hemming—This is used for garment hems to hold the folded edge in place. Hold the garment toward you, and move the needle from right to left. The hem is held over the fingers of the left hand. Pick up a thread from the fabric below the folded edge of the hem. Next, pick up a thread from the folded edge of the hem. Repeat until hem is complete.

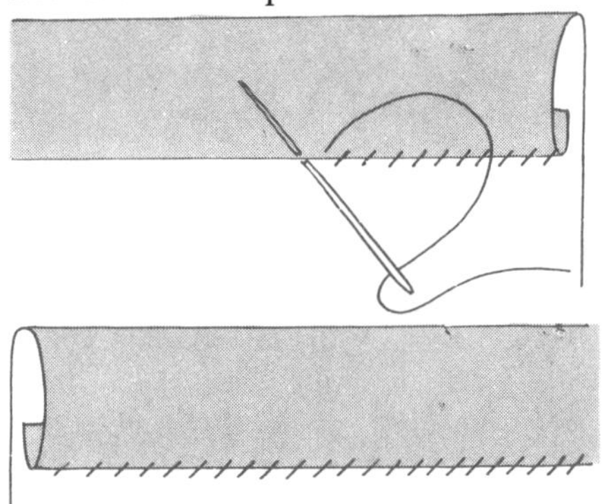

Hem-Stitching—This is a decorative way to finish hems on table linen. A few threads are drawn out at the required depth of the hem. Fold the hem, and miter the corners, tucking in the threads. Tack in place.

Work a hem-stitch. Bring the needle and thread to the edge of the drawn threads. Push the needle behind three threads, then bring the end around and behind them again. Bring the needle out through the thread loop, so a knot is formed. Repeat. Some hem-stitches can also be done on the machine.

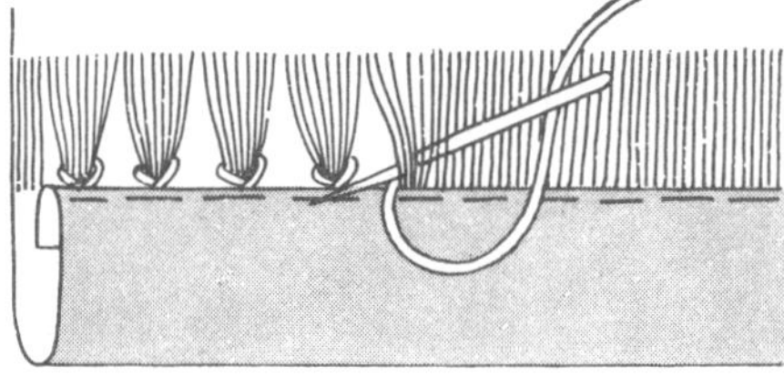

Herringbone-Stitch—This is sometimes called a *catch-stitch.* It is used over an edge to hold it flat. Work the needle from left to right over folded or raw edges. This forms criss-cross stitches. Hold the edge away from you as you work.

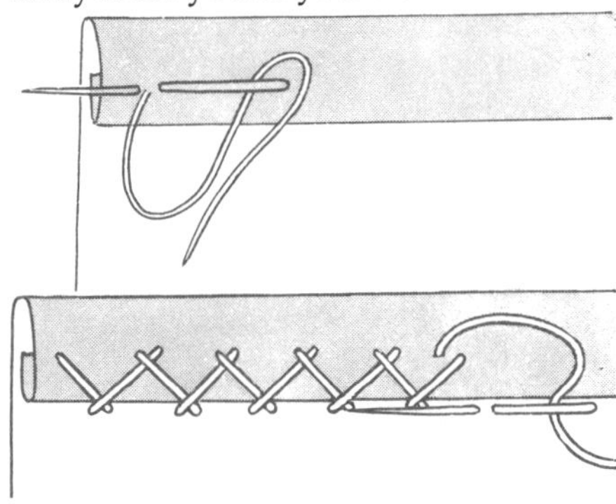

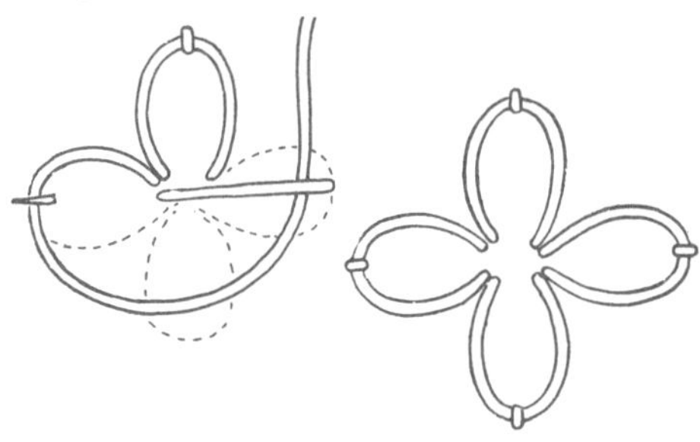

Lazy-Daisy Stitch—This is a variation of the chain-stitch. It is a detached chain-stitch. Groups of these stitches are often made together to form flowers in simple embroidery designs.

Overcasting—This is a quick way to finish raw edges by hand. It is often worked on single fabric. The thread is taken over the edge of the cloth, all the way along. Stitches should be small and evenly spaced. Zigzag or step-stitches may be used on zigzag machines. Consult your sewing-machine handbook.

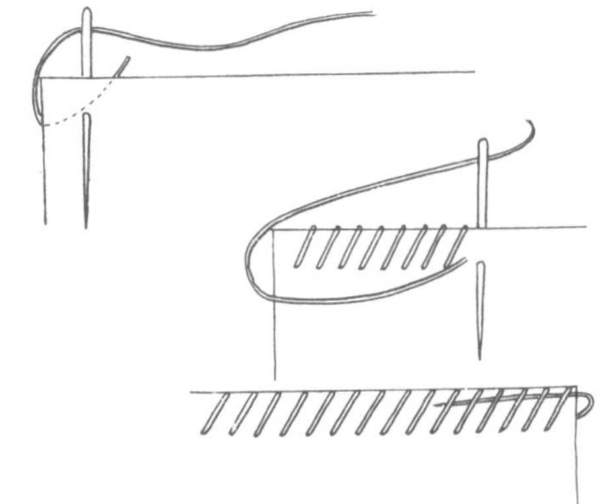

Pin-Stitch—This is a simple, decorative way to finish hems on lingerie and fine table linen. It is usually worked from the right-side or on a hem that has been tacked and pressed. Stitches are pulled firmly to give a punched-hole effect.

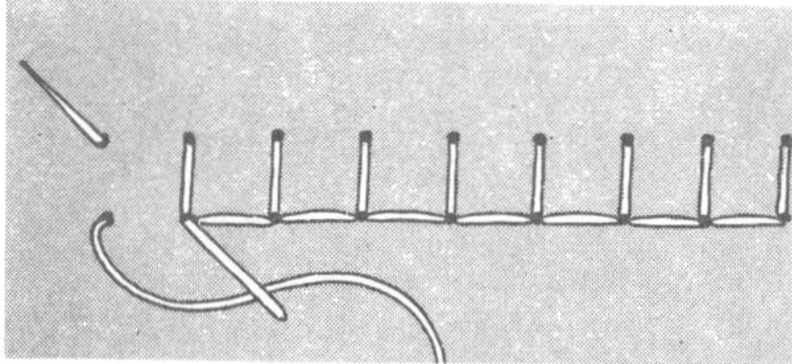

Satin-Stitch—This decorative stitch is used in hand-embroidery and appliqué. Insert the needle at one edge of the design, then at the opposite edge. Return to the starting edge by passing the needle underneath the material. Stitches should be close together and parallel. This can fill in a design of flowers, leaves and other things on a garment. It can also be made on a zigzag machine, so check your sewing-machine handbook.

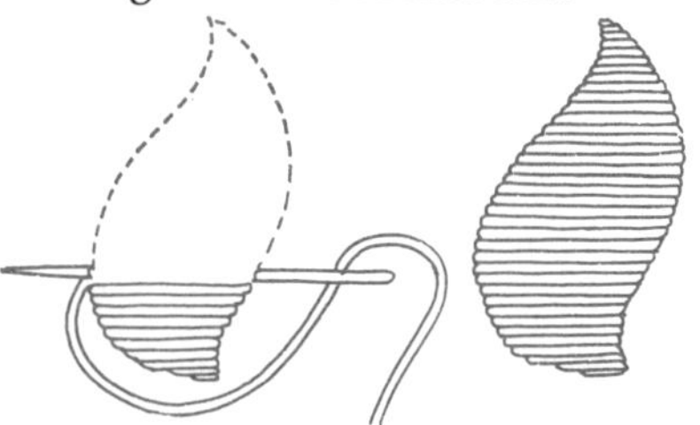

Shell Hemming—This is a variation of hemming used on fine, sheer lingerie fabrics. It is worked from right to left on the wrong-side. Make a narrow, folded hem. Press it in place. Attach thread with one or two back-stitches. Sew a few hemming stitches. Take the needle and thread completely over the hem. Pull the loop tight. Repeat along the hem, making sure the shells are regular and even in size.

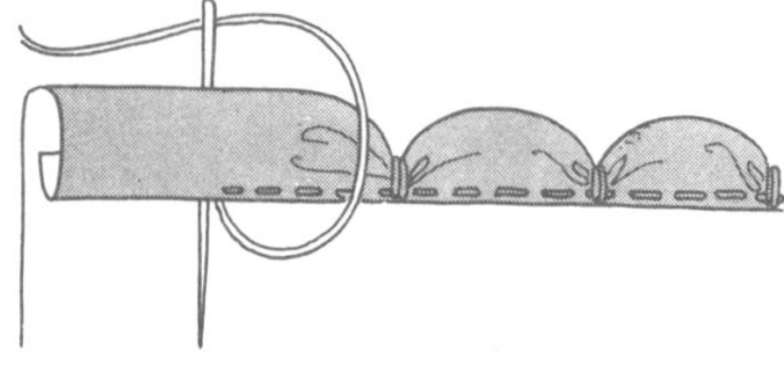

Slip-Stitch—This is used for sewing a hem when stitching needs to be invisible on both sides. Pick up a single thread of fabric below the fold. Push the needle through fold for about 1/4 inch. Repeat.

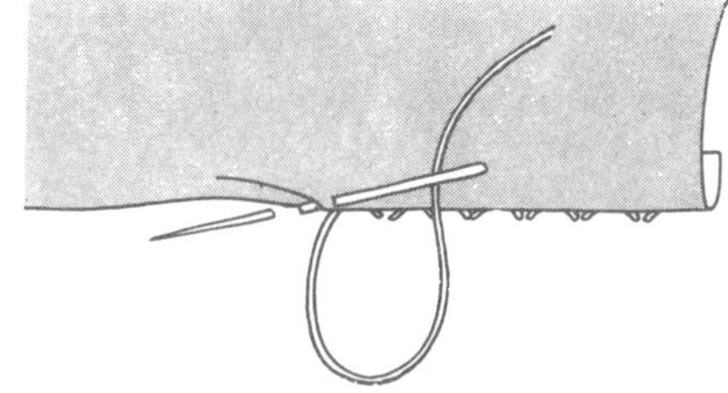

Stem-Stitch—This is a stitch for outlining designs. Keep the thread *below* the needle. The needle is brought out exactly where the previous stitch finished. A row of back-stitches shows on the wrong-side.

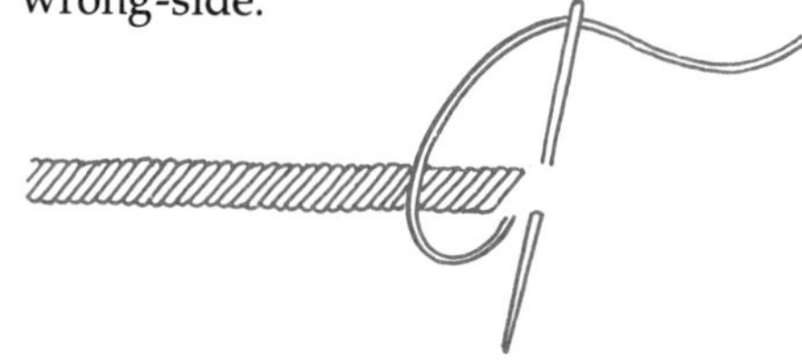

Smocking—This decorates rows of gathering with rows of hand-embroidery. Carefully prepare the garment fabric, and gather evenly. Many stitches are used for smocking.

Cable Smocking—Work the needle from left to right along a row of dots. Bring the needle out. Pick up one dot with the thread above the needle, and gather up. Pick up the next dot with thread below the needle. Repeat the process until complete.

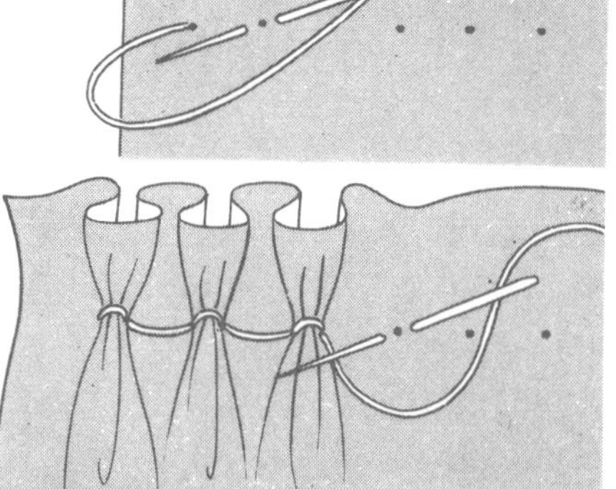

Honeycomb Smocking—Work the needle from right to left. Alternate between two rows of dots. Bring the needle out on the first dot on the left. Using short stitches, pick up the first and second dots. Gather material together. Take a second stitch through the same dots. Push the needle out on the third dot in the row below. Pick up the second and third dots. Draw together, then take the second stitch though the same dots. Repeat the process until finished.

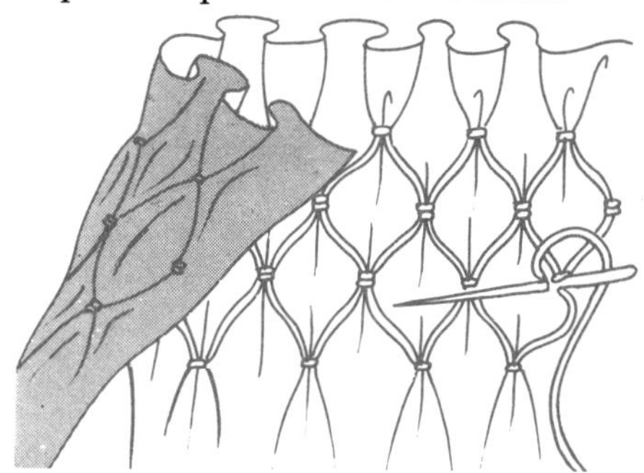

NEEDLES

You need a needle suited to the fabric and thread. Fine, delicate fabrics require fine needles. Heavy fabrics need thicker needles. With hand sewing, it is easy to select the correct needle. With machine sewing, the appropriate needle may be forgotten. Often the sewing-machine needle is left in the machine until it breaks, then it is replaced with the same type. When only natural-fiber fabrics were available, needle selection did not matter as much.

Today, with many man-made fabrics available, it is different. Man-made fabrics blunt needles quickly. Select a new needle for *each* new garment or outfit you make. If you do not do this, you may damage the next garment you sew.

A blunt needle can ruin a fine fabric. When sewing jersey fabric or silky, woven fabrics with little stretch, use a ball-point needle. These eliminate missed stitches and reduce the risk of snagging the fabric as the needle pierces it.

The eye of the needle must be large enough to accommodate the thread used. If it is not, the needle may bend, and the thread will snarl and break. When possible, buy the best-quality needle you can afford. Poor-quality sewing-machine needles are not economical. They do not last long and give unsatisfactory results.

Thread

Why are there different types of thread? Natural fabrics need to be sewn with natural thread and man-made fabrics with man-made thread.

The thread you use should have the same characteristics as the fabric being sewn. If not, the stitching and fabric will not be compatible in wearing, washing or cleaning. Natural fabrics—wool, cotton, linen and silk—shrink, even if only slightly. If a cotton thread is used, the same thing happens. Any variation between fabric and thread shrinkage is almost unnoticeable.

If a man-made thread is used for these fabrics, the results may be disastrous. Cotton and linen need a high temperature setting for ironing. If too-hot an iron is placed on a man-made thread, it melts. The result is no seams! If you use a

Needle and Thread Chart

Fabrics	Type	Thread	Machine Needle	Hand Needle	Stitches Per inch
WOVEN FABRICS					
Very Sheer Chiffon, Tulle Net	Natural and man-made	Mercerized Cotton 90-100 Silk A	9	10	16
Sheer Voile, Organdy Lace	Natural and man-made	Mercerized Cotton 70-80 Silk A	9-11	9	14-16
Lightweight Gingham, Muslin, Taffeta, Silk	Natural and man-made	Mercerized Cotton 60 Silk A	9-11	8-9	12-14
Mediumweight Poplin, Cotton, Corduroy, Linen	Natural and man-made	Mercerized Cotton 50 Silk A	11-14	7-8	10-14
Heavyweight Denim, Twill Canvas, Tweed	Natural and man-made	Mercerized Cotton 24, 30, 36 Silk A	14-18	4-5	8-10
STRETCH FABRICS Use stretch-stitch when possible.	Lightweight natural	Mercerized Cotton 50, 60 Silk A	9-11 Ball- or unipoint	9-10 Ball- or unipoint	12-16 stitches per inch
	Heavyweight natural	Mercerized Cotton 40 Silk A	16-18 Ball- or unipoint	4-5 Ball- or unipoint	8-10 stitches per inch
	Man-made	Cotton-covered polyester	16-18 Ball- or unipoint	4-5 Ball- or unipoint	8-10 stitches per inch
SPECIAL FABRICS Leather, PVC	Natural and man-made	Mercerized Cotton 40-50 Silk A	14-16	5-6	10-12
BUTTON SEWING		Silk Twist D 100% long-staple polyester buttonhole twist	6-7		
EMBROIDERY		Silk Twist D 100% long-staple polyester buttonhole twist, cotton-covered polyester, top-stitching and buttonhole twist	6-7	9-10	

natural thread on fabric that does not shrink, seams will pucker when the garment is washed. These seams may be pressed with care and attention. But the same thing happens again when the garment is washed. This does not happen if a man-made thread is used.

Many man-made fabrics are also stretch fabrics. Synthetic thread has a certain amount of give to allow seams to stretch. It is better to use a stretch-stitch and stretch thread.

PRESSING AND IRONING

Pressing produces a professional finish on a garment. It is necessary from the preparation stage until the garment is complete. Pressing is *not* ironing. In pressing, the iron is lifted, set down, lifted and set down again. It is not moved back and forth on the garment, like ironing. Pressing is done for the entire garment.

For many fabrics, your hand must bear most of the iron's weight. This keeps the surface from becoming distorted or flattened. A pressing cloth is needed because steam makes it possible to mold fabrics.

KNOWLEDGE OF FABRIC

There are certain points to consider about fabric before pressing. These include the *weight, thickness, texture* and *fiber content* of the fabric. When fabric is a blend, follow instructions for the fiber that needs the *lowest* iron temperature.

Cotton—Moisture may be used, but press fabric until dry. Use steam, then press without it. Use a pressing cloth on the right-side when pressing a textured or dull fabric. Chintz and other glossy cottons are pressed dry on the right-side to keep the shine.

Most cotton is pressed or ironed with a hot iron while slightly damp. The fabric must be completely dry when finished or mildew may occur. Some drip-dry and minimum-iron cottons are improved by light pressing of seams and edges. For lightweight cotton, use the heat setting for silk. For heavyweight cotton, use the heat setting for linen.

Linen—Follow the rules for cotton, but increase heat and moisture. For lightweight linen, use the heat setting for cotton. For heavyweight linen, use the heat setting for linen.

Rayon—This needs low heat. Use a steam iron and a light, *dry* pressing cloth. Press on the wrong-side.

Wool—Never subject wool to extremes of moisture, heat or pressure. Do not press it when it is wet or dry. It must be *damp.* A moist heat is needed, and a wool pressing cloth is preferable.

For lightweight wool, use the heat setting for wool. For heavyweight wool, use the heat setting between wool and cotton. Use a heavier iron.

If the wool pile is flattened, raise it with a small, stiff brush. Do this *immediately* after pressing. Use two press cloths for wool. Put a dry one immediately against the surface of the fabric being pressed. Put a damp one on top. This keeps press marks or shine from appearing.

Silk and Man-Made Fabrics—It is not necessary to use moisture when pressing these fabrics. If moisture is needed, use only a minimal amount. A pressing cloth is not usually needed, but keep a fine cotton one ready to protect fabric.

When moisture is needed, test the fabric to see if water spots it. Tissue paper placed between the iron and fabric prevents this. Use a low iron temperature. Man-made fibers melt if too high a heat is used. Silk becomes brittle.

Velvet—Steam velvet and napped fabrics instead of pressing. The surface of the pile needs protection, so use a velvet board with upstanding wires. The fabric is placed pile-side down on the board. Press it lightly on the wrong-side with a slightly damp cloth.

If a velvet board is not available, use the iron in a vertical position. Put a damp cloth over the sole plate. The wrong-side of the velvet is passed back and forth across the surface of the iron plate. The steam passing through the fabric presses the velvet without flattening the pile.

When pressing velveteen or corduroy, use the same method. Press corduroy on the right-side. Use a piece of self-fabric, pile-side down, as a press cloth. The piles interlock. If pressing is kept light, no flattening occurs.

Lace—Press lace on several layers of terrycloth, with right-side down. The textured surface sinks into the fabric. Use a dry pressing cloth. Set the iron temperature according to fabric type. Test a spare piece of fabric first. Press lightly to avoid distortion.

PVC and Laminated Fabrics—Do not use an iron. Hammer with the end of a wooden rolling pin to flatten seams.

Elastic Fabrics—These need no pressing or ironing.

Stretch Fabrics—Do *not* stretch these fabrics while pressing. Press seams from the wrong-side during sewing. Iron lightly on the wrong-side to remove wrinkles.

Knit Fabrics—Press in the direction of ribbing. Use a damp cloth on the wrong-side. Avoid stretching during pressing.

Fur Fabrics—Do not press real fur. To press seams, hems and facings, place the fur fabric between two thick, soft towels.

BASIC PRESSING

Shrink and press fabric that is not preshrunk *before* cutting. You will press each stage as you make up a garment, so keep the iron ready.

Gather all your pressing equipment, and clean the iron if necessary. Use some fabric scraps for tests. Scraps should be large enough for *before* and *after* pressing comparisons.

See how the garment fabric stands up to heat, steam and moisture. *Never* use too much of any of these.

Use a pressing cloth suitable for the fabric. For wool, use a light, firm, wool cloth. For cotton or cotton blends, use a firm, cotton cloth. *Never* use a wet press cloth. Start with it slightly damp. Add more moisture with a sponge as needed. If more moisture is needed on certain areas, use a small brush to wet the cloth.

Never press over pins. Take out as many tacking threads as possible before pressing. Press on the wrong-side of the fabric. When you must press on the right-side, use a pressing cloth.

Try to press with or along the grain of the fabric. The fabric may stretch if you do not.

Irons have heat settings for different fabrics, so use them. *Never* overpress or you will ruin the fabric and garment.

Use a seam roll under seams, and press from the wrong-side. Use a tailor's ham, seam roll or end of a sleeve board for darts.

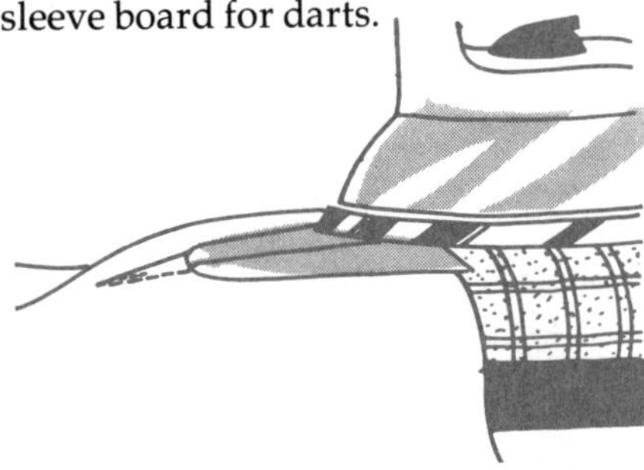

Use brown-paper strips under seam allowances, darts or pleats. This keeps ridges from appearing on the right-side during pressing. Strips

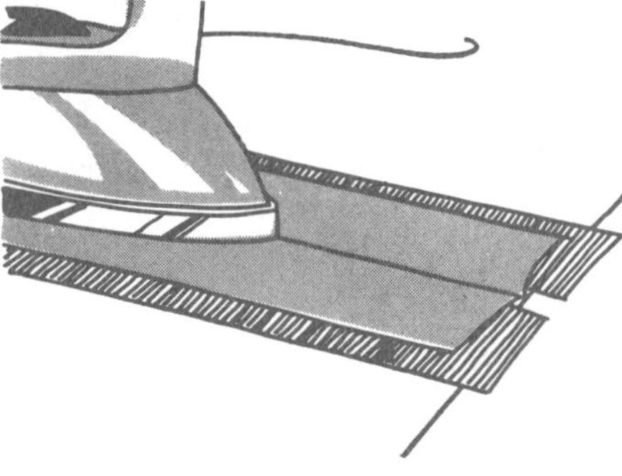

should be wider than the area to be pressed. For seams in heavy fabric, dampen strips slightly before pressing.

Press seams and darts after stitching or before stitching to another section of the garment. Save time by pressing several seams and darts at the same time.

Keep the weight of the iron in your hand. Work with the tip of the iron, using only light pressure. Do not allow the full weight of the iron to rest on the fabric. Heavier pressure is needed only for firmly woven fabrics or those that are crease-resistant.

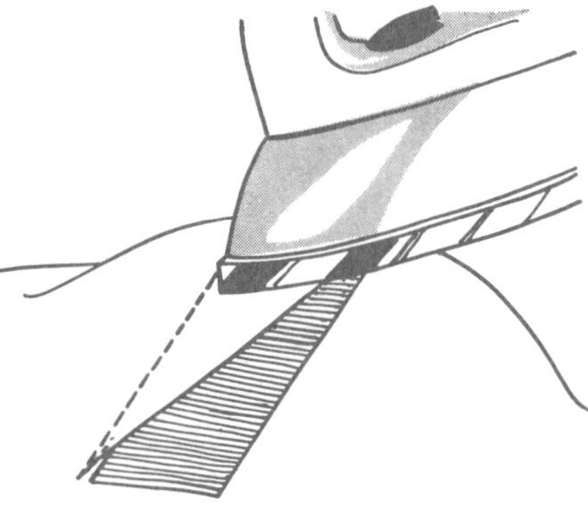

Do not press creases or sharp edges until you are certain their position is correct. Press darts, side seams and hems. Darts and tacks are pressed along the stitching line, then pressed to one side.

If a shiny or flattened area appears on the fabric, hold it over steam to revive it.

Use an iron-holder so the iron is not left flat on the ironing board. Turn the iron off and unplug it when pressing is finished. Install a socket that lights up a red warning light when the iron is on.

BASIC IRONING

Have ironing equipment ready. An iron with a non-stick sole plate makes the gliding action of ironing easier. Aerosol starch and mist water sprayers are also helpful.

Have fabric in the correct state of dampness for ironing. Iron double parts, such as collars and cuffs, first. Start on the wrong-side. Iron on the wrong-side for a mat finish and on the right-side for a glossy finish. Iron with or along the grain of the fabric when possible.

PRESSING PART OF A GARMENT

Open Seams—Push the tip of the iron along open seams. Place a seam roll or brown paper under the seam edges. Press firmly on the wrong-side for a flat finish.

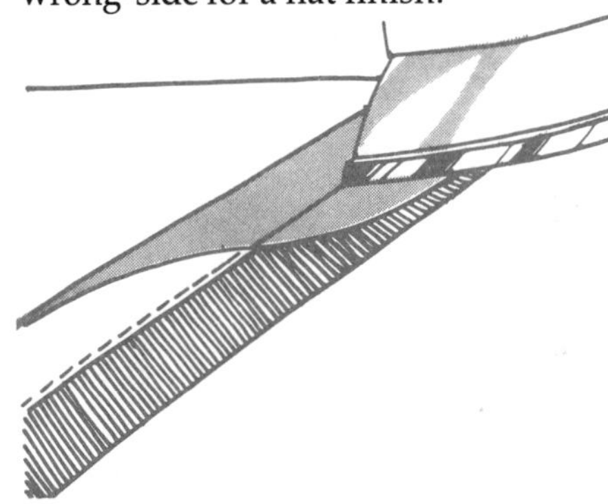

Enclosed Seams—Press the stitching line, trim off excess fabric and layer, if necessary. Press the seam open over a seam roll or sleeve board. Turn and press lightly on the wrong-side. Push the seam away from the edge. It will not show from the right-side.

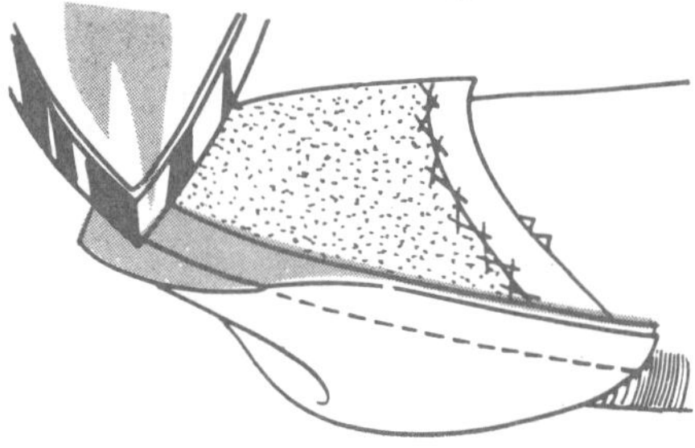

Curved Seams—Press along the stitching line. Clip seam allowances so they lie flat. Press the seam open over a seam roll, tailor's ham or sleeve board.

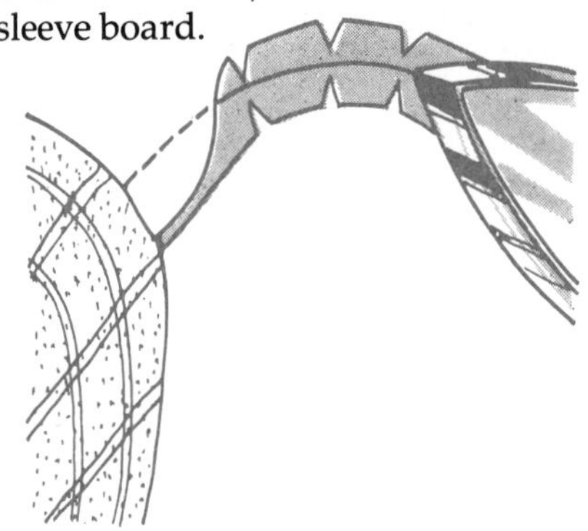

Eased Seams—Press slightly gathered seams in wool and other fabrics to shrink excess fullness. Use a damp cloth and steam iron, with the seam over a curved surface. Steam the fabric by holding the iron *over* the seam, not on it. Repeat several times if necessary.

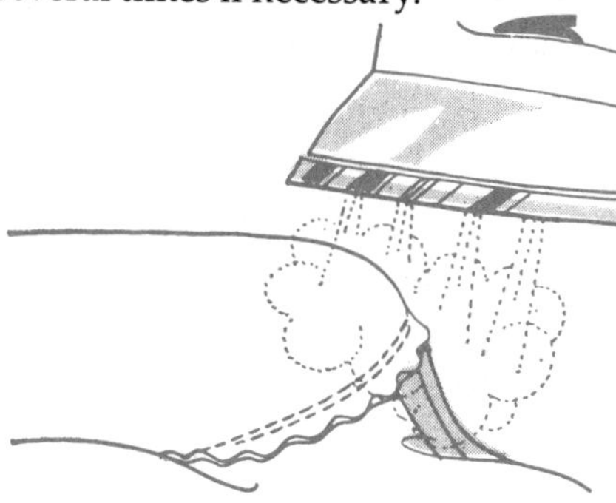

French Seams—Press firmly from the wrong-side. Lift the seam and push the tip of the iron along to remove wrinkles.

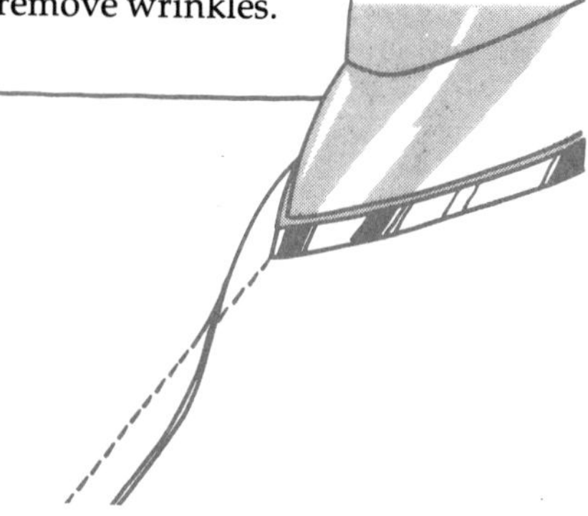

Waist Seams—Press open or press edges up toward the bodice.

Darts—Press as for a French seam. If darts are cut or trimmed, press them as open seams. Press them over a slightly rounded surface. First press the stitching line like any seam. The iron should not go beyond the point or a crease will appear on the right-side.

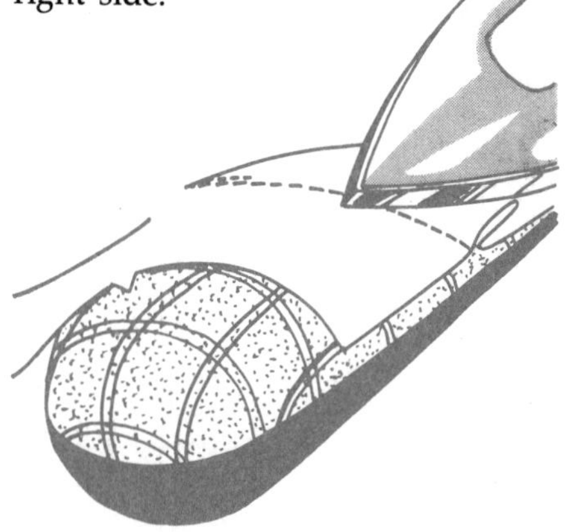

Open the garment out. Press the dart lightly from the right-side, starting at the wider end. Press underarm and elbow darts down.

Press waist darts toward the center front. Press center-back and shoulder darts toward the neckline.

Tucks—Do not use much steam or stitching lines may pucker. Press on the wrong-side. Rub the wrong-side of pin-tucked fabric over the upturned sole plate of the iron. This makes tucks stay upright.

Pleats—Remove all pins, but leave tacking threads in place. Use a fine thread for tacking pleats. With the garment right-side down on the ironing board, arrange pleats. Use a chair to support any of the garment that hangs off the board. Press lightly over a damp pressing cloth, or use a steam iron and dry cloth.

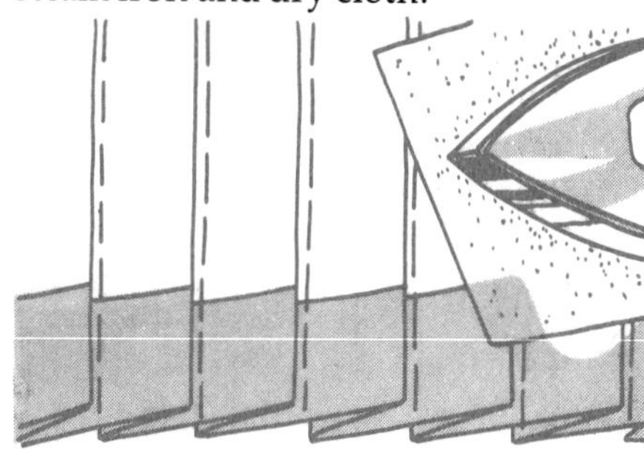

Hold the garment up, or try it on to see if pleats hang correctly. Put strips of brown paper under the folds. Then press heavily to set sharp creases.

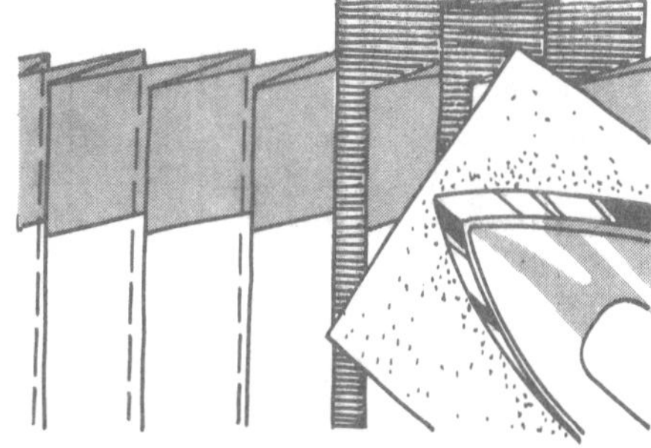

Remove all tacking, and rearrange pleats with the wrong-side down on the ironing board. Pin pleats in place if necessary. Press carefully and lightly, then let the fabric remain there until it is completely dry.

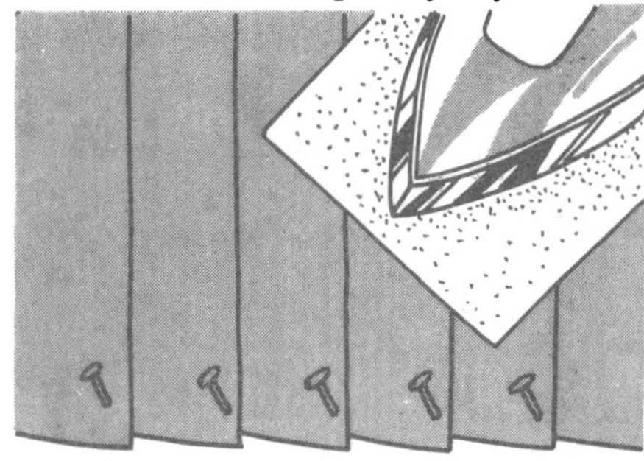

Sleeves—With wrong-side out, arrange the sleeve head over the sleeve board or tailor's ham. Press the seam toward the armhole, moving it around the board as you work.

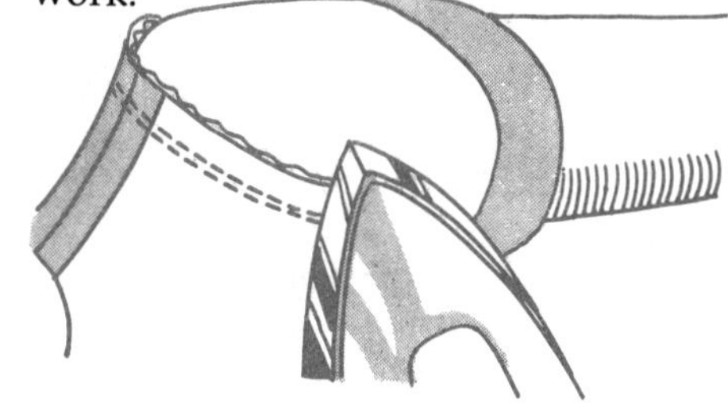

Gathers—Hold the rows of stitching in your left hand. From the wrong-side, push the point of the iron into the folds toward the stitches. Do not crease the folds.

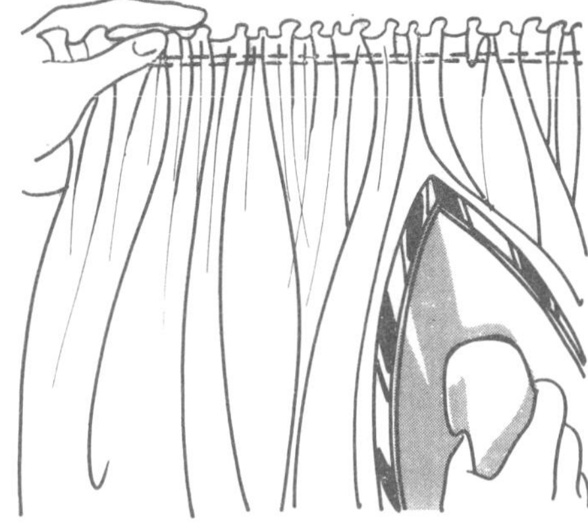

Fastenings—Avoid pressing over snaps, hooks and eyes or buttons. Impressions will be made on the garment. Press around them.

For zippers, place the opening right-side down on a thick, soft cloth on the ironing board. Press carefully on the wrong-side. Use little moisture or puckers may form. When pressing from the right-side, place strips of brown paper between the zipper and placket edges.

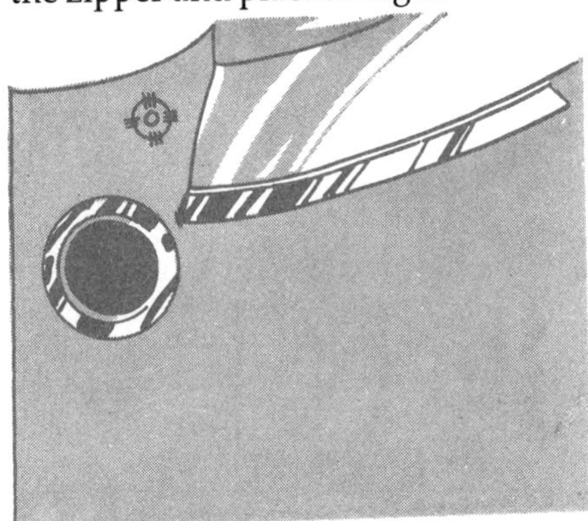

Hems—Remove all pins and tacking from the finished hem. Press the lower edge from the wrong-side of the garment. Use a damp pressing cloth or steam. Pound the edge with the back of a clothes brush if a crisp edge is required. Press the top of the hem lightly or a ridge will form on the right-side.

If a soft, lower edge is preferred, steam the hem without letting the weight of the iron rest on the fabric. Gently pat the edge with the back of a clothes brush to set it in place. Let the fabric dry completely.

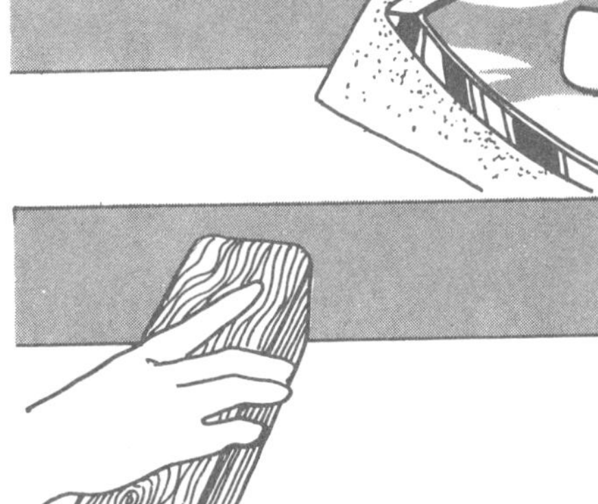

FINAL PRESSING

Although you have pressed the garment during sewing, it is important to touch-up the finished article. This does not correct careless sewing, but improves the final appearance.

Do this with the garment on a dress form if possible. It can also be done on a hanger. Wire clothes hangers are not good because they mark the shoulder and do not allow clothes to hang well.

Steam and pull small sections in shape where necessary. Put soft, crumpled, tissue paper inside to pad curves until fabric dries. Let it dry completely before taking the garment from the dress form or hanger. Press in the following order to avoid creasing the areas already touched up.

1. Collars and facings.
2. Sleeves.
3. Bodice and waist seam.
4. Skirt.
5. Belts and trim.

CARE AND REPAIR OF CLOTHES

Care of Clothes

Being well-groomed is important, even with today's casual clothes. Be sure your clothes are clean and well-cared for to get the maximum value out of them. Time spent organizing a routine for caring for clothes pays off. There is no last-minute panic when getting ready in the morning.

CARE OF WARDROBE

Arrange enough storage space for your clothes. Clothes can become crushed and soiled in storage. Take out seasonal clothes you are not wearing. Clean them and put them away. Arrange hanging and drawer space so similar items are together. Some people prefer storing complete outfits in one place. Each outfit is accompanied by accessories.

Allow air to circulate in the storage area or clothes may smell musty. Use a moth-repellent with little odor.

Keep a small basket of supplies where clothes are stored for repairing and mending. If these items are kept someplace else, you may not take care of problems.

ROUTINE

Set aside a few minutes every evening to care for clothes and accessories used that day. Prepare for the next day, too. Make note of any items needing repair. Set aside a regular time for mending. Deal with minor problems as they arise.

Hang up all garments after wearing them. Always brush outdoor clothes after wearing. Close fastenings, and let clothes air before putting them away. Use good-quality hangers.

Wipe greasy collars and necklines with a grease solvent. Use a commercial cleaner on a pad. Air the clothes and room after doing this. Deal with any stains or spots immediately. Do not allow them to set. Put out clothes and accessories for the next day.

MINOR PROBLEMS

Buttons and Buttonholes—Sew on lost or loose buttons. Buttons can unravel easily, so check for threads that might pull loose.

Lint and Pilling—Remove lint or pilling by winding sticky tape around your hand, keeping sticky-side out. Rub tape over the fabric surface. A special clothes brush also does this job. With knits, remove pilling with a special scraper.

Hems—Resew the complete hem on a garment if it comes undone in one place. Make emergency repairs with double-sided, sticky tape.

Pulled Threads—Do not cut pulled threads. Ease them back in place with a pin. If loops are left, pull these to the wrong-side where they will not show. A needle threader is a good tool for doing this.

Tears and Holes—Darn or patch tears and holes. An emergency repair can be made to a tear by ironing on a piece of special mending tape.

Pressing—Use an iron and ironing board. Have clean pressing cloths, a sleeve board and a clothes brush ready.

Pants—Shake and brush thoroughly. Press carefully, paying attention to creases. Soap may be rubbed along the crease line on the wrong-side to make sharper creases when pressed in the normal way. This also works for pleats in skirts.

If pants are shiny, sponge with a solution of vinegar and water. Use about 2 tablespoons of vinegar to 2 cups of water. Wring out a cloth in clear water, and rinse the area. Use a damp cloth under the iron, and steam lightly on both sides of the fabric.

If pants are baggy, shrink the fabric back in shape by placing a damp cloth over the area. Stroke the iron over the top to steam the fibers. Let the garment dry completely before wear.

Suits, Jackets and Dresses—Brush, sponge and press thoroughly. Take care of shiny and baggy areas as above.

Knits—If collars and cuffs stretch out of shape, wash the garment carefully and dry flat. You can also have the garment dry-cleaned. Sew a few rows of shirring elastic in the wrong-side of the rib to give it stretch again.

WASHING CLOTHES

Before washing, sort clothes into piles of whites and colors, according to fiber content. Most washable fabrics have care labeling. Keep these labels available when you purchase a fabric. They are normally sewn in purchased clothes.

When sewing at home, sew a label in the garment for future reference. When fabric is a blend, choose the washing process for the one needing the mildest treatment.

Detergents—Use the detergent according to instructions. Use less rather than more. Dissolve the detergent completely in water before adding clothes.

Bleaching—Most protein stains, such as blood, urine and food, can be removed by soaking in an enzyme presoak. Follow instructions on the package. Use a mild solution of bleach to remove some stains and whiten some white fabrics. Follow instructions about dilution and soaking.

Hand-Washing—Use lots of water at the correct temperature so clothes do not have to be moved around vigorously. Rinse thoroughly.

Machine-Washing—Do not overload the machine. Use correct washing temperatures, and sort loads carefully.

Laundromat—Do not try to wash large, mixed loads because a machine has a large capacity. The washing temperature may be hot, so wash only fabrics that can take high temperatures. Use the recommended amount of detergent.

Rinsing—Thoroughly rinse all fabrics. Most washing machines do this correctly. Hand-washing may be inadequately rinsed.

Finishes—Fabric softeners are effective when used in the rinse water for towels, diapers and some wool. Starch is effective for stiffening cotton and linen. Spray-on starch is useful for small areas such as collars and cuffs.

Burns and Scorches—For slight burn marks, use a mild borax solution. Wring out a clean cloth in the solution, and rub the mark with it. Repeat a few times, and rinse the same way with a clean damp cloth. Washable fabrics may be soaked immediately in cold milk.

Color Bleeding—Test fabrics for color fastness before washing with others. If a lot of color is lost in washing, add 2 tablespoons of white vinegar to the final-rinse water. If a color bleeds from one area of a garment to another, there is no effective remedy.

Iron Marks—These are brown, rusty-looking marks that can be removed by pouring salt on the stain. Soak the salt in lemon juice. Let it soak in the fabric for about one hour, then rinse well.

Shrinkage—Wool shrinks if washed incorrectly, and shrinkage cannot be corrected. Some man-made fibers shrink, so keep these slightly stretched while drying. Hang the garment to drip-dry after weighting it at the hem.

DRY-CLEANING

The label on a purchased garment gives instructions about caring for it. Before buying fabric, see if it needs dry-cleaning. Sew a label in the finished garment to indicate care instructions.

Not all fabrics can be dry-cleaned. Felt, velvet, laminated fabrics, leather, suede and other fabrics with special finishes may present problems. Ask your dry-cleaner if you are in doubt.

Do-It-Yourself Dry-Cleaning—This service is found in many laundromats. The results can be disappointing, but it is inexpensive. There is usually no pressing service available, so clothes may be clean but not in good shape. Professional pressing is usually worth paying for on tailored garments.

Dry-Cleaning—Remove buckles and belts before taking a garment to the cleaners. Make any repairs. Attach a note explaining any known stains. If the fabric is thin and limp after dry-cleaning, ask to have it "sized."

STAIN REMOVAL

The longer a stain is on a fabric, the more difficult it is to remove. Always take prompt action on stains. If the garment is dry-cleaned, explain the type of stain so appropriate measures can be taken.

Small stains can often be dealt with at home, using inexpensive cleaners. Keep a multipurpose stain remover at home. You can choose from liquids, powders and aerosols. Carefully follow directions for best results.

Other useful cleaning substances include ammonia, enzyme presoaks, hydrogen peroxide, bleach and vinegar.

Removing Spots and Stains—Test the cleaner on a bit of fabric first. Hold the stained area taut over the sink, and pour a suitable cleaner through the fabric several times. Rinse well, and wash in the normal way.

Another method is to spread the stained area over a thick pad. Dampen a clean sponge with the cleaner. Rub it over the stain in several applications. Work from the outer edge of the stain to avoid spreading the stain. Smudge the edges to avoid a hard line around the stain.

Repairs

MINOR PROBLEMS

Buttons and Buttonholes—Worn buttonholes can be made into bound buttonholes. You will need to use larger buttons. This is only worth doing on a valuable garment. Buttonholes on purchased clothes can be strengthened by stitching over them with a buttonhole-stitch.

A button may be torn off a garment, leaving a weakened area. Stitch a piece of fabric or tape over it on the wrong-side. Loops for buttons often break. Replace them with a new thread loop.

Collars and Cuffs—Shirt collars may wear through along the neck fold. Stiffened collars cannot be removed and reattached because of the stiffening slots. Other collars can be turned to prolong the life of the shirt.

Remove a collar and use the underneath facing as a new top collar. Or cut a piece from the shirttail to make a new collar.

Cuffs may fray or get dirt ingrained along the edges. A single cuff can be remade by shortening it slightly. A double cuff can have the worn place darned. Remove it, and replace it the other way around. Then the darned part is hidden in the fold.

You can make a patch from a shirttail. You can also add new contrasting cuffs and collar.

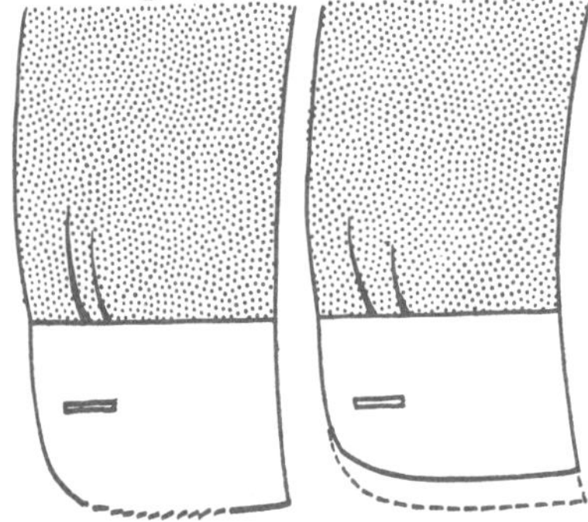

Pockets—It is possible to buy standard-size, ready-made linings for pockets. Or the pocket area can be opened and a new cotton lining stitched in. Make a pattern from the old one. A quick repair can be made to a pocket with a small hole in the bottom. Machine-stitch across the lining just above it.

Elastic—Open a few stitches of the casing. Pull out old elastic and cut a new piece the same length. Thread the elastic through a bodkin or attach a small safety pin to one end. Pull the elastic through the casing. Oversew the ends firmly, and restitch the casing.

STAIN	DRY-CLEANABLE FABRICS	WASHABLE FABRICS
Beer	Hold fabric taut. Pour water or hydrogen peroxide through the spot.	Soak washable wool or silk in 2 tablespoons hydrogen peroxide to 1 gallon water.
Blood	Pour solution of liquid detergent and water through the spot. Apply vinegar solution, and rinse well.	Soak in warm solution of water and enzyme presoak.
Chewing gum	Apply ice or cool in freezer to make gum brittle. Scrape off gum with back of knife. Treat area with cleaning fluid.	Same treatment as dry-cleanable articles.
Chocolate	Treat spot with warm water, then apply a borax solution. Rinse.	Soak in warm solution of water and enzyme detergent. Treat wool with hydrogen peroxide.
Coffee, Tea	Treat immediately with warm water. Apply vinegar.	Wash immediately in hot water, or soak in solution of water and enzyme presoak.
Fruit juice	Pour cold water through stain. Treat with weak solution of detergent or vinegar. Rinse well.	Wash immediately in normal wash. Treat persistent stains with white vinegar. If necessary, bleach with hydrogen peroxide.
Grass	Treat with alcohol, and dry-clean.	Treat with alcohol. Treat persistent stains with hydrogen peroxide.
Grease	Apply carbon tetrachloride.	Apply carbon tetrachloride.
Ink (Ball-point)	Dry-clean.	Treat with alcohol or carbon tetrachloride.
Ink (Blue/Black)	Same treatment as for washable articles.	Pour water through stain and wash normally. If stain persists, dry-clean.
Mildew	Treat with mild solution of hydrochloric acid. Dry-clean.	Treat with hydrogen peroxide. Wash frequently and expose to sunlight.
Perspiration	Treat with vinegar solution. Dry-clean.	Soak in solution of enzyme detergent. If stain persists, soak in vinegar solution.
Shoe polish	Treat with carbon tetrachloride or turpentine.	Wash normally in warm water, with some ammonia added. Rinse and rewash.
Wine	Sponge with cold water. Immediately treat with detergent solution. If stain dries, dry-clean.	If wet, soak in cold water, then soak in solution of enzyme detergent. If dried-in, soak in detergent and hot water, and wash normally. If stain persists, dry-clean.

Worn Edges—If the edge of a garment is frayed, sew a contrasting or matching binding over it. Use leather for heavy fabrics and braid or ribbon on others.

Darning and patching sometimes seem unnecessary. But as clothes and fabrics increase in cost, repair them whenever possible.

DARNING

It is possible to darn a hole in knit and woven fabrics. You create a new piece to fill the hole. Choose a suitable thread close to the original fabric in color, texture and thickness. A darn should be as invisible as possible. Use a long, fine darning needle and a darning mushroom.

When making a garment, sew a few extra strands of wool in a seam.

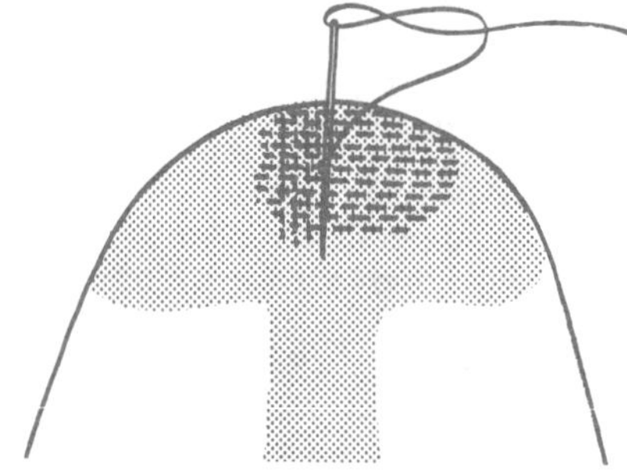

These are good for darning the garment later if needed. On woven fabrics, a few threads may be pulled out of a hidden seam allowance. You can also darn with the sewing machine.

Darning Thin Places—Chalk around the weakened area on the wrong-side of the fabric. Using small running stitches, darn across the weft threads only. Space rows closely and evenly. If the thread shrinks, leave a small loop at the end of each row. For weak fabric, darn across the other way at right angles to the first rows.

Darning Holes in Woven Fabrics—This is also called *reweaving*. It is a difficult, tedious job but worth doing on expensive fabrics and garments.

Put the damaged area in an embroidery hoop. Work from the wrong-side. Study the fabric with a magnifying glass to see how it is woven. Pull some matching threads from a hidden seam allowance in the garment.

Using a long, fine darning needle, weave a thread across the whole damaged area. Weave it over and under existing threads. Leave a short length at each end of the row on the wrong-side. Use a new thread for each row. Repeat across at right angles to the first rows. When finished, trim all the thread ends to about 1/8 inch. Press the area carefully on both sides.

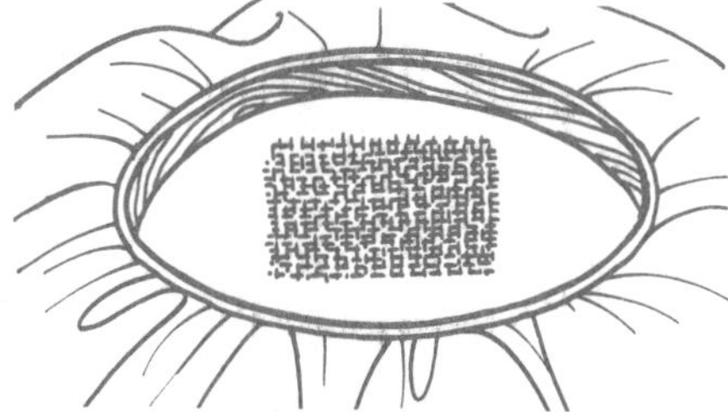

Darning Cuts in Woven Fabrics—First, close the edges of the cut or tear with a herringbone-stitch. See the section on *Stitches and Threads*, page 67. Darn as described in the previous method.

Darning Tears—Patch a large, jagged tear. If it is a straight or L-shape tear, it can be darned. A tiny tear can be held together with a herringbone-stitch.

Use a herringbone-stitch to hold edges of tears together. Darn an area about 3/8 inch around the tear. As a guide, outline the area with chalk or trace tacking before darning. Darn with small, even running-stitches along the weft and the slit. Darn at right angles to the first rows.

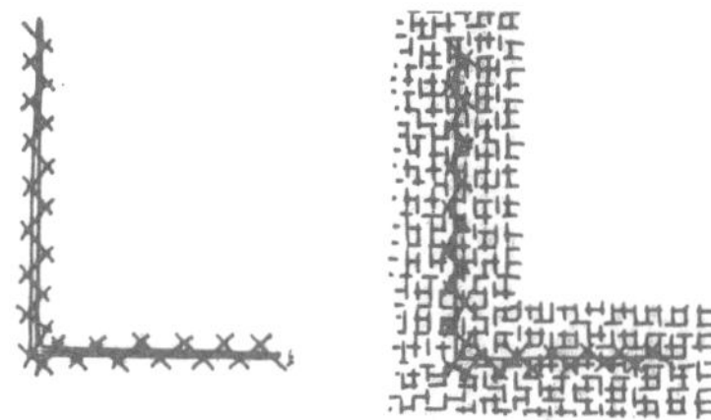

Darn a tear on the cross grain, as shown below.

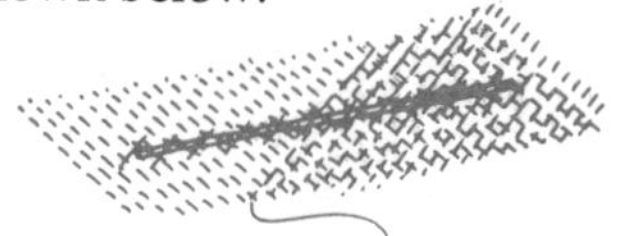

Darning Holes—New warp and weft threads must be formed across a hole on knit or woven fabric. Trim the edges of the hole, and place the area over a darning mushroom. Darn the entire area, not just the hole, for strength. Work on the right-side, and sew in new warp threads first. Turn the article, and weave new weft threads over and under the warps.

PATCHING

A large hole or worn patch is difficult to darn. Patch it with a piece of fabric. Unless a decorative fabric is desired, choose fabric of a similar weight, type and color. Use matching thread.

When making a garment, save a few fabric scraps for patching purposes. Fade it to match the worn garment by washing it in water with baking powder.

A suitable piece of fabric may be obtained from a hem or facing. The hem or facing can be patched with a scrap of some other fabric. Use wide, white, cotton tape for patching sheets, dishtowels and other items. Or save an old article to patch similar ones. Cut patches on the same grain as the area to be patched. Patches are usually square or oblong and big enough to cover the weakened area.

Print Patch—This is used for print fabrics. Cut a patch, allowing a 1/4-inch finished edge all around. Match the pattern exactly to the fabric pattern.

Fold and press the edges on the wrong-side. Miter the corners, then pin and tack the patch in place.

Fold the fabric level with one edge of the patch. Oversew the two neatly together. Complete all four sides.

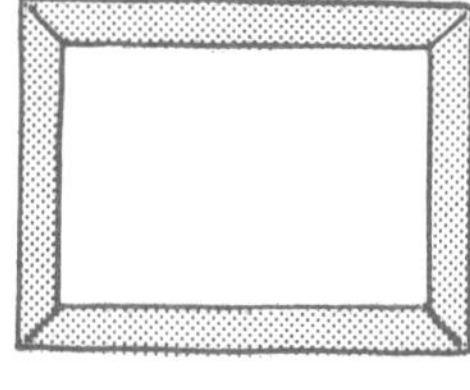

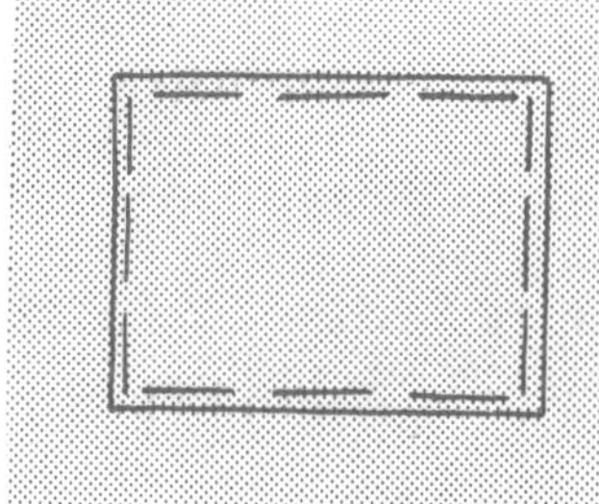

Trim away the worn area underneath to about 1/4 inch from the stitching. Blanket-stitch edges together.

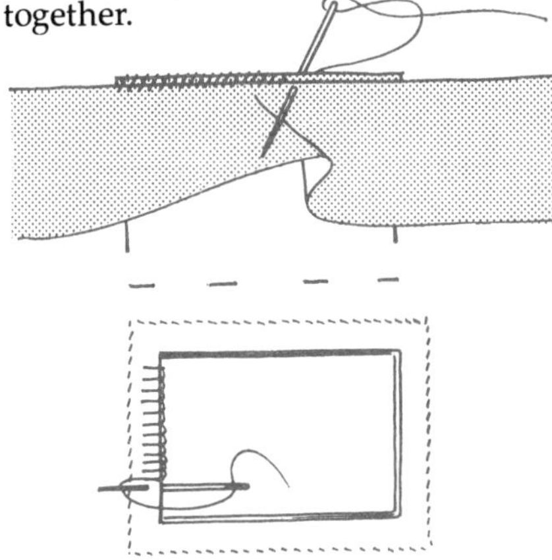

The zigzag-stitch and step-stitch on sewing machines are ideal for patching purposes. Check your sewing-machine handbook for instructions.

Cloth Patch—This patch is used for outer garments, such as flannel trousers. Tack around the outline for the patch on the garment. Cut away the worn part to within 1/4 inch of the tacking. Snip diagonally into corners.

Cut a suitable patch with 1/4-inch finished edges. Press in place. The grain and nap must match the garment exactly.

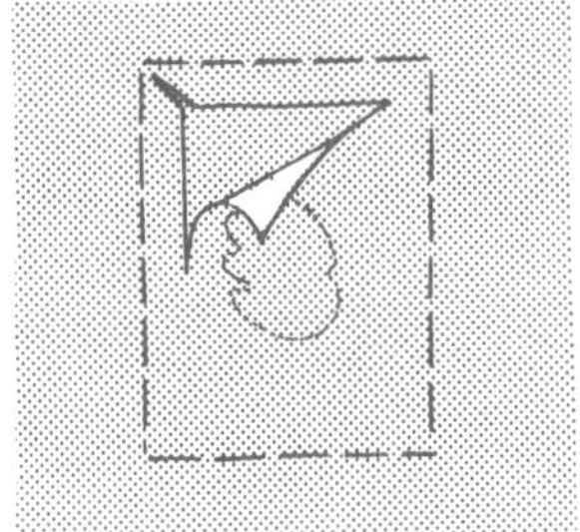

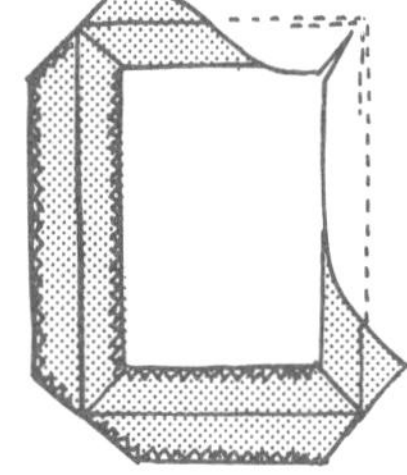

Pin and tack the patch in position. Slip-stitch the edges of the patch to the garment. Remove the first tacking.

From the wrong-side, back-stitch or machine-stitch along the slip-stitching. Press the edges, then finish them.

Decorative Patch—A decorative patch can be used on children's clothes, jeans and lingerie. Use a contrasting color or design, a cut-out or an embroidered motif. Appliqué the piece over the worn area. Leather or suede patches on jackets are herringbone-stitched or hemmed around the edges.

Patching Machine-Knit Fabric—Patching can be done on lock-stitch or stockinette-type fabrics.

Cut a round or oval patch. Tack it on the right-side, matching the direction of the knitting.

Using suitable thread, buttonhole-stitch the edge of the patch to the garment. On the wrong-side, cut away the weak part to within 1/4 inch of the stitching. Buttonhole-stitch this edge to the patch.

For machine-patching, refer to your sewing-machine handbook. There are many stitches that may be used for applying patches to machine-knit fabrics.

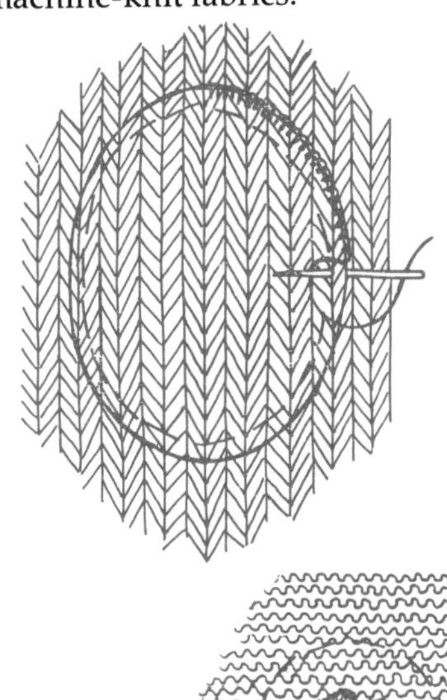

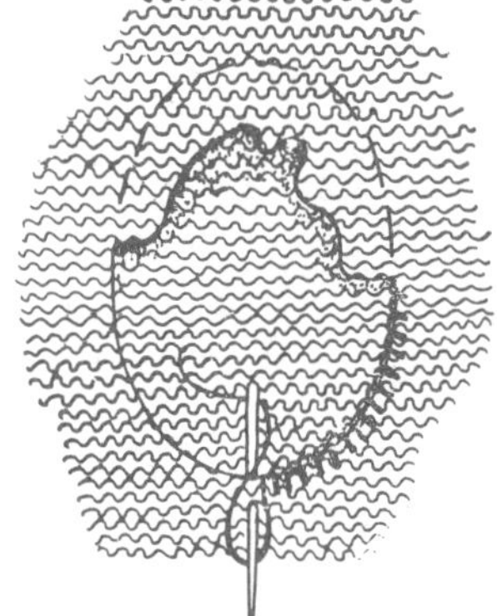

Patching Wrong-Side—This strong patch can be used on aprons, overalls and household linen.

Cut a suitable patch, allowing 1/4 inch for finished edges. Press the finished edges to the right-side. Miter the corners.

Pin and tack the patch in place on the wrong-side. Machine-stitch close to the edge. Cut away the weakened fabric to within 1/4 inch of the machine-stitching.

Snip 1/8 inch into the corners. Fold under the raw edges. Pin, tack and machine-stitch close to the fold.

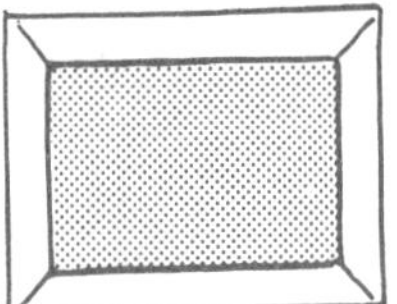

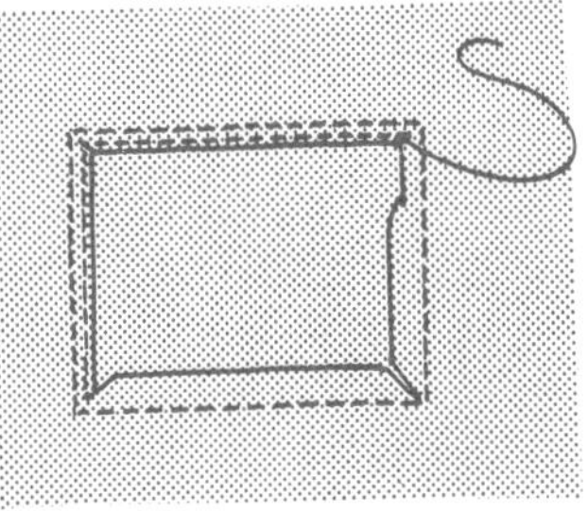

Flannel Patch—This patch can be used for thin wool and some knits.

Cut a matching piece of fabric for the patch, with no finished edges. Tack this in position on the wrong-side. Herringbone-stitch in position. Trim away the worn area underneath. Herringbone-stitch the edges to the patch on the right-side. On knit fabrics and blankets, cut the patch in a round or oval shape.

Machine-Darned Patch—Use this patch on lingerie and household linen. Use fine machine-embroidery thread.

Cut a suitable patch 1/8 inch larger than the hole. Tack it to the wrong-side. Tack or chalk around the outline of the hole as a guide. Machine-darn around the patch so stitching is 1/8 inch over raw edges.

Get Sewing

Sewing Techniques from A to Z

ORDER OF MAKING A GARMENT

Follow the instructions included in the pattern. If you do not have the pattern instructions, follow the order given below for a dress. Modify the order for different garments. Remember to fit and press the garment carefully during sewing.

STITCHING DIRECTION OF SEAMS

Unless pattern instructions say otherwise, follow these rules.
Side Seams—Sew from armhole to waist in bodice. Sew from hem to waist of skirt.
Shoulder Seams—Stitch from neck to armholes.
Darts—Stitch from the widest to the narrowest part.
Sleeve—Sew from the shoulder to the wrist.

GENERAL ORDER OF CONSTRUCTION

1. Stitch tucks.
2. Sew all darts, and press.
3. Make and attach pockets.
4. Sew seams, remove tacking and press. Leave in center-front and center-back tacking lines.
5. Attach facings to button-through designs.
6. Make buttonholes or buttonloops, or put in a zipper.
7. Make pleats and gathers.
8. Make the collar, cuffs and belt.
9. Sew or iron on interfacing. Stitch facings to neck and opening edges, and attach the collar.
10. Stitch, press and tack in sleeves. Try on the garment. Adjust the fit of the sleeves, then remove them.
11. Attach cuffs to sleeves or finish sleeve edges.
12. Set-in sleeves and finish armhole seams. Press.
13. Attach bodice to skirt.
14. Try on the garment and adjust the fit. Finish the fastenings and hem the garment.
15. Press garment, remove tacking and complete the finishing.
16. Attach any trim. Sew in a care label.

BELTS AND BUCKLES

Belts

A belt usually completes an outfit. Belts can be made in many shapes and styles. They can alter the appearance of a garment.

Belts can be wide or narrow, buckled or tied, above or below the waistine. A belt may emphasize a tiny waist or detract from a plump one. It may be brightly trimmed or embroidered. A belt can have an eye-catching buckle and become the main decorative feature of an outfit. Hand- or machine-embroidery, top-stitching, sequins or beads can add interest to a belt.

Separates can be teamed up with a belt. Old styles can be updated with a new belt. Many ready-made belts can be purchased, but handmade belts are more exclusive.

Try the shape and size of a belt. Practice with a piece of paper or fabric. Measure around the body at the point where the belt will be worn. This is *not* always the natural waistline.

Cut the required amount of fabric. Allow about 8 inches for overlapping and fastening. The wider the belt, the longer the length needed.

TIE BELT

Tie belts are often used on children's clothes. They may be any width. They can be cut from fabric on the straight grain or bias, or made from purchased ribbon. Experiment with a piece of cord around the waist. It will help you decide on the total length required. Include enough for the bow and its ends.

Cut a piece of fabric twice the required width, plus 1 inch for seam allowances. Ends may be left straight or shaped to points.

Interfacing is often added at the waistline area to prevent curling. Cut interfacing 1 inch shorter than the actual waist measurement, and half the width of the fabric.

Place interfacing on the wrong-side of the fabric, inside the seam allowance. Tack or baste in position 5/8 inch from the cut edges. Trim interfacing to the stitching.

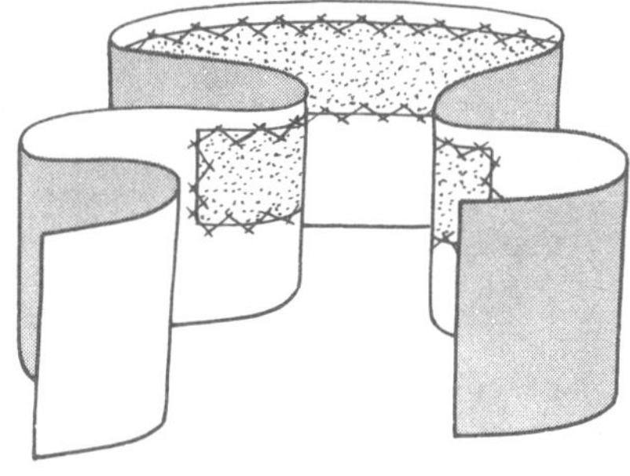

Slip-stitch interfacing in position with tiny stitches on the wrong-side. With right-sides together, fold the belt in half lengthwise. Pin and tack all around. If the belt is narrow, lay a piece of strong thread or cord inside. Secure it at one end.

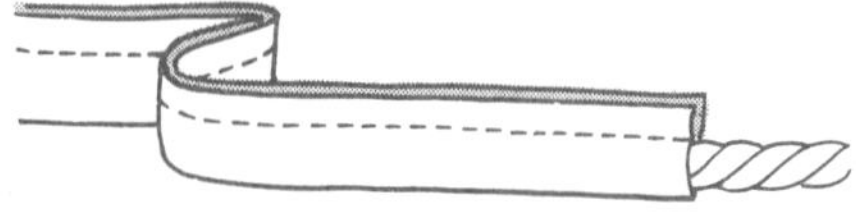

Machine-stitch along the seam line. Leave a 4-inch opening in the center of one side for turning. Remove tacking.

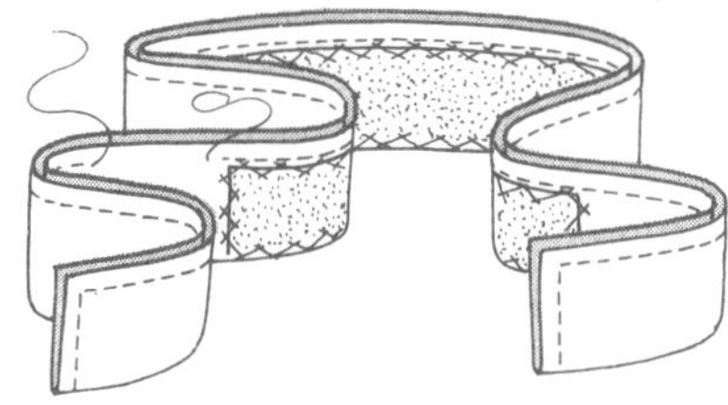

Trim seam allowances and corners. Turn the belt to the right-side. This is done with the help of a thick, blunt knitting needle. Use the point of the needle to push out corners for a neat finish. Turn a narrow belt with the thread or cord, then remove it.

Roll seamed edges of the belt between thumb and fingers to move the seam to the edge of the belt. Tack to hold in position. Slip-stitch the opening edges together, then top-stitch all around. Press lightly. Remove tacking, and press again.

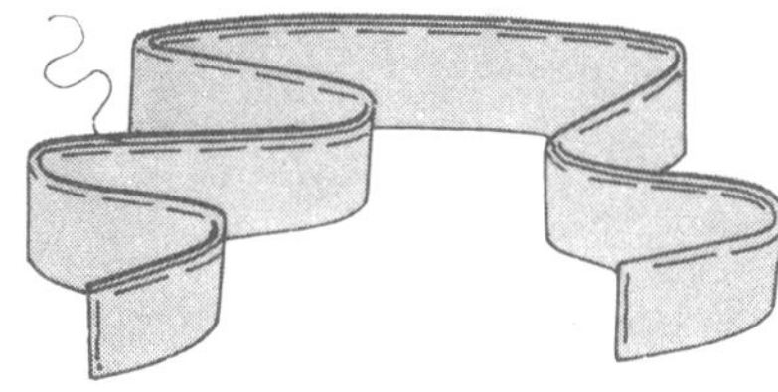

RIBBON BELT

Use good-quality, firmly woven ribbon of the required width. If thick enough, it may be used singly. Usually two pieces are lined with interfacing for stiffness.

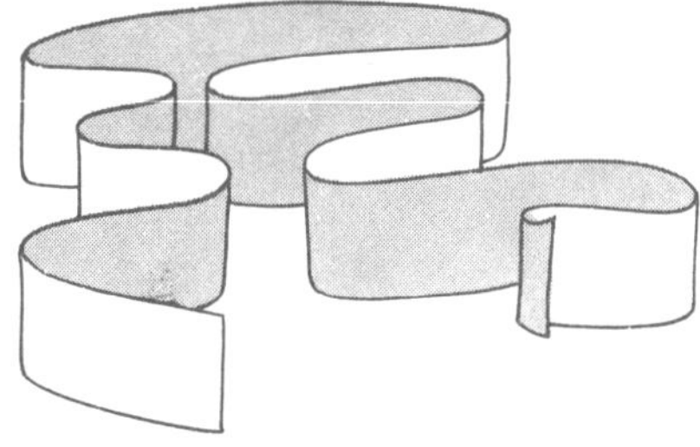

Cut ribbon to the required length. Cut an extra piece of ribbon the length of waistline, less 2-1/2 inches. This is for the facing. Cut a piece of iron-on interfacing slightly narrower than the ribbon. Make this the exact length of the extra-facing ribbon.

Iron interfacing on the facing ribbon, and trim ends to a curve.

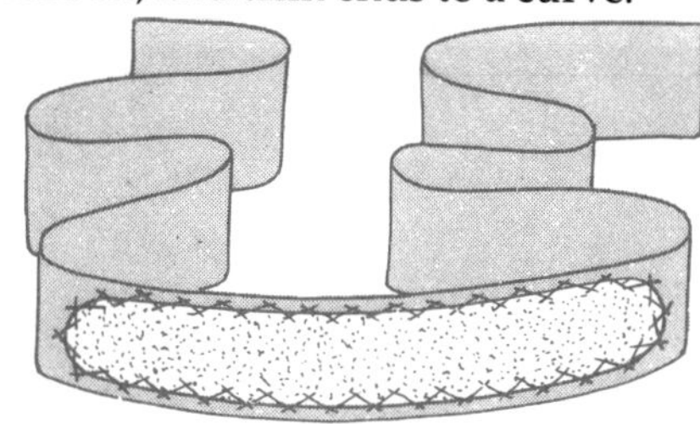

Center the faced-ribbon lining on the waist area of the ribbon. Tack in position with the interfacing inside.

Machine-stitch the stiffened facing ribbon to the ribbon belt inside the edges. Fasten threads securely. Trim the belt ends to a point to prevent fraying.

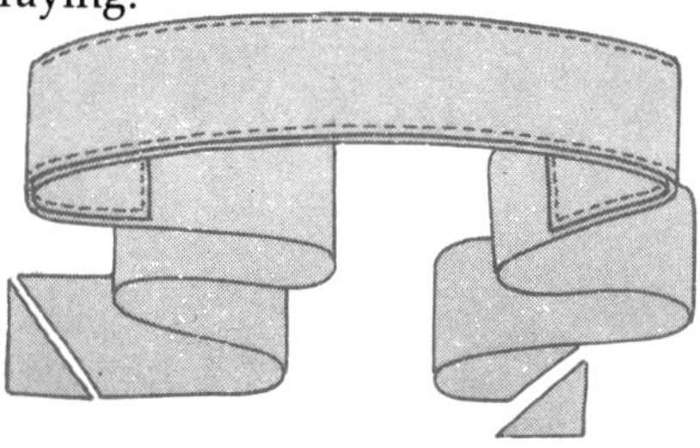

STRAIGHT, STIFFENED BELT

This is a popular way to make a belt from fabric. Organdy, canvas, iron-on interfacing or purchased belting may be used for stiffening. It depends on the weight of the fabric.

Buckles or hooks and eyes are often used for fastening stiffened belts. See the section on *Belt Fastenings*, page 114. The method below uses purchased belting.

The width of belting should be the same as for the finished belt. Cut belting to the size of the waistline, plus 8 inches for seam allowances and overlap.

Trim belting to a point at one end.

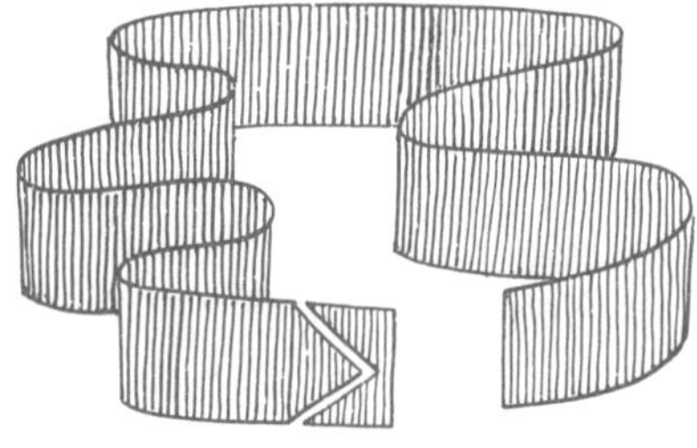

Cut a fabric strip on the lengthwise grain. Make it twice the width of the belting, plus 3/8 inch, and the length of the belting, plus 3/8 inch.

With right-sides together, fold the

strip in half lengthwise. Stitch across one end only. Trim and press the seam.

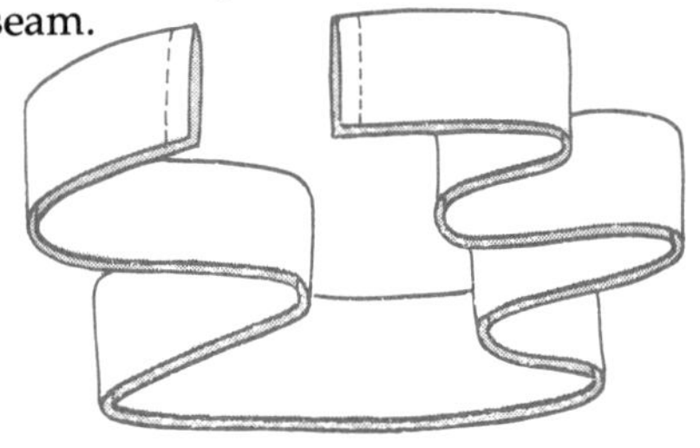

Place the pointed end of the belting in the pointed end of the belt. Pin one raw edge along the length of the belt. Tack in place.

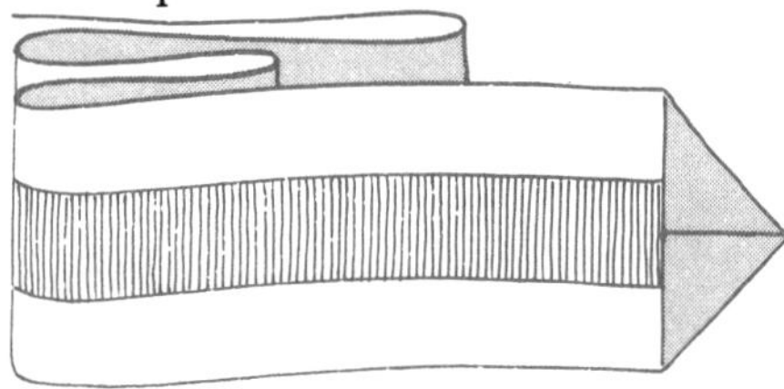

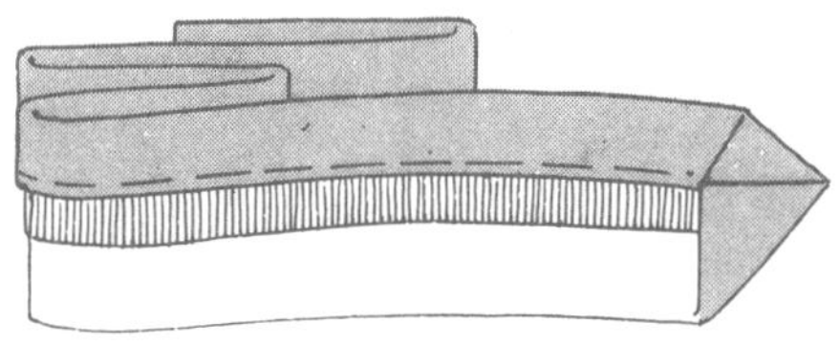

Pin the other edge over the top. If this edge is a selvage, it may be pinned and tacked without finishing the edge.

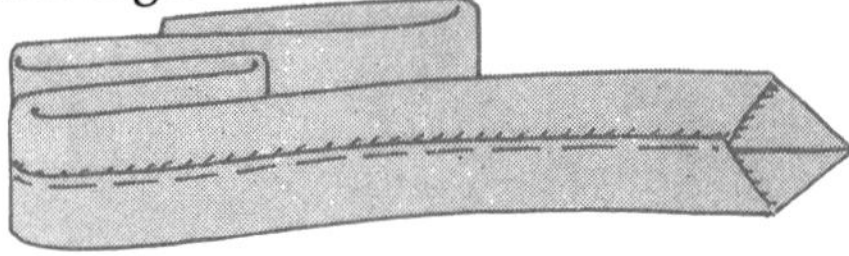

Slip-stitch edges in place neatly and invisibly. Sew a buckle to the straight end of the belt, or finish it with hooks and eyes.

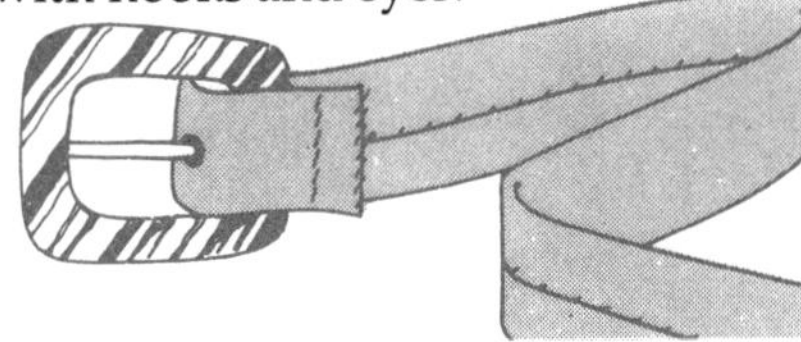

CONTOUR BELT

Contour belts are usually stiffened belts cut on a curve. They fit close to the body on the line of the garment. Ready-made belting is not usually suitable. Interfacing, such as organdy, canvas, bonded interfacing or buckram, is needed. Use one or two layers, according to the stiffness required.

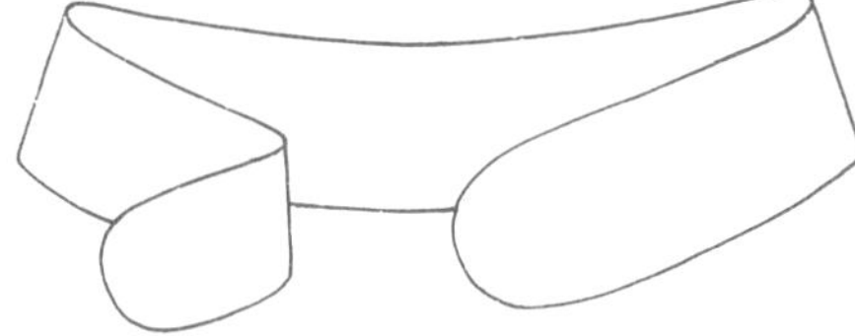

Cut the pattern in the desired shape. Cut two pieces of fabric on the lengthwise grain. Use the paper pattern. Allow a 5/8-inch seam allowance.

Pin two layers of interfacing together. Trace the outline of the pattern on the interfacing. Within this outline, stitch rows of stitching 1/4 inch apart. Cut along the outline.

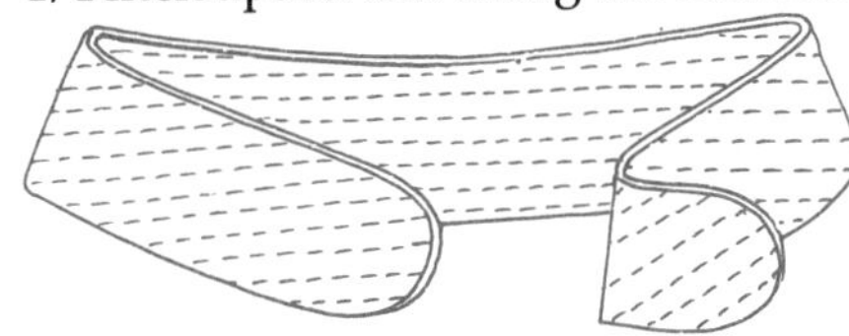

Stitch a piece of bias tape along the inner curved edge to prevent stretching. Stay-stitch around the two pieces of belt fabric to help them keep their shape.

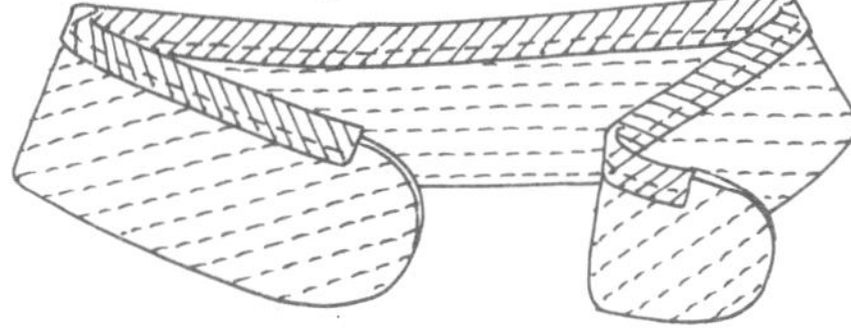

Pin the prepared interfacing to the wrong-side of one piece of belt fabric. Fold in the seam allowance. Sew it to the interfacing with long running-stitches.

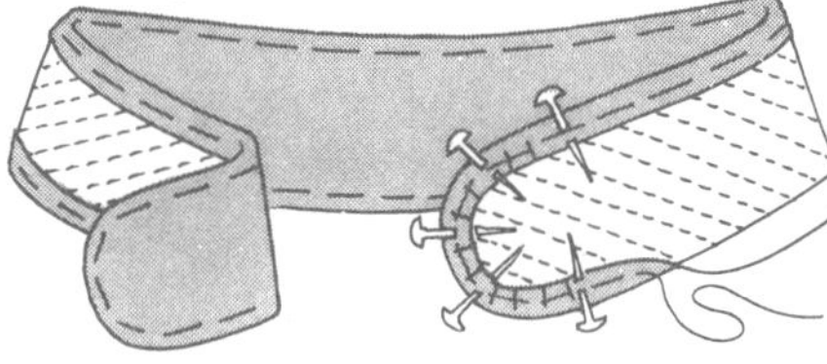

Turn the seam allowances to the wrong-side on the other piece of fabric. Tack and press, and trim to 3/8 inch.

Carefully pin this facing to the interfaced belt. Slip-stitch in place.

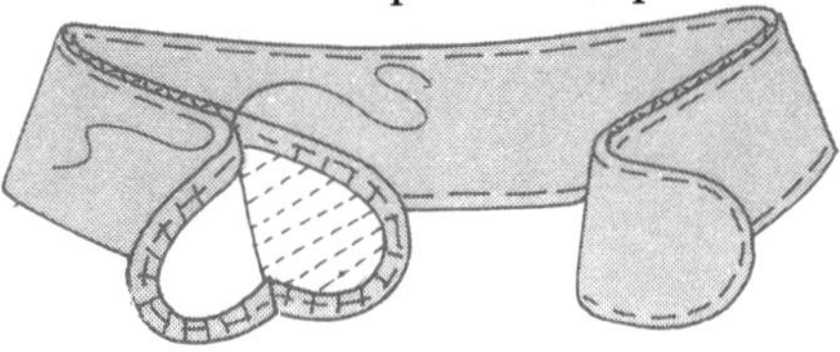

Remove tacking, and top-stitch if required. Sew on fastenings.

STRAIGHT, SOFT BELT

Soft, pliable belts look effective on evening wear and day wear with round lines. These belts may be made from many weights of fabric, including real and imitation leather. Lightweight interfacing is used to prevent creasing.

Cut the fabric to the required length of the belt, plus 9 inches for the overlap and seam allowances. Cut the interfacing and belt backing 3/4 inch narrower than the fabric and exactly the same length. The narrower backing allows the edges of the belt to roll slightly. This brings the seams to the wrong-side of the belt instead of to the edge.

Cut all strips on an angle at one end. Baste or tack interfacing to the wrong-side of the backing fabric 5/8 inch from edges. Trim the interfacing close to stitching.

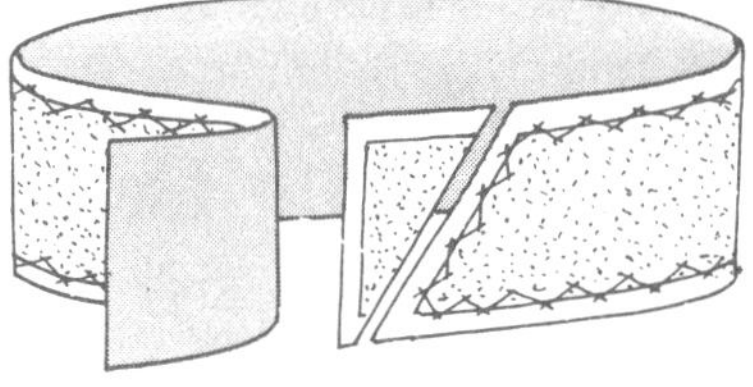

Place the belt and backing with right-sides together. Pin and tack all around. The belt is slightly wider than the backing, so keep edges together.

Stitch along both sides of the belt 5/8 inch from edges. Trim allowances, and press them toward the backing. Turn the belt to the

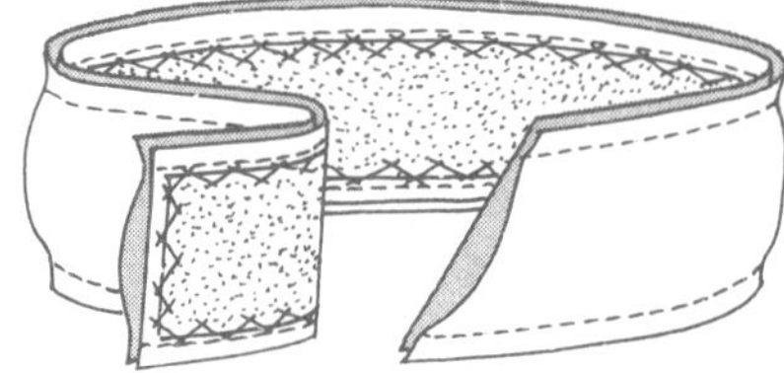

right-side and press. Turn in slanted edges, and slip-stitch together.

The buckle should be narrower than the belt width so the belt fabric settles into soft folds. See the section on *Belt Fastenings*, page 114.

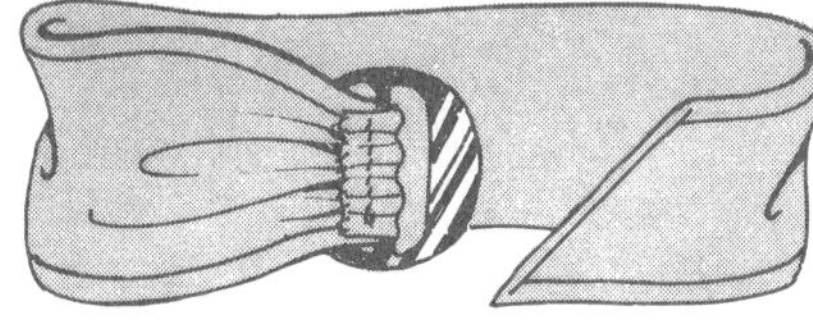

CUMMERBUND

This is worn by men and women to dress up evening wear. It also provides a decorative link between two garments, such as pants and shirt, or blouse and skirt.

A cummerbund is a wide belt that covers the whole midriff. It shapes itself easily to the body. It is cut on the cross or bias of the fabric.

Cut a length of fabric and lining on the true cross grain. It should be the length of the measurement around the midriff, plus 1 inch. Cut it 9 inches wide. Treat fabric and lining as one.

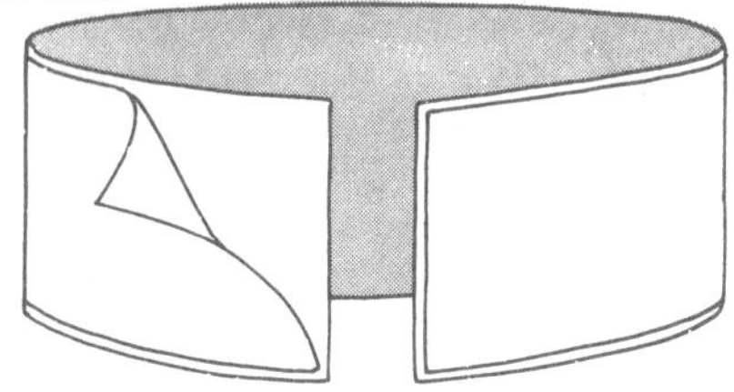

Turn in 1/4 inch on the two long sides. Machine-stitch close to the edge. Turn in another 1 inch. Tack

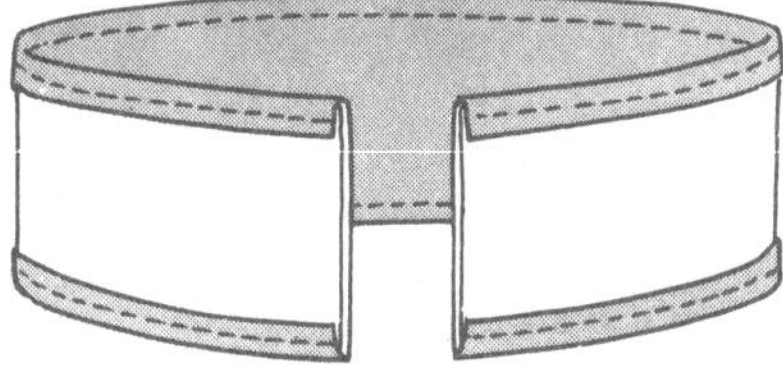

lightly in place and press. Make a row of gathers 1/2 inch inside each end. Draw the gathers up to the required depth, and fasten ends securely. Make two more rows of gathers at each side of belt about 3/4 inch apart. These will be positioned at the side seams.

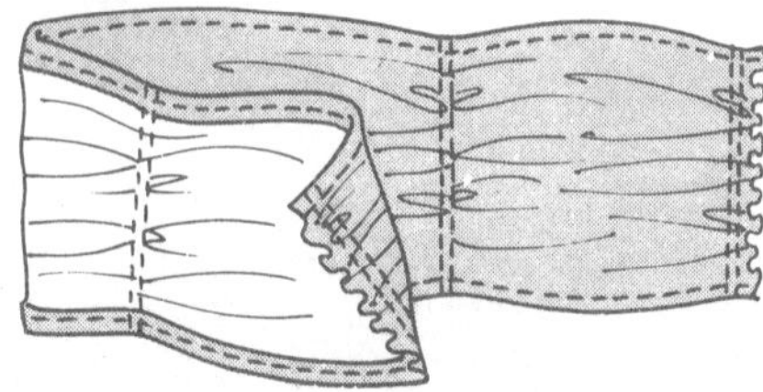

Cut four pieces of boning 1/2 inch narrower than the belt. Make a casing with seam binding. Center the

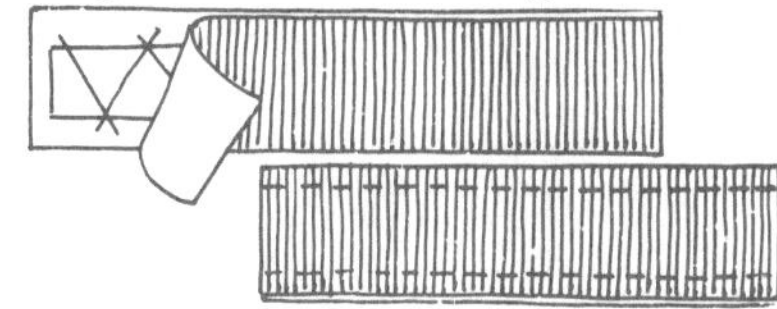

covered bones over the gather lines on the wrong-side. Slip-stitch them in place.

Cut a piece of 1-inch-wide grosgrain ribbon an inch longer than the width of the belt. Sew the ribbon on the right-side at either end along the gathering lines. Allow the ends to extend 1/2 inch at either end of the stitching rows.

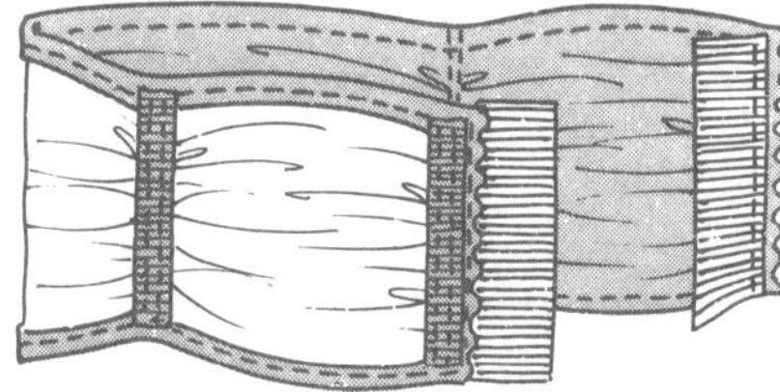

Turn in grosgrain ends, then fold ribbon to the wrong-side. Slip-stitch it in place. Attach hooks to the grosgrain at one end and eyes at the other end. Edges should meet exactly and evenly at the center back when fastened.

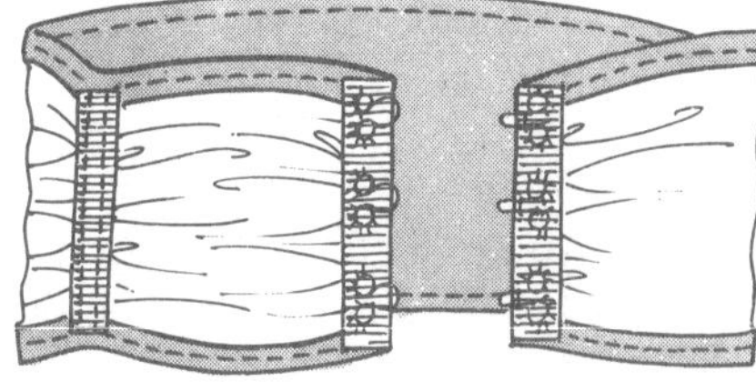

BELT LOOPS

Belt loops are needed to keep a belt at the garment waist or hip line during wear. Carriers should be long enough for the belt to slide through easily, usually 1/4 to 1/2 inch wider than the belt. This depends on the thickness of the fabric.

Mark the position of loops on the garment. Note the width of the finished belt. On childen's clothes, belts may be fixed to the waistline in one place.

Thread Loops—Use a double strand of thread. Match color and type to the fabric.

On the wrong-side of the garment, attach thread to the seam allowance. Attach it half the width of the belt away from the waist seam or waistline. Bring the thread through the seam. Make at least four large bar tacks. Finish the same distance away from the waistline on the other side.

Tacks will be longer than the width of the belt and will appear slack. See if the belt passes through the carriers easily. The tacks form the body of the loops.

Work a buttonhole-stitch to cover the tacks from end to end. When complete, thread ends through the seam, and secure on the wrong-side.

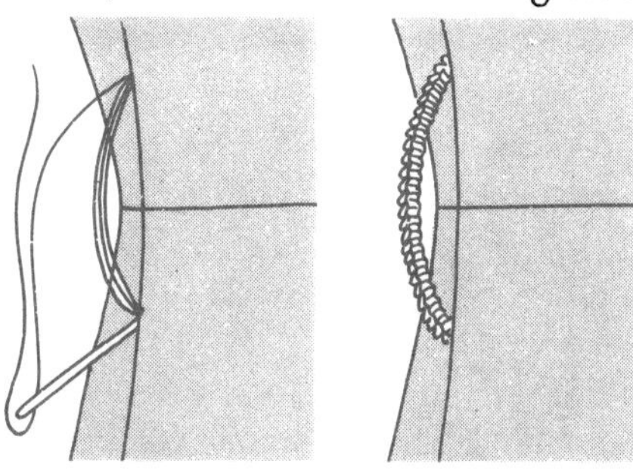

Rouleau Carriers—Make fabric tubes 2 inches longer than the belt width. Make an opening on either side of the waistline in the side seam of the garment. Insert rouleau loop ends. Position each carrier so the loop is 1/2 inch wider than the belt. Pin in position.

Slide the belt through to see if the carriers are big enough. Restitch the section of seam, including the rouleau, *twice* for extra strength.

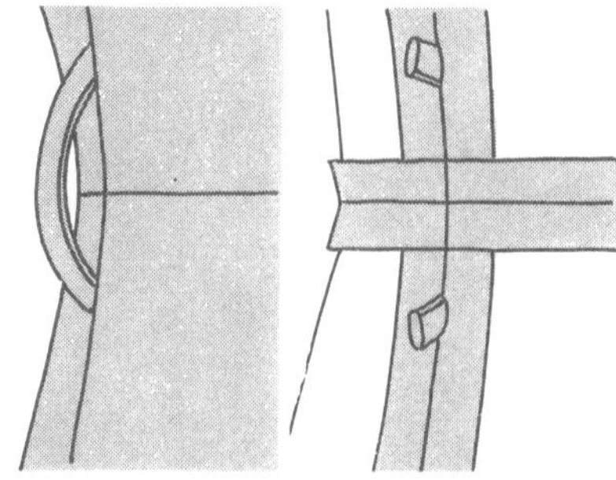

In another method, belt carriers are used as a feature of the garment. Ends are top-stitched in place. Stitching may be done with matching or contrasting thread.

Make lengths of tubing 1-3/4 inches longer than the belt width. Turn under 1/4 inch at each end and press.

Pin carriers on the side seams at either side of the waistline. Use more loops, if desired. Pass the belt through the carriers before stitching to make sure it pulls through smoothly. Stitch carriers securely in place.

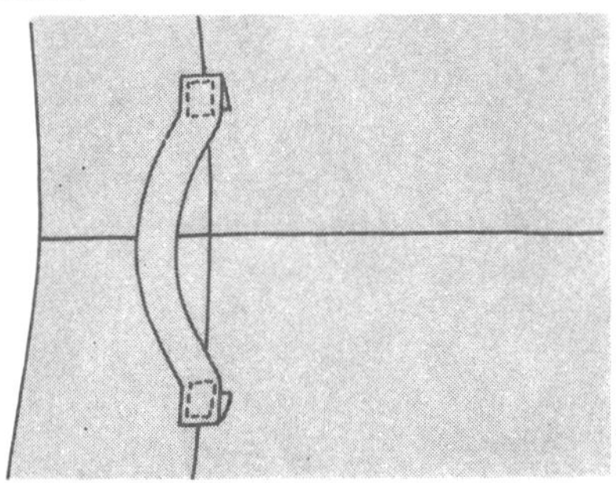

Buckles

Buckles are a secure way to fasten belts. Many types of buckles are available. They can be metal, wood, plastic or fabric-covered. They can be designed to catch the eye or be unnoticeable. Kits are available to cover buckles with fabric.

Buckles may be the slide type, prong-and-eyelet type or clasp type. Each is attached to the belt in a different way. To determine where to place a buckle, try on the finished belt. Mark the center front.

SLIDE BUCKLE

This buckle is often used for a straight, soft belt. Trim the unfinished end so it extends 1 inch beyond the center-front mark. Stitch 1/4 inch from the raw edges, then overcast.

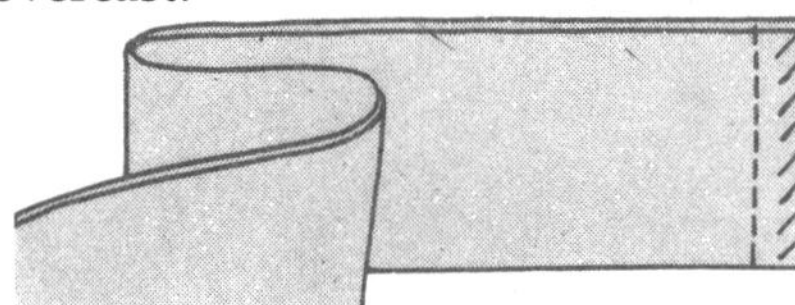

Make small pleats. Fit this end around the bar of a buckle narrower than the belt width. Slip-stitch end securely in place. Snaps may be attached to keep a soft belt closed. Put the belt on, and mark the positions for snaps. Do not make the fitting too tight or snaps pop open.

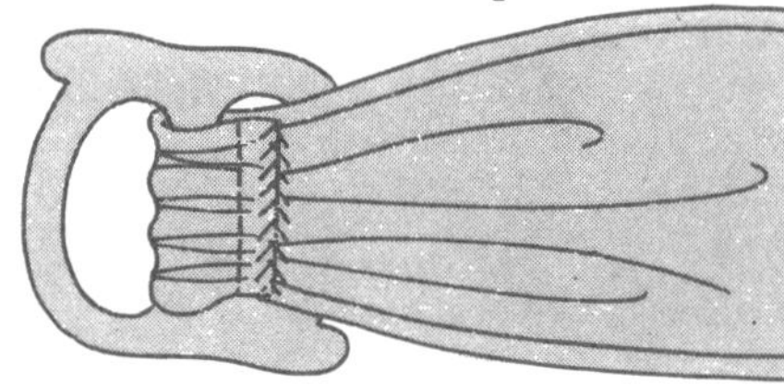

PRONG-AND-EYELET BUCKLE

Trim the unfinished end of the belt so it extends 2 inches beyond the center-front mark. Stitch 1/4 inch from the raw edges, then overcast.

Make a hole for the prong of the buckle at the center-prong mark.

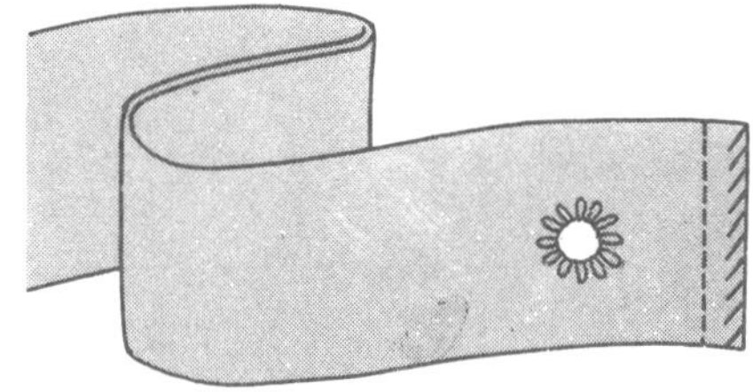

Overcast raw edges. Push the prong through the hole, and fold down the end of the belt. Stitch it firmly in place.

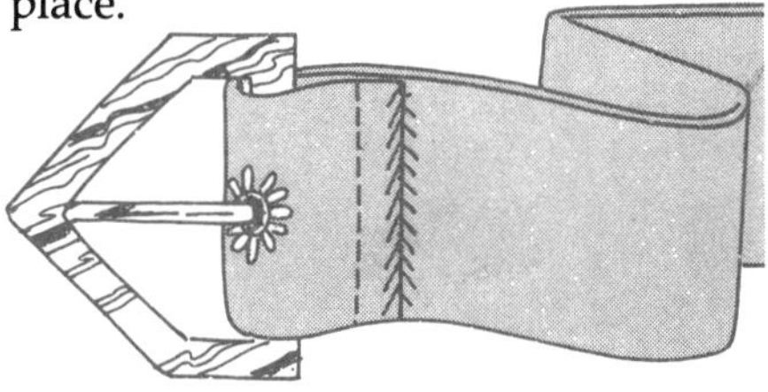

Make an eyelet at the other end of the belt. Place it at the center-front marking. Put one or two on either side for adjustment.

An inexpensive kit can be purchased to put metal eyelets in belts. Eyelets can also be stitched by hand.

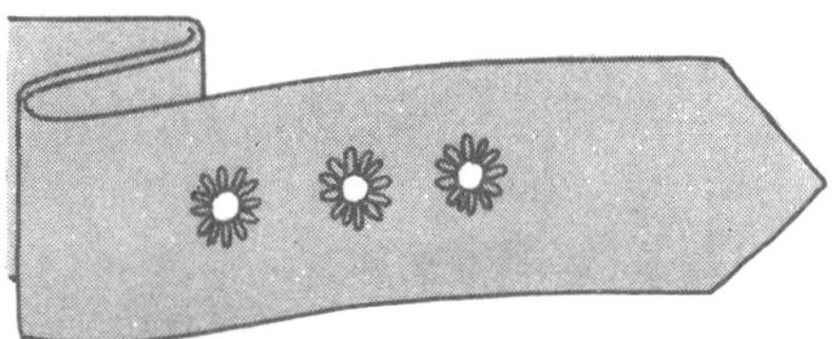

For handmade eyelets, mark the position of the holes. Sew around the marks with rings of tiny stitches. Use stab-stitches on thick fabrics. Pierce holes in the centers with an awl or stiletto. Satin-stitch or buttonhole-stitch around the edges.

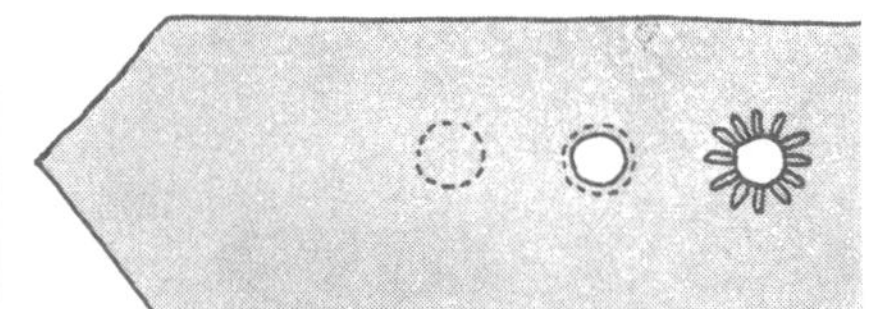

CLASP

Slip the unfinished belt ends through the buckle and its bar. Fold back the ends. Try the belt on, and trim the excess to 7/8 to 1-3/4 inches.

Remove the buckle, and stitch across each end 1/4 inch from the edge. Overcast and replace the two buckle pieces. Turn back the belt ends, and slip-stitch securely in place.

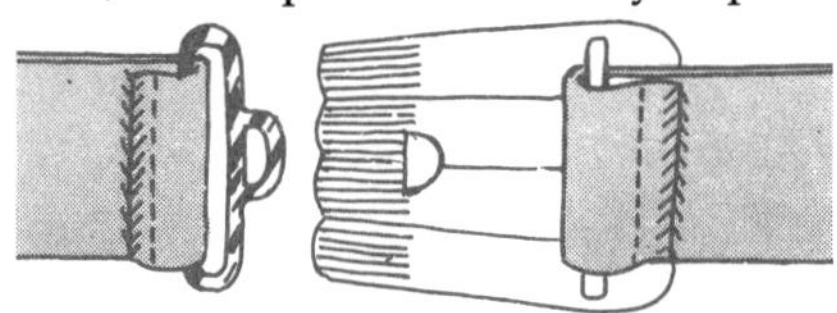

HOOKS AND EYES

Use these for securing closely fitting belts. With snaps, they can hold the loose end of a belt in place. They may be used with a slide buckle. On their own they can fasten a cummerbund, contour belt or ready-tied ribbon belt.

Fasten a belt with a bow or decoration on the front with hooks and eyes at the back. Sew them securely to the belt. Place hooks and eyes far enough from the end so they do not show.

TOUCH-AND-CLOSE TAPE

Velcro is a commercially made nylon tape that fastens by means of loops and piles on two separate strips. It is useful on belts for children and the handicapped. It also holds a loose belt end in place. Follow manufacturer's instructions for use.

BINDING AND PIPING

Binding

Binding is used to finish and strengthen the raw edges on fine or mediumweight fabrics. Binding usually shows on the right-side and wrong-side. It may be used in contrasting colors.

Bias binding, also called *bias tape,* can be purchased in many widths and colors. It can also be made from pieces of fabric left when the garment is cut out. If cut on the true cross grain, bias binding can be stretched when sewing. It fits neatly around curves.

Bias bindings are used for armholes, necklines, waistlines and curved seam edges. Straight bindings, such as ribbon, Paris binding, seam binding and braid, are used unfolded on straight edges. They do not stretch around curves.

For bound openings, see the section on *Openings,* page 135. For bound hems, see the section on *Hems,* page 122. For bound buttonholes, see the section on *Buttons and Buttonholes,* page 92.

CUTTING BIAS BINDING

True-Bias Strips—Take a square or rectangle of fabric. The weft is the thread running *across* the fabric. It has some stretch or give. Fold one corner of the fabric over. The weft edge should lie along the lengthwise thread.

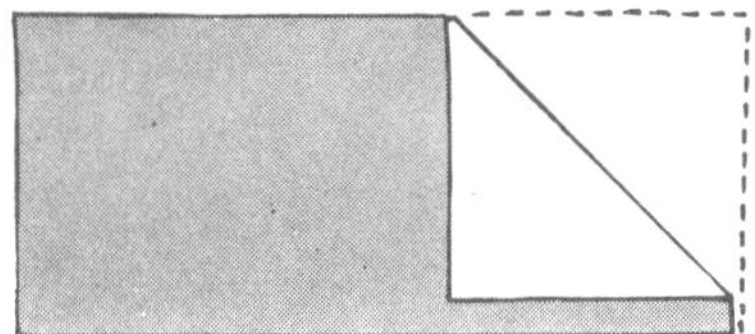

Mark the fold with a line of pins. Press and remove pins, then open the flap out. Use a ruler as a guide for the width of the bias. Using pins or tailor's chalk, make lines parallel to the fold line pressed on the fabric.

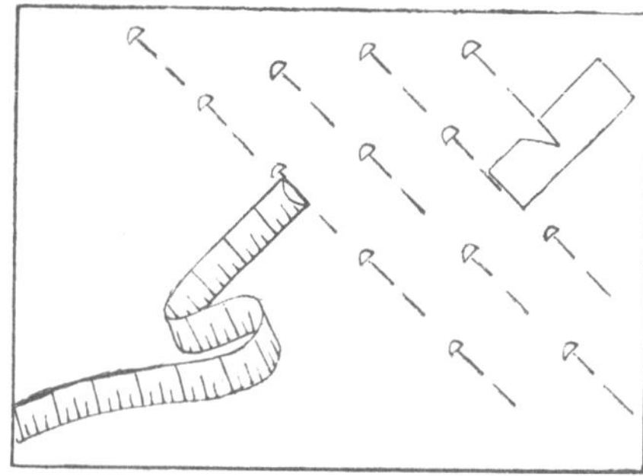

Calculate the required width of strips. For a single width, measure twice to four times the finished width, plus two seam allowances. For a double width, measure four to six times the finished width, plus two seam allowances.

Measure the distance between each length of bias with a ruler. Cut along the lines marked. After cutting required strips of bias, sew them together.

Continuous Bias—When long strips of bias are required, another method is recommended. Prepare a rectangle of fabric on the straight grain. On the wrong-side, mark a bias line from an upper corner to the opposite, lower side. Using the line as a guide, make parallel lines the width required until the length is sufficient.

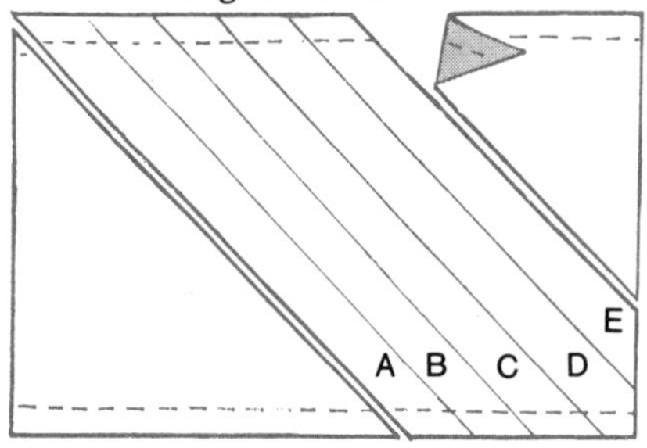

Mark a 1/4-inch seam allowance on both ends. Place right-sides together, so the lines on the lengthwise edges match. Pin the edges, and stitch together. This forms a tube.

Press the seam open. Cut along a line around the tube, starting at the first line. Continue until the strip has been cut.

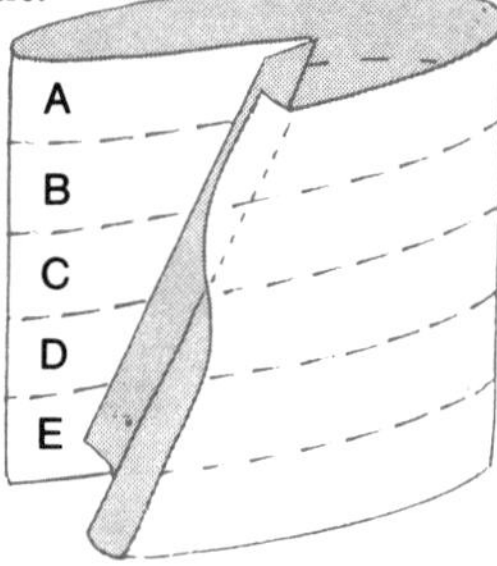

JOINING TRUE-BIAS STRIPS

Place bias strips flat on the table with right-sides up. Cut short ends

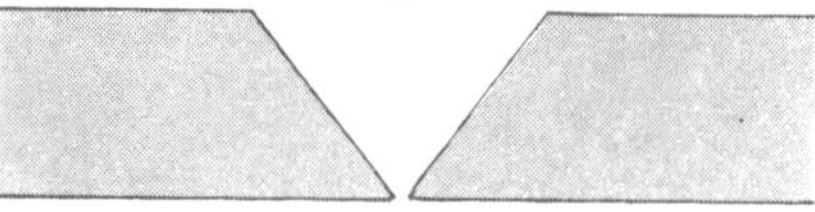

parallel with the grain. Put right-sides together and overlap

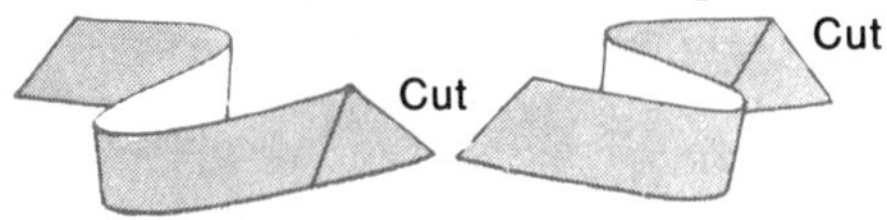

parallel to the grain. Put right-sides together and overlap corners for the depth of the seam. Place the bias edges together.

Tack along the seam line between the angles formed by the overlapping corners. Machine-stitch along the seam line. Remove tacking.

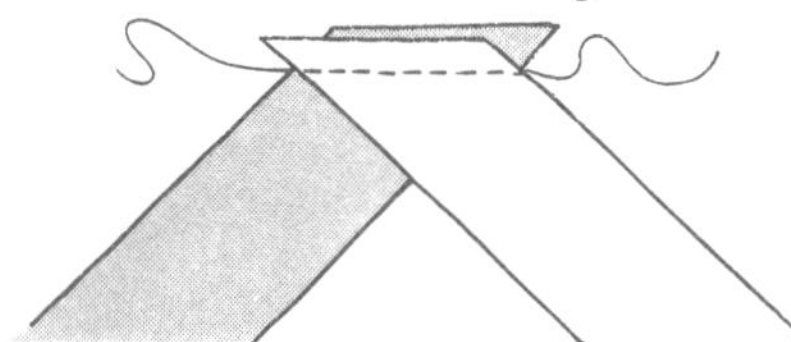

Press the seam allowance flat, and cut off protruding ends. Repeat this process until you have the required length of bias binding.

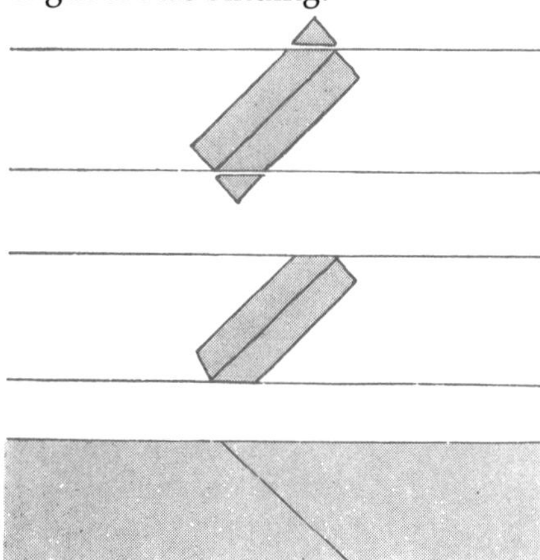

COMMON BIAS-BINDING FAULTS

Uneven Joins—The joins may be uneven when the bias is completed. This is caused by putting edges of the fabric together for joining without overlapping the seam allowance.

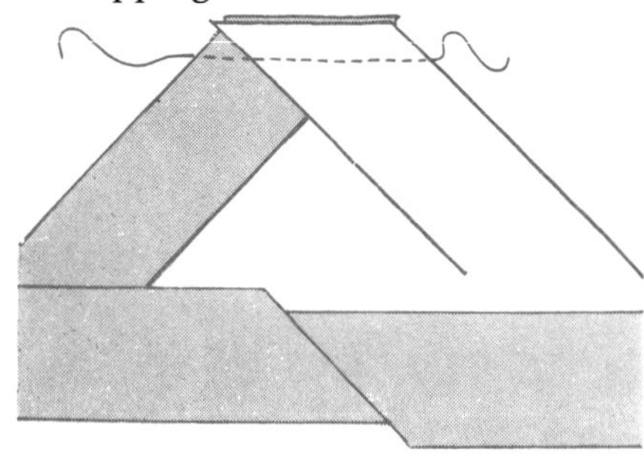

Crooked Bias—This can be caused by the fabric not being at right angles when joined.

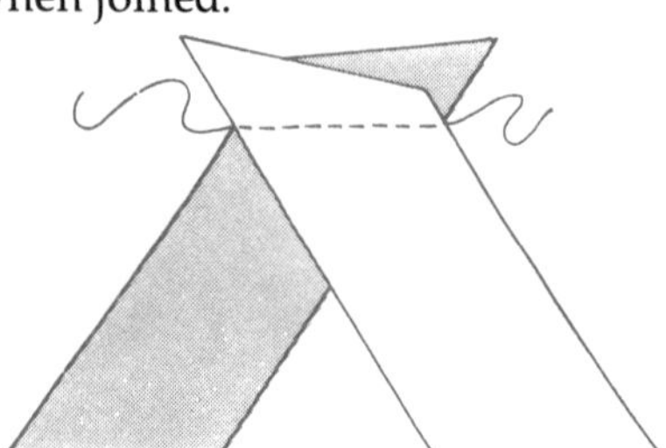

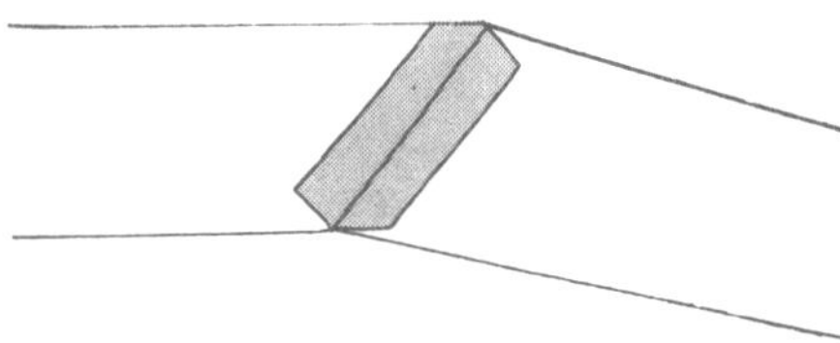

Joins in Opposite Directions— Always cut and place the ends of the bias strips parallel to each other before sewing together.

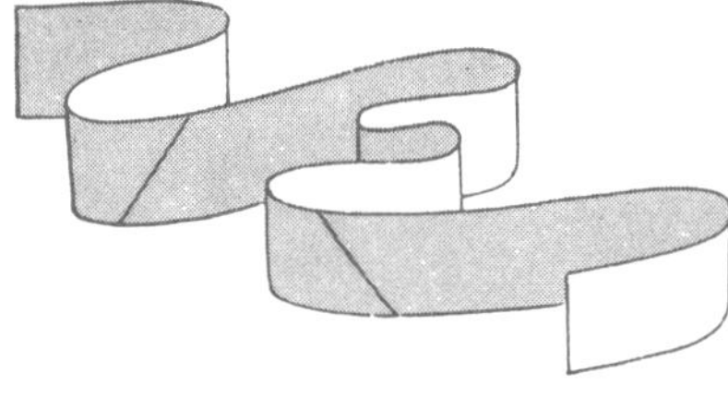

Stripes in Opposite Directions— Do not mix right-sides and wrong-sides of woven fabric, or use fabric from the opposite bias.

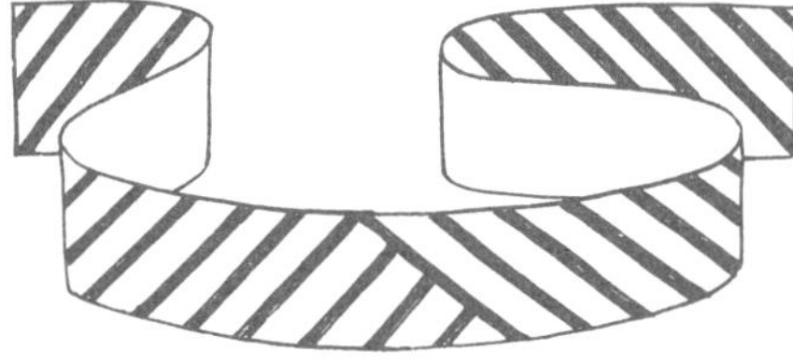

Material Grains in Different Directions—This is caused when the right-side and wrong-side are confused.

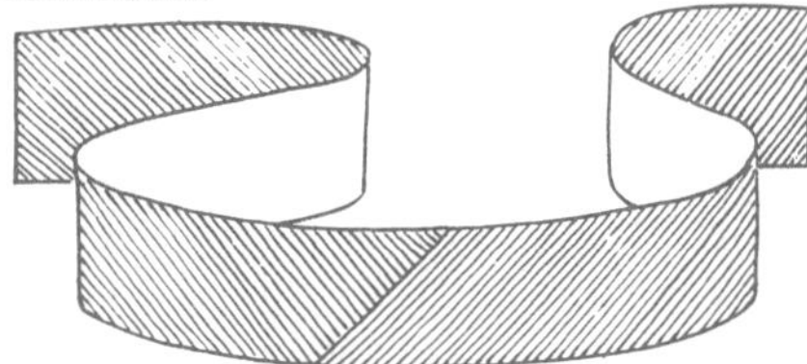

SHAPE BEFORE SEWING

Strips cut from fabric must have seam allowances and fold lines pressed in. Binding fits better if it is stretched and pressed in shape to remove slack. Purchased bias tape has been preshrunk, but can still be shaped.

Folding—Fold the cut strip in half lenthwise, with wrong-sides together. Press lightly. For single

binding, open it out. Fold the cut edges to the center. Press again.

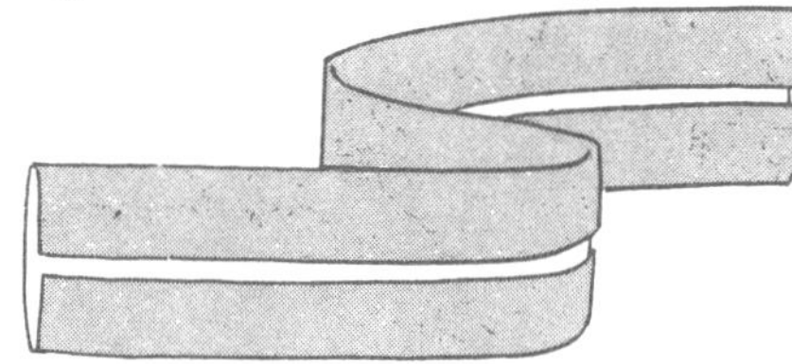

Shaping—Pin one end of the strip to the ironing board. Stretch the binding in the shape of the edge to be bound. Press lightly, using a steam iron. Let it cool before using.

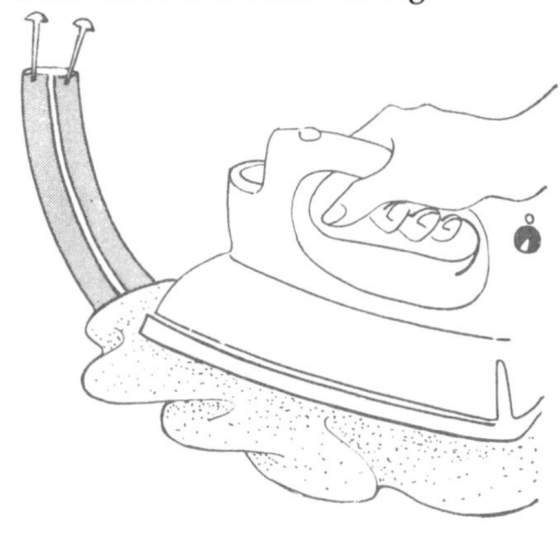

BINDING EDGES

Before making raw edges, trim the seam allowance to 1/4 inch on stretchy fabrics. Stay-stitch inside the seam allowance, leaving slightly narrower edges.

Choose a suitable-size binding for the garment. On a small garment, use a narrow width. A fabric that frays badly may need a wide binding to enclose all raw edges. Binding must match the fabric for washing, such as cotton binding on cotton fabric.

If using pieced bias strips, place joins in the binding out of sight when possible. Leave about 2 inches of binding at the beginning and end to finish ends neatly. When completed, binding should be a regular depth along its length. It may be applied to the wrong-side and folded over to cover stitching. It can be decoratively stitched by hand or machine.

Single Binding—This is used for straight edges. With the true bias cut from the fabric, press an edge on both sides. Make this the length of the fabric on the wrong-side. With purchased tape, the turned edges are already made.

Fold the bias in half, with wrong-sides facing, and press. Unfold it. With right-sides facing, place the bias along the edge of the garment. The raw edge of bias should meet the raw edge of garment. Leave 2 inches free at each end.

Tack above the crease line of the binding. Machine-stitch in the crease line, and remove tacking.

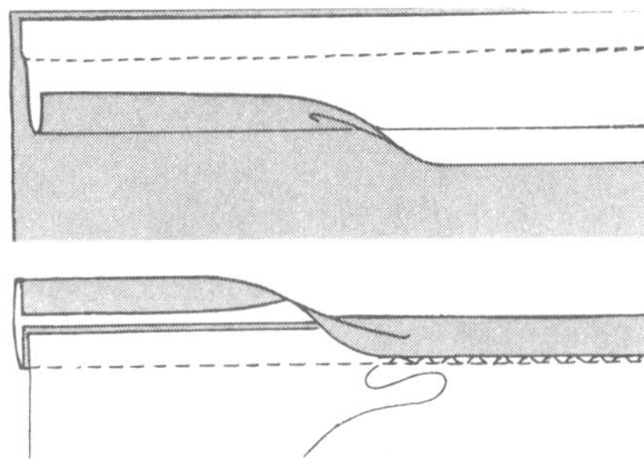

Turn the bias to the wrong-side of the garment. The edge of the strip should be turned under. Slip-stitch the bias to the garment over the seam line. Pick up machine-stitches rather

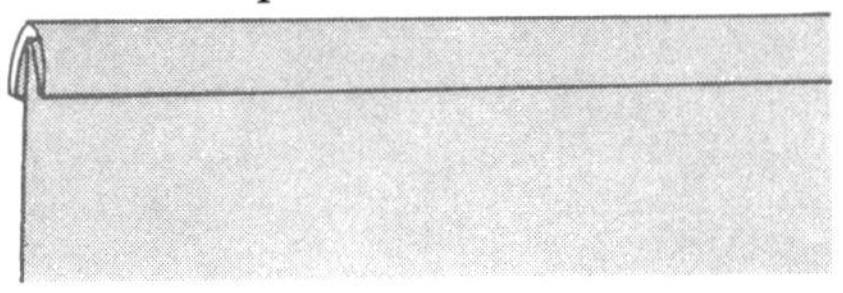

than fabric. Stitches are not visible on the right-side. Press the binding.

Curved Edges—Place binding on the garment as instructed for a straight edge. Stretch or ease the binding around the curve without stretching the garment.

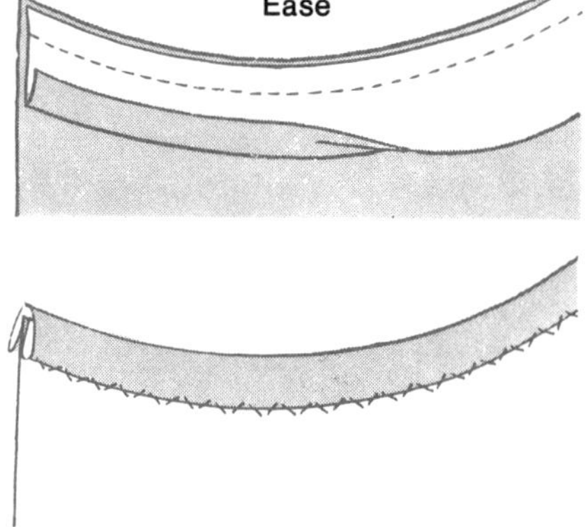

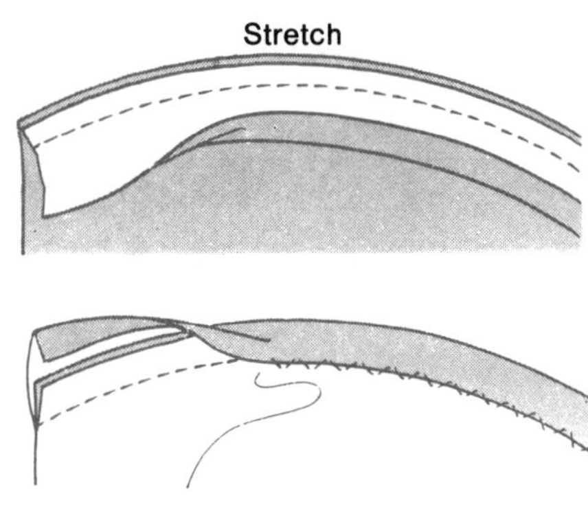

Double Binding—Sometimes called *French* or *rouleau binding,* this method is used for sheer fabrics.

Trim the seam allowance. Cut bias strips 6 times the finished width, plus 1/4 inch. This allows for the way binding becomes narrower when stretched.

Fold the strip in half lengthwise, with wrong-sides together. Press the fold without stretching. Shape the strip to match the edge of the garment.

Divide the double strip lengthwise, equally in thirds. Press. Pin, tack and stitch the strip to the edge, as for single binding.

Quick Method—This is an easy method used by professionals. Fold bias in half lengthwise, with wrong-sides facing. Press a crease. Place bias edges along the garment edge on the right-side of garment. Tack along the seam line and machine-stitch. Turn the fold of the bias to the wrong-side, and slip-stitch in place.

Binding may also be tacked in position on the wrong-side. The fold extends beyond the stitching line. Machine-stitch binding from the right-side in the line formed by the seam.

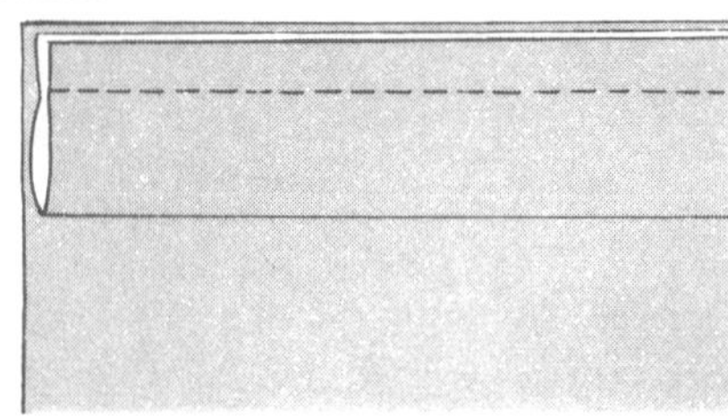

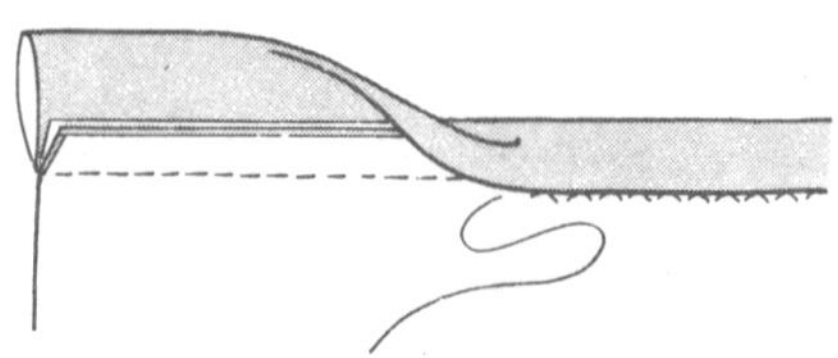

Special attachments are available for machines to apply and stitch binding in one action. Follow instructions carefully.

Machine-Stitching—Another method leaves a row of stitching showing on the right-side and wrong-side. This means careful creasing of the folds. It is used on garments that are bound all around or when there are many edges to bind. It works well with purchased bias tape and Paris or seam binding.

Prepare the bias strip, but fold one half slightly wider than the other. Place binding over the raw edges with the narrower half on the right-side.

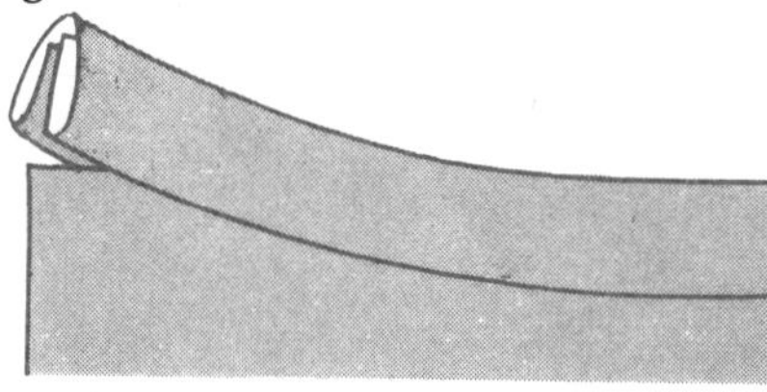

Pin and tack through all thicknesses. Machine-stitch about 1/8 inch from the inner edge. Stitch from the right-side. The slightly wider half will be caught by the stitching along its length. Remove tacking, and press from the wrong-side.

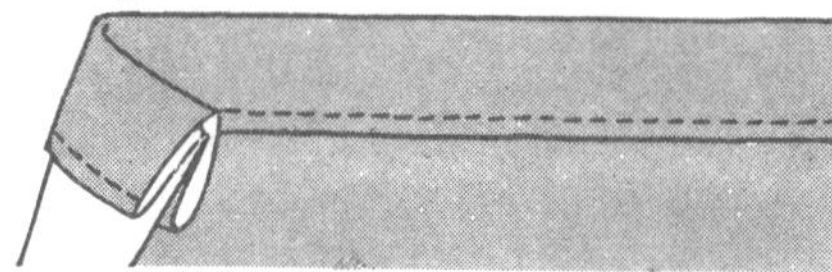

Corners—For *outside corners,* use the following method. Stitch binding to the garment as far as the seam allowance at the corner. Back-stitch

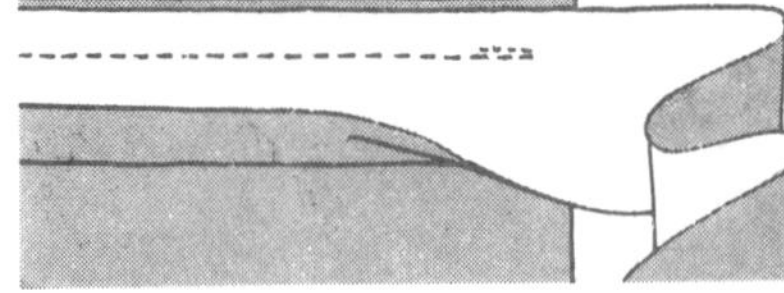

for strength. Fold the strip diagonally at the corner. Pin, tack and stitch along the outer seam line to the edge of the garment.

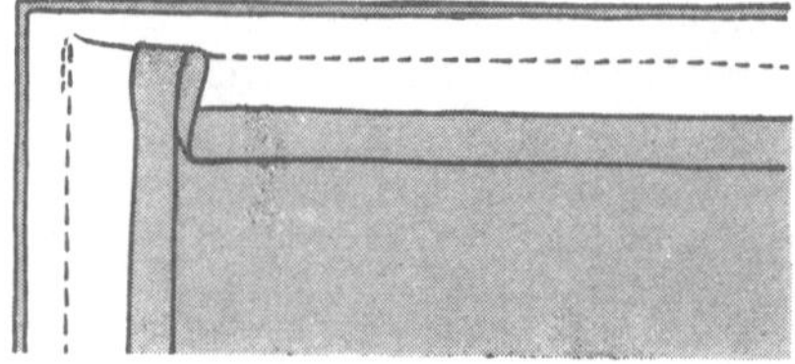

Turn the binding to the inside. This forms a miter at the corner on the right-side. On the wrong-side,

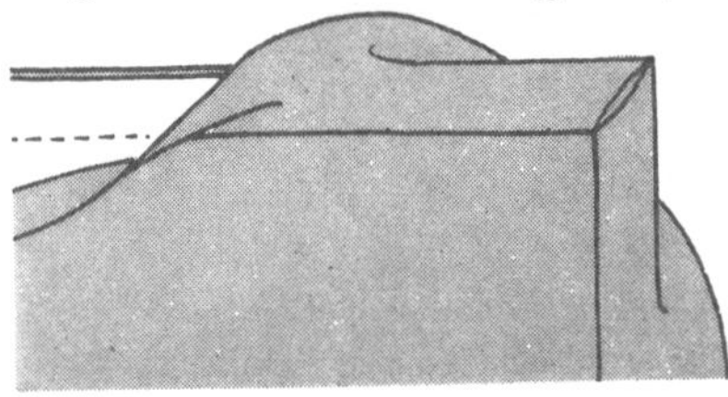

make a second folded miter in the other direction. This avoids excess bulk. Pin and slip-stitch binding. Miter folds in place.

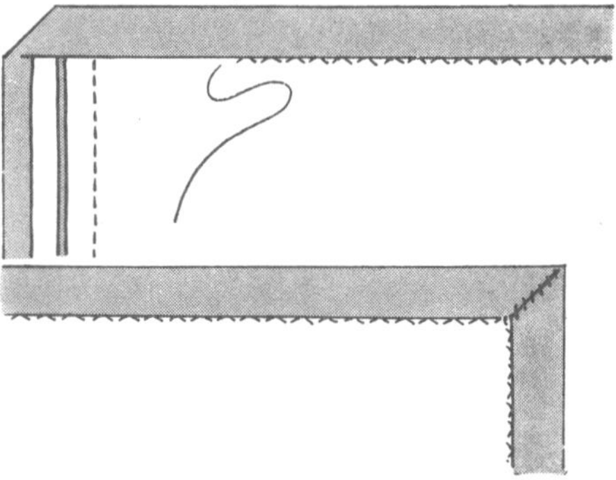

For *inside corners,* use the following method. Stay-stitch the garment corner and clip. Pull out the clipped

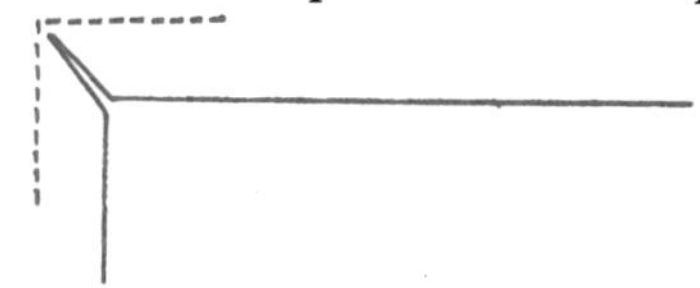

edges. Pin and tack binding to the right-side, the same as the single binding method. Stitch from the wrong-side of the garment.

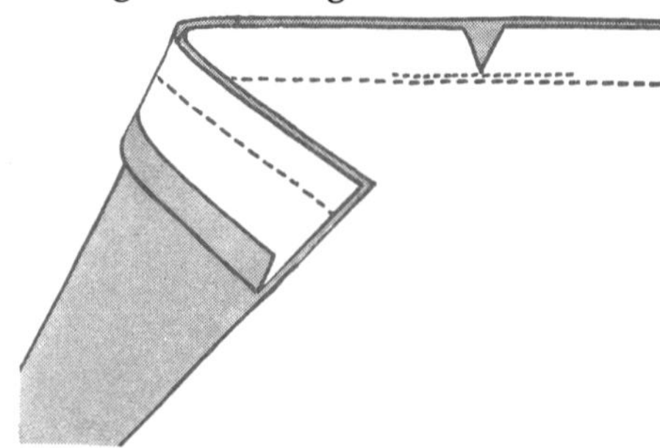

Make a miter on the right-side. Pull the fold to the wrong-side through the clipped edges. Turn the binding over the seam. Make a miter in the opposite direction.

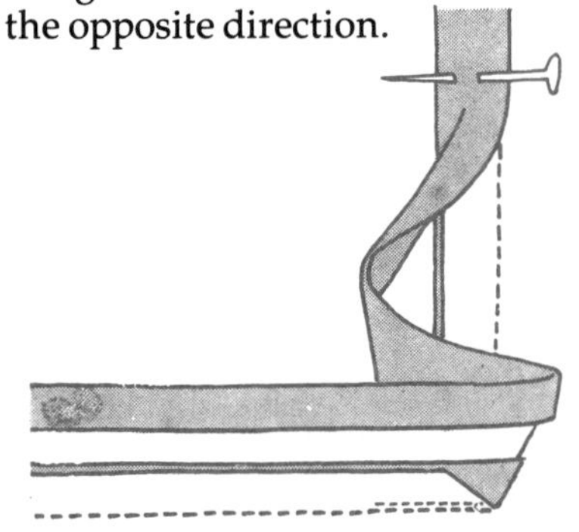

Pin and tack the binding in place. Slip-stitch the miter folds and the binding. Remove tacking and press.

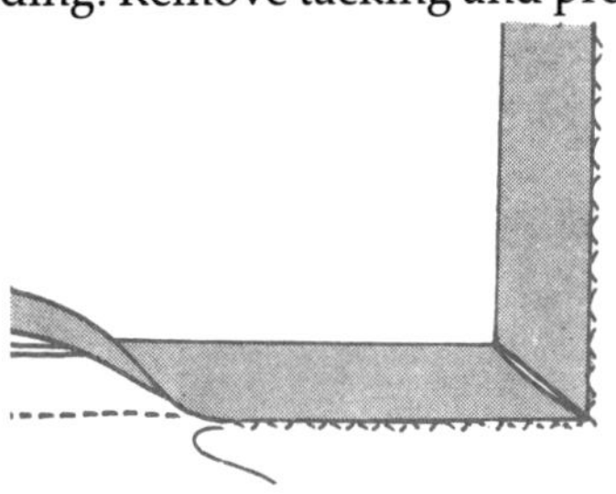

Joining—It may be necessary to join binding while sewing it to the garment, such as on an armhole.

Use this method for single or double binding. Stop stitching about 1 inch before the joining place. Fold the garment so the strip ends are at right angles.

Stitch the ends together on the straight grain, close to the garment. Do not catch the garment in the stitching. Trim and press the seam.

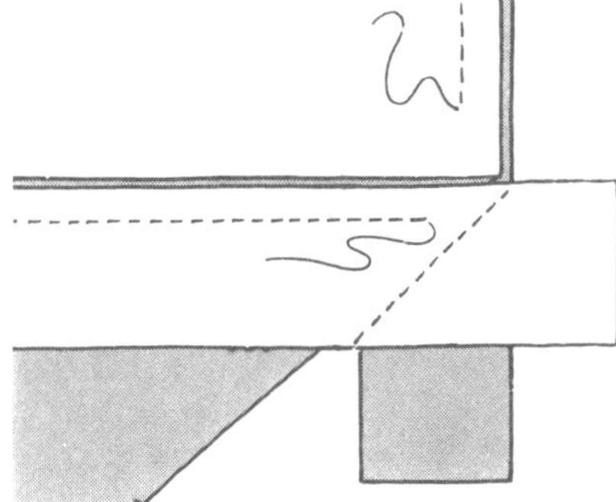

Trim the seam allowance at the seam. Press it open. Continue stitching the binding to the garment.

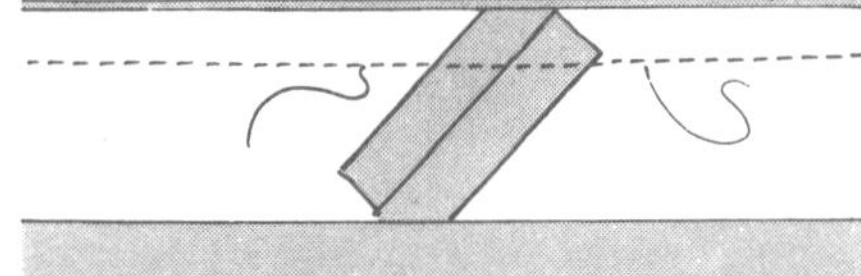

A quick method is to stitch to within about 2 inches of the joining place. Leave extra binding on both ends. Trim one end on the straight grain to 1/4 inch. Trim the other end the same way. It should overlap by 1/2 inch. Fold under 1/4 inch on this end. Press and pin or tack the folded end over the other end. Continue stitching over the joining area. Slip-stitch the ends for neatness.

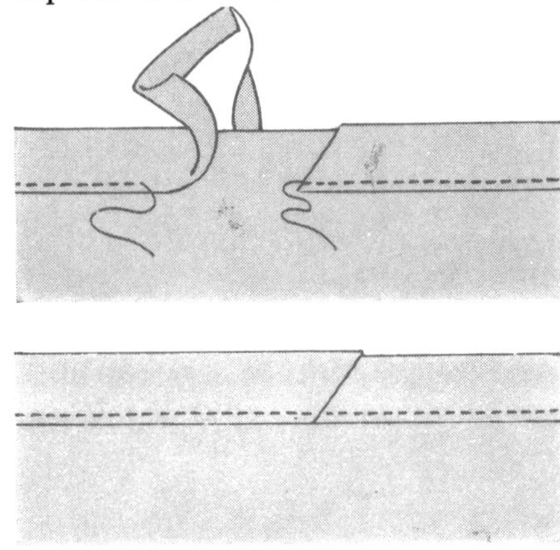

Ending—When binding ends at an opening or seam edge, finish it at the ends. Complete the facing or fastening first.

For single and double binding, use the following method. Stitch the binding to the garment. Continue

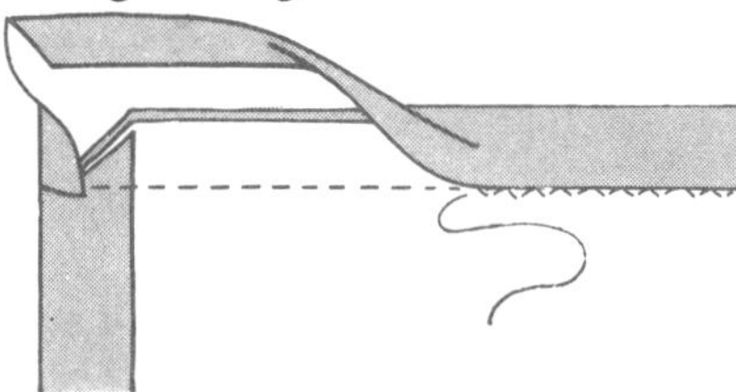

stitching beyond the edge of the garment. Trim the binding to 1/4 inch beyond the garment edge. Fold it under. Trim off the corner of the garment seam allowance. Turn the binding to the wrong-side, and pin in place. Slip-stitch, including the open end.

Piping

Piping is used with or without an inner cord. It outlines a style line or collar for decorative effect. It is often used in soft furnishings such as cushions, loose covers and decorations.

Piping is made from a piece of straight or bias fabric. It is held in place by two pieces of a seam. On the edge of a garment, it is stitched between the facing and garment edge.

Without Cord—For a piped edge without cord, mark seam lines on the garment edge and facing. Measure the edge to be piped. Cut a piece of piping fabric slightly longer than this measurement. The fabric should be twice the width of the finished piping, plus two seam allowances. The strip must be bias cut and preshaped if the edge is curved.

Fold wrong-sides together along the length. Press and tack 1/4 inch from the folded edge for 1/4-inch piping. Place the strip between the right-sides of the seam edges with raw edges together.

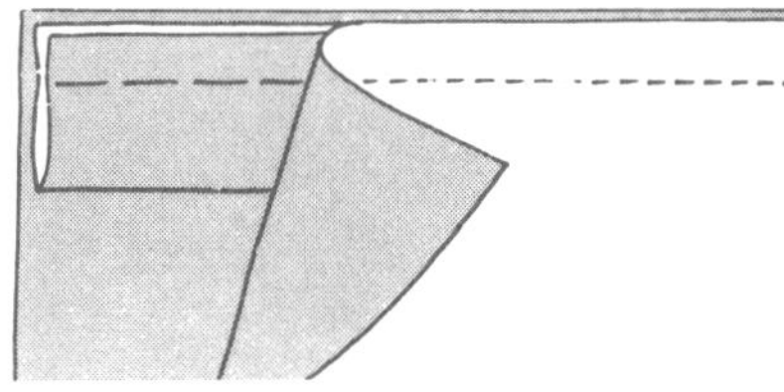

Piping should be an even depth when seen from the right-side. Machine-stitch along the seam line. Remove tacking, and clip curves.

Press on the wrong-side. Turn right-side out, and press again. Complete the facing.

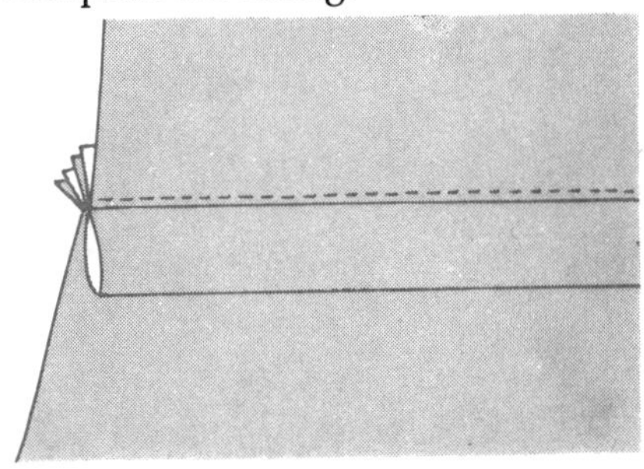

For a lapped seam, prepare the piping strip as above. Turn under the seam allowance on the edge to be top-stitched, and press.

Pin and tack this to the strip 1/8 to 1/4 inch from the fold. Place the

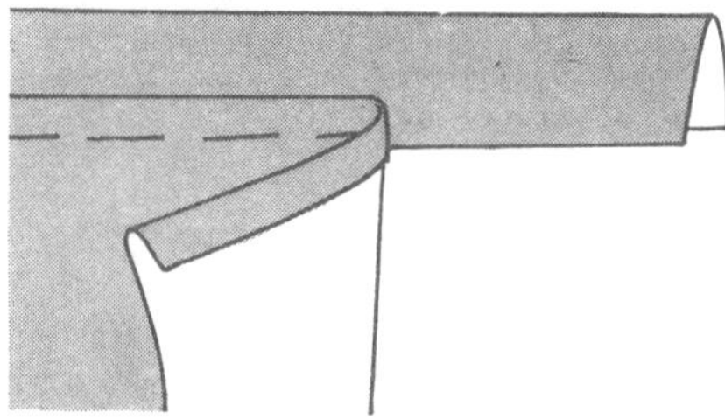

fitting lines of the two garment pieces together. Pin, tack and top-stitch on the fitting line. Remove tacking and press.

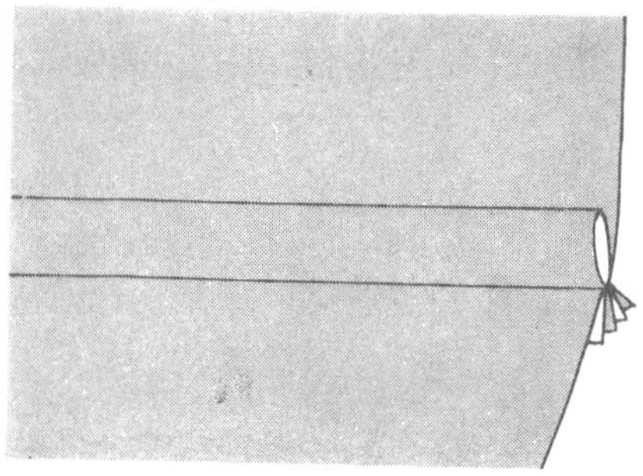

With Cord—Buy cord suitable for the weight of the fabric and style of the garment. Preshrink it before use. Bias strips or braid are suitable for enclosing cord. Use the zipper foot to stitch close to the cord, especially if fabric is bulky.

Fold the piping strip in half lengthwise. Do not press the fold. Place the cord in the covering. Pin and tack close to the cord.

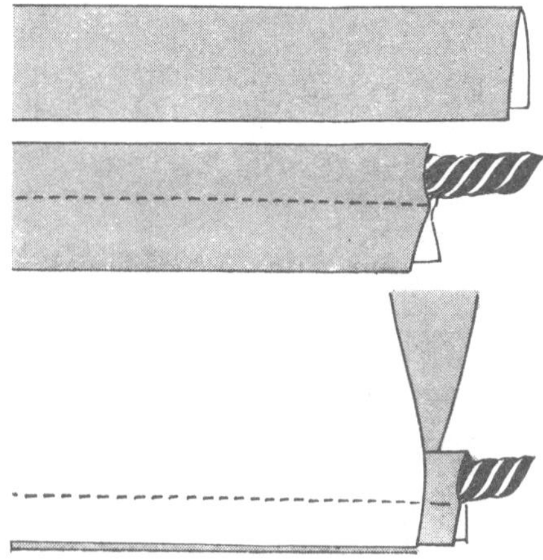

Place the covered cord between the seam edges. The cord should be just above the seam line. Pin, tack and machine-stitch close to the cord.

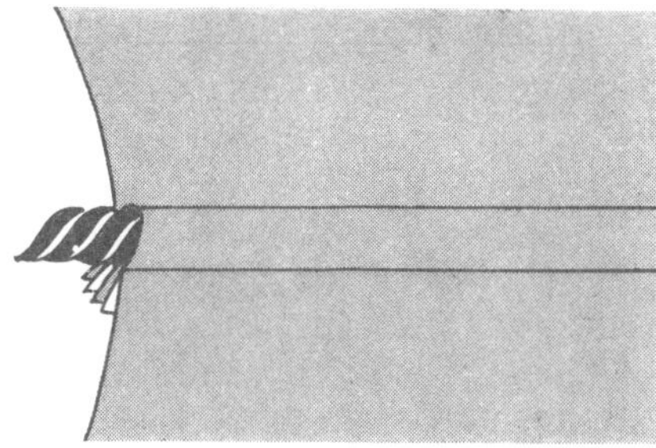

BUTTONS AND BUTTONHOLES

Buttons

The appearance of a dress can change when buttons are added. Zippers and elastic are common, but buttons are still used for practical *and* decorative purposes. Buttons may be important to the design or draw attention to a pocket or tab.

Buttons of plastic, leather, metal and wood are available. You can complete any look with matching or contrasting buttons. Use washable buttons on a washable garment.

CHOICE

Read the section on *Buttonholes*, beginning on page 94, before buying buttons.

On a pattern, the number and size of buttons is suggested. Buttons can make the garment more individual. Keep in mind the size of the wearer, the fabric and design of the garment. Decide how the buttons will be fastened—with buttonholes, loops, frogs. Try several groupings.

Pin on buttons or paper disks of various sizes and colors, in different groupings. This lets you see the effect before making the buttonholes.

Buy good-quality buttons, even for an inexpensive garment. Consider covering uncovered buttons with matching fabric.

If you have altered your pattern, the number, size and placement of buttons may also need adjusting. Be aware of any changes you must make.

ABOUT BUTTONS

Buying Buttons—Buy your buttons *before* you make your buttonholes. You may have to search to find the correct size in the correct color.

Always buy the number of buttons your pattern suggests, *plus* one or two more. It is expensive to replace all the buttons if any are lost.

Look for strength in the buttons you choose. Buy the best quality you can afford. Plastic buttons with shanks may break. Unless they are molded in one piece, do not buy them. Metal buttons are ideal because they are long-lasting and durable.

Button Position—Place buttonholes where they take the most stress. Set them at a fitted waistline or the fullest part of the bust, or the opening will gape.

Altering—If you must alter the length of the garment, evenly space buttonholes between the top and bottom position.

Belted Garment—If the garment is belted, do not place buttonholes too close to the belt. Buttons catch on the belt, and pull the opening out of shape.

Large Buttonholes—Space large buttonholes farther apart than small ones. Large buttonholes spaced too close together look unbalanced.

You may choose buttons larger than the pattern suggests. *Never* move the buttonhole in from the position shown on the pattern. If you do, it alters the center line on the garment and throws it out of balance. Instead, extend the edges of the fabric to make room for the larger-button size. If necessary, do this on the overlap and underlap. Make this alteration to the pattern *before* the garment section is cut out.

Interface Buttonholes—Interface buttonholes for support. If you do not, they may tear and fray with wear.

Make Test Buttonholes—Make test buttonholes on a scrap of garment fabric before making them on the garment. This avoids spoiling the garment if any problems arise.

Use a scrap of the fabric large enough to handle and a piece of interfacing. Put them together. Do not test the fabric alone or the thickness will not be the same. The test will be inaccurate.

You may have to use a different method if the fabric frays or is too bulky. Discover problems at the testing stage to avoid spoiling the garment.

Finished Buttonholes—Buttonholes should look slim and neat when finished. They are usually only about 1/4 inch wide. On fine fabrics they may be narrower.

MEASURING BUTTONS

The size of the button determines the size of the buttonhole. The minimum length of the buttonhole must be equal to the diameter of the button, plus the thickness. Allow 1/8 inch to make room for the shank and fabric bulk.

It is easy to find the correct length of a buttonhole. Wrap a piece of paper about 1/4 inch wide around the button at its widest point. Pin it together where ends meet. Remove the paper without unfastening it. Flatten paper on the fold opposite the pin. The measurement from the fold to the pin, *plus* 1/8 inch, is the length of buttonhole.

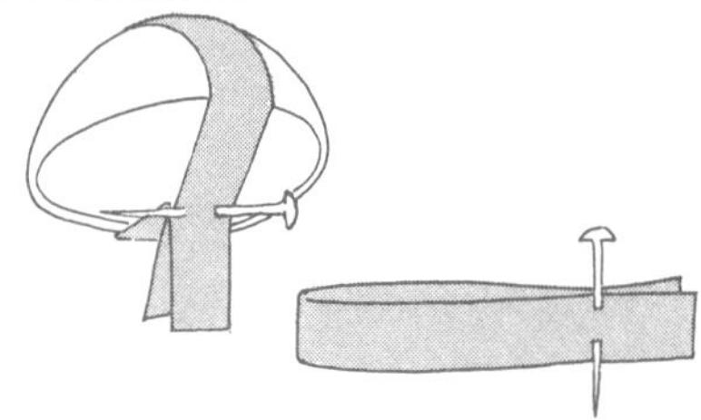

Make buttonholes slightly larger than the button for easy fastening and to prevent wear. Thick buttons need more space in the buttonhole. Allow about 1/8 inch for round buttonholes and 3/8 inch for piped buttonholes. Leave 1/8 inch for hand-sewn buttonholes and 1/4 inch for machine-sewn buttonholes.

POSITION OF BUTTONS

Space buttons close enough together so openings do not gape when closed. Buttons must be exactly opposite the buttonholes. Secure points of stress, such as a fitted waistline or fullest part of the figure, with a fastening of the same kind.

On a belted garment, space buttons above and below the belt. *Never* stitch buttons to a hem.

Make buttonholes first. Try on the garment, and pin it closed. Match the center-front line.

Place a pin through the center of the buttonhole in the underlayer. For horizontal buttonholes, mark the end of the buttonhole nearest the opening. Sew the button in the center of this spot on the center-front line.

For vertical buttonholes, mark 1/8 inch below the top of the buttonhole. Do this on the center-front line.

Separate the two layers of garment. Mark button placement, and sew on the buttons. Remove the pins.

If buttons are an important feature, sew them on with a few stitches first. Try on the garment, and check button placement. Sew buttons exactly in position.

To sew buttons on a garment, use a double strand of strong thread about 18 inches long. Pull it through beeswax to make it easier to work through buttons and cloth. Thread will be less likely to form knots.

Begin sewing each button with two or three back-stitches on the right-side. You can use shiny thread for a decorative effect.

BUTTONS WITHOUT SHANKS

Position buttons about half their diameter from the edge of the garment or where indicated on the pattern. Attach thread at the place where the button is sewn. Use two or three back-stitches on the right-side. Place the center of the button over the thread fastening.

Determine the length of shank required, according to the thickness of the material. The thicker the material, the larger the shank. The shank should be the thickness of the garment edge with the buttonhole. You can use a matchstick to help make buttonholes. One matchstick makes a shank about 1/8 inch long. Place the stick across the top of the button.

Pass thread across the stick and through the second hole of the button to the back of the fabric. Repeat this until enough thread has been sewn for strength.

Remove the matchstick. Place the needle and thread between the button and fabric. Ease the button to the end of the shank.

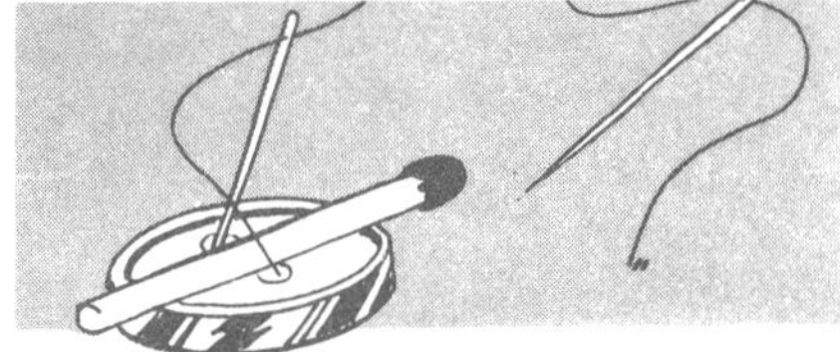

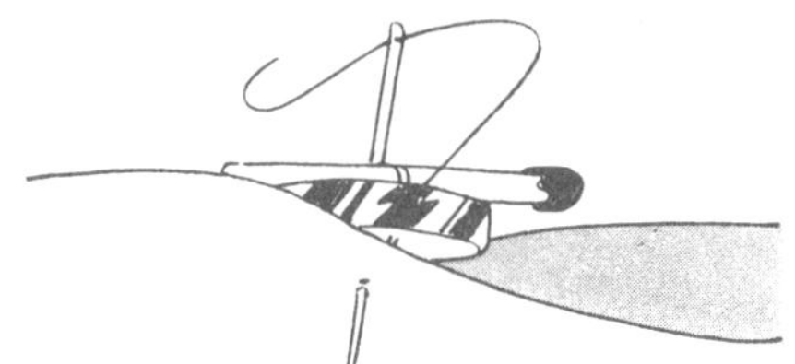

Wind thread around the stem of the stitches three or four times for strength. Take the needle to the back of the fabric, and finish securely.

For thick or delicate fabrics see the section on *Reinforced Buttons,* page 94.

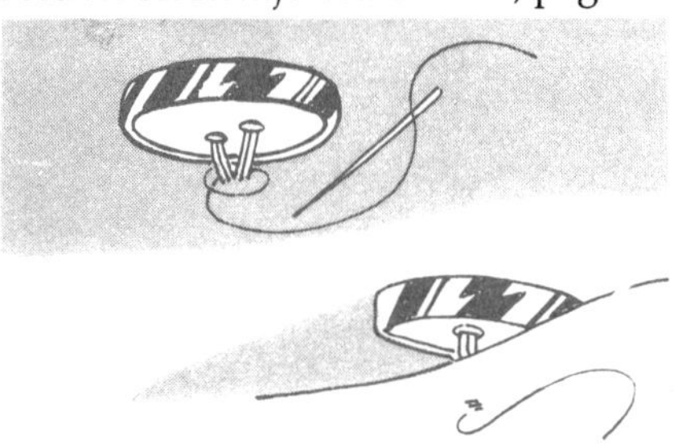

BUTTONS WITH SHANKS

Place buttons with shanks at right angles to the buttonholes. Hand-stitch buttons the same way as two-hole buttons. Push the needle through shank holes, then down and up through fabric.

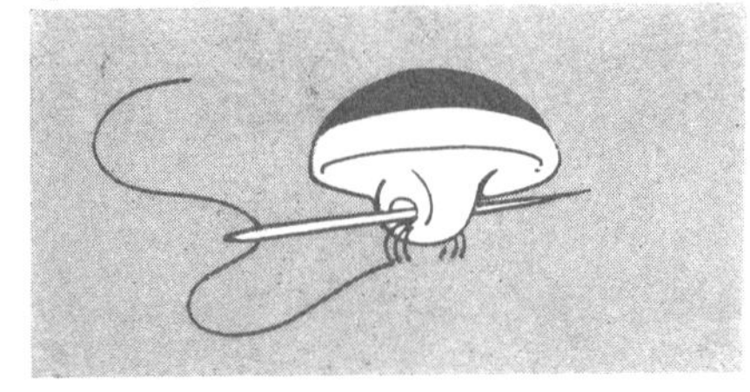

On overalls, make buttons with detachable shanks for laundering. Eyelets are made, and shanks are pushed through these. Toggles secure them on the wrong-side.

BUTTONS WITH FOUR HOLES

These can be sewn as two-hole buttons. Back-stitches lie parallel on the wrong-side of fabric.

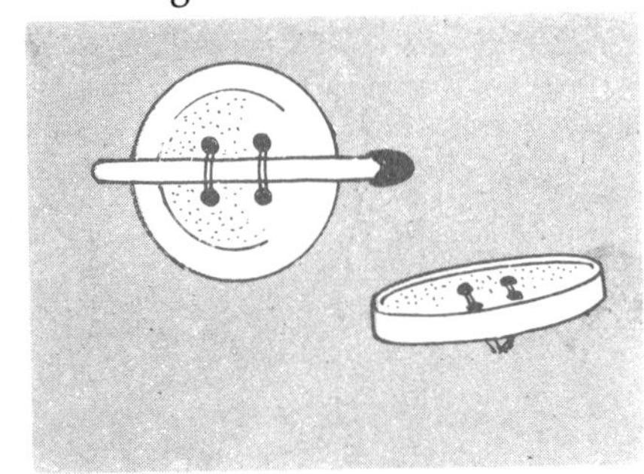

There are many ways thread can be stitched through holes. Use the same method for each button on a garment.

Crossover-stitching is used on buttons with a sunken center, such as men's pants buttons. Arrowhead-stitching is decorative if stitched with shiny thread.

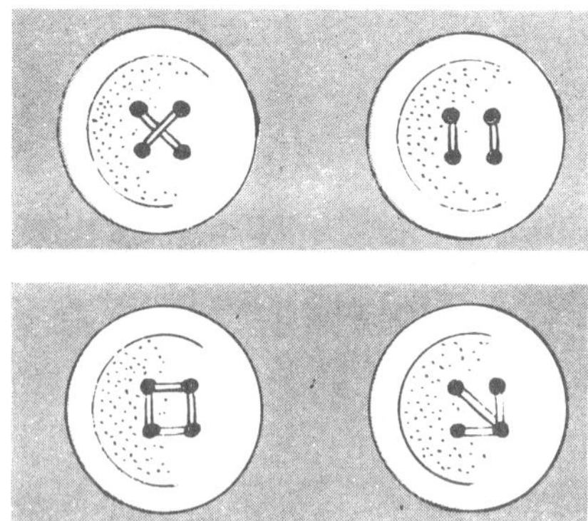

COVERED BUTTONS

These are usually made in self-fabric. They may be any size from tiny satin wedding-dress buttons to large ones for a coat. They are made commercially or at home from a kit. They have a shank or a padded fabric back sewn like a shank.

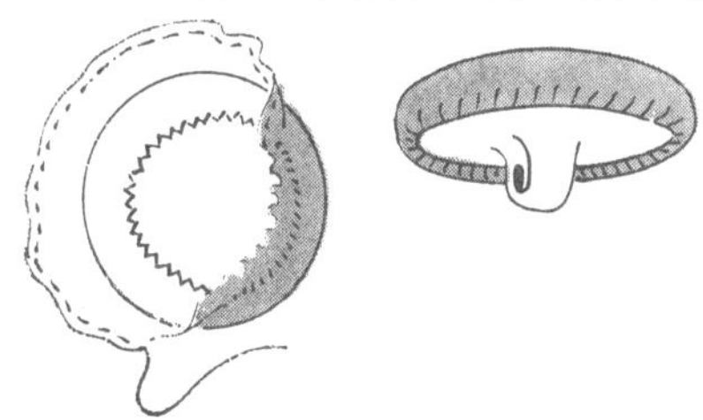

REINFORCED BUTTONS

These are often necessary on coats or suits where buttons get a lot of use. They are also found on delicate fabrics that might be torn by the pull of a button.

On thick fabrics, put a small, flat button underneath the button on the inside of the garment. Sew through both, making a shank on the right-side only. On delicate fabric, place a small, folded square of ribbon between the garment and facing underneath the button. Sew through all layers.

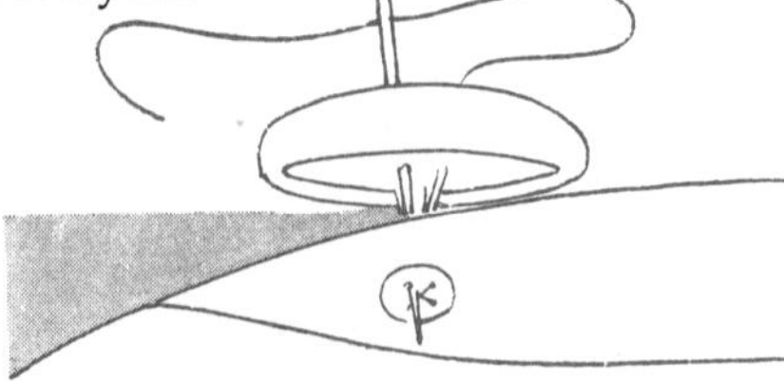

LINK BUTTONS

These types of fastenings are used instead of cuff links. They sometimes fasten the neck of capes.

Measure how long the thread needs to be for the cuff or cape to close neatly. Make two or three loops of thread this length between the two buttons. Do a buttonhole-stitch over them along most of the link. Knot the ends securely.

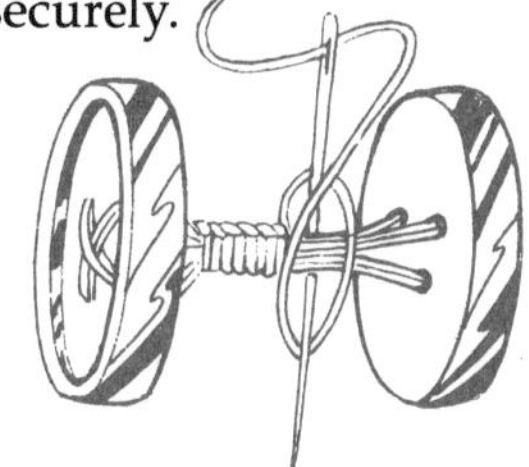

JEWELED BUTTONS

If the button has sharp edges or is a rough, irregular shape, sew it directly to the buttonhole. Sew snaps underneath to fasten the opening.

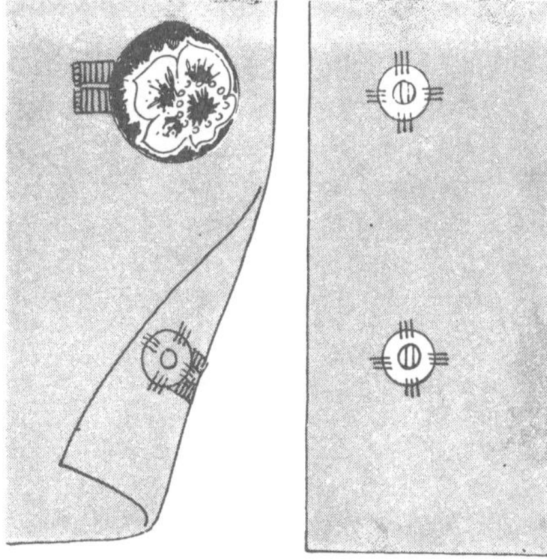

CHINESE BALLS

These are often used as decoration only. They may be used as the buttons in frog fastenings if made from strong cord. Sew them the same way as jeweled buttons if they are used at an opening. They are made from matching or contrasting cord, braid or rouleau. They can be less expensive than purchased buttons.

Use cord, braid or bias tape. If making a small button, cut a piece of cord 9 inches long. Loop the cord.

Loop it again, putting it under the first loop. Make a third loop. Weave

it through the other two loops. Loops remain open when working them.

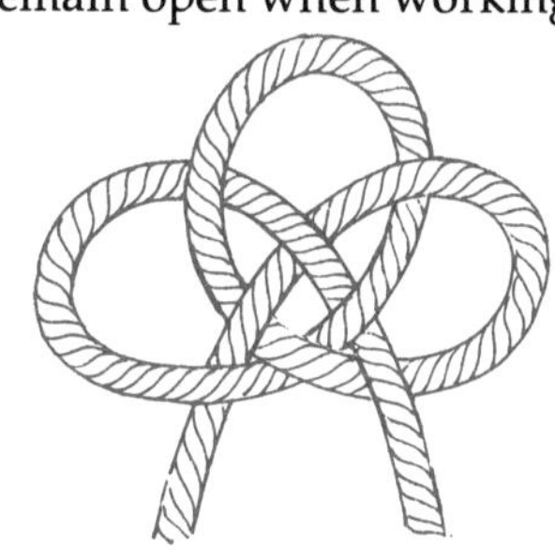

Ease the loops together, and shape them into a ball. Cut the ends, then sew them flat to the underside of the ball.

Buttonholes

Buttons are usually matched to buttonholes for a garment closing. *Buttonholes* are small slots, cut and finished in the fabric. They are large enough for the button to pass through.

Buttonholes must be neat to look smart. Poorly finished ones spoil the look of a garment. Buttonholes are placed so the distance between the buttonhole end and the garment opening is half the button width. Buttonholes may be positioned vertically, horizontally or at an angle, as a fashion detail.

Horizontal Buttonholes—The straight-across buttonhole is the most popular. It takes a lot of wear and tear. When sewn by hand, it is made with a straight end and a round end nearest the opening.

Vertical Buttonholes—The straight up-and-down buttonhole is suitable when there is little strain at the opening. This buttonhole may be more suited to the style of the garment, such as a loose-fitting top.

If worked by hand, these buttonholes may have round or square ends. Round-end buttonholes are often used on fine fabrics. These include delicate underwear, nightwear, evening wear and baby garments. Use the style of the garment and fabric as a guide to the type of buttonhole.

BOUND BUTTONHOLES

These give a professional, couture look to coats, suits and dresses. Use them when the fabric is good quality and the design is distinctive.

There are several ways to make bound buttonholes. Construction depends on the skill of the sewer and the type of fabric used.

One-Piece Bound Buttonholes— Make these buttonholes before the facing is attached. They are made through the fabric and interfacing only.

Cut a strip of fabric on the straight or bias grain. It should be 2 inches wider and 1 inch longer than the buttonhole. Bias pieces are preferable. They allow more ease when buttoning and unbuttoning.

These can be a decorative feature if made in a checked or striped fabric. Fabric on the bias has give. It reduces the risk of fabric pieces pulling away and the buttonhole fraying.

Mark the center of each strip with tailor's chalk. Transfer size markings with tacking lines. Center the fabric strip over the buttonhole. Position right-sides together, and tack all around.

Machine-stitch along the lines on the long sides. Each line must be exactly the same length. Stitch twice for strength. Tie thread ends on the wrong-side.

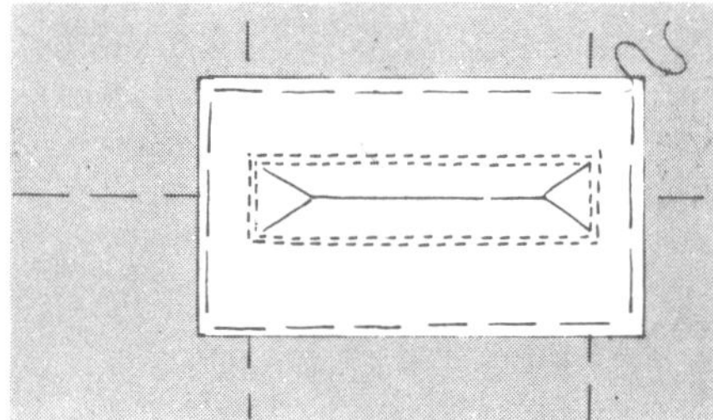

On the right-side, fold the edges of the binding toward the buttonhole center. Press one after the other. From the wrong-side, slash along the center of the binding between the stitching lines. Use small sharp scissors. Stop 1/4 inch from each end. A pin placed 1/4 inch in from each end prevents overcutting.

Do the same on the garment side. If the slash is too long, the triangles at either end are too small to handle. Buttonholes will be weak in these places.

From the ends of the slash, clip diagonally to each corner. Be careful

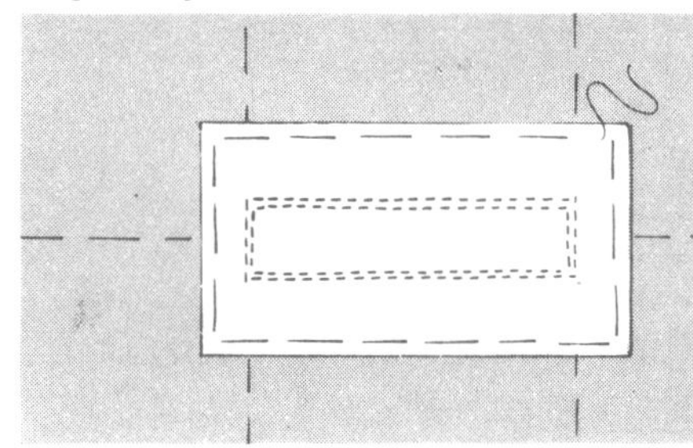

not to cut any stitches. Remove tacking-stitches, and push binding through the opening. Press away from the opening. Make an inverted pleat at both ends. Folds meet exactly in the center of the slit. Tack folds together.

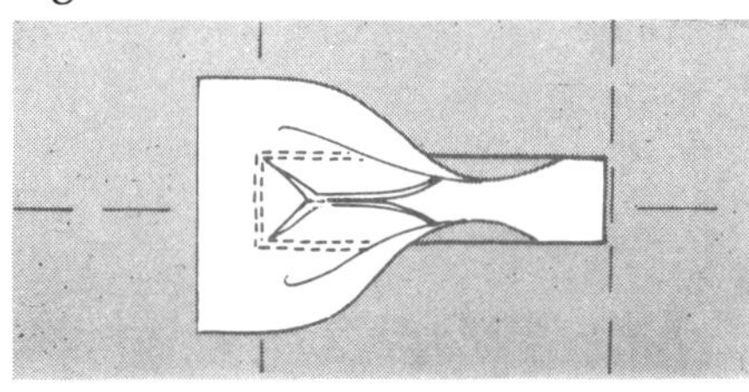

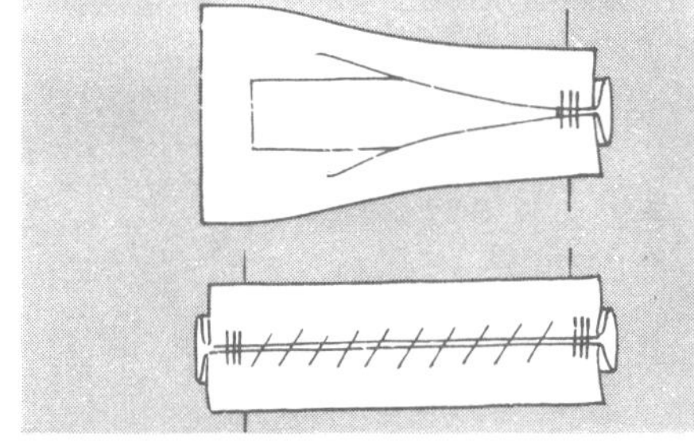

With the right-side of the garment facing you, fold the back edge of the opening. This exposes a corner triangle. Machine-stitch across the base of the triangle using short stitches. Stitch each triangle twice. Carefully tie thread ends. Trim

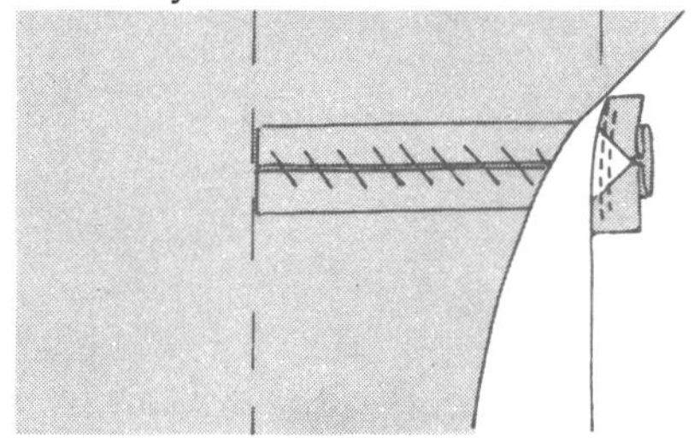

binding and catch-stitch edges to the interfacing.

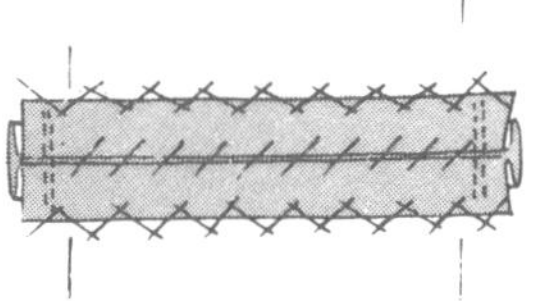

To finish, pin and tack the facing to the garment through all layers of fabric and interfacing. Place pins across each end of the buttonhole to mark size on the facing.

Make a slash on the facing between pins. Clip the center of each slash.

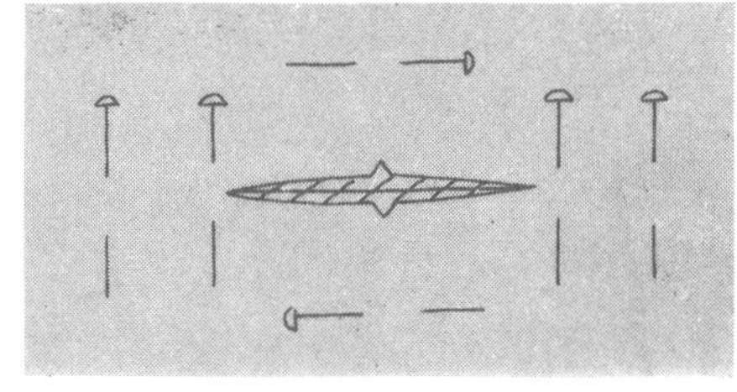

Turn in the edges, and slip-stitch the facing to the buttonhole on the wrong-side. This makes an oval shape.

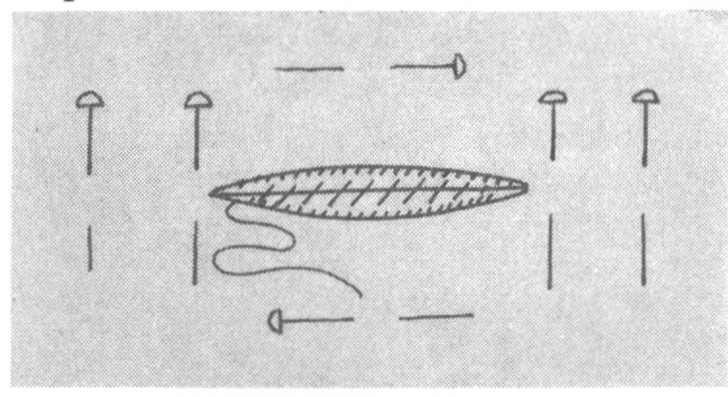

Two Piece or Piped— This buttonhole is made before the facing is attached. It is made through the fabric and interfacing only. It is a quick, easy method for firmly woven fabrics.

Cut a piece of fabric 1 inch wide and twice the length of the buttonhole, plus 1 inch. Iron interfacing to the wrong-side.

Fold in half along the length, with wrong-sides together. Carefully tack 1/8 inch from the folded edge. Trim the edges to 1/8 inch from the stitching.

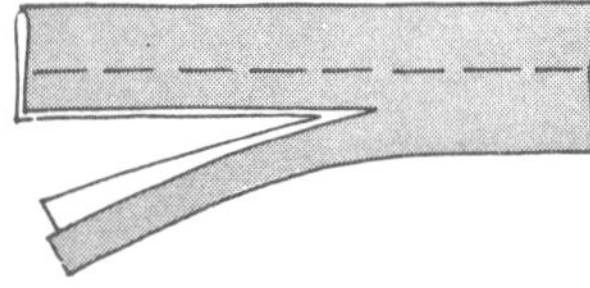

Place two strips on the right-side, with the cut edges along the center line of the buttonholes. Leave 1/4 inch at each end. Tack in place.

Machine-stitch in place with double rows of stitching over the original tacking on each strip. Begin stitching in the center of each strip.

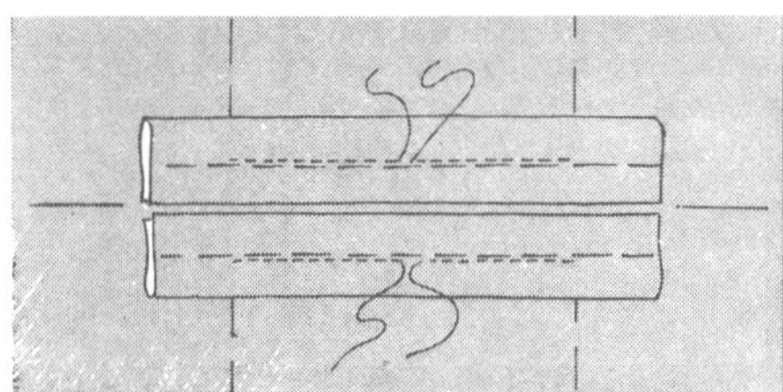

From the wrong-side, cut buttonholes between the rows of stitching. Cut the corners, turn the strips through and press. Oversew folded edges together.

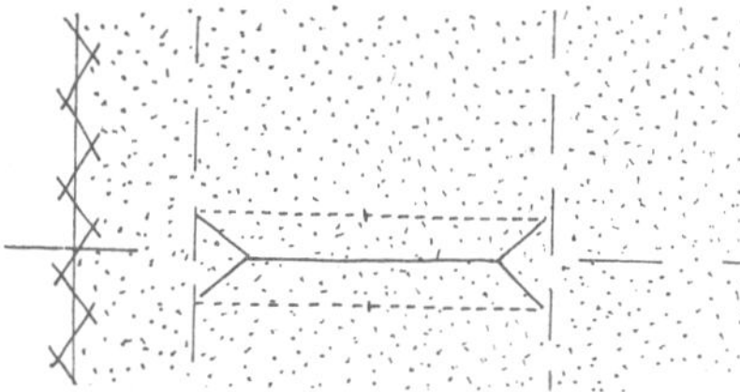

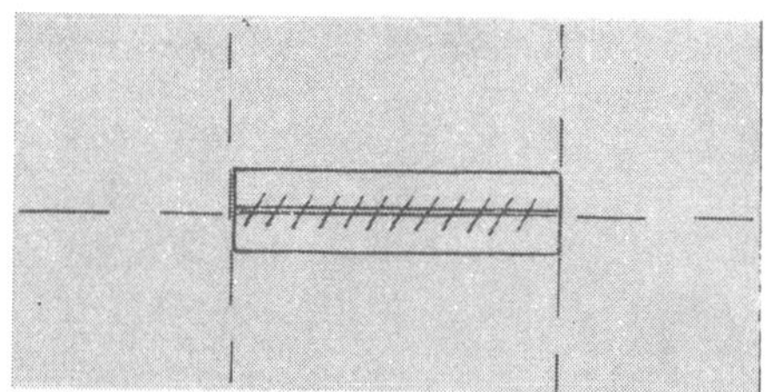

Finish as for one-piece bound buttonholes. Or cut a slit in the facing, turn under the edges, and hem in place.

Window Method—This is probably the easiest method. It is good for bulky or easily frayed fabrics. It may help to interface afterward with this method.

Repeat the stages of the one-piece method. Use pieces of lighter fabric, instead of self-fabric. Turn the

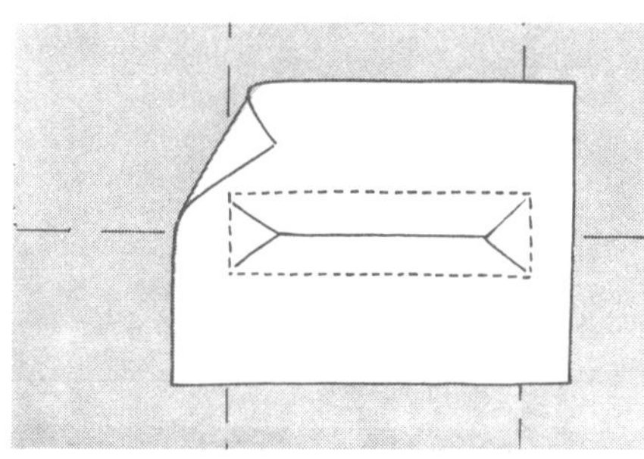

binding through to the wrong-side. Press all around to form a window opening. Make sure the organza is not visible from the right-side.

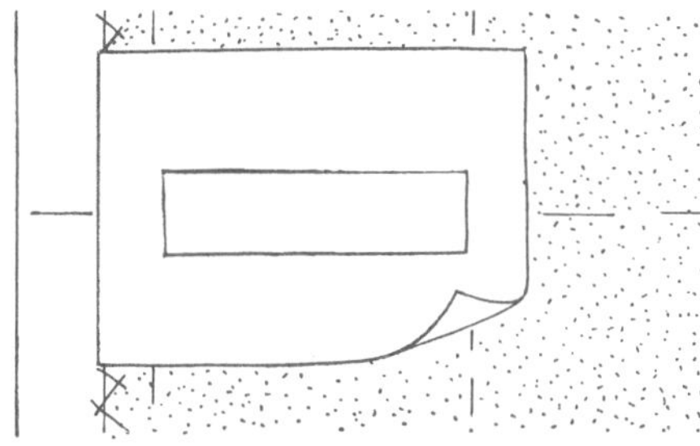

Cut straight strips of fabric about 2 inches wide, 1 inch longer than the buttonhole. This may be on the bias or grain. Place two strips together, right-sides facing. Machine-baste along the exact center line, using the longest machine-stitch.

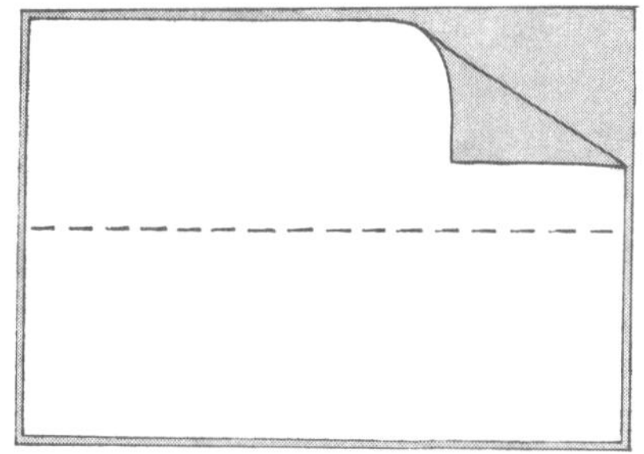

Fold each piece of fabric back, with wrong-sides together. Press the resulting seam. Position the tacked

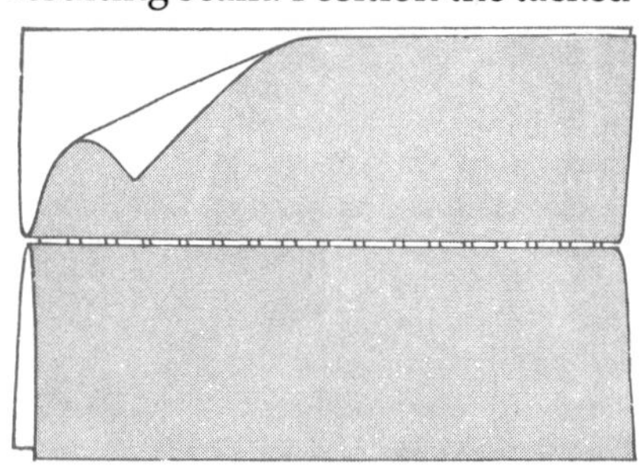

pieces of fabric over the window on the wrong-side of the garment. Center the seam. Secure with a pin at either end.

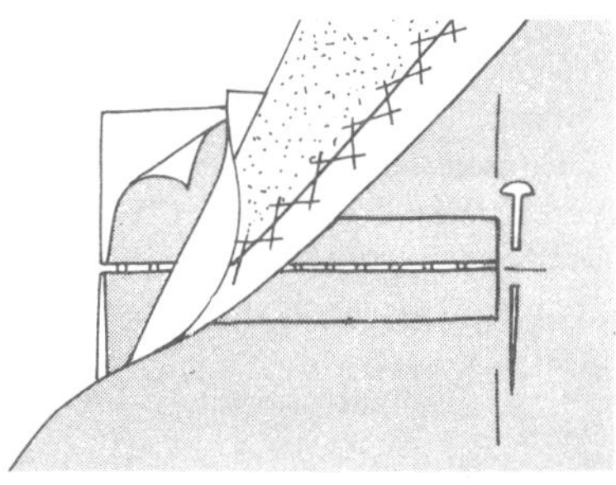

Turn garment fabric back from the buttonhole to show the seam. Use about 15 stitches per inch. Stitch through the seam and binding on the long side of buttonhole, a little beyond the seam at each end. Stitch

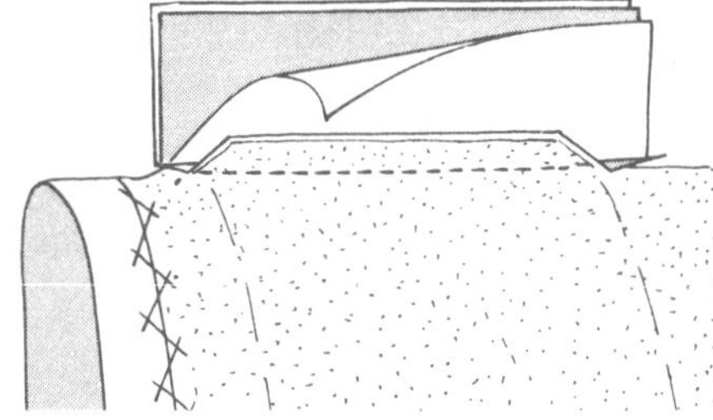

the triangular ends in the same way. Secure thread ends and press.

Finish the facing the same way as the windows are constructed. Follow the first three stages of the window method on the facing. Slip-stitch windows over buttonholes on the wrong-side.

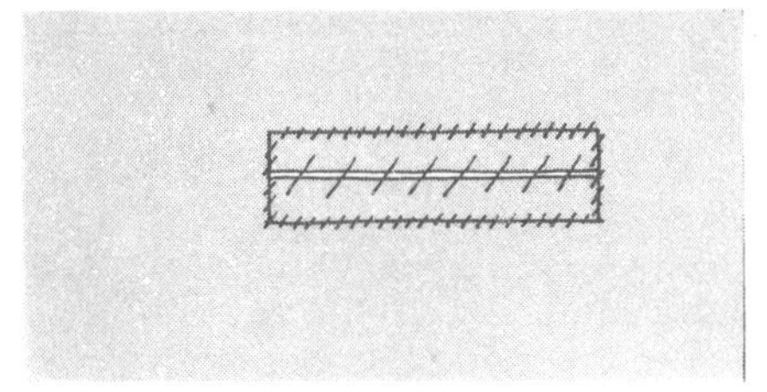

SLOT BUTTONHOLES

These are also called *seam buttonholes.* They are small openings in a seam near the garment edge. Slots may also be made in other seams for belts.

Mark the position for openings in the seam. Pin and tack. Place strips of seam tape or ribbon at the seam line. These should be about 1 inch longer than slot on marking. Stitch along each edge on both seam allowances.

Stitch the seam. Back-stitch at both ends of each slot. Press the seam

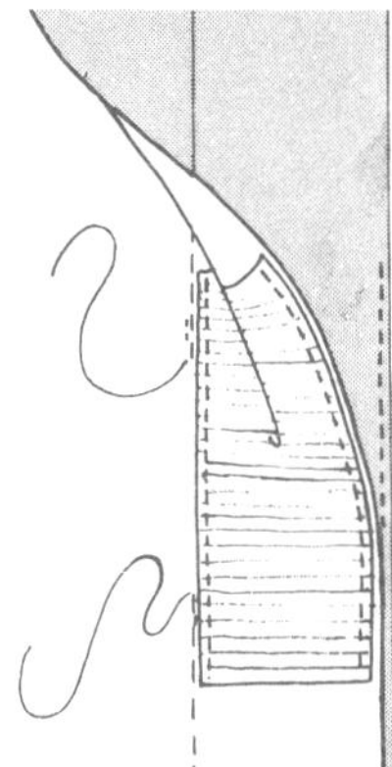

open. Work bar tacks at each end of the slot on the wrong-side of the fabric. Stitches should not show on the right-side of the fabric. Remove tacking-stitches from each opening.

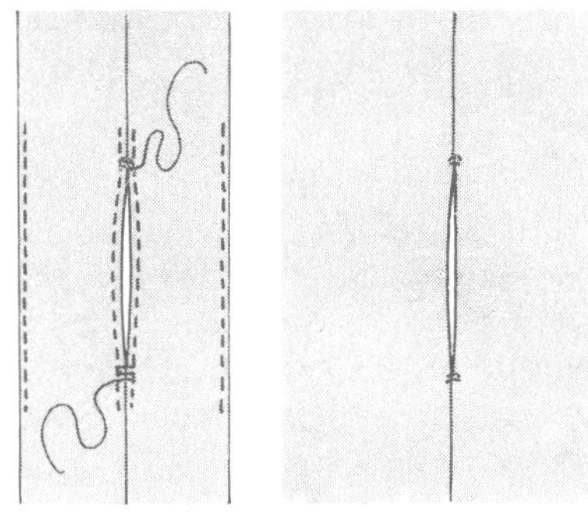

HAND-SEWN BUTTONHOLES

These are best for fine, dainty, light fabrics. They are also good for underwear and baby garments. They are stronger than bound buttonholes.

Badly sewn buttonholes that are not level or stitched evenly are noticeable on a garment. Practice first on a scrap of fabric.

Horizontal buttonholes usually have fan-shape stitches at the end nearest the garment opening. A bar tack is made at the other. Vertical buttonholes usually have bar tacks at both ends. They are sewn through all layers of fabric and interfacing when the garment is finished.

Mark the buttonhole as described in the section on *Bound Buttonholes,* page 95. Place a pin at either end of the rectangle. Slash along the exact center line. Pins prevent the slash from going too far. Remove pins. For extra strength, place a line of stitching in a rectangle 1/8 inch from the slit.

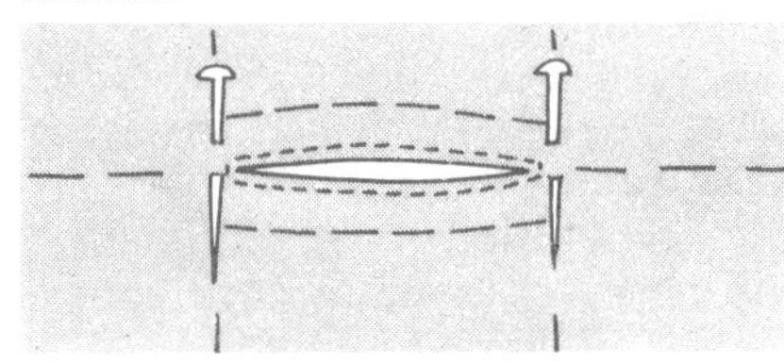

On fabrics that fray, overcast the edges of the slit. Do both processes neatly or thick, lumpy stitching shows on the finished buttonhole.

Starting at the right-side, work buttonhole-stitches to the end of the first side. Use a 20-inch length of thread. If a longer thread is used, it may be difficult to manipulate. This causes twisting and knotting.

Insert the needle in the slash from the right-side. Bring it out a little outside the stitching line. Bring the thread around under the point from the eye of the needle. Draw the needle through the fabric to form a knot at the edge of the slash.

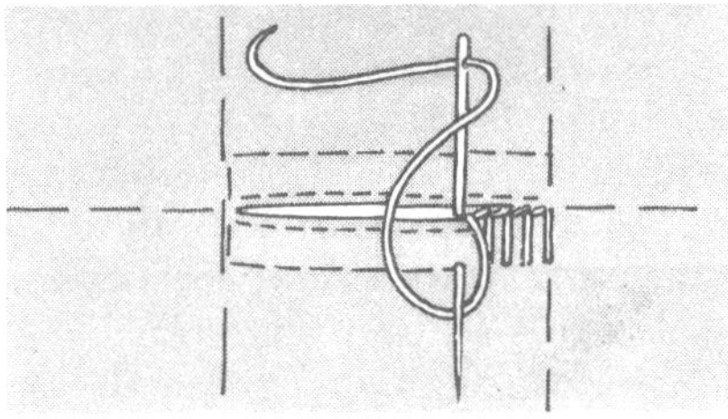

Continue along the slit to one end. Make a fan-shape around the end. Continue in a buttonhole-stitch along the other side.

Keep stitches even and close together to cover the cut edge. Do not pull the knots too tight because it buckles the fabric edge.

Make several stitches across the end covering the last stitches to form a bar tack. Work buttonhole-stitches through fabric and bar tack. Finish neatly and securely. If the straight effect is preferred, finish both ends in a bar tack. The fan usually looks daintier.

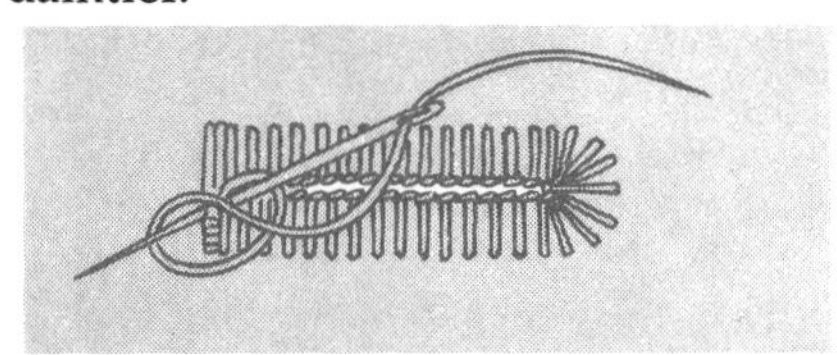

MACHINE-STITCHED BUTTONHOLES

Machine-stitched buttonholes give a crisp, long-wearing finish. They are good for casual or semicasual wear and tailored garments. A sewing machine can make beautiful buttonholes. Set the machine accurately, and stitch slowly and carefully.

These buttonholes are suitable for casual, washable clothes. They can be made on zigzag machines and straight-stitch machines with a buttonhole attachment.

A buttonhole attachment has a set of templates in various sizes. A template is selected and inserted in the attachment. Buttonholes will be uniform in length. The templates are various sizes, in oval and keyhole shapes.

Mark the length and placement of the buttonholes on the fabric. Use interfacing as close as possible to the fabric color.

Follow instructions from your sewing-machine handbook. This gives the setting for length and width of the stitch required to make a satin-stitch. On some machines, buttonholes are worked automatically.

Follow the setting instructions. Often the machine can stitch the buttonhole without the operator having to turn the fabric.

Make a test sample. As fabrics vary, so does the machine setting. Use the same number of fabric layers on the test sample as for the final buttonhole. When you set a satin-stitch, fabric runs through the machine without having to move the fabric.

If the work requires pulling, the stitch has not been set correctly. This results in stitches piling up and a lumpy buttonhole.

Strong, neat buttonholes may be worked with the stitch not larger than a satin-stitch. A strong buttonhole can be made by running a strand of thread under the stitches while sewing. Most zigzag machines have an extra sewing foot for buttonholes that allows this.

Attach the facing and interfacing, and trace buttonhole markings. Stitch the buttonholes, following machine instructions. For extra-strong buttonholes, stitch a second time.

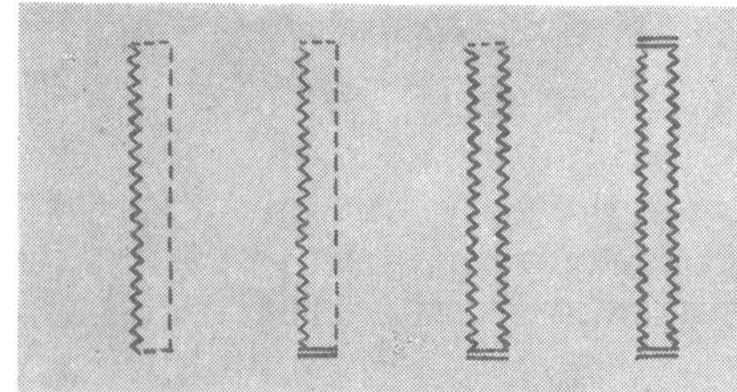

CORDED BUTTONHOLES

These buttonholes do not stretch but are strong and wear well. The final appearance is a raised buttonhole. For bound buttonholes, use the two-piece method. Fold the fabric strips around a piece of fine cord or twine. Stitch close to it, using a piping or zigzag foot.

Using the one-piece method, follow the diagrams below. For

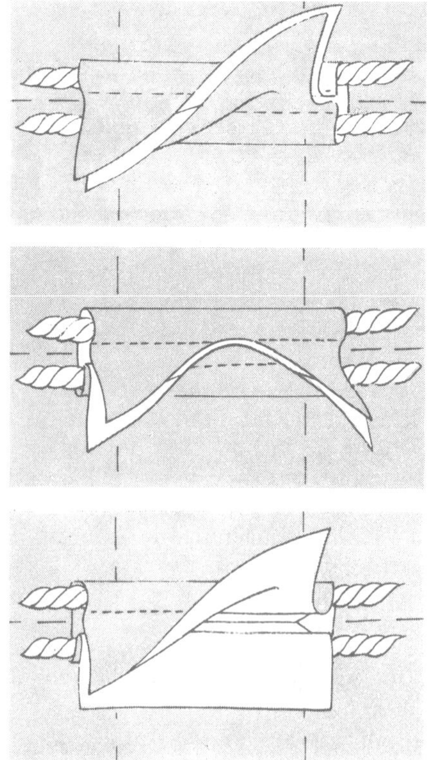

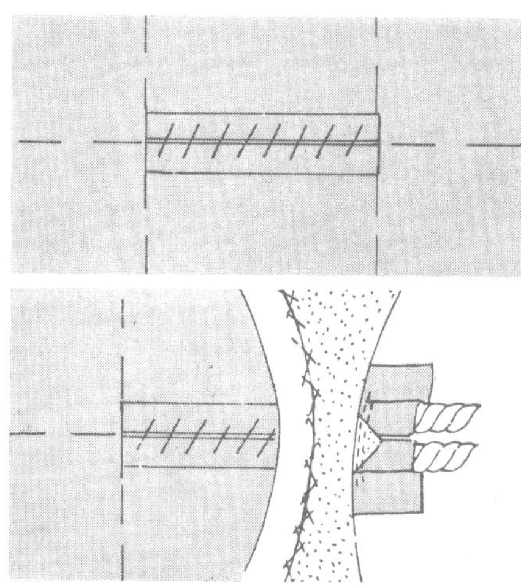

hand-sewn buttonholes, pin a piece of thread around the slot. Secure it at one end and work a buttonhole-stitch over this. Finish with a bar tack at the end with the pin. Cut off the ends of the cord.

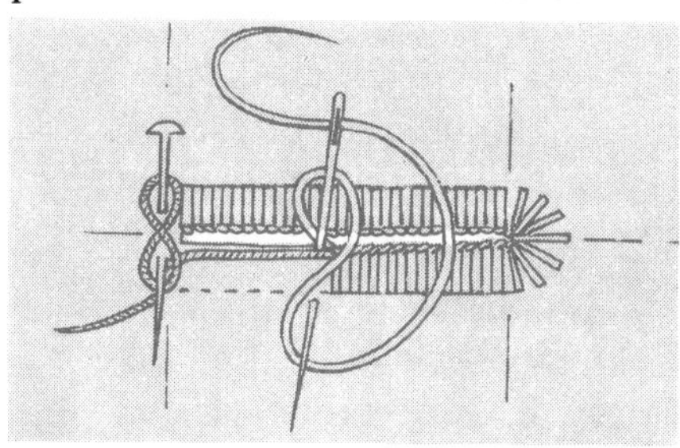

For machine-sewn buttonholes, follow machine instructions. There may be a special sewing foot to use.

TAILOR'S BUTTONHOLES

A tailor's buttonhole looks like a keyhole buttonhole. It is sewn the same way as a hand-stitched buttonhole. It is used on tailored coats and suits made from thick fabrics. It is also used on casual-wear fabric, such as drill, canvas or denim.

The hole at the end takes the strain of the fabric. A button shank keeps fabric from dragging. Use an awl, sharp stiletto or leather punch. Make a hole at the end of the buttonhole marking nearest the opening edge.

Place a pin across the opposite end of the marking and slash. Overcast cut edges all around.

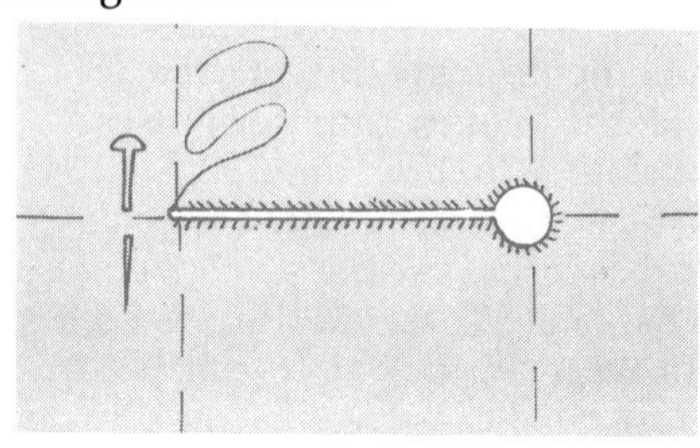

Work the buttonhole-stitch. Finish the straight end with long stitches to form a bar tack. Work the buttonhole-stitch through fabric and across bars. Finish securely.

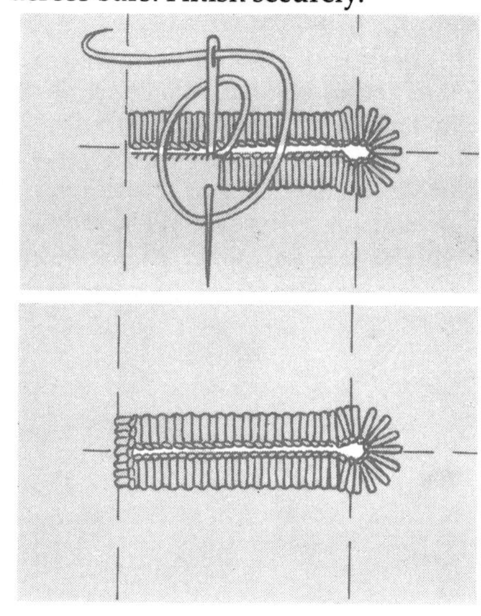

INTERFACING

Choose a suitable interfacing to go with the fabric. A light fabric needs light interfacing. Interfacing gives the buttonhole strength and support.

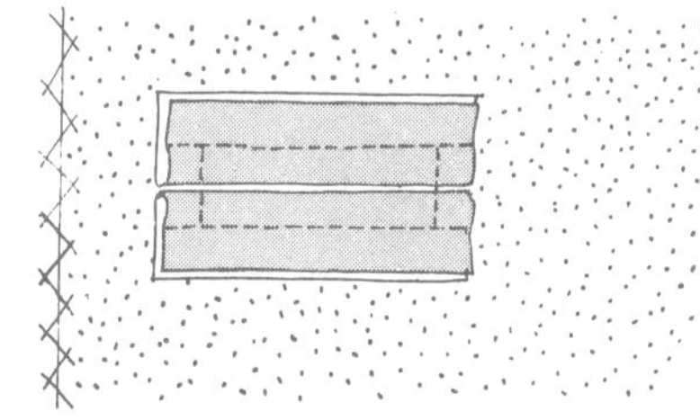

For heavier fabric, a heavier interfacing is used.

A buttonhole is made through fabric and lining *before* interfacing is attached. A slot slightly longer than the buttonhole is cut in the interfacing. When placed in position, the bound buttonhole is pulled through to the wrong-side. The interfacing is slip-stitched to it all around.

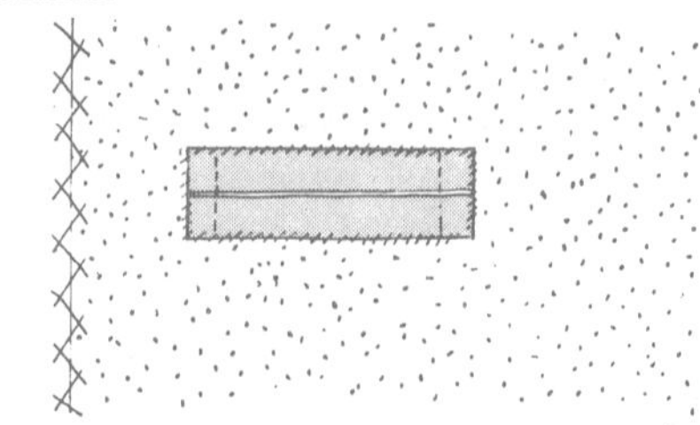

On many garments, only a small area around the buttonhole position needs to be supported. This should be about 3/4 inch wider and larger than the actual buttonhole. A piece of interfacing is cut and tacked over the buttonhole position on the wrong-side of the fabric. The two layers are treated as one.

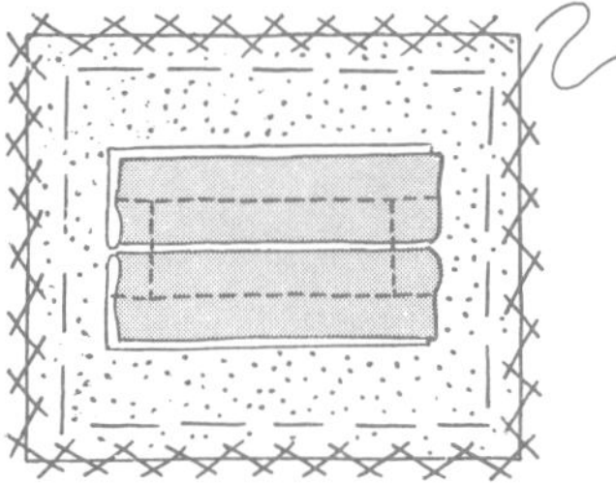

POSITIONING

Usually the top buttonhole is placed half the width of the button, plus 1/4 inch, below the neckline edge. On a dress with a front opening, the last buttonhole is 3-1/4 to 5 inches from the bottom. It is *never* on the hem.

Mark the position of the buttonholes with basting. If the fabric is delicate, tack the lines by hand. Do not mark the fabric. Mark the center-front line. Mark horizontal and vertical lines for positioning and length of buttonholes.

Make markings for the position of the buttonhole on the *right-side* of the fabric. The buttonholes follow the grain line exactly if the garment is cut on the straight grain.

For single-breasted, center-front openings, the center-front line of the underlap is the position for buttons. The center-front line of the overlap is the position for the buttonholes.

For double-breasted garments, place buttons at equal distances on either side of the center-front line on the underlap. Mark buttonholes in corresponding positions from the center line of the overlap.

On most patterns, buttonhole positions are shown by a single line. This line has a short line at right angles on one end for horizontal buttonholes and at both ends for vertical ones.

Horizontal Buttonholes—These begin about 1/8 inch to the side of the button nearest the closure. This allows for the strain or pull caused by body movement at the closure point. Use this position for buttonholes where the closure must take considerable strain.

Vertical Buttonholes—Start these slightly above the point where the button is attached and exactly on the center line. The strain is taken at the top of the buttonhole. Use vertical buttonholes only on openings where there is not much strain.

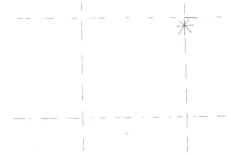

COLLARS

Collars can be the focal point of the garment. They are always in view, so it is necessary to cut, stitch and fit them perfectly. Many different collars are used in dress design, but they are all adaptations of a few basic shapes.

Some collars rise from the neckline and turn down to create a roll. The roll must be smooth, without any rippling or twisting. The underside of a rolled collar should never show.

Interfacing may be needed to keep the shape and body of a collar. The type of interfacing used depends on the weight of the fabric and design of the collar.

Making Collars

Check the size of the collar against the neckline if pattern alterations have been made. Carefully follow pattern layout instructions. The direction of the grain on the collar is important.

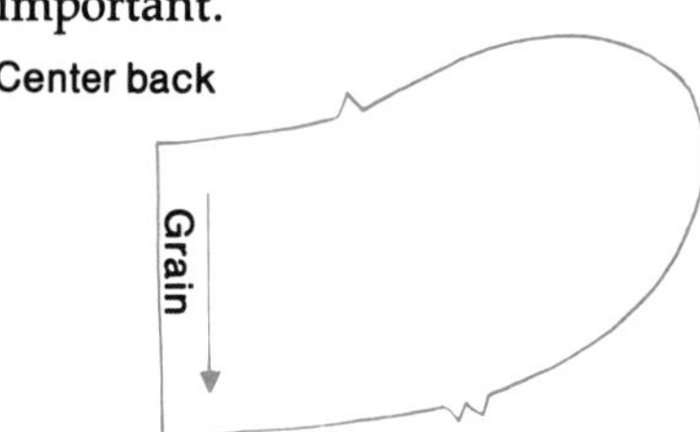

For a collar with a shaped neckline, the grain should run parallel with the center back. Straight collars are cut on the straight grain or the true cross grain.

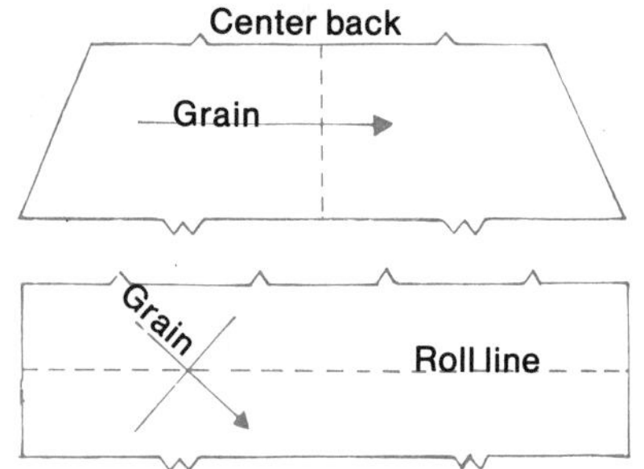

Cut interfacing the same size and shape as the collar. Or cut interfacing to fit inside the stitching line for thick fabrics. Interfacing is hand-stitched to the fitting line on the wrong-side of the collar. Non-woven interfacing is excellent because it does not stretch. Cut woven interfacing on the same grain as the collar.

Transfer pattern markings to the collar and undercollar. Include center-front, center-back and shoulder lines. Pin and tack interfacing to the wrong-side of the collar. Trim the interfacing close to tacking on the neck edge or use iron-on interfacing. Trim or miter corners inside the seam line on the interfacing to reduce bulk.

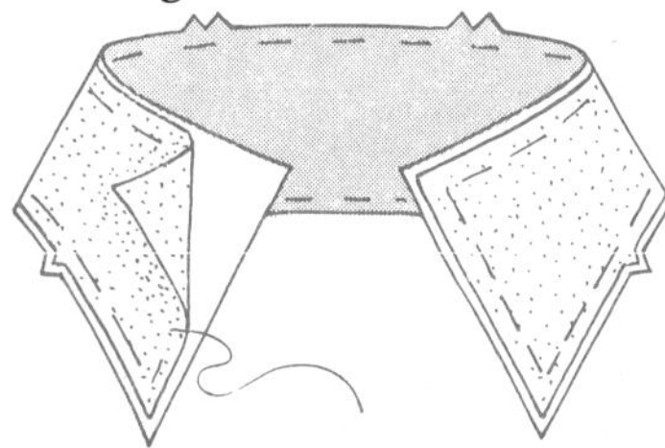

Place the right-side of the undercollar on the right-side of the collar. Match fitting marks. Pin and tack, leaving the neck edge open.

Machine-stitch the three layers together in the direction of the straight grain. Leave the neck edge open. Start at the collar center and stitch to one end. Repeat for the other half, overlapping a few stitches.

If the interfacing is hand-stitched, machine-stitch the collar and undercollar off the edge of the interfacing. On a pointed collar, sew one stitch across the corner to make it easier to turn.

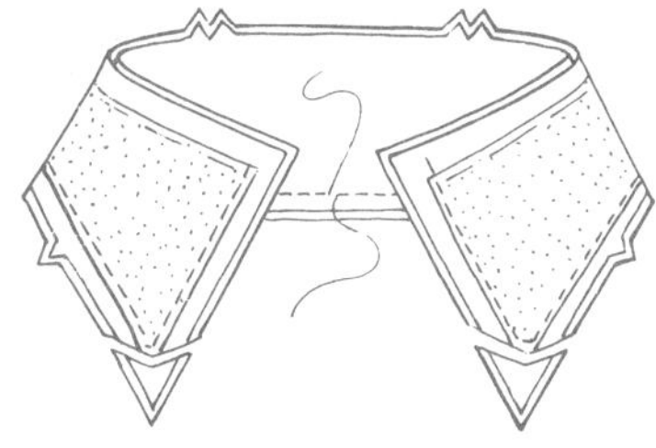

Press the stitching, and trim the interfacing close to machine-stitching. Trim the undercollar seam allowance to 1/8 inch. Trim collar seam allowance to 1/4 inch. This is called *layering*. It eliminates the thick ridge at the edge of the finished collar.

Clip curved collars almost to stitching about every 1/2 inch along edges. For pointed collars, snip edges diagonally across the points. Cut corners back.

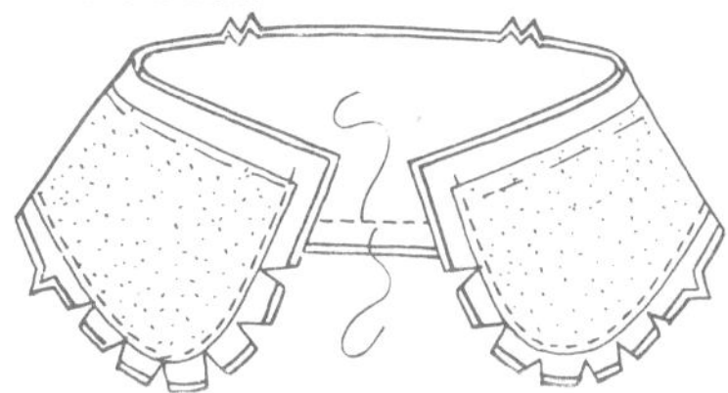

Turn the collar so the right-side of the fabric is outside. Use a knitting needle on the inside to push out the points. A pin or needle can be used outside to pull out corners.

Separate the neck edges, and press the seam open from the inside. Roll

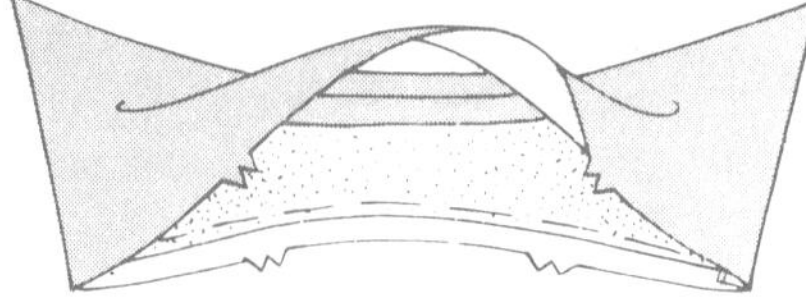

the collar edges, curves and points gently between fingers and thumbs. Do this until the stitching is visible at the edge. Pull the undercollar slightly until the stitching is not visible from the top. Tack, press and top-stitch, if required.

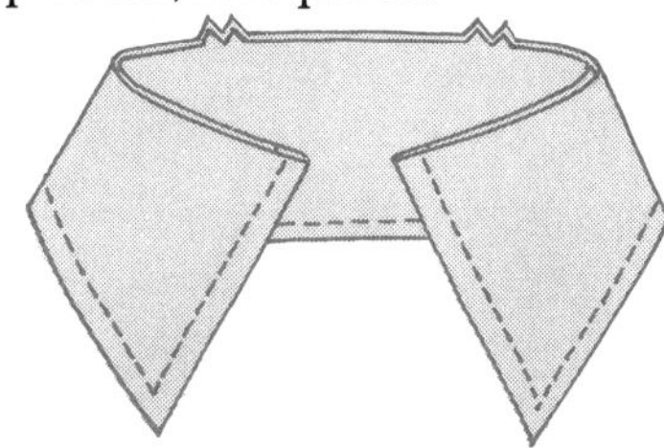

ATTACHING COLLARS

A flat, shaped collar is attached with a facing. A standing or rolled collar is stitched directly to the garment without added bulk. Collars on shirts sometimes combine both methods. The fronts of the neck are faced, but the collar is hemmed at the back. Tailored shirts are usually attached to a band, so the collar rolls over at the top of the band.

Whichever method you use, position the collar accurately on the garment. Match notches and balance points exactly. Be sure the collar is symmetrical at the center front.

Put together and tack two-piece collars before pinning them to the garment. This prevents a wide gap from developing at the center front or center back.

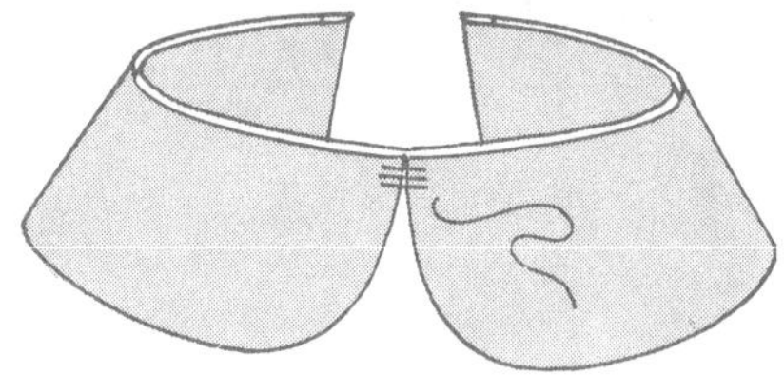

Types of Collars

FLAT COLLAR

This collar is also called a *Peter Pan collar.* It is one of the easiest to make because it has a curved neck edge. It may vary in width or be made in two pieces with a tiny gap at both back and front. It can have a curved, pointed or scalloped edge. There is little roll because it lies flat on the bodice. The collar and undercollar are cut from the same pattern piece.

Attach flat collars cut in one piece without a facing if the neckline is worn fastened. Otherwise hemming-stitches show. Usually a facing is used.

Collar without Facing—Separate the neck edges of the collar and undercollar. Pin the undercollar to the right-side of the garment at the neckline. Carefully match pattern markings. Gently ease where necessary and tack.

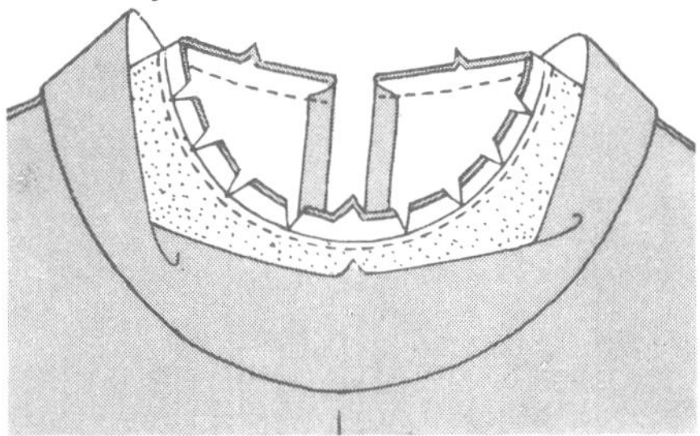

Machine-stitch along the fitting line. Press well and remove tacking. Trim the seam allowances to remove bulk. Clip curves where necessary. Press seam allowances up into the collar.

Roll the collar over your hand so the upper collar is slightly stretched. Turn under the seam allowance on the neck edge of the upper collar. Tack the folded edge down to cover stitching. Match balance points. Hem neatly in place, picking up original machine-stitches.

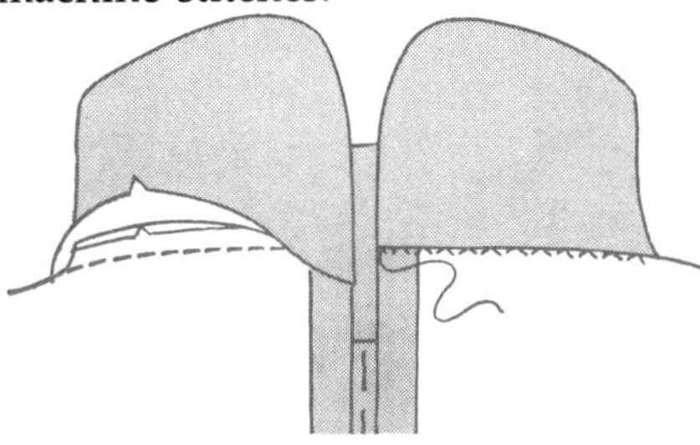

Bias-Strip-Facing Collar—Pin and tack the collar in place. Cut a piece of bias tape or matching fabric on the cross grain. Make it the length of the collar. With right-sides together, pin and tack the tape on the neck edge fitting line. Machine-stitch through all layers along the fitting line.

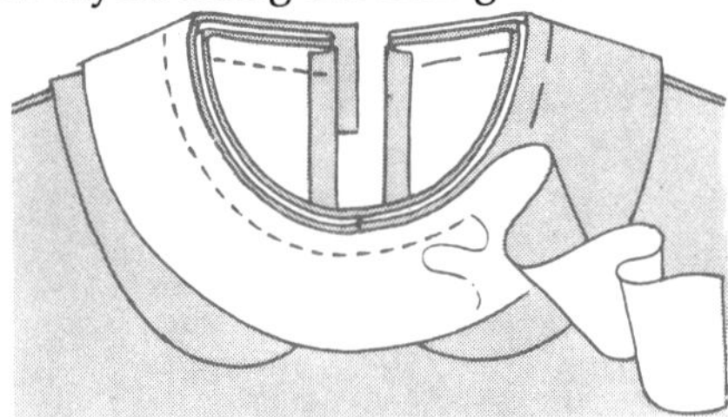

Remove tacking. Trim seam allowances to avoid bulk. Press the raw edges and bias strip away from the collar. Turn the bias strip on the wrong-side, and fold under the raw edge. Tack and hem in place.

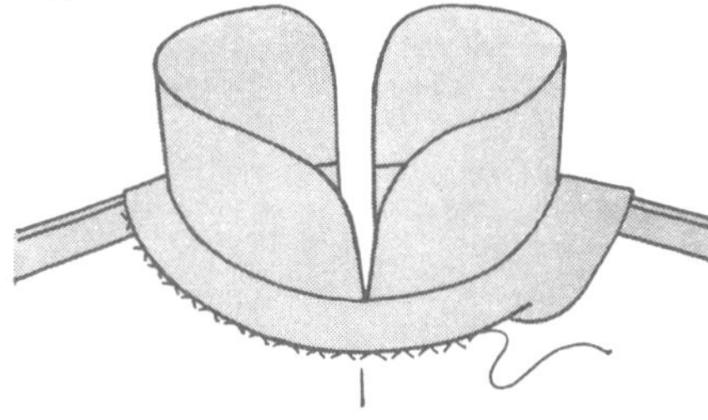

Shaped-Facing Collar—Prepare the facing by turning under the notched edge. Stitch the edge as shown in the pattern instructions. Pin and tack the facing to the neck edge over the collar, with right-sides together.

Machine-stitch along the fitting line. Trim and clip seams. Press the

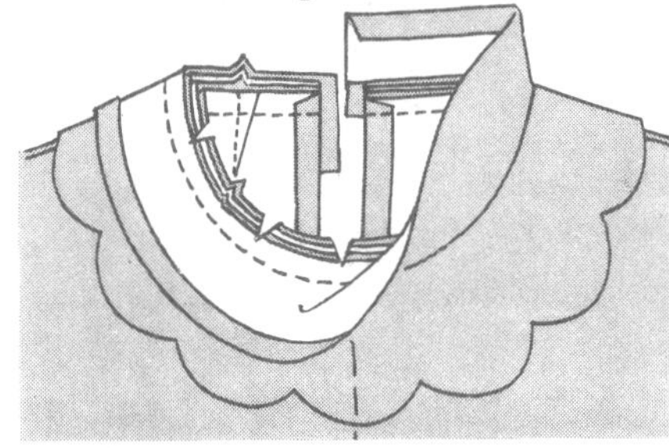

facing to the inside. Hem or slip-stitch the facing in place, at shoulder seams only.

ROLLED COLLAR

Light to medium fabrics may have collars with a shaped stand. There is a pronounced roll around the neck. The collar may stand away from the neck. It is usually cut on the bias in one piece. Rolled collars usually have a two-piece undercollar and a slightly larger upper collar. Both collar pieces are cut on the cross grain.

Construction Method—Prepare the bodice. Make the collar following pattern instructions. The undercollar may need stretching to fit. Press the upper collar so the seam is not visible at the edge.

Shape the collar to make the roll line. Tack the neck edges together while it is in this position. Stitch thread in a marking line along the roll line.

Self-Facing Collar—Stay-stitch the garment neck edge and self-facing. Pin and tack the collar to the garment, with right-sides together.

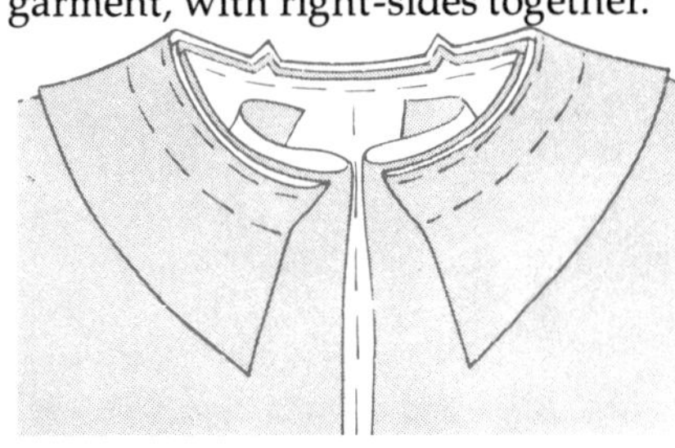

Join the back neck facing to the garment. Finish the notched edge by turning under the seam allowance, and edge-stitch it.

Pin and tack the facing over the collar. Machine-stitch along the fitting line, with the facing-side up.

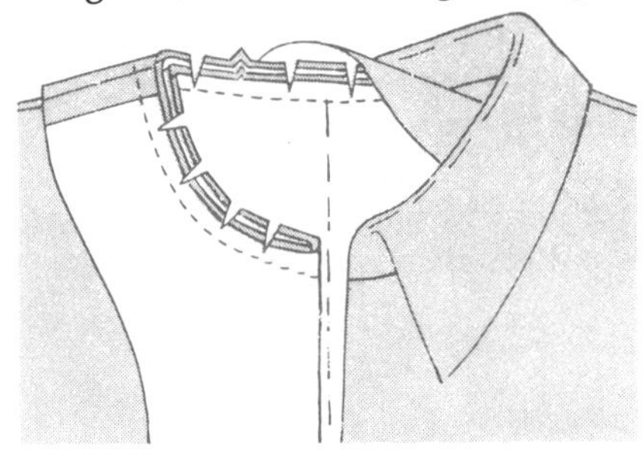

Trim seam allowances, layering to avoid bulk. Clip through all thicknesses almost to the stitching. Press the facing to the inside. Tack close to the neck seam. Slip-stitch the facing in place at the shoulder seams. Remove the trace thread from the roll line.

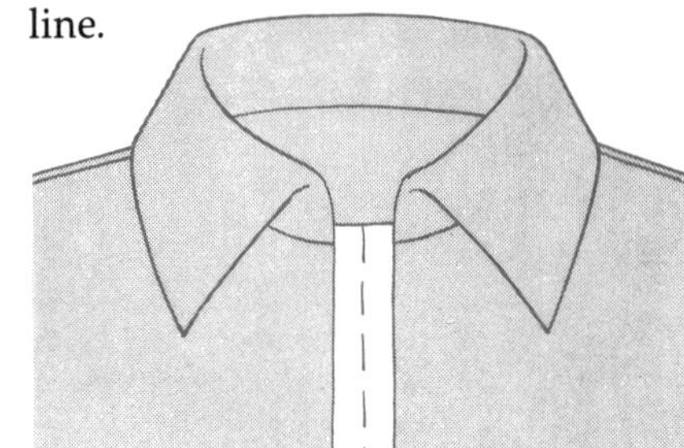

NOTCHED COLLAR

Sometimes called a *convertible collar,* this is a rolled collar with lapels. It has a front opening, and usually one edge laps over the other.

Tailoring techniques may be needed if thick fabric is chosen. For light fabric, make the collar, and attach it the same way as a rolled collar.

For medium fabrics, join the two undercollar sections together. Iron or sew on interfacing. Pin, tack and stitch the undercollar to the garment neck edge. Match notches. Clip curves almost to the stitching. Trim seam allowances, and press the seam open.

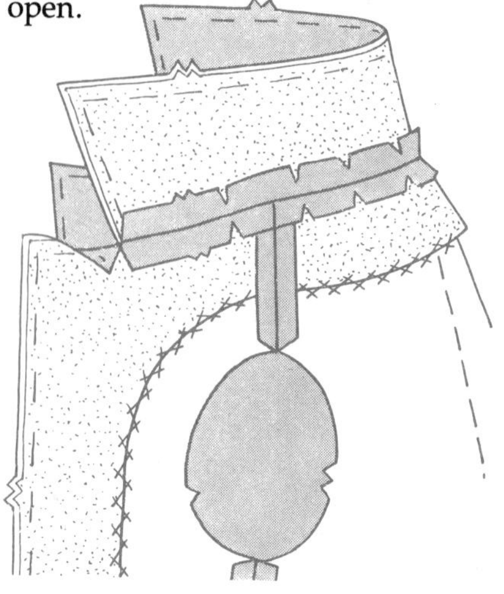

Pin, tack and stitch the upper collar to the neck edge of the facing. Clip edges where necessary, and press the seam open. Finish the unstitched edge of facing as directed in pattern instructions.

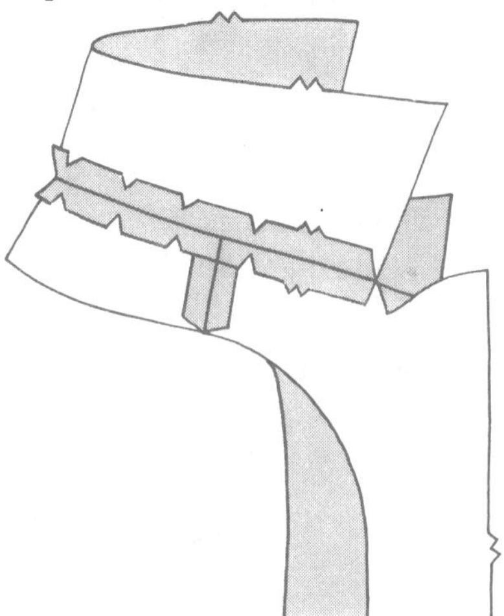

Pin and tack together the garment and the completed collar. Have right-sides together at the neck seam only. Try on the garment without sewing other seams.

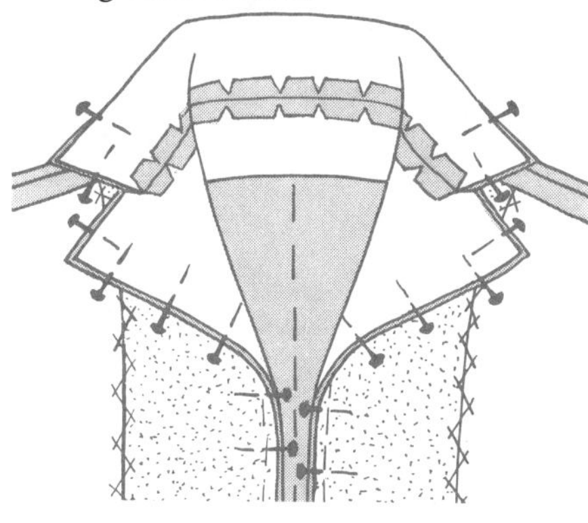

Shape the collar so it has a smooth roll and sits well on the garment. The garment and undercollar seam allowances should not show beyond the collar and facing. Pin the edges of the collar together to hold the required position.

Tack and stitch collar pieces together. Ease and stretch where necessary. Starting at the neck seam, stitch the facing and garment together along the fitting line. At the corners, take one stitch across the point.

Trim seam allowances, layering to avoid bulk. Press the seams open; then press in the direction they need to be turned.

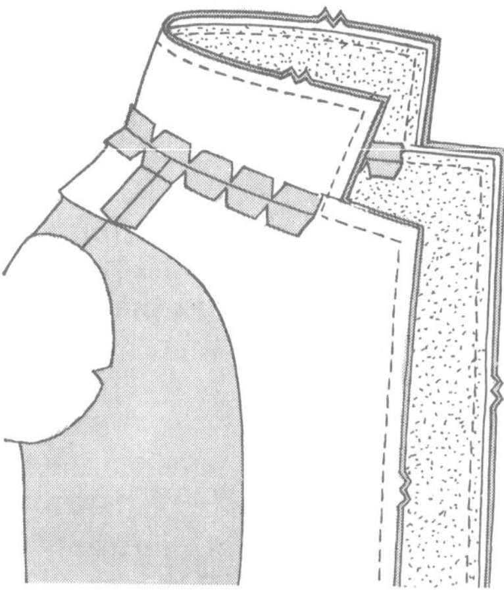

Turn the collar to the right-side and press. Try on the garment and check the way the collar and lapels roll. Pin the roll to hold it in place. Pin again above the neck seam.

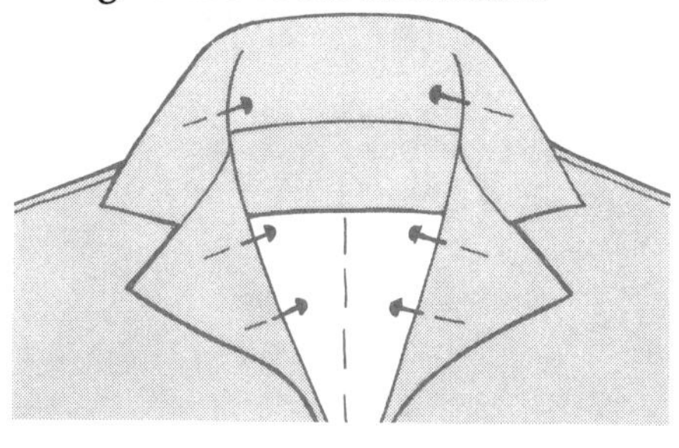

Slightly ease the upper collar over at the edge to hide the seam. Ease the facing edge over on the top of each lapel the same way.

Lift the facing, and blind-stitch the neck seams loosely together. Anchor the facing in place at the garment seams. Remove all pins and tacking, and press.

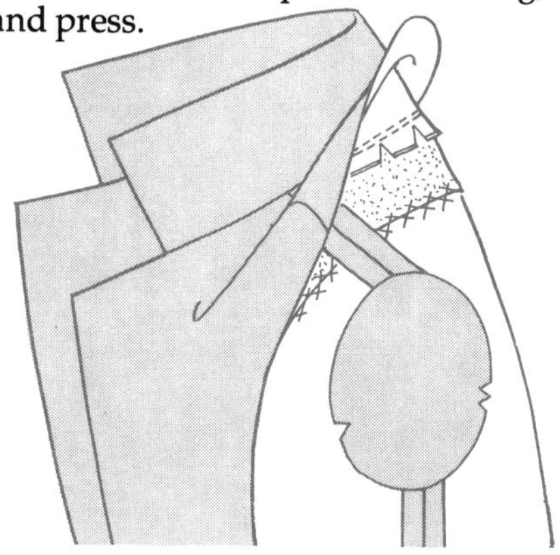

SHAWL COLLAR

This is another kind of roll collar. The upper collar and lapels are cut in one piece. This collar is found on dressing gowns and wrap-around coats. The edge of the collar may be curved, notched or scalloped.

Join the two pieces of the undercollar, and press the seam open. Iron on or catch-stitch

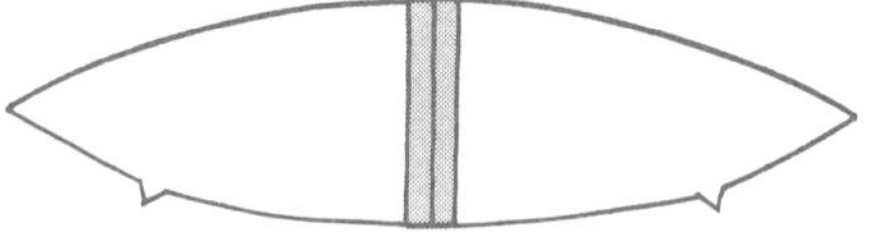

non-woven interfacing to the wrong-side of the undercollar and garment along seam lines.

Pin, tack and stitch the undercollar to the garment neck edge. Ease and clip along the curved edge. Try the garment on to check the fit.

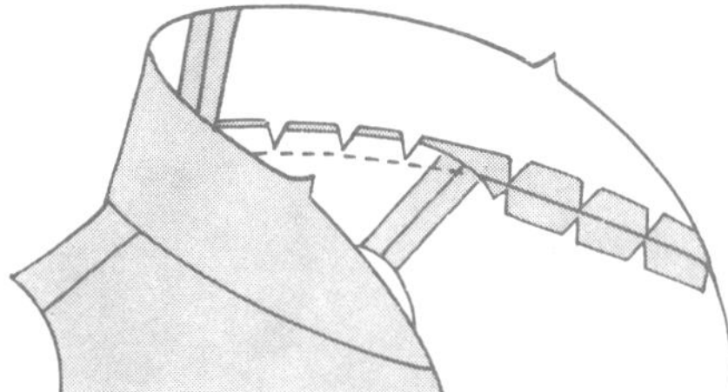

Join the upper collar and facing at the center back. Press the seam open. Turn the seam allowance under on the unstitched edge of this piece. Clip curves to make them lie flat. Stitch, trim and press.

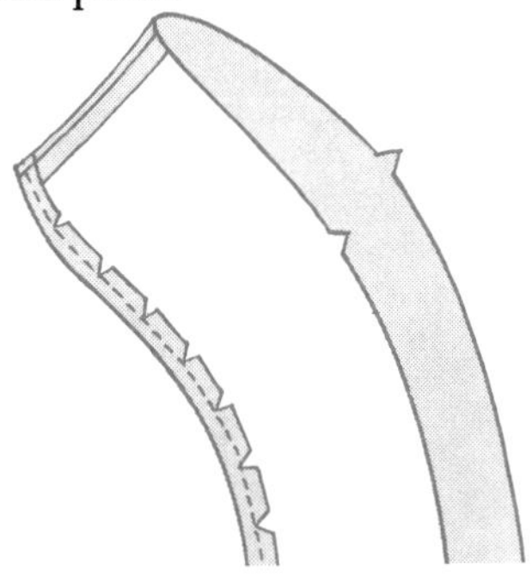

With right-sides together, pin and tack the facing to the undercollar and front of the garment. Match notches and ease to fit. Stitch along the seam line. Clip curves and trim seam allowances. Press. Turn the facing to inside and press again. Slip-stitch the facing over the back-neck seam.

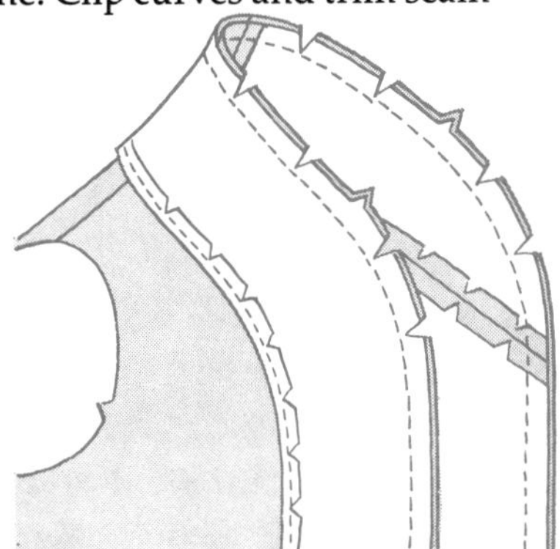

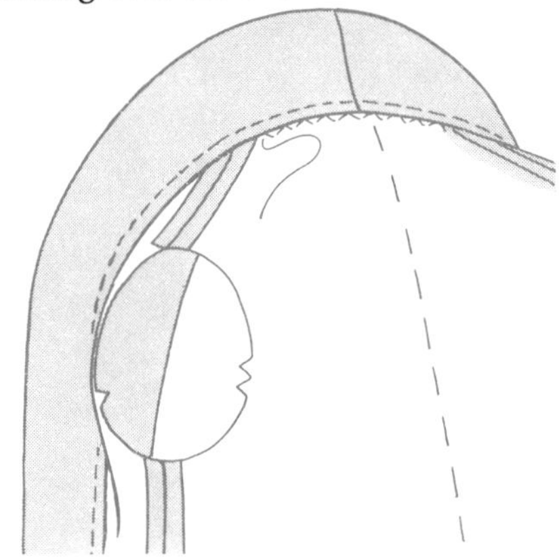

COLLAR WITH STAND

Shirt and tailored-blouse collars are sewn to a band that is attached to the neck edge of the garment. These collars have little roll and are often buttoned up to the neck at the front.

Make the collar and top-stitch, if desired. Measure the neck size and adjust pattern piece, if necessary.

Trim the interfacing for the band. Catch-stitch or iron it to one piece of the band in the seam line. Pin and tack it to the undercollar, with right-sides together.

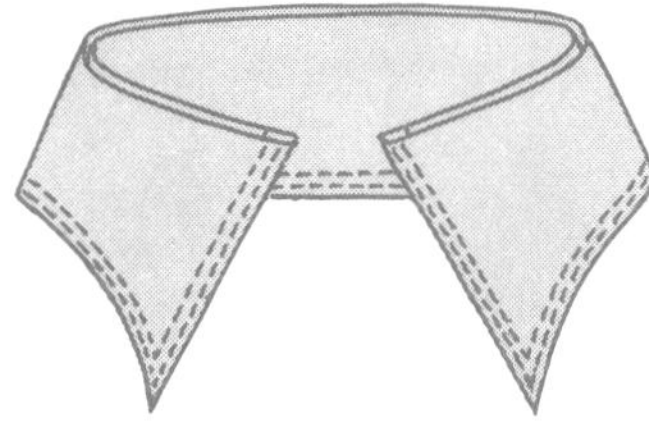

Pin and tack the other band piece to the upper collar, with right-sides together. Clip the seam allowance as necessary so it lies flat.

Stitch ends and upper edges together along the seam line. Stitch to within 5/8 inch of the neck edges. Leave neck edges open.

Trim seam allowances, layering to reduce bulk. Clip almost to the stitching so seam lies flat.

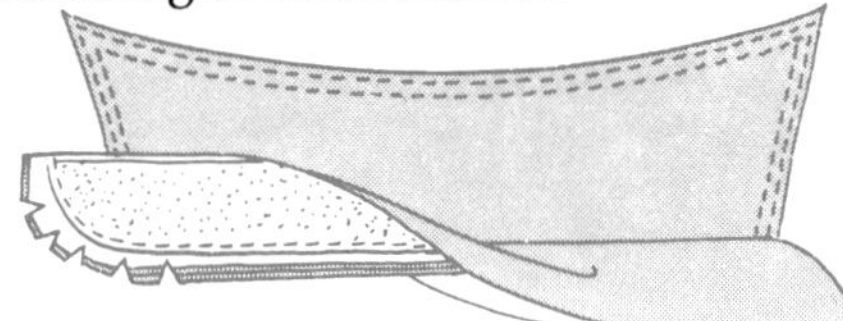

Press the band away from the collar so the collar is enclosed in the band at the neck edge. Prepare the garment, including the front opening. Stay-stitch the garment neck edge.

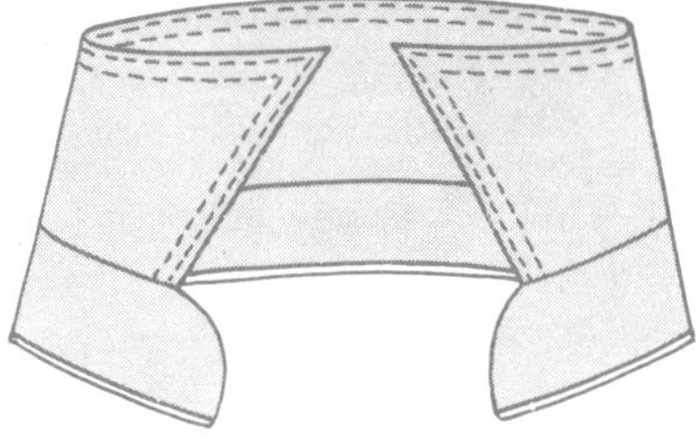

With right-sides together, pin and tack the interfaced band to the garment neck edge. If necessary, clip it so it lies flat.

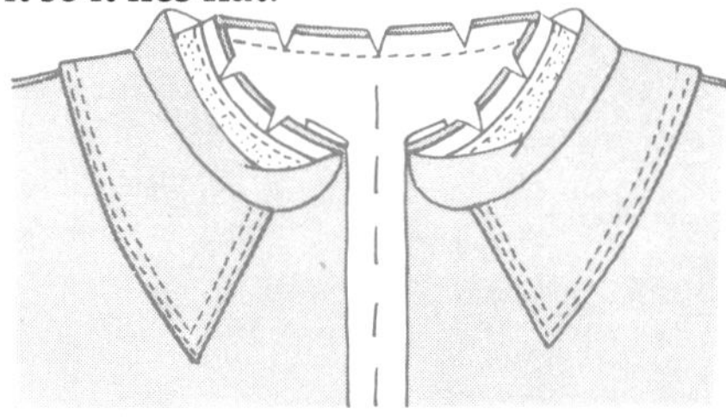

Stitch, trim and layer seam allowances to reduce bulk. Press seam allowances toward the band on the front edge. Trim. Pin the folded edge over the seam, and slip-stitch in place.

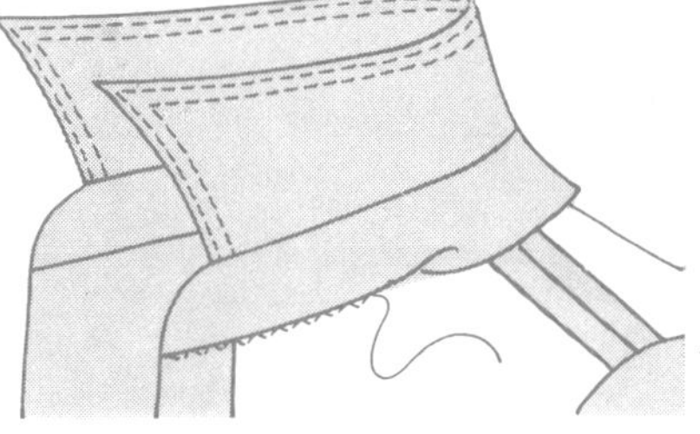

STANDING COLLAR

This collar is also known as a *Mandarin collar.* It can take many forms, according to the style of the garment. It is often attached so the collar finishes the neck edge. It may be fitted stiff and close to the neck or take a softer, looser shape. It may be cut in one or two sections, and have a straight or curved finished edge.

COLLARS

Interface one collar section. Use non-woven interfacing or cut a bias strip of woven interfacing. Iron it on or catch-stitch it in the seam line.

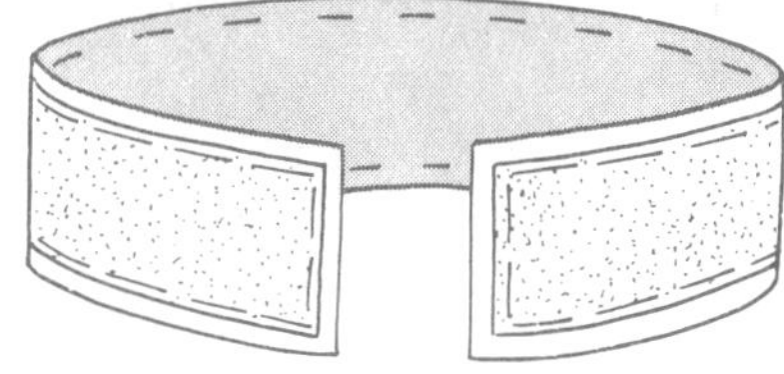

For a one-piece collar, fold it in half lengthwise with right-sides together. Stitch ends to within 5/8 inch of the neck edge. If the collar is two pieces, stitch around three sides but not the neck edge. Trim, turn and press the ends only. Do not press along the length.

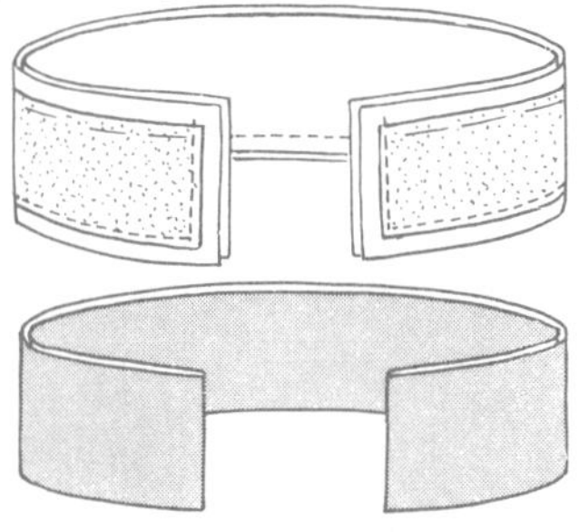

Prepare the garment by putting in the zipper or making buttonholes. Pin, tack and stitch the interfaced side of the collar to the garment neck edge. Clip seam allowances as necessary. Layer to remove bulk.

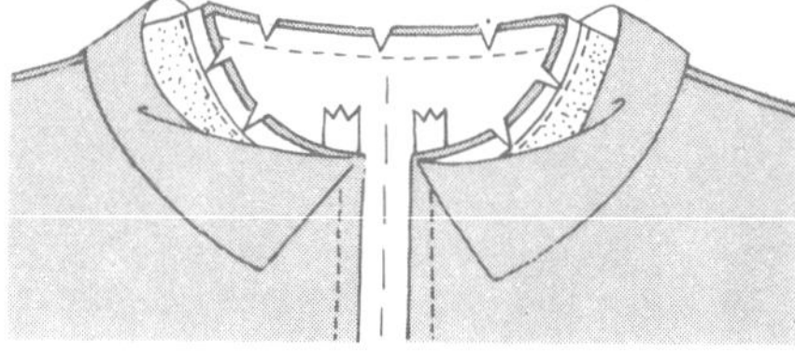

Press the seam open, and press it toward the collar. Trim most of the seam allowance off the remaining collar edge at the neck. Turn the seam line under, and tack it down over the seam. Slip-stitch it in place. Pick up machine-stitches rather than fabric.

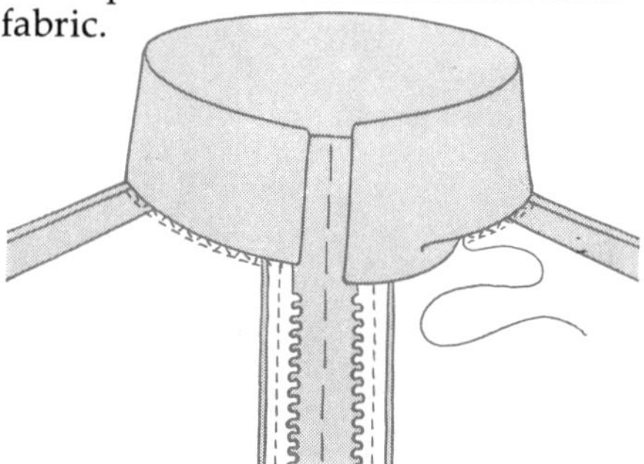

The collar may be top-stitched. It is usually fastened with hooks and eyes.

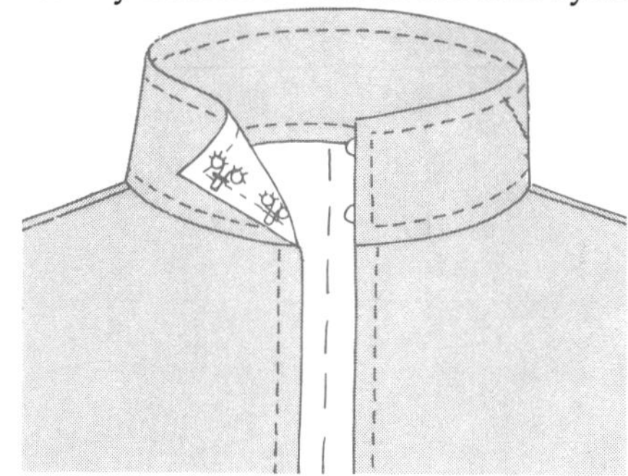

BIAS-TURNOVER COLLAR

This is another type of standing collar. It is often confused with a rolled collar because there is a roll at the neck. It is better known as a *turtleneck.* If cut high and close to the neck, it is also called a *funnel collar.* The collar is one piece and must be cut on the cross grain to make a smooth roll.

Stay-stitch the bodice neck edge. Interface and face the bodice as in the pattern instructions. Make buttonholes or put in a zipper.

Attach light interfacing to half of the collar. Extend it over the fold line by 5/8 inch. Iron on or catch-stitch it in the seam lines. Fold the right-sides

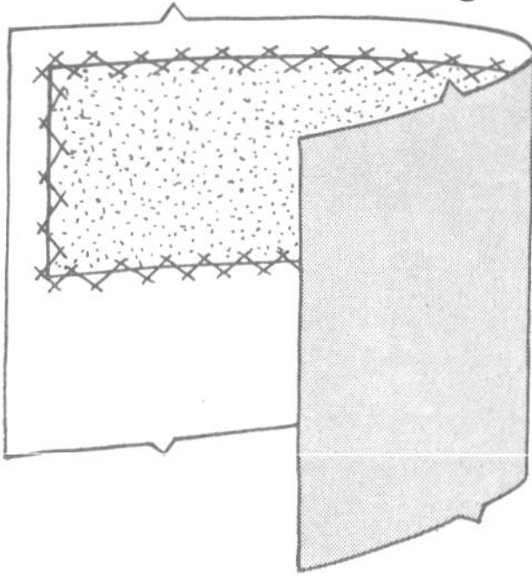

of the collar together. Stitch both ends to within 5/8 inch of the neck edge.

Trim seam allowances, press and turn the collar to the right-side. Press the ends only on the right-side, not along the length.

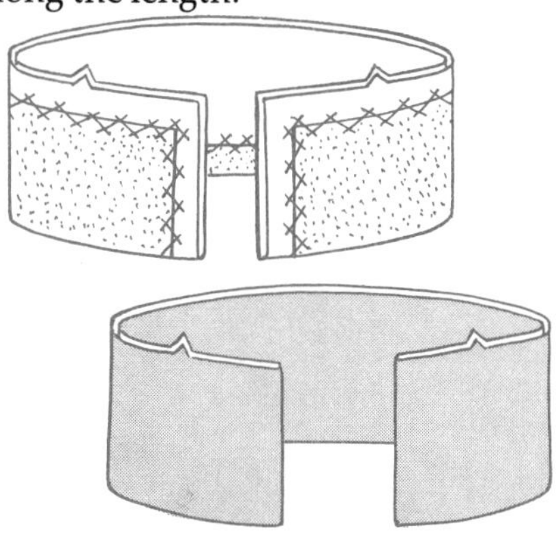

Pin and tack the interfaced collar piece to the neck of the garment, with right-sides together. Match notches.

Clip seam allowances and ease the collar for a good fit. Stitch and trim seam allowances, layering to reduce bulk. Press edges toward the collar.

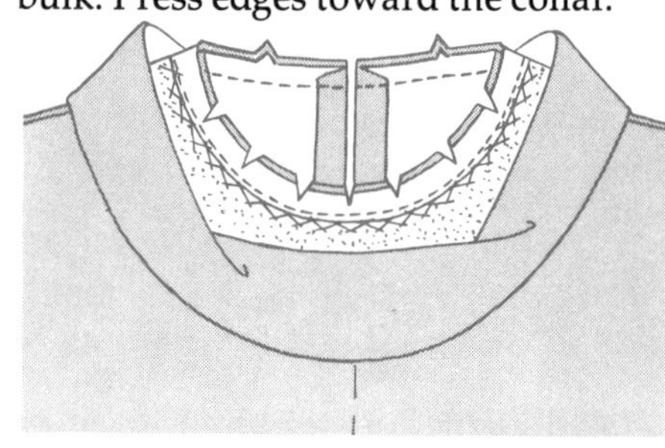

Fold the collar in place. Try on the garment to check fit. Ease the collar over to make a smooth roll line. Sew a thread trace line through all the layers.

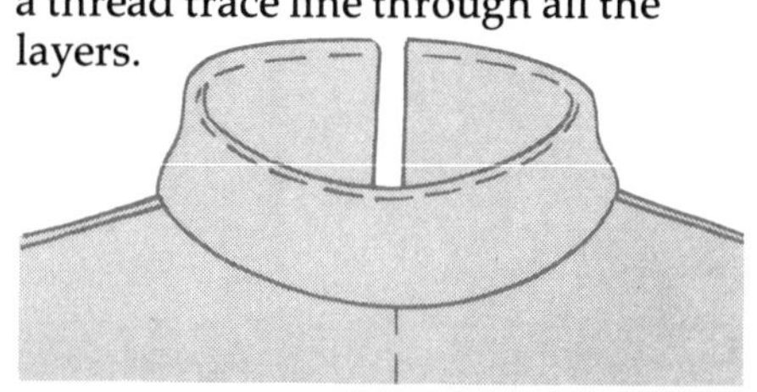

Remove, trim and turn in the raw edge so it covers the seam. Slip-stitch it in place, and remove all tacking.

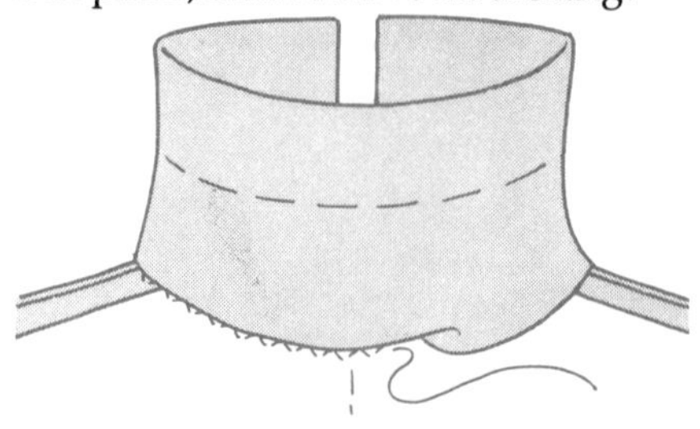

Turn the collar over, and add hooks and eyes as required.

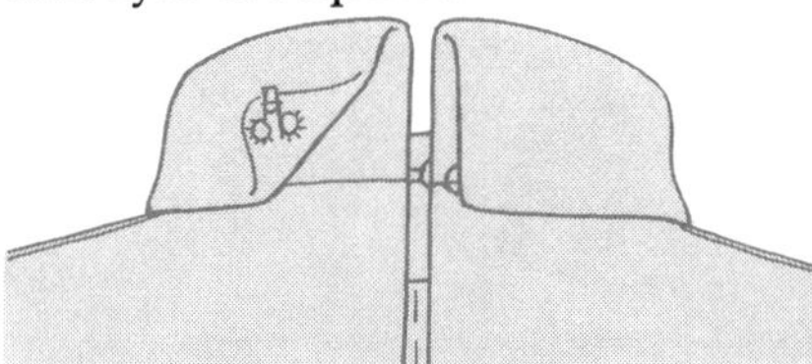

CUFFS

Most cuffs are made of two layers of fabric and one layer of interfacing. All three pieces are cut on the bias. Iron-on interfacing may be used. Trim seam edges, layer and press toward the cuff.

Cuffs are sewn on a sleeve before the sleeve is permanently sewn in place. If there is no opening at the bottom of the sleeve, the cuff must be large enough for the hand to go through. If cuffs are fastened or lapped over, a facing or placket finishes the opening in the sleeve.

Pin a sleeve in the garment to check whether the finished length of sleeve, plus cuff, is correct. Try the fit of the cuff around the wrist.

For buttoned cuffs, make bound buttonholes before stitching cuff sections together. Or complete the cuffs, and sew buttonholes by hand or machine.

Prepare sleeves by machine-stitching, trimming, finishing and pressing seams. Complete plackets or faced openings, if necessary.

On gathered sleeves, sew two rows of gathering-stitches around the bottom of the sleeves. Sew one row along the fitting line and one row 1/4 inch nearer the raw edges.

TURNED-BACK CUFF

Straight-Band Cuff—Place the ends of the cuff with right-sides together. Pin, tack and machine-stitch. Press the seam open. Fold the cuff in half, with right-sides outside. Interface one half, if required.

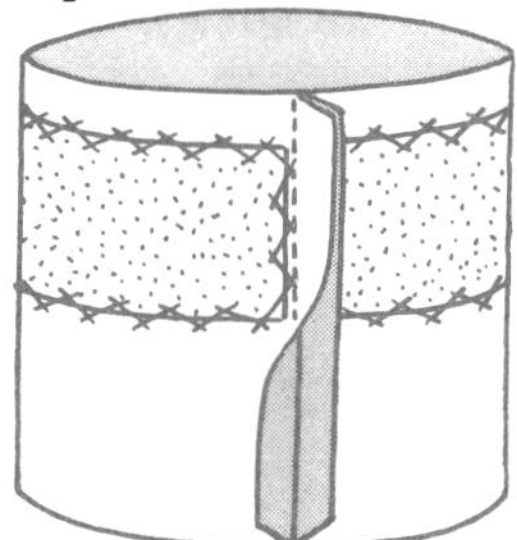

Stitch the raw edges together. Join cuffs on the wrong-side of the sleeve.

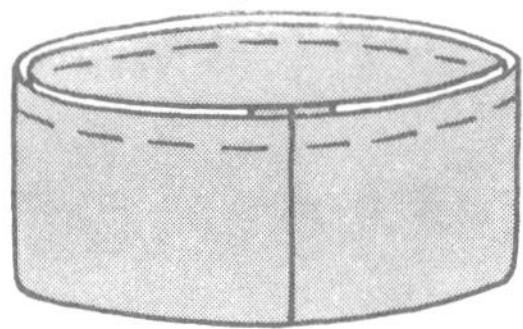

Seams should meet. Machine-stitch seams with two rows of stitching.

Overcast edges, and press flat. Cover with seam binding, then remove tacking. Turn the cuff back to the right-side of the sleeve.

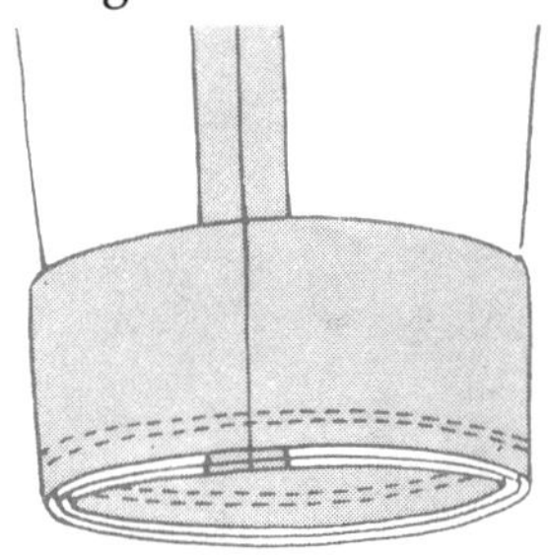

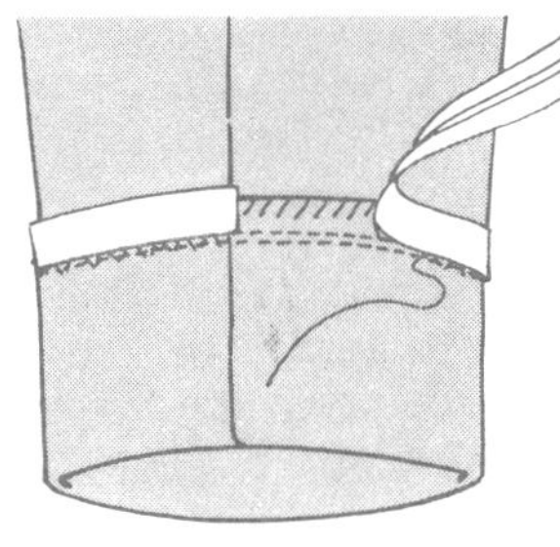

Shaped Cuff—Sew or iron interfacing between the top cuff and undercuff, inside the seam allowance. Spread the cuff open. Hide the seam by rolling the top edge slightly over. Tack the edge. Press to hold it in position.

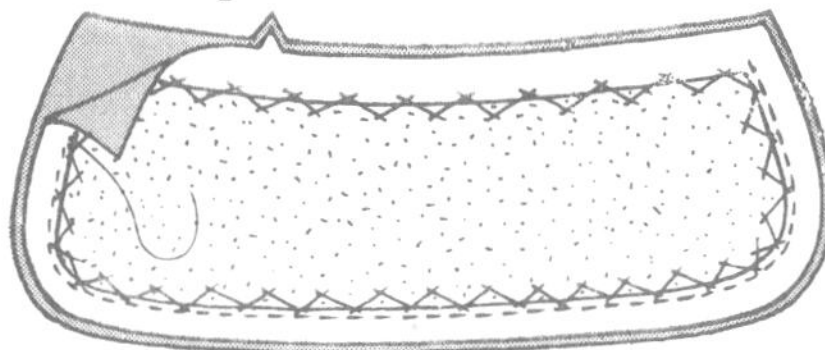

Turn the cuff to the right-side. Press the seam on the undercuff. Tack and machine-stitch the raw edges together.

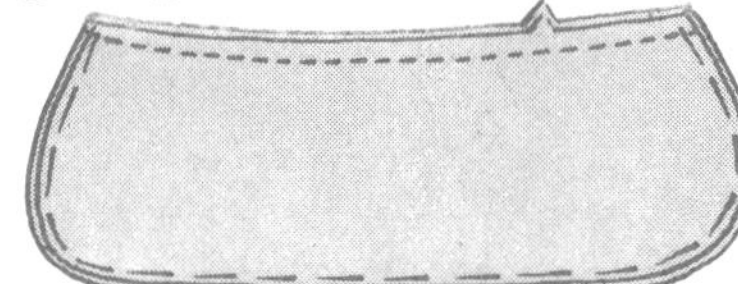

Put the right-side of the cuff to the wrong-side of the sleeve. Match markings. Tack and machine-stitch them together. Remove the tacking and press. Tack and stitch a bias strip

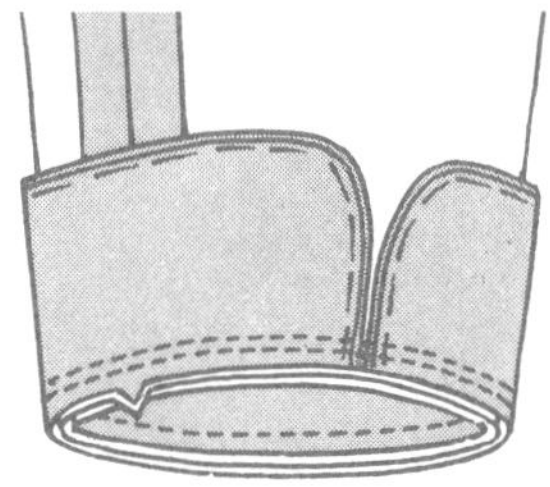

on the cuff side of the edge. Remove tacking and press.

Crease the cuff away from the sleeve. Machine-stitch the fold of the bias on the right-side of the sleeve.

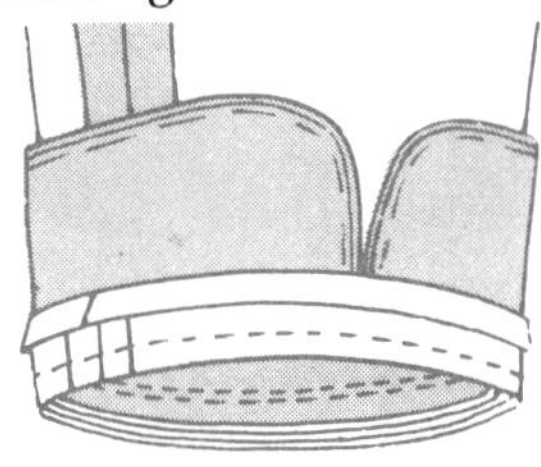

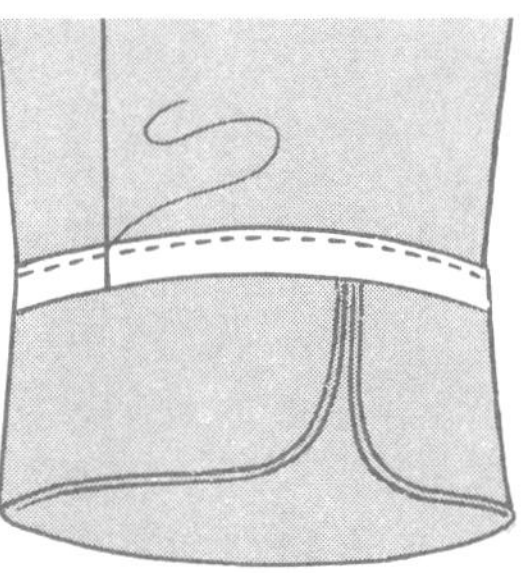

Cuff Shaped with Band—Sew or iron interfacing to the band or cuff. Tack and machine-stitch the top cuff and undercuff together. Remove tacking.

Ease the top piece over to hide the edge seam. Machine-stitch the short ends. Cut corners and turn to the right-side. Press seams toward the undercuff. Machine-stitch raw edges together.

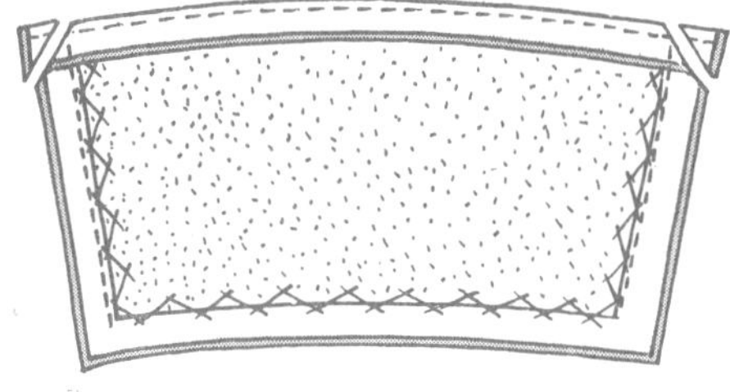

Put the right-side of one band to the right-side of the cuff. Tack and machine-stitch them together. Put the right-side of the other band to the undercuff. Use the first row of stitching as a guide to help position the band. Machine-stitch to the ends and down the sides.

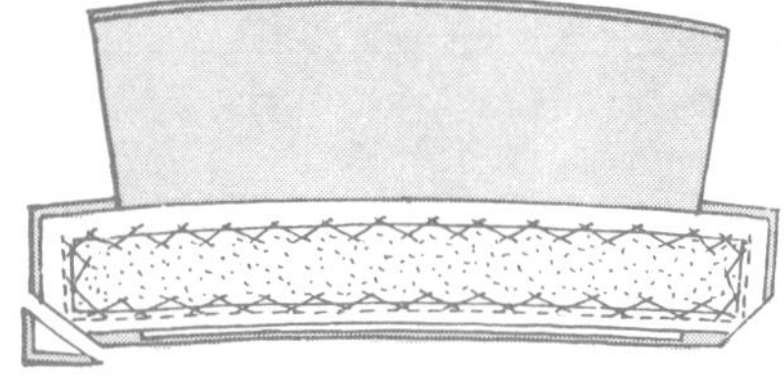

Cut the corners, and turn the band to the right-side. Place the right-side of the band to the wrong-side of the sleeve. Machine-stitch in place. Fold

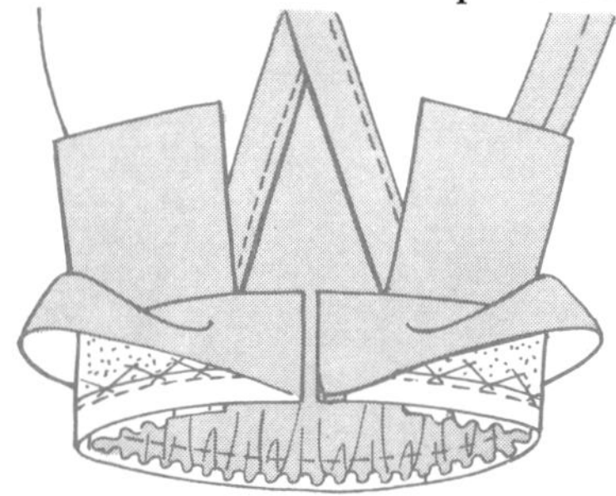

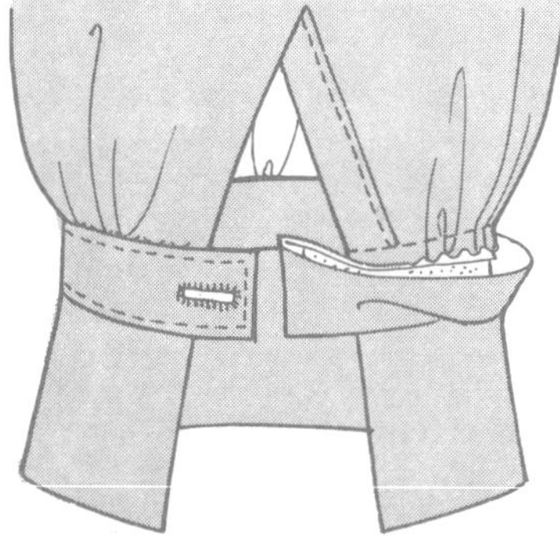

the cuff and the band away from the sleeve. Turn the loose edge of the band to cover the stitching. Edge-stitch it to the sleeve.

Cuff Cut-in-One with Sleeve— Interface the cuff area before sewing the sleeve seam. Use bias-cut or iron-on interfacing. Make it equal to the length of the cuff and twice the depth, plus two seam allowances.

Catch-stitch the interfacing at the fold line and roll line. Or use iron-on interfacing. Machine-stitch the sleeve

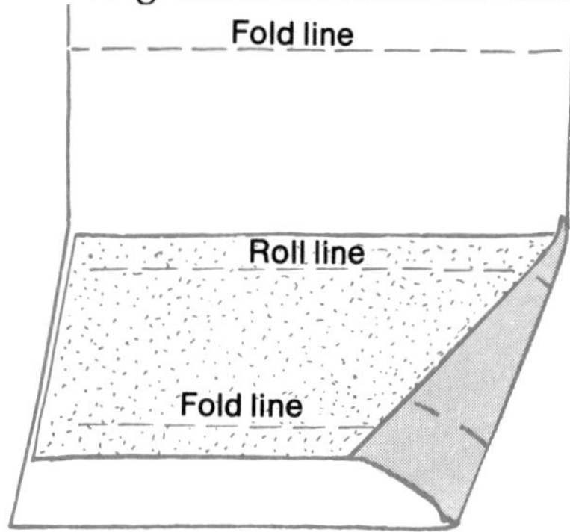

seam. The cuff area is usually tapered out at the bottom edge so the cuff turns back easily. Press seams open.

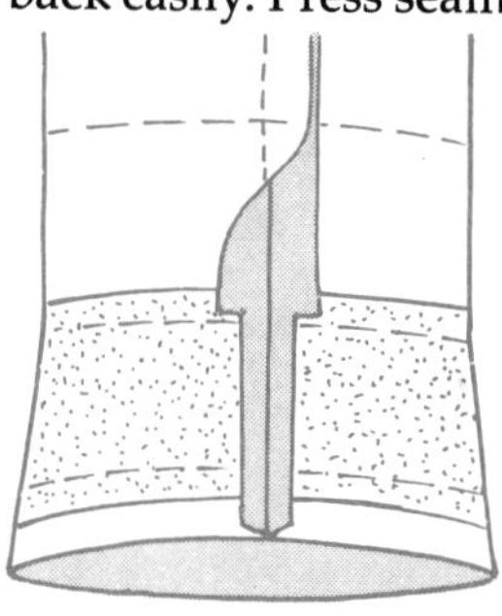

Turn up the bottom edge. Top-stitch or finish by machine. Turn the cuff inside along the fold line. Tack close to the fold.

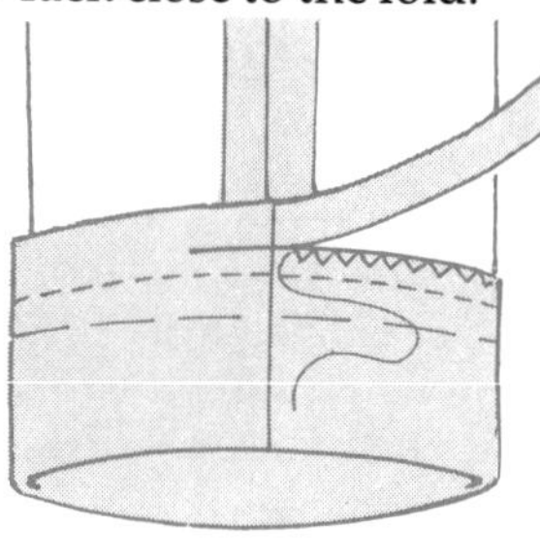

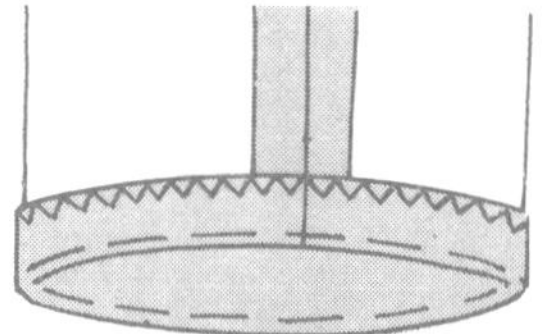

Roll the folded edge over on the right-side of the sleeve. This forms a cuff. Tack through all the layers to keep the rolled edge in place. Hem the edge to the inside of the sleeve, and press lightly.

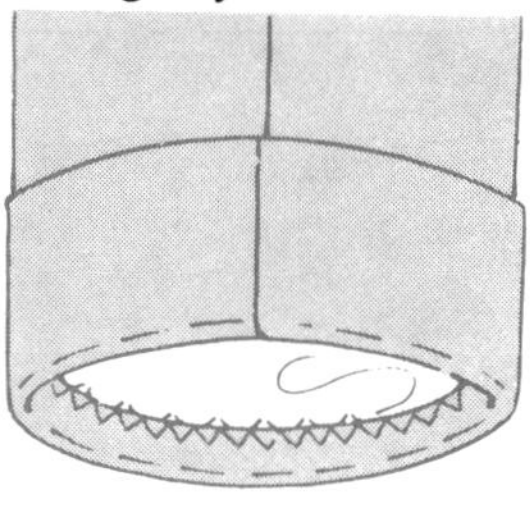

EXTENDED CUFF

Band Cuff— Adjust the sleeve edge to fit the wrist. It should be close, with enough room to push the hand through. Cut the rectangle of fabric to this length, plus two seam allowances. Make it twice the finished cuff depth, plus two finished edges.

Sew or iron interfacing to half of the cuff along the length. With right-sides together, join the short ends of the band. Press the seam open.

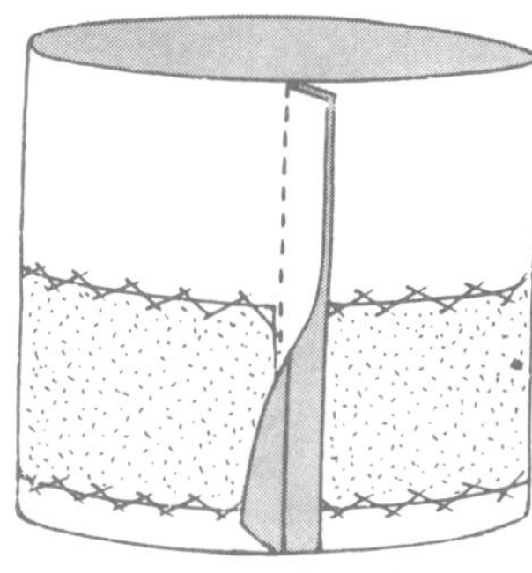

Place the right-side of the interfaced half to the right-side of the sleeve edge. Pin, tack and machine-stitch.

Trim and layer the seam. Press the

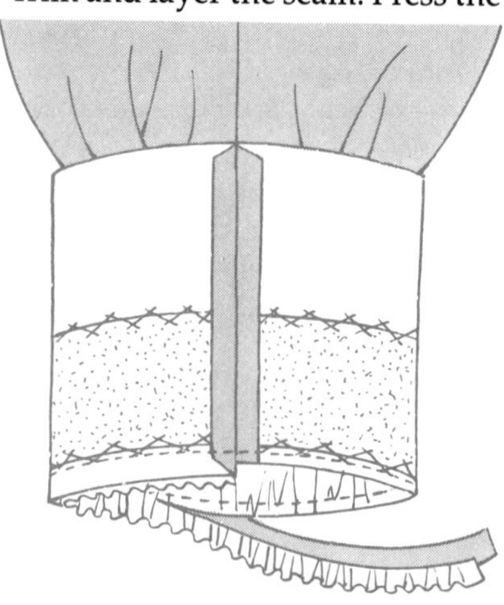

seam allowance in the cuff area. Turn the cuff to the inside along the fold line, with wrong-sides together.

Tack close to the fold. Trim the remaining seam allowance. Turn under the edge and hem in place.

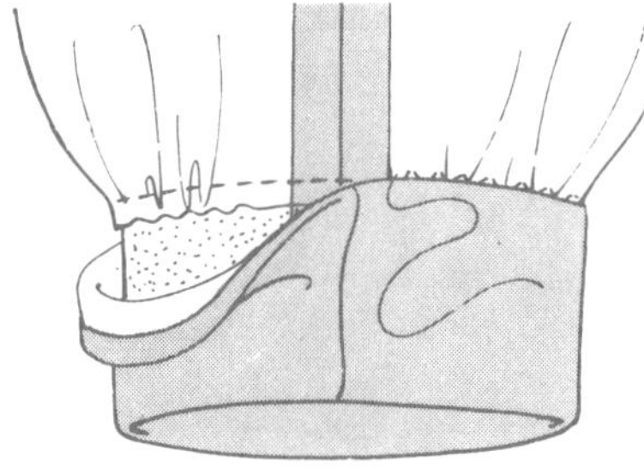

Pick up machine-stitching as you sew. Remove tacking and press.

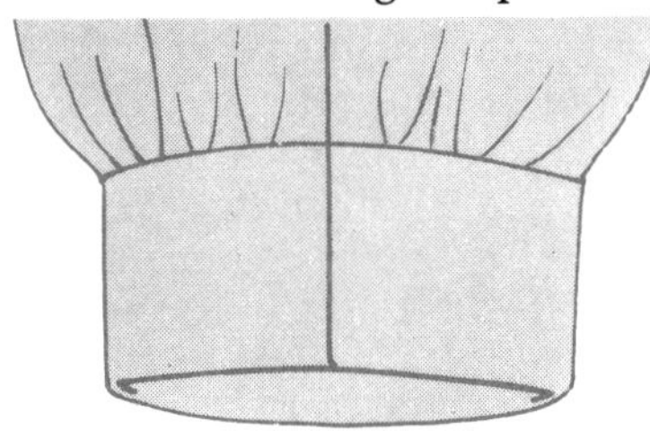

Alternative Method—If the sleeve has full gathers, the cuff is attached *before* sewing the sleeve or cuffs. It is easier to machine-stitch gathers in place along a flat surface. Sew sleeve and cuff seams in one continuous seam.

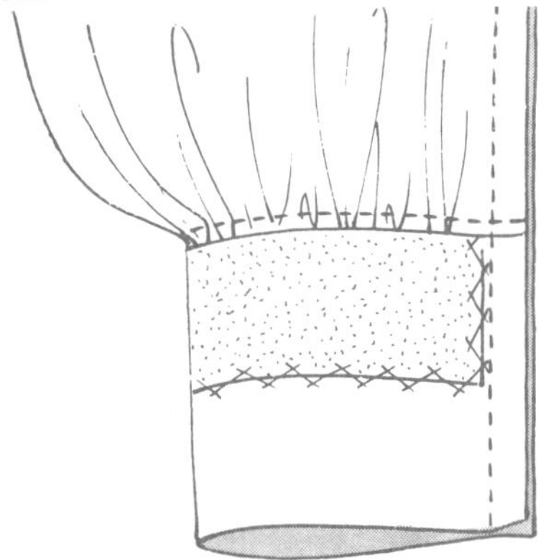

Lapped-Over Cuff—Full-length, gathered or pleated sleeves are usually sewn in a lapped cuff that fastens with a button and buttonhole. This kind of cuff fits the wrist snugly. There must be an opening in the sleeve so the hand can push through. The opening is finished with a placket or facing before the cuff is attached. The two sleeves have openings on opposite sides.

Continuous-Lap Placket—
Stay-stitch the slashed area, stitching one stitch across the point. Slash open.

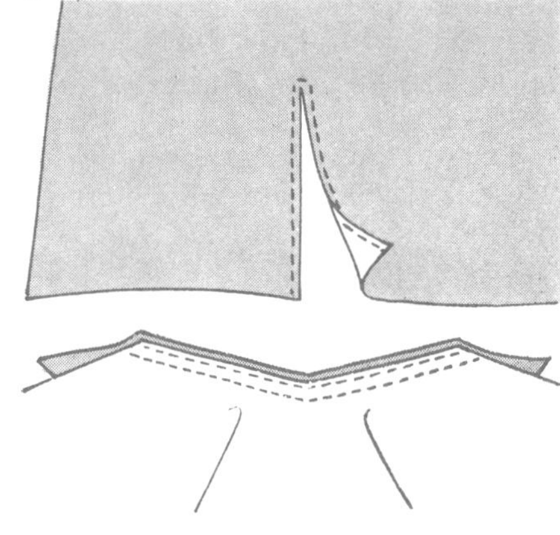

Cut a strip of the garment fabric 1-1/4 inches wide, and twice the length of the slashed opening. Cut along a selvage if possible.

Stretch out the slash. Place the right-side of the strip on the right-side of the sleeve. Pin, tack and machine-stitch close to stay-stitching, with sleeve-side up. Pivot at the corner.

Press the strip. Turn it over to enclose the raw edges. Slip-stitch the selvage in place to cover machine-stitching or stitch through all layers.

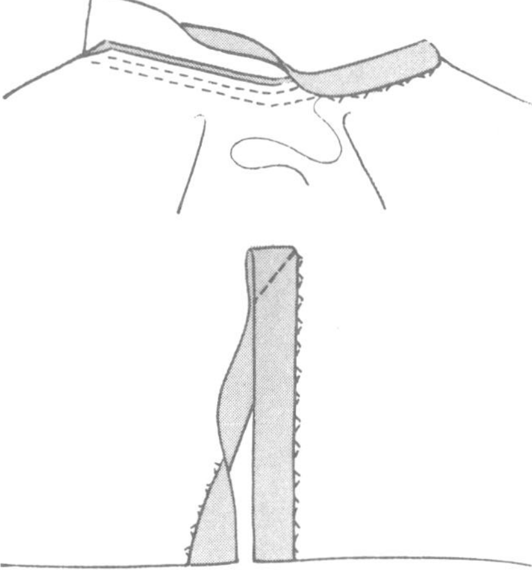

Turn the lap to the inside of the sleeve. Stitch diagonally at the top to reinforce the point of the slash.

Faced-Opening Cuff—Cut a strip of garment fabric. Make it 3 inches wide and the length of the opening, plus two seam allowances. Turn under and edge-stitch two long sides and one short side.

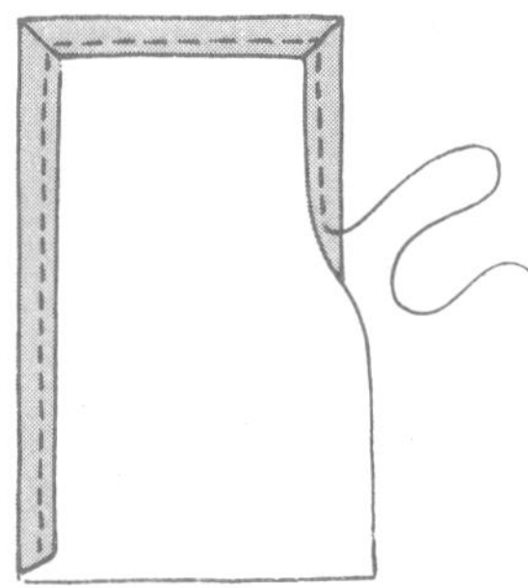

Center the facing over the slash markings, with right-sides together. Machine-stitch along stitching lines. Take one stitch across the point, then slash open.

Pull the facing through to the wrong-side of the sleeve. Catch-stitch the facing to the sleeve without stitches showing on the right-side.

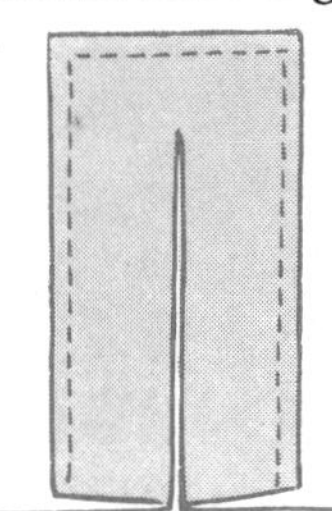

Method for Lapped Cuff—Prepare the opening with a placket or facing as before. Make bound buttonholes if required.

Sew or iron interfacing to the underside of the cuff. Fold the cuff in half along its length, with right-sides together. Machine-stitch the ends to within 5/8 inch of the notch. Trim, layer and press seams.

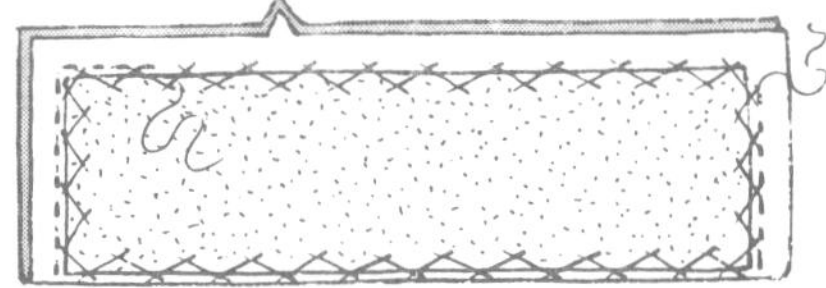

Turn the cuff right-side out. Fold back the front lap of the placket.

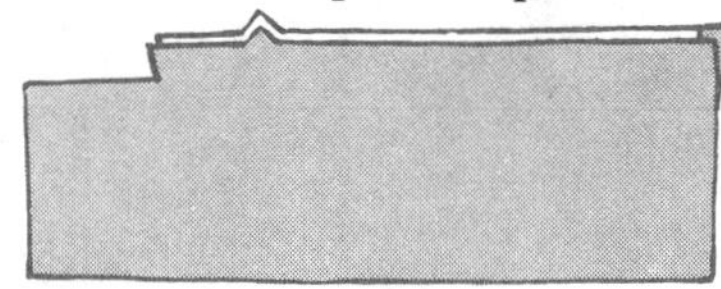

Place the cuff edge level with the fold.

Pin and tack the right-side of the upper cuff to the right-side of the sleeve. Match notches. The back lap must extend beyond the placket as marked in the pattern.

Machine-stitch from the gathered side. Press, trim and turn the cuff to extend the sleeve. Tack the folded edge of the cuff.

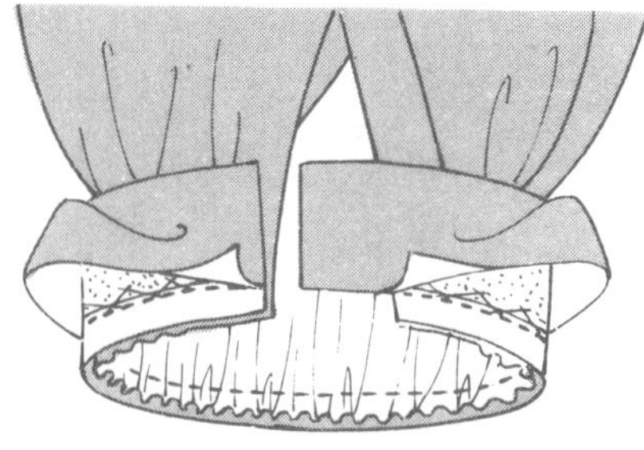

Trim the remaining seam allowance. Fold under and slip-stitch in place over machine-stitching inside the sleeve.

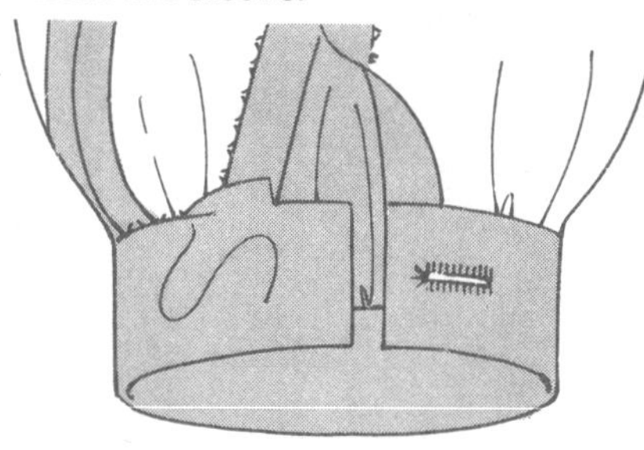

Try the cuff around the wrist to find the correct position for the button. Sew on the button. If bound buttonholes have not been made, sew a buttonhole by hand or machine. You can also use a snap under a button for closure.

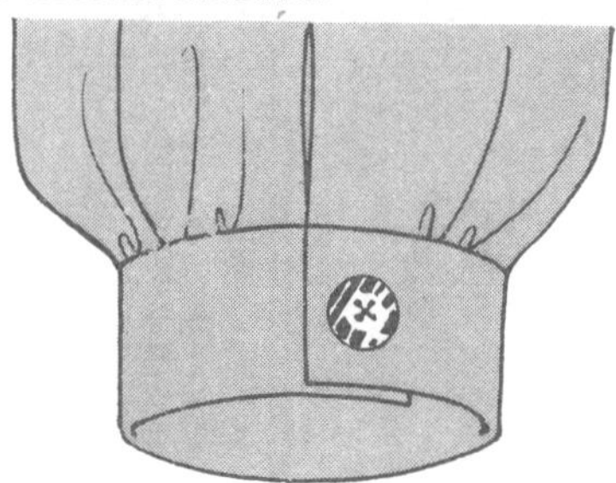

SHIRT-SLEEVE CUFF

On crisply tailored shirts, the sleeve opening is usually finished with a stitched placket. The cuff is top-stitched.

Shirt-Sleeve Placket—This is a neat, flat, stitched placket. It uses two pieces of self-fabric.

Stay-stitch the sleeve opening with tiny stitches. Slash along the marked line and out to each corner. Use sharp, pointed scissors.

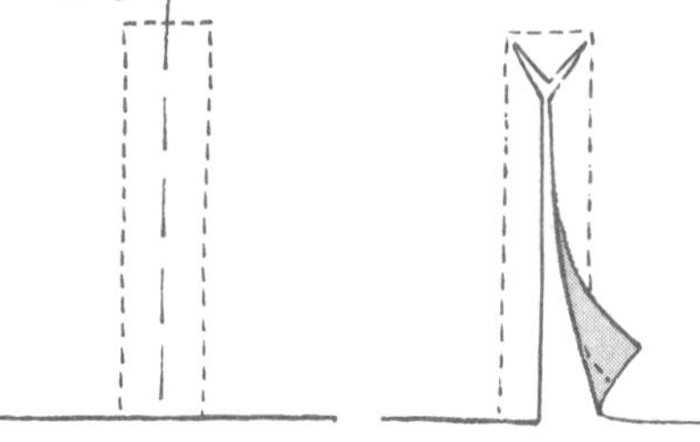

Place the right-side of the underlap placket to the wrong-side of the opening edge nearest the sleeve seam. Tack, machine-stitch and press.

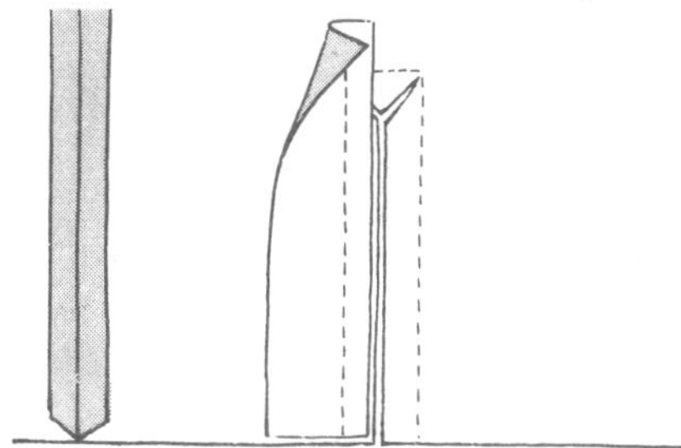

Turn the binding to enclose the raw edge. Fold under the edge, press it and top-stitch from the right-side.

Repeat with the overlap piece of placket on the other edge of the opening. Stitch it to the top end of the slash. Turn to the right-side, fold and

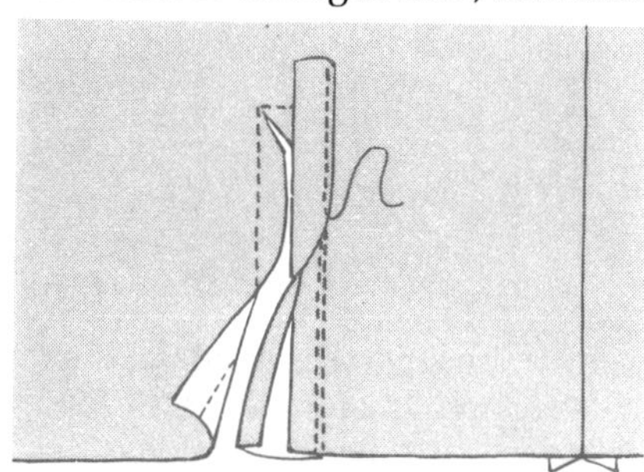

press along the fold lines to form a miter. Pin the overlap over machine-stitching.

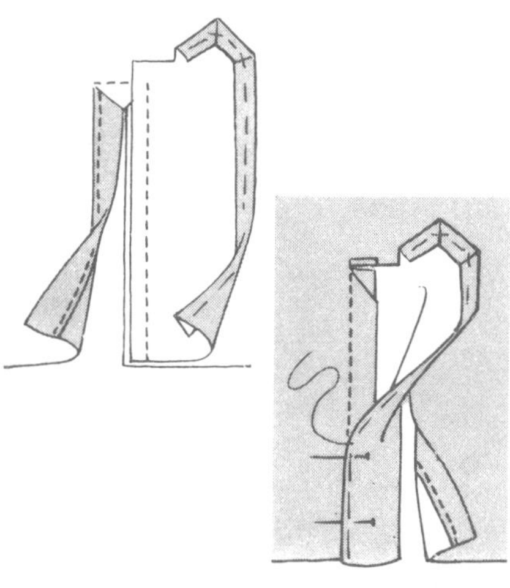

Top-stitch the outside fold of the overlap to the top of the opening. Tie threads securely. Stitch across the placket, including the point of the slash and the top of the underlap.

Leave the needle in the fabric when you finish stitching. Turn the garment. Top-stitch the remaining edges of the overlap. Tie off the thread ends.

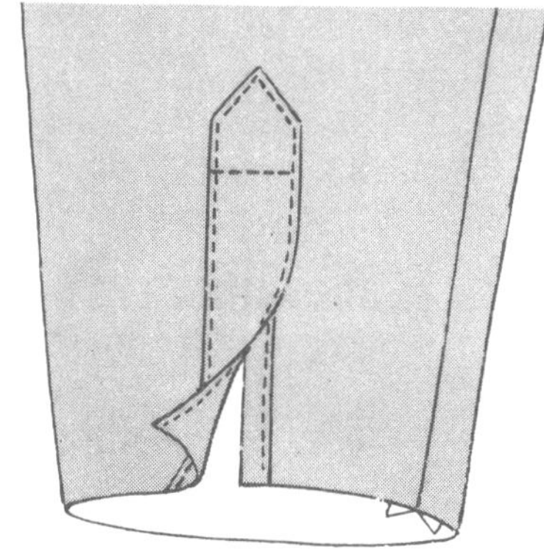

Method for Shirt Cuff—Finish the sleeve opening with a shirt sleeve placket. Sew or iron interfacing to half the cuff, inside the seam line. Fold the cuff lengthwise, with right-sides together. Tack and machine-stitch along the seam line. End stitching 5/8 inch from the long notched edge.

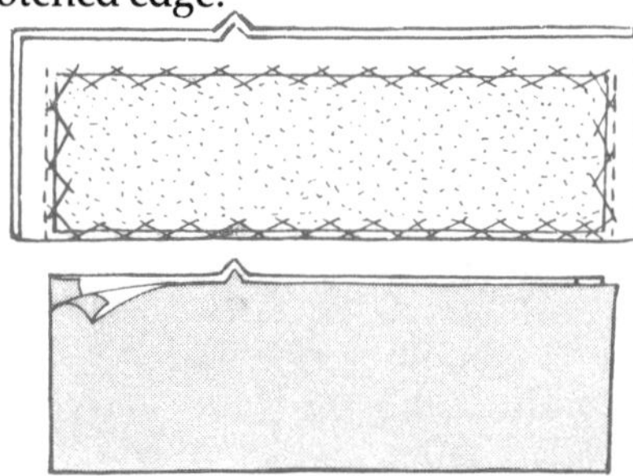

Put the wrong-side of the gathered sleeve edge to the non-interfaced half of the cuff. Edges of the placket must be level with the cuff edges.

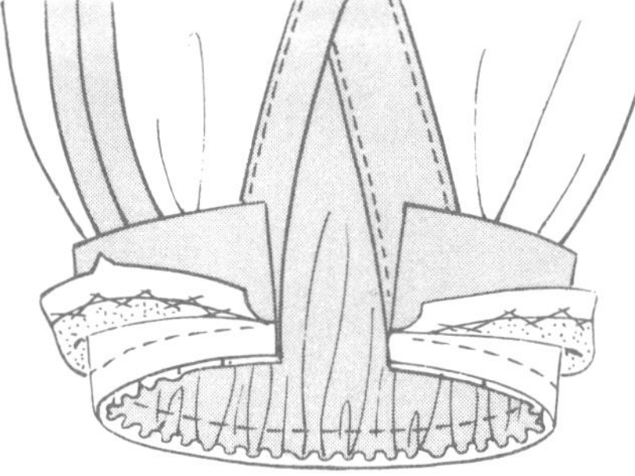

Stitch along the seam line. Trim and layer the finished edges. Turn the cuff over the sleeve edge. Fold under the edges on the remaining raw edge, and tack in place.

Top-stitch around the cuff close to the edge. Sew a second row 1/4 inch farther in. Remove tacking and press. Sew on a button, and finish the buttonhole.

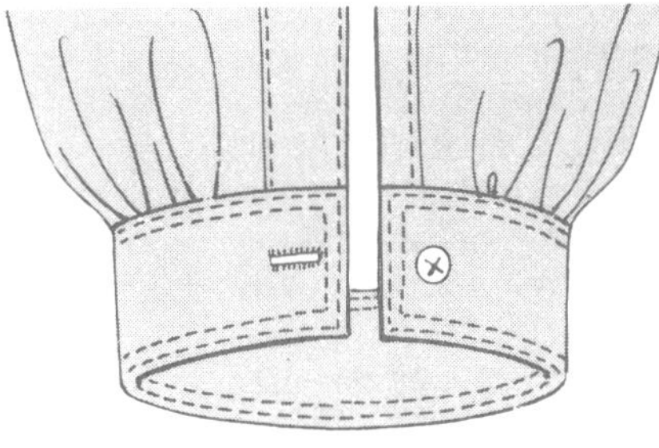

CUFF FINISHED WITH TOUCH-AND-CLOSE TAPE

You can attach a loose-band cuff to a long, full sleeve. It can be fit snugly by using touch-and-close tape. Interface cuffs to help them keep their shape.

Make and attach the band cuff as above. Or sew or iron interfacing to the wrong-side of the cuff piece. Gather the lower edge of the unseamed sleeve. Adjust it to the length of the cuff.

With right-sides together, pin, tack and machine-stitch the cuff to the sleeve edge along the seam line. Stitch from the sleeve side.

Remove tacking, trim seam allowances and press finished edges toward the cuff. Fold the sleeve and cuff in half lengthwise. Match notches and cuff seam.

Machine-stitch along the seam line. Press stitching and remove tacking. Trim and finish the sleeve seam allowances. Press the seam open.

Trim the cuff seam allowance. Press the lower edge of the cuff under along the seam line. Hem it to the cuff seam, picking up machine-stitches. Press.

Try on the sleeve. Make a fold in the cuff so it fits snugly but not tightly. Make the fold on the outside of the wrist, overlapped toward the back. Mark the folds.

Cut two 2-inch strips, and hem them in place. Use double thread, because stitching takes the strain when putting on and taking off the garment. Sew on buttons if desired.

LINKED CUFF

There are two types of linked cuffs. A *button-linked cuff* has a band cuff that extends beyond the edges of the sleeve opening. It is fastened with linked buttons on a cuff through two buttonholes. A *French cuff* has a similar cuff but is made deeper and folds back on itself. Linked buttons or cuff links hold it closed through four buttonholes.

Machine-stitch or sew buttonholes by hand because four bound buttonholes are bulky. Sometimes the buttonholes that show are bound and the two underneath are stitched.

Button-Linked Cuff—Sew or iron interfacing to the cuff. Put the right-side of the cuff to the wrong-side of the sleeve. Tack and stitch them together.

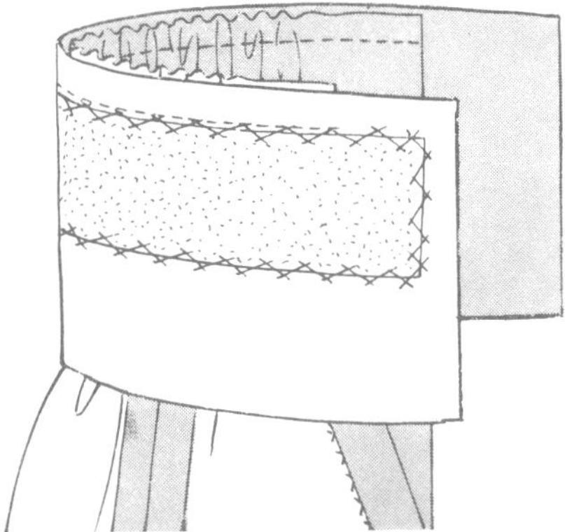

Fold the cuff with right-sides together. Machine-stitch the ends, and remove tacking.

Cut the corners, and turn the cuff to the right-side. Turn the loose edge

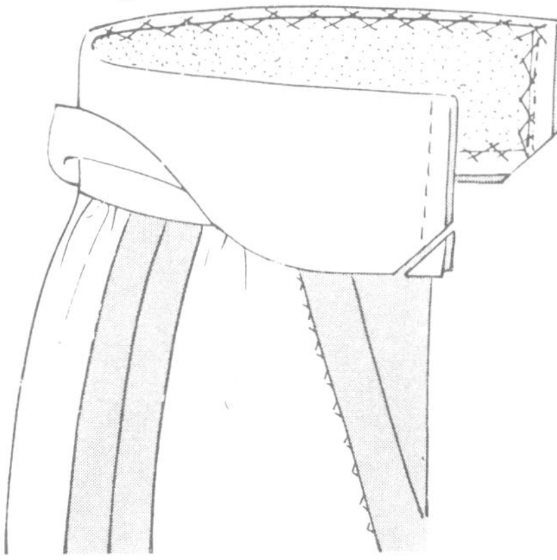

of cuff in to cover the first row of machine-stitching. Edge-stitch.

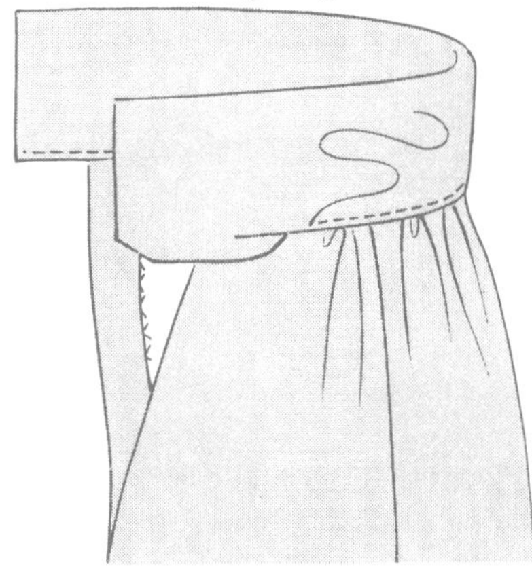

French Cuff—The underneath layer of the cuff is on top when folded back. Interfacing is sewn or ironed to the *underneath* cuff piece. Make two bound buttonholes for the top cuff, if preferred.

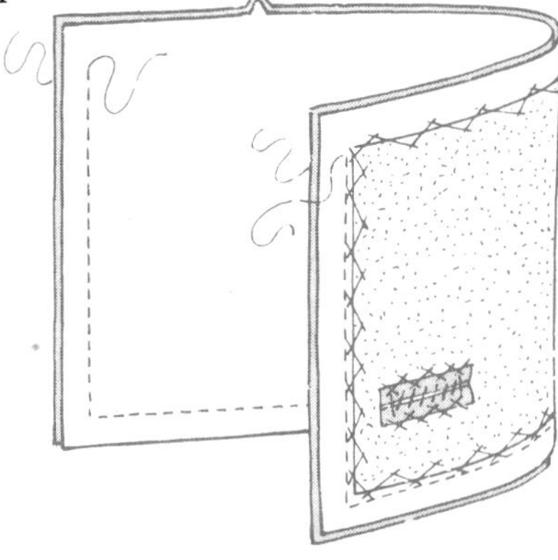

Stitch the cuff sections with right-sides together. End 5/8 inch from the notched edges. Trim and layer the seam allowance. Turn the cuff right-side out and press.

Finish as for a button-linked cuff. Fold the cuff back along the roll line.

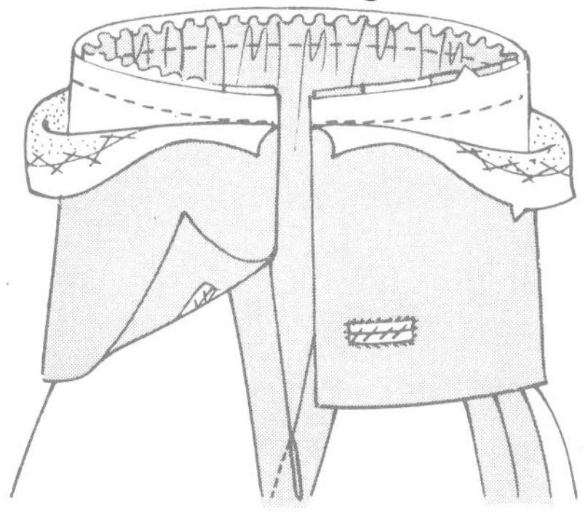

Sew the remaining two buttonholes by hand or machine. Press the cuff

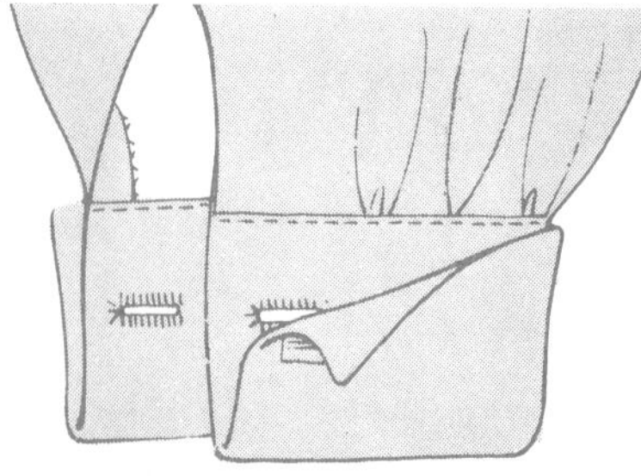

lightly. Fasten with cuff links or linked buttons.

DETACHABLE CUFF

These cuffs are made for garments that need to be dry-cleaned, or to add contrast to an outfit. Usually interfacing is left out, although many interfacings are washable.

Detachable cuffs can be made in many shapes, sizes and styles. They can turn back over the end of a sleeve or existing cuff. They may extend below a jacket sleeve to look like a shirt cuff. If they turn back, they need to be tapered. One edge fits inside the sleeve and the other edge fits over the sleeve.

Inside Sleeve—Make the cuff in the usual way. When it is turned to the right-side, press seam allowances under on the remaining raw edge. Slip-stitch this edge. Attach the cuff

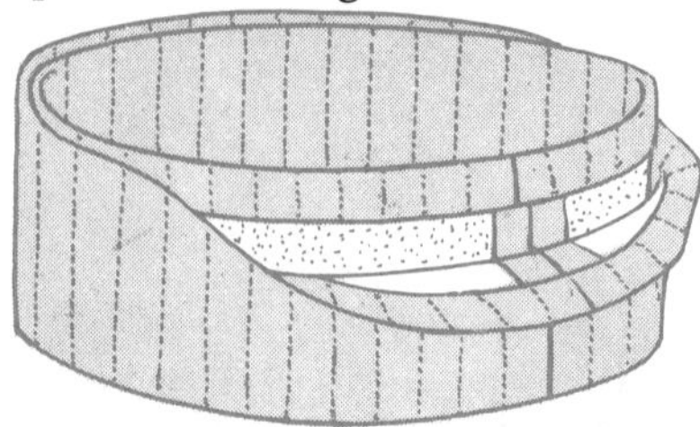

to the inside of the sleeve with snaps or touch-and-close tape. Or slip-stitch it in place.

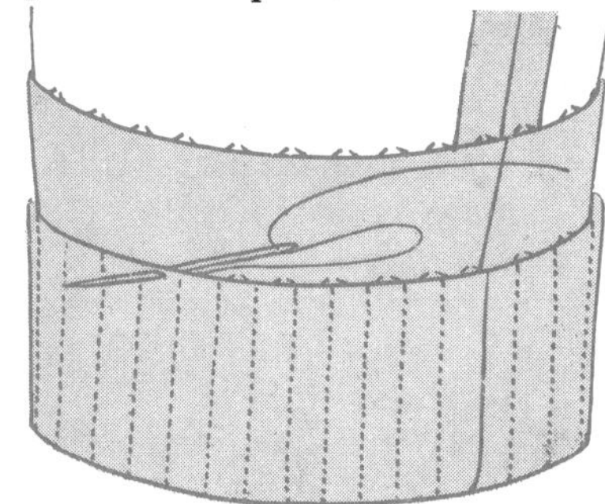

Outside Sleeve—These are often made with a slit. They are easier to turn over the sleeve edge.

Stitch each end of the cuff with right-sides together. Trim, layer and press. Turn cuff to the right-side and press again.

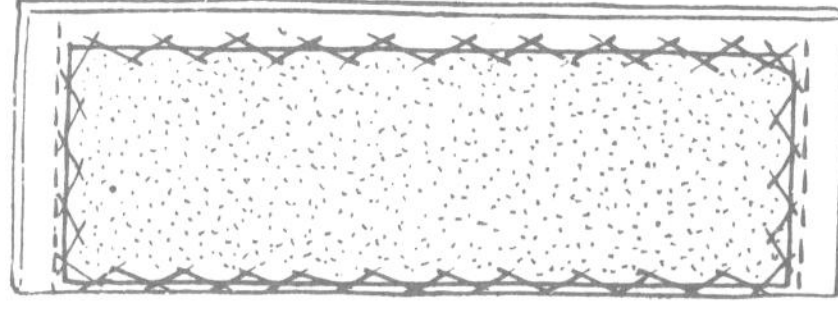

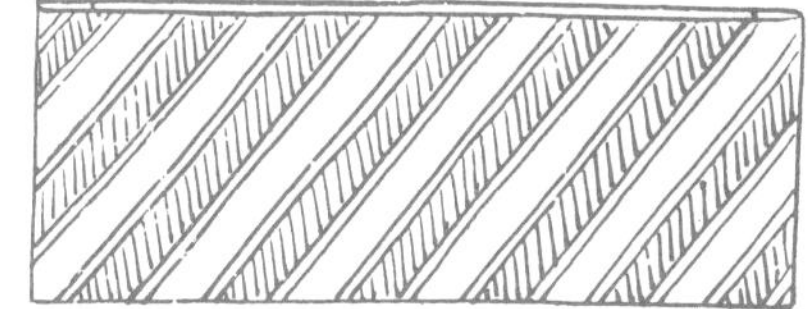

Slip-stitch the two ends of the cuff together about 1/3 of the way. Leave a slit. Cut a bias strip to fit around the inside of the sleeve. Tack the raw edges together. Bind them with the bias strip.

Fold the cuff over the sleeve edge. Be sure it is the right depth on the outside. Fasten the cuff to the inside of the sleeve with snaps or touch-and-close tape. Or slip-stitch it in place. Roll the cuff over the sleeve edge again, and press lightly. A heavy cuff can be held in place on the outside with catch-stitches between the undercuff and outer sleeve.

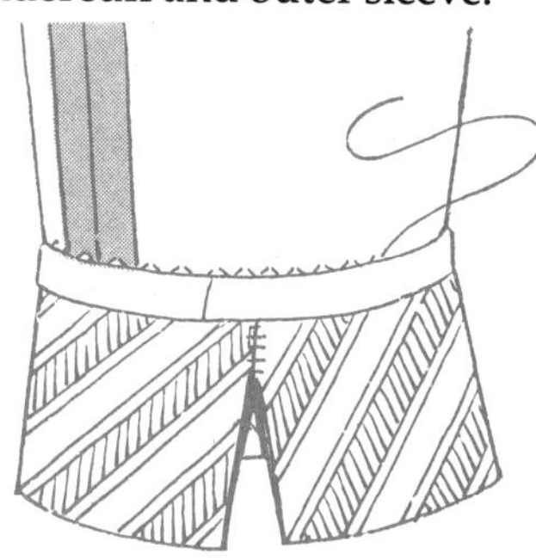

DARTS

Darts are tapered folds of fabric stitched on the wrong-side of a garment section. They control fullness and turn flat fabric into shapes to fit the body. Darts are usually the first construction detail completed when making a garment. They are important to the finished fit and shape.

Darts must be carefully sewn and pressed for a smooth, round effect. Placement and stitching of some darts may be part of the design.

On the bodice front, darts shape the bust. They also provide neat fitting for the midriff, the back shoulders, and the waist of skirts and pants. They are also used at the elbow and sometimes the back neckline and bodice-front shoulder line. They taper toward, but do not quite reach, the fullest points of the figure. Adjustments may be made to pattern darts to fit individual figures. Tall figures need longer darts. Move skirt darts to match if vertical bodice darts are altered.
altered.

STRAIGHT DART

Examine pattern markings to check the position and shape of darts. Transfer markings to the fabric with tailor's chalk or tailor's tacks. Mark the symbols for matching the sides and end of each dart. Left and right sides of a garment usually have darts that match in length and placement.

Fold fabric so the dart side markings match. The point of the dart should be on the fold. Place pins at right angles to the fold. Tack close to the stitching line, try on and adjust for fit.

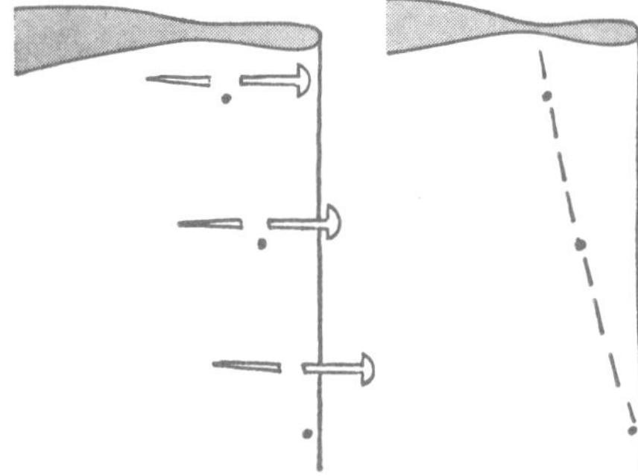

Machine-stitch along the stitching line. Start at the wide end, and taper to nothing at the point. Run the last two or three stitches along the fold at the point so puckers do not appear on the right-side.

Smooth the line of stitching between finger and thumb. Sew ends through stitches on the underside at the tapered point, and remove tacking.

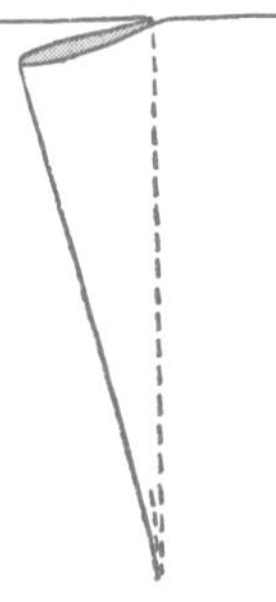

Press on the wrong-side along each side of the stitching. Press the dart to one side over a curved surface. This helps retain shape and smoothness. Vertical darts are usually pressed toward the center of the garment. Horizontal darts are pressed down. Check pattern instructions. Deep darts on thick fabrics are trimmed, opened and pressed flat. Edges can be overcast.

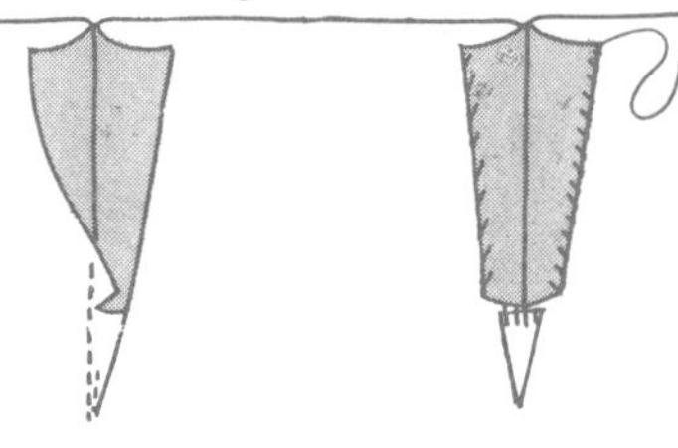

CURVED DART

This dart curves out at the waistline of a dress bodice front and curves in on pants and skirt fronts. It is stitched in a similar way to a straight dart.

Fold the center line of the dart. Pin and tack the outer, curved lines.

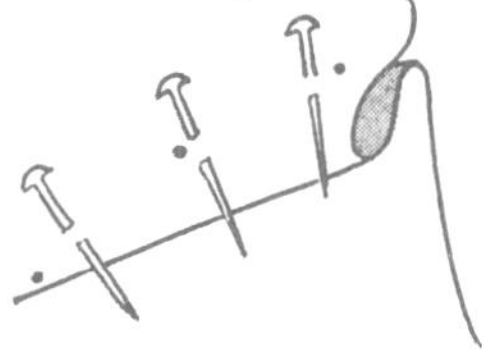

These are indicated on the pattern piece with broken lines. Machine-stitch outer curved lines, and remove tacking. Sew ends to a tapered point.

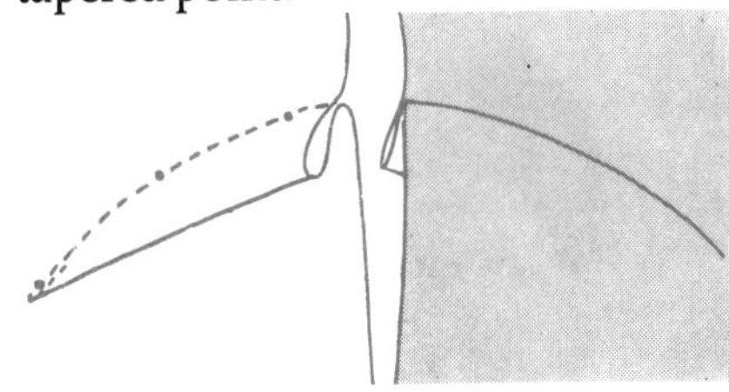

Slash the dart through the center of the fold. Press open. Overcast edges to give a finished appearance. Tie threads at the wide end.

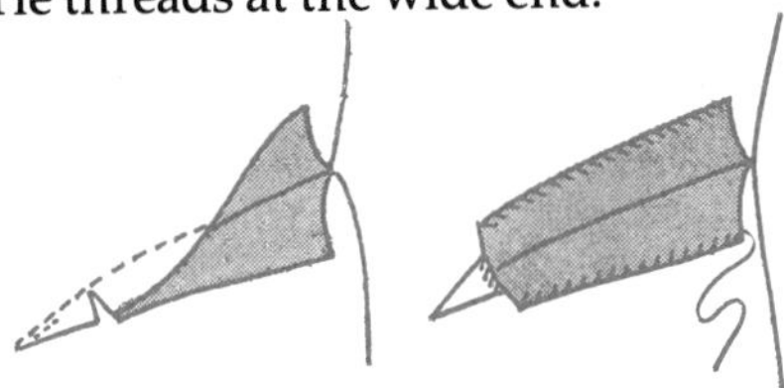

SHAPED, BIAS DART

This is also called a *French dart.* It is slashed first, then pinned, tacked and machine-stitched. It is used on A-line dresses. Darts begin at the hip level and curve up to fit the bust, skimming the waistline. The center-line marking may not be indicated because it is a slashed line.

Reinforce the dart by running a line of stay-stitching down each side of the dart. This stitching is inside the outer-marking line. Slash where

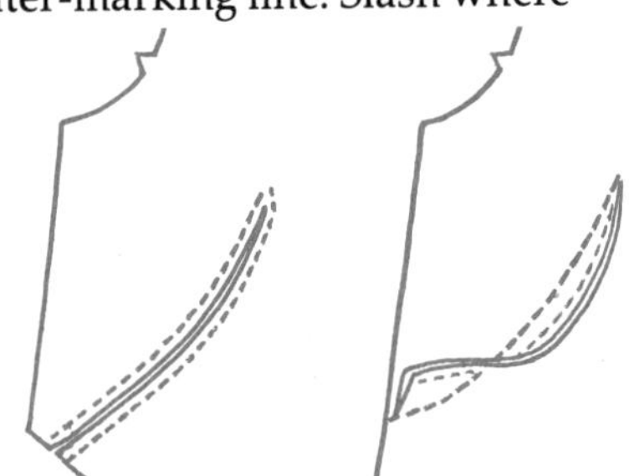

indicated. Turn to the wrong-side of the fabric. Place the broken outer-marking lines together and pin. Ease or stretch may be indicated on the pattern, usually between two medium dots. Ease and stretch the fabric so one side matches the other. Pin and tack.

Machine-stitch the dart. Remove tacking and press. For heavy fabrics, press open, and clip if necessary.

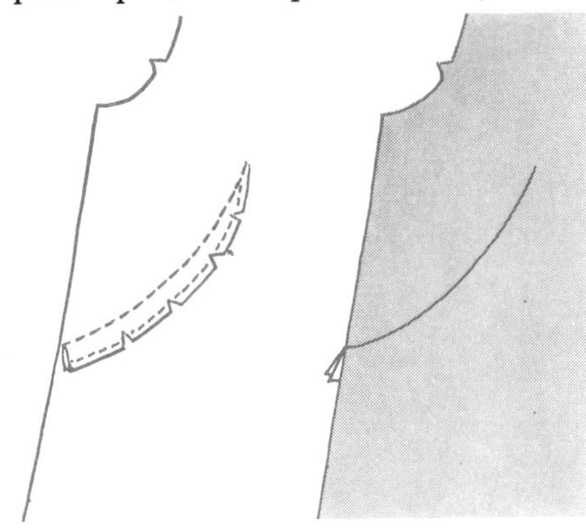

DOUBLE-POINTED DART

This dart is also called a *concave dart.* It is found at the waistline of a fitted dress where the bodice and skirt are cut from one piece. It is also found on close-fitting blouses.

Work on the wrong-side of the fabric. Fold along the center lines, pin and tack outer-marking lines together. Place pins at right angles to the fold.

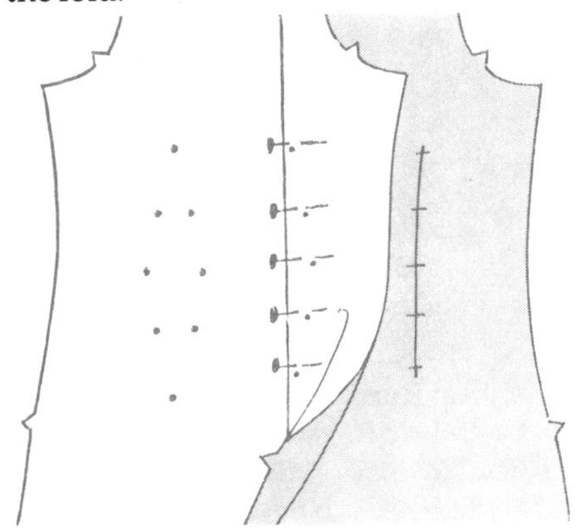

Machine-stitch the dart. Start at the center, and stitch to the point. Go two or three stitches beyond the fold.

Snip or cut into the fold of the dart at the center point. Snip either side of the center point. Press the dart toward the center of the garment. Sew ends into the underside stitches of dart points.

To keep material from dragging on the right-side of double-ended darts, snip the widest part of the dart. A *double-ended dart* consists of two darts meeting at the wide end. It is usually sewn in the middle of a garment piece, such as the back of a blouse or dress. It is sewn away from the garment edge. Beginning at one tapered point, stitch to the other tapered point. Knot both ends. See illustration. Allow the split dart to spread. Overcast edges.

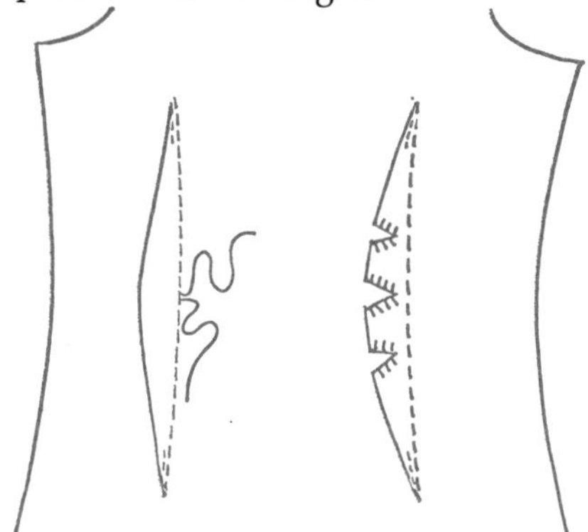

DART TUCK

This dart is a combination of a dart and tuck. It can be used on blouses, dresses or shirts, at or above the waist edge. The narrowest part of the dart is at the edge of the fabric. It widens out as it goes in to release fullness. Dart tucks may also be double-ended.

Work on the wrong-side of the garment. Fold the dart on the center line. Pin and tack. Stitch along the

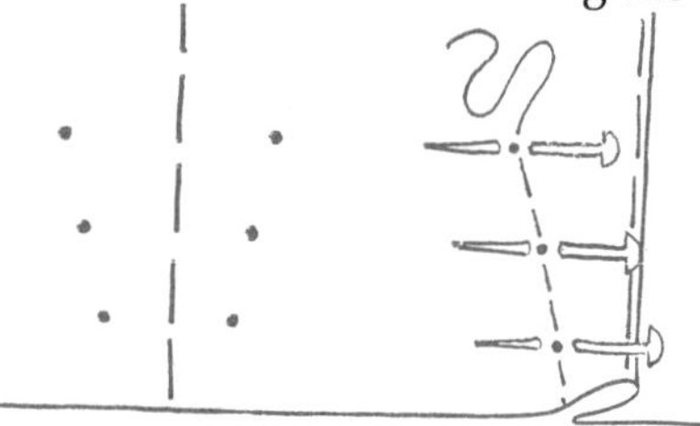

stitching line from the outside edge of the fabric inward. Back-stitch to finish.

Straight-stitch across the end to the fold line for firmness. Remove tacking. Press the dart toward the center of the garment. Never press the released fullness.

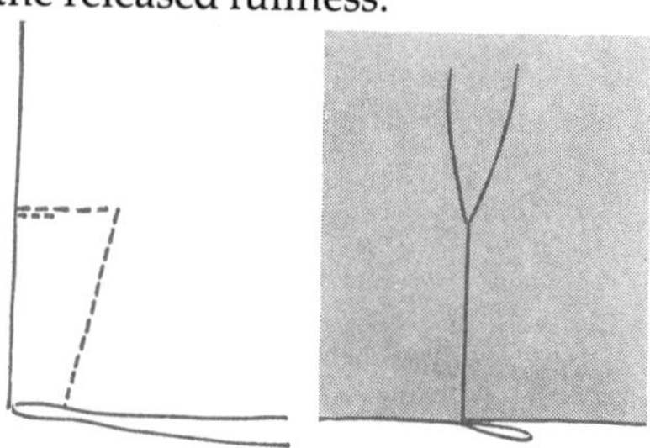

DART SEAM

This dart is found on the underarm of some dresses.

Cut or slash the solid line. Stay-stitch inside the balance marks.

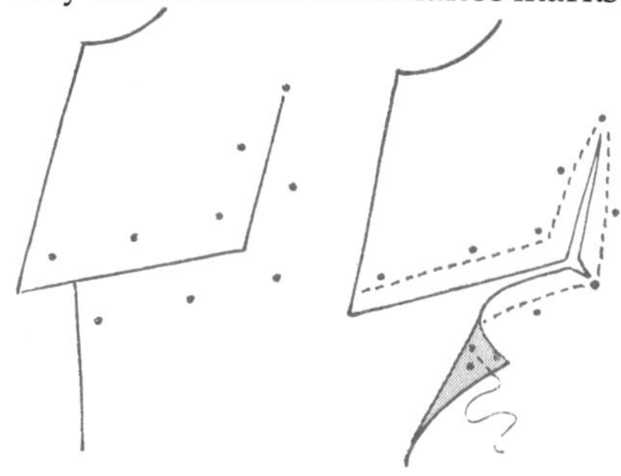

Match construction dots by pinning broken lines together. Work with the full-side up. Tack the seam line, and remove pins.

Machine-stitch the seam line. Leave the needle in the work and pivot at the corners. Remove tacking. Fasten the ends by sewing threads in stitches on underside. Press the dart down toward the center.

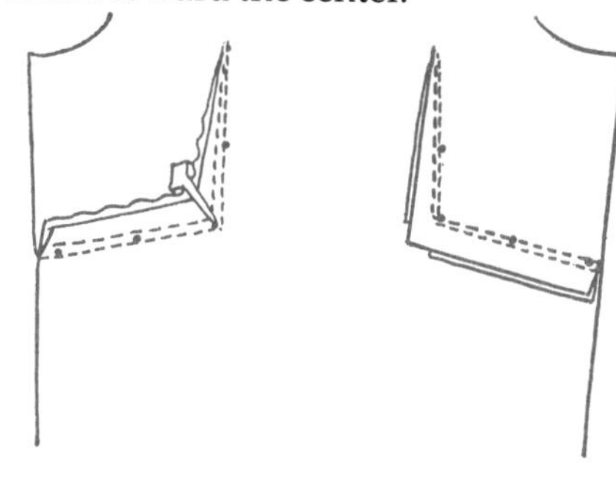

FACINGS

Facings are used to finish a garment, to reinforce an edge and to help a garment retain its shape. They show on one side only.

Facings are usually turned to the wrong-side and are unseen from the right-side. When applied to the right-side of the garment, it is called a *conspicuous facing.* It may be a decorative feature.

The facing is usually cut from self-fabric in the same shape as the edge. It is sewn to the edge. Interfacing may help create a professional, well-tailored look.

Bias tape is sometimes used as a facing on small areas of delicate fabrics. All other facings have a finished edge because the edge shows inside the garment.

For strength and to prevent stretching, stay-stitch the garment edge before attaching the facing. If alterations have been made, alter the facings.

GENERAL INSTRUCTIONS

Cutting—To face a straight edge, use a piece of fabric on the cross or straight grain. For shaped facings, match the grain on the facing to the grain on that part of the garment. The width should be enough to give a neat, flat finish.

Interfacing—Choose a suitable weight and type of interfacing for the fabric and style. If woven interfacing is used, cut it on the same grain as the facing and garment.

Attaching Facing—Place the facing edge and garment edge together. Match notches and center lines with right-sides together. Stitch along the fitting line. Trim, layer, snip and press the seam.

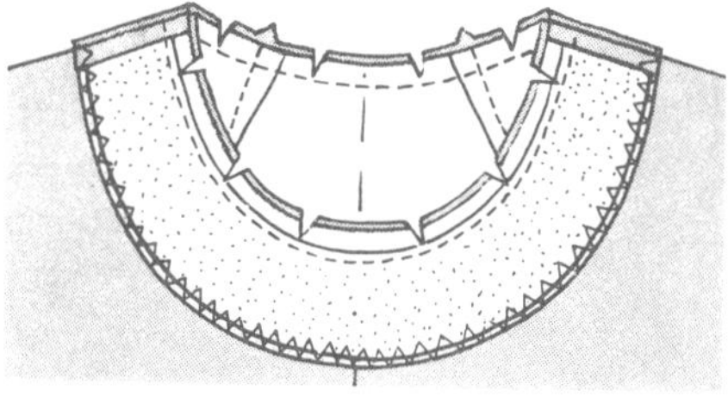

Turn the facing to the wrong-side. Roll the seamed edge so the join is slightly to the inside of the garment. Tack close to this edge and press.

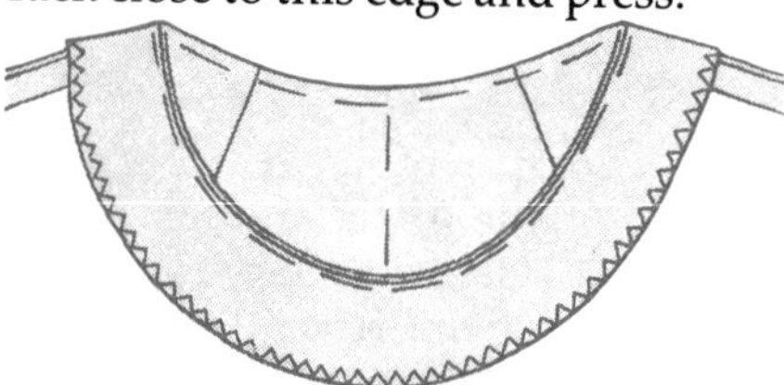

Understitching—This helps keep the facing from rolling to the right-side. Clip or notch seam allowances on curves, then layer or grade. Press finished edges toward the facing. With the facing lying flat, machine-stitch or back-stitch close to the seam line. Sew through all layers. Turn the facing to the wrong-side of the garment. Press the edge.

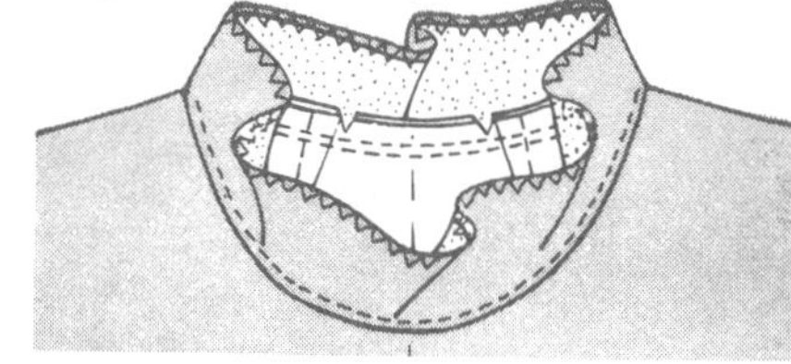

Finishing—The finished, free edge of the facing is slip-stitched to the lining. For an unlined garment, it is attached only at the seams.

STRAIGHT FACING

This is used on straight hems or down the front of cardigan jackets and button skirts. Cut the facing as long as the edge, plus finished edges. It must also be the width of the finished facing, plus finished edges. Cut it on the straight or cross grain.

With right-sides together, pin and tack the facing to the garment. If facing shows on the right-side, put the right-side of the facing to the wrong-side of the garment.

Machine-stitch along the fitting line. Remove tacking, trim seams and press.

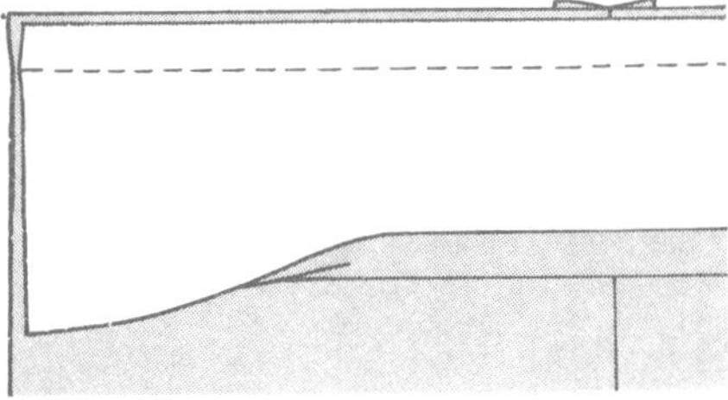

Understitch and turn the facing to the wrong-side. Roll the seamed edge between thumb and finger to make a clean edge, then tack it and press flat. Stitch facing down on the wrong-side at the seams to keep it in place.

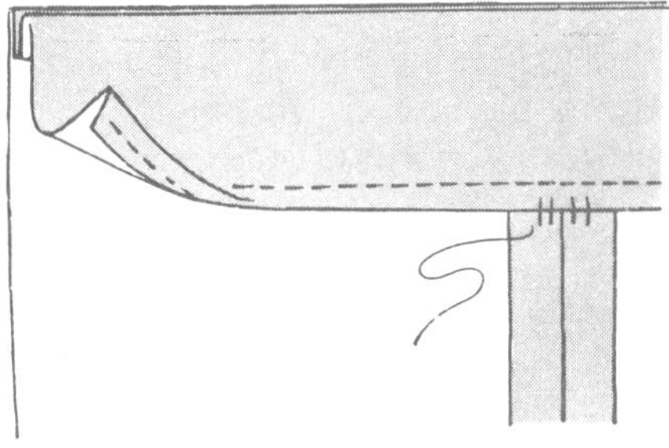

Turning Corner—Miter corners so they lie flat. See illustration.

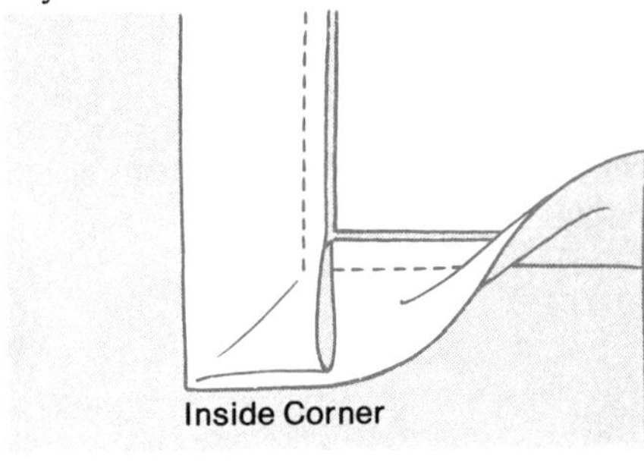

Inside Corner

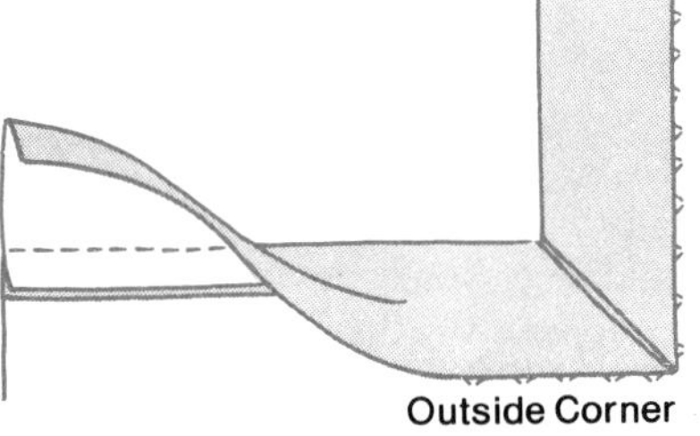

Outside Corner

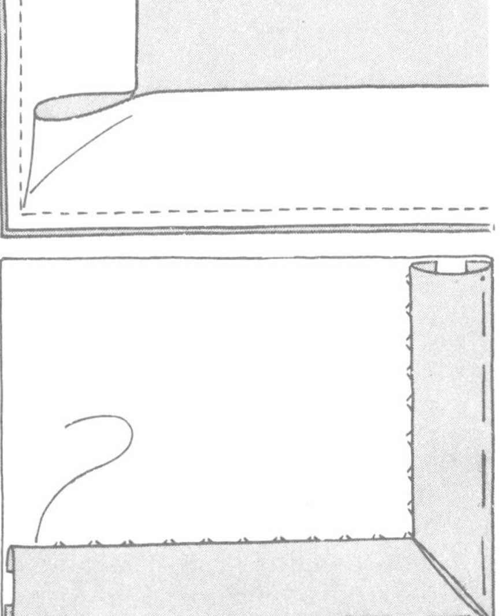

BIAS FACING

This may be cut from self-fabric or lining, or use purchased bias tape. A thinner fabric reduces bulk if the garment is thick. Put in the zipper before sewing on the facing.

Cut a bias strip four times the finished width required. Allow a little extra for the strip to narrow as it is stretched. Double-fold bias tape is suitable if folds are pressed open.

Fold the strip in half lengthwise. Press lightly, and shape it to the curve of the garment edge. Complete as for double or French binding. Turn the strip completely to the wrong-side of the garment so it does not show. Slip-stitch it in place.

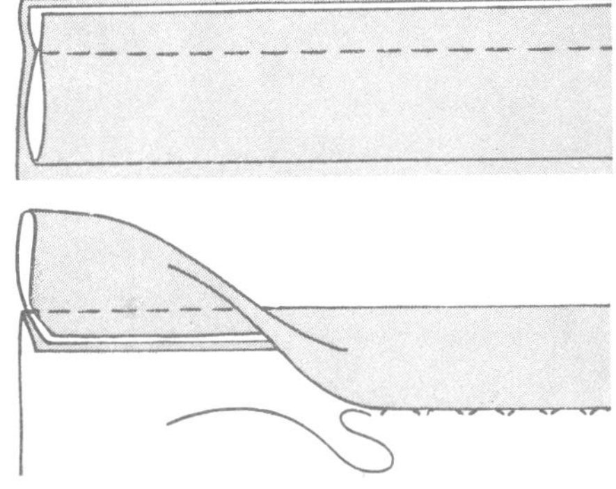

SHAPED FACING

A separate pattern piece is usually included for shaped facings that finish armholes and necklines, if necessary. The facing matches the shape of the edge to be faced. It is wide enough to lie flat. Neck and armhole facings are usually attached after the garment is made and the openings completed.

Armhole—Mark fitting lines on the garment and facing. To prepare the facing, stitch, trim and press the underarm seam. Turn under the unnotched edge. Edge-stitch or overcast it on the machine.

Tack bias binding over the seam line on the wrong-side of the garment. This prevents stretching.

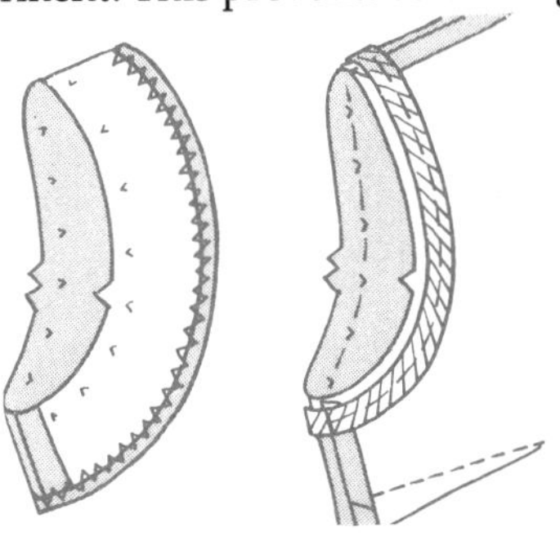

Put the facing on the garment, right-sides together. Match side seams and balance marks. Pin, tack and machine-stitch along the seam line, facing-side up.

Remove tacking. Trim, layer and clip the seam. Press and understitch.

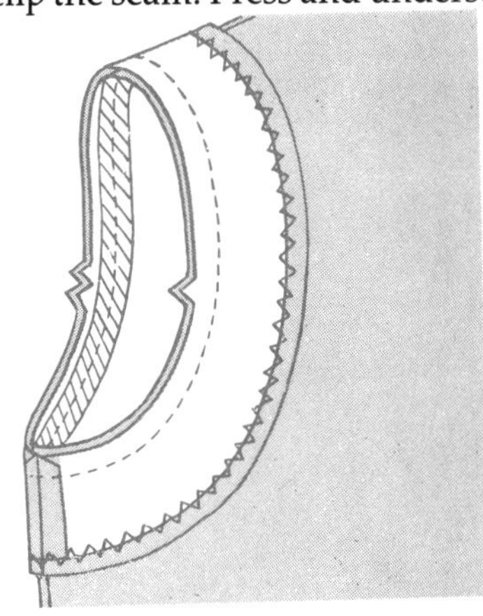

Turn the facing to the wrong-side and press again. A few catch-stitches on the underside of the facing at the seam allowance holds it flat. It keeps it from rolling to the outside.

Turn the bodice inside-out. Slip-stitch the facing to the lining. If there is no lining, tack the facing at the seams.

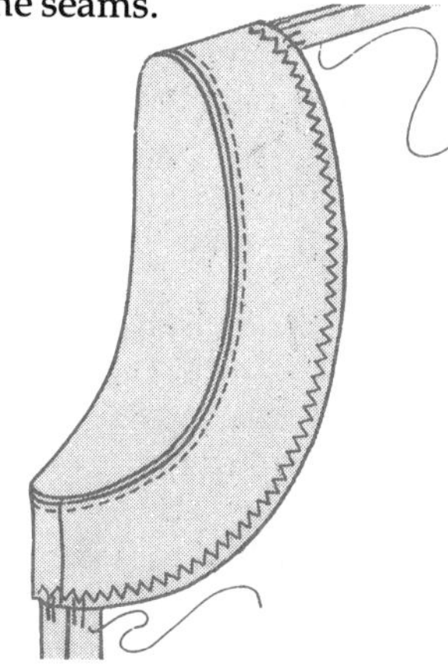

FACING AS PART OF GARMENT

Where an opening edge is straight, it can have a fold-back facing. This is cut in one with the bodice so there is no seam at the edge. Faced edges of this type are often overlapped for fastening. The center and overlap pattern markings are transferred to the fabric.

Cut and attach interfacing according to pattern instructions. Stitch interfacing to the fold line on the wrong-side. Use long, running-stitches. Catch-stitch along the other edge of the interfacing to hold it flat.

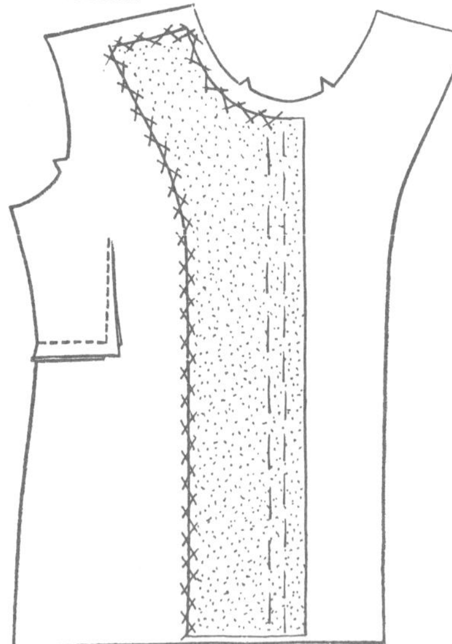

Turn the facing to the wrong-side along the fold line. Attach extra pieces of shaped facing. Add seam binding to the fold line and neck seam for reinforcement.

At the neck seam, center the binding on the seam line. Pin and tack it in place. On the fold line, pin the binding to the seam allowance of the interfacing that extends beyond the fold line. Machine-stitch it in place close to the binding edge.

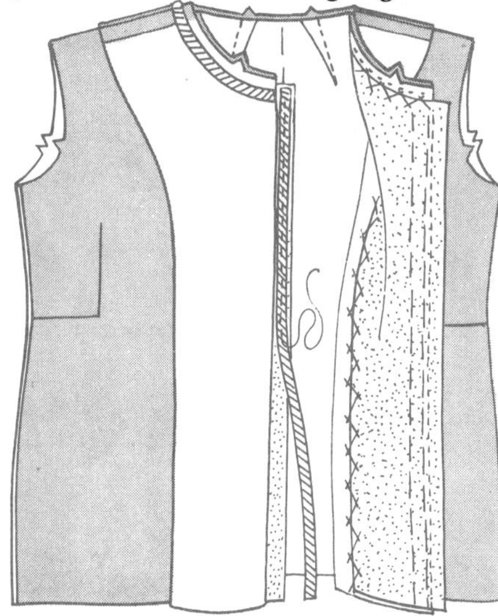

Pin, tack and stitch the facing to garment at the neck edge. Do not stitch the fold line. Trim, layer and clip the seam allowance. Remove tacking and press.

Understitch and turn the facing to the inside. Slightly roll the seamed edge between thumb and finger. The seam should not show from the right-side of the garment. Press.

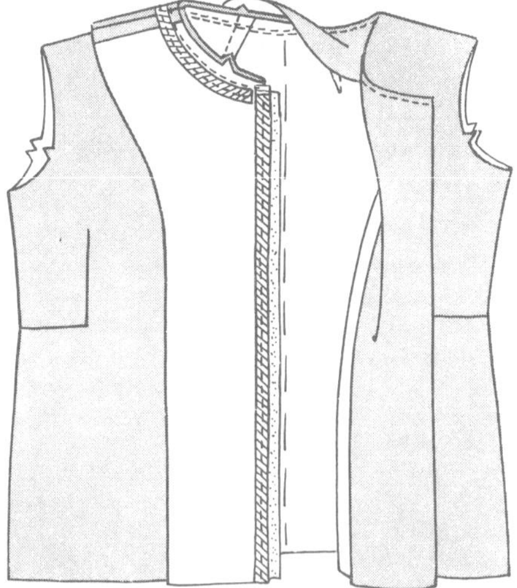

Lift the facing. Catch-stitch the facing and seam allowances to hold the facing flat. Finish the raw edge of the facing by turning it under and edge-stitching. Catch-stitch the facing in place at the shoulder seams, back-neck darts or wherever needed.

FASTENINGS

Almost all garments need openings and fastenings of some kind. Fastenings allow the garment to be put on and taken off. They keep openings in position while the garment is being worn.

There are many ways garments can be fastened. Openings can be finished for durability, decoration and comfort. Fastenings may be the main fashion detail, or they can be concealed. They should be washable or dry-cleanable. Use a fastener suited in type and size to the garment, fabric and type of opening. If the fasteners are *not* part of the garment decoration, they should not be visible.

Sew fastenings after the opening has been finished and pressed. Sew loops and bound buttonholes first.

The following instructions are for ladies' garments. Men's garments fasten on the opposite side.

LOOPS

Thread Loop— A thread loop is often used with a small button at the neck edge. It is hidden by the collar. The loop should be as long as the diameter of the button, plus its thickness. On children's wear, sew thread loops inside the overlapping part of an opening. Thread loops may be made a feature of a garment. They can be worked in groups down the edge of an opening.

Use buttonhole twist or double thread in a color matching the fabric or buttons. Finish loops with a blanket- or buttonhole-stitch.

Put a thin card behind the position of loop. Place pins in position as

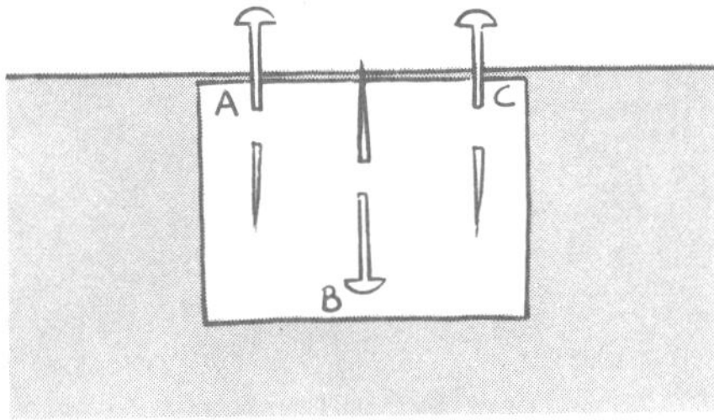

shown in the diagram. Fasten thread with a double-stitch at one pin. Sew the thread back and forth from pin A to pin C. Pass the thread around pin B and finish off at pin C. Continue

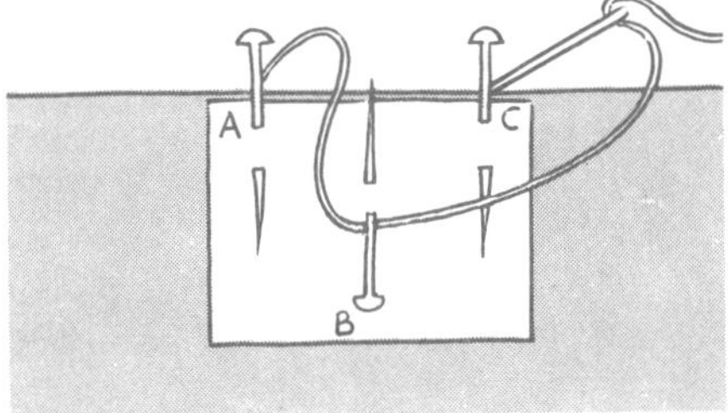

for the required number of strands.

Remove the card. Turn the loop around and sew with buttonhole- or blanket-stitch over the strands.

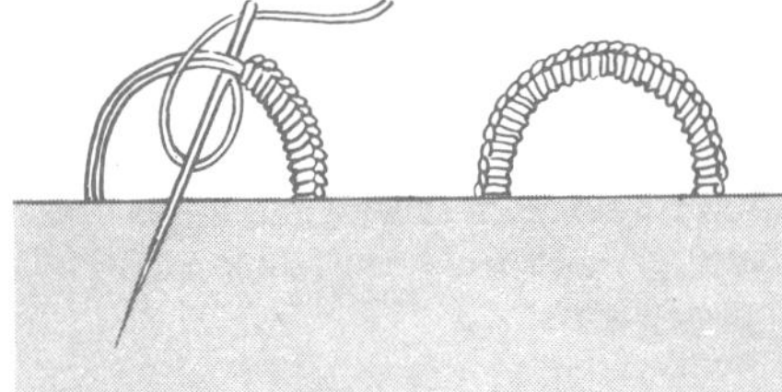

Belt-Carrier Loop—Work a loop at the waist for a belt carrier or as an eye for a metal hook. Make thread chains instead of loops. These are also suitable for lingerie strap holders.

Mark the garment where the chain begins on the shoulder seam near the armhole. Sew one or two tiny stitches to secure thread.

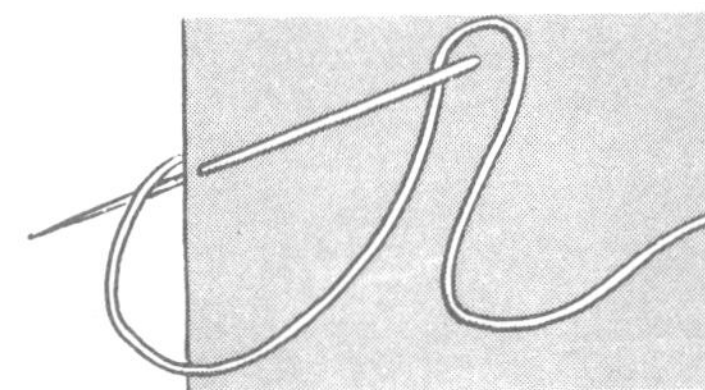

On the right-side, make a loop by taking another tiny stitch. Hold the

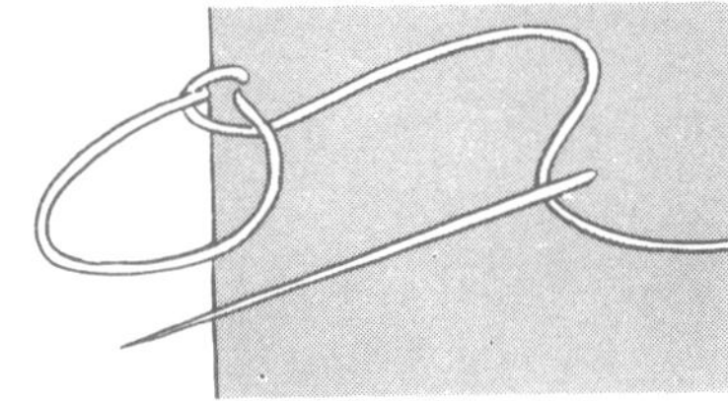

needle and thread in your right hand. Slip your thumb and first two fingers of the left hand through the loop of thread. Pick up another loop of thread. Pull it through the first. Repeat several times, tightening as you work.

Make enough loops for a chain 1-1/2 inches long. Push the needle through the last loop. Pull it tightly to form a knot.

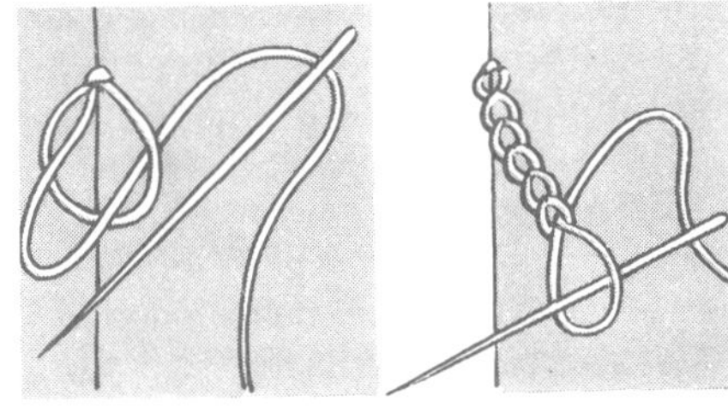

Sew the ball part of the snap to this end of the chain. Sew the socket part of the snap to the garment.

Rouleau Loop—These are attractive with covered buttons. Loops are fabric tubes made from bias strips. The seam allowance or a length of piping cord fills the tube.

Cut bias strips of fabric. Short lengths are good for single-spaced loops. Often loops are made from one long, continuous strip.

The width of the strip needs to be twice the finished width, plus the seam allowance. Make a few test loops to get the correct width for the fabric and garment. Fold strips in half lengthwise, with right-sides together and tack.

Machine-stitch along the length of the strip, stretching the strip slightly. Remove tacking. Trim the finished edge so it is less than the width of the stitched tube. Leave enough fabric to pad out the tube.

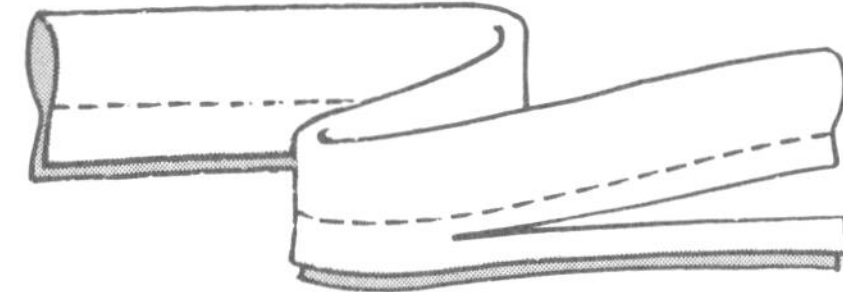

Attach thread to one end of the rouleau. Thread it through a bodkin.

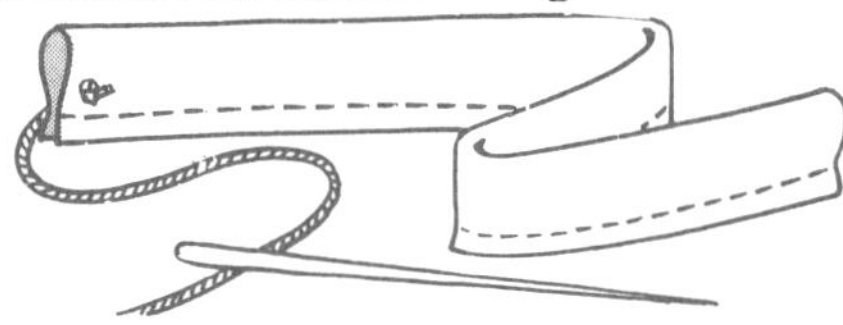

Carefully push the bodkin through the tube, and ease fabric along the

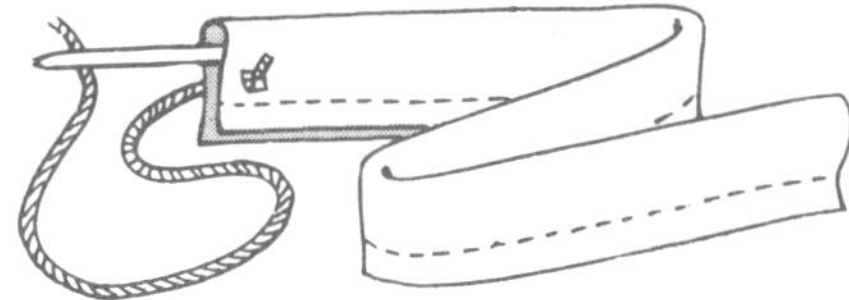

thread. Pull the length of tube inside out. Remove the thread.

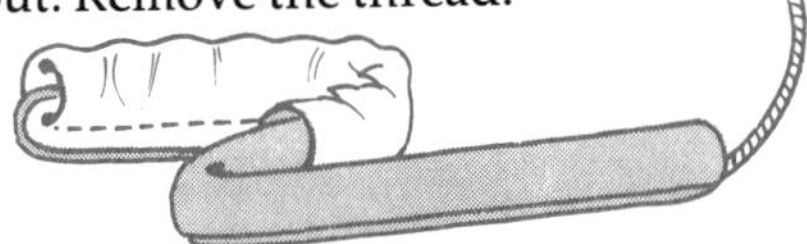

The seam thread may break if the rouleau is pulled quickly when turning. It is possible to stitch the bias strip with a narrow zigzag or stretch-stitch without stretching the fabric while stitching.

Corded, Rouleau Loop—Cut a bias strip of fabric to fit around the cord, plus seam allowances. Cut a piece of cord at least twice the length of the bias strip. Mark the center point.

Place the cord on the right-side of the strip. Put the two raw edges together. Move the fabric so one end of the fabric is over the center mark on the cord. Tack the fabric in place.

Use a zipper or piping foot. Stitch across the center mark and along the long edge close to the cord. Remove

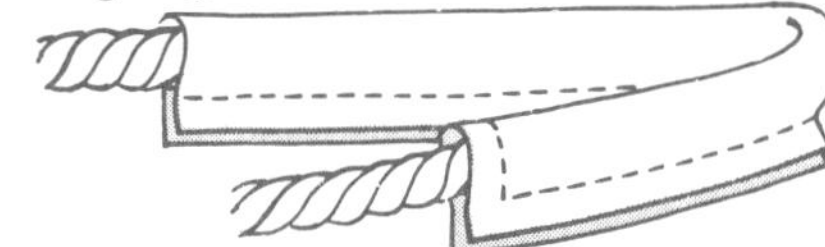

tacking and trim the seam allowance. Pull the enclosed cord out slowly, so the free cord fills the tube. Trim off

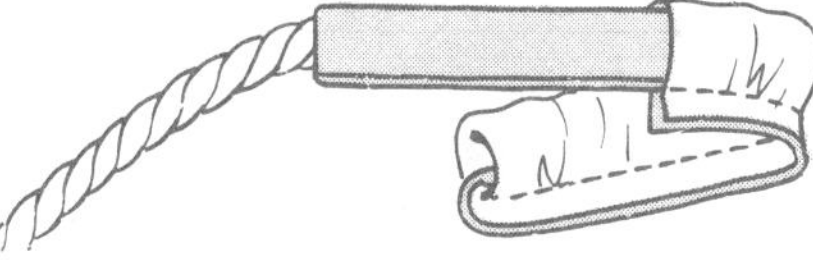

the stitched end and any excess cord.

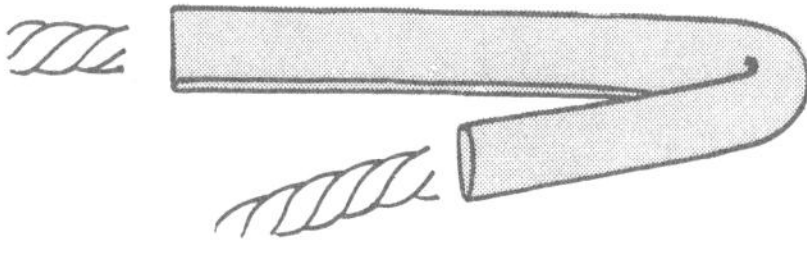

Placing Rouleau Loop—Space single loops along an opening. When a long row of closely spaced loops is needed, use a continuous piece of tubing.

For single loops, the loop should extend beyond the edge of the garment about half the diameter of the button, plus the thickness of the tubing. The distance between A and C in the diagram is about the diameter of the button, plus twice the thickness of the tubing.

Mark the width and depth of the loop on the raw edge on the right-side of the garment opening. Place loop between pins A, B and C, with the seam of the loop on top. Tack along the seam line.

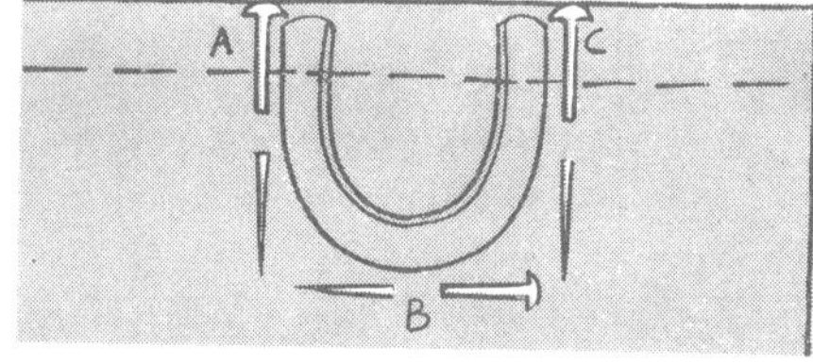

Put the facing and garment right-sides together with raw edges meeting. Tack, then stitch along the seam line.

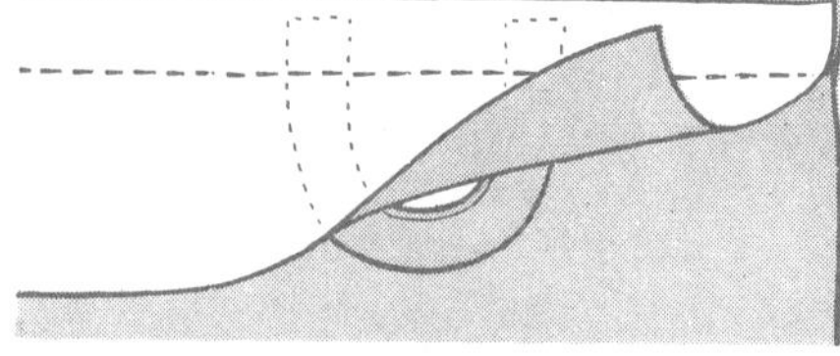

Remove tacking. Turn the facing to the wrong-side of the garment. Tack and understitch the turned edge on the inner edge of the right-side of the facing. Remove tacking.

Turn the raw edge of facing under 1/4 inch to the wrong-side. Edge-stitch along the edge to finish.

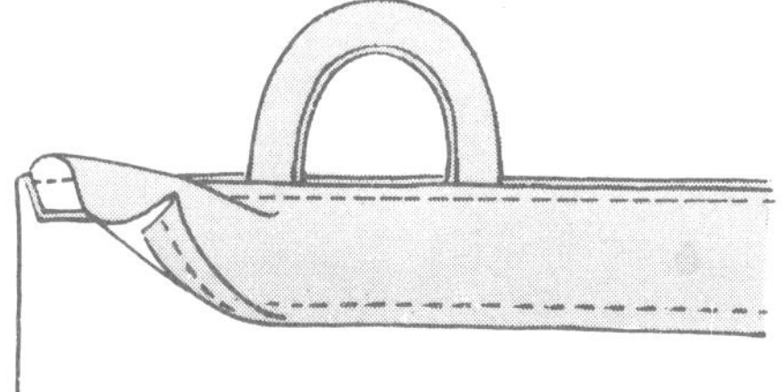

For continuous loops, use a long piece of prepared tubing. Pin a series of loops of the correct size in place. Stitch along the seam line. Trim the short loops in the seam allowance. This avoids extra bulk at the edge of the garment.

Ribbon, Braid Loop—Ribbon or braid can be used for loops in the same way as rouleau tubes. Enclose them in the facing, or add them to the edge after the garment is made.

Cut a piece of ribbon 1-1/4 times the diameter of the button, plus finished edges. Fold the ribbon in half and crease. Fold the finished edges and crease in place.

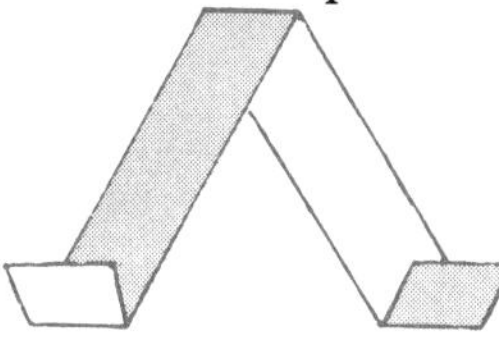

Mark the position for a single loop. Pin and tack the ribbon in place on the wrong-side, close to the edge. Sew each loop in place on the wrong-side. Or stitch on the right-side close to the garment edge.

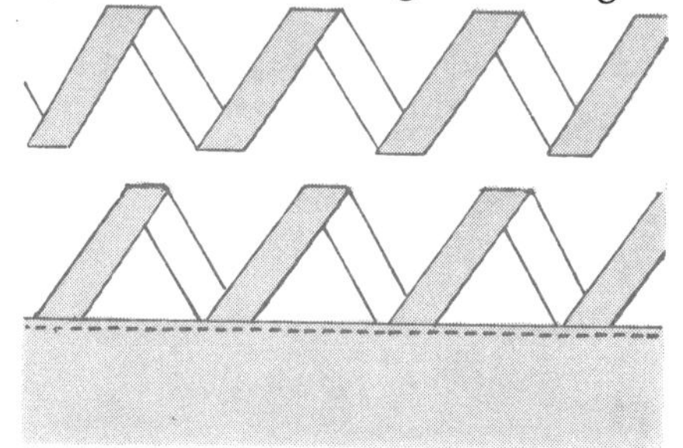

EYELETS

Eyelets are round openings made in the fabric for lacing, drawstrings, buckles, studs or cuff links. There are special kits available to make and finish eyelets.

Eyelets are suitable only for firmly woven, strong material. Do not use them on fine or filmy fabric. Make narrow laces from rouleau tubes, ribbon, braid or cord. White shoelaces can be dyed to match a garment.

Hand-Sewn—Mark the position for eyelets on the fabric with tailor's chalk. Make two long tacking-stitches forming a cross on these marks.

Sew a circle of small running-stitches around the mark for the eyelet. This reinforces the circle and keeps the fabric from stretching. Punch the correct-size hole in the fabric with an awl or stiletto, or cut with scissors.

Use a double thread and leave about 1 inch for finishing. Bring the needle through the fabric from the wrong-side, outside the circle of stitches. Work around the eyelet with close buttonhole-stitches. Finish by tying threads securely on the wrong-side.

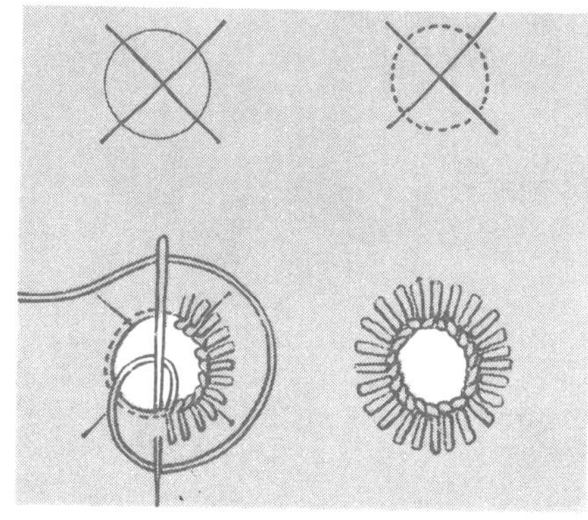

Eyelets may be made on some sewing machines. Refer to your sewing-machine handbook for instructions.

FROG FASTENINGS

Frog fastenings are often used with Chinese ball buttons. These fastenings are made from fabric rouleau or cord. The loop extends beyond the edge of the opening and over the button.

Practice first with a piece of string. Then make the frog on paper before sewing to the garment. Make the loops with the seam of rouleau strip facing you. This is the wrong-side of

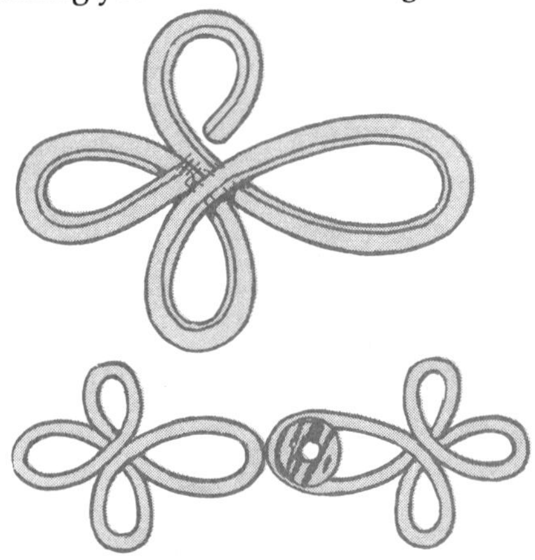

the finished fastening. Tack each loop with tiny stitches. Sew it with stitches that do not show on the right-side of the garment.

HOOKS AND EYES

These are often used to secure waistbands and neck edges. If the strain on the waistband or neck edge is great, use heavy-duty hooks.

Stitch hooks to the wrong-side of the overlap. The edge of the hook is always in line with the edge of the garment.

Attach the edge of the hook to the garment with two stitches under the hook. Secure the shaft of the hook above loops with two stitches across it. Pass the needle under the fabric, then begin sewing around the loops.

Buttonhole-, blanket-, or overcast-stitch around the two loops of the hook. Three types of eyes can be used with the hook—the metal loop, metal bar and worked bar.

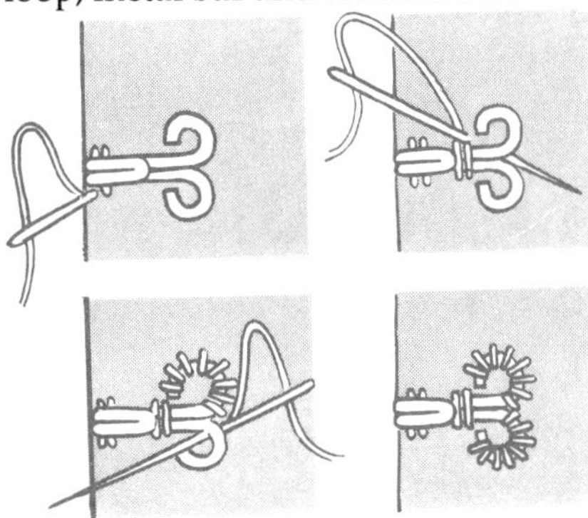

Metal Loop—This loop is used for openings in edges that meet and do not overlap. Sew the metal loop to the wrong-side of the edge of the garment, opposite the hook. Place enough of the loop over the edge for the hook to fasten in it. Secure ends over the edge of the garment at each side of the loop. Buttonhole-stitch loops in position.

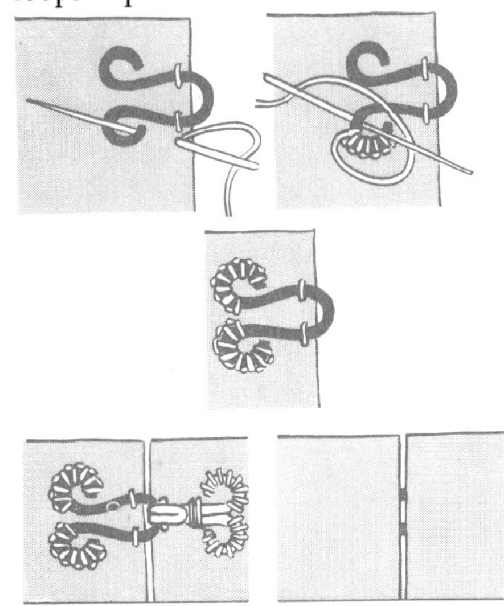

Metal Bar—This is used for openings where edges overlap. Sew the bar to the right-side of underwrap. Buttonhole-stitch around the loop.

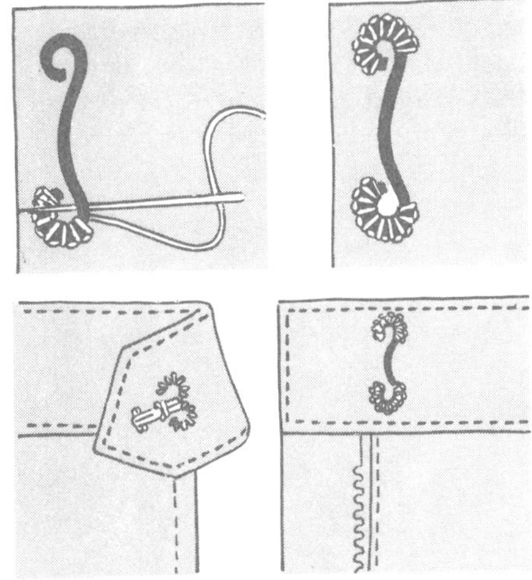

Hand-Worked Bar—This may be used instead of a metal bar. It can also be used for edges that meet. For overlapped fastenings, the bar lies straight on the material. If a bar is used on edges that meet, strands form a loop.

Attach thread with a double-stitch. Make a straight bar tack across the fabric. Only a few threads of the fabric are picked up. The needle is taken back to the other end of the stitch.

Sew the required number of bar tacks. Heavy fabric needs more bar tacks than a fine fabric. Work a close buttonhole-stitch across the bars from side to side.

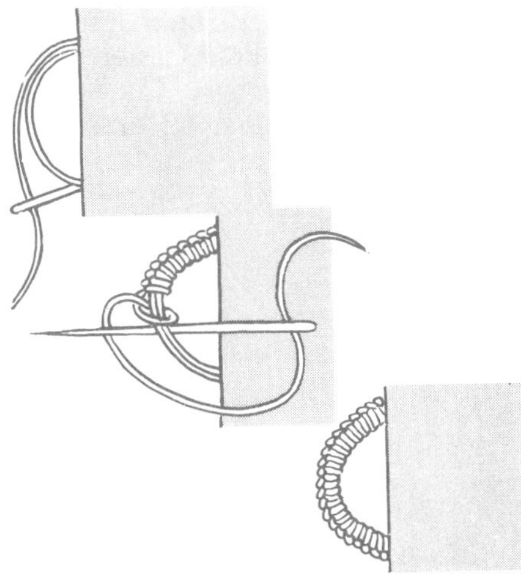

Covered Bar—Cover bars with matching thread so fastenings are less obvious. Sew buttonhole-stitches close together until the metal is hidden.

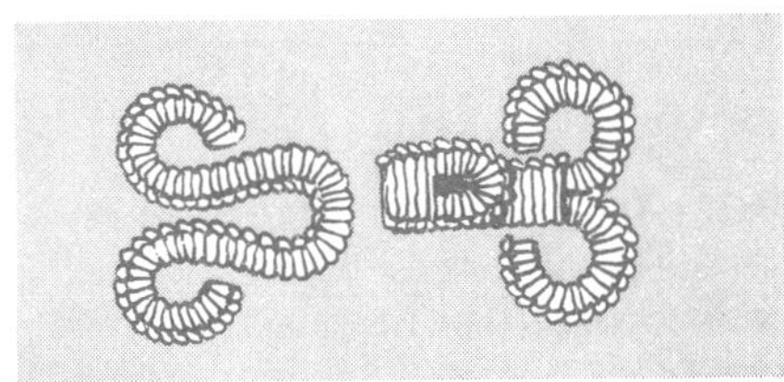

SNAPS

Snaps are often used on overlapping openings where there is little strain. When there is no overlap, or where stand-up-neckline edges meet, use a floating or extended snap.

Snaps are made in two parts. One part is thick with a hole. The other part has a flattened base and a knob in the middle. The thick section with

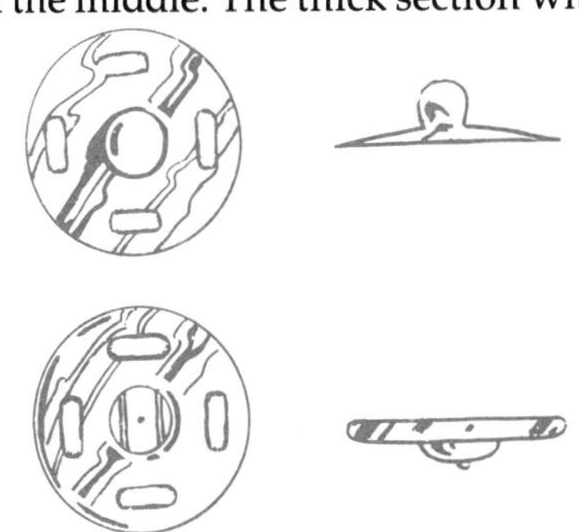

a hole is sewn to the right-side of the underwrap. The part with knob and flat base is sewn on the wrong-side of the overwrap.

Sew the ball part on first. Rub the knob with tailor's chalk. Press it in the other edge of the opening. Sew the socket part exactly on that spot.

Use double-stitches to fasten on and off under the edge of the fastener. Buttonhole-stitch or oversew fasteners in place. Use the same number of stitches in each hole.

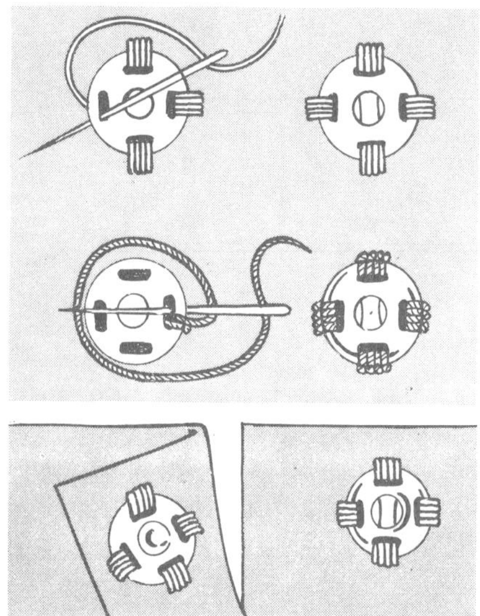

Extended Snap—Sew the ball part on the inside of one edge. Sew the socket part to the other edge through one hole only. It will extend beyond the edge. Where the metal parts show on an important garment, cover them with fabric.

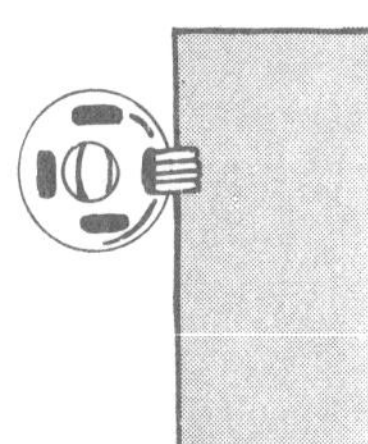

Covered Snap—Cut two circles of fabric about twice the diameter of the snap. Sew running-stitches around the edge. Put the two parts of the snap face down on the wrong-side of the circles. Push the knob of the ball part through the fabric. Close the two parts of the snap together. Gather up the running-stitches and fasten them securely.

TAPES AND TIES

Turn the tape end over so the raw edge meets the selvage edge. Make a crease across the tape as shown in the illustration. Turn the diagonal fold back.

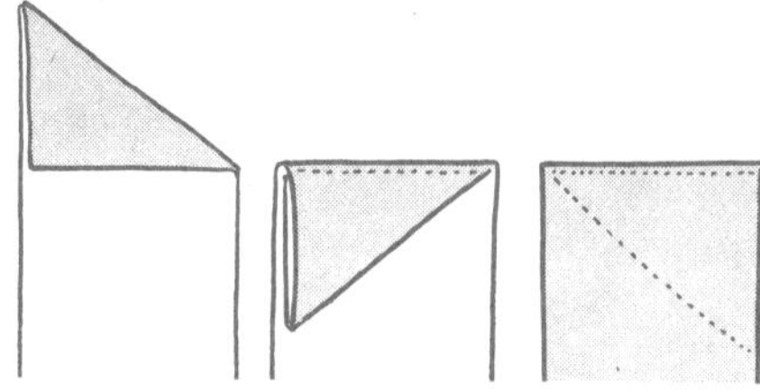

To attach the tape, place the finished edge on the edge of the garment. Pin in place as shown. Hem

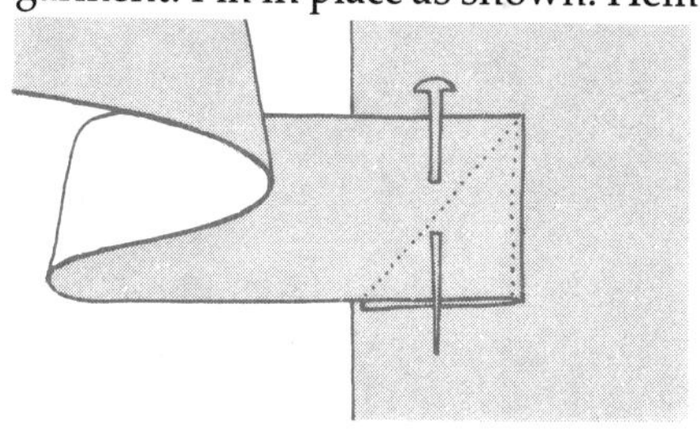

three of the inner edges. Do not fasten the thread, but turn the tape back. Make it level with the edge of the garment as shown in the diagram. Oversew the edges.

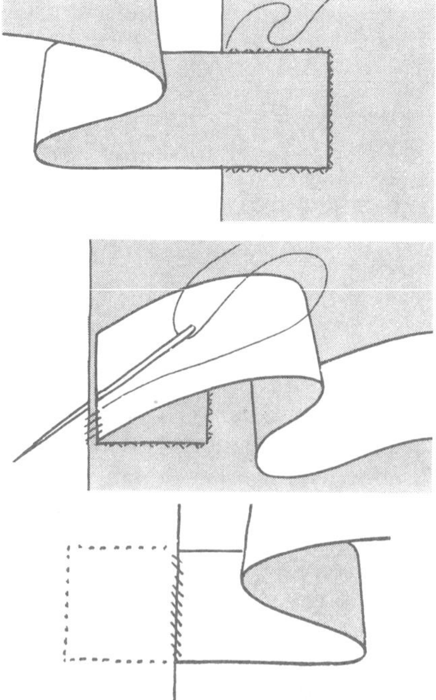

When overlapping edges with a tie fastening, make the tape as instructed above. One tie is stitched to the right-side of the underlapping edge. One tie is stitched to the wrong-side of the overlapping edge. Place one tape on the wrong-side of the overlap. The raw edge is down in the place required. Pin in place.

Back-stitch or machine-stitch around the square as shown in the diagram. Finish the free end of the

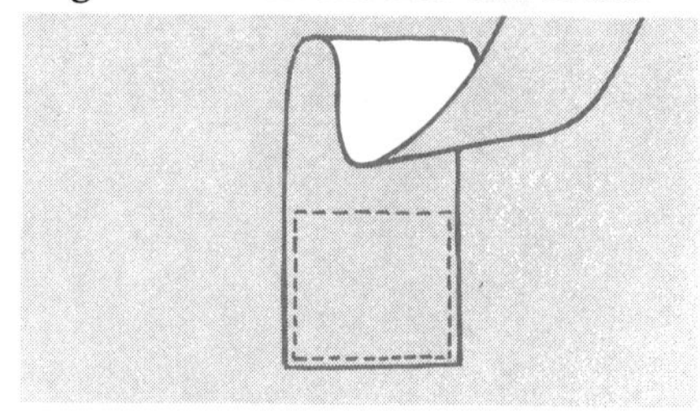

tape. Make a narrow hem on the wrong-side. Small knots or a

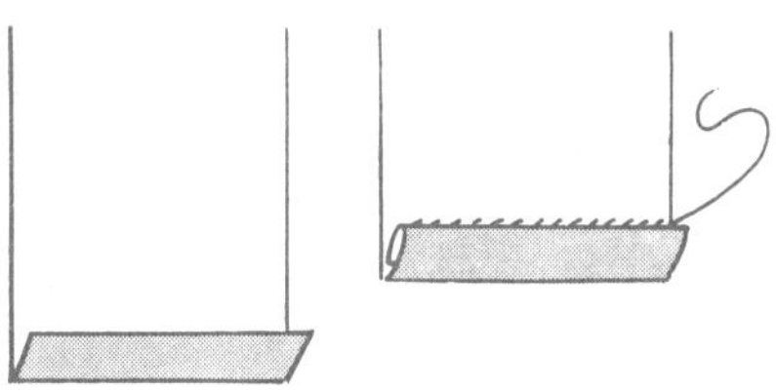

hand-stitched roll may be formed at the end.

Ribbon is attached the same way as tape. The free end of ribbon is not hemmed. Cut the ribbon to shape, as shown.

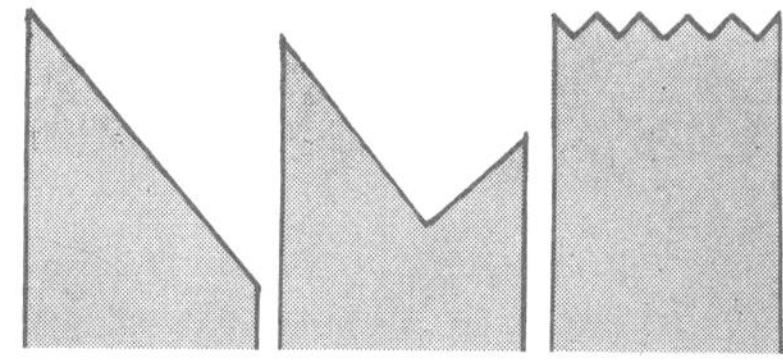

Touch-and-Close Tape—This nylon tape is made as two strips. One strip is covered with tiny burrs that act like hooks and eyes. When pressed together, the two strips stick together until pulled apart.

Tape is made in a variety of colors and widths. It can be cut to size because it does not fray. It is useful on loose-fitting garments. Do not use it where there is much strain or on thin fabric. Use it on detachable features such as bows, hoods and beading.

Stitch the tape in place by machine. A small zigzag-stitch can be used. If stitching should not show on the right-side, slip-stitch the tape on the wrong-side of the overlap.

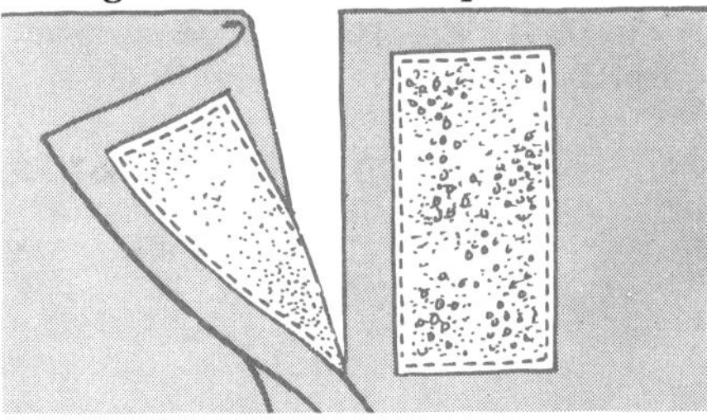

GATHERING AND SHIRRING

Gathers are small, soft folds used for skirts, blouses, sleeves, yokes, frills and children's clothes. They are made with running-stitches to ease material and control fullness. They can be made by hand or by machine. Gathers are marked on patterns to indicate their position. Details are given about how much material is taken up in a row of gathering.

Divide the area to be gathered into sections. Leave gathering threads in until the final stitching is complete.

Shirring, also called *ruching*, is several rows of gathers, or gathers and fine elastic. If elastic is used, shirring can be used on areas where the size is adjustable, such as waist and neck cuffs. Shirring may be decorated with smocking or other embroidery.

Gathering

HANDMADE

Use a long, double thread. Sew a row of running-stitches on the right-side along the line to be gathered. Sew another row 1/4 inch away. Leave thread free at both ends.

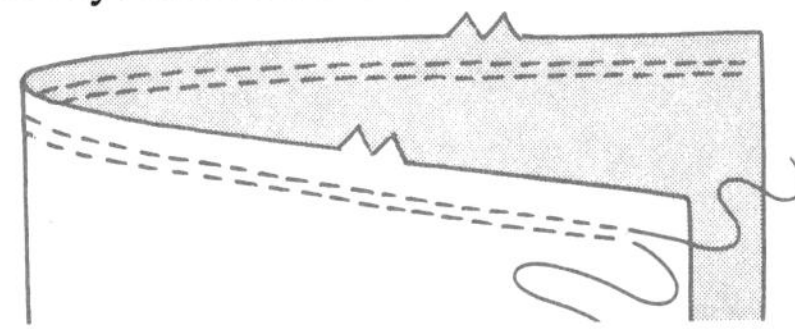

Ease fabric along the thread gently from both ends. Ease the piece of

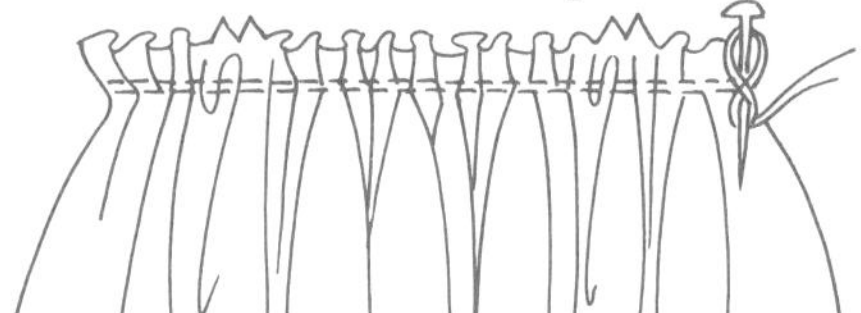

gathered fabric to the correct length before finishing. Make several firm stitches at each end when you finish.

MACHINE-MADE

This produces an even effect, and gathers are easy to distribute. On delicate fabric, use a fine needle and thread to avoid damage. Some machines gather automatically with the aid of a gathering foot. Check your sewing-machine handbook for instructions. Do not use this method when precision is needed.

Set machine-stitch length to the longest stitch. Loosen the top tension. Machine-stitch two or more rows of evenly spaced stitching. Draw up the bobbin thread. A heavy thread on the bobbin keeps thread from breaking.

Ease the bobbin thread through the fabric. Evenly distribute fullness from both ends. Wind each end of the drawn-up thread around a pin placed at right angles to the stitching.

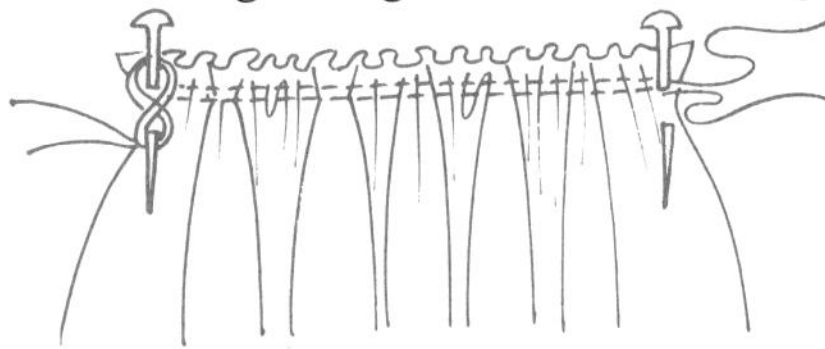

Work gathers until they are even, then fasten thread ends. Make several back-stitches to secure the gathers.

Gathers may also be done on the sewing machine. Sew two rows of zigzag-stitching over cord. Draw cords to the required length. This method avoids placing strain on the thread. It is quick, efficient and simple.

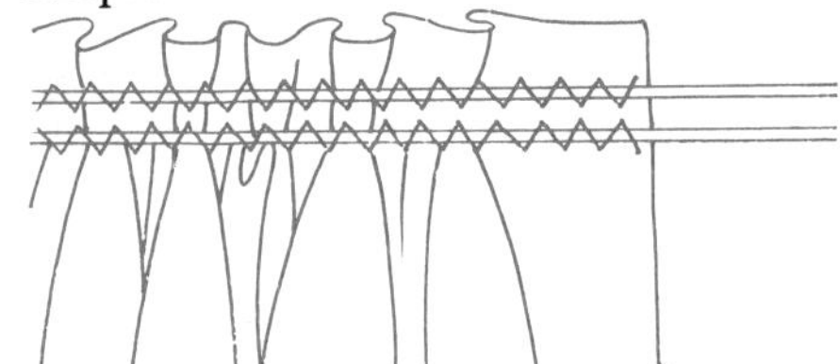

GAGING

Many rows of hand gathers hold a large amount of fabric in a small area. This is called *gaging*. It is the method used for smocking. Sew running-stitches on the right-side. Take a longer stitch under the surface. Keep all the stitches in line.

Gaging is easy to do on dotted or checked fabric. Special iron-on transfers can be used to make guide dots on other fabrics.

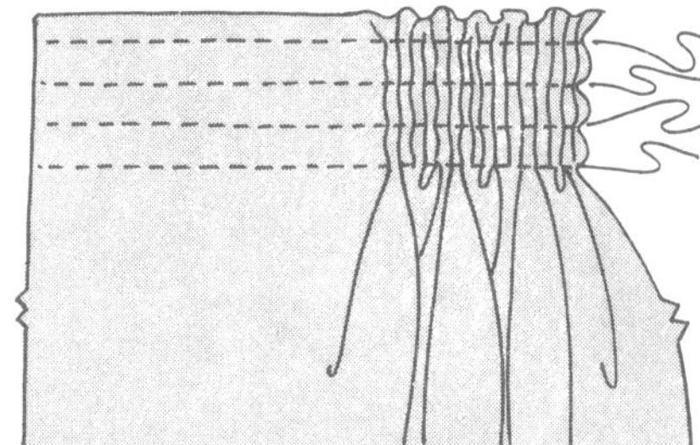

With Elastic—This is a simple way to stitch elastic directly to the garment at sleeve edges. Use elastic about 1/4 inch wide. Sew from the wrong-side.

Pin the end of the elastic in place. Stitch with a zigzag-stitch over the elastic, stretching it while you sew. Set the stitch so stitches fall *between* the elastic cords. This keeps the elastic from being pierced and later broken.

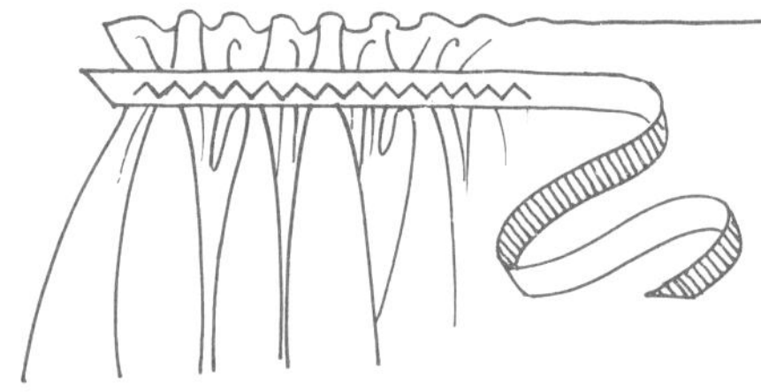

Shirring

HAND-SHIRRING

Sew several rows of evenly spaced gathers, and pull them together. Sew off thread ends, or knot them in pairs.

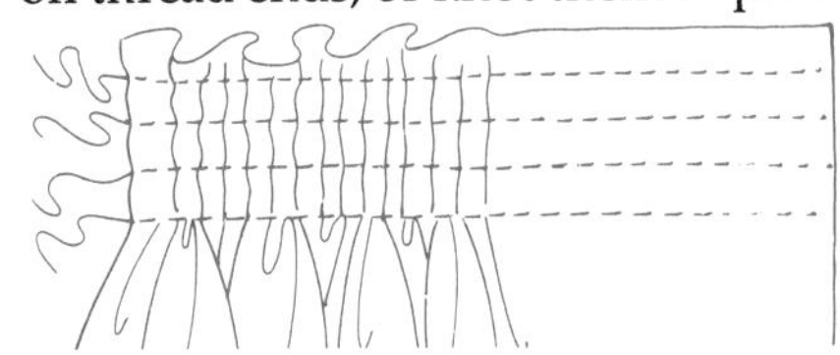

Threads may break in wear, so hand-shirring is usually backed with a piece of fabric. Cut a piece of self-fabric on the straight grain. Turn in the edges, and tack it to the wrong-side over the shirred area. Hem to the gathers.

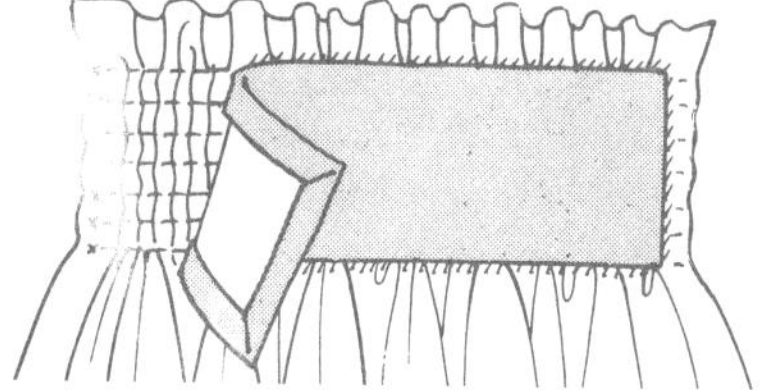

MACHINE-SHIRRING

There are two ways to do this. Shirring elastic, which is fine tubular elastic on a reel, is used on the machine bobbin. Wind it evenly, but do not stretch it.

Set the machine to a long straight-stitch. Test the top tension on a scrap of garment fabric. It may need to be tightened. Stitch two or three rows, holding the fabric flat. Fabric should gather back to half the original length.

Mark the place where the rows of stitching are sewn. Machine-stitch from the right-side with a long straight-stitch. Hold the fabric taut. Place fabric on greaseproof paper to keep it flat while stitching. The paper can be torn away later. Stitch several evenly spaced rows, keeping fabric flat.

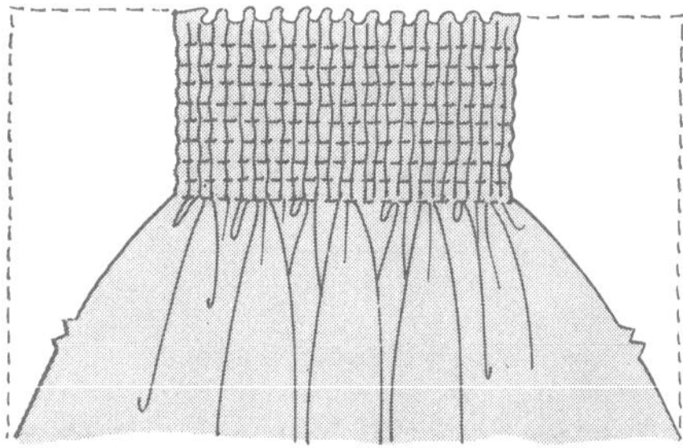

Use your sewing machine for the second method of shirring with a buttonhole foot. This foot usually has two parallel grooves along the underside. Place the fabric in position, ready to sew. Use a long, double strand of shirring elastic. Place one strand in each groove of the foot.

Use a three-step zigzag-stitch to sew the shirring elastic directly to the fabric. Pull elastic to gather the fabric while stitching. Hold the elastic at the back when starting to sew. This keeps the fabric running smoothly under the foot. The more the elastic is pulled at the front, the more the fabric is gathered.

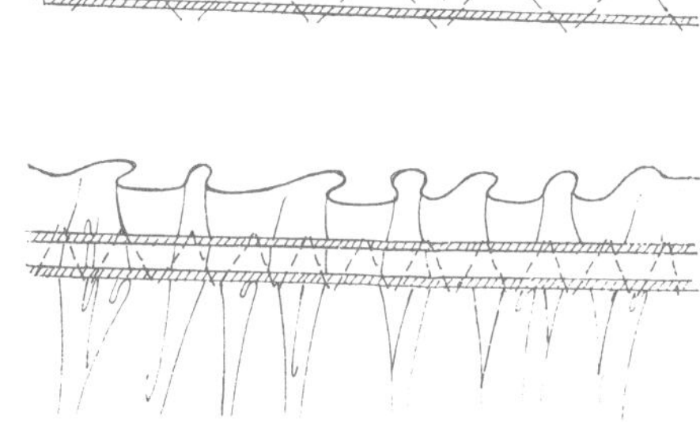

DECORATIVE SHIRRING

Set the sewing machine for shirring. Use a three-step zigzag-, serpentine- or other similar stitch.

Place greaseproof paper under the fabric to keep elastic from gathering during sewing. Sew parallel rows of stitching until the required depth of shirring is achieved. Sew in the ends

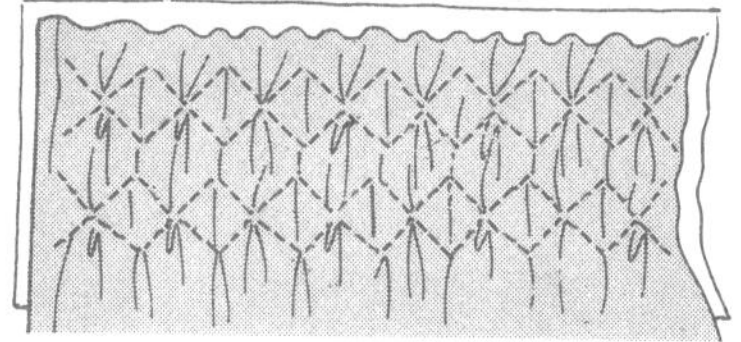

of the elastic. Tear away the paper. Remove tiny pieces of paper with tweezers.

Experienced sewers may want to match the pattern on the rows of stitching. Join the points of the stitches in one row to the points in the next row. Stitch slowly and carefully. Make stitching in decorative shirring more obvious by using contrasting colors or double thread in the needle.

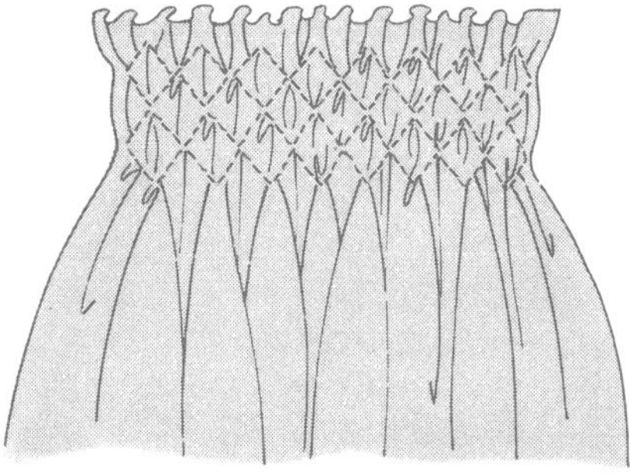

GATHERED RUCHING

This trim is gathered to form frills. It can be used as a decorative edging for children's clothes. It can be done on women's garments when a feminine effect is desired.

Use a ribbon or fabric that has been hemmed along the raw edge. Make running-stitches through the center of the fabric or ribbon. Ease fabric on the thread, and make gathers even. Tack or baste the

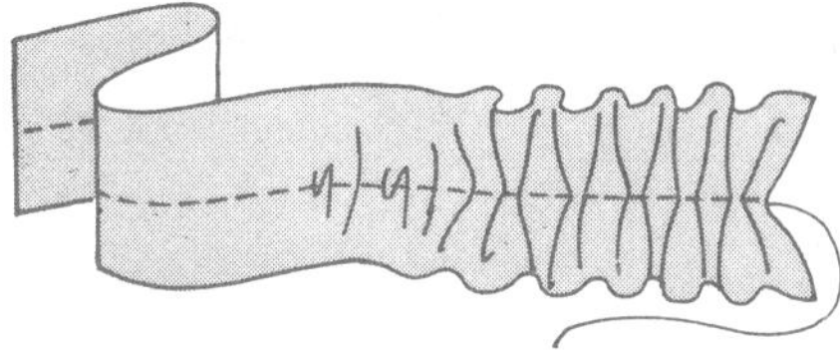

ruching to the garment where required. Machine-stitch along the

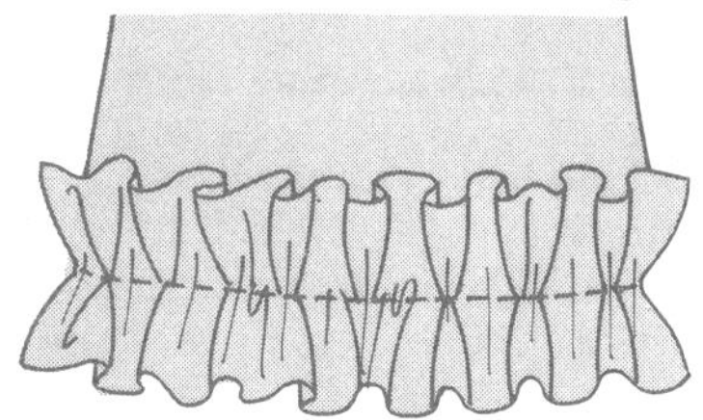

line of gathering-stitches, and remove tacking.

SHELL-GATHERED RUCHING

Cut a 2-inch-wide bias strip. Fold the bias strip in half lengthwise, with right-sides together. Tack along the edges. Machine-stitch and remove tacking.

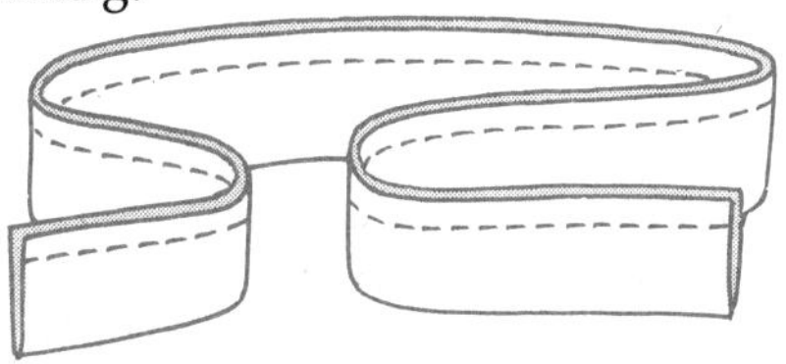

Turn the bias strip inside-out, forming a tube 7/8 inch wide. The seam should be down the center.

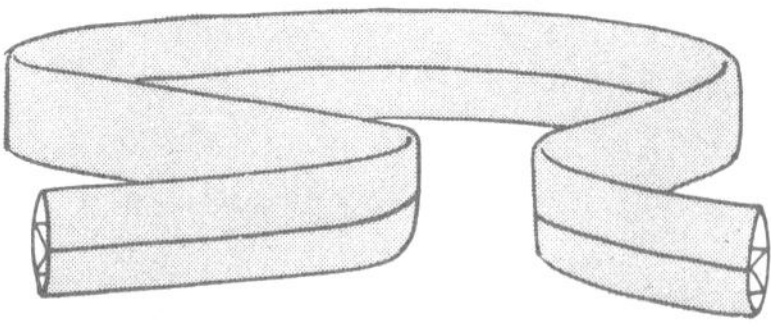

Insert running-stitches diagonally from edge to edge on the tubing. Stitches should not go over the edges of the fabric.

Gently ease the thread to gather the tubing, forming shells of equal proportions. When complete, attach

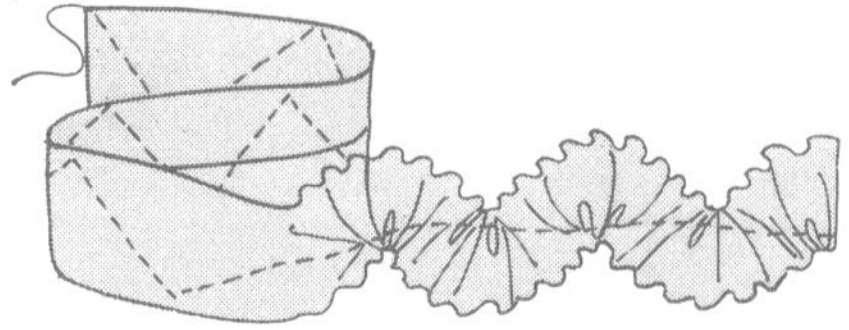

the shell-gathered ruching to the garment with slip-stitches or machine-stitches.

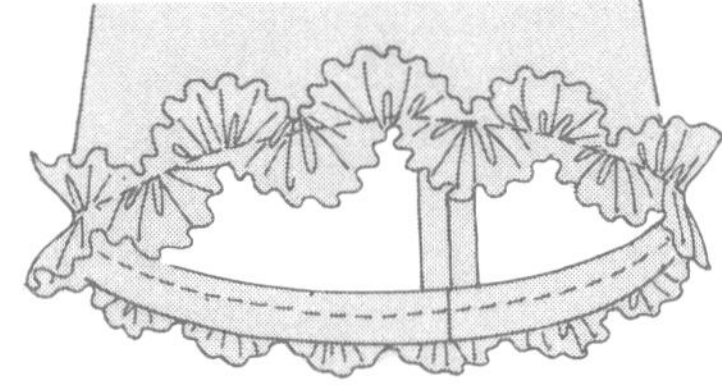

GODETS AND GUSSETS

Godets

A godet is a shaped piece of self-fabric or contrasting fabric. It is inset in a garment to add extra width. The most common type is shaped like a slice of pie. Godets can also be semicircular, oblong or pleated. They make tight garments easy to wear. They are an interesting, eye-catching style detail. If a pattern does not include godets, they can be added in seams, darts or slashes in sleeves or skirts.

Godets can be used to add extra weight. Tack seam binding along the

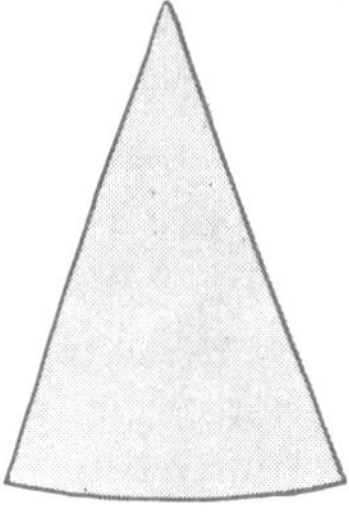

seam lines of the garment piece. If the fabric can stretch out of shape, tack the godet to the garment piece along the top. Let it hang for a day or two. Then pin, tack and stitch the godet in place where it falls. It will always hang well.

Level the godet with the edge of the garment, and finish the hem. For godets in a seam or dart, end stitching at the pattern markings. Tie off threads securely, and complete as above.

For godets in a slash, stay-stitch around the slash. Tack a piece of lining over the right-side of the point as reinforcement. Clip to the

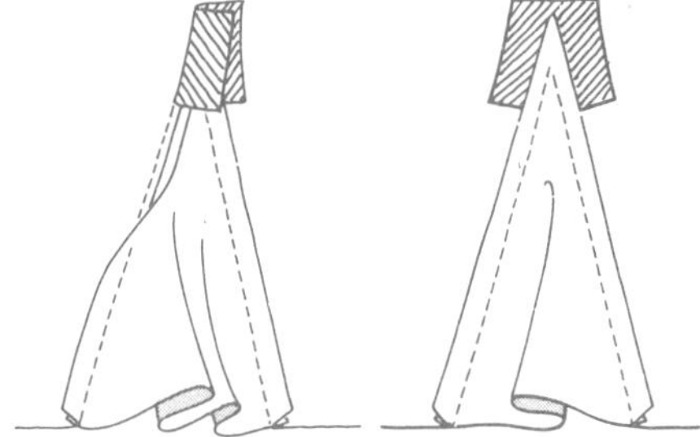

stitching at the point, then turn to the wrong-side. Pin, tack and stitch the inset along the slashed seam line.

Press the godet. In a slash, press the seam allowance away from the godet. In a dart, slash the fold of the dart, and press the point flat.

Clip the godet seam allowance about 1 inch below the point. Press edges as shown in the illustration.

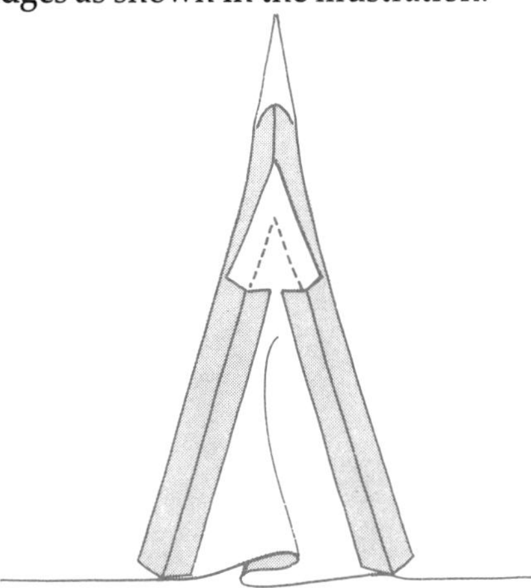

Top-stitch near the garment edge, if desired. Allow the garment to hang for a day or two, then finish the hem.

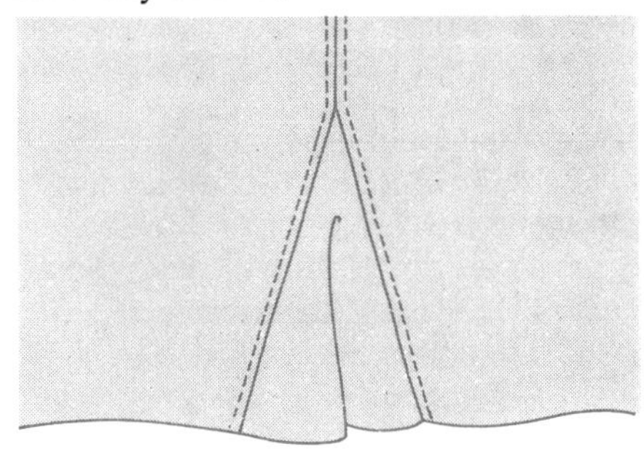

Gussets

Gussets are set in a slash or seam of a garment. They allow ease of movement at underarms or crotch. They may be cut separately or as an extension of a garment piece. These are called *combination gussets.*

Gussets are usually cut as a triangle or diamond-shape piece of self-fabric. They are stitched so they fit without being obvious. For a new pattern, make up the gussets in inexpensive fabric as a test. Adjust the size and placing of the gussets as needed.

CONSTRUCTION METHOD

Reinforce slash points with lengths of seam binding or a square of lining cut on the cross grain.

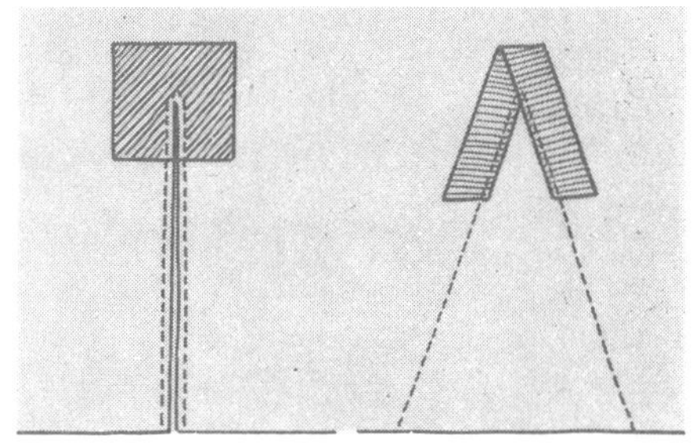

A square of iron-on interfacing may also be used. Press it to the wrong-side of the points of the slashes. Cut the slash to within 1/4 inch of the points. Tack the gusset, and try the fit of the garment and gusset. Make any alterations, then remove the gusset.

Slash to the stitching line at the points. If the gusset contains a dart or seam, stitch and finish it. With right-sides together, pin and tack the gusset to the garment. Stitch the same way as triangular gussets. Then press seam allowances away from the gusset. Clip as necessary, and trim the reinforcemnt square.

Gussets may have a lining for reinforcement. Slip-stitch this in place with edges turned under or left flat. Finish it with the gusset seam allowances.

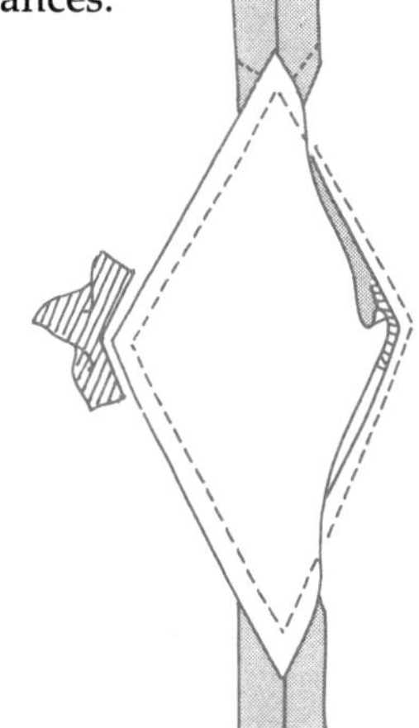

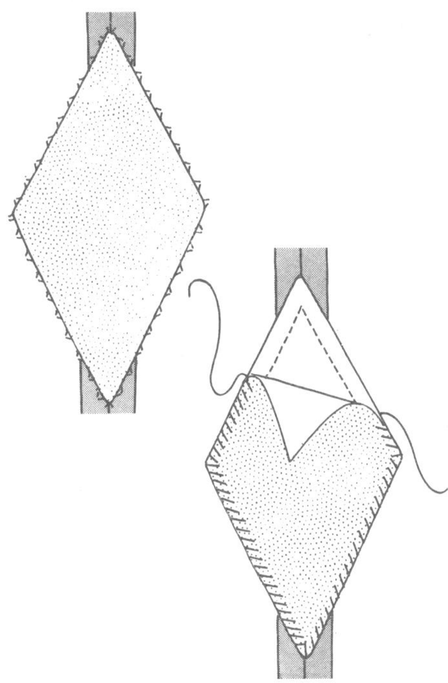

TRIANGULAR GUSSETS

With right-sides together, pin and tack gussets in the slash. From the garment side, machine-stitch along the seam line. Pivot at the point. Press seam allowances away from the gusset. Trim edges of the reinforcement squares. If a triangular gusset is set in the underarm, stitch the underarm bodice seam and sleeve in one long seam.

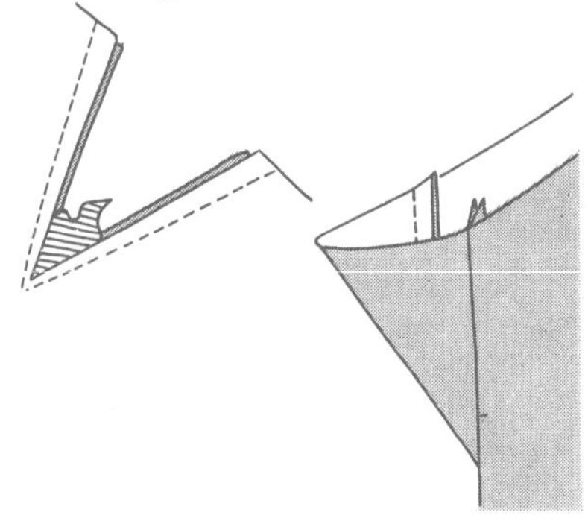

HEMS

A hem is usually a double fold turned to the wrong-side of a garment edge. It finishes the edge neatly and helps the garment hang well.

The hemline length and finish of the edge are important to the style and appearance of a garment. Hemline placement varies according to the type of garment and its fashion. The length should be flattering to the wearer.

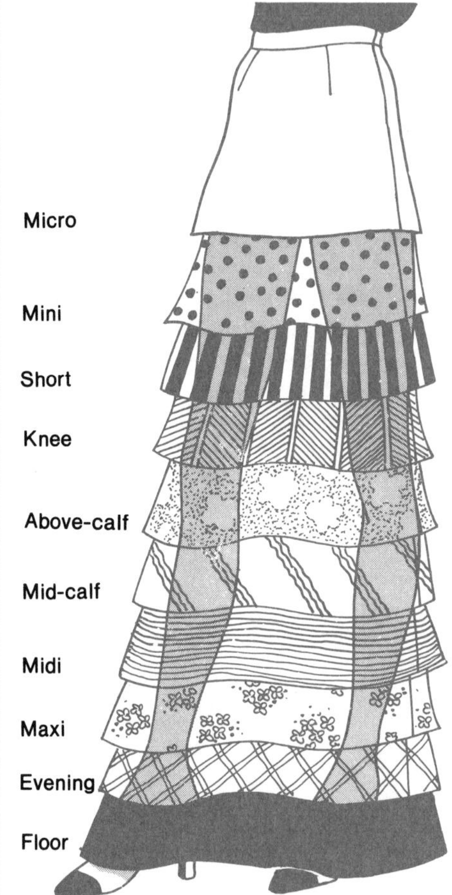

To determine the depth of a hem, consider the fabric and style of the garment. Adjustments may have to be made for striped fabric and pleated edges. Unless the hem is a decorative feature, it should be unobtrusive.

PERFECT HEM

Match seam lines when pinning the hem in place. Adjust fullness between the seams. Skirt or dress hems have a professional look when bulk and fullness are eliminated. When edge fullness is adjusted, shrink with an iron. Put heavy cardboard between the hem and the dress so only the hem shrinks.

When using tape on a hem edge, use *bias* tape. Hemming-stitches take up only one thread of the fabric. They are not visible on the right-side of the garment.

When preparing a hem, be sure the garment is an even length all around. Insert pins in the hem vertically to keep fullness evenly distributed.

Press any seams in the hemline before hemming. Ask a friend to help adjust your hem, or use a hem marker or yardstick.

When making a hem, check pattern instructions. For a flared style—heavy, knit or stretch fabrics—a narrow hem is needed. Make wide hems for lightweight, flimsy fabrics, and straight or floor-length garments.

Gauzy fabrics should have fine, rolled finishes or deep hems. Consider the type of garment and the position of the hem before you decide which finish to use.

Let your height help determine the hem depth. Tall figures can carry a deeper hem than short ones. Deep hems worn by short figures make the garment look out of proportion.

Narrow, 1/4-inch hems stitched by machine are quick and easy for long-wearing garments. These include children's clothes, nightwear, jeans, aprons and shirts.

HEM DEPTH	
Straight skirt	2 to 3 inches
A-line skirt	1-3/4 inches
Flared hem	1/2 to 3/4 inch
Circular hem, sheer	1/8 inch
Blouse hem	1/2 to 1-1/2 inches
Jacket or sleeve hem	3/4 to 1-3/4 inches

MARKING HEM

Make any fitting alterations to the garment, then let it hang for 24 hours. Try the garment on with the appropriate underwear, shoes and belt. Fasten all openings.

A second person needs to mark the hem. The wearer stands on a chair so the hang of the garment can be seen. Decide on the length of the hemline. Place a line of pins around the garment at this level, 2 to 3 inches apart. If the edge is uneven, measure up from the table using a hem marker or yardstick.

Pin up the hem along the line of pins to see if the length is correct. If necessary, experiment to get the correct length. Keep the edge level all around. Leave the line of pins marking the edge, but remove the others. Let the hem down again, and take off the garment.

TURNING UP HEM

Lay the garment on a flat surface. Trim the seam allowance on the hem.

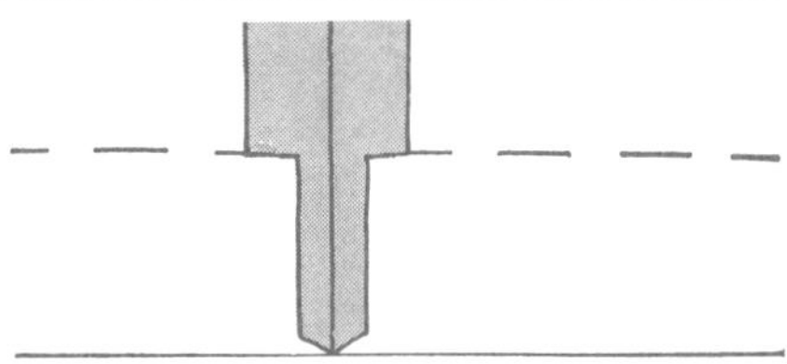

Tack the hem up 1/4 inch from the final hemline. Press the folded edge only. Work on the wrong-side of the fabric in short sections. This keeps the hemline from stretching.

Use a tape measure or hem gage to mark the hem depth, plus the finished edge. Mark with tailor's chalk or pins. Trim excess fabric along this line. On transparent

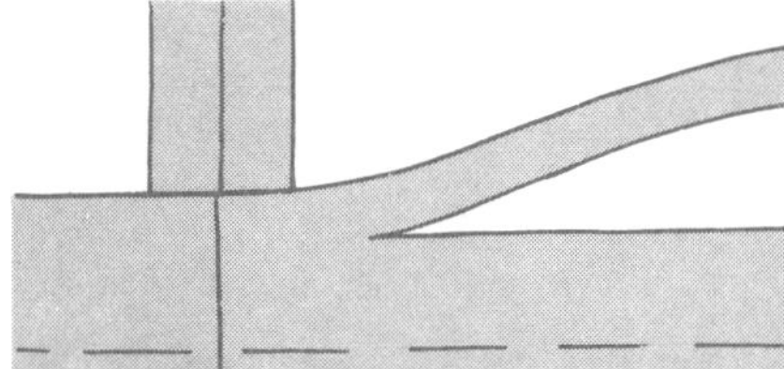

fabrics, hems are made with two folds the same depth to hide raw edges.

HEM FULLNESS

Hem fullness can be treated in different ways, according to the type of fabric and hem being used.

Shrinking—Shrink wool, cotton and linen that is not preshrunk. Sew a line of ease-stitching around the free edge of the hem.

Pull up the ease thread at intervals to evenly adjust fullness. Put a dry cloth between the hem and garment. Use a damp cloth over the hem. Press well to shrink excess fabric. Repeat if necessary, then allow to dry. Remove ease-stitching.

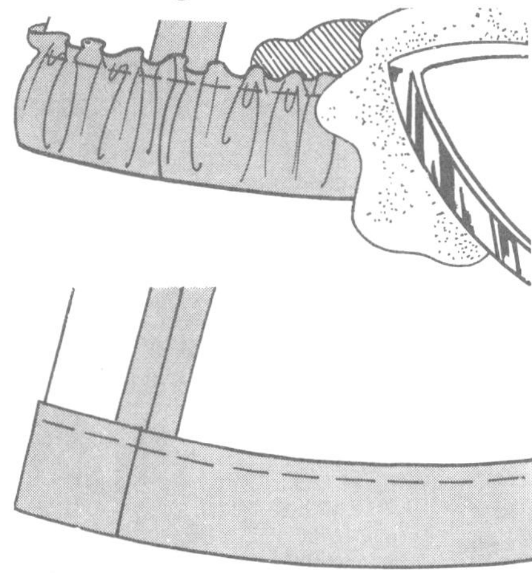

Pleats—Make small pleats, tucks or darts all around the hem. Leave the tacked edge competely flat. Space pleats around the hem. On thick fabric, trim away the surplus material in pleats. Finish the edges.

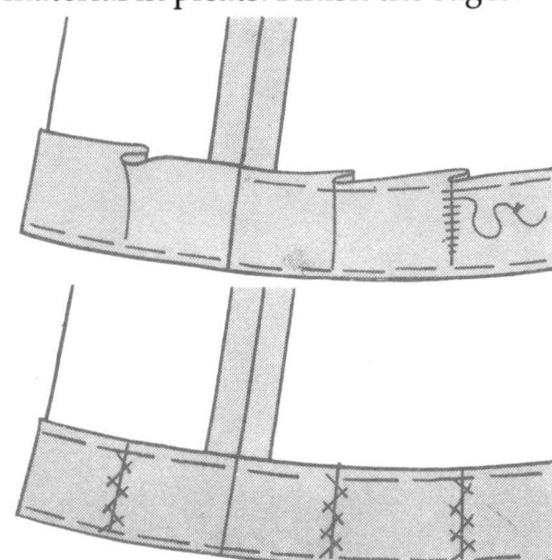

Gathers—Machine-stitch a row of ease-stitching or gathering by hand. Pull up the thread at intervals to evenly adjust fullness. Lift and gently pull with a pin. Repeat this process in other areas of the hem.

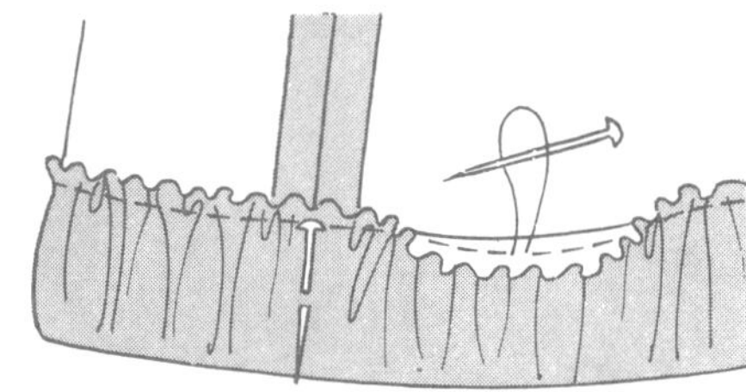

If there is a raw edge, turn it under and stitch. Stitching can be used as an ease thread if there are 10 stitches to the inch. If a raw edge will be

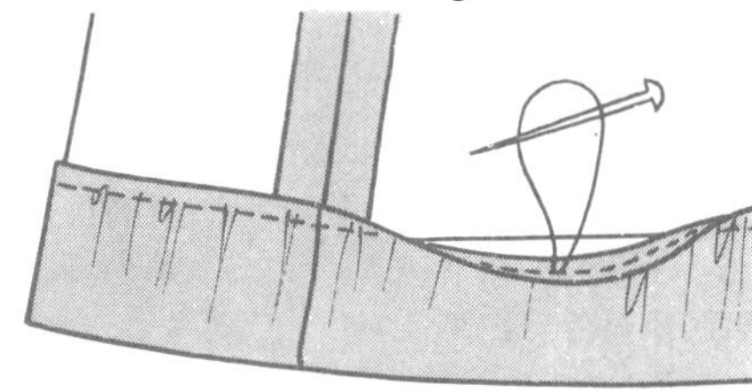

covered with tape, an ease thread can be put in. Adjust it before stitching tape to the hem. If a skirt or dress does not have too much fullness, use a seam thread on the hem as an ease thread.

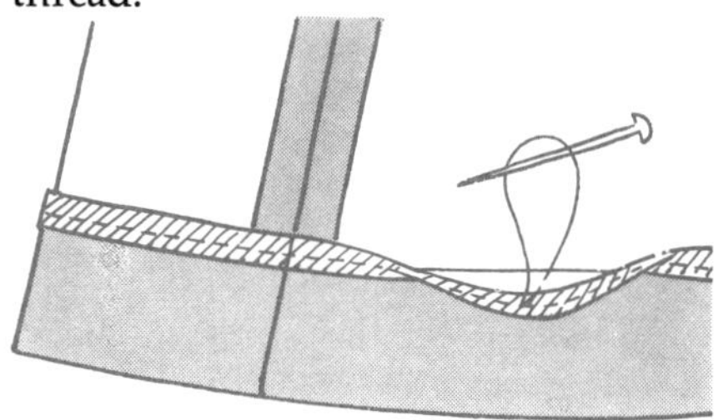

CORNERS IN HEM

A hem may join a facing at the corners of a button-through skirt or on the front edges of a jacket. Miter corners to eliminate bulk and make corners lie flat.

Fold the fabric as shown in the illustration below. Press, open out and trim as shown. Fold under the

edges on three sides and press. Turn hems to the wrong-side, and oversew them at the corner joint. Stitch the hems.

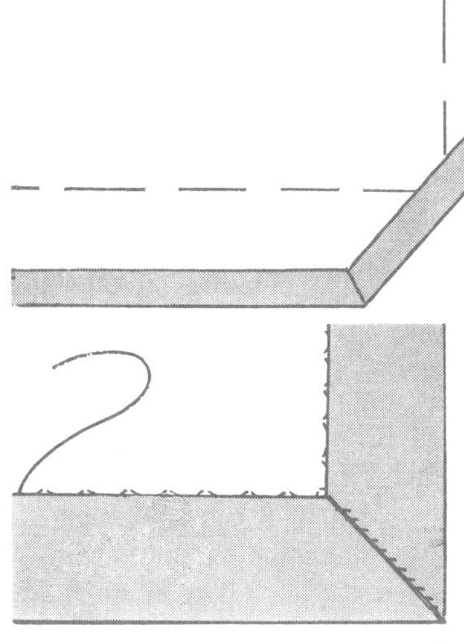

FINISHES FOR RAW EDGES

Finish raw edges before sewing a hem to a garment. Keep the depth of the hem even. For fine fabrics, turn up the raw edge 1/4 inch. Pin, tack and press in position.

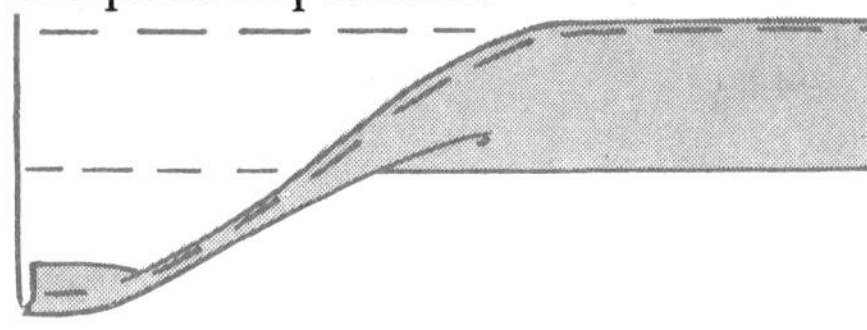

For light fabrics, turn over edges and machine-stitch with a straight- or zigzag-stitch. For fabrics that fray,

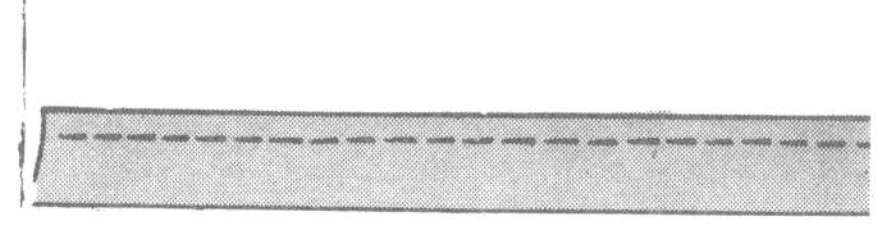

stitch 1/4 inch from the raw edge. Trim with pinking shears.

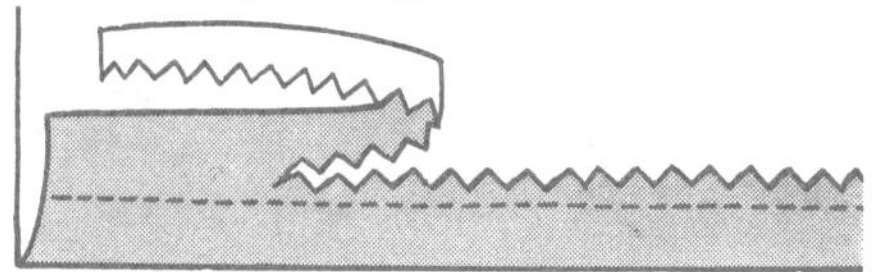

For medium fabrics, overcast edges by hand or machine. Make stitches small and close together. If the material frays badly, work a row of straight machine-stitches, then trim closely. Overcast by machine-stitching.

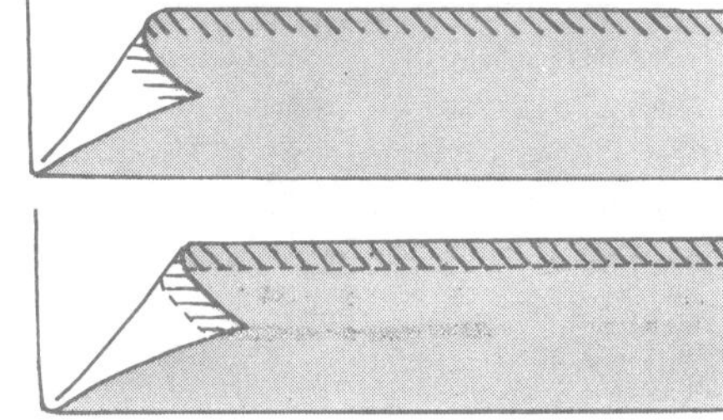

Enclose heavy fabrics in a bias strip on the edge of the hem. This can be made from lining fabric or one fold of bias tape, trimmed to reduce width. Sew the usual way from the right-side. Roll binding to the wrong-side. Instead of turning it in, let it lie flat. Work a slip-stitch along the join from the right-side to reduce bulk.

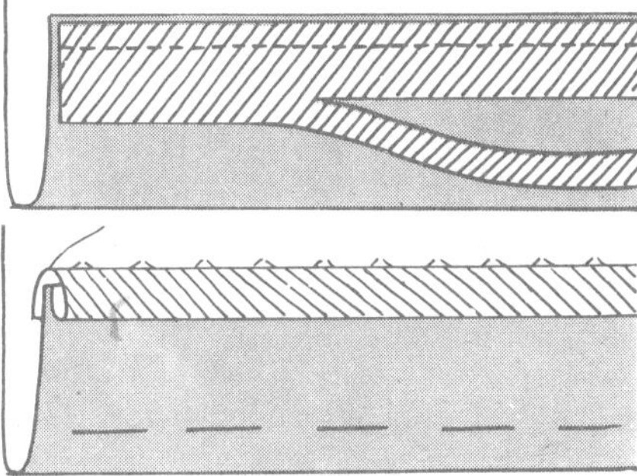

SEWING HEM TO GARMENT

Plain Hem—Press the finished edge of the hem, dealing with any fullness. Working with the garment flat on a table, tack the hem to the garment. Tack it near the line that marks the hem edge for sheer fabric, and 1/2 inch away for all other fabrics.

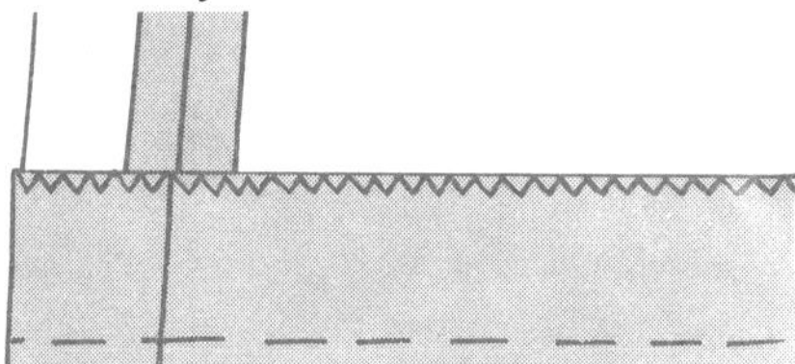

On hems of fine fabric, turn the finished edge toward you. Take the smallest stitch in the garment. Pick up one thread of the fabric. Run the needle 1/4 inch through the fold on the hem.

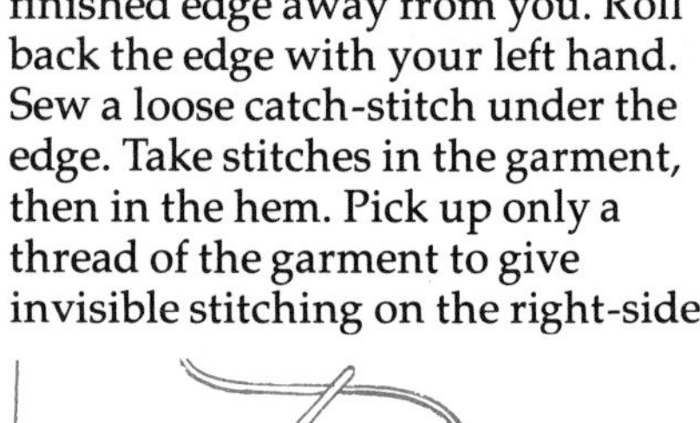

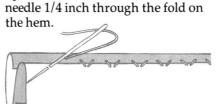

For other fabrics, work with the finished edge away from you. Roll back the edge with your left hand. Sew a loose catch-stitch under the edge. Take stitches in the garment, then in the hem. Pick up only a thread of the garment to give invisible stitching on the right-side.

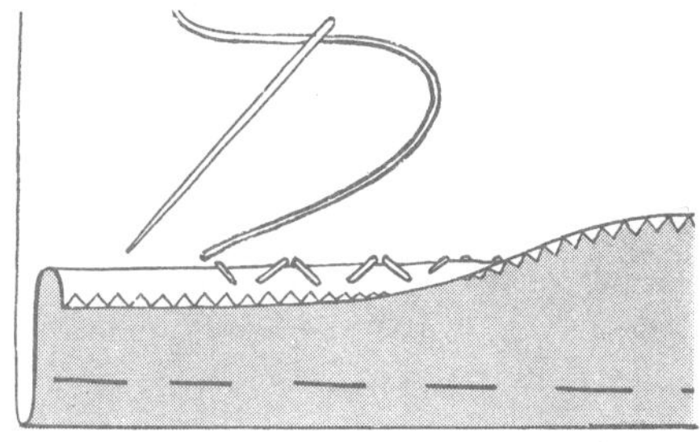

Remove tacking before pressing.

PRESSING HEM

Remove all pins and tacking. Press the hem from the wrong-side of the garment. If there is extra fullness, shrink it.

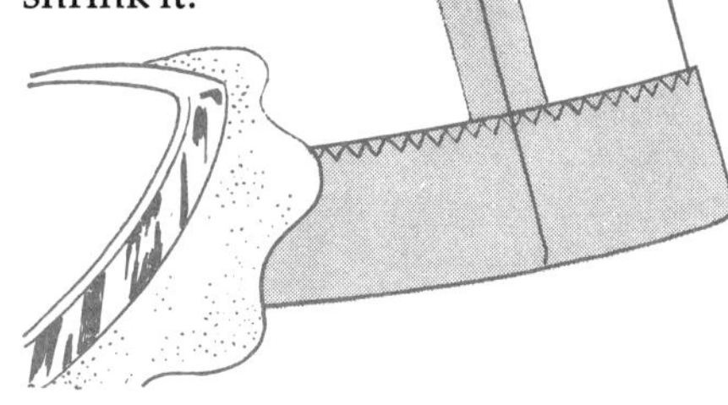

For soft-edge hems, hold the steam 2 to 3 inches above the hem. Steam it well. Pound the hem lightly with a ruler or back of a clothes brush for shaping. Do not let the iron touch the hem. Let the hem dry.

For sharp-edge hems, press the hem from the wrong-side to within 1/4 inch of the stitched edge. Pound it well if a sharp-edge crease is required. Press lightly from the right-side.

For a pleated hem, press seams before hemming, especially where a seam occurs at a fold. For hems on pleated skirts, see the section on *Pleats*, page 138.

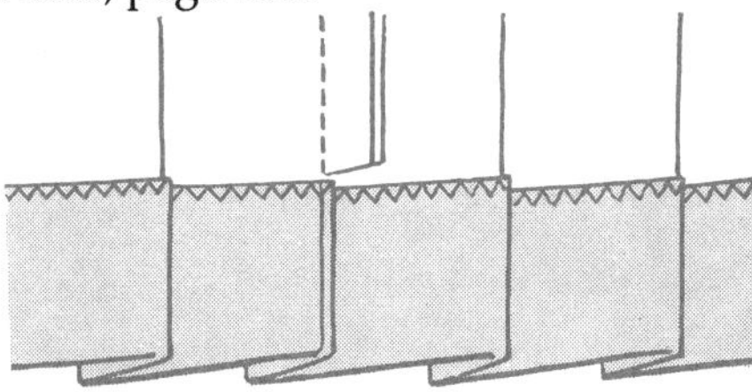

TYPES OF HEMS

Catch-Stitch Hem—This hem lies flat without using tape. It is suitable for heavy wool and other fabrics. It can be used on lined coats.

Sew from left to right. Catch a thread of the fabric in the hem. Push the needle from right to left above the hem edge. Pick up the thread in the garment below the hem edge. Push the needle from right to left. Do not pull the stitching of the hem too tight. Repeat until the hem is completed, then remove tacking and press.

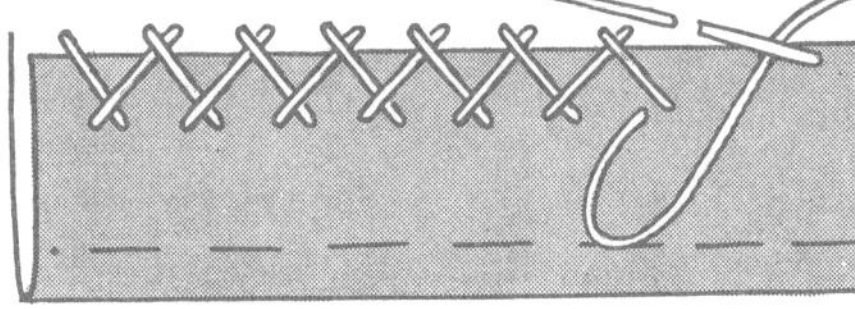

Tailor's Hem—This is useful for jersey and soft wool fabrics. Use about 8 stitches to the inch. Stitch the raw edge of the hem, then pink the edge. If the fabric frays, use seam tape or overcast it rather than pinking the material.

Pull to ease stitching. Sew the hem 5/8 inch from the pinked edge. Fold the hem back against the outside of the garment. Slip-stitch the hem, pushing the needle into the stitched line. Pick up one thread of the garment material. Take another thread on the stitching line, followed by one stitch in the fold. Repeat until the hem is complete. Remove tacking, and press the hem.

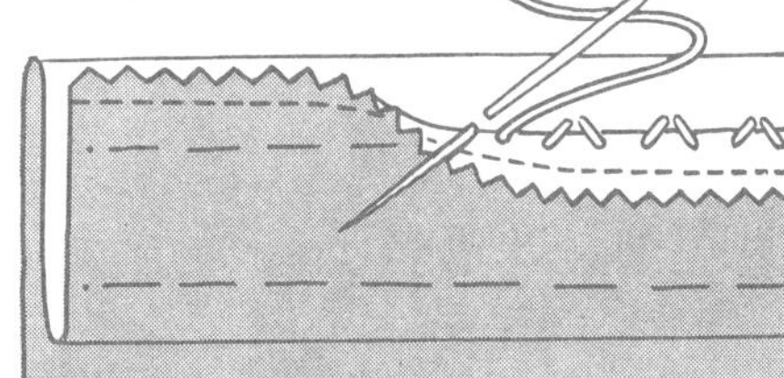

Lock-Stitch Hem—This is a strong, long-wearing hem, sewn from left to right. Attach thread in the edge of the hem at the side of the garment. Take a stitch through one thread of the garment fabric.

Take another stitch through one thread of the garment 1/4 inch from the starting point. Follow this with another on the hem.

Pass the needle over the loop as indicated in the illustration below. Repeat the process until the hem is complete. Remove all tacking and press.

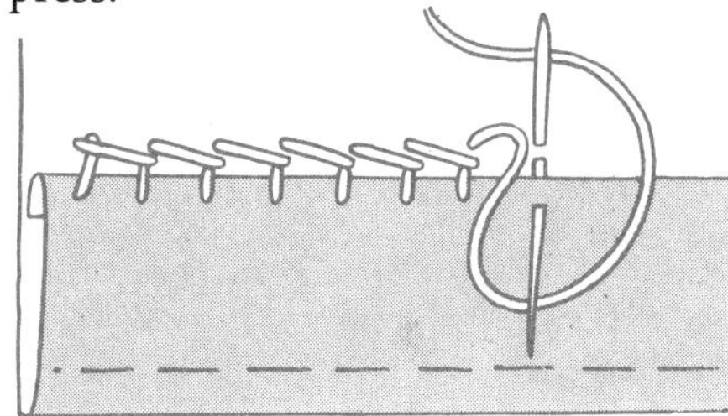

Slip-Stitch Hem—This hem is suitable for firmly woven cotton, light or medium fabrics and silk.

Turn raw edges under about 1/4 inch. Pin in position. Stitch, using 8 stitches per inch.

Slip-stitch the hem to the garment by picking up a single thread below the folded edge of the hem. Slip the needle into the fold about 1/4 inch. Bring out the needle, and pick up another single thread below the fold. Slip the needle in the fold edge again. Repeat until hem is completed, remove tacking and press.

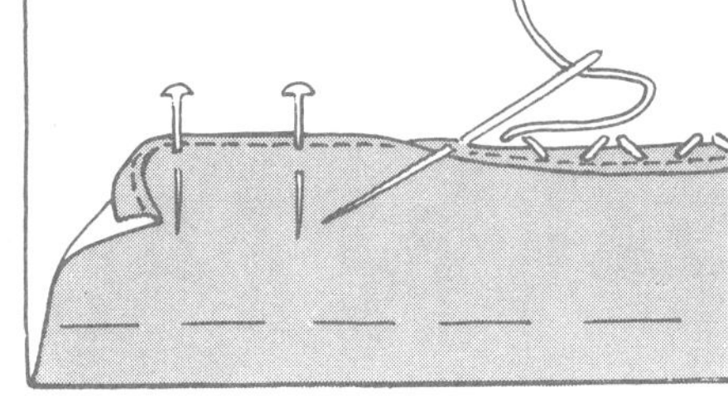

Stitched-Edge Hem—This is a neat edge for hems that cannot be rolled. Turn under the edge and machine-stitch. Turn the edge again, hem with an invisible hem-stitch and press.

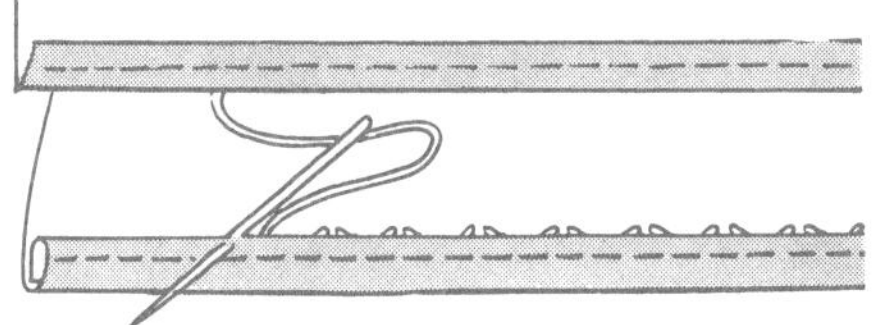

There are two other ways to finish this hem. Pink the raw edge, turn up the edge and press. Machine-stitch as

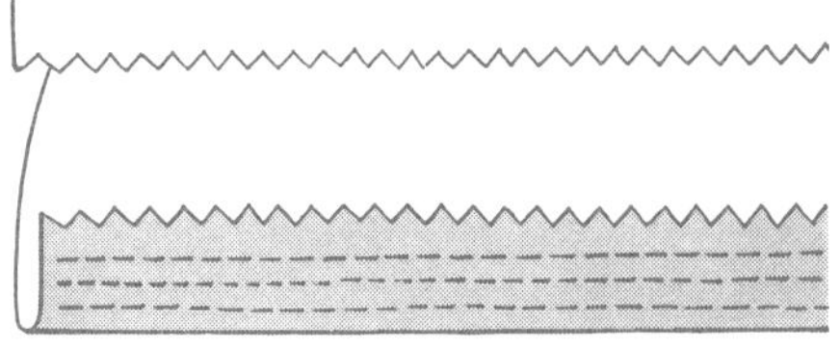

required. Or turn the raw edge and stitch, then turn and stitch a second time. Press.

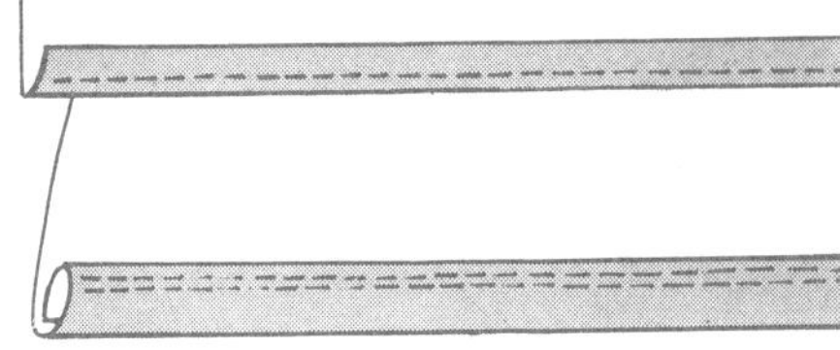

Narrow, Machine-Stitched Hem—This hem gives a neat, flat edge on fabrics that do not fray.

Use a narrow hemming foot or rolled-hemming foot on the machine. Refer to your sewing-machine handbook. When

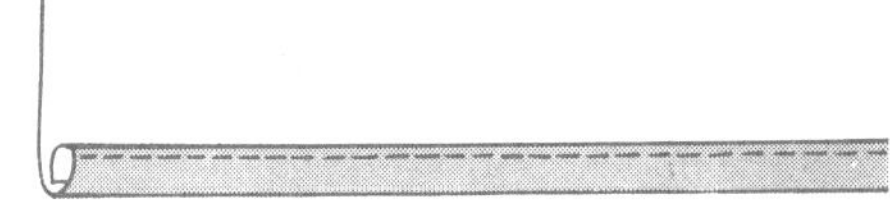

the narrow-hemming foot is used, the material is turned twice and stitched in one step. When the rolled-hemming foot is used, the fabric is coiled in a roll, then zigzagged in place.

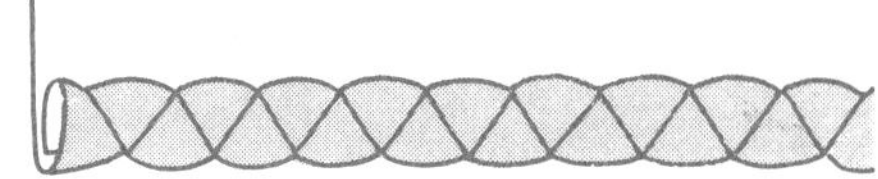

Blouse-Edge Hem—Blouse hems should not show a ridge when tucked into a close-fitting skirt. To avoid this, make a line of stitching around the lower edge of the blouse about 1/2 inch from the edge. Add another row 1/4 inch away. Pink the

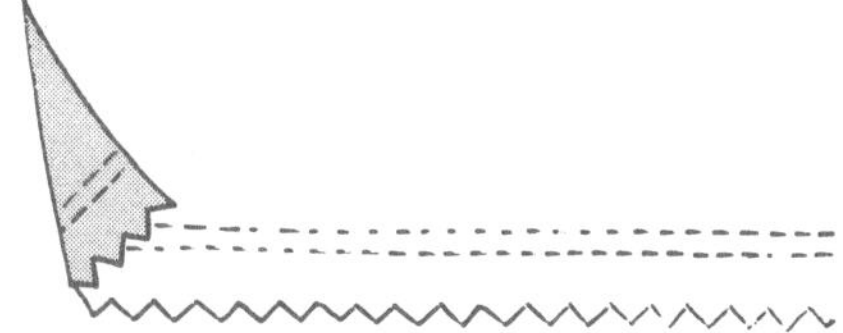

edge. If the fabric frays, turn the raw edge under about 1/4 inch, and stitch around it twice.

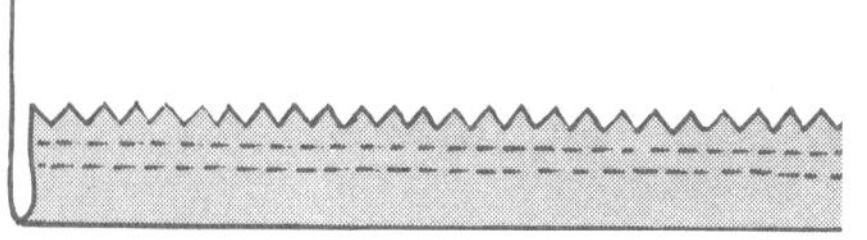

The edge may be overcast with a narrow zigzag-stitch over fine cord. Trim the fabric.

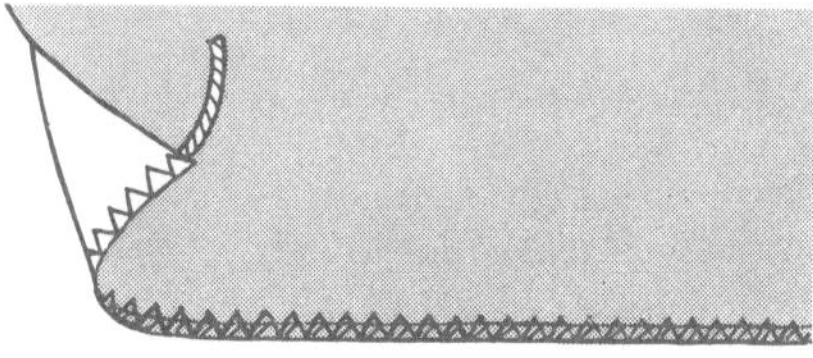

Machine Blind-Stitched Hem—Some sewing machines have a special guide for this stitch to use on thick fabrics. Follow your sewing-machine handbook for details.

Make the hem even, and tack the edge. Trim the hem edge to the required depth, then overcast the raw edge to finish it. Prepare the machine for blind hemming by attaching the special foot.

Put the garment hem in the machine as shown. Sew carefully. Catch only one thread in the fold of the garment or stitching will show on the right-side.

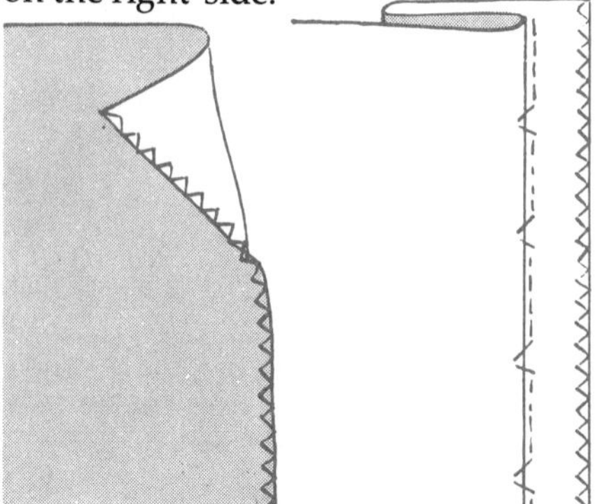

Rolled, Stitched Hem—This is suitable for light, fine fabrics. It is a neat hem for lingerie and the edges of frills.

Stitch 1/4 inch from the edge. Trim close to the stitching edge. Between thumb and forefinger, roll the edge for a few inches. Make a roll about 1/8 inch deep.

Sew the roll in position with a slip-stitch. If the hem puckers, snip machine-stitching at intervals.

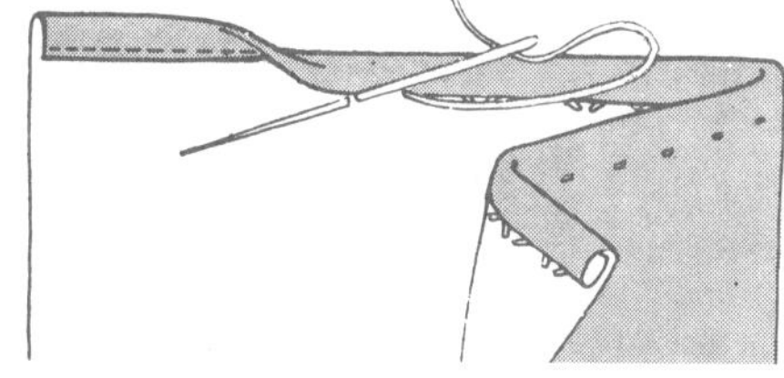

Quick, Hand-Rolled Hem—Fold the hem edge under from 1/8 to 1/4 inch. Take a small stitch on the edge of the fold. Then make a tiny stitch in the fabric ahead of and at an angle to the first. Repeat the stitches.

This produces a line of zigzagging.

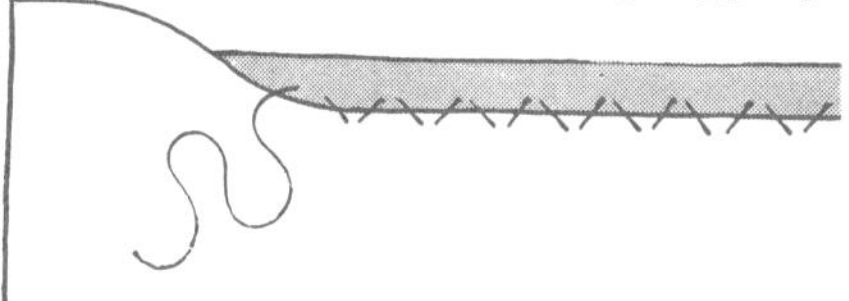

Make several stitches. Hold the turned edge at the beginning of the stitches with one hand. Use the other hand to pull up the thread. The edge forms a roll.

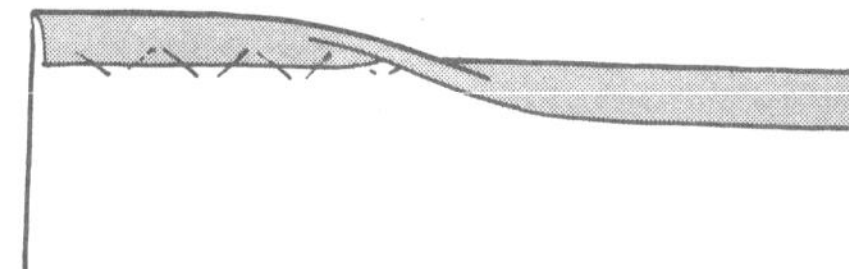

Taped Hem—This hem uses seam binding or bias tape. It is suitable for cotton, wool, fabrics that fray and heavy man-made fabric.

Sewing 8 stitches per inch, stitch around the hem edge. Pull the thread up to ease fullness so the hem lies flat. Stitch tape 1/4 inch from the hem edge. Press tape gently, pin in position and tack. Hem the tape to the garment. Remove tacking and press.

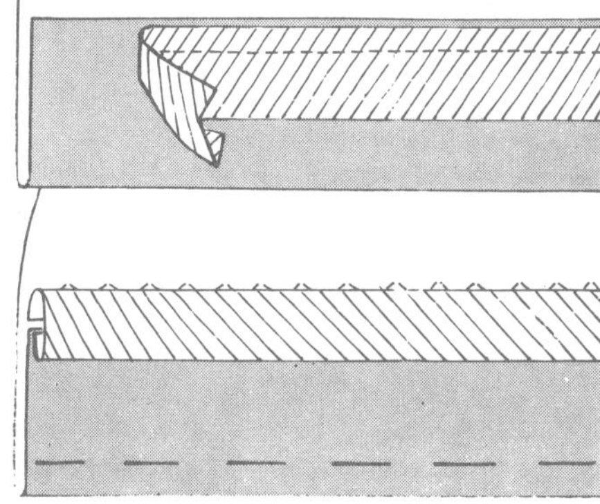

Bound Hem—This is a quick method to use when there is no fabric to turn up. Use it when a bound edge that shows on the right-side is acceptable, such as aprons and children's clothes.

Try on the garment. Cut the hem to the right length. Bind the cut edge, using bias tape or cross-grain strips cut from the garment fabric. See the section on *Binding and Piping,* page 87, for details.

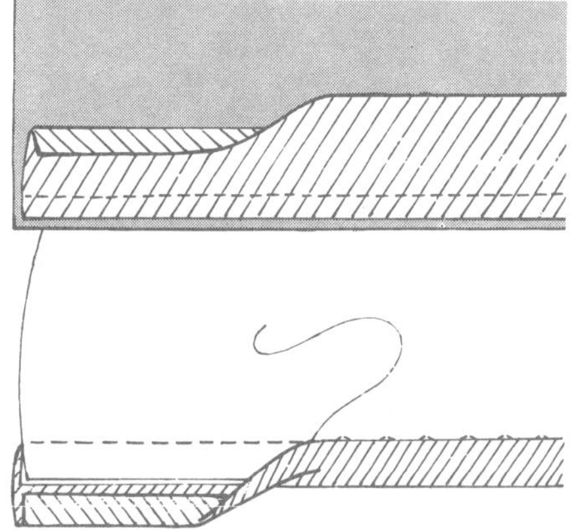

Faced, False Hem—This is useful for lengthening a garment by letting down the original folded hem. It can also be used on the right-side as a decorative feature.

Cut facing from bias fabric or use wide bias tape. Turn the tape under, and stitch one raw edge. Stitch the other raw edge to the garment edge. Place tape and edge with right-sides together. Sew together like a plain open seam.

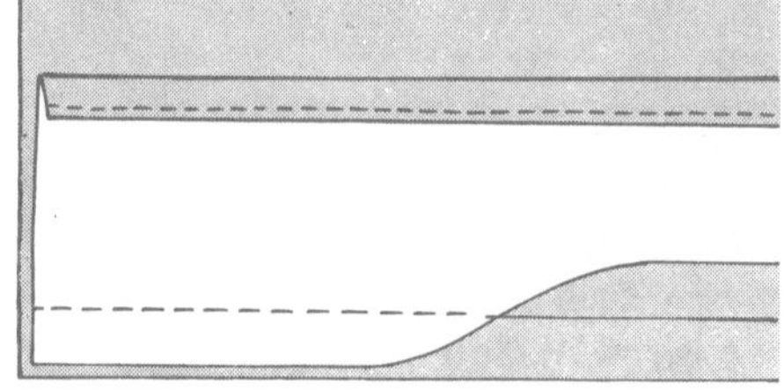

Press the seam open. Turn the facing to the inside part of the garment to the depth of the seam. Pin and tack. Slip-stitch the facing in position. Remove tacking and press.

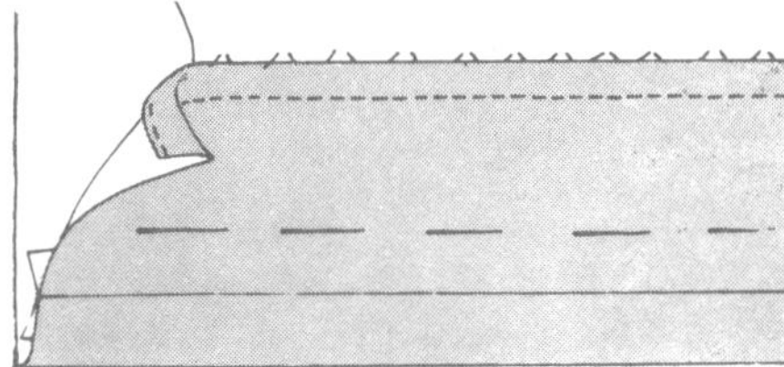

Gathered, Circular Hem—This is used for a gathered hem on a circular skirt. The narrower the hem, the less fullness there will be.

Turn the raw edge under. Pin, tack and stitch, using 8 stitches per inch. Pull the bobbin thread from both ends. Ease fabric slightly to adjust excess.

Steam-press the garment hem so it

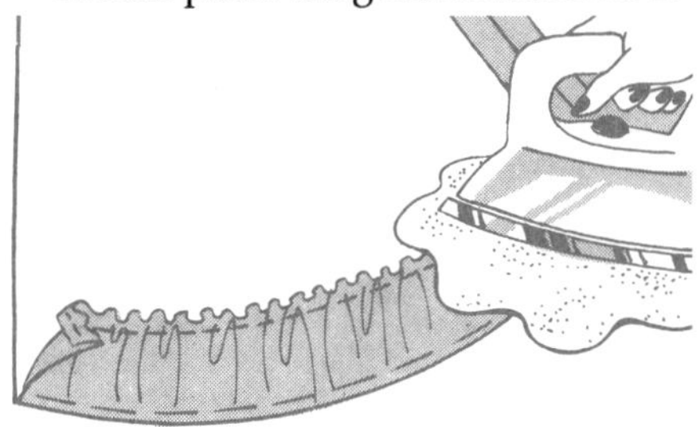

shrinks. Pin and tack hem in place. Remove tacking and press.

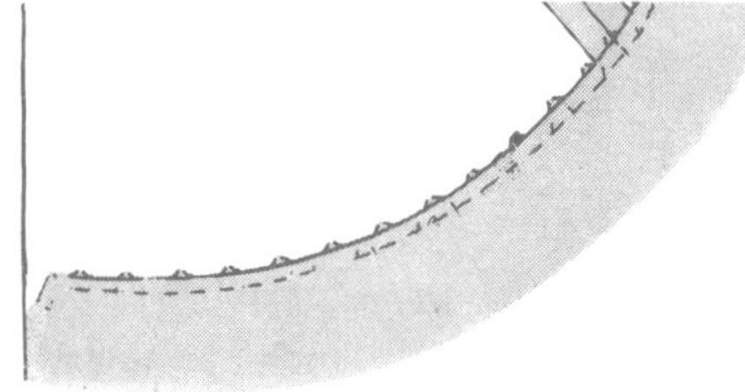

Circular Hem with Tape—This method is used on circular skirts made from thick fabric. With 8 stitches to the inch, stitch around the raw edge. Pull the two ends of the bobbin thread and gather evenly. Steam fullness to shrink surplus fabric. Stitch bias tape to the edge. Pin and tack the tape to the garment. Hem with a blind- or hem-stitch and press.

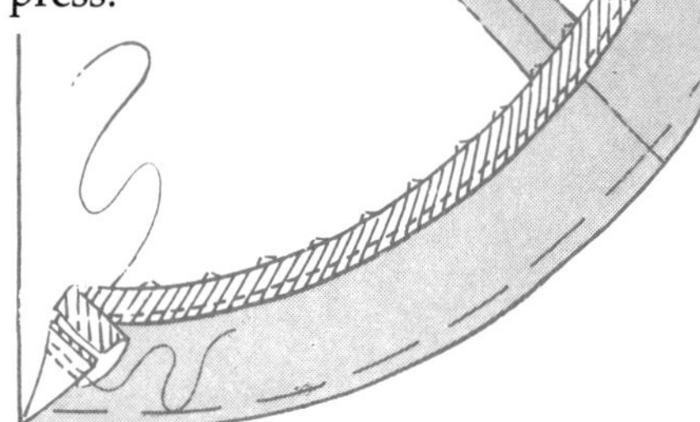

Hem on Sheer Fabric—If a plain hem is desired, make the first and second folds almost equal in width. The raw edge cannot be seen through the fabric from the right-side. A stitched hem may also be used.

Mark the hemline on the wrong-side. Fold the excess fabric to the wrong-side along the marked line. Press.

Stitch as close to the edge as possible, using a fine needle and short stitches. Trim away surplus material close to the stitching. Turn

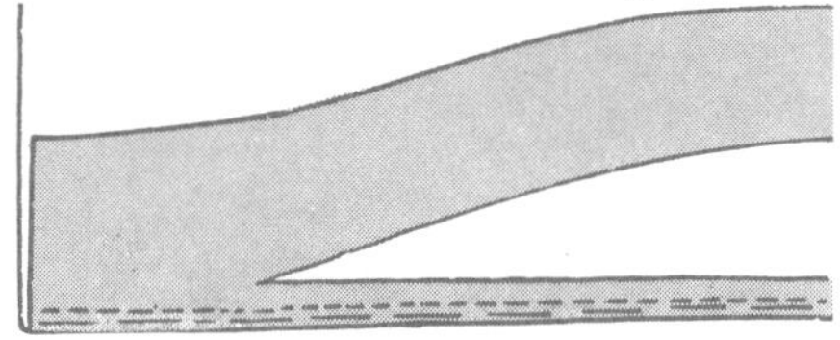

the stitched edge to the wrong-side and press.

Stitch close to the edge. There should be two rows of stitching on the wrong-side and one row on the right-side. Press.

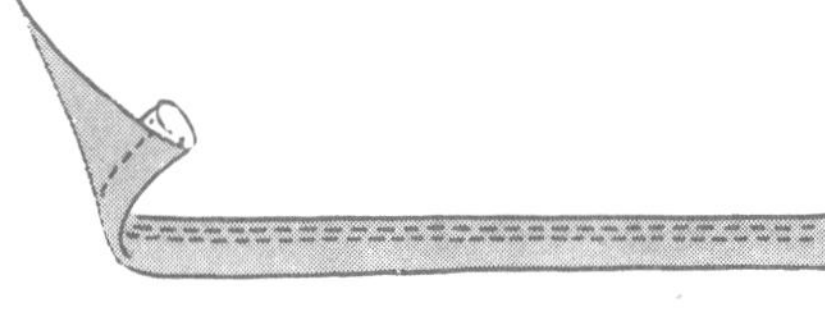

Hand-Stitched Shell Hem—This type of hem gives a decorative finish for cuffs, collars, baby clothes and lingerie.

Tack a narrow hem, then sew a 1/2-inch hem with running-stitches. Another method shows fewer stitches on the right-side. Hem the edge down, taking two stitches every 1/2 inch.

Take two stitches over the edge, and pull the thread tight. Repeat the two stitches at evenly spaced intervals.

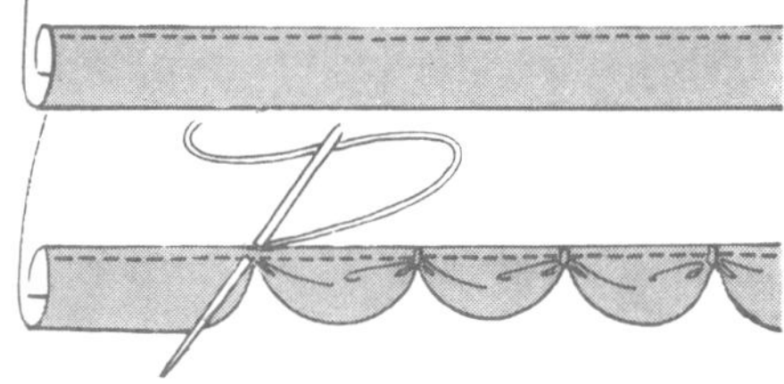

Machine-Stitched Shell Hem—This can be done with a sewing machine using a blind- or stretch blind-hem-stitch.

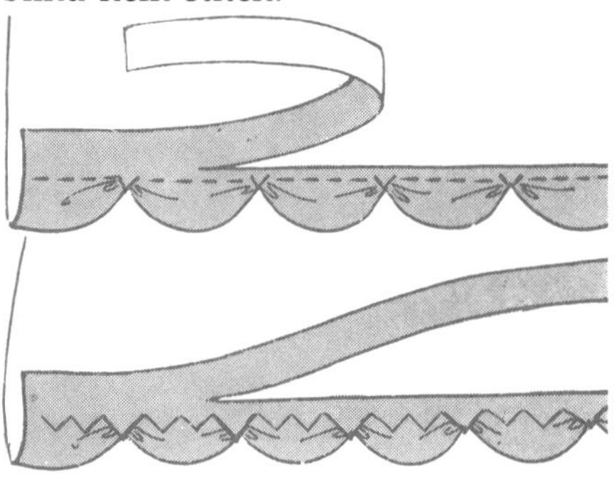

Embroidered Hem—Use this for sheer fabrics. It is a pretty hem for baby clothes, fine table linen and evening dresses.

Mark the exact length of the hem. Turn up the surplus, and tack near the folded edge. On paper, design a simple pattern, then trace it lightly on the right-side. Sew around the design with a zigzag-stitch. Satin-stitch by hand or machine over the design on the right-side. On the wrong-side, trim close to the stitching.

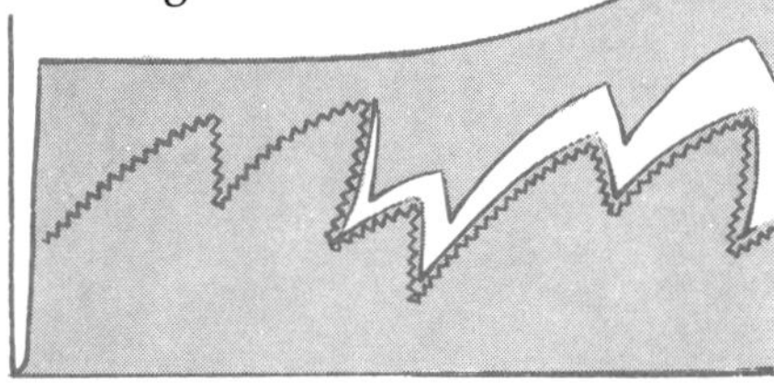

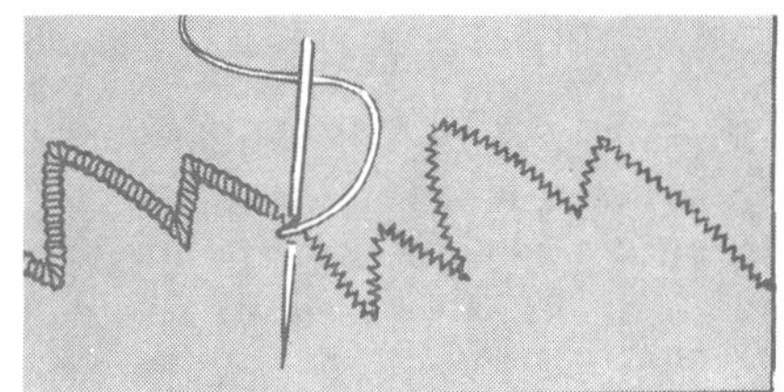

Pin-Stitched Hem—This stitching gives a punched-hole effect. Stitches are pulled tight during sewing. It is used on lingerie, especially curved edges.

Pin and tack the hem, then press to get sharp edges. Work from right to left, preferably from the right-side.

Make a back-stitch in the fabric below the hem. Put the needle back

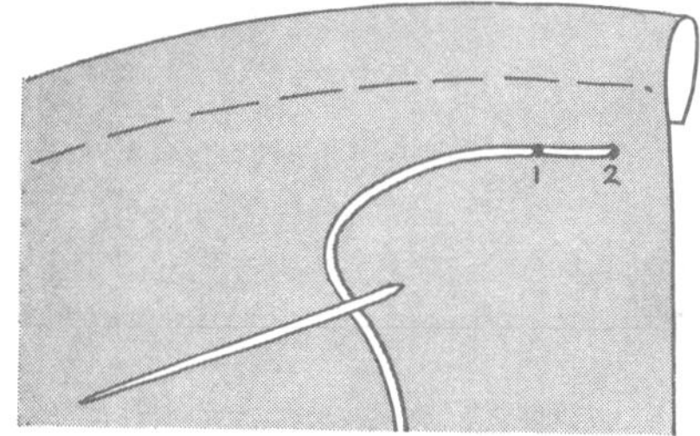

in hole 2. Bring it out above the first hole. Put the needle in hole 1 again.

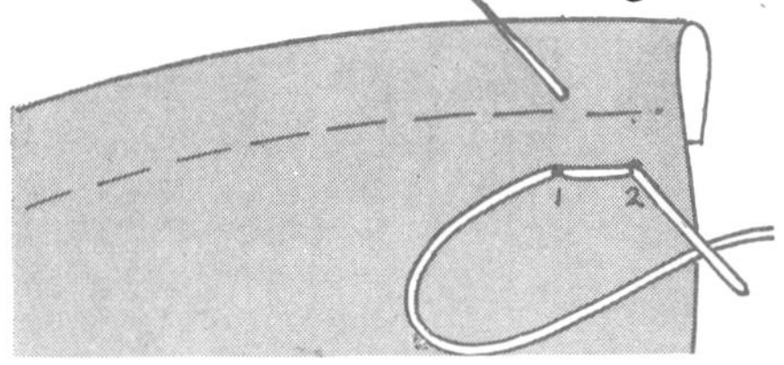

Take a small stitch forward, pulling firmly. Repeat.

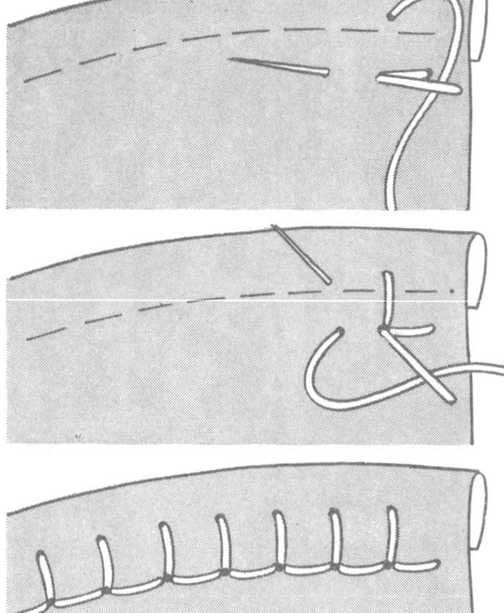

Lettuce-Edge Hem—With many fine, stretchy, jersey fabrics a conventional hem is not desirable or attractive. For a pretty, flouncy hem, do a lettuce hem. It looks like crinkly leaves of lettuce.

Tack a 1/4-inch hem. Stretch the fabric as you tack, so tacking is loose. Set the sewing machine on zigzag.

Make some test samples. This helps make stitching on the garment perfect. Have the right-side of the garment up. Let the stitch fall on the fold with the left swing of the stitch, then off the fold with the right swing. Stretch the fabric during stitching. If you make tests before you start, you will find the correct stitch length for the fabric.

Enclose the edge with zigzag-stitches. When the fabric "relaxes" after sewing, it flutes. After sewing, use fine embroidery scissors to remove tacking. Carefully trim away excess fabric on the wrong-side.

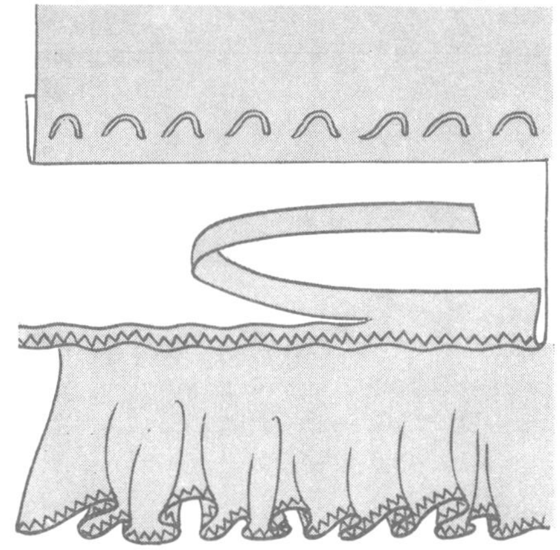

Hem on Lace—Mark the length of the hem. Trim lace about 3/8 inch below the marks. Stitch flat horsehair

braid at the edge of the skirt, below the marked length on the right-side.

Turn on the marks. Catch the free edge of the horsehair braid to the dress with long hemming stitches.

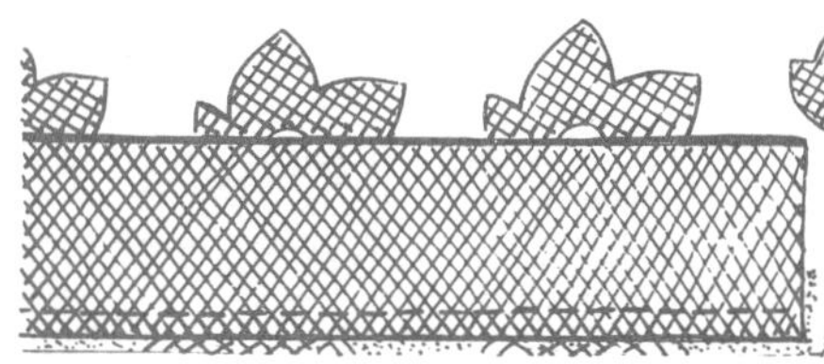

Use narrow braid for hems that fall straight. Use wide braid for hems that stand out crisply.

Stiffened Hem—Full-length evening dresses may need stiffened hems to add stiffness without weight. There are two methods of making this type of hem.

Put horsehair braid on the outside of the skirt, 3/8 inch over the lower edge. Lap the ends, then stitch. Turn

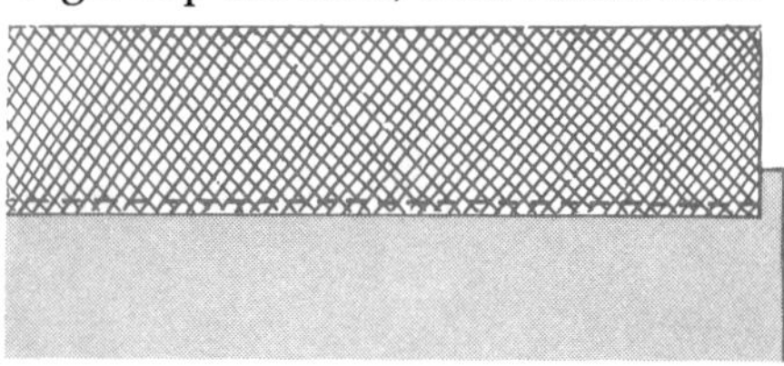

the horsehair braid to the inside. Roll the skirt fabric inside for 1/8 inch. Hem in position, then press.

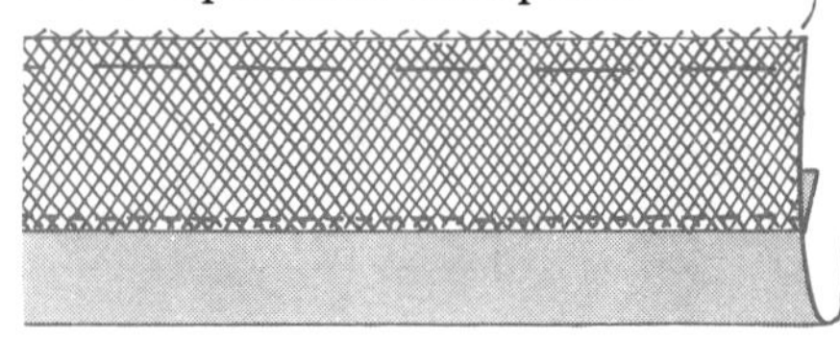

With the second method, horsehair braid is covered by the hem. It is usually 1/4 inch narrower than the hem depth. Put braid 1/4 inch above the lower edge of the skirt, along bottom edge of the braid. Remove tacking. Turn 1/4 inch of skirt material to the inside over the horsehair braid. Tack and stitch, then remove tacking.

Stitch the horsehair to the fabric about 1/2 inch from the top of the

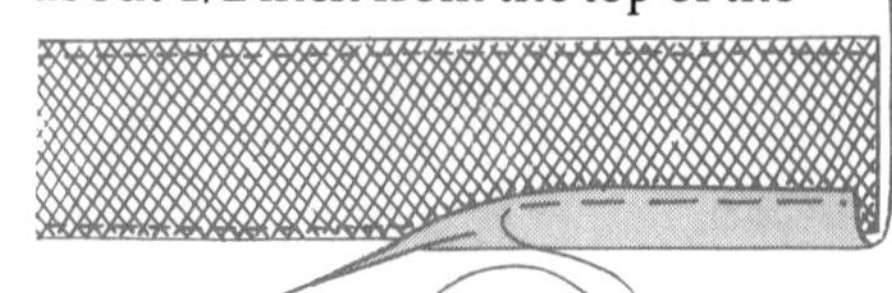

hem. Turn the hem to the inside. Pin, tack, then hem in position. Remove tacking and press.

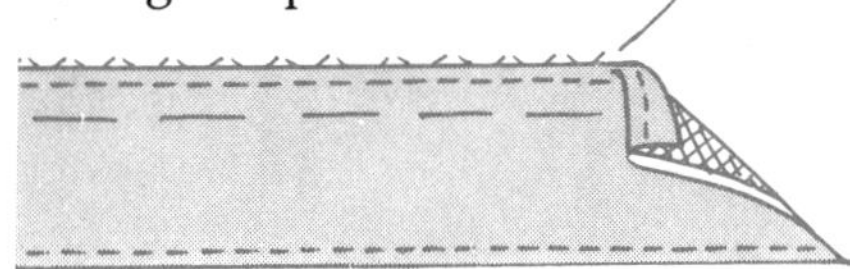

INTERFACING AND LINING

Interfacing

In most garments, an extra layer of fabric is needed for openings, belts, collars, cuffs and pocket flaps. This adds strength and crispness or body to the garment. Special woven and non-woven fabrics are used for interfacing. Interfacing is usually placed between two layers of fabric or between fabric and lining. It can be sewn or bonded to the garment or facing. The finished appearance of a garment is improved by the correct use of interfacing. It can make sewing easier, too.

Soft interfacing helps give a gentle roll to a collar. Firmer interfacing prevents edges from stretching. Use a lighter-weight interfacing than the fabric.

NON-WOVEN INTERFACING

This is made by fusing fibers without weaving. There is no grain, so it does not fray. It is easy to cut and sew and can be cut out economically. Interfacing is usually washable, drip-dry, crease-resistant and does not shrink. It is perfect for fabrics made from man-made or natural fibers.

Non-woven interfacing is unaffected by dry-cleaning. It is available in many weights and can be used with every type of fabric. It is even possible to make it up alone as a foundation petticoat.

Choose interfacing slightly stiffer than the fabric. This does not mean the interfacing is heavier, only stiffer. Take a piece of fabric to the store and try it with the interfacing. There are many interfacing weights available.

- *Super soft* can be used with silk, man-made jersey and soft wool. It is suitable for dresses, light jackets, evening gowns, dresses and skirts.
- *Lightweight* can be used with cotton, linen, wool, rayon, satin and minimum-iron fabrics. It is suitable for jackets, coats, dresses and skirts.

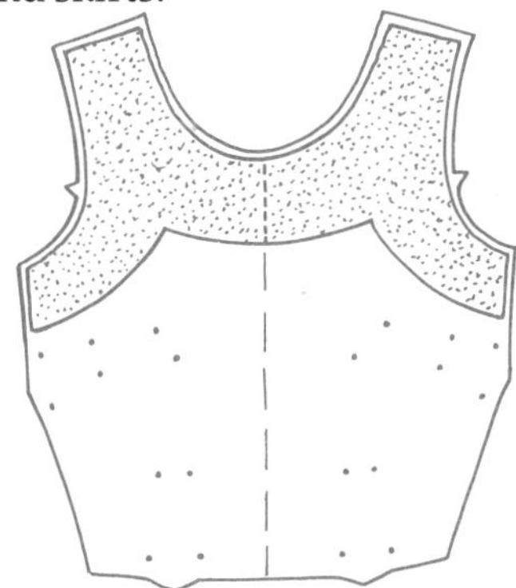

- *Extra-lightweight* can be used with silk, lawn, chiffon, voile and similar fabrics. It is suitable for white and colored fabrics where interfacing is visible or shows through. It is fluorescent white and non-yellowing.

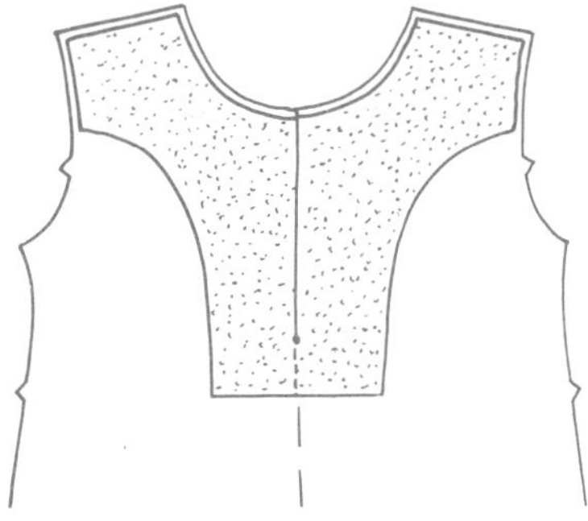

- *Mediumweight* contains nylon and can be used with white and colored fabrics, wool mixtures, flannel, suiting, satin and brocade. It is suitable for bridal wear, vests, tailored dresses, suits and lapels.

- *Heavyweight* can be used with heavy wool, velvet, upholstery, heavier satin and corduroy. It is suitable for evening gowns, coats and bridal wear.

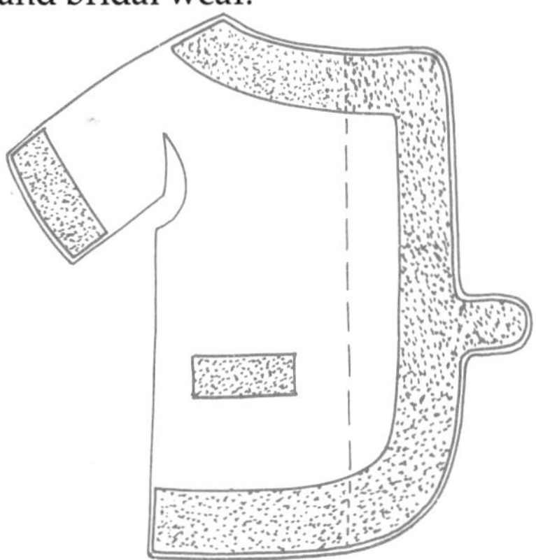

- *Iron-on* can be used with most fabrics. It is suitable for small areas like cuffs, collars, pockets and waistbands. Iron-on is cut from a pattern piece and pressed on the wrong-side of the fabric with an iron. The adhesive should not show through the fabric on the right-side. Before applying it to the fabric, test it on a scrap.

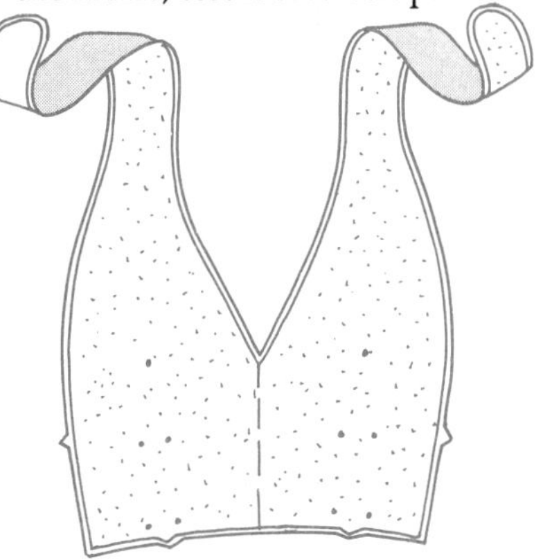

WOVEN INTERFACING

Many fabrics can be used for interfacing. Some are specially made for this use. Some canvas types are suitable only for tailored garments. They are put on the wrong-side of the garment fabric, inside the seam line.

Most woven interfacings need to be preshrunk and have the grain straightened before pieces are cut out. The grain on the garment and the grain on the interfacing must be the same. The interfacing may pull the garment out of shape.

Follow pattern instructions about the type of interfacing to buy. Feel the fabric and interfacing together in the store before you buy them.

For light fabric, such as jersey, soft brocade, poplin and fine wool, use fine lawn or organdy. For ultra-light fabric, such as silk, voile or see-through fabrics, use silk organza, net, soft organdy or fine lawn.

With medium fabrics, such as wool, rayon blends, gabardine and corduroy, use cotton. Tailored garments need soft canvas or wool canvas. For heavy fabrics, such as suitweight cotton, linen or wool, use cotton.

USING INTERFACING

Cut the interfacing from the pattern pieces as described in the instructions. Interfacing does not show when the garment is worn. Joins may be made in interfacing to avoid buying large quantities.

Overlap the iron-on type so pieces match on the fitting lines, then press together. Machine-stitch woven and non-woven pieces together. Trim so the final piece is the correct size.

Interfacing is usually slip-basted or bonded in place before garment pieces are joined. It may or may not be stitched with the seams. Heavy interfacing may have the seam allowance trimmed away so it lies inside seam lines.

Where the facing of an opening is cut in one with the garment, interfacing is cut beyond the fold line. An extra-strong edge results when the facing is folded back.

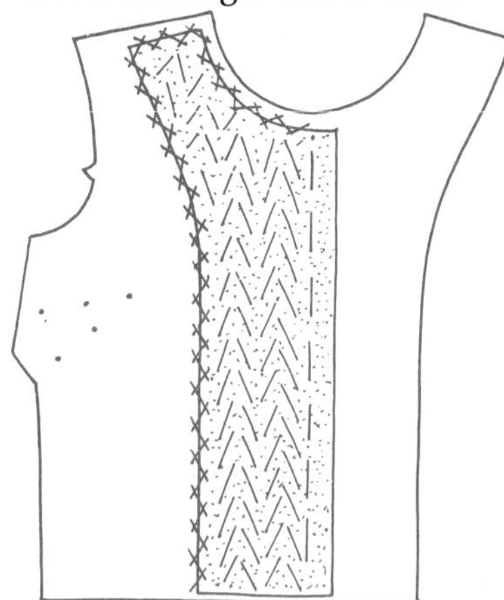

Place fabric to be interfaced on a flat surface, wrong-side up. Pin and baste in position. The garment piece may be shaped, such as with darts. Lay it over a shaped area like your knee before fixing the interfacing. Basting stitches are removed later. Catch-stitch loosely along any folds that will not be stitched. Follow instructions when using iron-on interfacing.

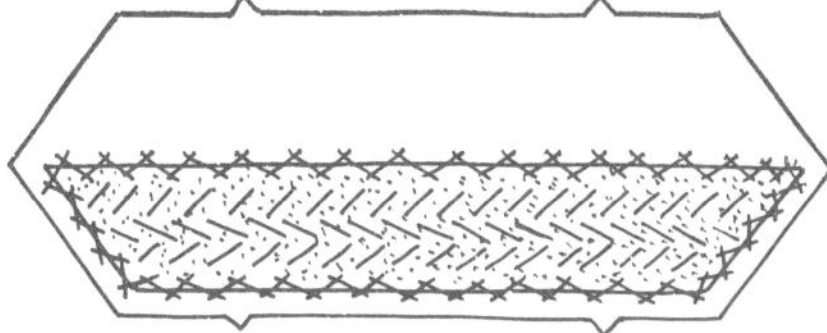

Lining

Lining is used on the inside of garments to give them body. It helps them hang well and keep their shape. The garment does not come in contact with the body and lasts longer. Special anti-static lining may be used to stop clinging.

On sheer fabric, add a lining for modesty. A lining usually finishes the inside of a garment and helps prevent creasing. An additional layer is added to avoid wrinkling or stabilize a garment section. The addition of this layer is called *mounting, underlaying* or *underlining*. It is *not* interfacing. The extra layer may also add warmth. Mounting does not hide raw edges, so a separate lining is also used.

Jackets, coats and skirts can be interfaced in small areas. A mounting and separate lining are also made with different materials for each one. The order of construction is:

- Mount underlining on the fabric.
- Interface areas.
- Make the garment.
- Make the lining.
- Join the lining to the garment.

Lining fabric should be durable enough to last for the life of the garment. It should be suitable for washing or dry-cleaning with the garment.

MOUNTED LINING

Mounted lining is also known as *underlining, underlaying* and *backing*. It is an easy way to line garments. The lining and garment fabric are sewn as one layer. Many fabrics are improved by mounting, especially if they are loosely woven. Good-quality wool, and self-lined and bonded fabric do not need it.

Mounting fabric should be suitable for use with the garment fabric. Mounting fabric is usually lighter and softer. If it is too thin, the garment is droopy, with a poor silhouette. Ordinary lining fabrics are not always suitable for mounting.

Professional seamstresses use silk, but it can make a garment expensive. There are other fabrics to use:

- Chiffon for embroidered chiffon evening dresses.
- Net for lace.
- Organza for silk, cotton and fine wool.
- Mull or lawn for dresses and blouses.
- Rayon or taffeta for some dresses and suits.
- Fine cotton for thick wool and tweed.
- Fine jersey for stretchy fabrics.

Construction Method—Pin the pattern on the fabric. Cut out the garment pieces. Remove pins, and put the pattern and fabric pieces on the lining material. Repin and cut out.

Transfer markings to the mounting fabric. Remove the pattern, and place lining and fabric with wrong-sides together. Tack the center of the fabric and lining to hold it together, or press if using iron-on interfacing.

Place the two layers of dart sections together. Stitch down the center of the dart to the point to assemble the dart. Place extra rows of tacking at equal intervals to hold the lining and fabric together.

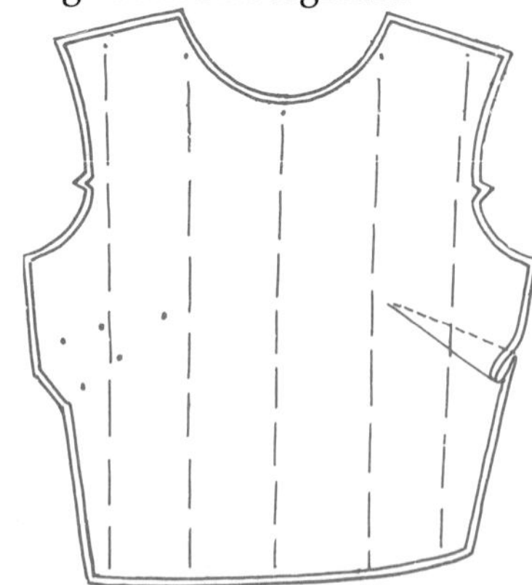

Tack 1/2 inch from the edge all around. When machine-stitching on seam lines, there will be four layers of fabric. Use 8 to 10 stitches per inch.

Trim and finish seam edges by

oversewing. Machine-finishing can make thick edges that show through.

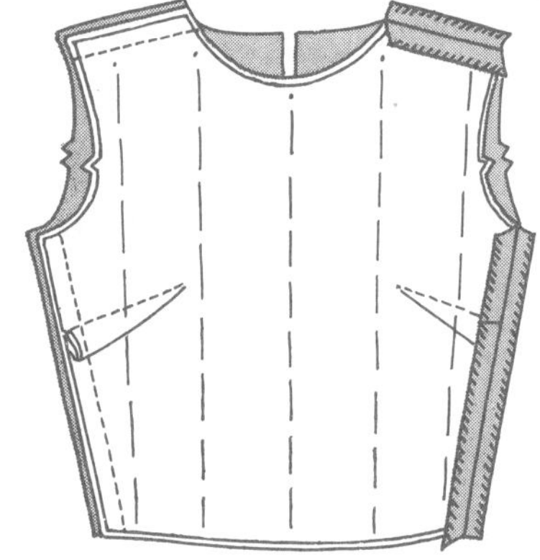

Understitch facings loosely to seam allowances only.

Before turning up the hem, stitch lining and fabric together below the fold line. Sew the finished hem to the

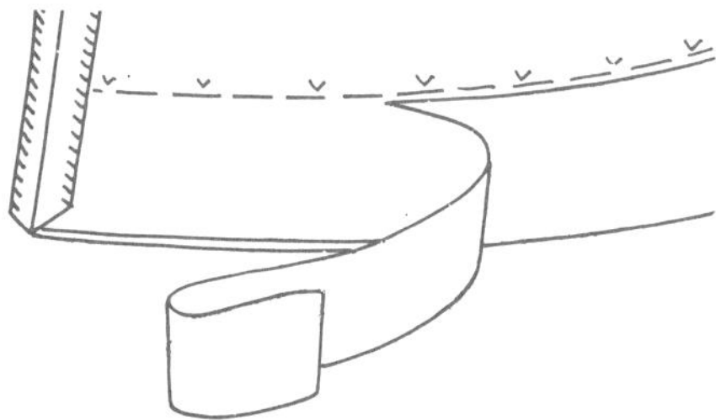

lining only, so stitching does not show on the right-side.

SEPARATE LINING

A separate lining improves the appearance of a garment. It makes rough fabrics more comfortable to wear. If the garment is worn unfastened, a matching or patterned lining can make a coat or jacket more attractive.

Lining may be temporarily hand-stitched in place at neck and armholes or permanently stitched by machine. Professional seamstresses make sections of the lining. Each one is hand-sewn in place to avoid extra bulk. It makes the lining wear better. Whichever method you use, lining should not restrict movement in the garment. If additional warmth is needed in coats, use a satin lining coated with tiny particles of metal.

If the garment is to be dry-cleaned, use a lining that can be dry-cleaned.

If the garment is made from jersey fabric, use a jersey lining. Choose an anti-static lining for man-made fabrics.

General Construction Method—For a vest, jacket, coat or skirt, make it the normal way. Interface small areas. Use the pattern to cut out the lining, then transfer markings. Make the lining the way you make the garment, but without interfacings.

Stitch the front-shoulder dart from shoulder to the second dot, about 4 inches down from the shoulder. Press darts toward armholes.

The garment may be fitted with darts at the waistline. Clip the waistline *after* machine-stitching, but *before* pressing. Sew the lining together as you sew the garment. Then sew darts and seams.

Machine-stitch or hand-sew the lining to the garment. Press under

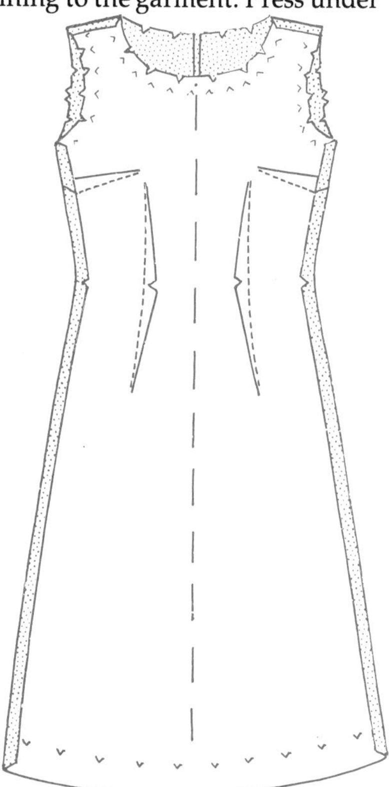

1/2 inch at the lower edge of the garment lining and sleeve lining. Press front and back neckline edges to the wrong-side along the seam line. Snip curved edges to within 1/8 inch of seam line. This allows the curved, turned seam allowance to lay flat.

Turn the front part of the lining back. The lining and garment side seams can be sewn together with running-stitches. Begin 2 inches below the armhole. Sew to 3-1/4 inches above the hem. Remove pins.

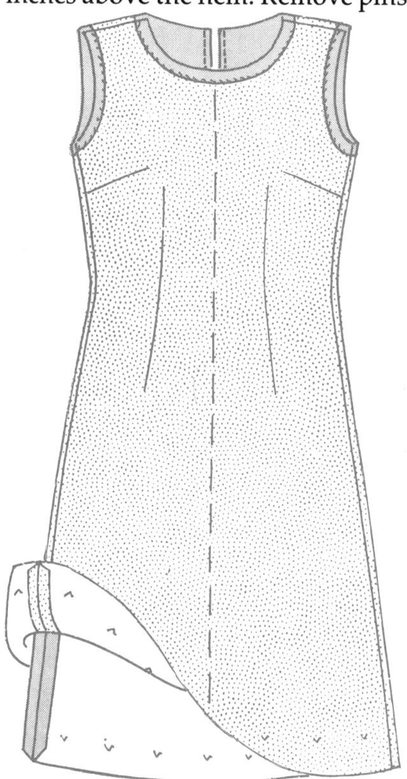

Slip the sleeve lining over the garment sleeve. Match the shoulder seams. Pin the back neckline and front edges of the lining over the garment facings. Hem the lining to the facings.

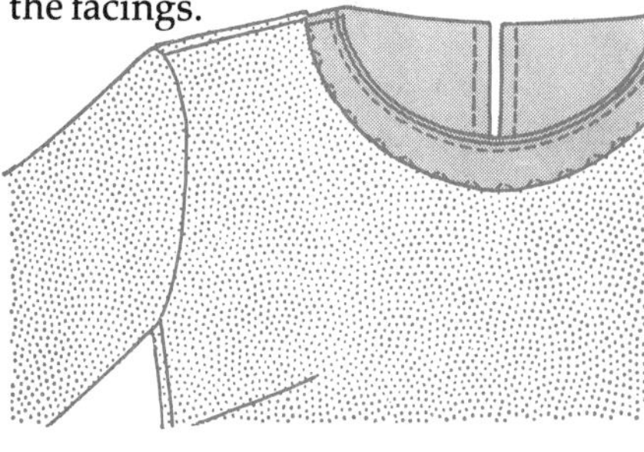

Try on the garment. Tack the lining to the garment just above the hem. A skirt or dress lining may be slip-stitched in place over the garment hem or attached at the seams. The bottom edge of the lining hangs free.

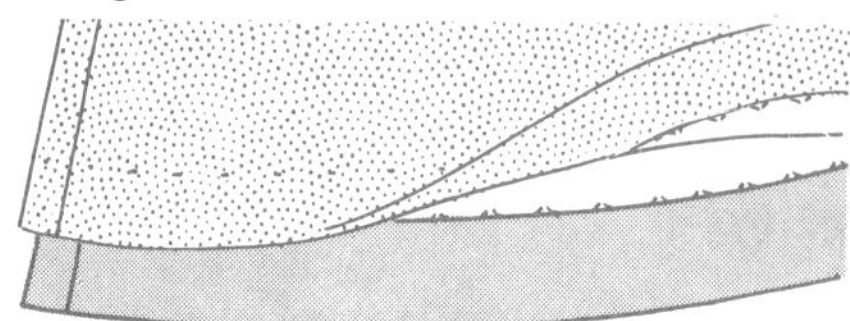

To finish hems and corners on jackets and button-through skirts, see the section on *Hems*, page 122.

Couture Method—This method is for experienced sewers. Pin, tack and machine-stitch darts and seams in the sleeves and sleeve linings. Turn the hem allowance on the sleeve lining to the wrong-side and press. Pin and tack the lining and sleeve together at the hem. Slip-stitch, then remove tacking.

Tack the lining and sleeve together at the armhole end. If gathering is

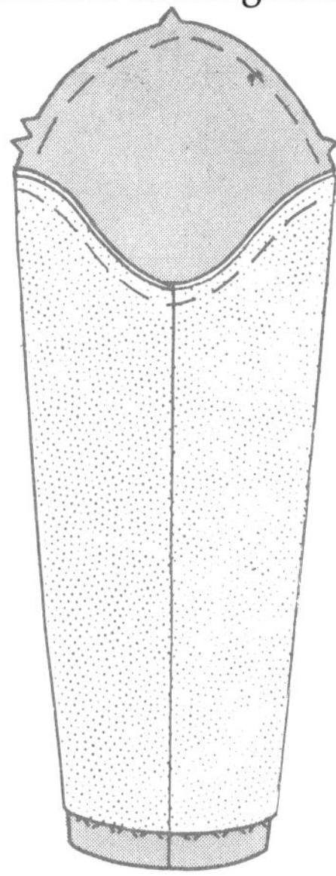

necessary, sew gathering thread through both thicknesses.

Make the garment bodice. Sew the sleeve in the normal way. Attach the

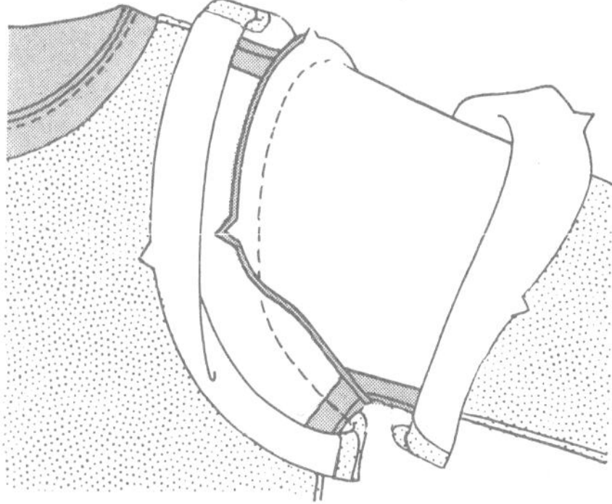

lining to the bodice. Turn the lining seam allowance under at the armholes. Tack it over the armhole seam to hide the raw edges.

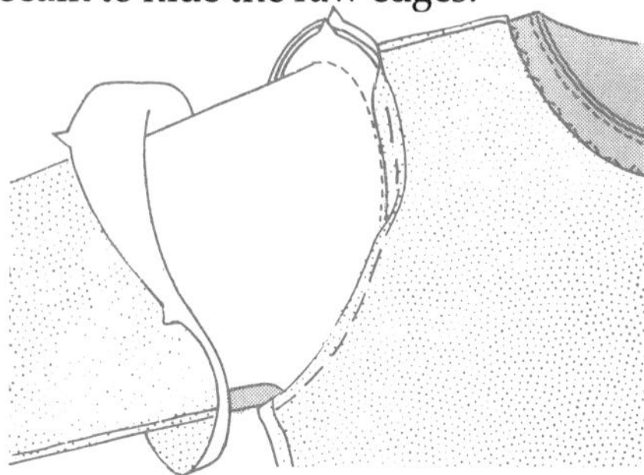

Try on the garment to make sure it is comfortable to wear. Slip-stitch the sleeve lining to the bodice lining. Remove tacking and press.

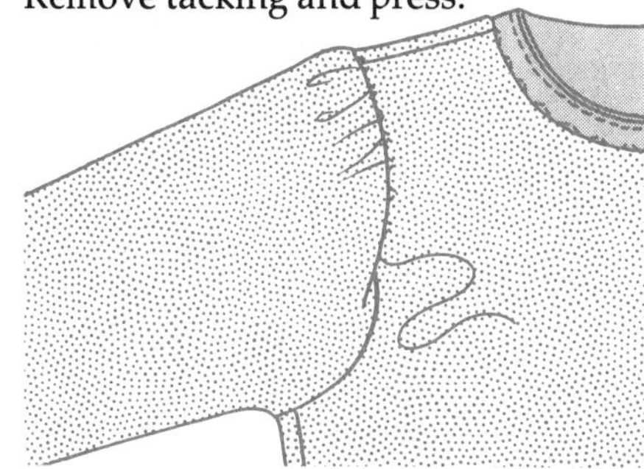

SKIRTS

Line a skirt with a separate lining or half-lining. Use a half-lining for the back and front. It ends below the hip level to prevent sitting out and bagginess. For skirts with pleats or slit openings, leave a slit in the lining or cut it away in that area.

Use strong, good-quality lining for skirts. Make the skirt and complete the zipper or placket. Make fitting alterations as necessary. Transfer alterations to the lining pattern.

Make and fit the lining. Press it and try it inside the finished skirt for length. Finish the lining hem.

Place skirt and lining with wrong-sides together. Pin and tack the waist edge. Fold the lining under around the opening, and slip-stitch it to the skirt.

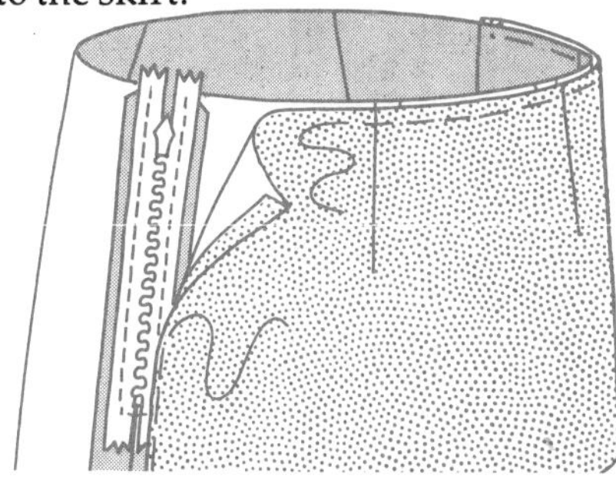

Machine-stitch the skirt and lining together on the fitting line at the waist. Complete the waistband.

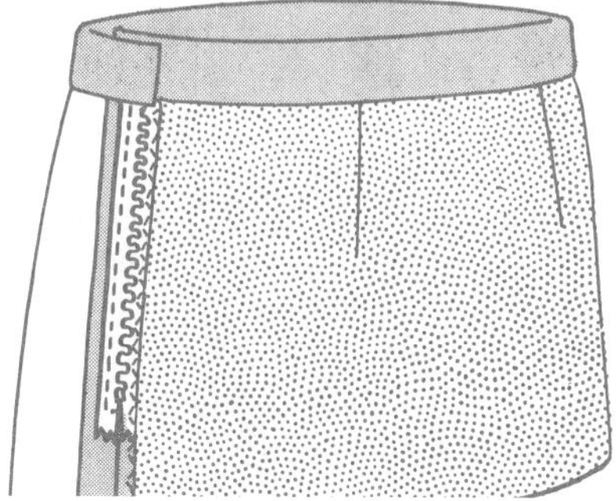

Attach the lining hem to the side seams of the skirt with bar tacks.

CHOOSING FABRIC AND LINING

Garment fabric	Lining fabric
Silk	Silk
Cotton	Cotton lawn
Batiste	Cotton lawn
Silk chiffon	Silk
Brocade	Rayon satin
Crepe	Silk
Light wool	Silk
Heavy wool	Satin
Corduroy	Satin
Cashmere	Silk
Lace	Light satin, silk
Thick coating	Special coat-weight satin or fur fabric
Lawn	Taffeta
Denim	Cotton lawn
Wool gabardine	Coat-weight lining
Fur	Coat-weight lining
Suede or Leather	Coat-weight lining

NECKLINES

The neckline is an important part of a garment. When a garment has no collar, you can finish the neckline with a facing or binding. Sew it accurately for an elegant appearance. A facing pattern is usually shaped to fit a neckline. It is usually included in the pattern.

If a facing pattern is not included, cut the facing strip on the bias. When the inside curve of a neckline is bound, stretch the bias in a curve. Press the facing before attaching it.

Stay-stitch the neckline before construction. Most necklines keep their shape better if they are interfaced.

Reinforce the neck edge with facing. There are many shapes—square, front-V, boat-shape, round or standing. The method of fitting the facing is similar to the one given on the next page.

A facing may be fitted on the right-side of the garment as part of the design. It may be contrasting fabric or stitched with contrasting thread as a decoration.

GENERAL CONSTRUCTION METHOD

Stay-stitch the neck edge by machine. Sew each piece next to the seam line, inside the seam allowance. This prevents stretching during sewing. Interface the facing. See the section on *Interfacing and Lining,* page 129, for details.

Pin and tack the bodice pieces together. Match balance markings. Try on and adjust for fit. Stitch and press any darts. Sew the bodice pieces together along the seam line and press. Insert a zipper if required.

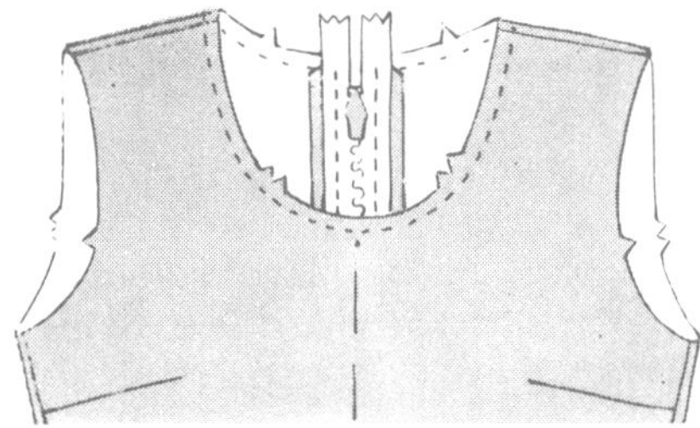

Prepare the facing by pinning pieces with right-sides together. Match pattern notches. Tack and machine-stitch along the seam line. Trim seam allowances to 3/8 inch, and press the seam open. Finish

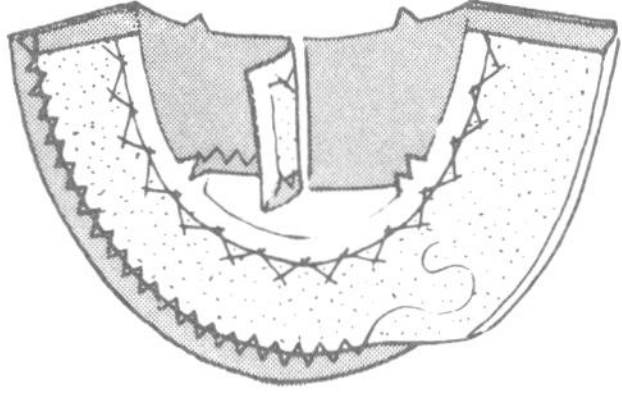

outer edges of the facing. See the section on *Seams,* page 149, for details.

With the bodice right-side out, pin the facing wrong-side out to the neck edge. Match pattern notches and shoulder seams exactly, then tack in place.

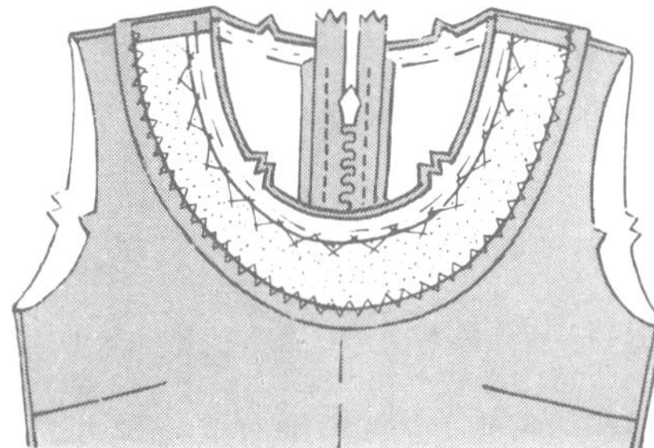

Stitch along the seam line around the neck edge, pivoting at corners. Make straight lines or smooth curves according to the style. Clip curves or corners in the seam allowance.

Trim the facing seam allowance to 1/8 inch and the bodice seam allowance to 1/4 inch. Press the seam

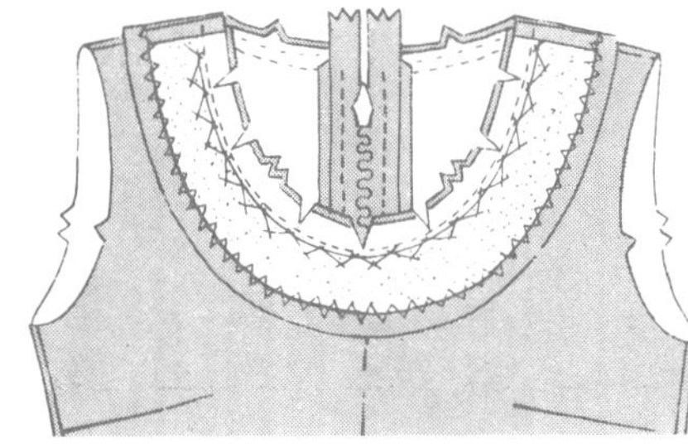

and turn to the wrong-side. Press the seam allowance up on the wrong-side of the facing. Stitch along the facing close to the neck seam through all layers. Understitching keeps the facing from rolling to the right-side.

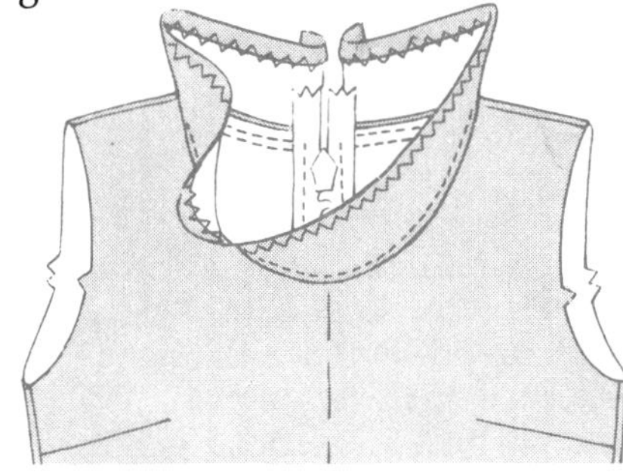

Fold the facing to the wrong-side of the bodice. Roll the edge so it falls inside and does not show from the right-side. Tack around the neck edge through all layers. Press the facing.

Attach the free edge of the facing to the seam allowances of the shoulder seams, not the bodice. Fold

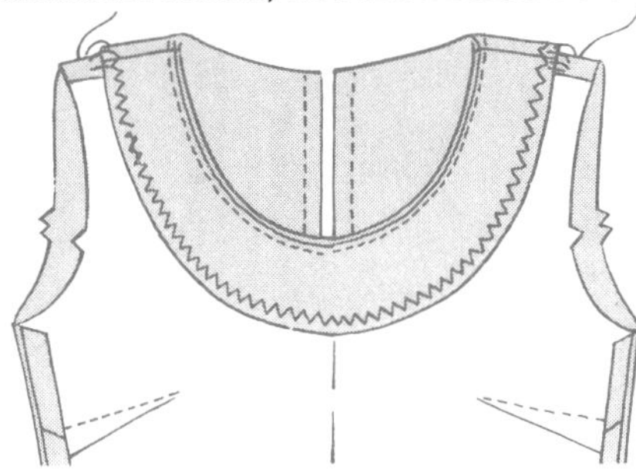

the ends of the facing under. Slip-stitch the facing to the zipper tape, at least 1/8 inch from the teeth. Press. Sew a hook and eye on the facing above the zipper.

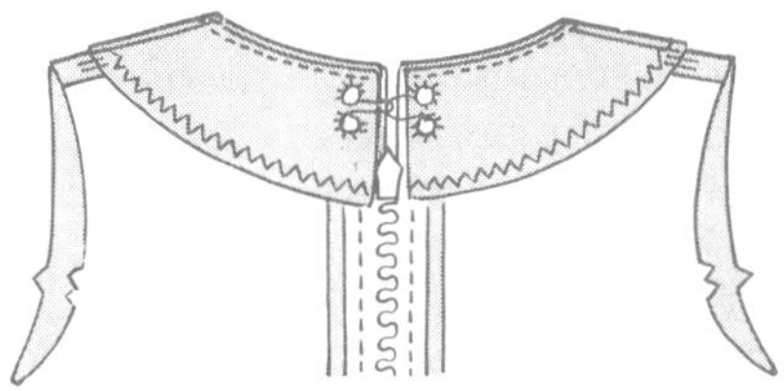

SLASHED, V-SHAPE FACING

A pattern is usually marked to indicate the slashed opening of a garment. Attach the facing to the garment before slashing. Place right-sides together. Pin and tack the facing to the garment. The facing should cover the marked slash area.

For reinforcement, tack a short length of fabric or seam binding over the facing at the point of the V. Stitch

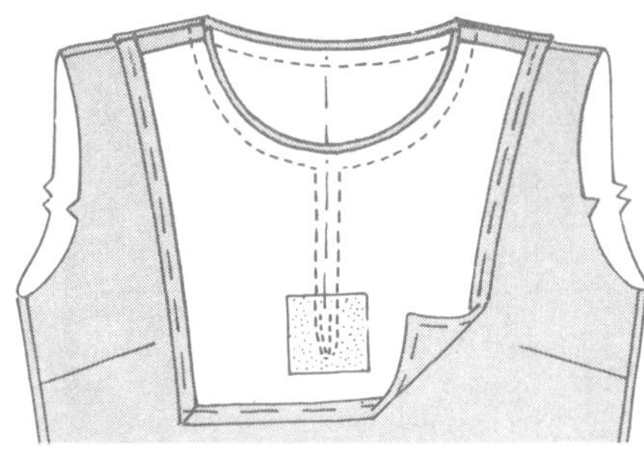

the facing to the neckline edge. Continue stitching down the front 1/4 inch from the center. Taper stitching to a point at the lower end of the opening. Make one stitch across the point before starting along the second side.

Machine-stitch a second time around the point using a fine stitch. Cut or slash between stitched lines down to the point. Remove the tacking, and turn the facing to the inside part of the garment.

Understitch the facing, and catch-stitch it at the seams. See the section on *Facings,* page 112, for details.

Press the facing to the wrong-side of the garment. Tack or slip-stitch the facing invisibly to the garment.

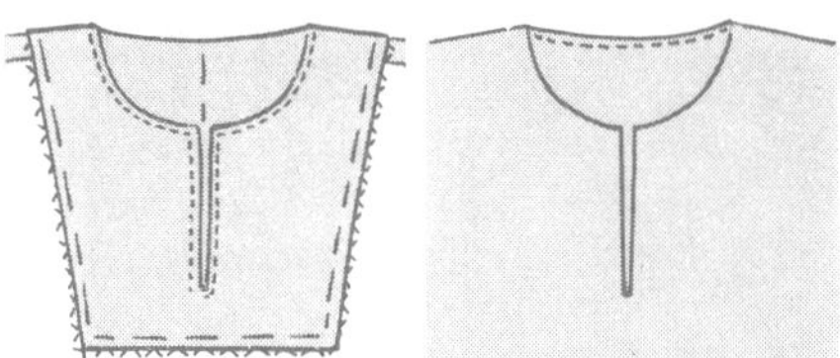

COLLARLESS CARDIGAN OR JACKET

This type of garment usually has fold-back facings and a front opening. Tape the neck and front edges to keep them from stretching during sewing or wear.

Stay-stitch the neck edge. Mark the center-front and front-fold lines. Attach the interfacing. See the section on *Interfacing and Lining,* page 129, for details.

Pin, tack and stitch the bodice shoulder seams. Ease where marked. Trim the shoulder seam allowances to 1/2 inch, and press open.

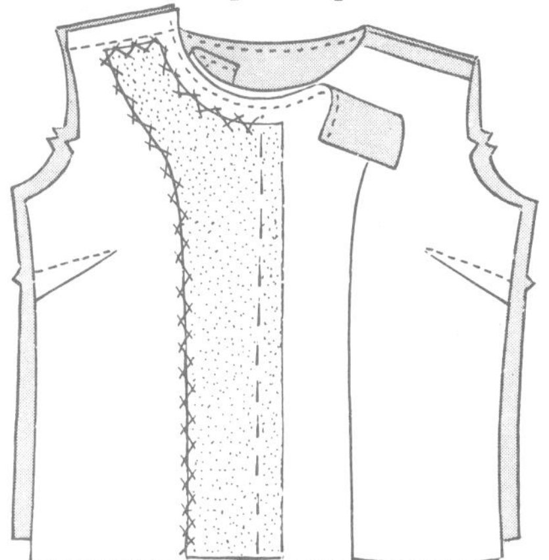

Pin, tack and stitch the back-neck facing to the front facings at the shoulders. Press the seams open, and trim seam allowances. Finish the free edge of the facing.

With the bodice right-side out, fold back the facings along the front fold lines. The facing will be wrong-side up. Be sure the back-neck facing is in place, with the wrong-side out.

Pin and tack along the seam line around the neck edge. Tack a strip of fabric or seam binding over the seam lines from the shoulder to the bottom of the front opening. Catch-stitch the binding fabric in place down the front. Stitch around the neck edge along the seam line, and complete as for shaped facing.

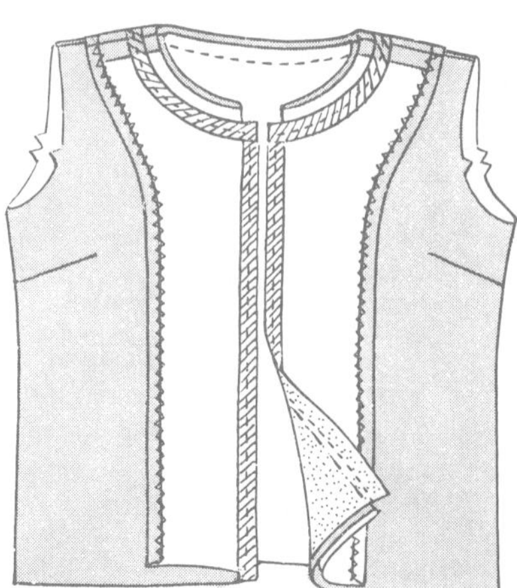

BOUND, PIPED OR CORDED NECKLINE

Binding can be used to finish necklines, particularly curved shapes where bias binding stretches to fit. A cross-grain strip can be cut from the garment fabric. Bias tape in matching or contrasting colors may also be used. Fill the binding with cord to make a piped edge. See the section on *Binding and Piping,* page 87, for details.

UNFACED BATEAU NECKLINE

This is also called a *boat-shape neckline.* It is a simple finish and used on loosely fitted dresses and cover-ups that have no neck fastening.

Stay-stitch the bodice neck edges outside the seam line. Stitch and press bodice darts, then tack the bodice together for fitting. Make any necessary alterations so the neckline is the right size and lies flat.

Machine-stitch and press the shoulder and side seams. Press under 1/8 inch of the seam allowance of the neckline and shoulder seam. Fold neck edges to the wrong-side along the seam line. Press shoulder seams flat.

Slip-stitch the edge of the hem to the bodice. Pick up one thread each time so stitches do not show on the right-side. Remove tacking, turn right-side out and press.

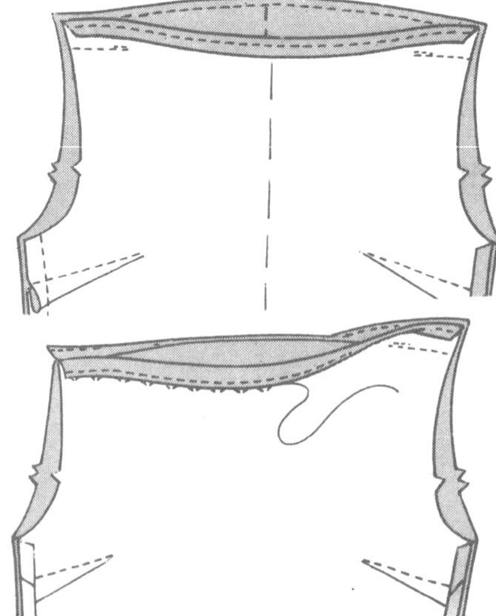

COWL NECKLINE

The soft drape of a cowl neckline is formed by setting in a yoke cut on the cross grain. The yoke is usually lined to give it body so it drapes well. Fabric cut on the straight grain is added to support the neck area.

Mount the lining on the yoke sections. See the section on *Interfacing and Lining,* page 129, for details. Pin and tack the mounted yoke sections at the shoulders. Machine-stitch. Press, clip and trim the seams.

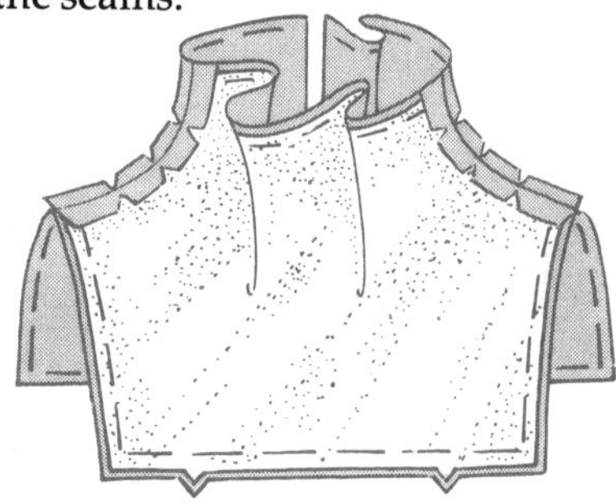

Tack seam binding over the back-opening seam lines as marked on the pattern. Attach a prepared facing to the neck edge. Roll it to the inside, and press lightly.

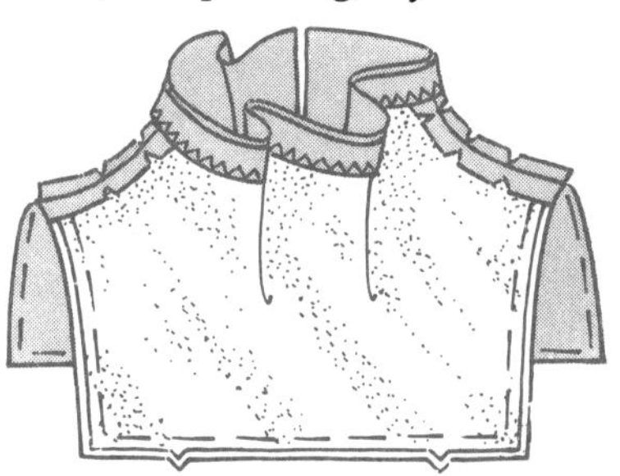

Stitch darts in the back of the stay piece, then press toward the center back. Join the shoulder seams of the stay pieces. Bind the top edge of the stay pieces with bias binding.

Tack the stay piece to the yoke, with wrong-sides together. Tape and stitch the yoke to the garment. Finish corners carefully.

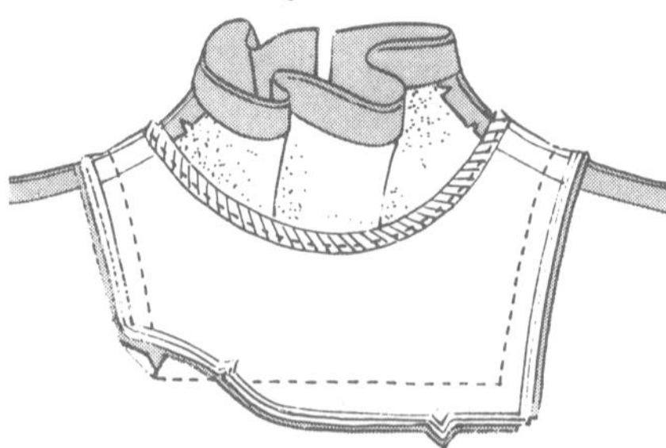

Pin in the back-neck zipper. Blind-stitch the facing to the lining fabric. Some fabrics need a weight attached to pull the cowl into soft drapes. Experiment to find the right size and place for the weight.

COMBINATION FACING

The combination facing is also called the *one-piece-neckline-and-armhole facing.* A one-piece facing finishes the neckline and armholes. For thick fabrics, cut the facing from lining fabric. The method differs according to the width of the shoulder.

Shoulders Wider than 2 Inches— Stay-stitch the neck and armhole edges. Attach interfacing, if required.

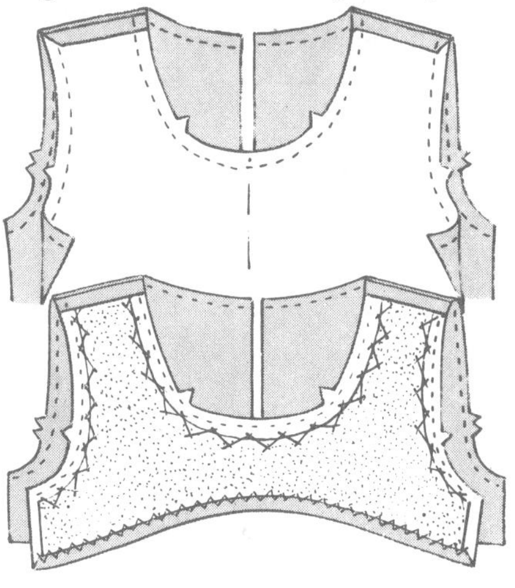

Pin, tack and machine-stitch the garment and facing shoulder seams separately. Press open and trim. Finish long, unnotched facing edges because they are not stitched to the garment.

With right-sides together, pin and tack the facing to the garment. Carefully match the balance marks on the neck and armhole edges. Machine-stitch along the seam allowances, and clip curves.

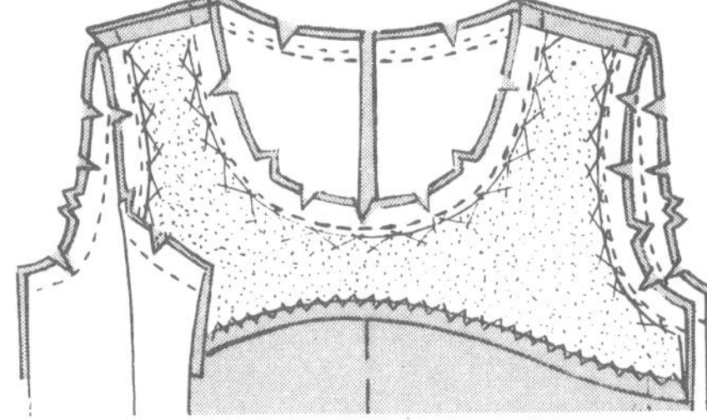

Press seams and turn right-side out by pushing your hand between the facing and garment. Pull back sections through.

Understitch the facing to the seam allowances on neck and armhole edges. Pin and tack side seams. Machine-stitch along the seam line up to, and including, the facing. Press seams open.

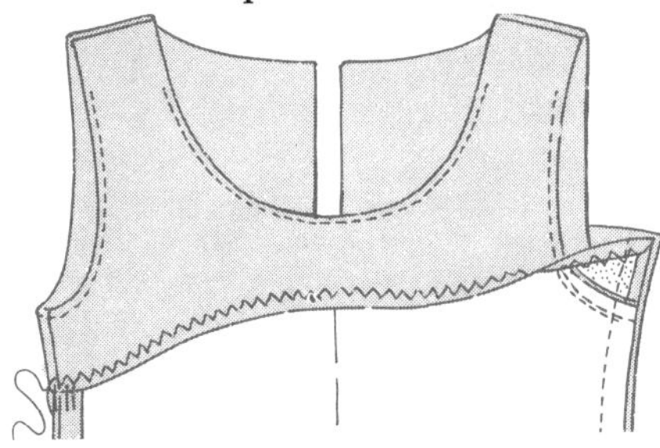

Tack the facing in place. Press and catch-stitch the facing to the seam allowance at the side seams only.

Shoulders Narrower than 2 Inches— Shoulder seams are finished as the final stage. It is impossible to pull the facing through the narrow openings on the shoulders.

Stay-stitch and interface the neck and armholes. Prepare the bodice and facing, but do *not* stitch the shoulder seams.

Make a tiny, temporary tuck in the garment at the shoulders. The facing is slightly smaller and later hidden. Put right-sides together. Pin, tack

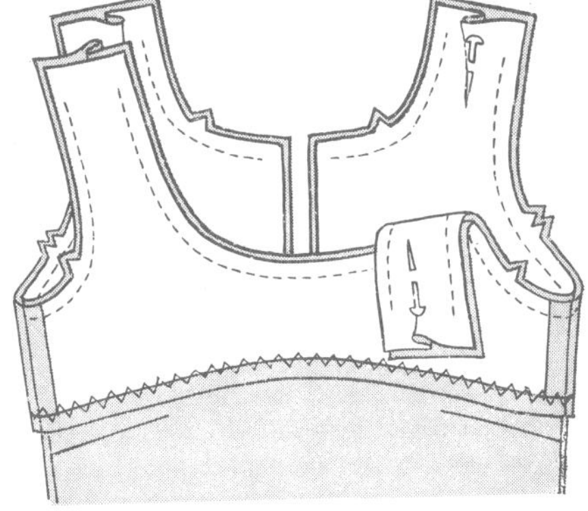

and machine-stitch the facing to the garment along the neck and armhole seam lines. Trim and layer or grade seam allowances. Clip curves and trim corners.

Remove the pins in the temporary tucks. Understitch the facing to the seam allowances. Fold the facing back; and stitch the bodice shoulder seams. Sew machine threads securely at both ends. Press the seam flat.

Trim the seam allowances on the facing to 1/4 inch. Press under along the seam line. Sew the folded edges together with tiny stitches, and press.

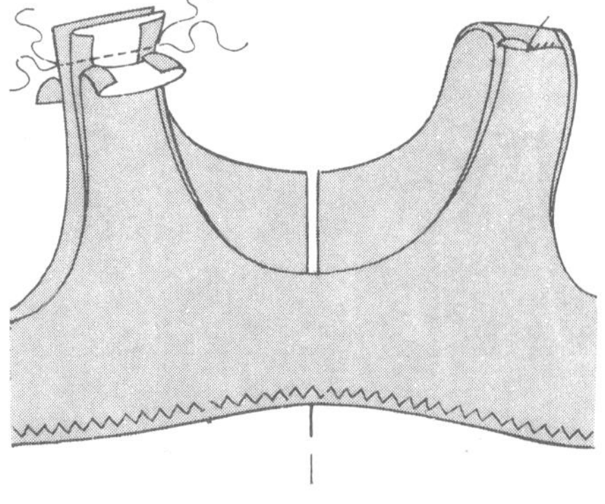

OPENINGS

Openings are needed for putting on and taking off clothes. There are several ways to finish openings. The choice depends on the type of fabric and the placement of the opening or placket in the garment.

Make the opening as neat and invisible as possible, unless it is a focal point of the style. Some openings are made so two edges overlap. This is called a *wrap.*

CONTINUOUS WRAP

A continuous wrap is also called a *continuous-strip opening.* It can be used on fine, thin material. It has been adapted for side openings on pajamas, shorts and shirts, and for wrist openings on long sleeves. It is fastened with hooks and eyes, buttons and buttonholes, or snaps. The opening can be made in a slash or seam.

Cut a piece of fabric twice the length of the opening and 2 to 3 inches wide. Match the grain with the edge to be bound.

Pull the garment edges of the opening apart so they lie in a straight line. Put the right-side of the binding to the right-side of the opening, with raw edges together.

Tack 3/8 inch from the raw edges. Machine-stitch with the garment-side up. Pivot at the point of slash, passing fullness behind the needle.

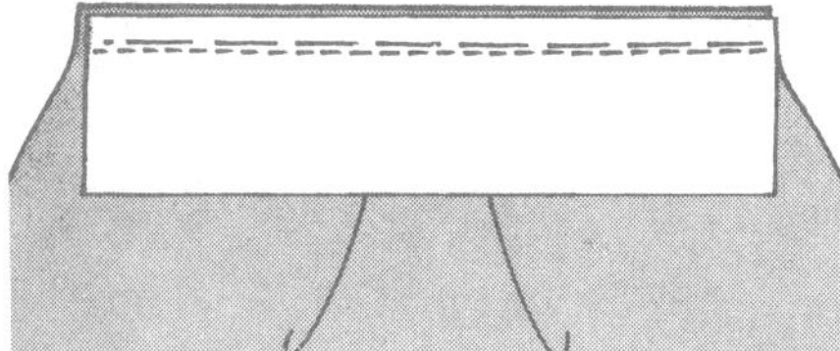

Turn under 1/4 inch on the free edge of the binding. Fold over the raw edges of the opening. Tack the folded edge above the first stitching. Hem in position, picking up every machine-stitch across the middle section of the strip.

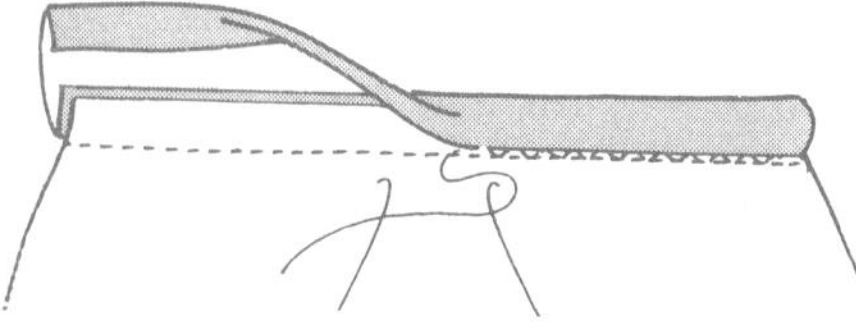

Fold the front part of the opening back along the stitching line. Press.

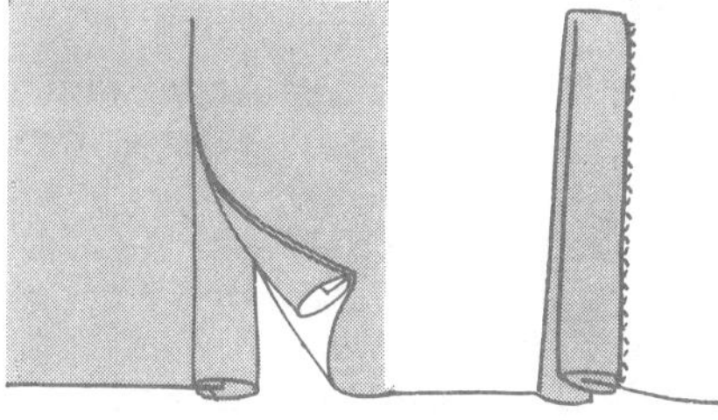

Remove all tacking, and sew on fastenings.

ALTERNATIVE-WRAP OPENING

Follow the method described above until the folded edge has been tacked above the first set of stitching.

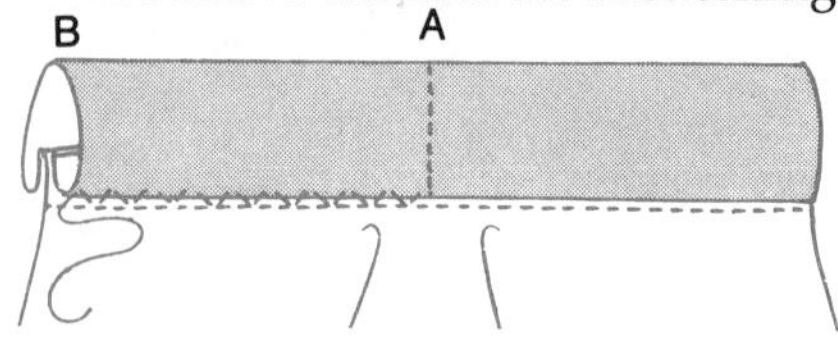

Hem the back portion only. Cut away the back of the unhemmed portion of the wrap. Turn back the

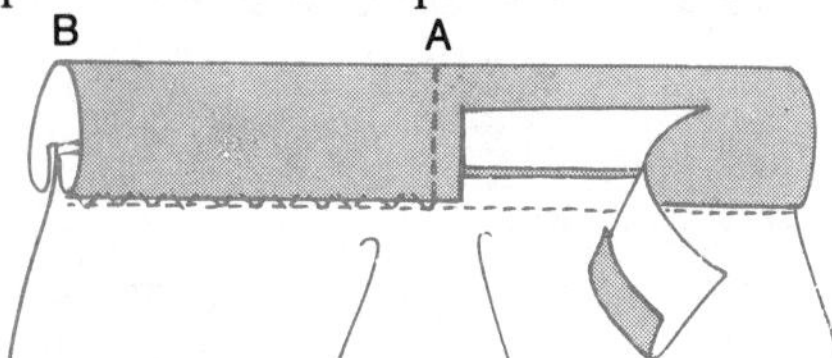

front part of the wrap. Tack the outer edge from the right-side. Tack the inner edge from the wrong-side of

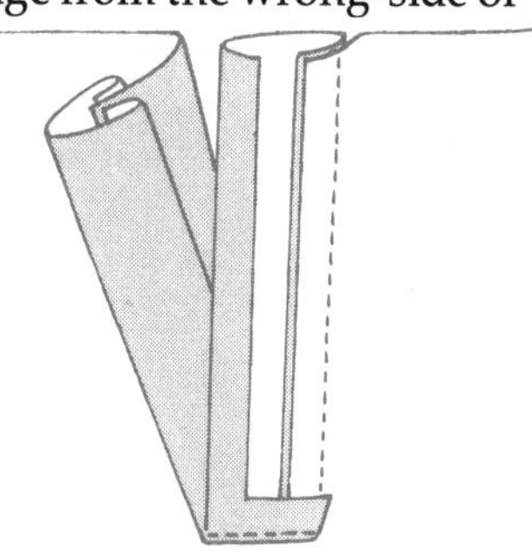

the garment. Machine-stitch the rectangle.

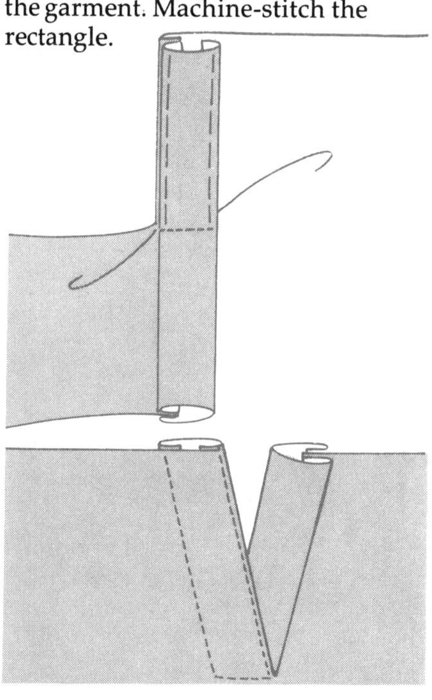

Openings without a wrap are usually faced or bound. These openings are not as strong as those with a wrap.

FACED-SLIT OPENING

A faced opening can be for front or back-neck openings and wrist openings on long sleeves set in a band. They are also for zippers when there are no seams. Fastenings often used with this opening are loops and buttons, hooks and eyes, zippers and link buttons.

Mark the position of the opening on the garment with tacking-stitches. Cut the facing section the length of the opening, plus 2 inches, and 2 inches in width.

Mark the opening on the facing with a line of tacking. Pin the edges

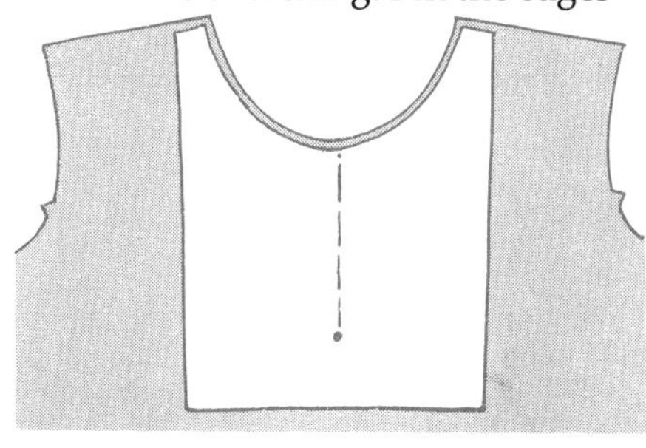

of the facing to the wrong-side. Tack and edge-stitch to finish.

Put the right-sides of the facing and garment together. Tacking lines lie over one another. Add a small square of lining material at the point for reinforcement. Put pins through tacking lines to find the correct position. Tack both thicknesses of fabric together along the tacking line.

Machine- or back-stitch 1/4 inch from the top of the marked opening to form a point. Slope stitches inward so a V-shape is formed. Sew a second row of stitching at the point for extra strength. Snip in the line of tacking between the stitches. Clip to the point.

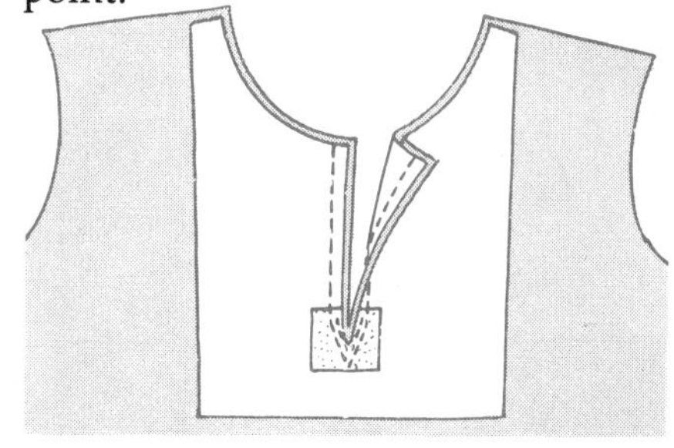

Turn the facing to the wrong-side. Pin and tack around the opening, and press. Top-stitch around the edges of opening on the right-side.

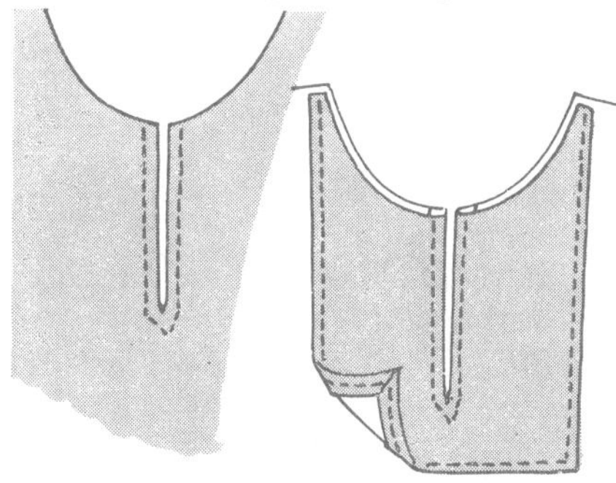

DECORATIVE, FACED OPENINGS

Conspicuous-Slit Opening—This is similar to the slit opening. The facing may have a shaped outer edge and be turned on the right-side of the garment.

Turn under the outer edge of the facing. Tack and press in place. Place the right-side of the facing to the wrong-side of the garment. Pin and tack in place. Machine-stitch around the slit and garment edge along the seam line.

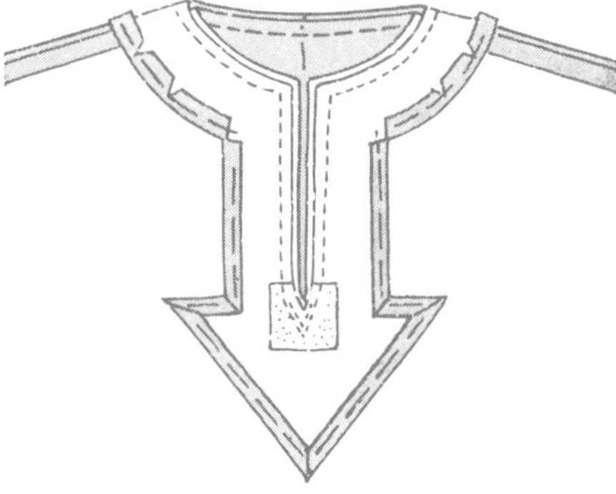

Turn to the right-side of the garment. See the section on *Facings*, page 112, for details. Machine-stitch around the outer edge to hold it in position. Use a straight- or decorative stitch. Press.

Bound Opening—This is used for front and back-neck openings. It can be fastened with loops, hooks and eyes, and link buttons. A decorative binding strip can be attached to make the opening attractive.

Cut the opening to the required length. Cut carefully if the opening is cut on the bias.

Cut a piece of material on the cross grain. It is twice the length of the opening and approximately 1 inch wide. With right-sides together, place binding to the opening, with raw edges together. Pin in place.

Tack to within 1 inch of the end of the opening on the first side. Then fasten off. Pin and tack the second side to the point. Machine-stitch and finish securely. The end of the opening should have 2 inches unstitched.

Finish the end by hand. Use small back-stitches. Taper the edge toward the end. Make a 1/4-inch turn to the

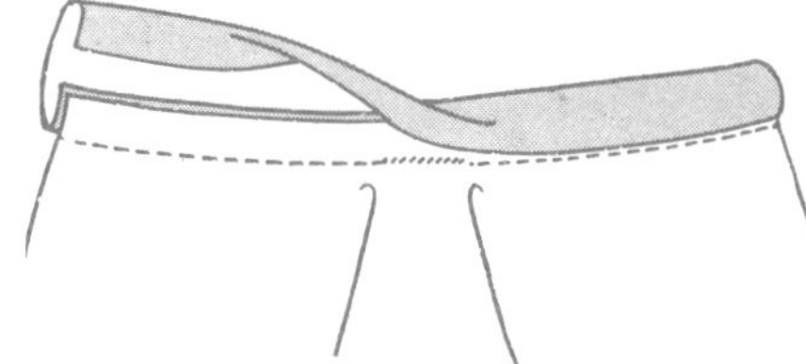

wrong-side along the free edge of the binding fabric. Turn binding fabric to the wrong-side of the garment. Tack the folded edge above the first stitching.

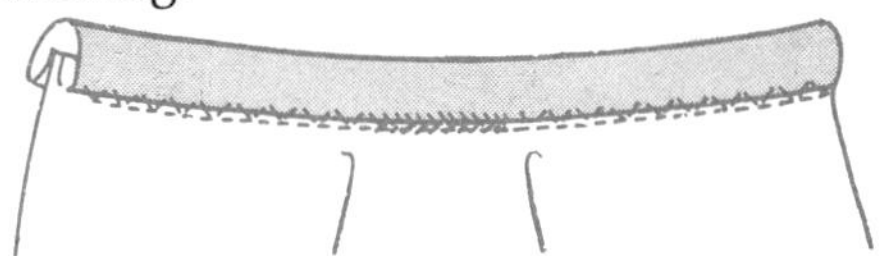

The finished edge should be slightly deeper than 1/4 inch toward the end of the opening. The bend of the binding will then lie flat.

Slip-stitch the binding in place on the wrong-side of the fabric. Remove all tacking, press and sew on fastenings.

PLEATS

Pleats are decorative folds in the fabric. They control fullness and give extra width to a garment. They are used in skirts, dresses, blouses, jackets and pants. Pleats are often made from three layers of material that hang from a supporting band. Or they are stitched for part of their length for a tailored fit.

A pleat can be made wider at the bottom to give better shape to a garment. Pleats also make it hang well. This improves the appearance of the garment. Pleats may be top-stitched down from the waistband. This prevents strain on the release point when the garment is worn. Soft pleats are left unpressed. For a crisp look, folds are firmly pressed.

Pleats may be included in a garment section, such as the back pleat in a blouse. These are made before the sections are joined. Skirt pleats are made after side seams have been sewn and finished. Seams are hidden under a pleat when possible. It is usually easier to complete the garment hem *before* pleats are made.

There are a few basic pleats, with many variations. Whatever method you choose, the fabric should be firm and closely woven.

GENERAL CONSTRUCTION METHOD

Preparation—Spread the fabric on a large, flat surface where pleats can lie flat. Accuracy is vital for perfect pleats, so spend time making them.

Mark all fold lines clearly. Pleats on patterns are marked with a solid line for folds and creases. Pleat folds are lapped to a broken line on the pattern. Arrows are shown in the direction in which pleats lap.

Transfer marked lines of the pattern to the wrong-side of the fabric. Tack fold and lap lines in different-colored threads to prevent confusion.

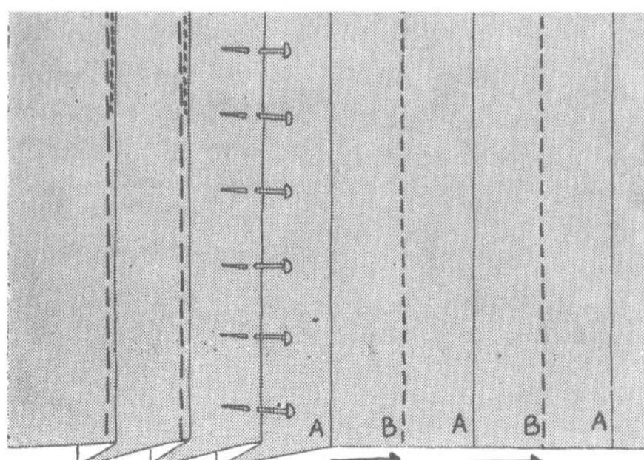

Turn the fabric to the right-side, and lap fold lines to the broken lines. Keep upper edges even so pleats hang correctly.

Pin and tack folds, then press gently. Use strong thread for tacking so it can be left in until pleats are pressed. Stitch pleats as instructed on the pattern. Complete the hem first, if possible. After fitting, press pleats with a damp cloth, and remove tacking.

Stitch pleats from the bottom up.

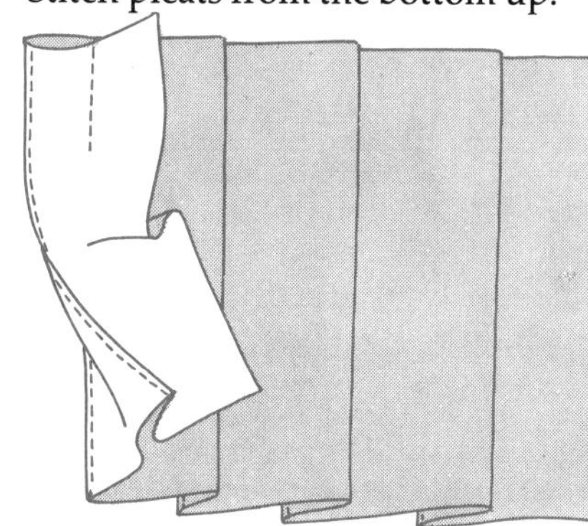

Stitching down may cause material to stretch and become distorted. If the fabric is crease-resistant, edge-stitch the underfold of each pleat.

Fitting—Try on the skirt before stitching the pleats. It is not always possible to get the size correct on the first attempt.

Tack pleats with a piece of tape along the waistline so the skirt hangs properly during fitting. If the

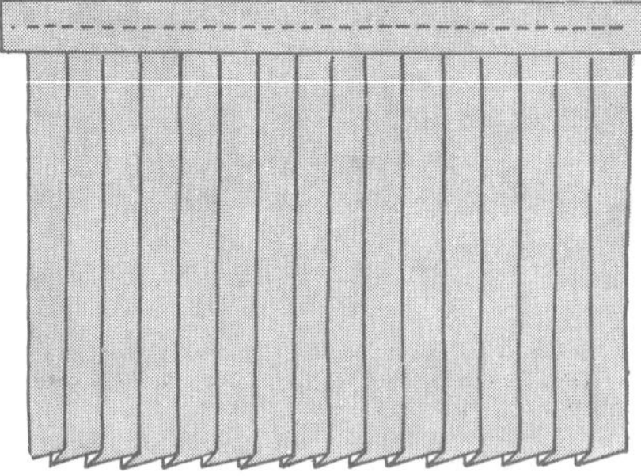

waistline does not fit, remove the tape and make tiny adjustments to each pleat. For straight pleats, keep

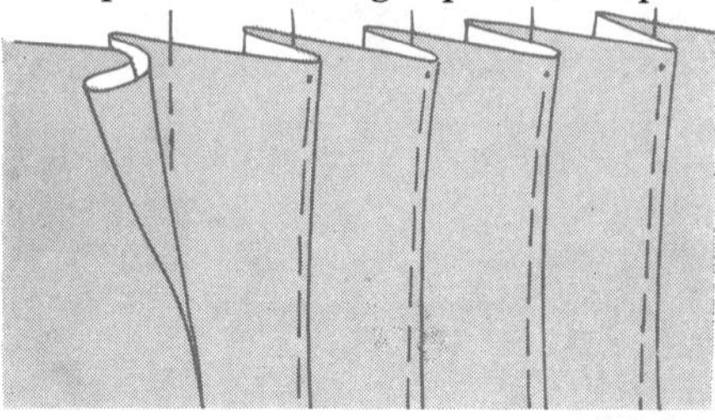

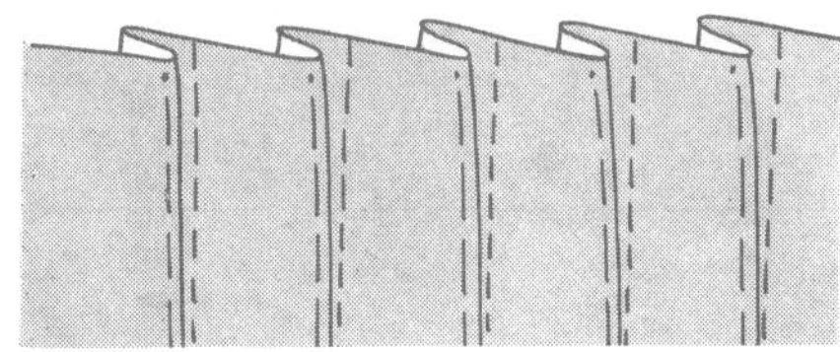

the edge of the pleat on the straight grain of the fabric.

Complete the pleats, zipper and hem. Tack another piece of tape around the waistline. Try on the skirt before stitching it to the waistband or bodice. Slightly raise or lower the skirt at the waist until the pleats hang perfectly. Adjust the seam line for the waist as necessary. Complete the garment.

Finishing Edges on Unpressed Pleats—The skirt can be made before the hem is completed. Remove tacking so pleats hang in soft folds.

Finishing Edges on Pressed Pleats—Press the pleats on the right-side and wrong-side. Make the garment. Remove enough tacking so the bottom edge lies flat for hemming. Leave placement lines in the garment, and complete the hem. Press pleats, then remove all tacking.

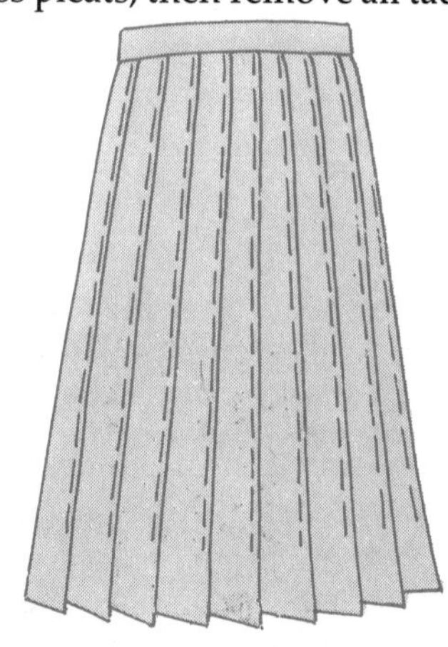

Finishing Edges on Top-Stitched Pleats—When fitting is complete, carefully press pleats on both sides. Machine-stitch around the waistline, 1/8 inch above the seam line. This holds the top of the pleats securely in place.

Top-stitch on the right-side, 1/8 inch from the edge of each pleat. Stitch down to the pattern marking or to the level most flattering to your figure. Make sure the end points of the machine-stitching are in line across the skirt. For extra strength, pivot the fabric. Sew one or two stitches across each pleat at the end

of the stitching. Complete the hem, press and remove tacking.

For durable creasing on springy material, continue top-stitching for the full length of pleats. Do not stitch the pleat edge to the garment. Stitch inside folds this way, too.

HEMMING PLEATED SKIRT

A narrow hem, not more than 1-1/8 to 2-1/2 inches, is used. On a straight skirt, fold up the hem and tack it before pleating.

Tack through all layers of fabric. This marks the arrangement of the pleat. Undo some of the pleat

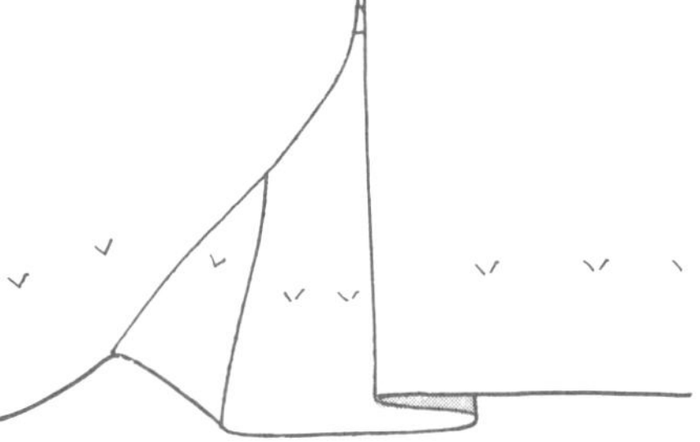

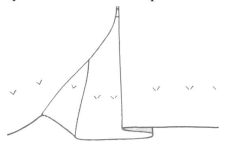

stitching. Trim away seam allowances to the depth of the completed hem. Press edges open below this point, and cut to 1/4 inch.

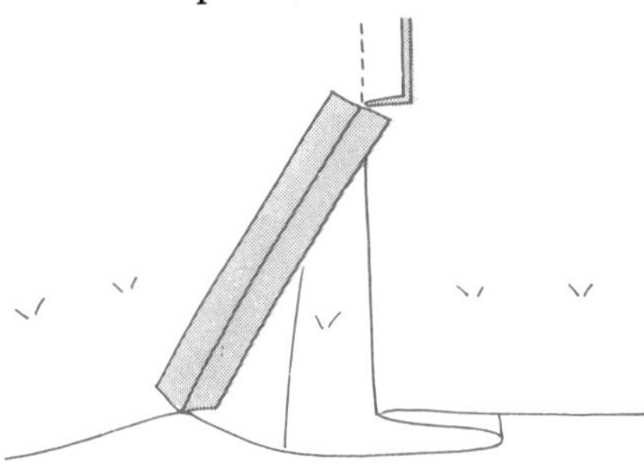

Turn up the hem and finish.

Refold pleats, and tack in place.

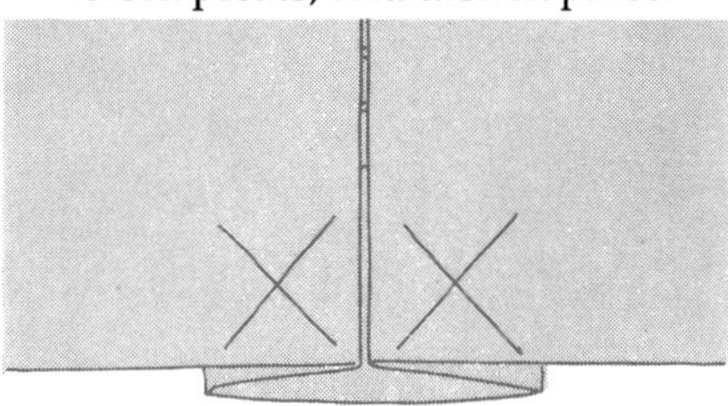

Press and stitch the fold of a pleat on the hem section if it is a seamed pleat. Or stitch all the way along the fold. This keeps the pleat or pleats hanging in place when wearing the

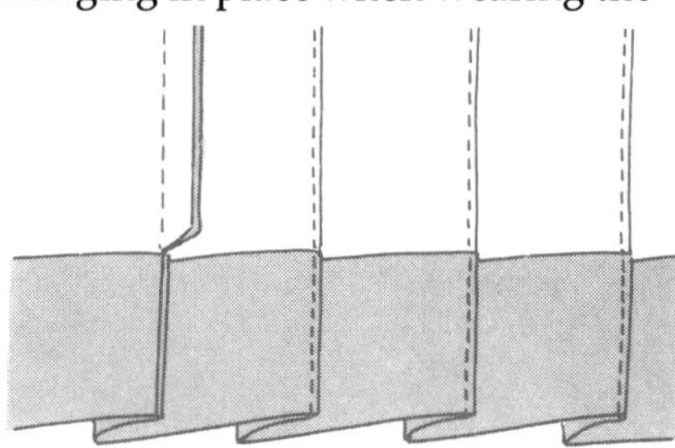

garment. Remove tacking, and gently press the skirt.

PLEATS WITH SEAM

Place fabric with right-sides together, fold to fold. Tack along the length of the pleat. Stitch to the

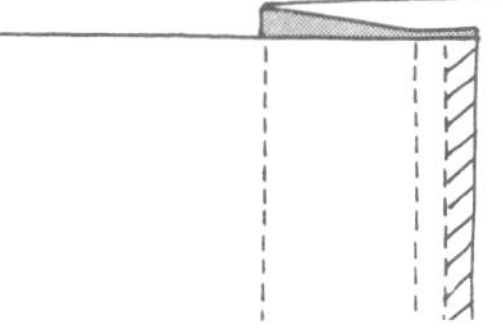

length of the fitted portion of the pleat.

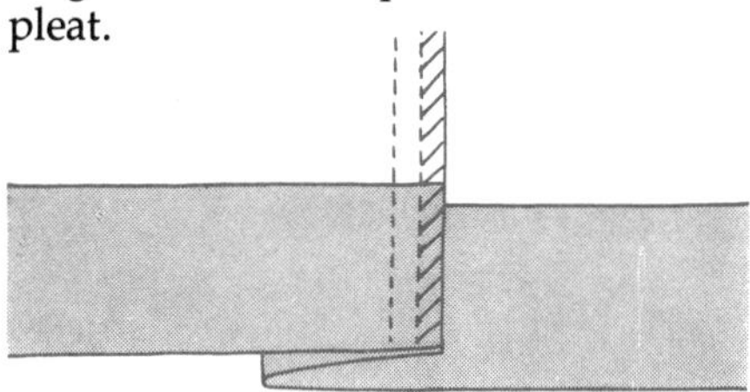

Place the fabric right-side down. The fold of the pleat lies over the stitched area. Pin and tack the pleat in position.

Press the pleat. Use a piece of thick paper between the pleat and garment. This keeps the pleat line from marking the right-side.

BINDING UPPER PLEAT

This method of binding is used to reduce bulk in heavy materials. It also gives a good fit to the garment. Snip an area 1/2 inch on each side of the stitched line and 1/2 inch above the end of stitching. Overcast or bind

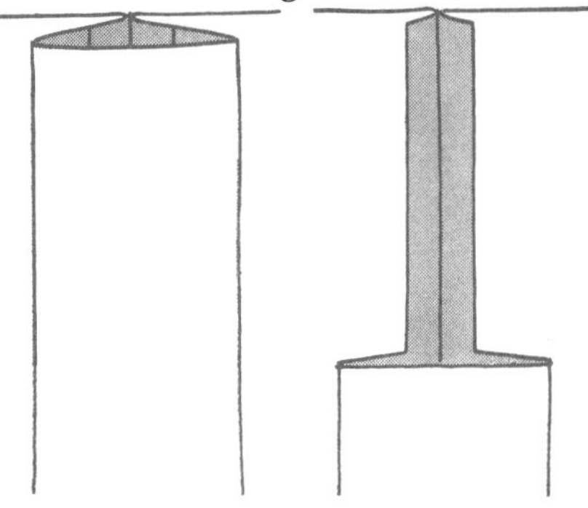

raw edges. Stitch a length of binding over the raw edges of the top of the pleat.

To give added support to the pleat, add straight binding to each end of the upper pleat. Attach other ends to the waist of the skirt.

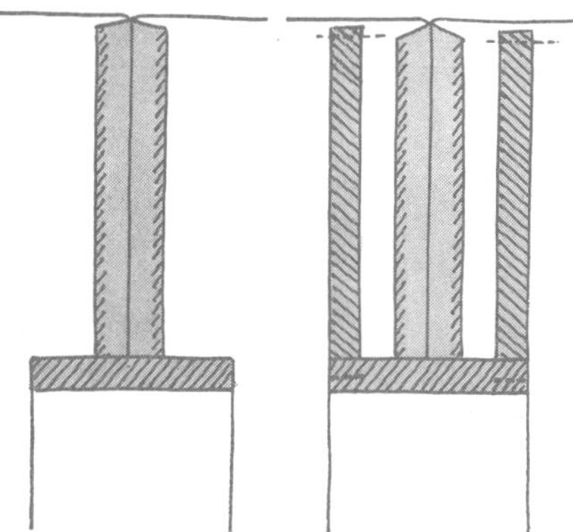

LINING UPPER PLEAT

Cut away the top area as indicated. This is the upper part of the pleat, the finished raw edges. Make a rectangle

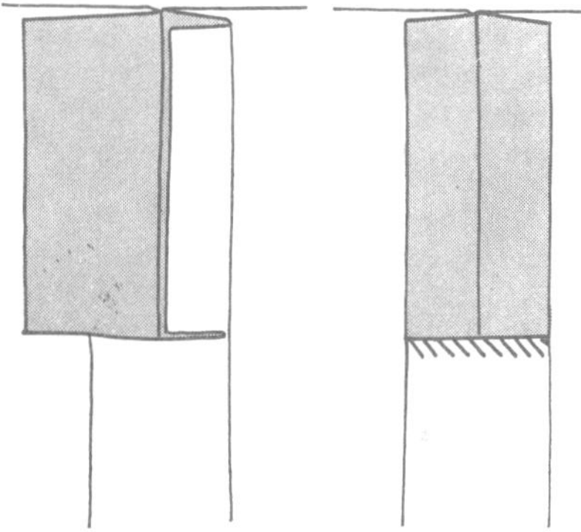

of lining 1 inch wider and 1/2 inch longer than the section already cut away. Fold and tack a 1/2-inch edge on the wrong-side.

Put the wrong-side of the lining to the inside of the pleat. Tack in position. Oversew the lining to the cut edge of the pleat. Hem the lower edge to the inner thickness of the pleat.

PLEAT STYLES

Pleats are made in many sizes. Most pleats can be straight or shaped, used singly or in groups.

Knife Pleat—These are folds turned in one direction. Mark the fold and placement line with pins or tailor's chalk. Use a ruler to place and evenly space pleats.

Create a fold line for each pleat. Press down to the placement or lap

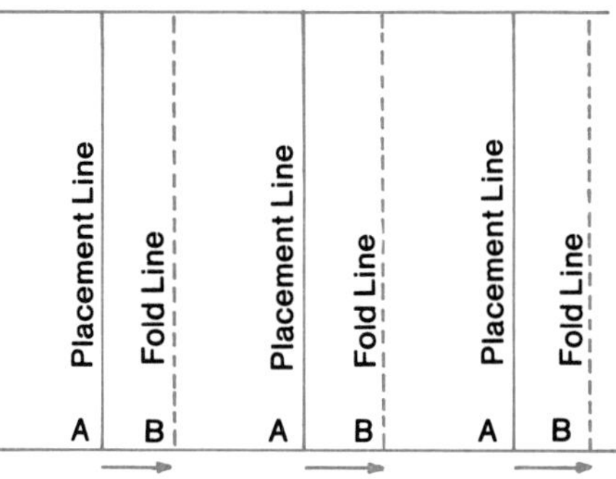

line. Pin the pleat at the placement

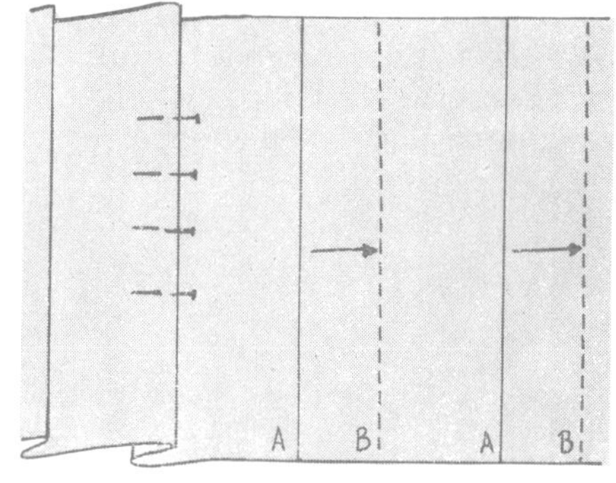

line. Tack the pleat in position. Stitch through all layers of material to the hip line or depth required. Tack

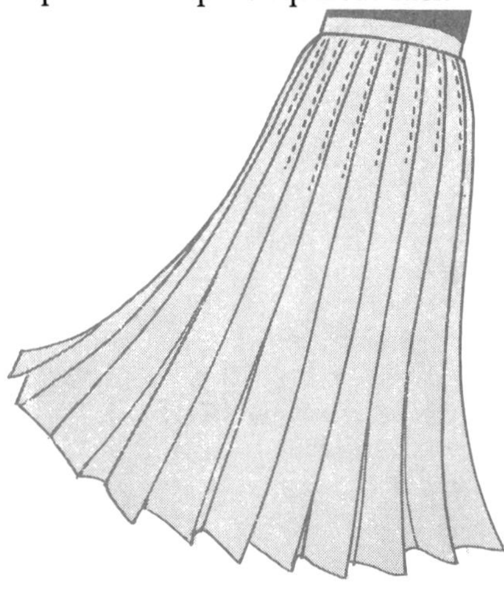

across the pleats at the waistline and

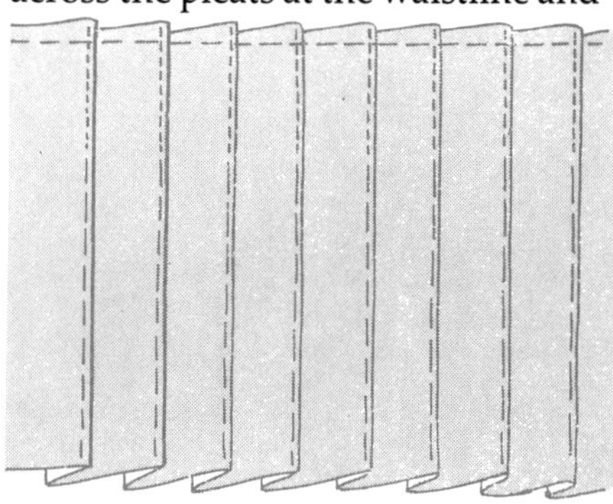

press. Remove tacking except at the waistline.

Box Pleat—These are made with folds in opposite directions.

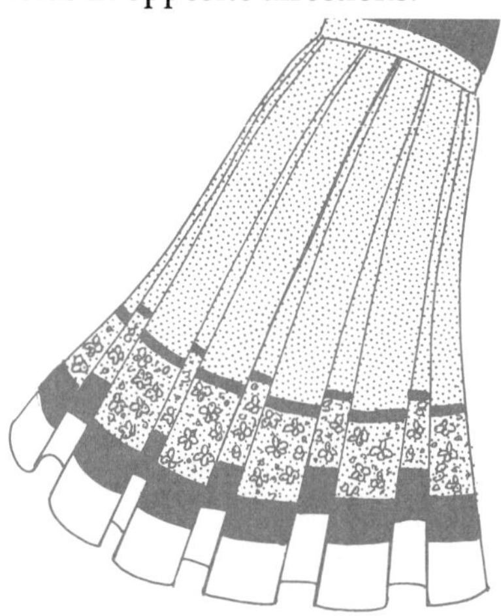

Underfolds meet at the center of the pleat.

Mark the fold and placement line with pins or tailor's chalk. Use a ruler so pleats are evenly spaced.

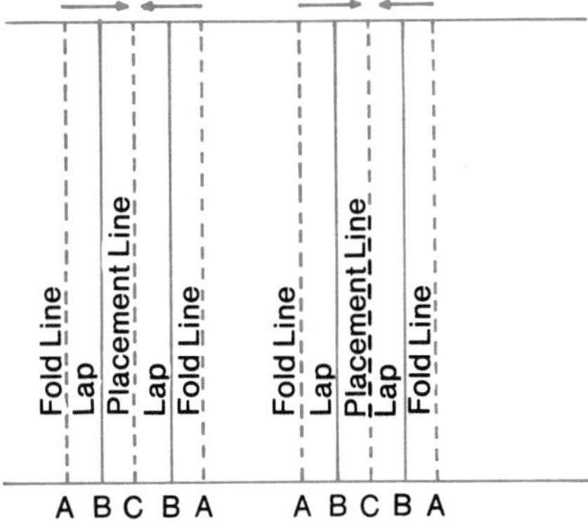

Crease the fold lines to the placement lines. Pin each pleat, and tack in

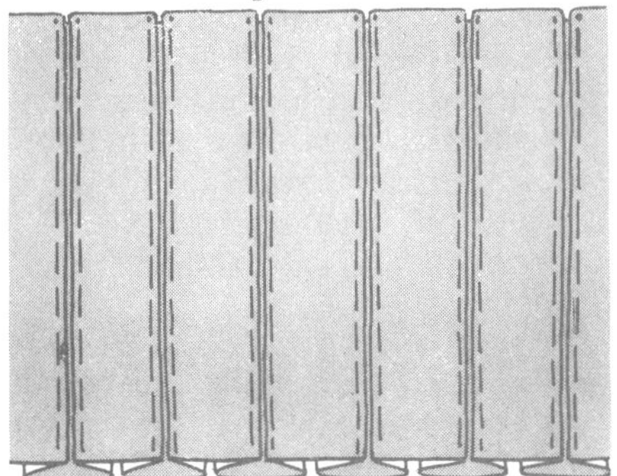

position. Stitch through all fabric layers.

Tack across the pleats at the waistline and press. Remove all tacking except at the waistline.

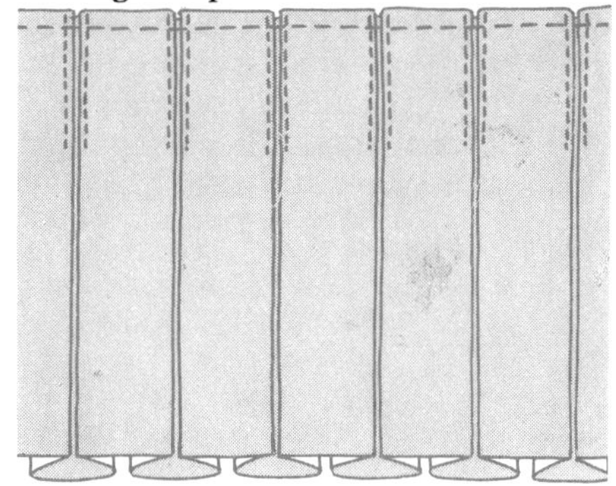

Inverted Pleat—These are box pleats in reverse. Often two appear on the

back and front of a skirt. Two pleats are turned toward each other.

Mark the fold line, center line and placement line with pins or tailor's

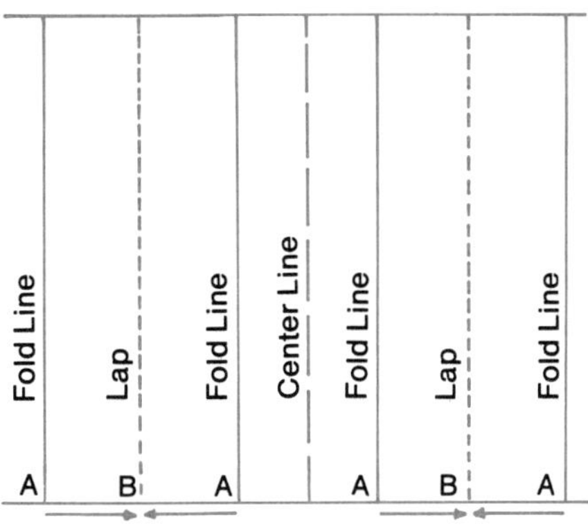

chalk. Create the fold lines of the pleat. Press down to the placement line.

Pin pleats at the placement line, and tack in position. Stitch through all layers of material. Top-stitch the upper part of the pleats. Press and

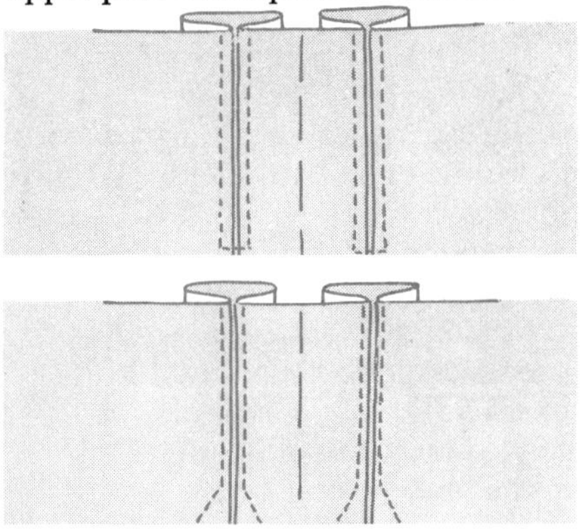

remove tacking. Press again for a crisp finish.

Kick Pleat—There are several ways to make a pleat in the center-back or

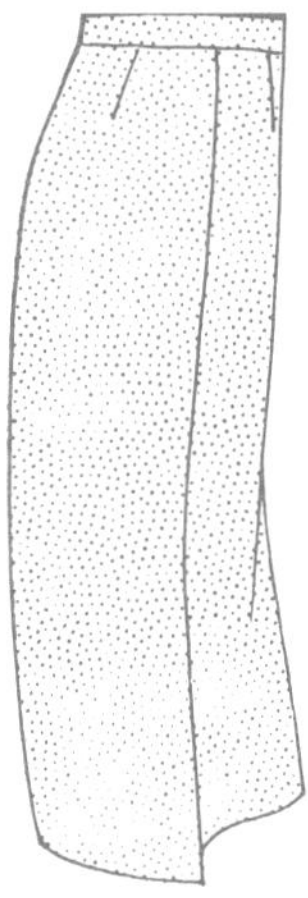

front seam of a skirt. Some patterns are cut with an extension in the seam allowance for a simple, folded pleat.

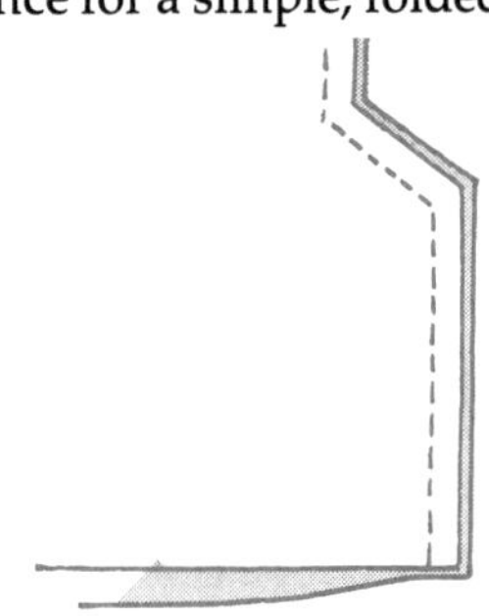

Mark the original seam line of the pattern on the material. This is the pleat line. Mark the top length of the pleat on the original seam line.

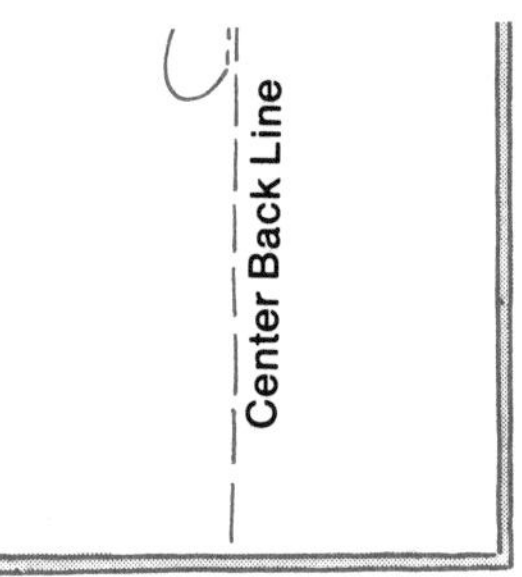

Place the skirt sections with right-sides together. Tack a pleat line to the top mark where the pleat ends. Continue up the original seam line to the waist.

Machine-stitch a 5/8-inch seam along the raw edge of the pleat extension. Continue up to the waistline along the original seam line. The extension may also be carried up to the waistline, as shown in the illustrations.

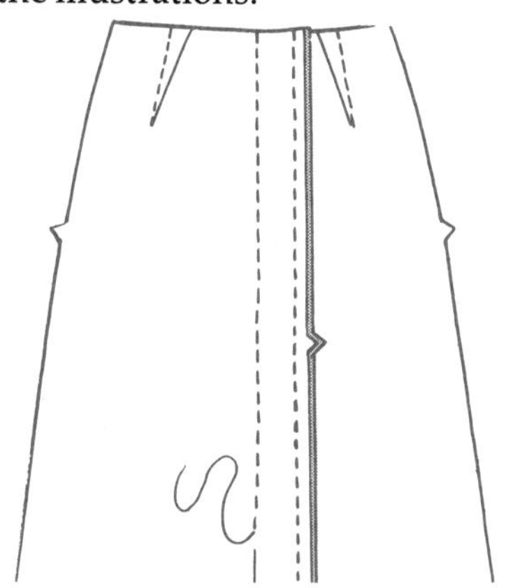

Press the seam to the left, and machine-stitch to the waistline. Remove tacking from the pleat on the original seam line.

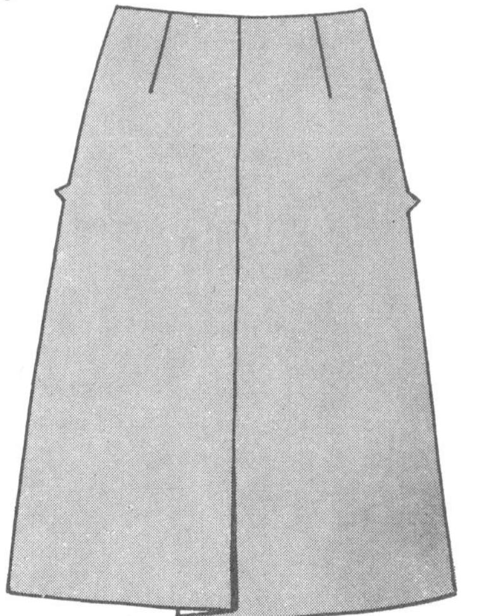

Sunray, Accordion Pleats—Sunray pleats taper in at the waist. Accordion pleats are the same width at both top and bottom. These pleats have folds that stand up instead of lying flat. It is almost impossible to make these at home. They must be made professionally.

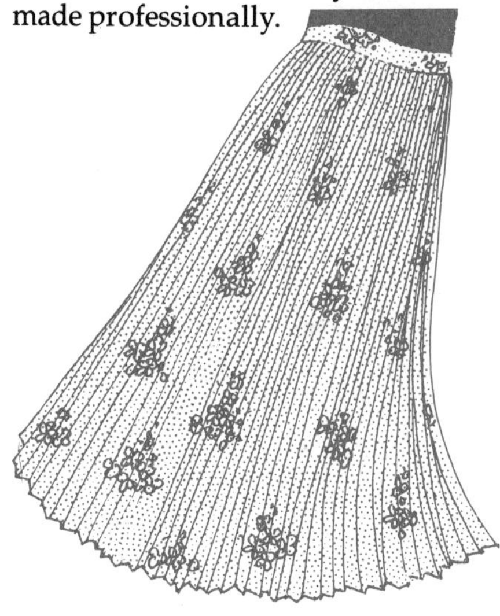

Dior Pleat—This is a type of kick pleat. It is also called a *false pleat.* Extra pieces of fabric are stitched in to provide fullness for ease when walking.

Cut and shape the seam allowance of the skirt sections. Mark the seam

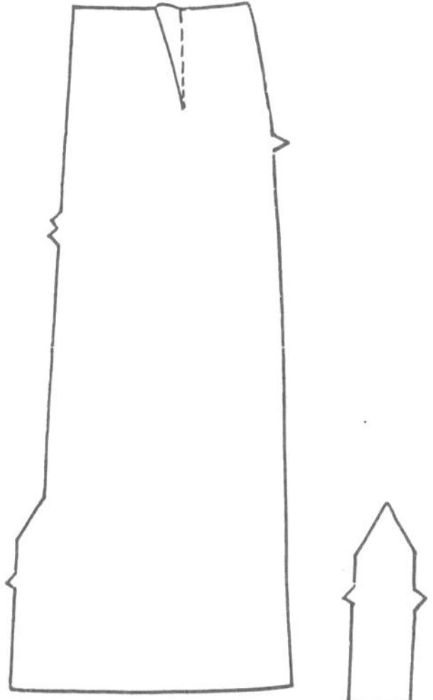

line on the skirt sections. Mark the length of the pleat along the seam line and tack it. Machine-stitch the rest of the seam line toward the waistline. Press seam allowances

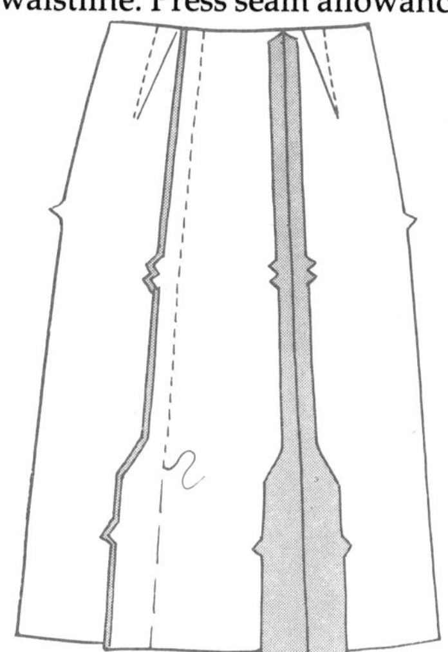

open. Cut the underlay of the pleat.

Pin, tack and machine-stitch the underlay to the seam allowance. Tack

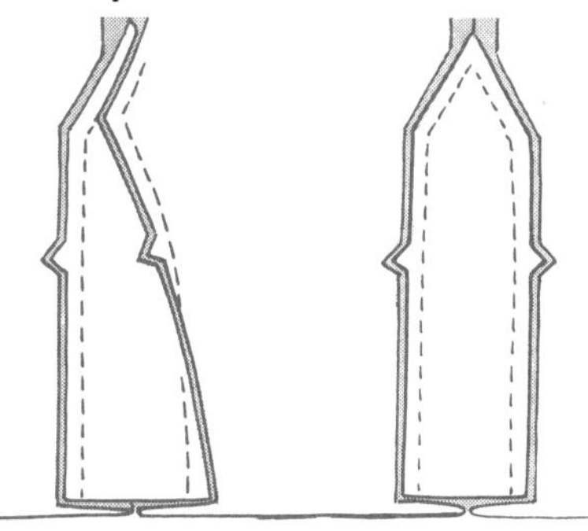

the upper end of the pleat to the skirt. Catch-stitch the edges at the top of the pleat to the skirt on the inside. Or turn the skirt to the right-side, and top-stitch through all thicknesses.

Remove tacking from the length of the pleat along the seam line. Press. When turning up the hem, have the underlay slightly shorter than the top of the pleat.

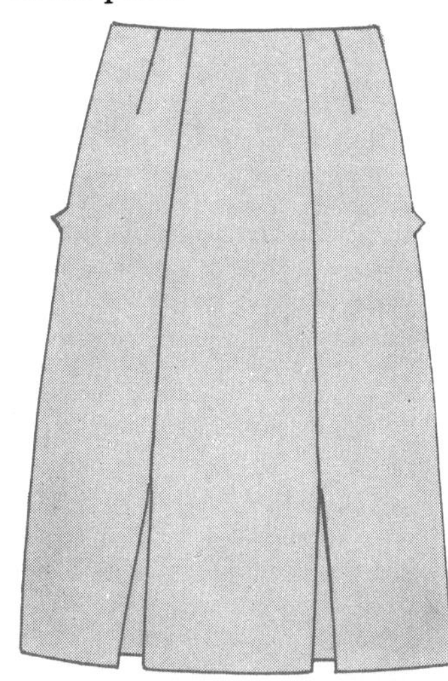

Double, Fan Pleats—*Double* pleats are set in straight skirts to provide more fullness. A wide piece of fabric is inserted. Keep pleats short or they will be bulky. One pleat is set over

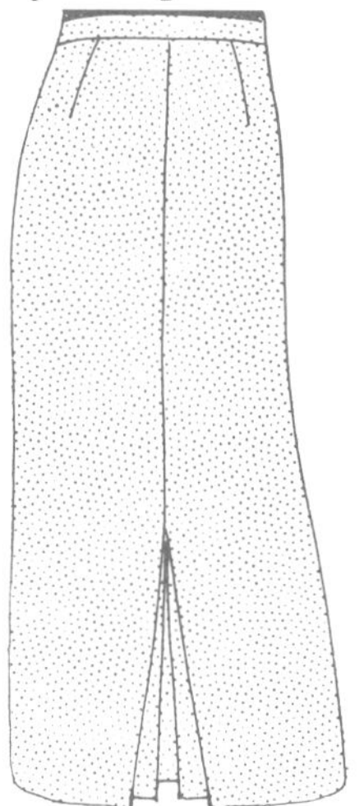

the other. *Fan* pleats are created by setting two or more pleats on top of each other. The width of each pleat is graded to avoid too much bulk. When pleats are pushed out during walking, they spring open, creating a fan effect. Fan pleating is pretty in evening dresses made of light, firm fabrics where pleats start just below the knee.

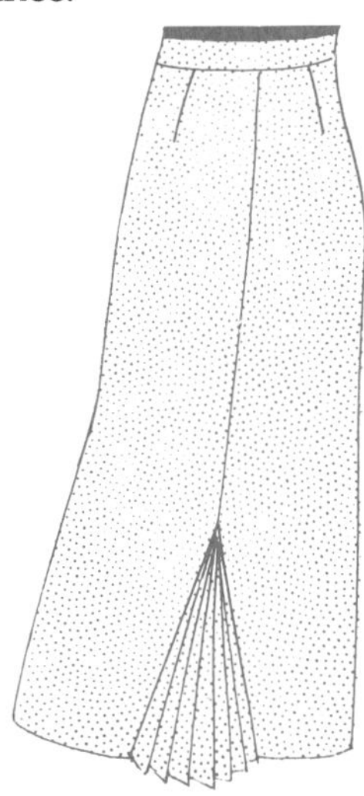

POCKETS

There are many types of pockets, both decorative and practical. Some are bags of lining material hidden inside the garment. Many are sewn on the outside as a feature of the design.

Pockets can be plain or decoratively stitched, in self-fabric or contrasting colors, textures and patterns. When used as decoration, place them correctly. Finish them carefully, or the appearance of the garment may be spoiled.

You can add a pocket to children's clothes, even if the pattern does not include one. Consider using pockets to hide burns, stains and flaws on ready-made articles. Outside pockets with large openings may need fastening for security. If fitting alterations are made, the pocket position may need to be moved.

Consider the type of fabric and the figure of the wearer when choosing pockets. Thick, tailored styles may look better with hidden pockets. Place pockets so large hips are not emphasized. Put pockets for decoration in the most flattering places. If the wearer sits most of the time, place skirt pockets lower down.

Figures vary in proportions. The number and size of pockets may need changing to enhance the final appearance. If in doubt, cut out pockets in paper. Experiment with them on the garment pieces or tacked garment. Adjust the size and shape, if necessary. If trying pockets on a completed garment, tack up the hem.

It may be easier to attach pockets to flat pieces of fabric. Add them at an early stage of making the garment.

Mark the final position of pockets by thread tracing. For symmetrical placing, transfer the markings from one-half of the garment to the other. Pin the two halves together with pattern notches matching.

Cut pockets on the straight or cross grain. Keep all corners true. Pockets or pocket flaps may need interfacing to help them keep their shape.

For welt, flap, patch and saddlebag pockets, match the material and garment grain. When stripes, plaids or checks appear in the fabric, match the pocket and garment design exactly. Do this for the crosswise *and* lengthwise grain. Cut pockets on the cross grain for an interesting effect.

Types of Pockets

IN-A-SEAM POCKET

This type of pocket is set in a seam or has a welt on the outside. One section of the bag is usually garment fabric, and one is lining.

Pockets can be made by using a narrow strip of garment fabric. Attach it to the upper-pocket-lining bag instead of making the section entirely of garment fabric. Pocket pieces may also be cut in one with the garment, as extensions of the seam allowance.

Cut two shaped pocket bags 8 by 4 inches wide. Or use pattern pieces. Tack and machine-stitch the lining-bag section to the front seam. Stitch 1/4 inch from the construction seam at the pocket opening. Match notches, and leave the seam allowance unstitched at the top and bottom edges. Tack and machine-stitch the fabric bag to the back seam edge behind the construction seam edge. Match notches.

Tack and stitch the lining and fabric-bag section together. Press toward the center front, and remove tacking.

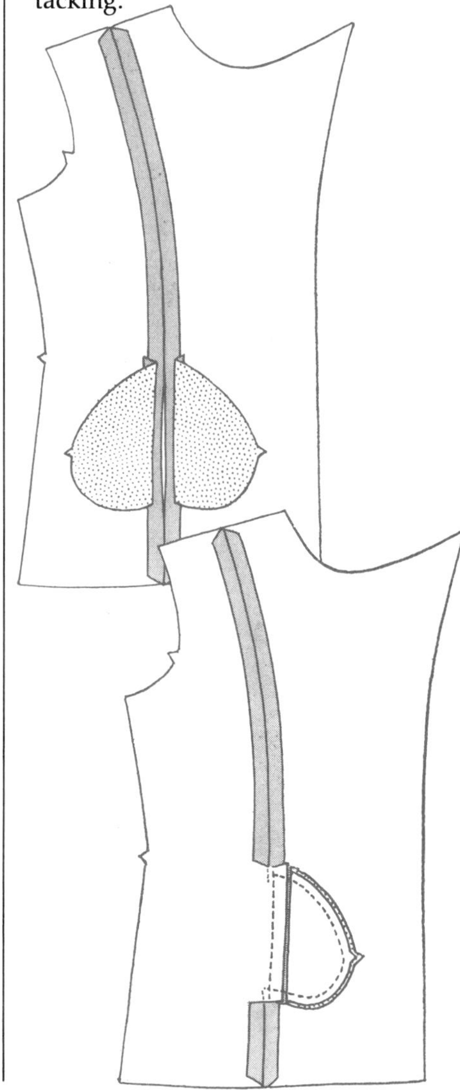

When a welt is visible on the right-side of a garment, both pocket bag pieces can be made from lining. Make a welt and put it between the lining and garment. Machine-stitch along the garment stitching line. See the section on *Welt Pockets*, page 146, for details.

The welt on the right-side of garment must be firmly sewn to the garment at the top and bottom.

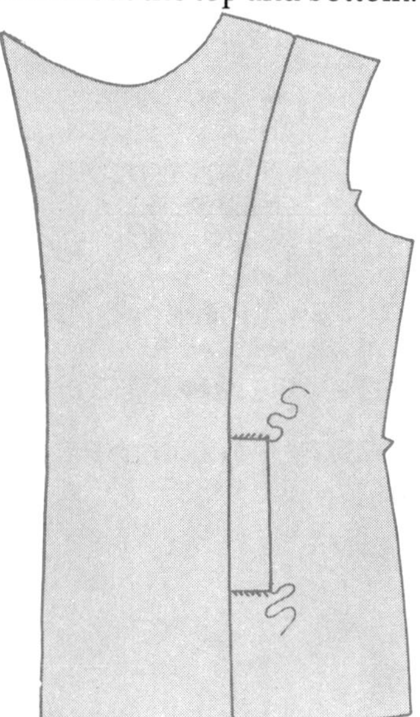

Catch-stitch the pocket and seam allowance together to hold the pocket in place inside.

POCKET INSIDE BODICE

This is sewn between the lining and garment facing. No pocket may be visible on the right-side of the garment. In this case, insert one at the facing edge between the garment and lining. It can be placed above the waistline in the buttonhole-side of the garment.

Cut two pocket pieces from lining using the pattern piece. Or make the pieces 7 to 8 inches by 4 inches, including seam allowances. Turn the straight edges to the wrong-side. Tack in place. Put the right-sides together, tack and machine-stitch.

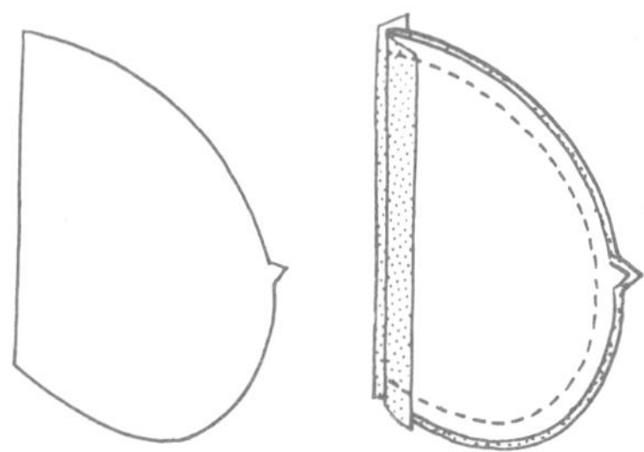

When the garment is lined, place the pocket between the lining and garment above the waistline. Tack one edge of the pocket to the facing edge of the garment. Tack the other edge to the matching facing edge of the lining. Slip-stitch the two edges. At the ends of the pocket, catch-stitch the facing edge at right angles. This holds the pocket firmly in position.

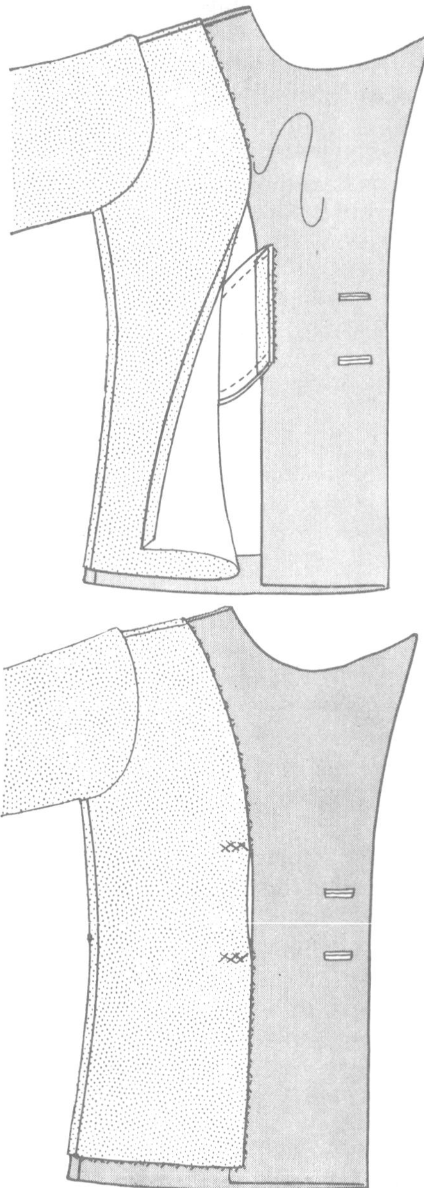

POCKET IN STYLE LINE

Pockets that appear in the design line of a garment are made before the garment is tacked together. A pocket may be made in one with the garment bodice or cut as part of pants or a skirt.

There are two ways to do this. For the first method, mark the position of

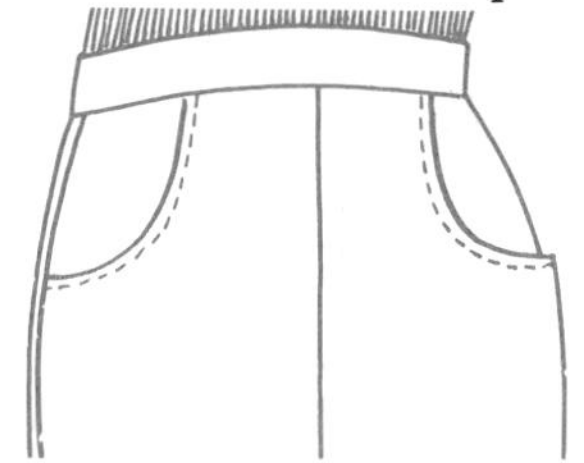

the edge of the pocket on the underlay piece. Put the facing and garment right-sides together. Tack and machine-stitch along the seam line. Snip and trim the edges, and press.

Turn the facing to the wrong-side. Roll the edge to bring the seam slightly to the wrong-side. Tack in place and press.

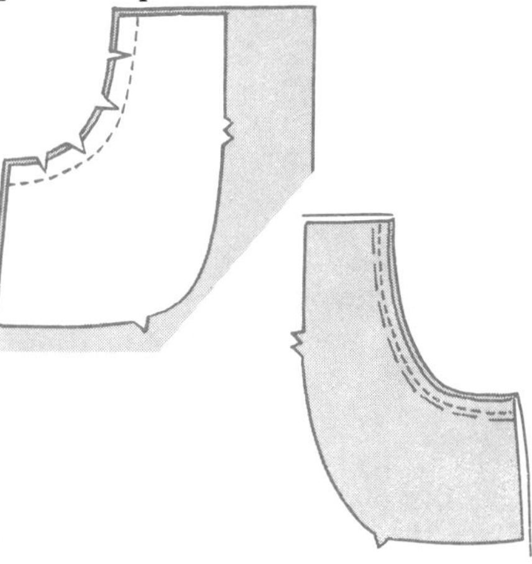

Place the wrong-side of the faced piece on the right-side of the underlay. Match the edge to the tacked line. Pin and tack in place.

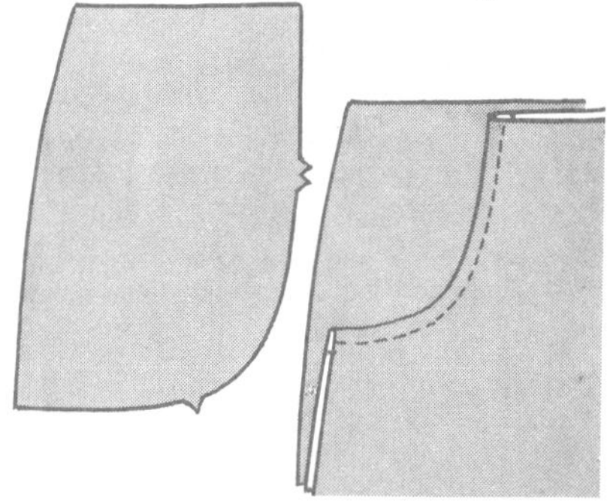

Pin and tack the facing to the underlay to make the pocket bag.

Machine-stitch the pocket bag along the seam line. Trim edges and finish securely.

The second method is to cut pocket sections from self-fabric. Some patterns include a pocket piece as an extension of the seam allowance.

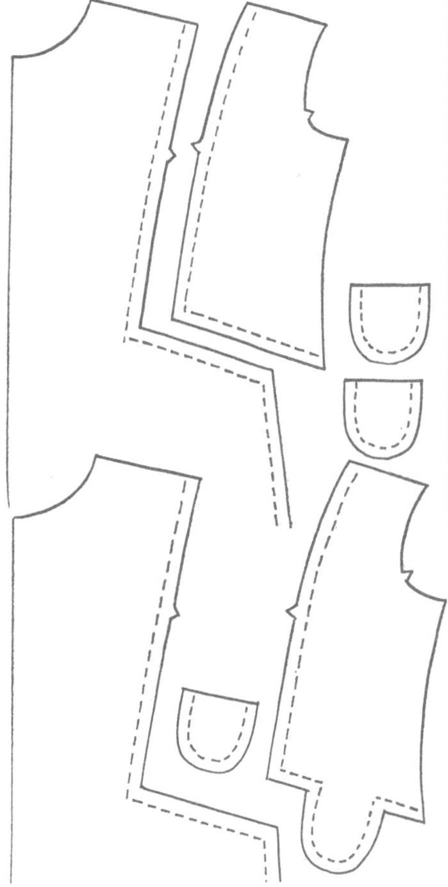

Tack along the outer seam line of the front part of the garment. Indicate pocket ends by cross-tacking on the tacking line. Tack the inner seam line of the side front section of the garment. Tack the pocket section in position. Stitch 1/4 inch below the garment seam line. The pocket seam edge is not visible when the pocket is completed.

Position seam binding on the wrong-side of the garment for strength. One edge should touch the seam line with the tape toward the raw edge. Hem the edges of the tape

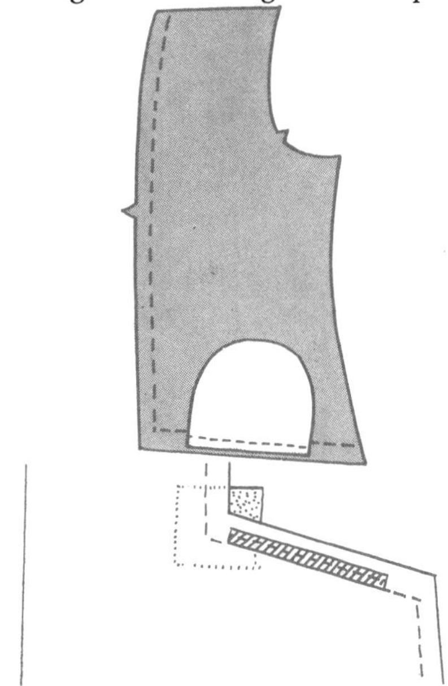

to the seam. Reinforce the inner corner, and tack along the seam line.

Tack a piece of light fabric, about 2 inches square, over the corner with right-sides together. The grain must be the same as the fabric grain. Machine-stitch a "V" from the edges to the point of the corner. Take one stitch across the corner but not through the tacking.

Turn the seam allowance to the wrong-side along the tacked line. Pull the extra square over so it forms folds. Cut the extra square level with the raw edge of the garment piece.

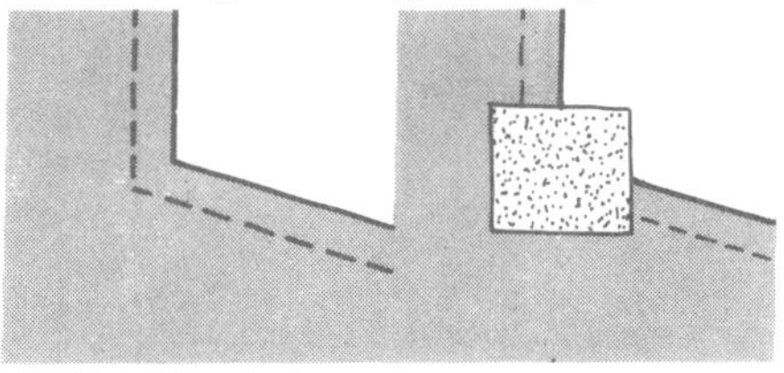

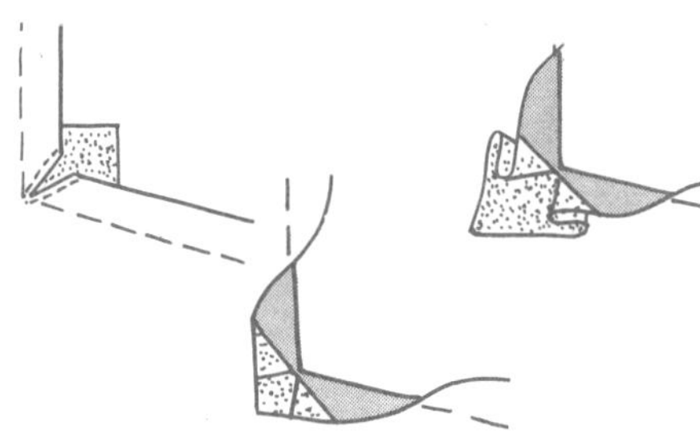

When the corner is reinforced, tack the pocket bag in place. Right-sides are facing. Machine-stitch about 1/4 inch in the seam allowance from the seam fold. When the pocket edge is complete, the bag edge is not visible.

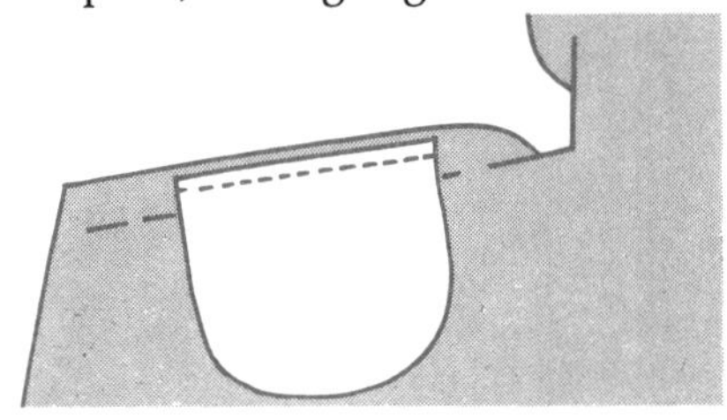

Turn the seam edge along the tacking at the seam line. Tack and steam press. Remove tacking, and press again to remove any tacking marks. Top-stitch the pocket opening across the top.

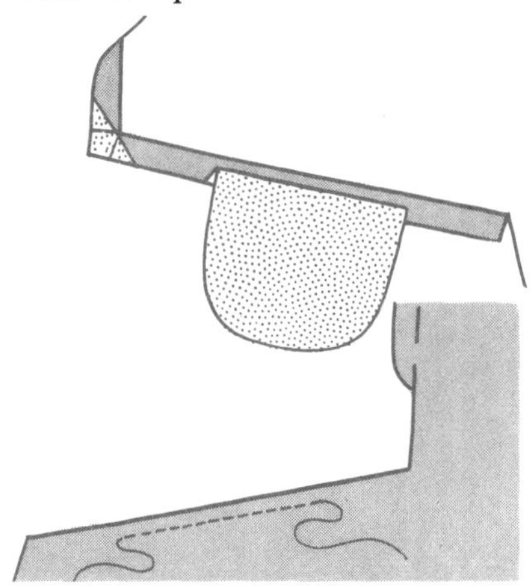

Turn the seam allowance. Tack it from the shoulder to the edge, then along to the underarm seam. Position sections as in the illustration above. Match stitching edges. Pin and tack edges in position for fitting.

When the bodice is fitted, machine-stitch the seam from the shoulder to the front pocket end.

Leave long threads to be pulled to the wrong-side and fastened.

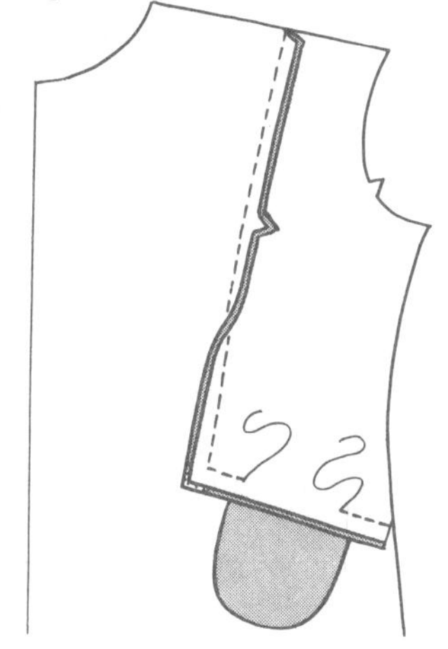

Pin together the two pocket sections. Tack and machine-stitch. Begin and end machine-stitching at the ends of the pocket opening. Remove all tacking. Complete

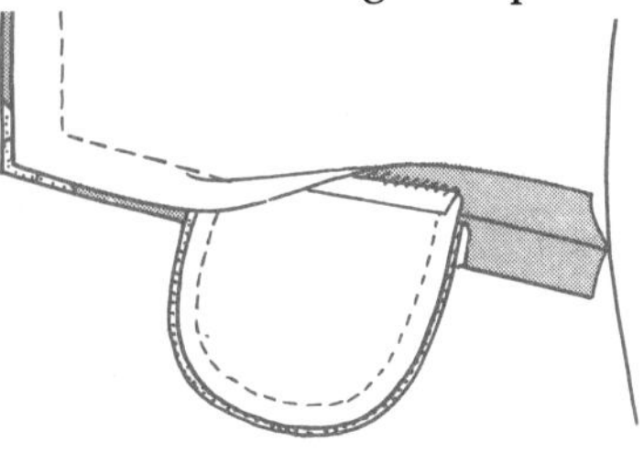

top-stitching from the side of the pocket end to the underarm seam.

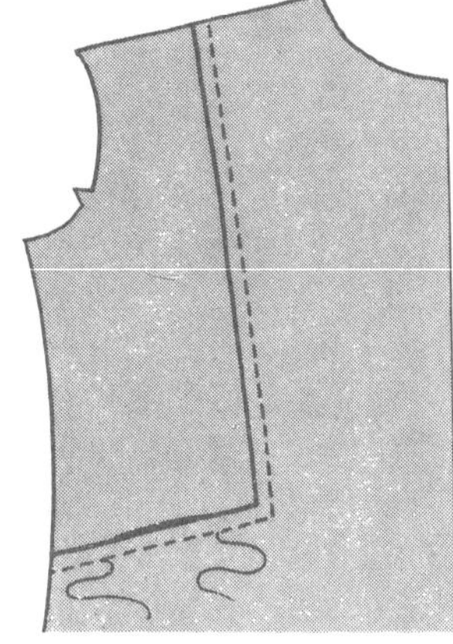

WELT POCKET

These pockets are inserted in a garment with a welt or flap showing. They are often used on jackets, coats and skirts.

Welts are usually left upstanding. Ends are secured to the garment. They may be above or below the pocket opening line. *Flaps* are normally attached at the top so they hang freely.

The method given below is for a *welt.* Directions for flaps are found below and also with the pattern.

Welts may be used as mock pockets for decoration. The grain of the welt must match the grain of the garment. Two thicknesses of fabric are usually used with interfacing. Welts may be cut from one piece of self-fabric with the top folded over or two pieces with a seam along the top. They are made like collars. See the section on *Collars,* page 99.

Cut the welt piece according to the pattern. Tack or iron interfacing to the wrong-side of the welt. Trim interfacing from seam allowances.

Place two welt pieces with wrong-sides together. Pin, tack and machine-stitch along the seam line. Trim and layer seam allowances. Turn right-side out. Roll the edge between fingers and thumb so the seam is not visible from the right-side. Tack near the edge and press. Top-stitch for decoration.

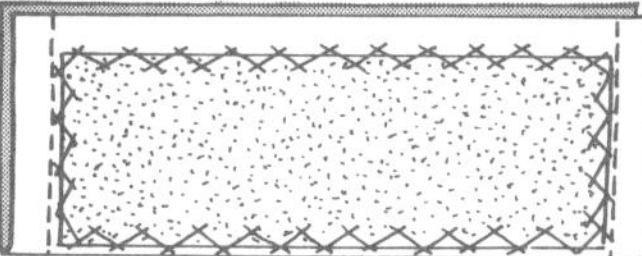

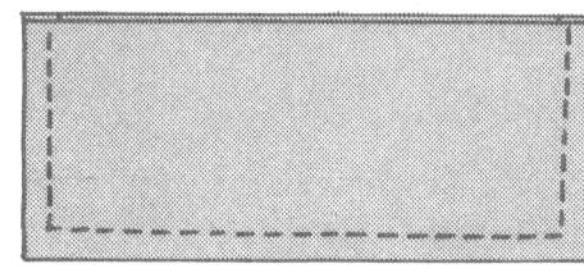

Mark the pocket position on the garment. Pin and tack the welt below the pocket mark with the cut edges along the pocket line.

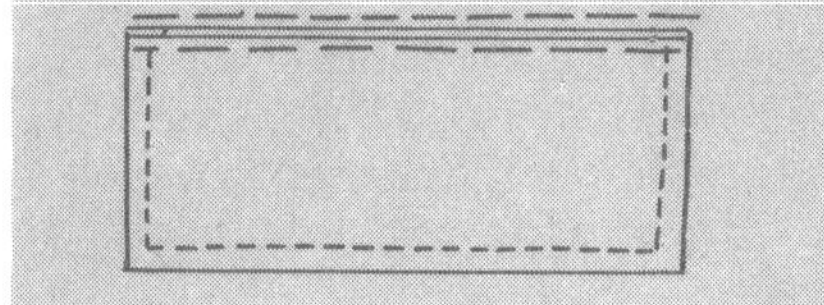

Cut two pocket bags. Place the lower section in the lining over the welt. Match stitching lines and tack. The upper section is fabric. It is sewn with the cut edge touching the edges of the welt and bag.

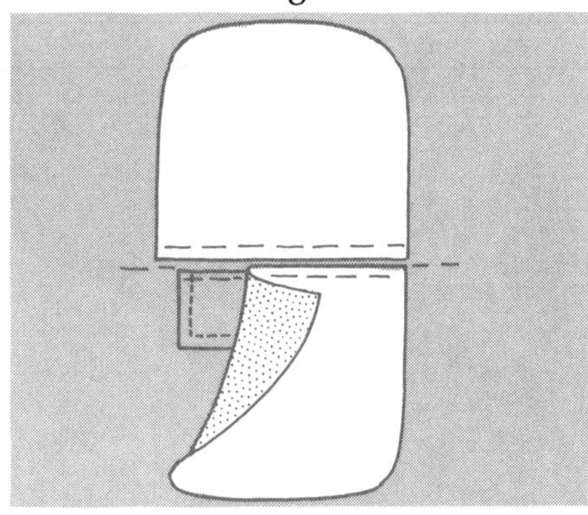

Tack and machine-stitch the lower section of the welt bag. Stitch back over 4 stitches on the stitching line for reinforcement.

Stitch the upper bag, ending three stitches from each end. Cut the pocket opening between raw edges of the bag section to within 1/4 inch of stitching ends. Cut diagonally to stitching ends.

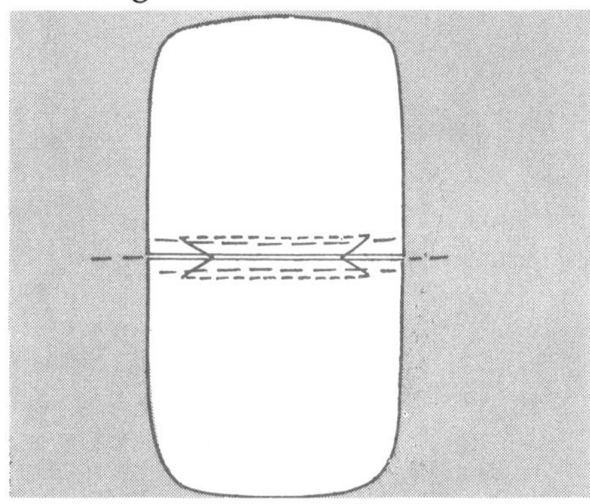

Pull the bag sections through to the wrong-side. Fold the welt in the position where it will fall when completed. Place pins at welt ends, through stitching ends of the upper bag.

Tack pocket bag sections together. Fold the garment away at one end of the pocket. Adjust the triangle at the end of the pocket opening. Stitch close to the pocket, across the triangle. Do the same for the other side.

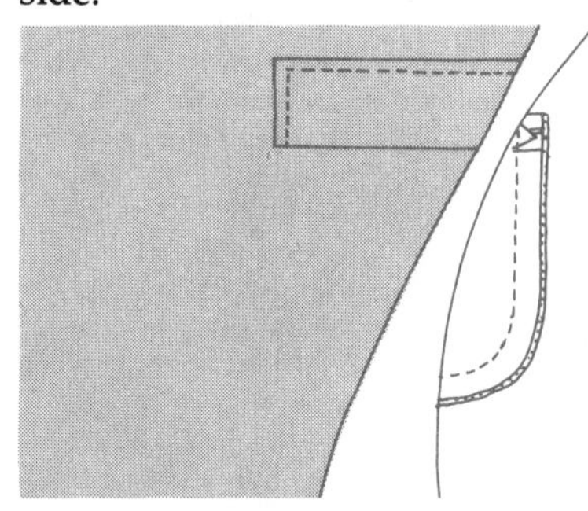

A flap can conceal a pocket opening. Stitch a strip of garment fabric to one section. It will be seen when the flap is moved. Flaps can be made in a shape to suit the garment. Use interlining to give extra body.

Cut two pieces of self-fabric for the flap. Interface and make up as for a welt. Mark the pocket line on the

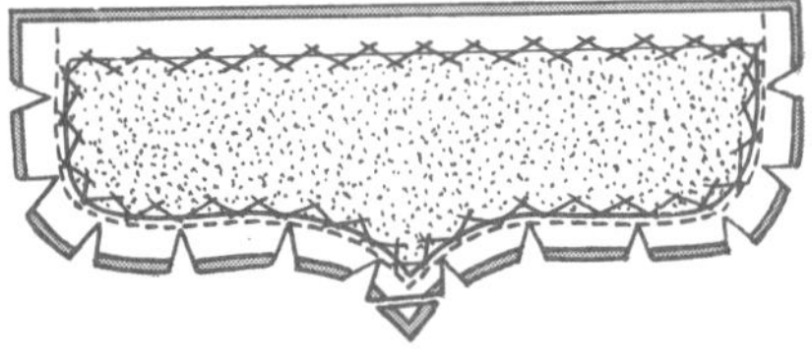

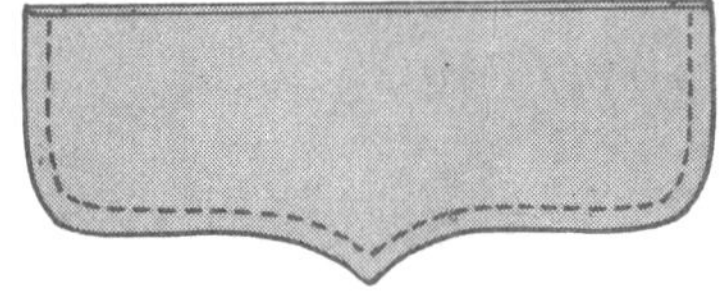

garment with thread tracing. Place the flap on the garment, with right-sides together and cut edges along the pocket line.

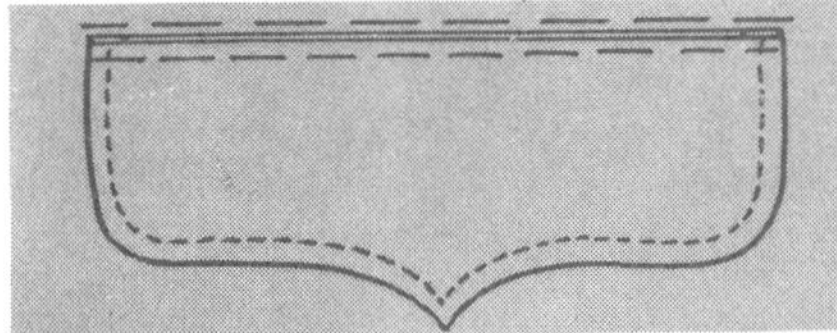

Tack in position 1/4 inch from the pocket line. Cut two pocket-bag pieces from lining. Also cut a strip of self-fabric 2 inches wide. Tack this strip to the lining. Machine-stitch the top and bottom edges. Catch-stitch the bottom edge to the lining.

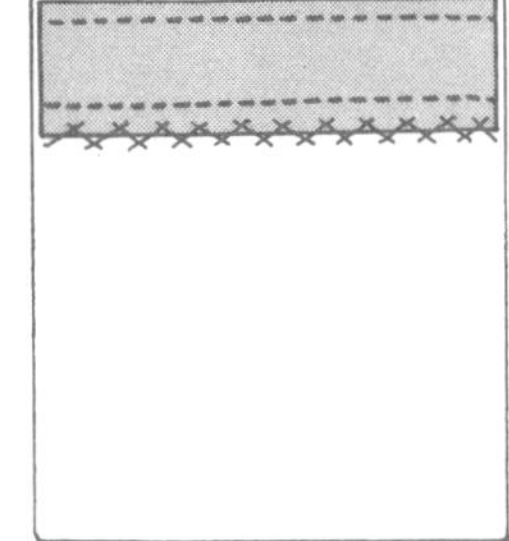

Cut a 2-inch strip of lining. Use this to bind the lower edge of the pocket opening, directly opposite the flap edge. Put the bag section over the flap with the self-fabric strip facing the flap. Tack in place, matching the bag edge to the flap edge. Stitch 1/4 inch from the cut edge. Stitch the bag and flap in position.

Put the cut edge of the binding to the lower edge of the tacking. It should touch the cut edges of the bag or flap. Tack in place. Machine-stitch the binding, making the seam line 2 or 3 stitches shorter than seam above. Remove tacking. Cut the garment between the edges of the bag section and facing to within 1/4 inch of the stitching ends. Cut diagonally out to the stitching ends.

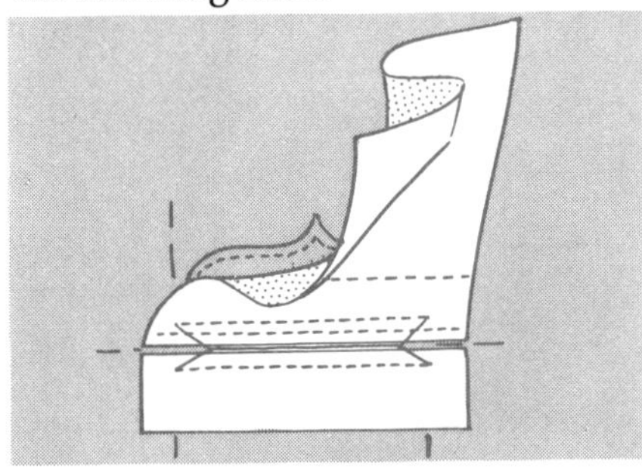

Pull the bag and binding sections through the opening to the wrong-side of the garment. The flap remains on the right-side. Bind the lower edge of the opening by folding a narrow section around the seam. Tack it in place. On the right-side, machine-stitch along the binding. Catch-stitch the raw edge to the garment.

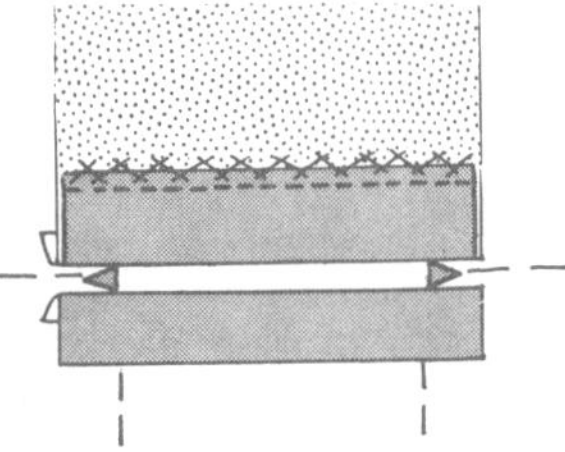

Fold the bag down over the bound edge. Fold the garment away from the open end of the pocket. Stitch a triangle in place in the arc. For decorative effect, tack the bag to garment. Machine-stitch on the right-side of the garment in matching or contrasting thread. Stitch down from the flap ends.

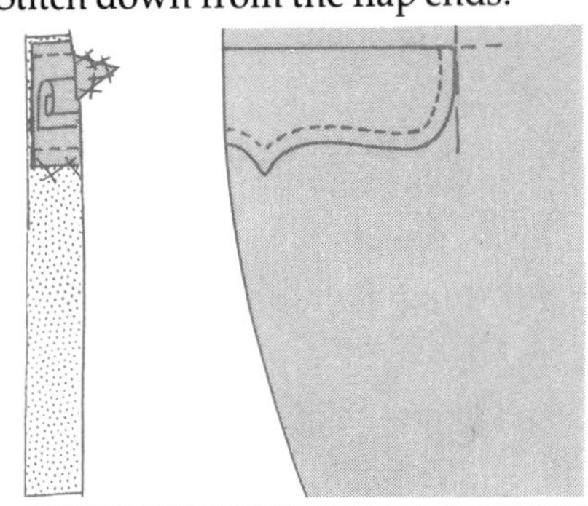

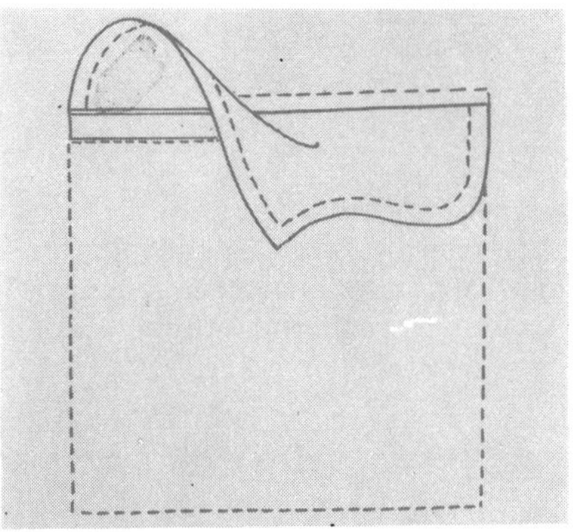

BOUND POCKET

One piece of fabric can be used to make a binding for pockets in thin and medium fabrics. Use piped or corded pockets for heavy, thick fabrics. Bound pockets are used on lined, tailored garments. They are made in a way similar to bound buttonholes.

Mark the *exact* position of the pocket on the garment with a straight line of thread tracing. Cut a piece of self-fabric on the straight grain. It is 2-1/2 inches deeper than the depth of the finished pocket and 2 inches wider.

With right-sides together, center this piece over the pocket line. Tack along the line. Machine-stitch an

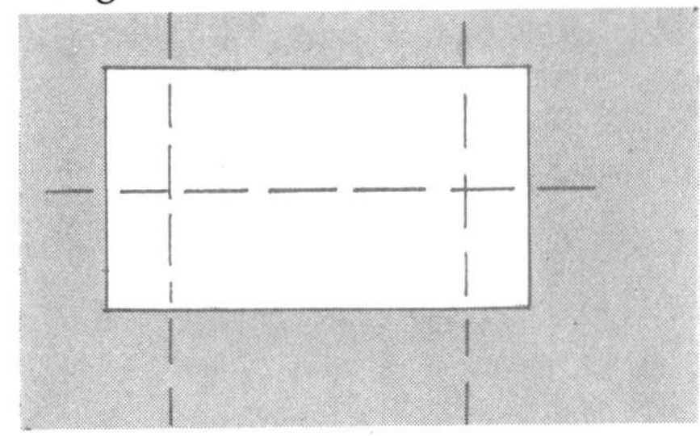

oblong 1/4 inch from the pocket line on both sides. It is easier to do this from the garment side.

Cut along the pocket line and out to the corners without cutting the machine-stitching. Pull the binding

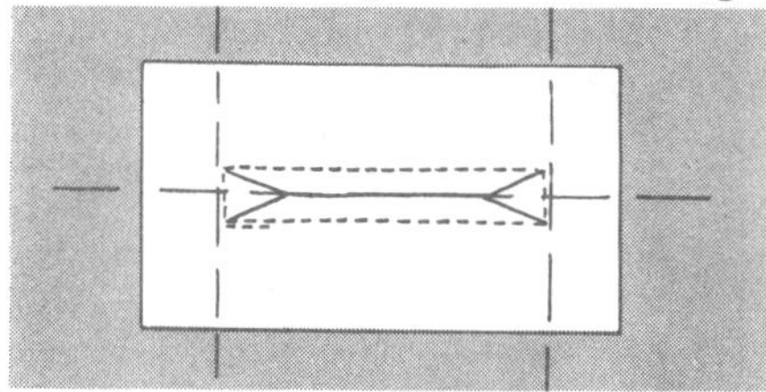

piece through the slit, leaving a neat shape on the right-side.

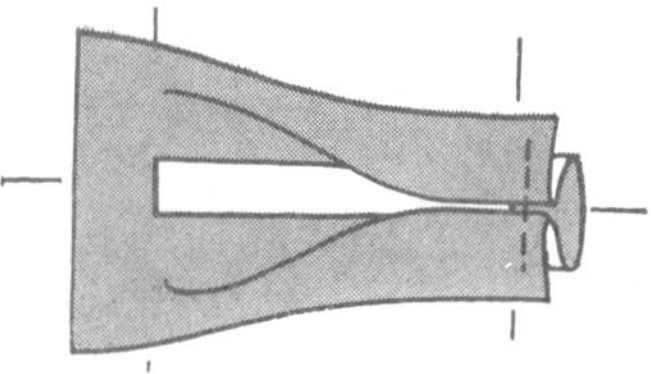

Fold the binding on the wrong-side. Oversew the folds, press and attach to the pocket. Place one pocket piece on the wrong-side of the garment. Tack in place.

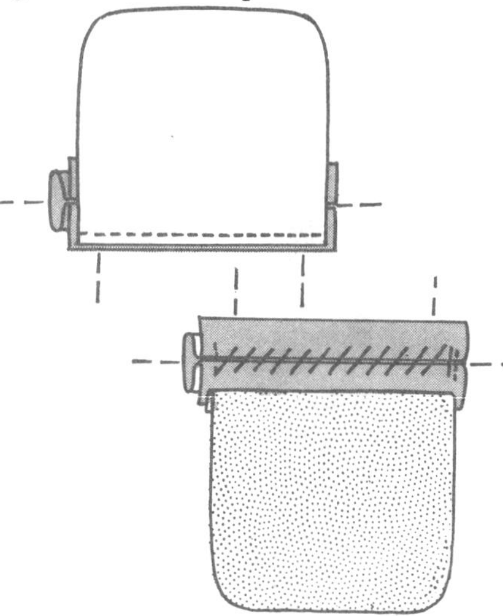

From the right-side of the garment, machine-stitch through all thicknesses just outside the binding. Press the pocket piece down. Put the other pocket piece over the first, with right-sides together. Tack in place.

From the right-side of the garment, stitch around the bound opening.

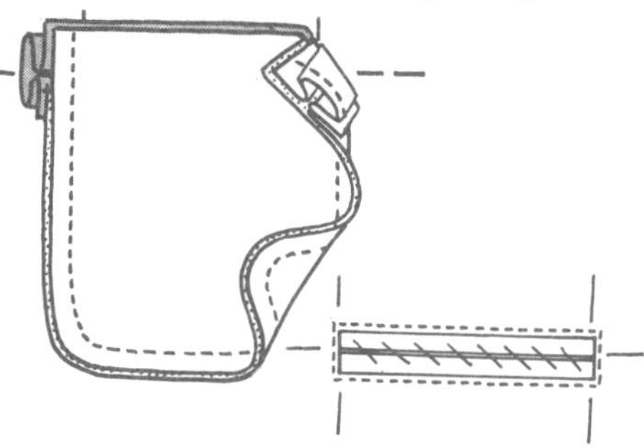

Pin, tack and machine-stitch the two pocket pieces together along the seam line. Do *not* stitch the pocket edges to the garment. In an unlined garment, raw edges can be bound for neatness.

CORDED POCKET

Bound openings can be made from two pieces of extra material, like a piped buttonhole. Cord can be inserted for interest and is sometimes used on a curved pocket. It may be finished at the end with decorative tacks. Self-fabric strips are usually cut on the true bias. A fine piping cord is used. See the section on *Binding and Piping,* page 87.

Cut two strips of true bias for each pocket. Fold the bias strip around the cord. Sew small running-stitches along the bias, enclosing the cord. Trim edges to 1/4 inch.

When the hem of the garment is complete, mark the pocket position on the garment with thread tracing.

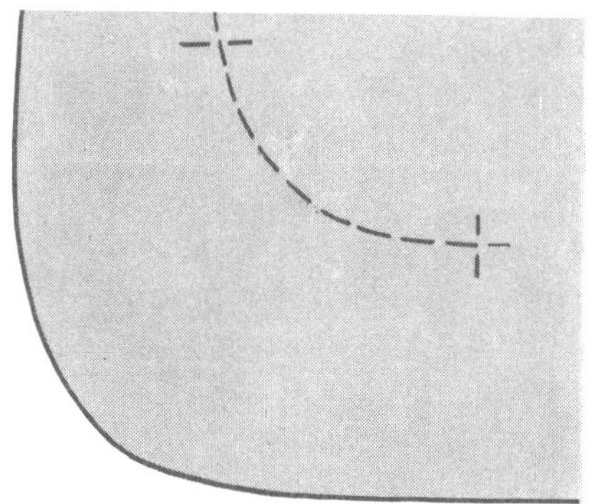

Place two prepared cord strips along the pocket position, with cut edges touching. Tack in place. Tack pocket ends at right angles to the pocket opening.

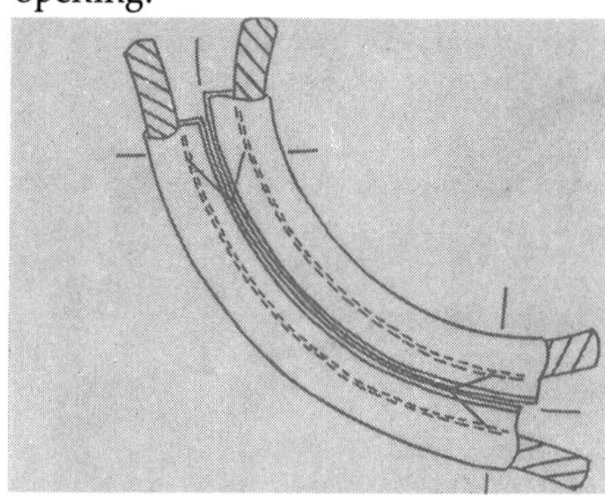

For curved pockets, ease the cord on the inner concave edge. Place the cord without stretching to the outer, convex edges.

Stitch near the cord, forming two parallel rows. Back-stitch ends to prevent tearing. Cut along the pocket line to within 1/4 inch of the end of the stitching. Cut diagonally to the stitching at the ends. Turn seams through the opening to the wrong-side.

Tack two cord edges together on the right-side along the length of the pocket. Press. Attach a pocket bag as

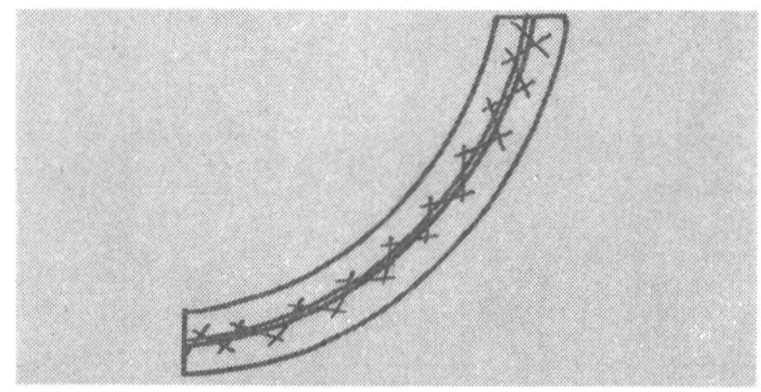

for bound pockets. Stitch decorative tacks at each end. See the section on *Stitches,* page 67.

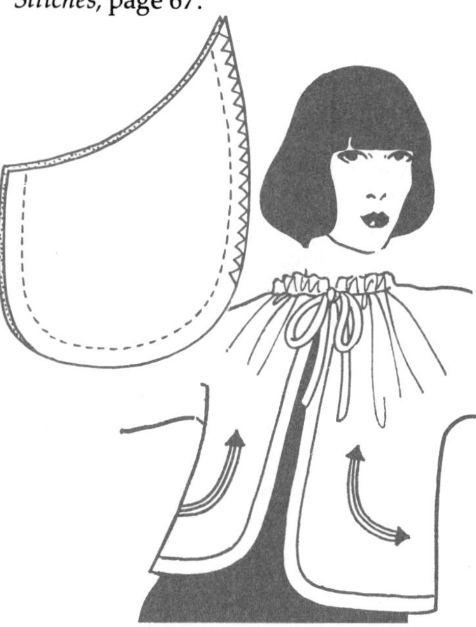

PATCH POCKET

These can be many shapes and sizes. They are usually made from a piece of fabric hemmed and stitched to the garment. They may be made from a piece of fabric folded in half to form a self-lining. They are stitched with wrong-sides together and turned to enclose raw edges. One edge is finished and left open.

These pockets may be lined or unlined, plain or decorative. Some have a box pleat down the center, gathers or a flap to cover the top edge. The pocket may be stitched down and have a zipper inserted at the opening.

Unlined Patch Pockets—Cut out the pocket piece. In a patch pocket, reinforce and strengthen the top edge with interfacing on the wrong-side of the material.

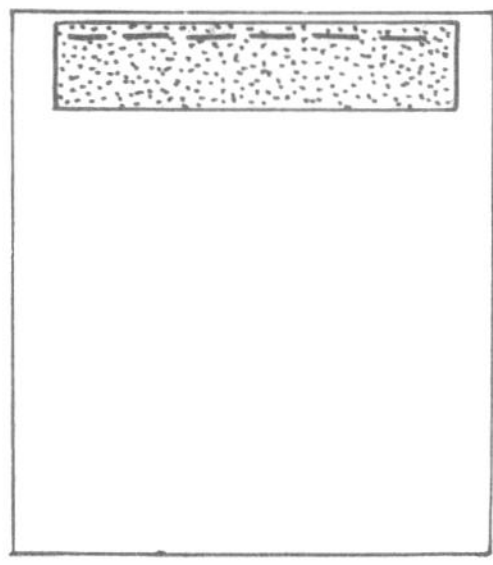

For a curved pocket, sew a row of gathering-stitches first. Cut a cardboard template the exact size and shape of the finished pocket. Gather the seam allowance over this. Press carefully. Remove the cardboard, and tack edges in place.

On a square pocket, miter the corners to lessen bulk where the seam or hem appears along two converging edges. Miter by tacking seam allowances. Fold over a corner of material so the fold touches the intersection of the two merging tackings. The grain of the top fabric should fall along the grain underneath. Tack along the fold and press.

Cut excess material to within 1/8 inch of the fold. Turn under the seam allowance on three sides. Put the folded edges of mitered corners together. Turn down the top edge of the pocket. Hem in place and press.

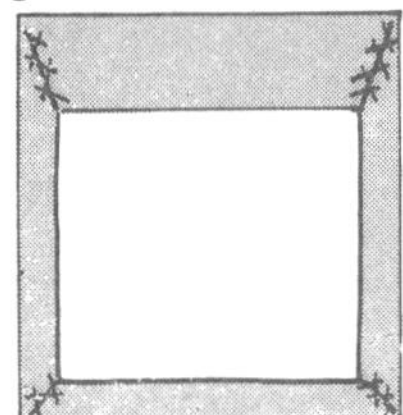

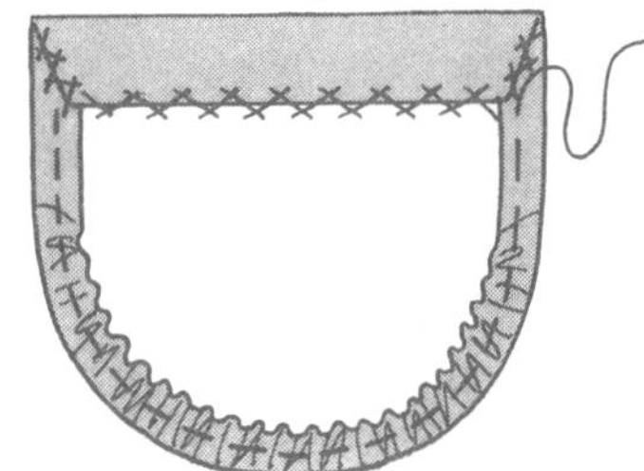

With thread tracing, mark the position of the pocket on the garment. Pin the pocket in place. Try on the garment and adjust the position if necessary. Tack in place.

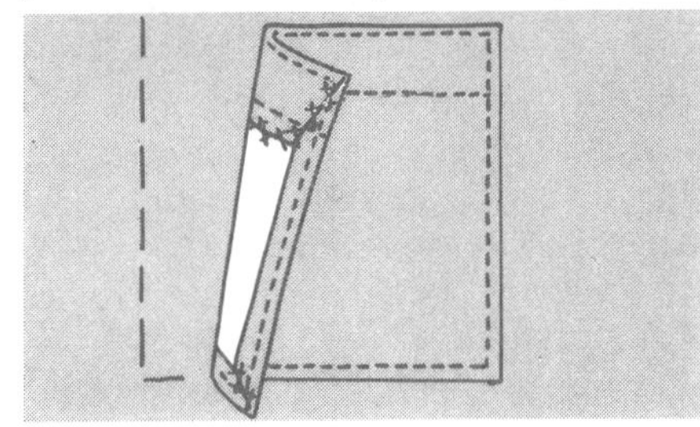

Back-stitch the pocket to the garment from the wrong-side. The stitches will not be visible on the right-side of the pocket. If a top-stitched finish is preferred, do this *before* attaching the pocket to the garment. A decorative stitch can be used.

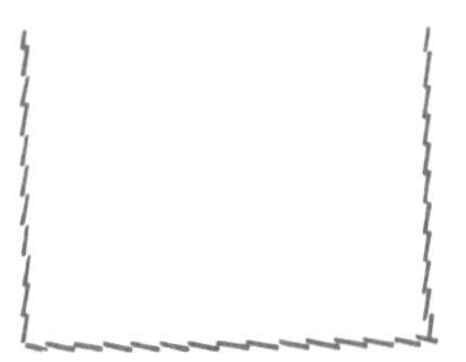

You can top-stitch the pocket from the right-side by hand or machine. It may be hard to get a good finish when stitching through several layers. Pay attention to stitch length, pressure and needle size.

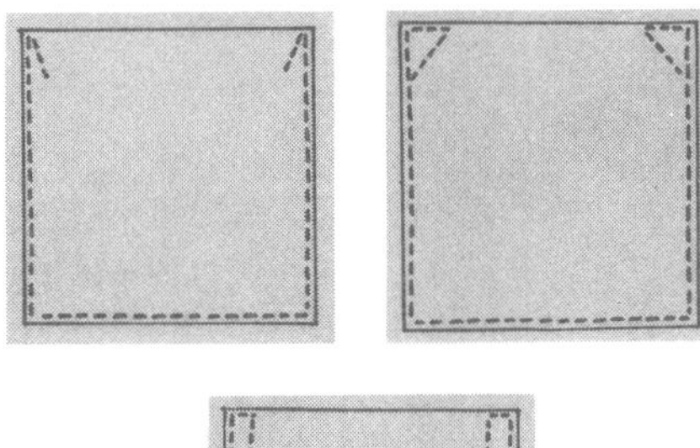

Lined Patch Pockets—Pockets in rough fabric need a lining for comfort and convenience. Cut the pocket piece from self-fabric, and cut a piece of lining. Trim away the lining above the pocket fold line.

Press the seam allowance under to the upper edge of the lining. With right-sides together, tack the lining to the pocket. Fold the top edges of the pocket along the fold line, over the lining. Beginning at the top of the hem facing, stitch down one side, across the bottom and up the other side.

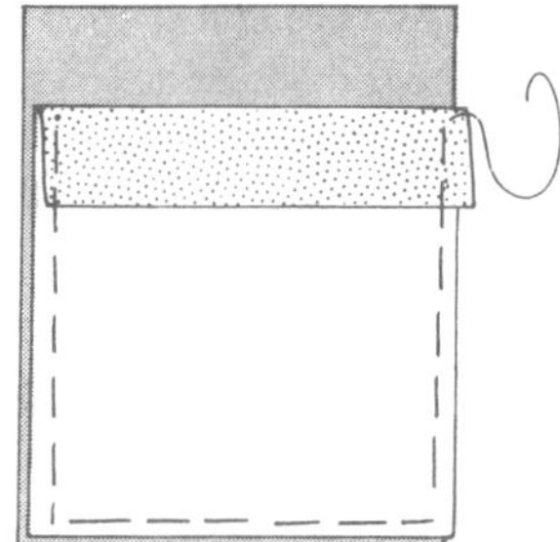

Trim the seam allowances, and turn right-side out. Close the pocket by hemming the lining to the fabric, then press.

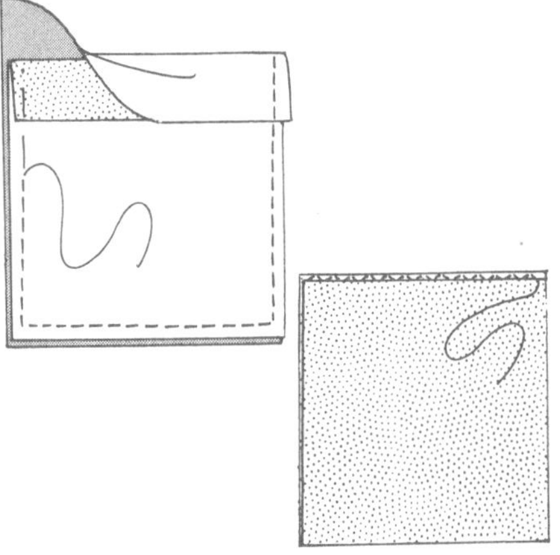

SEAMS

Seams hold sections of a garment in place, giving shape and emphasis to the style. Some seams are decorative as well as functional. If seams pucker, stretch or are crooked, undo them and resew them.

Test-sew a double layer of fabric for tension pressure and stitch length before sewing garment seams. Select the correct thread and needle for the fabric.

When sewing jersey or knit, consult your sewing-machine handbook for the correct stretch-stitch to use. If using a straight-stitch machine, stretch fabric slightly while sewing. This helps keep the seam from breaking during wear.

On a simple zigzag machine, stitch length depends on the thickness of the fabric. When the needle moves to the left or right, the fabric receives greater support from the needle plate at the point where the needle penetrates the fabric.

On some machines, there are many stitches to choose from. Consult your sewing-machine handbook. On jersey fabrics, a roller foot assists feeding the fabric. This foot is available for most machines.

Use a ball-point needle when sewing knit fabrics. These needles prevent fiber damage. Man-made fabrics blunt needles rapidly. Use a new one for each garment to avoid damaged seams and drawn threads.

For hand finishes, choose the correct stitch technique, and needle and thread for the fabric. Always attach thread securely, but not with knots. Knots come undone, tear delicate fabric and cause lumps in seams and hems when fabric is pressed.

GENERAL CONSTRUCTION METHOD

Learn what stitch size, type of stitch and type of thread to use for the fabric you choose. You need to know how to do certain stitches, such as tacking, joining and finishing. You should know some decorative stitches. Practice stitches before starting.

Seam Allowance—Garments cut from a paper pattern have a 5/8-inch seam allowance. Some fabrics and seams need bigger edges. Most sewing machines have a seam-guide attachment or lines marked on the plate. These keep seam allowances uniform during stitching.

Seam Width—This is the finished width of seams, such as a French seam. It varies with the type of fabric and seam.

Stay-Stitching—This is the first line of stitching on curved or stretchy edges. Sew it before pinning or tacking pieces together. It prevents stretching and acts as a guide when joining sections together. Machine-stitch a row of stitches about 1/8 inch away from the seam line along the seam allowance.

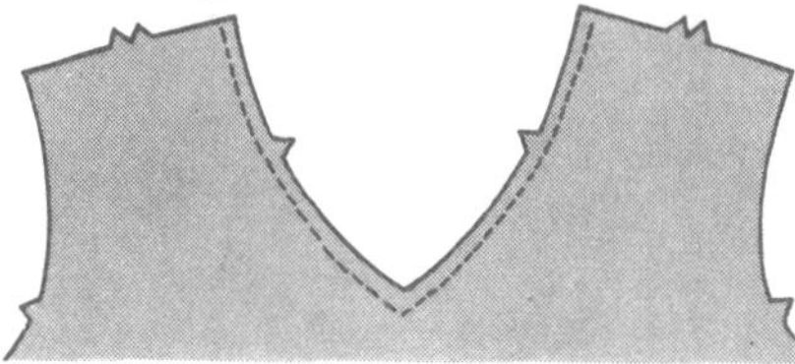

Pinning, Tacking—Experienced sewers sometimes machine-stitch seams after pinning them. Pins are placed along the seam allowance at right angles to the seam line.

Finishing Seam Threads—When beginning and finishing seam stitching, tie off top and bottom threads securely. Or back-stitch about 1/2 inch at each end. This leaves double stitching for extra strength.

When stitching ends in the middle of a seam, pull one of the threads through. Top and bottom threads will be together. Knot them or sew them in.

Pressing—Press the line of stitching before trimming, turning or opening the seam. Press again if necessary. Press garment seams as garment construction progresses.

Trimming—If fabric is bulky, trim excess seam allowance after stitching and pressing, before finishing. Enclosed seams are usually trimmed to 1/4 inch.

Layering, Grading—This trims two or more seam allowances that are turned together in one direction, such as the edge of a collar. It prevents bulky seams and ridges. Each layer is trimmed to a different width. The seam allowance on the most important piece is left the widest.

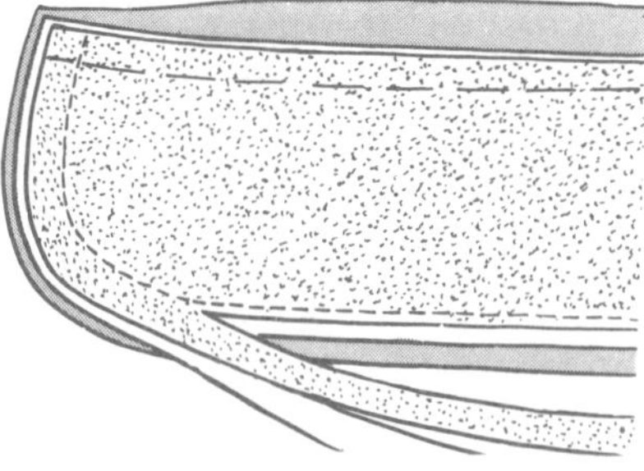

Notching, Clipping, Snipping—Curved seams must have the seam allowance cut in a special way so they lie flat. When the seam curves outward, cut small notches from the seam allowance. Do *not* cut seam stitches. On inward curves, snip about every 1/4 inch. When there are sharp angles in a seam, snip or trim the seam allowance. Inner corners usually have an extra line of stitching as reinforcement.

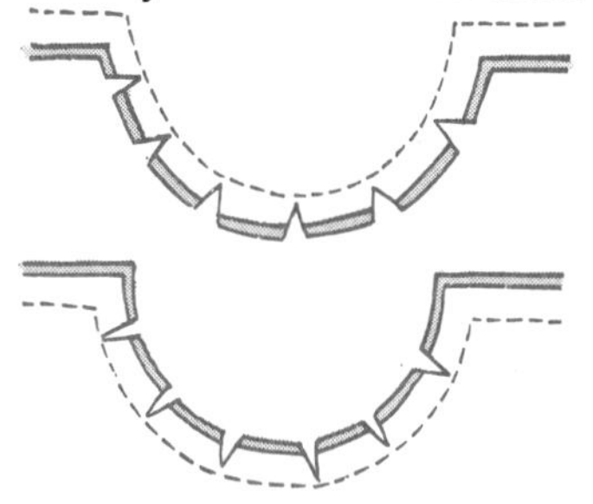

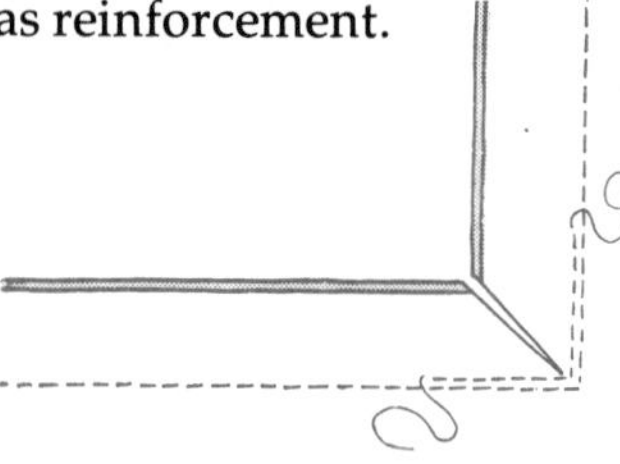

TYPES OF SEAMS

Plain, open seams are the most common. There are several variations of this type.

Plain, Open Seam—This is sewn from the wrong-side of the fabric. Little stitching shows on the right-side. It is used for side, shoulder and sleeve seams. The seam allowance is pressed open or to one side after stitching.

Place right-sides together. Pin and tack nearer the edge than the seam line. Machine-stitch along the seam line. Remove pins and tacking, and press the stitching. Finish, trim and press again.

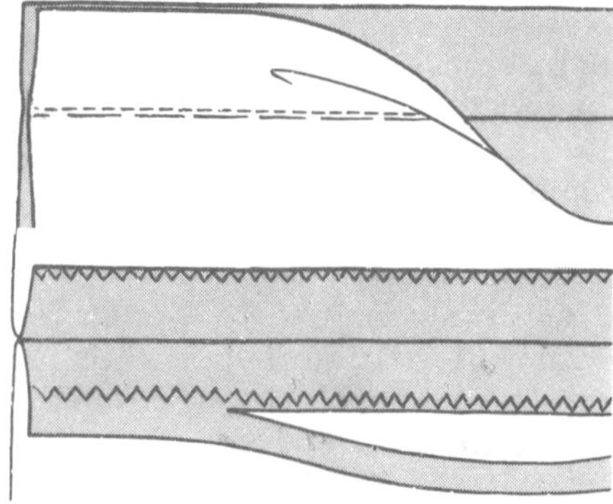

Plain Seam, Eased—You may need to ease one edge to fit the other when making a seam. First stitch through the single layer close to the seam line within the markings. Pull the thread until both sets of markings match.

Secure the thread end. Evenly space the tiny gathers, and tack them to keep them in place. Complete the seam as usual, machine-stitching with the eased side *up*.

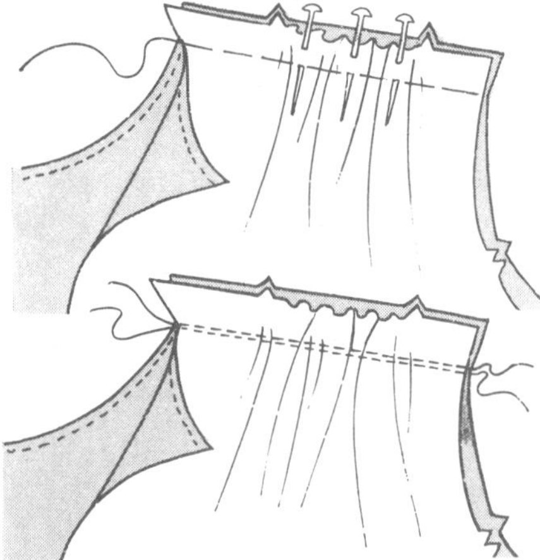

Plain, Intersecting, Crossed Seam— With right-sides together, pin the seams and press open. Push a pin through to match them exactly at the center. Pin each side of the seams and stitch. Trim corners to reduce bulk.

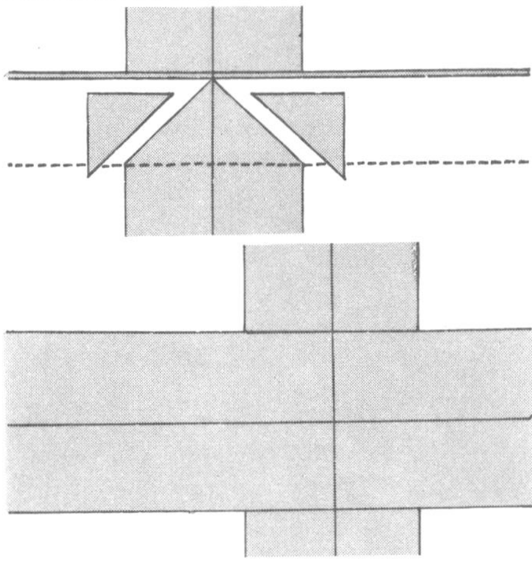

Plain Seam on Stretch Fabric—Use a stretch- or narrow zigzag-stitch. You can stitch the seam with a piece of tissue paper underneath to keep fabric from slipping during sewing.

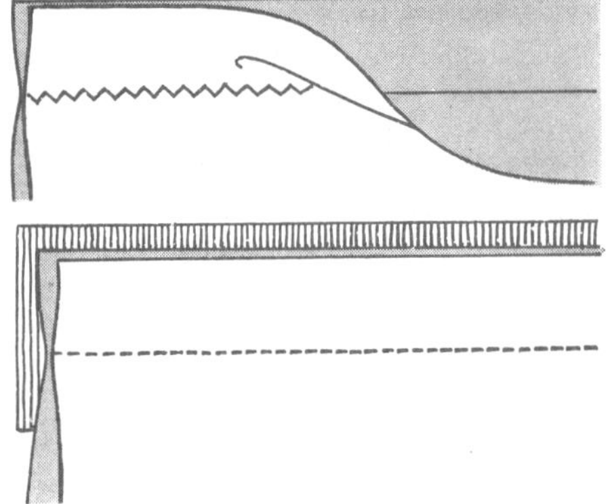

Plain Seam With Bias-Cut Edge— Place the straight edge on a flat surface. Pin and tack the bias edge to it. Stitch from the bias side without stretching.

Plain Seam, Joined at Corner— Reinforce the inner corner with a line of stitching next to the seam line, then clip to the point. With right-sides together, pin the two garment pieces with the clipped piece up. Tack and stitch along the seam line, pivoting at the corner.

Remove tacking and press the stitching. Press the seam open. Clip in from the outer corner and catch-stitch the trimmed inner edges. You can also press seam allowances toward the outer edge. Trim fullness and catch-stitch the trimmed edges together.

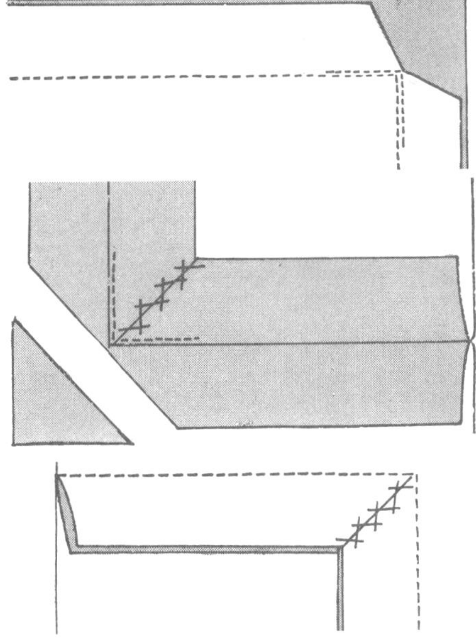

Plain Seam, Top-Stitched—This makes a plain, open seam visible from the right-side. Stitching can be done in matching or contrasting thread, and in a straight or decorative stitch. Press the seam to one side, then top-stitch from the right-side through all layers. One or more rows of stitching may be spaced as desired.

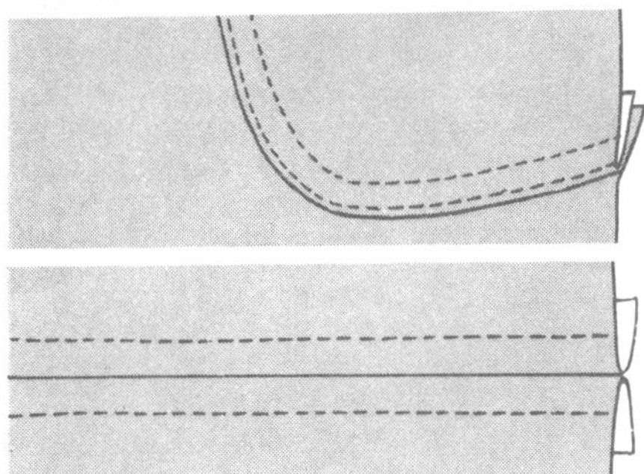

French Seam—This flat seam does not show from the right-side. It is often used for straight seams on sheer fabrics and fabrics that fray easily. Clothes that need frequent washing, such as blouses and lingerie, may also be made with French seams.

All raw edges are enclosed so no extra finishing is needed. Pin and tack the garment pieces with wrong-sides together. Start about 1/8 to 1/4 inch nearer the edge than the seam line. The width of French seams varies according to the thickness and fraying quality of the fabric. Stitch along the line, and carefully trim seam allowances. Press and remove tacking.

Fold the fabric with right-sides together. Roll the seam between fingers and thumb until the stitching is along the edge. Tack and press in place. Stitch along the seam line, keeping the seam an even width. Remove tacking and press.

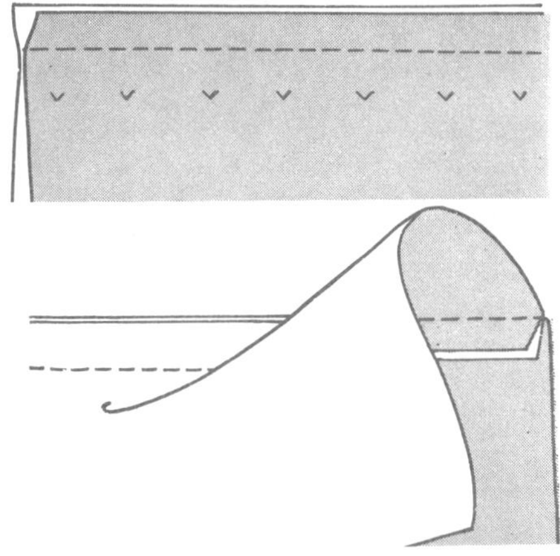

Mock-French Seam—This is another way to finish a plain seam. Prepare and sew a plain, open seam, but do not press it open. Turn in the seam allowances as shown, and press in place. Stitch 1/8 inch from the edge.

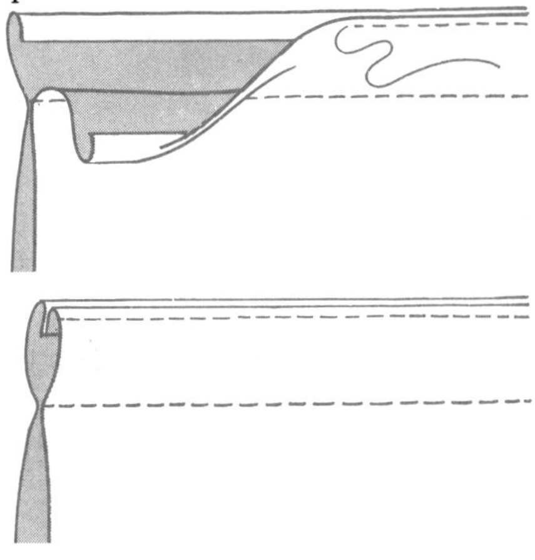

Lapped Seam—This type of seam is also called *top-stitched* or *overlaid.* It is visible on the right-side and is a strong seam. It is suitable for joining shaped sections, such as bodice yokes. Extra trim may be included when making a lapped seam. First decide which garment piece is to be the overlay and which the underlay. It is usual to lap the yoke on the bodice, or lap a plain flat section on a full one.

Mark the fitting lines on each section. Turn under the seam allowance on the overlay to the wrong-side. Press and tack in place. Clip curves if necessary. Prepare gathers, pleats and darts in the underlay. Place this piece on a flat surface, right-side up.

Pin and tack the folded edge of the overlay along the seam line of the underlay. Match balance marks and stitch 1/8 to 1/4 inch from the fold through all layers. Trim and finish the seam allowances on the wrong-side.

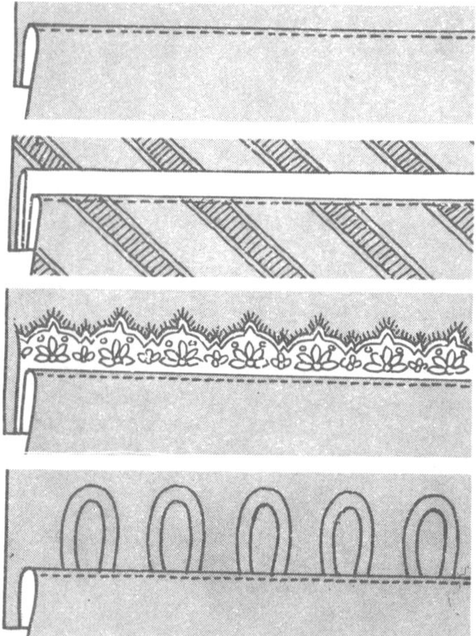

Run-and-Fell Seam—This is also called the *double-stitched seam.* It is the strongest type of seam. It lies flat with two rows of stitching on the right-side of the garment. It is not suitable for bulky fabrics.

Raw edges are enclosed so no extra finishing is required. There is no fraying during laundering. The width depends on the type of fabric. It can be as narrow as 1/8 inch on fine fabrics. The seam can also be made on the wrong-side. Only one row of stitching shows on the outside.

With wrong-sides together, stitch a plain seam. Press it to one side. If you

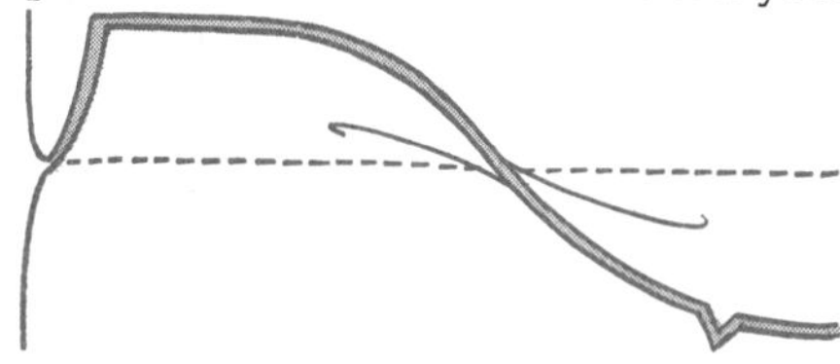

are making the seam on the inside of the garment, put right-sides together.

Trim the underneath seam allowance to 1/8 inch. Trim the upper seam allowance to 3/8 inch. Fold it and press it over the lower one. Stitch through all layers close to the folded edge. Press.

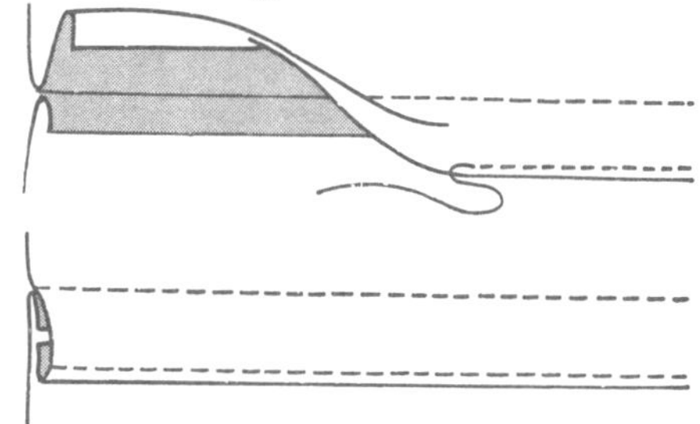

Channel Seam—This seam defines or outlines important style lines. A third layer of fabric is added to this seam. The extra piece may be a matching or contrasting color.

Mark the fitting lines on both sections. Trim seam allowances to 5/8 inch for a finished channel width of 5/8 inch. Turn seam allowances under, press and tack in position. Make a line of tacking down the center of the length of fabric to be inserted. If no pattern piece is given, cut a strip about 5/8 inch wider than the seam width.

With the strip right-side up, overlap the two folded edges, also right-side up. Keep folds along the tacking line. Pin and tack in place. Sew two straight rows of stitching through all layers. Each row should be 1/4 inch from the folded edge.

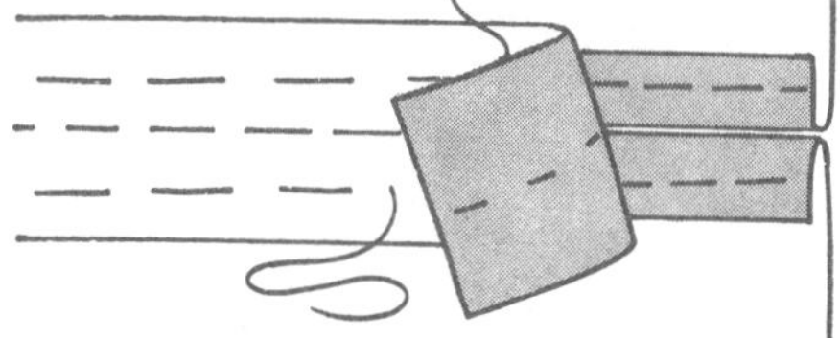

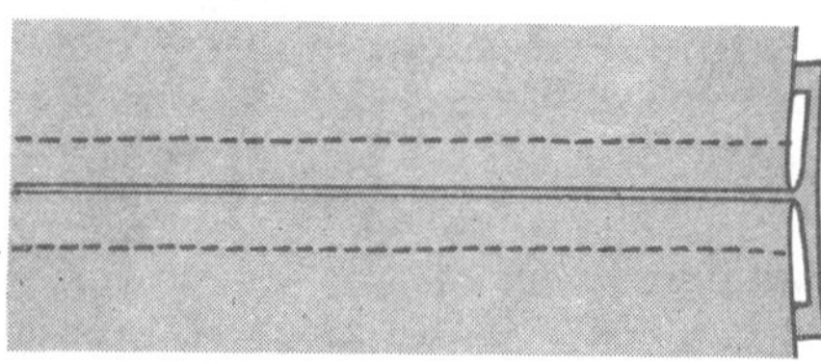

Remove tacking, finish raw edges and press on the wrong-side.

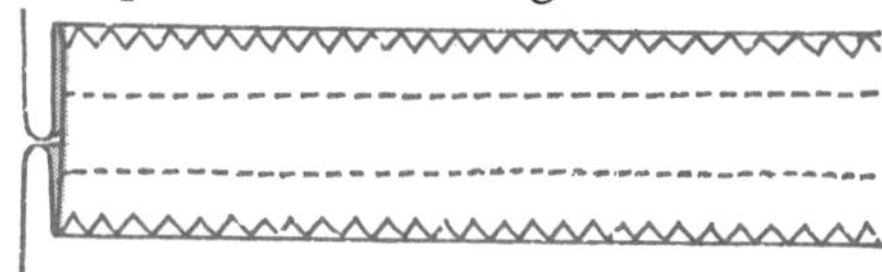

Piped, Corded Seam—Piping or cord may be added to seams during construction for decorative effect. Piping can be self-fabric, matching or contrasting bias binding. See the section on *Binding and Piping,* page 87.

Fold piping in half. Tack along its length. For corded piping, fold the binding around the cord, then tack in place.

To pipe or cord an open seam, tack piping to the right-side of one of the sections along the seam line. Place the right-side of the other fabric section over it. Stitch through all layers along the seam line.

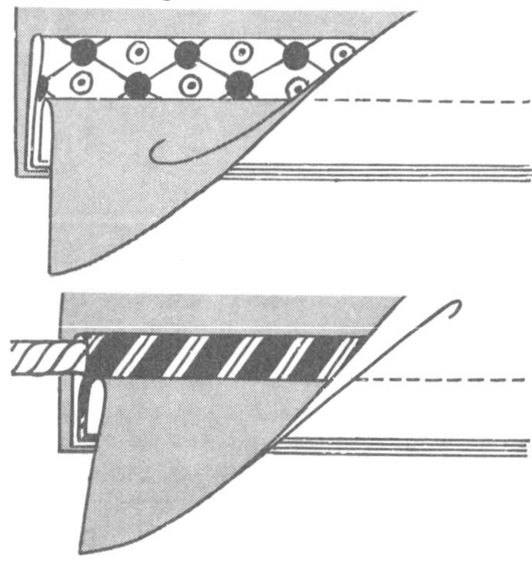

To pipe or cord a lapped seam, tack piping along the seam line of the underlay. Place the folded edge of the overlay on the piping. The required amount of piping should show on the right-side. Tack and machine-stitch.

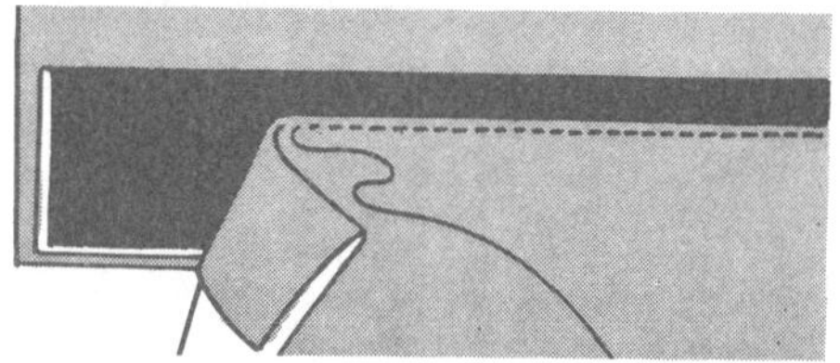

SEAM-FINISHING

Finish inside edges for a smart appearance and extra strength.

Pinked—Trim closely woven fabrics that do not fray with pinking shears.

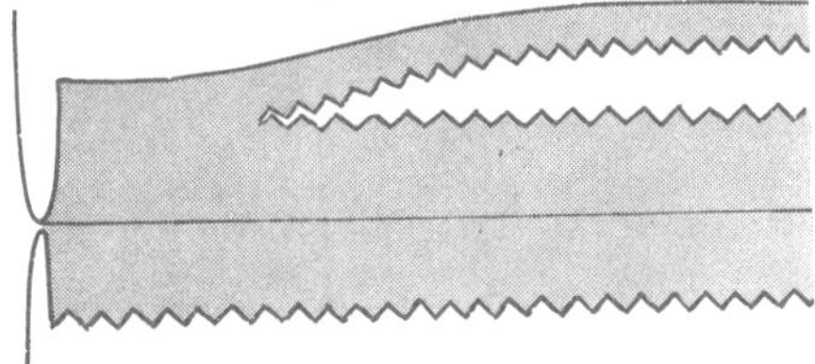

Pinked, Stitched—This is stronger than pinking alone. Machine-stitch 1/4 inch from the edge. Trim the edge with pinking shears.

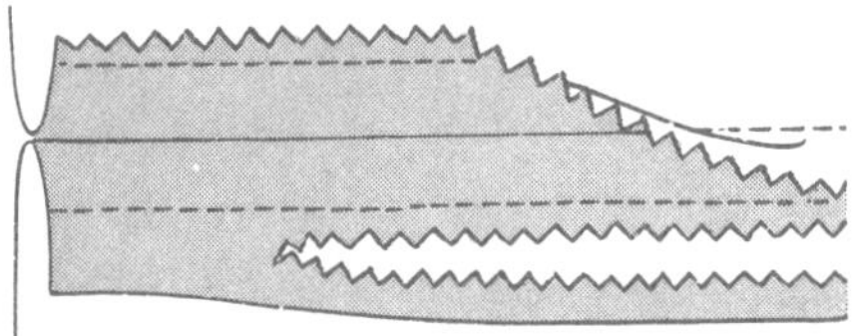

Machine-Overcast—Do a zigzag- or step-stitch test on a scrap of fabric. Stitch 1/2 inch from the seam line with a narrow zigzag-stitch. Carefully trim excess. Or trim excess

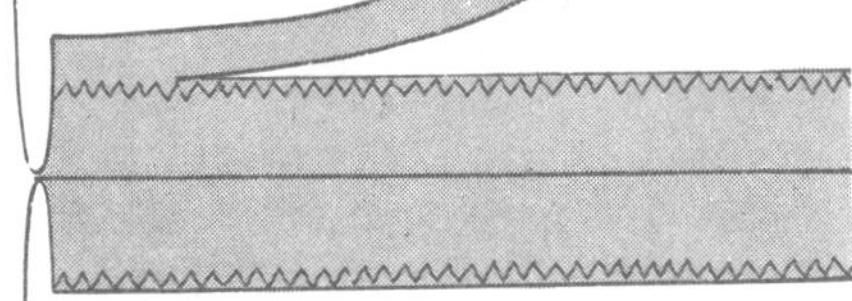

seam allowance and stitch a full-width zigzag- or step-stitch over the edges.

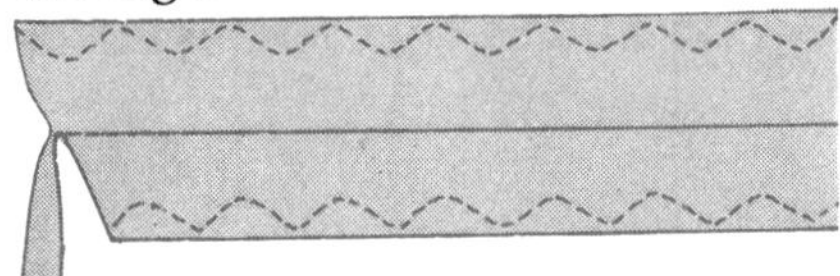

Hand-Overcast—This takes time but is suitable for most fabrics. It may be necessary if no sewing machine is available. Use a blanket- or overcasting-stitch. If the seam is pressed open, trim seam allowances evenly. Sew over both edges separately. If seam allowances are pressed to the same side, trim, then sew over both edges together. If the fabric frays, a line of stitching may be sewn along edges before overcasting by hand.

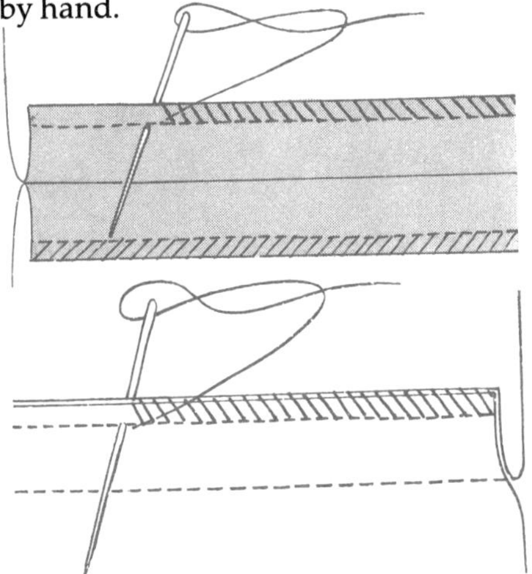

Rolled—This is only suitable on fine fabrics. It is a slow process. Trim the seam allowance to within 1/4 inch of the stitching. Roll the edges between fingers and thumb as you go. Overcast over the top of the roll. Catch overcasting in the machine-stitching.

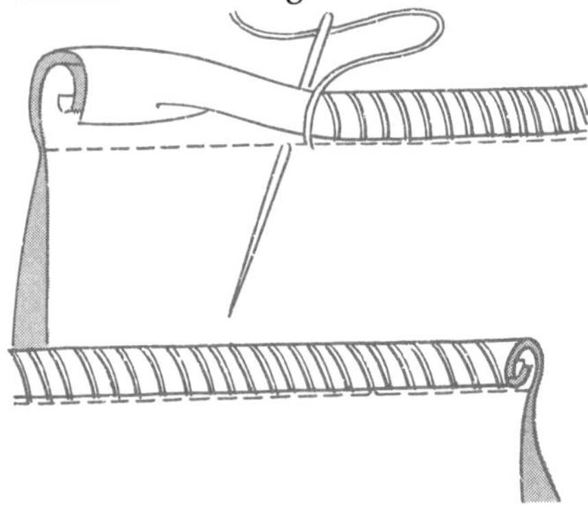

Bound—Use bias tape in a matching color to bind edges of heavy, thick, easily frayed fabrics. Bound seams look neat inside unlined jackets and coats where seam finishing is seen. See the section on *Binding and Piping*, page 87. Bias tape is necessary for curved seams, such as armholes. Paris or seam binding is used for straight seams.

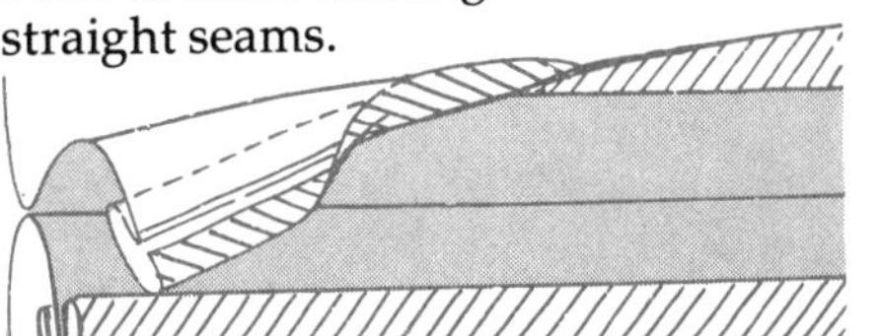

Seam-Bound—One seam allowance is used to bind the raw edge of the other. Trim one edge to within 1/8 to 1/4 inch of the stitching, depending on the thickness of the fabric. Fold and press under the edge of the other

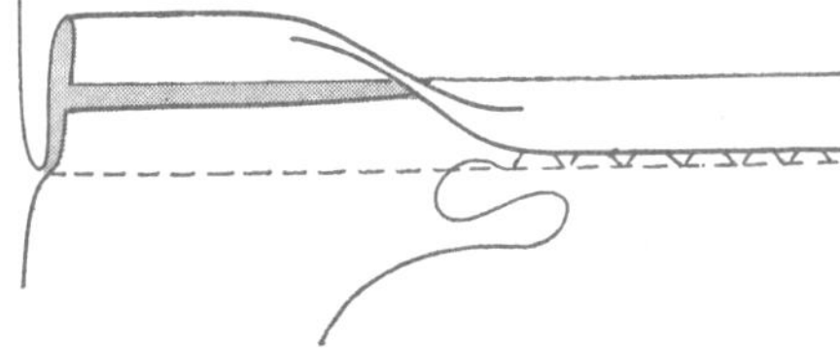

seam allowance. Slip-stitch it over the seam. Catch the stitches in the line of stitching.

Edge-Stitched—Use this method for light fabrics. Turn and press under the edges of the seam allowances, and stitch close to folds.

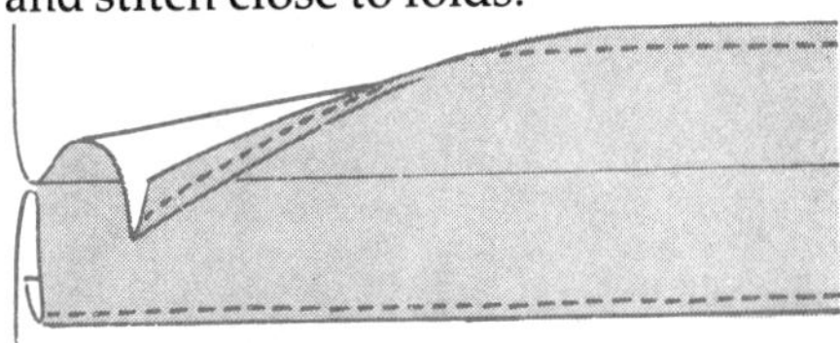

SLEEVES

There are many types of sleeves. They must fit comfortably and take strain and movement. The fit of a sleeve at the shoulder is important. The length and style of a sleeve is a matter of fashion. It may also be influenced by the fabric used.

Many sleeves are set in a round opening. Diagonal seams are used in some styles. Others have sleeves cut with the bodice. Sleeves are always an important part of a garment. Be careful when making, fitting and stitching sleeves. They must be cut on the straight grain or true bias in order to hang well.

Before stitching in sleeves, try the bodice to see if the armhole is comfortable. Make, finish and press sleeves before inserting them in the armhole. If finishing is left until after you sew the sleeve, the fabric weight makes handling difficult. The sleeve may pull out of shape.

SLEEVES

Set the right sleeve in the right armhole and the left sleeve in the left armhole.

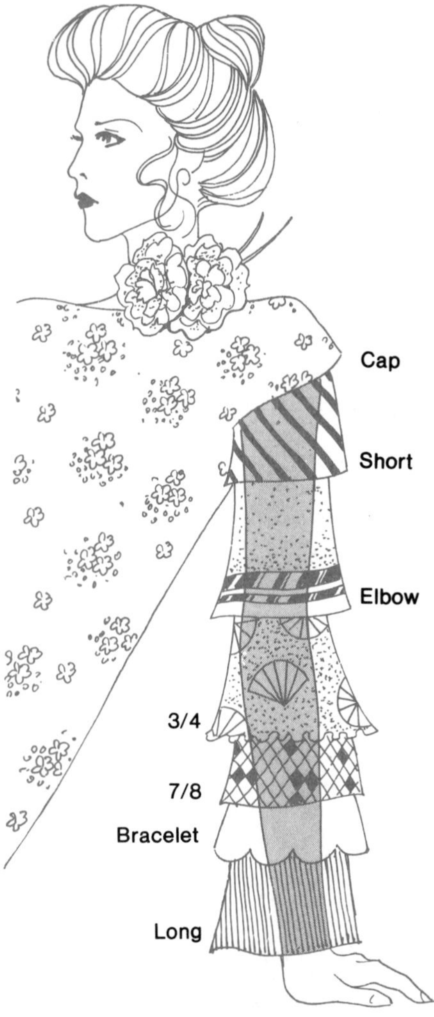

Darts or gathers may be included at the back of the elbow on long, tight sleeves. When the arm bends, it pulls up the back of the sleeve. Extra length is allowed for this at the back. The head of the sleeve is made slightly longer for comfort and ease of movement. There is a dip toward the front.

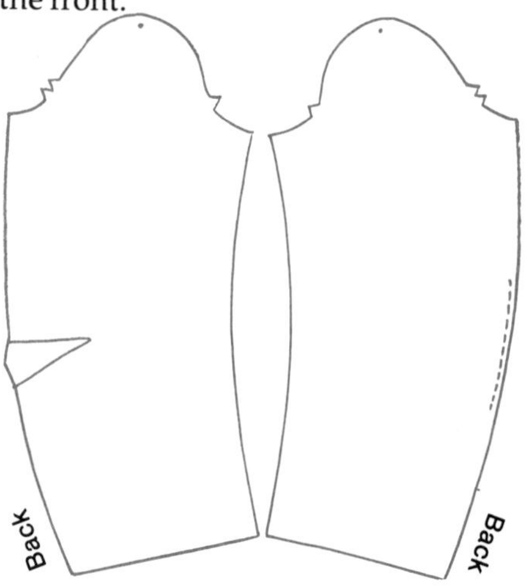

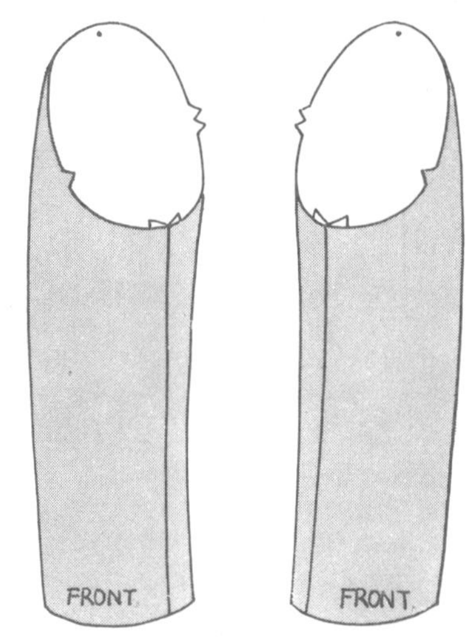

SETTING IN SLEEVES

Clearly mark all construction points. Ease-stitch the head of the

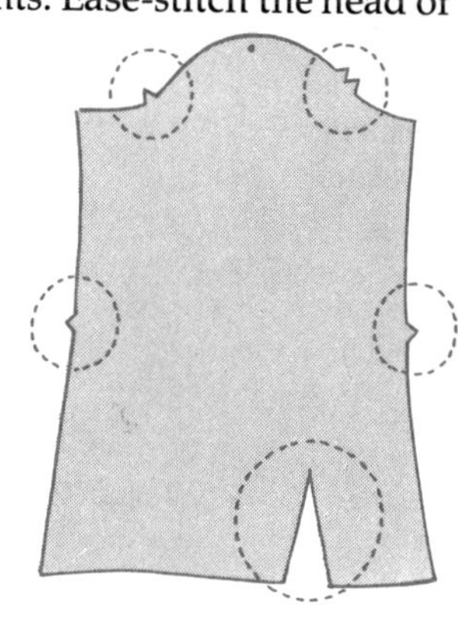

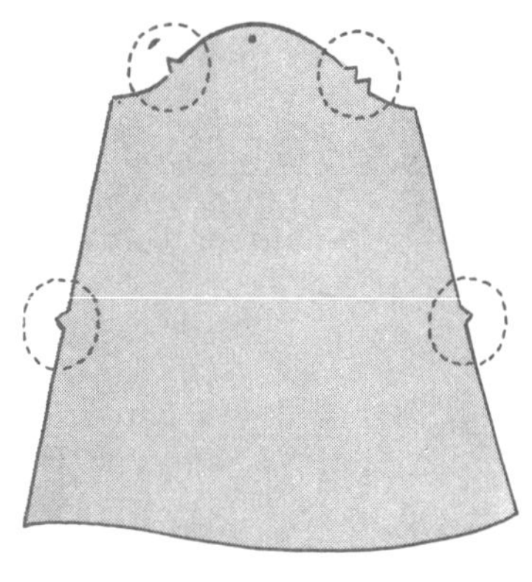

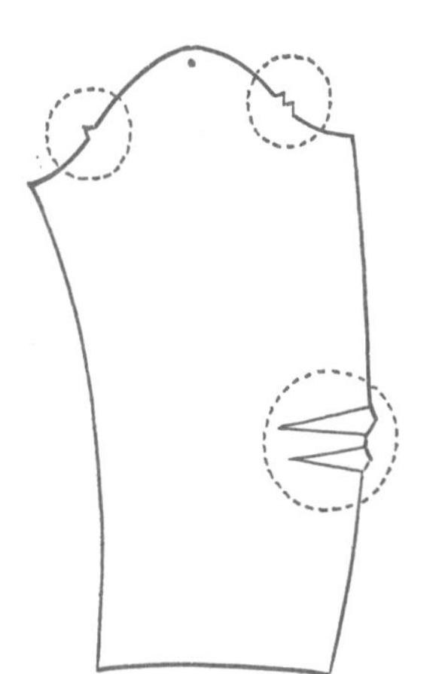

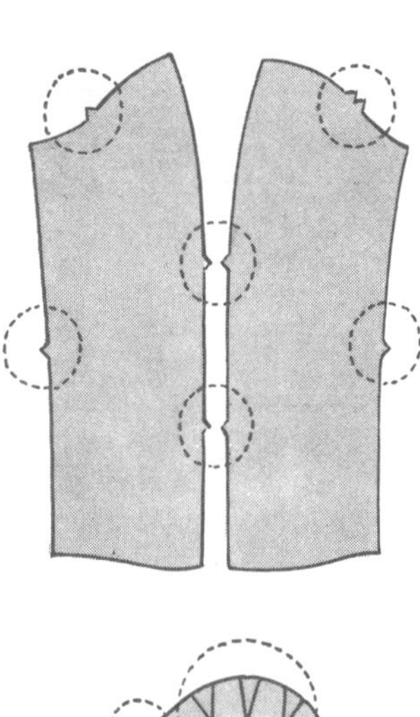

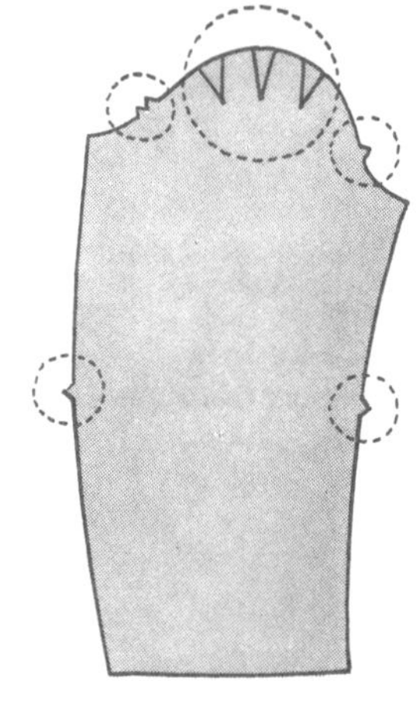

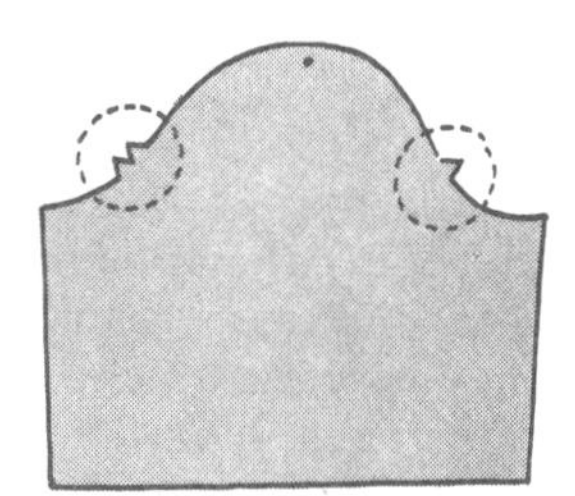

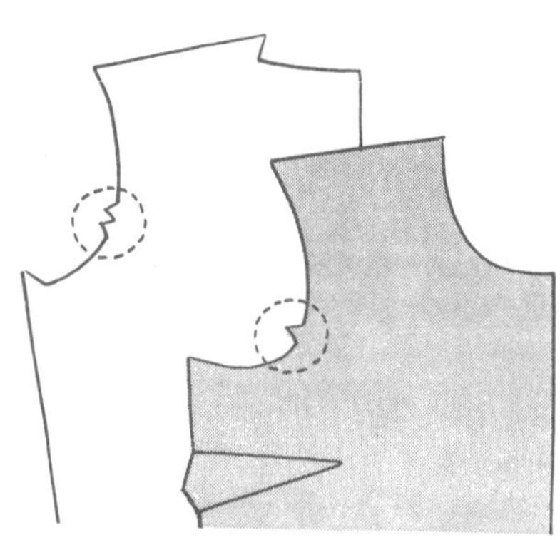

sleeve between construction marks. Sew one row of machine-stitches along the fitting line and another row 1/8 inch nearer to the edge in the seam allowance.

Before sewing, slacken the top tension on the machine. Use a strong, smooth thread on the bobbin. Leave long thread ends at the end of each row. Ease-stitching may also be done by hand.

If shrinkage of the sleeve head is needed, ease it away at this stage. Use a damp pressing cloth and soft pressing pad or roll. Next pin, tack and stitch the underarm seam. Press it open.

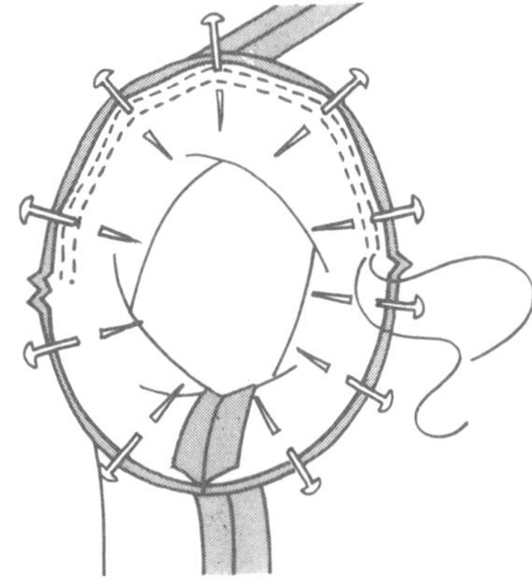

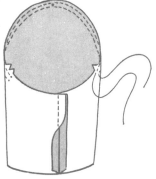

With right-sides together, pin sleeves to the armholes with the sleeve inside the bodice. First pin at the underarm and shoulder seams. Next, pin notches and other construction points. Always place pins at right angles to fabric edges, with pins pointing inward.

Arrange and ease fullness at the sleeve head by pulling bobbin threads, evenly distributing the fabric. Wind thread ends in a figure-8 around pins placed at either end of the ease to hold fabric.

From the sleeve side, pin and tack the sleeve to the bodice along the fitting lines. Tack the smooth underarm section, then the eased-head section. Be sure no tucks or gathers form while tacking.

The bias section between the notches at the sleeve head should appear crowded with the threads of the weave or the loops of knit. Try on the sleeve-bodice section, and make any necessary adjustments.

When the sleeve fits correctly, machine-stitch along the fitting line from the sleeve side. Start to one side of the matching underarm seams. Sew slowly to keep tucks and puckers from forming.

Let the machine carry the fabric through. Do not push or pull it because this causes a wavy seam line. Sew twice around the armhole, continuing beyond the starting point.

Remove all tacking, and lightly press seam allowances over the end of a sleeve board. Use the tip of the iron. This helps the allowance turn naturally into the sleeve.

Snip the sleeve allowance at intervals. Trim and finish edges if the garment is not lined.

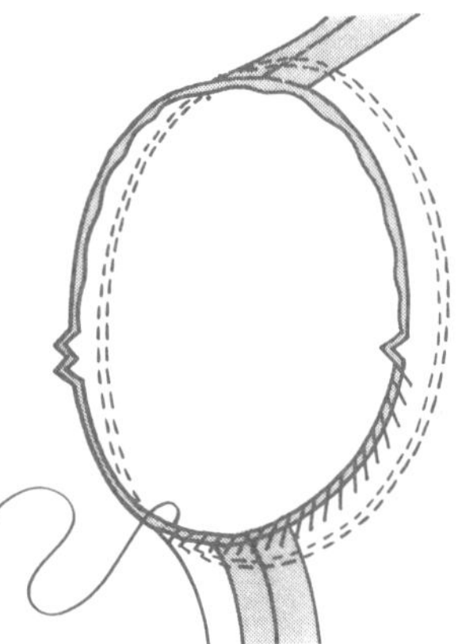

Turn the garment to the right-side. Let the sleeve hang down. Hold a closed fist under the shoulder seam. The sleeve should fall smoothly with no puckers or fullness in the head.

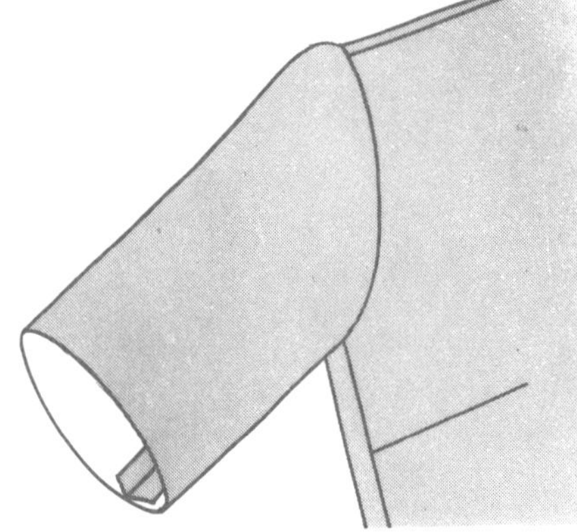

FINISHING ARMHOLE SEAMS

Machine-Overcasting—This is also called *blanket-stitching.* Set in the sleeve as previously instructed. Sew a second line of stitching 3/8 inch outside the first row in the seam allowance.

Trim the seam allowance above the second line of stitching. Overcast the raw edges.

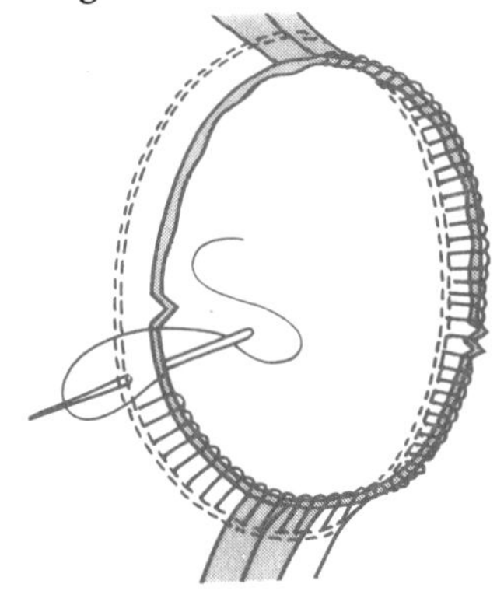

Binding—Place the right-side of the binding to the armhole seam allowance on the bodice side. Keep raw edges together. Tack 1/4 inch from the edge of the seam allowance to within 1 inch on each side of the seam. Overlap 1-3/4 inches of the crossway strip. Stitch under the tacking line from the strip side.

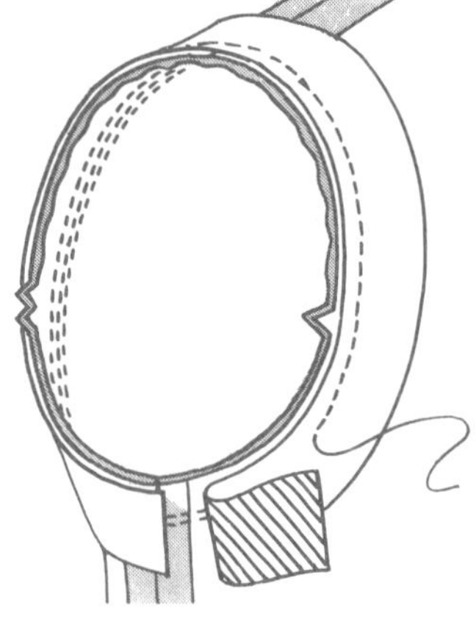

Remove tacking, and turn the crossway binding to the sleeve side of the armhole. Turn under the raw edges, pin and tack above the machine-stitching. Slip-stitch in position.

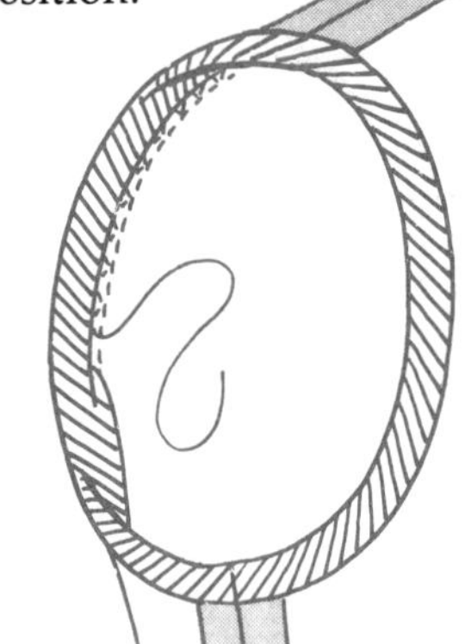

SLEEVES

French Seam—This is a useful seam for sleeves in material that frays easily and is too transparent for binding. Work the French seam as instructed in the section on *Seams*, page 151.

FITTING SLEEVES

When the sleeve is folded lengthwise through the center, the back-cap curve should be longer than the front-cap curve. Stitching lines of the underarm seams should meet. If this does not happen, you will have fitting difficulties when placing the sleeve in the armhole.

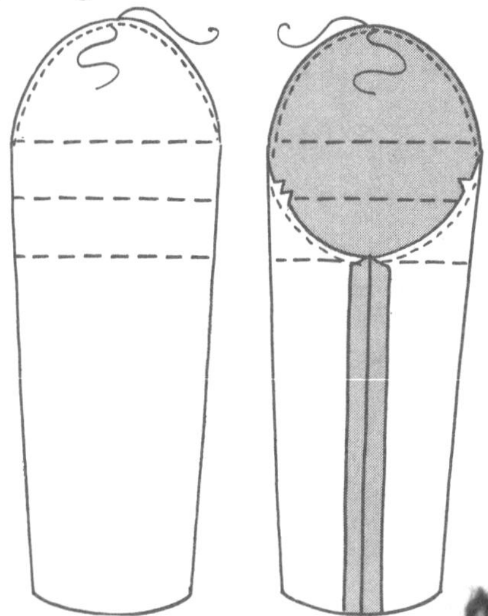

Tack darts and seams on the sleeve. Stitch these after the sleeve has been fitted properly. Try on the garment with the sleeve. Ease up the two threads at the cap head of the sleeve to position the sleeve. Tuck the seam allowance under.

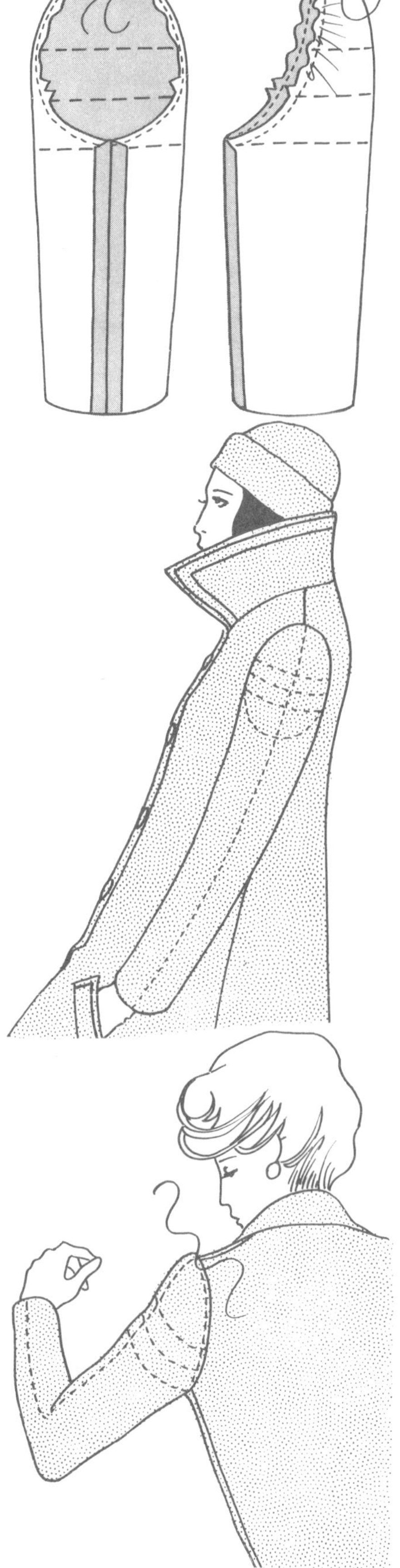

If a sleeve does not fit properly, check the following points.

Gathers at Elbow—These should be distributed evenly above and below the elbow bend.

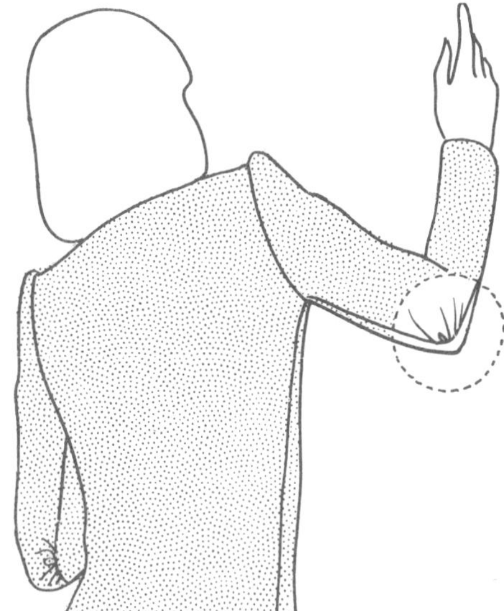

Darts at Elbow—If there is only one dart, it should fall at the elbow bend.

If there are two or more darts, they should fall evenly above and below the elbow bend.

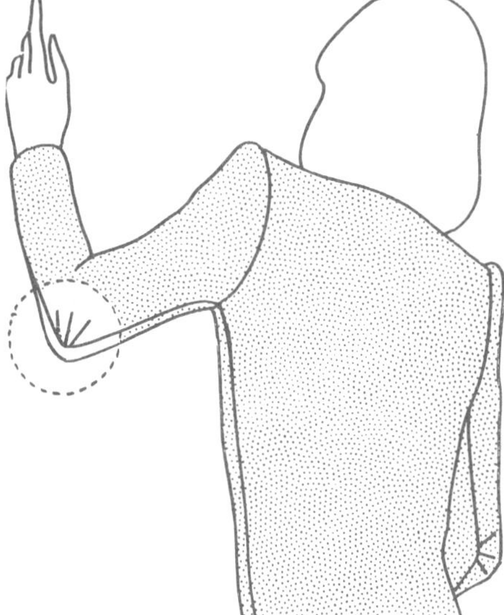

Back Seam—On a two-piece sleeve, back seams should be opposite each other across the width of the back.

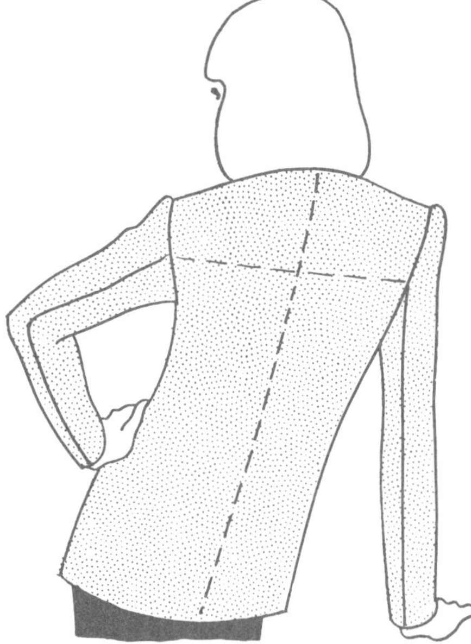

Gathers—When gathers are used at the head, they should finish at the same point on both front and back of garment. A line drawn between the ending of gathers at back and front is parallel to the floor.

Darts—If darts are used at the cap of the sleeve, the position of the two outside darts should be equal from the shoulder seam.

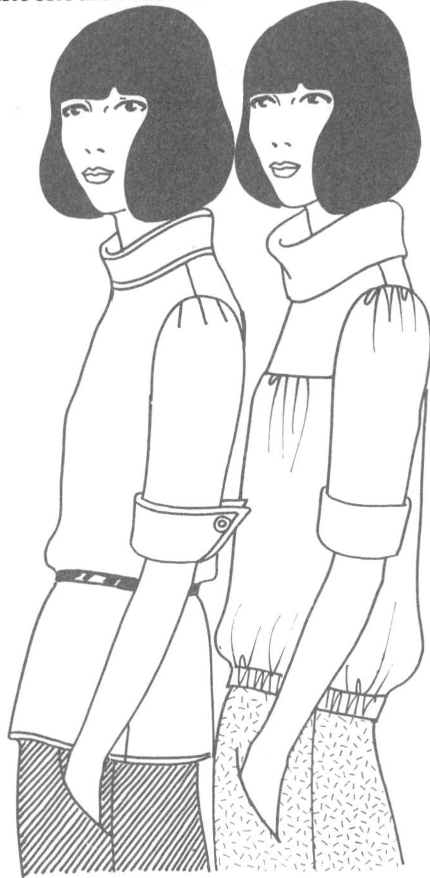

Wrinkles—Diagonal wrinkles on the highest part of the sleeve cap result from the cap being too short. Unpin the cap across the shoulder top. Let out the top part. Repin the sleeve to the garment.

If wrinkles are still visible, raise the underarm seam of the sleeve. Do this on the armhole of the garment from the underarm toward the width of the chest and back. When the sleeve is fitted, lower the sleeve stitching line at the underarm. Trim away extra seam allowance.

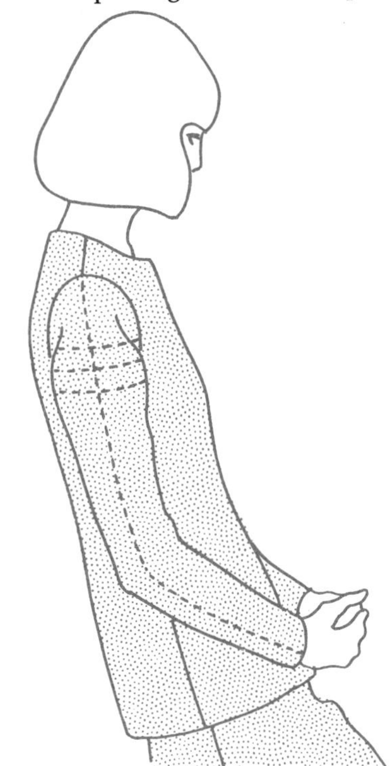

Diagonal wrinkles at the upper front and back arm can be fixed by lifting up the sleeve cap. This gives more ease around the armhole of the garment at the front and back.

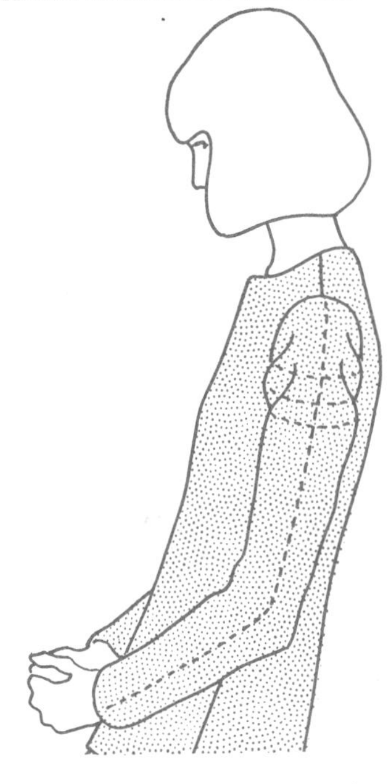

Underarm Sleeve Bend—When the underarm of the sleeve bends in toward the body underarm, the sleeve is too high at this point. Lower it by snipping under the armhole of the sleeve. Reposition the sleeve at the underarms.

If the underarm of a jacket bends out toward the arm under the armhole, the bodice is too high at this point. Trim the armhole slightly at the underarm, and reposition the sleeve.

Sleeve Length—The length for a coat or suit sleeve should be halfway between the wrist bend and thumb first-knuckle joint. The back edge of the sleeve should reach halfway between the wrist bone and the little-finger knuckle. The sleeve is slightly longer at the back edge than the front. This allows for the bend at the elbow. Close-fitting sleeves should be long on the wrist, and wide sleeves should be shorter.

Many people have one arm that is longer than the other. Measure the length of each sleeve accurately.

LINING SLEEVES

After garment sleeves are fitted correctly, tack the sleeve lining together. Stitch it to match the garment sleeve size. Fold the seam at the armhole of the lining to the wrong-side. Place an ease thread along the fold. Begin and end at the center top of the sleeve lining.

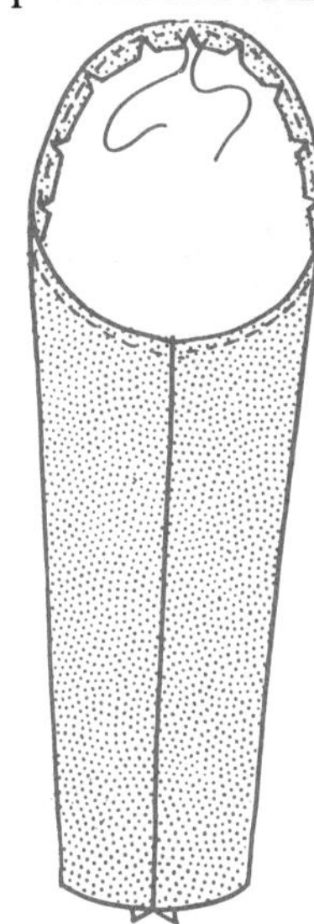

Ease surplus lining material in the seam allowance on the inside of the sleeve cap. Distribute it evenly. Match the correct sleeve lining to the garment sleeve. Turn the lining and garment sleeve wrong-side out.

Match the stitching edge of the sleeve to the stitching edge of the garment seam at the underarm. Pin in position. Match front sides of the lining and garment at underarm seams. Pin together. Stretch the garment sleeve a little so the lining is slack along the seam.

Tack seams together to within 2-1/2 inches of the folded edge at the wrist. Remove pins. Slip your hand

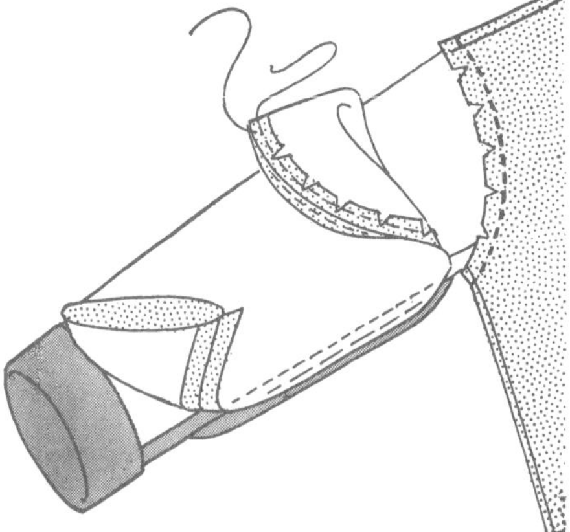

through the sleeve lining at the cap end. Hold lining and garment at the wrist. Turn the lining right-side out over the sleeve.

Match armhole seams and darts of the lining to the garment, and pin together. Pull the ease thread up at the sleeve cap of the lining. Adjust ease around the armhole edge.

Pin the armhole lining to the armhole of the bodice lining. Hide the stitching line, pin in place and tack. Slip-stitch the cap edge to the garment lining. Remove all tacking and press.

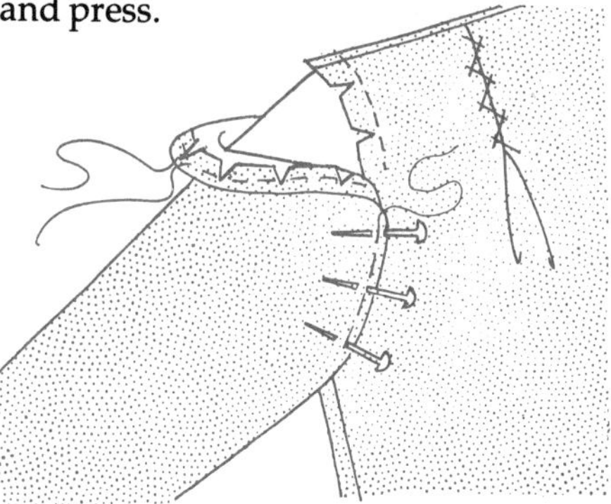

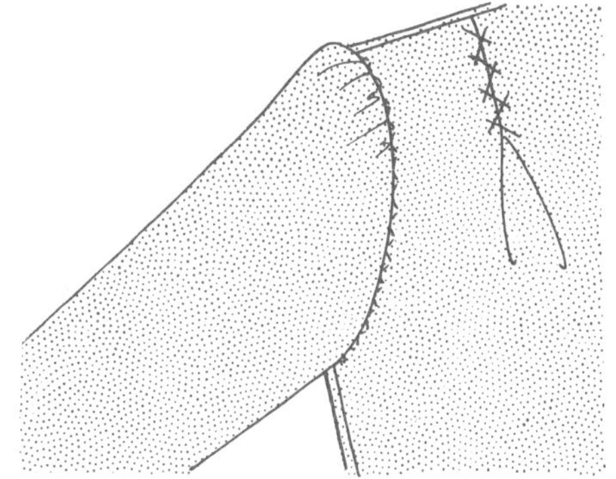

BASIC TYPES OF SLEEVES

Set-in Sleeve—The finished line depends on the amount of fullness in the sleeve and the amount of fabric in the cap of the sleeve. Follow the method given for setting in a sleeve. The only difference is the amount of fullness at the cap of the sleeve. For a full-sleeve cap, there is excess fabric to distribute along the head of the sleeve. The technique for fitting and setting in the sleeve is the same.

Pin, tack and stitch the front and back of a garment at the shoulder seams. Ease the fullness of the sleeve at the cap.

Machine-stitch the sleeve to the armhole. This is done with work completely flat. Pin and tack the side

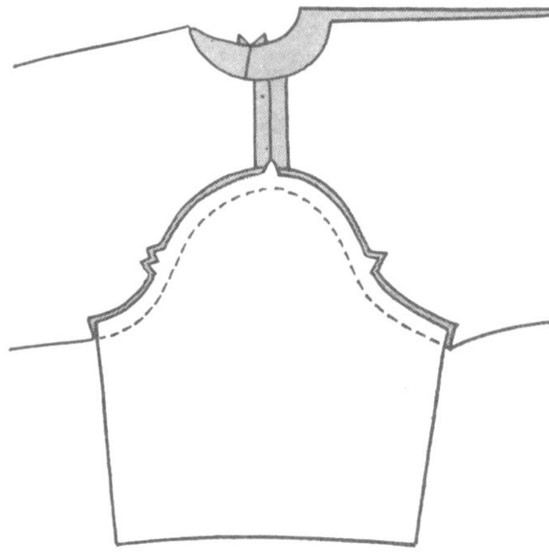

seams of the garment and underarm sleeve. Tack in one continuous seam. Machine-stitch, remove tacking and press.

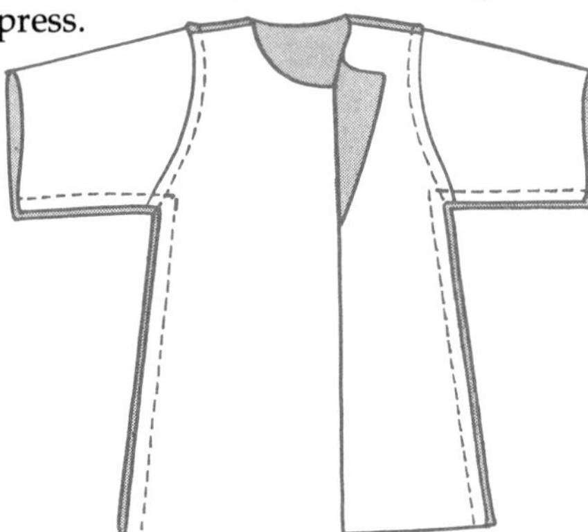

Raglan Sleeve—This sleeve is attached by a diagonal seam from the underarm to the neckline. It gives a smooth, round line and is comfortable to wear. It is ideal for shoulders that present fitting difficulties.

The seam and dart can fit the curve of the shoulder. The sleeve is often made in two pieces. A seam, instead of a dart, outlines the contour of the shoulder.

Pin and tack seams and darts. Machine-stitch, remove tacking and press the seam open. Match seams

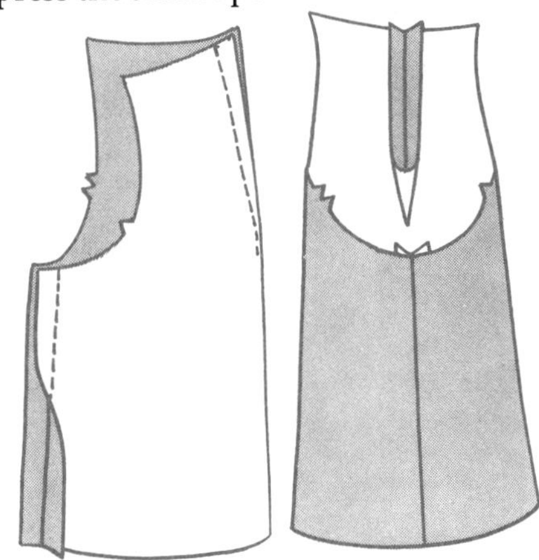

and pattern markings. Pin the sleeve in the armhole.

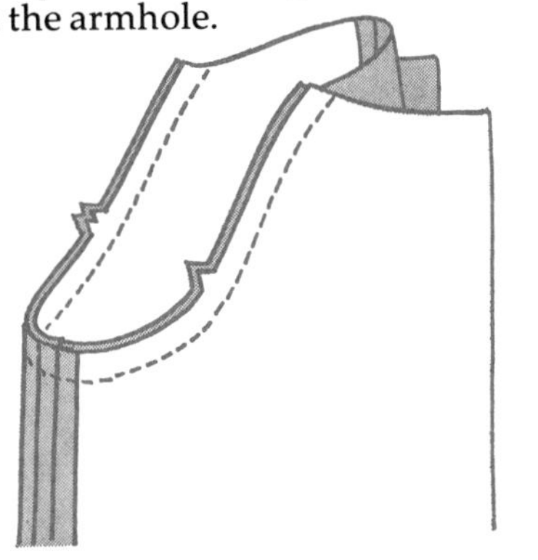

Tack and ease any fullness. Machine-stitch the sleeve to the garment along the seam line. Press the seam open from neckline to notches. Finish the underarm seam between notches with a second row of machine- and blanket-stitching.

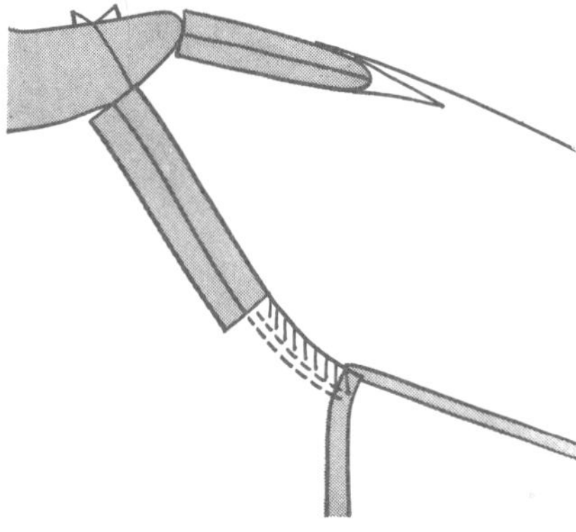

Another way to set in the raglan sleeve is to sew the sleeve in flat. Pin, tack and machine-stitch the sleeve to the bodice seams, then remove tacking.

Press seams open, and clip the seam allowance. Pin, tack and

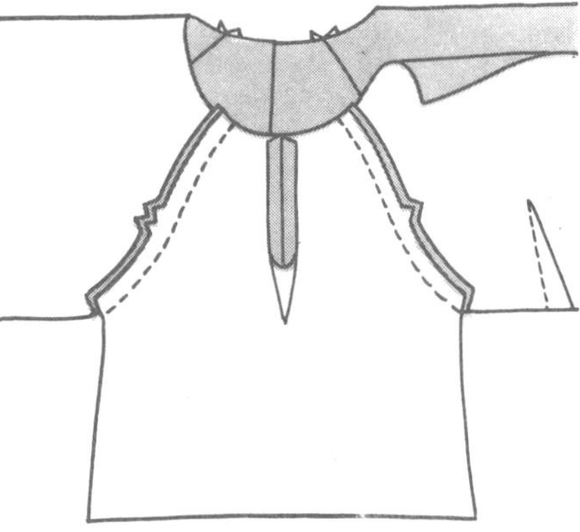

machine-stitch the sides of the dress and underarm sleeve seam, making one continuous seam.

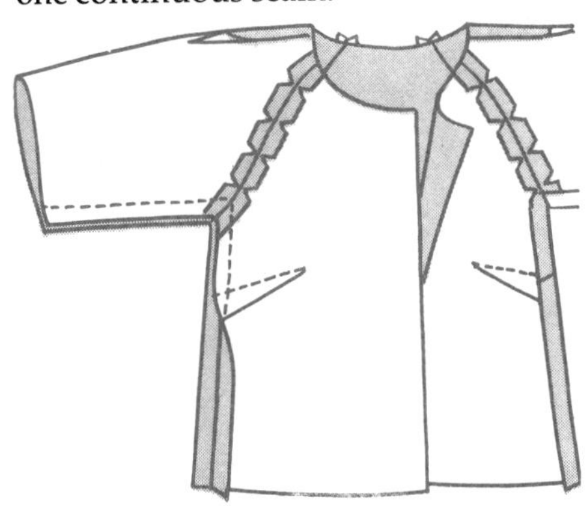

SLEEVE VARIATIONS

Bell Sleeve—The wrist edge of this sleeve is loose.

Tailored, Fitted Sleeve—Often used for heavier material, it is closely fitted to the arm and wrist. It is usually made in two pieces.

Puffed Sleeve—A sleeve gathered at the cap by the shoulder seam. It has the appearance of a puff. It is usually gathered on a cuff. On some styles, the cuff edge is puffed and the cap is smooth.

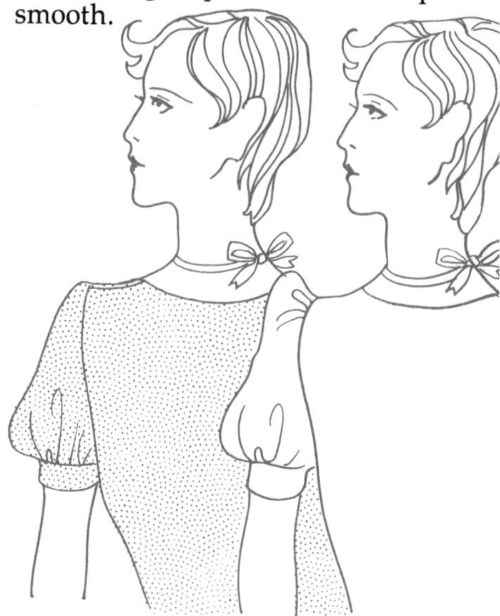

Cap Sleeve—This style extends from the shoulder and covers only the top part of the upperarm.

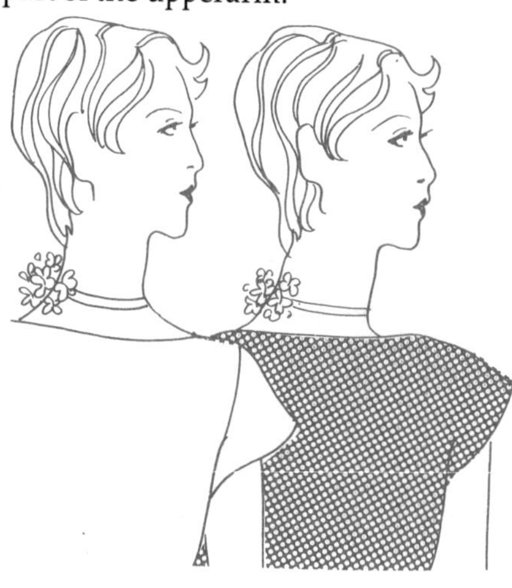

Long, Gathered Sleeve—This is a classic, elegant style gathered at the cap and cuff. It is set in as a standard sleeve.

Magyar Sleeve—This simple sleeve is an extension of the garment. The shoulder seam is continued along the curve of the arm. The underarm seam is also extended. Often the underarm seam is strengthened with seam tape.

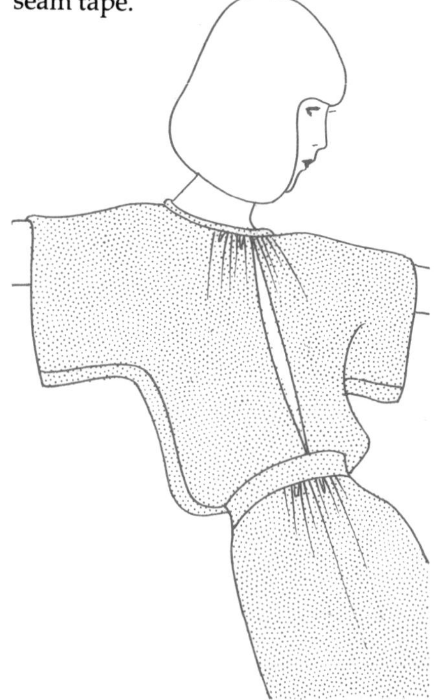

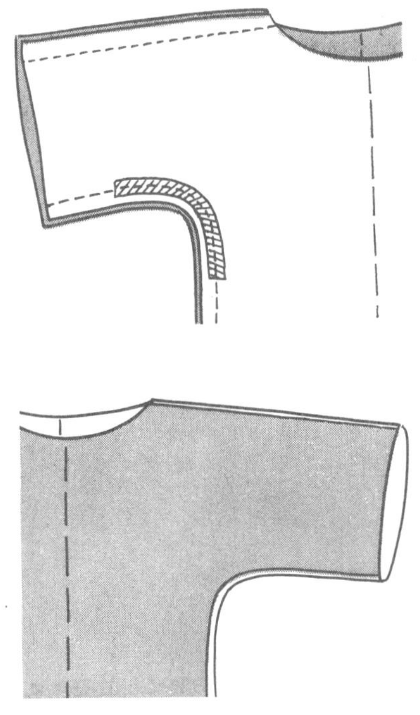

Kimono Sleeve—This often fits in a squared-off armhole, lower than the usual shoulder line. A gusset may be set in at the underarm for ease of movement.

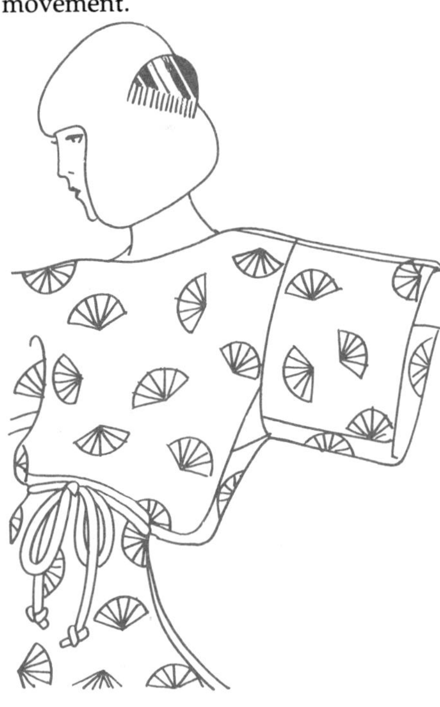

BOTTOM-EDGE FINISHES

For cuffs, see the section on *Cuffs*, page 105. There are many ways to finish the edges of sleeves. Finish sleeves before sewing them to the garment. Sleeves may be hemmed, but other finishes are possible. Long and short sleeves may be faced, bound or scalloped.

Faced Edging—See the section on *Facings*, page 112. With right-sides together, place the facing to the sleeve with raw edges together. Stitch 1/4 inch from the edge.

Turn the facing up along the stitched line. Pin and tack in place on the wrong-side. Turn under a

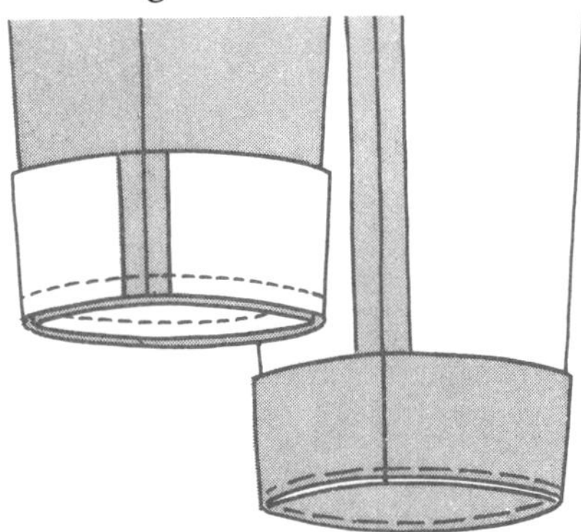

narrow hem on the free edge, pin and tack to the sleeve. Hem in place. Make sure the stitches do not pull or show on the right-side. Remove all tacking.

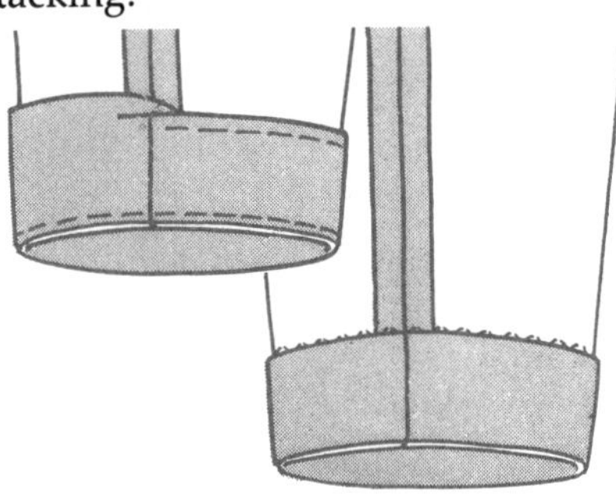

Bound Edging—See the section on *Binding and Piping*, page 92. Cut a crosswise strip twice the required finished width, plus two seam allowances.

Put the right-side of the binding to the right-side of the sleeve. Place raw edges together. Pin and tack 1/4 inch from the edges. Stretch binding material. Fold the turned edge over raw edges to the wrong-side of the sleeve. Tack above stitching, hem in place and remove all tacking.

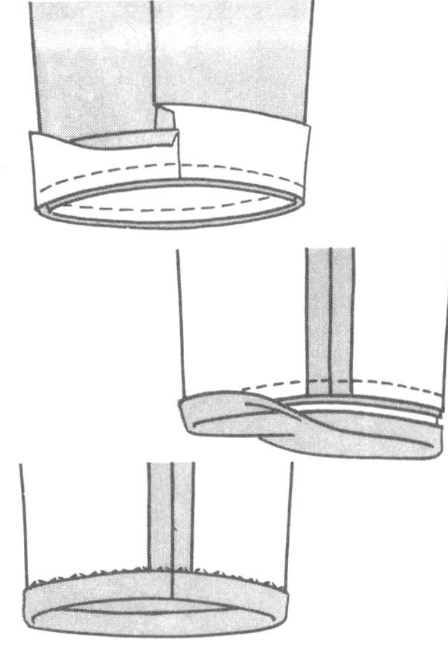

Scalloped Edging—Use a coin or compass, and a thin card. Draw a straight line on the card. Mark the size of scallops by drawing circles.

Draw a line through circles at the points of contact. Carefully cut out between lower curves. Trace the

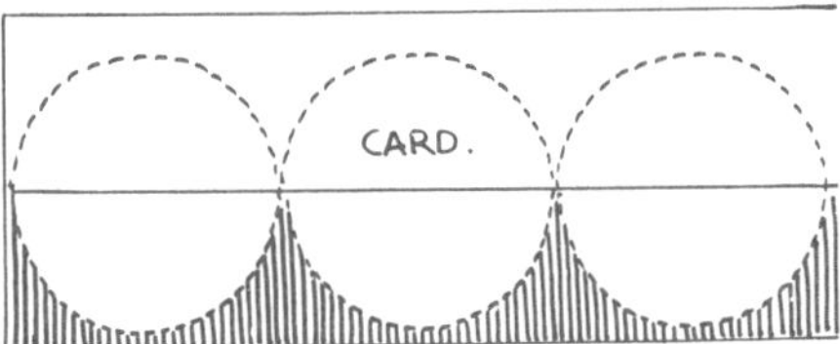

outline of the scallops on the wrong-side of the garment edge. The deepest part of the curve is the fitting line.

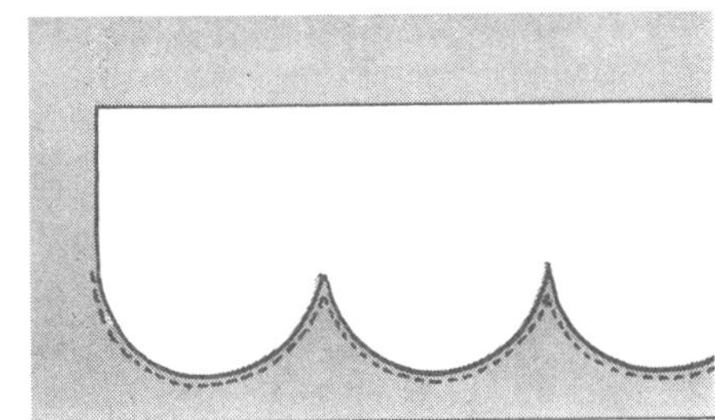

Put the right-side of the facing to the right-side of the sleeve. Tack with small stitches along the outline of scallops. Machine-stitch along the

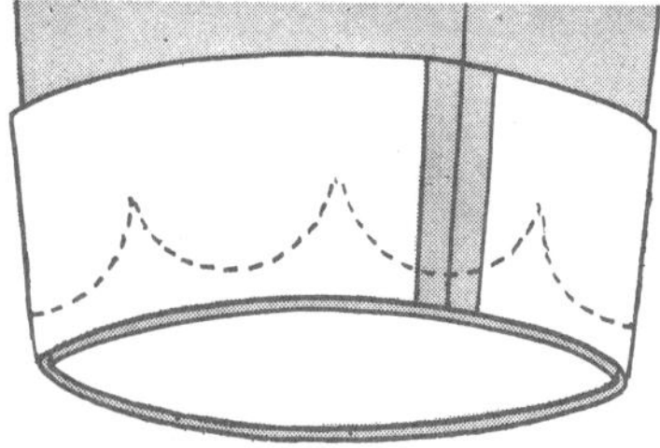

shaped outline. Remove all tacking and cut away seam allowances to 3/8 inch.

Trim edges and clip around the curves and into the points between the scallops. Do not cut stitching.

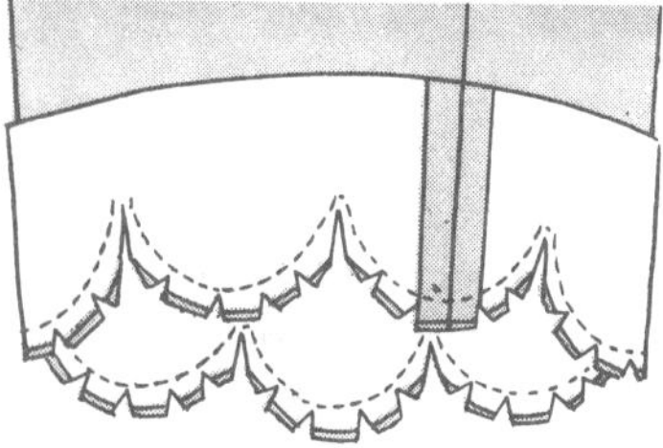

Turn the facing to the wrong-side of the sleeve. Use the round handle-end of a spoon to work around each curve. Be sure the seam lies exactly on the edge of each scallop. It helps to roll the seam between first finger and thumb to manipulate it into position. Tack the edge to hold it in place. Press and remove tacking.

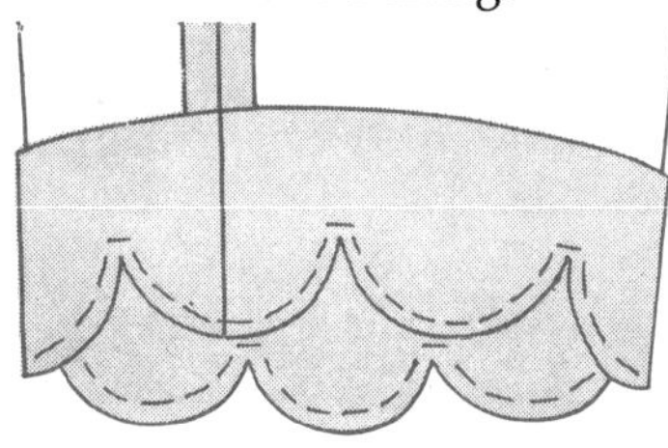

If the scallops are narrow and the facing is wide, slip-stitch the edge of the facing to the sleeve. If scallops are deep and the facing is shallow, turn the edge of the facing under. Finish it with small running-stitches.

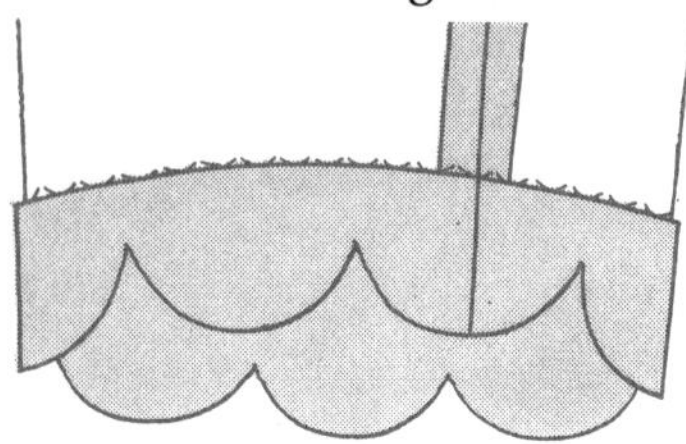

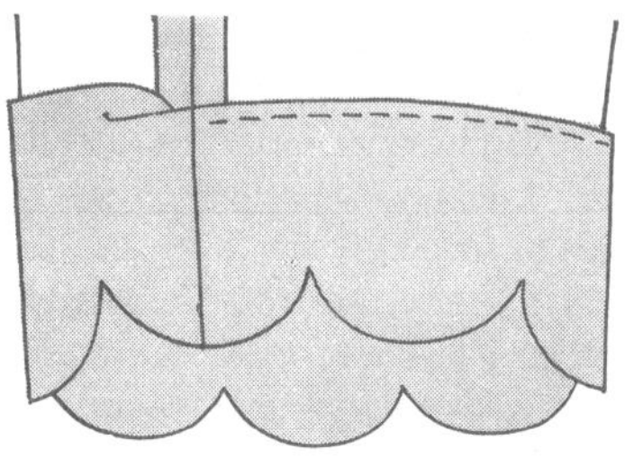

Adapted Facing—With right-sides together, put the facing to the sleeve edge with raw edges together. Pin, tack and stitch along the seam line.

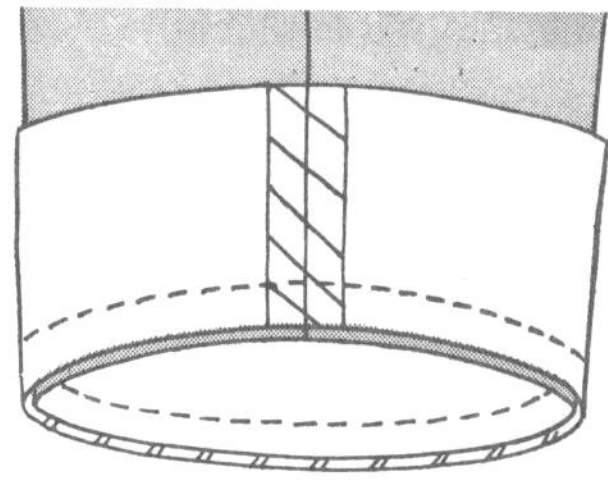

Turn the facing to the wrong-side of the sleeve. Leave 1/8 inch of the facing showing on the right-side. Tack in position.

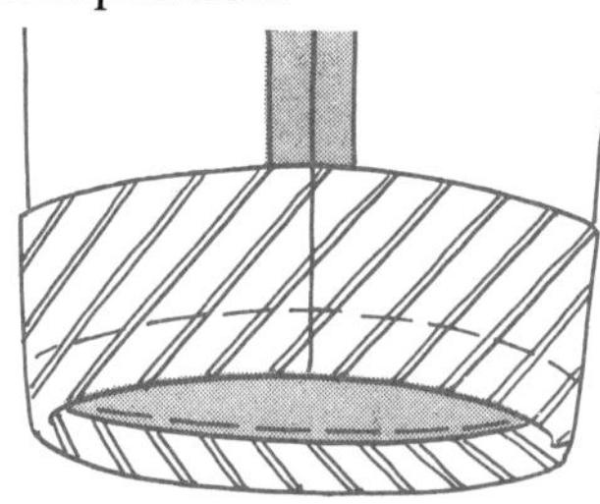

Edge-stitch the right-side of the facing along the seam line so it is barely visible. Turn up or overcast the free edge of the facing on the inside. Catch the facing to the seam, and remove all tacking.

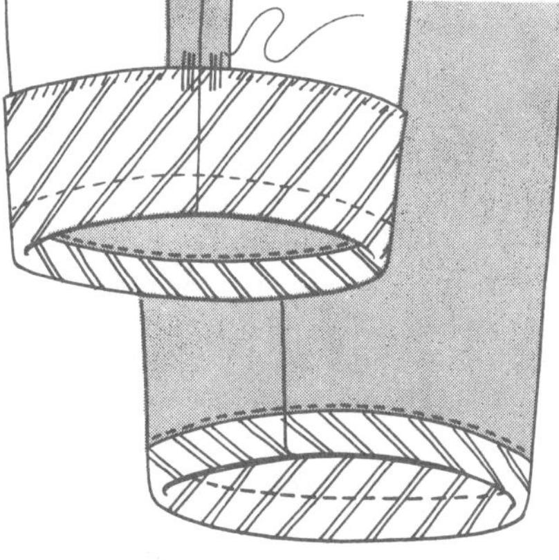

TUCKS

Tucks look like pleats but are stitched for all or part of their length. Tucks are made by a fold on the right-side of the garment. When tucks are only partly stitched, they are called *dart tucks.* They allow the rest of the fabric to fall in soft, unpressed pleats, such as on a bodice front.

Tucks are usually used as a decoration on yokes, cuffs, sleeves and bodice fronts. They may also be sewn in a skirt to allow lengthening later. This can be done on children's clothes or to hide a seam.

It looks best to have tucks run with the straight grain. Tucks can also be made on the cross grain. Sewn by hand or machine, tucks help control fullness and add decoration.

The width and spacing of tucks may vary, according to the type of fabric and style of the garment. Stitching is clearly seen on the right-side, so practice on fabric scraps first.

FABRIC CHOICE

Use a fabric with an obvious grain line that is easy to press in sharp creases. It is difficult to tuck thick fabrics. Tucking looks effective on fine material. Extra-decorative effects can be created by tucking on stripes.

WIDTH OF TUCKS

Narrow tucks are suitable on fine fabrics or short sections. Long or thick fabrics need wider folds. Try several widths of tucking on a piece of fabric to decide which width looks best. Do this before laying out pattern pieces. Garment sections to be tucked can be cut the correct size for tucking.

It is easier to tuck an area of fabric, then cut out the pattern piece. When the width of each tuck is determined, cut a cardboard template to mark the width exactly.

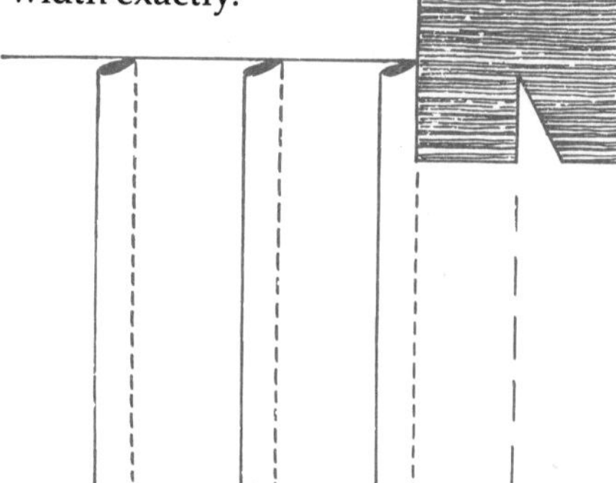

SPACING TUCKS

For the best effect, use tucks in a series of evenly spaced rows or in groups of three or more rows. Too-few rows look skimpy. A large area can create extra weight that pulls a garment out of shape.

Fine tucks often look best with about 1/2 inch between rows. Wide tucks may need more space because of the extra bulk of each fold. Practice spacing when practicing the width.

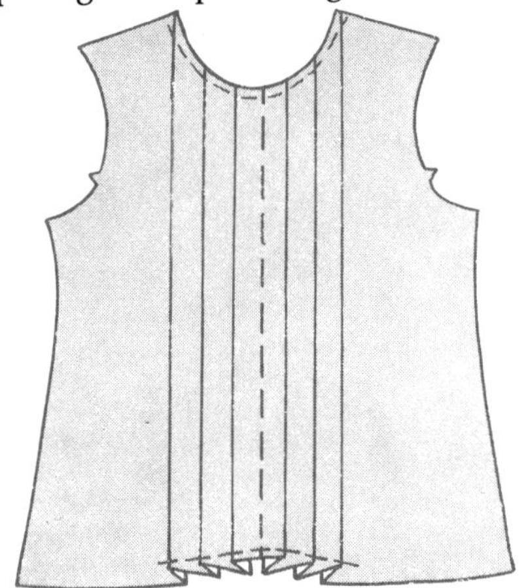

STITCHING TUCKS

Tucks may be sewn by hand or machine. Some machines make tucks automatically. Before stitching, decide the direction in which the tucks will be pressed.

Tucked edges are not stitched to the garment. The fold is pressed in place and secured by the seams at the ends. Test pressure, tension and stitch length before beginning. A straight-stitch is normally used, but decorative machine-stitches may also be suitable.

PRESSING TUCKS

Tucks may be pressed in one direction. On a center front, they are often pressed so each side faces out from the center.

Pin a tucked section to the ironing board with right-side up. Stretch it slightly so the folds stand up. Use a pressing cloth and an iron at a temperature suitable for the fabric. Press folds lightly in the required direction. Remove the fabric and turn it over. Press the stitching gently over a soft cloth.

GENERAL CONSTRUCTION METHOD

Mark the lines for the tucks using a template. It may be easier to mark and sew one tuck before marking the next. For wide tucks, tailor's tacks may be used along the length to mark fold lines.

Work from the left side of the fabric, toward the right. Pin and tack each tuck in place along its template length. Keep the grain straight so one thread runs along the edge of each tuck. Do not use too many pins.

Machine-stitch the tuck in place with suitable thread. If shrinkage occurs during washing, tucks will pucker and look irregular. Use the correct needle for the fabric. Be sure the stitch length, pressure and tension are also correct.

Remove tacking and press each tuck lightly along the stitching line. Press from the wrong-side of the fabric. Turn to the right-side and press tucks, using a damp cloth.

When tucks are complete, lay out pattern pieces in the usual manner. Pin and cut out pieces.

TYPES OF TUCKS

Blind Tuck—Each tuck overlaps the next so only one line of stitching is visible. Mark fold lines and overlap lines. Crease the fold line to the

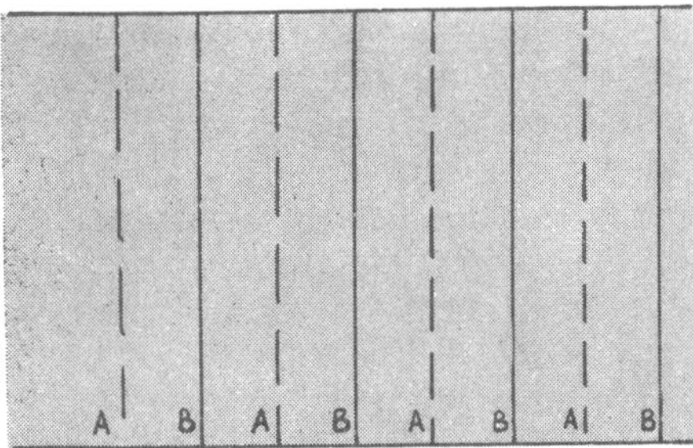

overlap line. Press and tack the tuck along its length. The folded edge is not stitched to the garment. Machine-stitch tucks and remove tacking. Repeat the process for all tucks.

Spaced Tuck—There is an even space between each tuck. Stitches are visible. Mark the fold line, overlap line and spaces. Crease the fold line

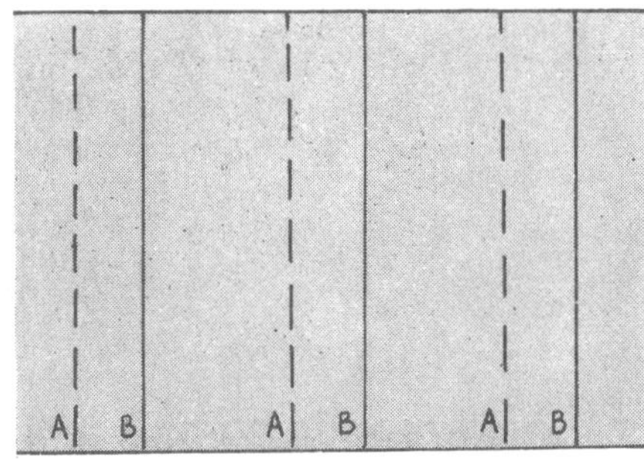

to the overlap line. Press and tack the tuck along its length. The folded edge is not stitched to the garment. Stitch tucks and remove tacking. Repeat the process for all tucks.

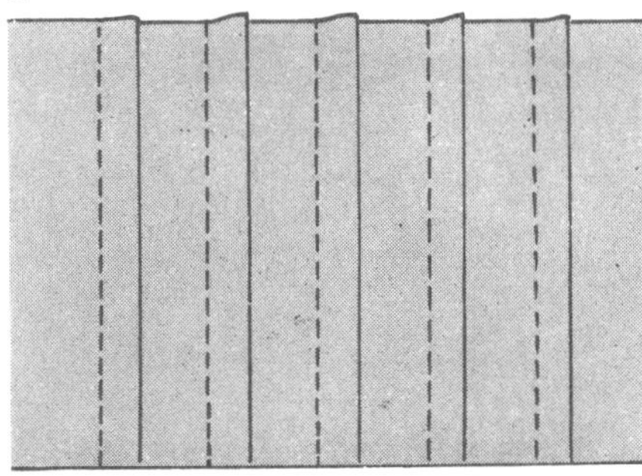

Pin Tuck—These tiny tucks are stitched closely to the edge of folds, but with spaces between them. Mark the fold line, overlap line and spaces.

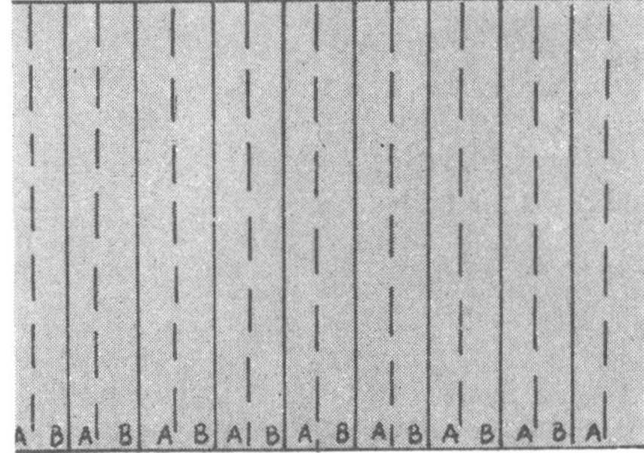

Crease the fold line to the overlap line. Press and tack the tuck along its length. The folded edge is not stitched to the garment. Stitch the tuck close to the edge of the fold. Repeat the process for all the tucks.

Remove tacking and press the tucks with a damp cloth to give a neat, crisp appearance.

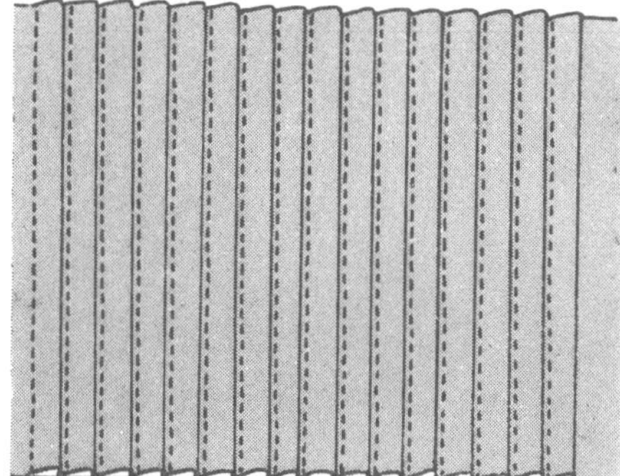

Corded Tuck—Enclose a cord in a tuck. Tack along the normal fold line of the tuck. Machine-stitch, using the zipper-foot attachment. If necessary, refer to your sewing-machine handbook about using a zipper foot for cording. Remove tacking.

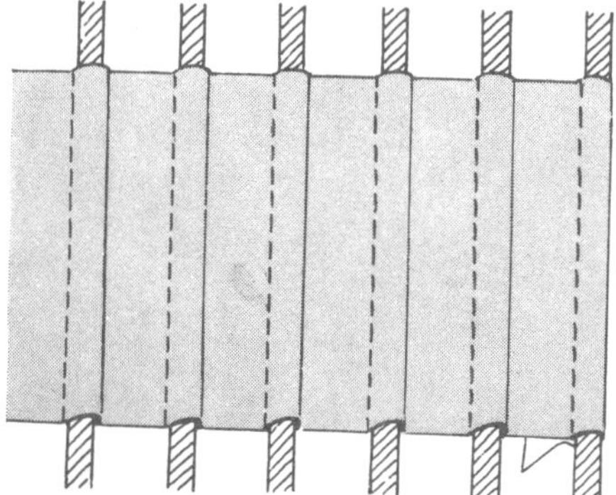

Crossed Tuck—These tucks run in one direction, like spaced tucks. Additional tucks run at right angles to, and across, the first section of tucks.

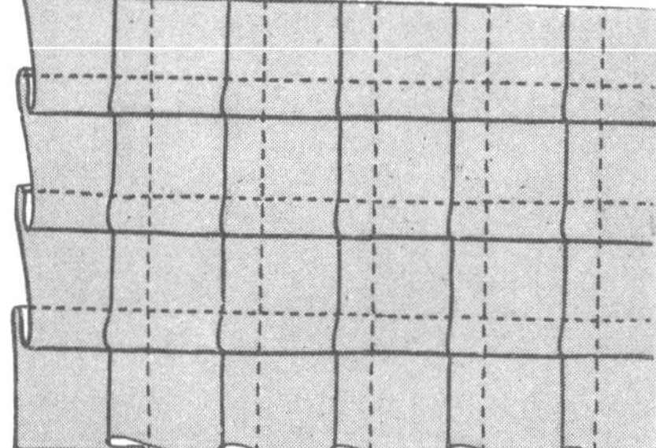

Grouped Tucks—Several lines of tucks are made close together. Tucks are stitched across the top, in one direction. Turn tucks in the opposite direction and stitch across. Repeat at intervals, turning the tucks in one direction and stitching across, then turning them in the opposite direction.

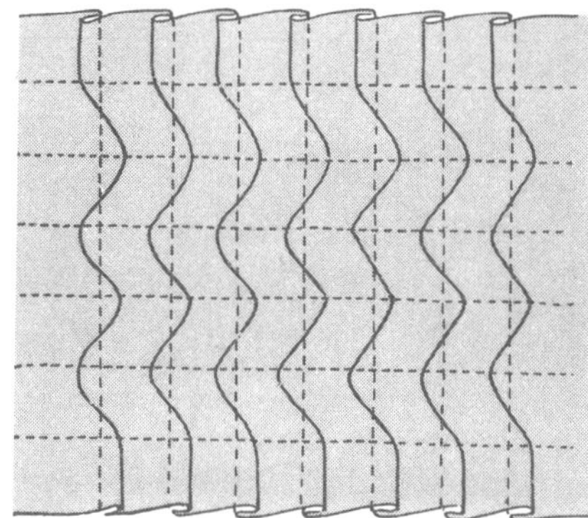

Overhand Tuck—Mark a design on the fabric. Over these lines, make tiny overhand-stitches. With the needle, catch a bit of the fabric with each stitch made. Use a contrasting or matching thread.

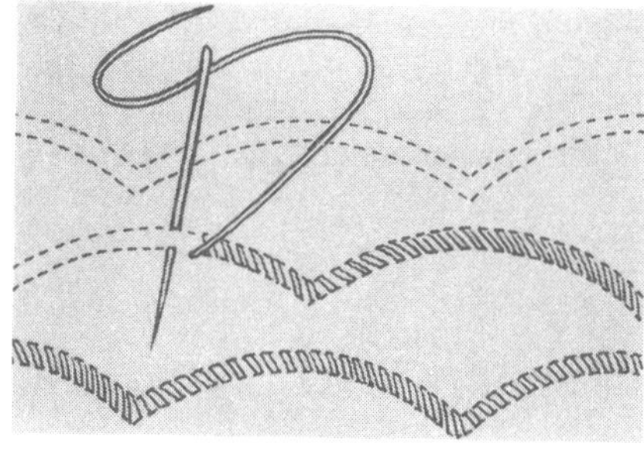

Machine-Stitched Pin Tuck—Refer to your sewing-machine handbook for instructions. Insert a twin needle and thread as directed. Use an all-purpose or tucking foot. Use the edge of an all-purpose foot or the grooves in a tucking foot as a guideline. Form rows of tucks as required.

For fancy pin tucks, the serpentine-stitch or the three-step zigzag-stitch is effective. On some machines, a scroll-stitch may be used to form elaborate, decorative cable tucks.

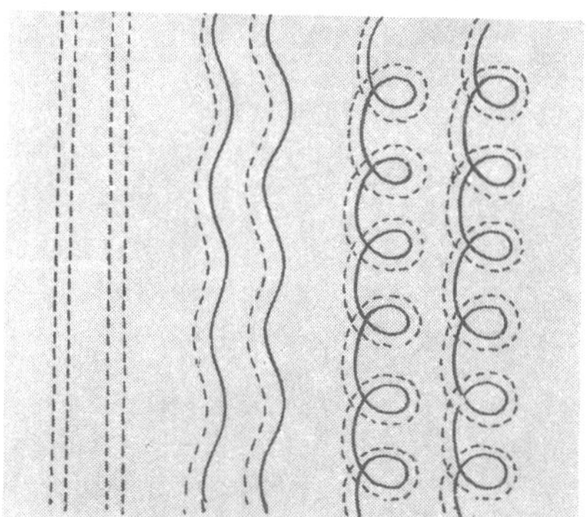

Machine-Stitched Shell Tuck—Prepare fabric as for spaced tucks. Use the blind-hem-stitch. Sew along the tacking line, allowing the wide zigzag part of the stitch sequence to fall over the edges of the fold. This holds the fabric edge at intervals to form shells. A cord may be included along the fold edge for extra decoration.

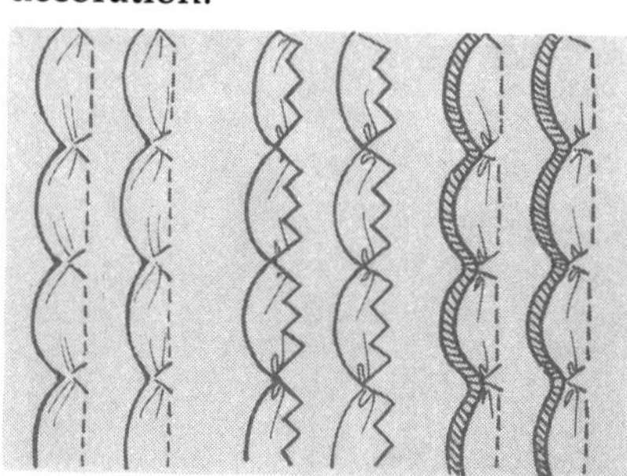

WAISTBANDS AND WAISTLINES

The waist of pants and skirts must be finished to hide raw edges and keep the waistline from stretching. When the top and bottom halves of a garment are joined at the waistline, there are several ways to complete the seam.

Waistbands

Fit and sew waistbands on skirts and pants so they fit snugly, without stretching, wrinkling or folding over. The width and type of band depends on the style of the garment and the fabric used.

Most waistbands, particularly on loosely woven fabrics, need interfacing to prevent stretching. Knit fabrics need elastic in the waist area for a good fit. Except on gathered skirts, the skirt is eased into the waistband to fit the curve of the waist.

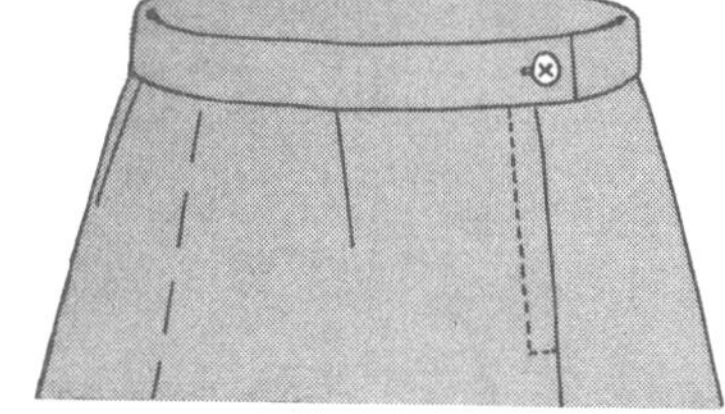

The waistband should be 1/2 to 1 inch larger than the waist measurement. When the waistband overlaps for fastening, allow an overlap of 1-3/4 inches.

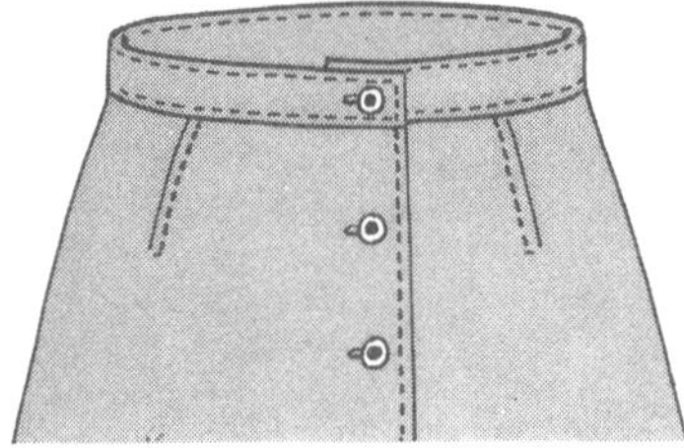

For side openings, the front overlaps the back. On front openings, the right overlaps the left. With back openings, the left may overlap the right.

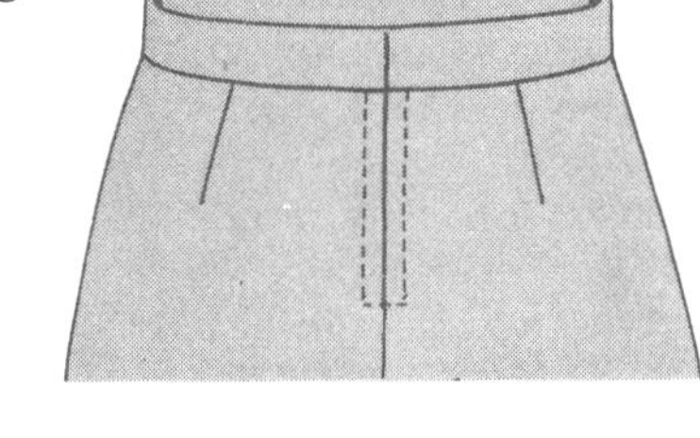

Hooks and eyes or buttons and buttonholes are used to fasten the overlapping area to the underlap. The overlap and underlap may extend on a button-through or wrap-around skirt. The two ends are tied to keep the garment in place around the body.

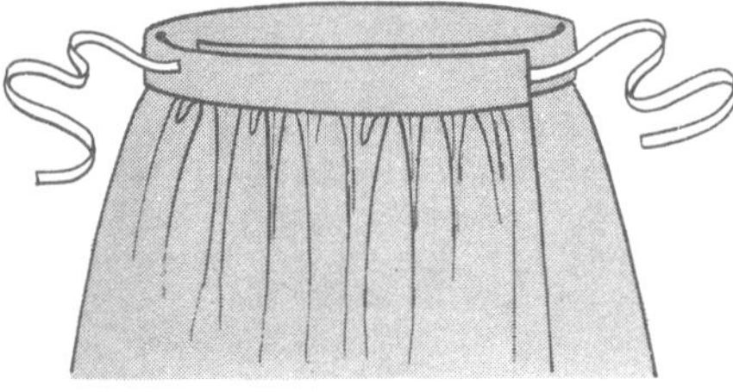

A zipper is usually put in *before* the waistband, and lining is added afterward. On some garments, a waistband of self-fabric is applied so stitching does not show on the right-side. Top-stitching may be used for strength or decoration.

SELF-FABRIC WAISTBAND

Cut a band of fabric the size of the waistline. Have an extra amount for seam allowances and overlap. Cut the width to twice the depth of the finished band, plus a seam allowance. Cut interfacing the length of the waistline and half the width of the waistband.

Place interfacing on the wrong-side of the waistband, and tack in place. Put the right-sides of

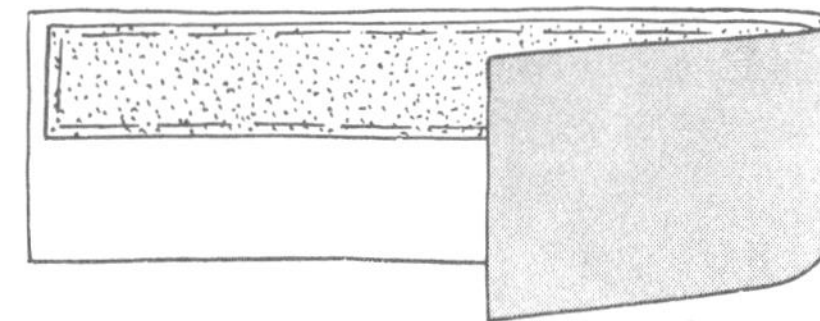

the garment and waistband together. Ease the skirt, then pin and tack in place.

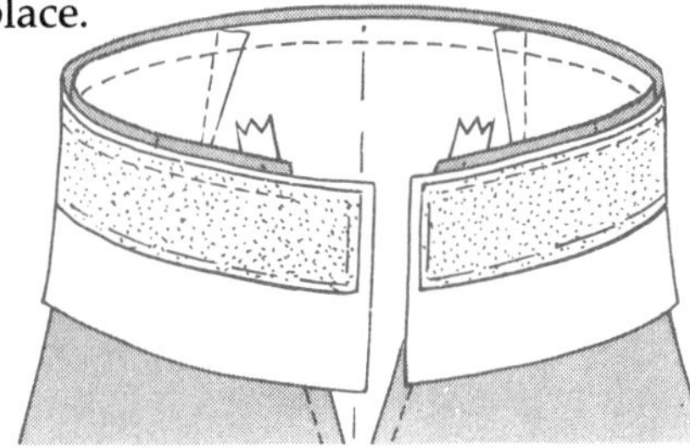

Machine-stitch the waistband to the skirt waist. Stitch along the ends of the waistband and remove tacking. Crease the band in half and press. Stitch the two ends, and shape the overlap to a point, if desired.

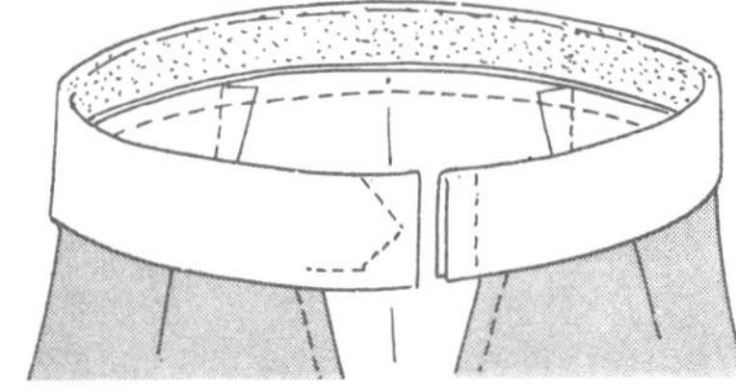

Turn the raw edges of the other half of the waistband under to the wrong-side of the garment. Slip-stitch the band in place so stitches are not visible on the right-side. Press the skirt waistband.

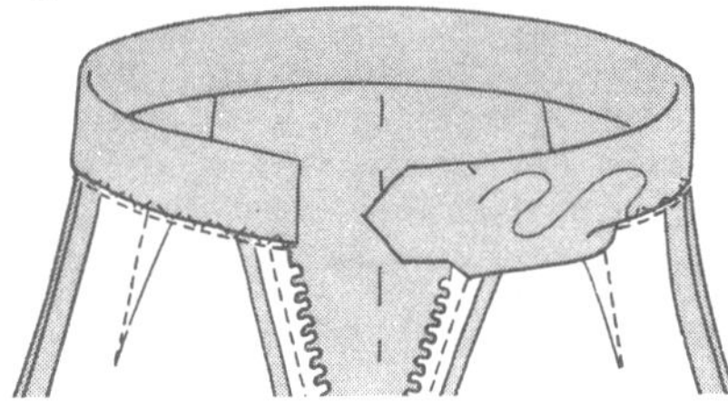

Sew hooks and eyes at the ends of the waistband to fasten the skirt top.

TAILORED WAISTBAND

Cut a waistband from self-fabric. Use one long selvage if possible or finish one long edge. Make the piece of fabric 3-1/4 inches longer than the waist and twice the width of the interfacing ribbon, plus two seam allowances.

Cut a piece of interfacing 1-1/4 inches shorter than the waistband.

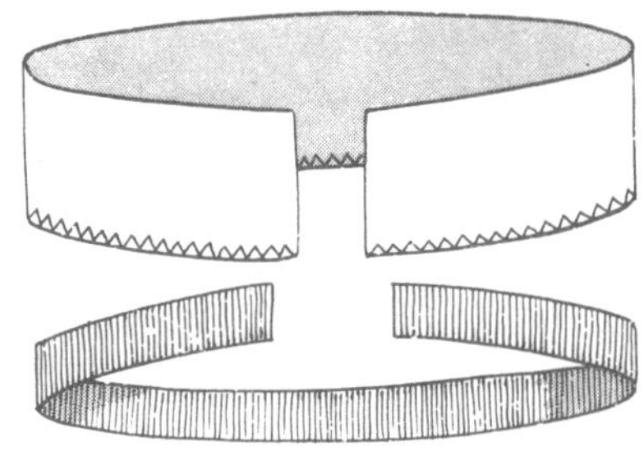

Mark the material along the lengthwise fold with tailor's chalk or long tacking-stitches before removing the pattern.

With right-sides together, ease the skirt onto the waistband. Leave a 3-inch underlap at one end. Pin, tack and machine-stitch along the seam line. Tack and machine-stitch the

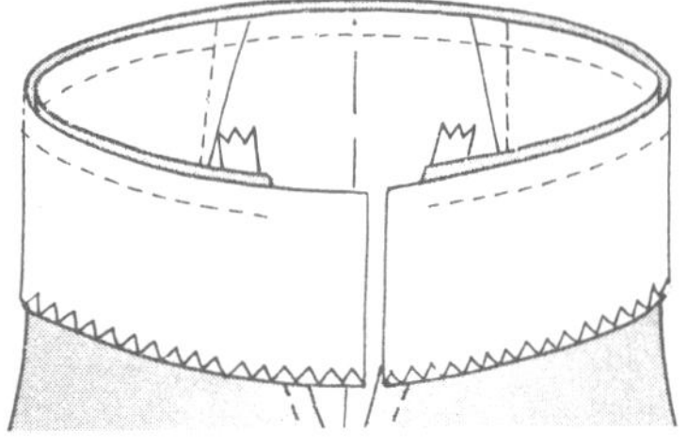

interfacing in place, just above this seam line. Leave 5/8 inch at each end of the waistband.

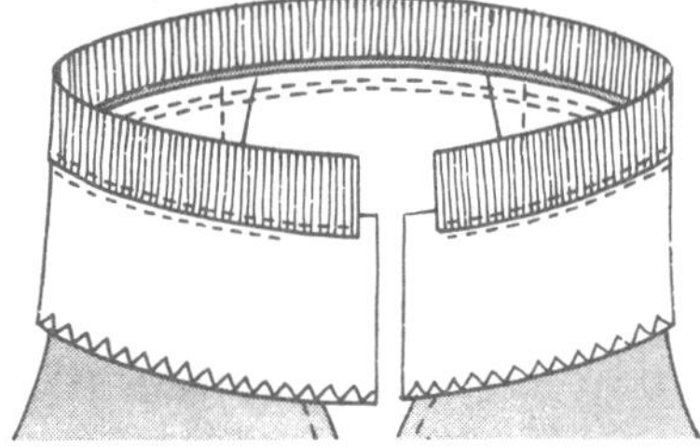

Turn in the ends, and press in place. Fold the waistband over the interfacing on the wrong-side of the skirt. Cut into the seam allowance of

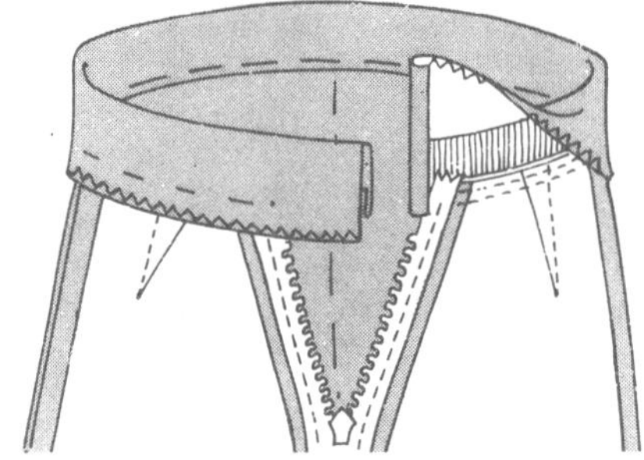

the waistband, level with the zipper tape. Turn under the seam allowance along the underlap extension, and hem around the extension.

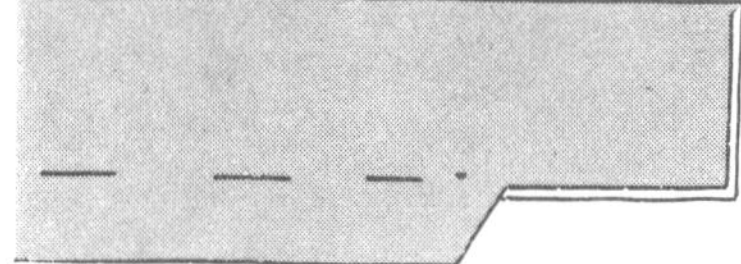

Tack the finished edge of the waistband in place around the waist. Stitch along the waist seam line through the skirt and inside the waistband, but not through the band on the right-side. Use a stab- or straight-stitch.

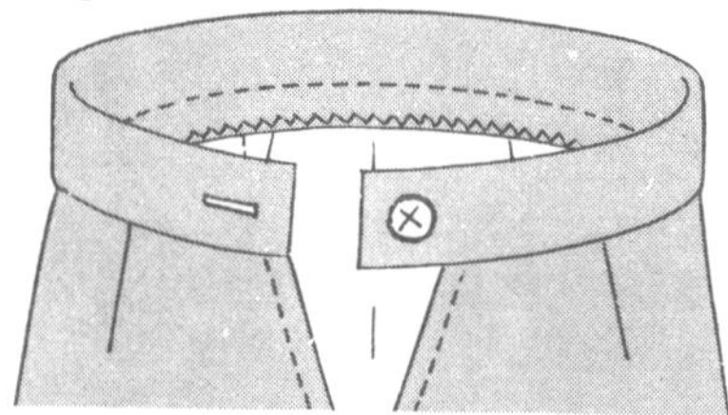

WAISTBAND WITH ELASTIC

It is necessary to put a piece of elastic in the back of a waistband on knit fabrics. This gives a smooth, flat front with slight gathers at the back to adjust to the stretch of the fabric. Back darts can be eliminated.

This method of attaching the waistband is similar to the one used for a tailored waistband. Interfacing at the back is replaced by elastic of the same width.

Measure interfacing, but cut a piece only half the needed length. Cut a piece of elastic the same width, but 2 inches shorter. Join the two together. Sew a 2-inch piece of interfacing to the elastic for the underlap.

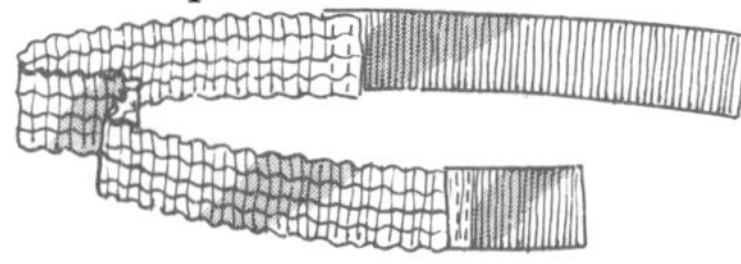

Sew the waistband and interfacing as before, but do not stitch the elastic.

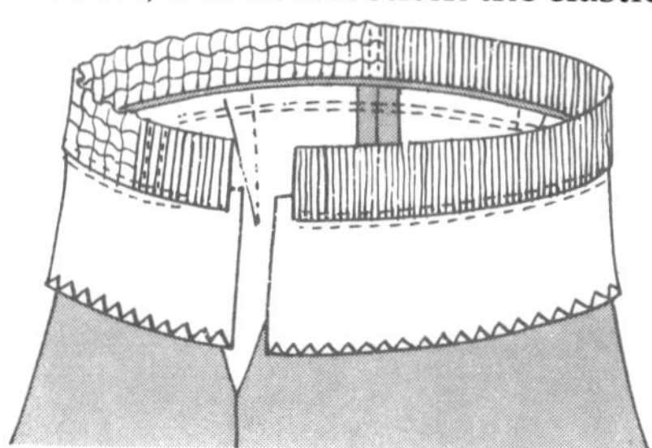

Fold the waistband over and complete it. Keep the elastic pulled flat. Waistbands for knit pants may be made with a piece of elastic replacing all interfacing.

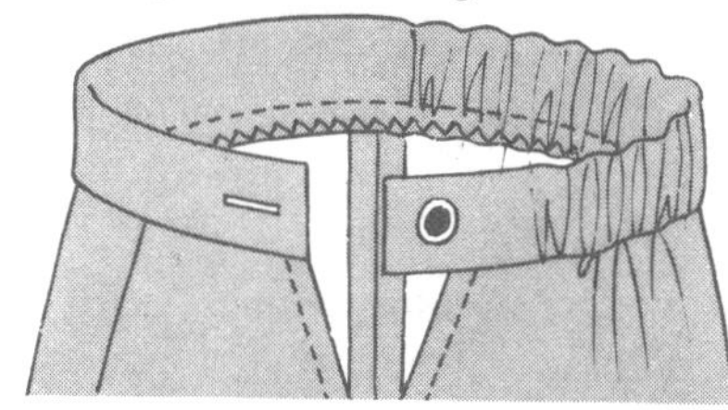

STITCHED WAISTBAND

This quick, strong method is used on jeans, children's clothes and other garments. Prepare the waistband with interfacing. Fold the band with right-sides together along the length. Stitch across the ends. Shape one end to a point first, if desired. Trim, turn to the right-side and press. Stitch the

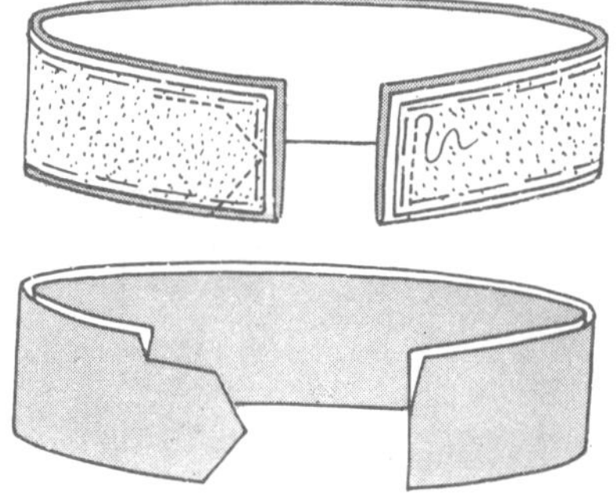

right-side of the band to the wrong-side of the garment along the seam line, easing as necessary.

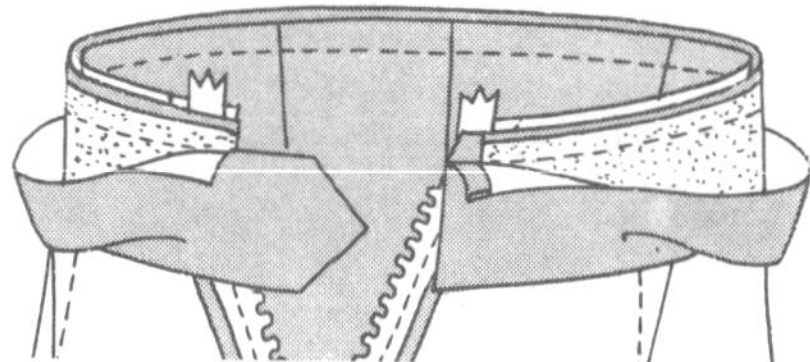

Press the seam up into the waistband. Turn in the other band seam allowance. Tack the folded edge in place on the right-side over the

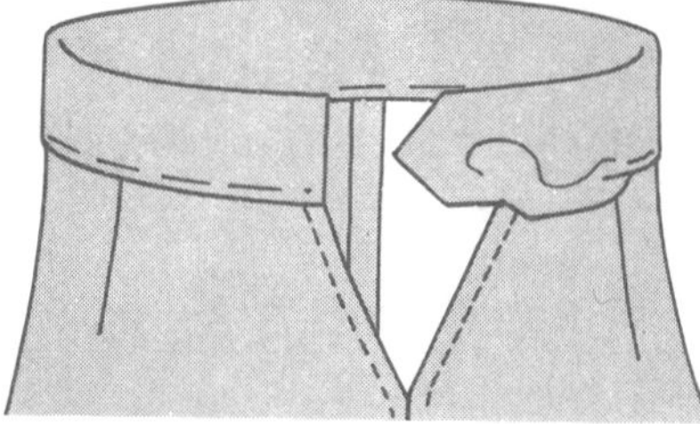

seam. Top-stitch around the band 1/8 to 1/4 inch from the edge. Use a straight- or fancy stitch in matching or contrasting thread.

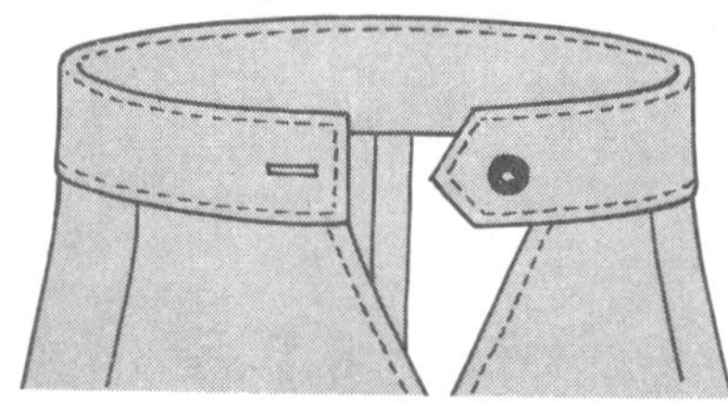

CONTOUR WAISTBAND

Some skirts and pants have shaped waistbands that are interfaced so they remain uncreased in wear. Reinforce the seam line of the long edges with bias tape. Cut two waistband pieces from the pattern piece. Interface one piece on the wrong-side. Trim the interfacing seam allowances.

Pin and tack the stretched bias tape over the seam lines along the two long edges of the interfaced piece.

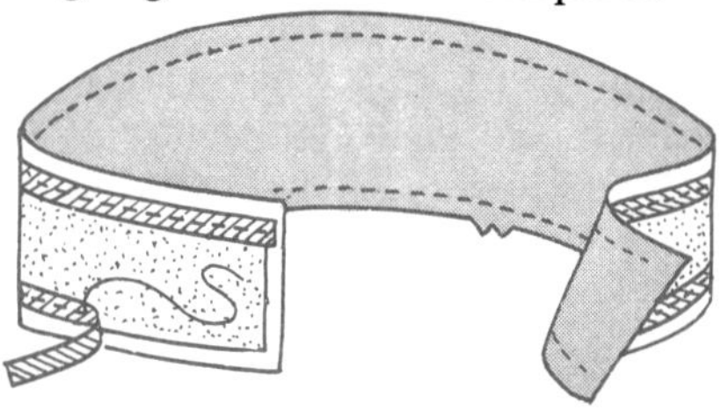

Pin, tack and stitch the two sections together around the two ends and the upper edge. Trim and layer the seam allowances. Press, turn to the right-side and press again.

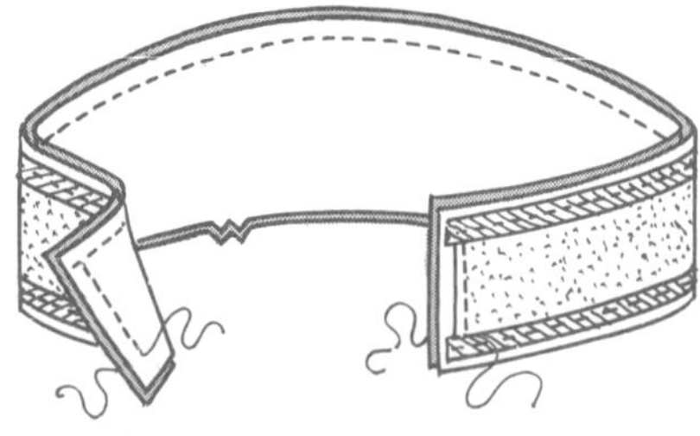

With right-sides together, pin, tack and stitch the waist edge of the band to the waist edge of the garment. Match balance marks, and ease the skirt onto the band.

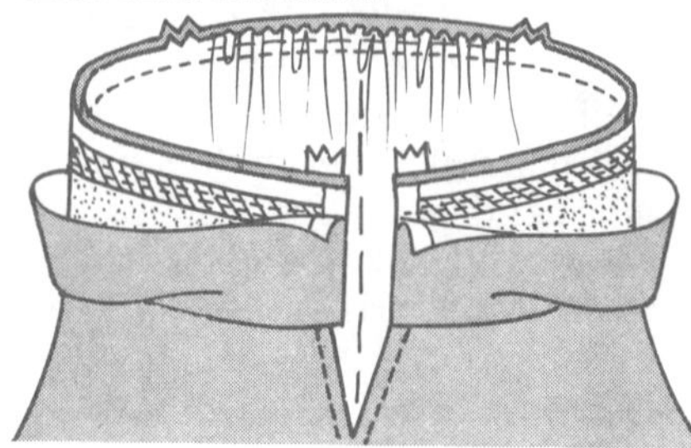

Trim and layer or grade seam allowances. Press them up into the waistband. Turn under the remaining seam allowance and slip-stitch it to the wrong-side of the garment. Catch the stitches of the seam underneath. Hem across the

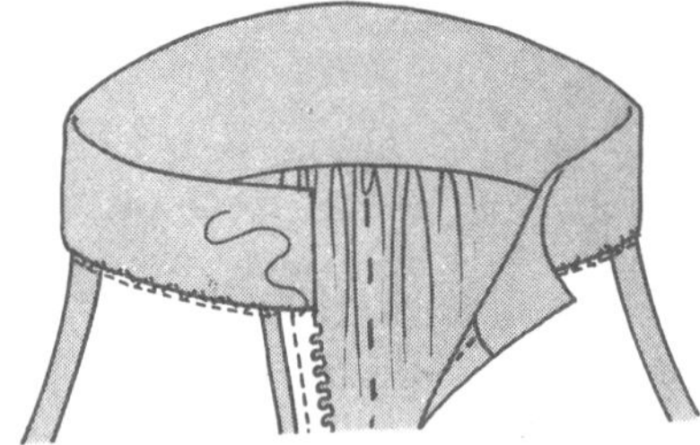

underlap and press. Sew on hooks and eyes as fastening.

WAIST EDGE WITHOUT BAND

Some styles of skirts and pants are finished at the top with only a facing. Fabric or bias tape may be used for facing.

Faced with Fabric—When using a self-fabric facing, interface it or reinforce the waist edge to prevent stretching.

Complete the garment and tack in any lining. Prepare the facing in the usual way. See the section on *Facings*, page 112.

Cut the facing and interfacing pieces according to the pattern. Sew the facing pieces together and interface. Finish the lower edge of the facing by overcasting or turning under, then stitching.

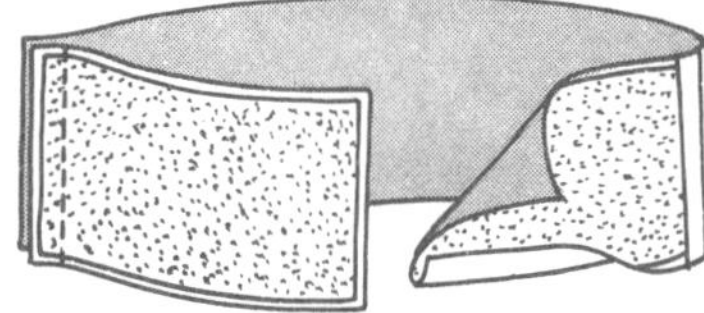

With right-sides together, pin, tack and stitch the facing to the garment waist edge. Match balance marks and ease the skirt on the band. Trim and

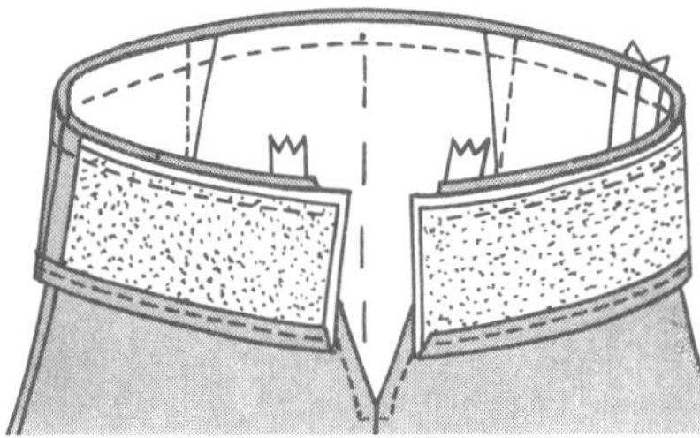

layer seam allowances. Clip edges without cutting stitches.

Understitch the facing, turn to the wrong-side of the skirt, and press the edge. Turn the ends under, avoiding the zipper, and hem the folds to the zipper tape.

Loosely catch-stitch the finished edge of the facing to seam allowances and darts to keep it in place. Sew a hook and eye at the top of the zipper to take any strain.

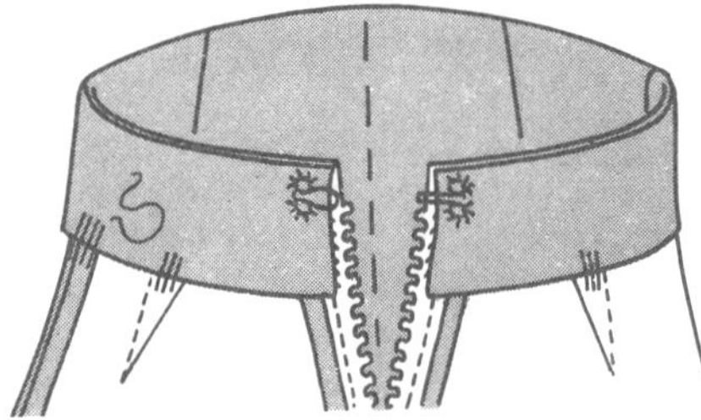

Waistlines

Bodices and skirts may be joined in several ways. One of the easiest ways is to sew them together with a plain, inconspicuous seam reinforced with ribbon. A waistband may be an inset type, a shaped belt inserted to fit snugly to the body curves, or a casing filled with elastic or a drawstring.

WAISTLINE WITH PLAIN SEAM

Complete the skirt. Stay-stitch the waist edge above the seam line. Complete the bodice, and stay-stitch below the seam line. With right-sides

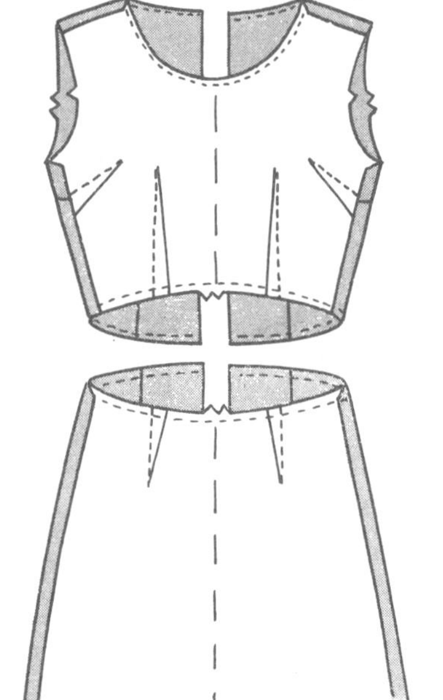

facing, pin the waist edges of the skirt and bodice together. Carefully match balance marks, notches and opening edges.

Try the garment on. Adjust the fit if necessary. Tack and stitch along the seam line, easing if required.

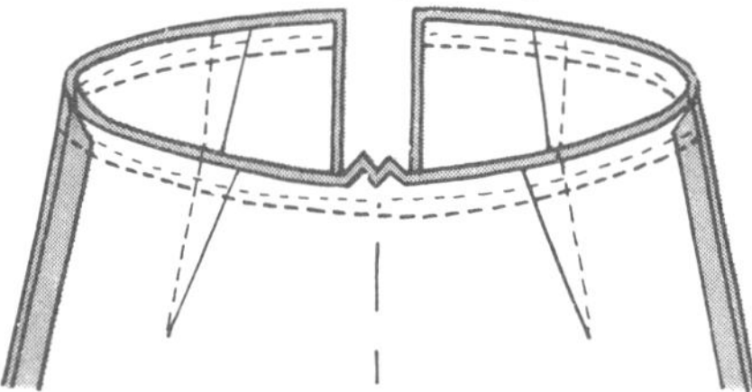

Remove tacking, and pull the bodice up, still wrong-side out. Press seam

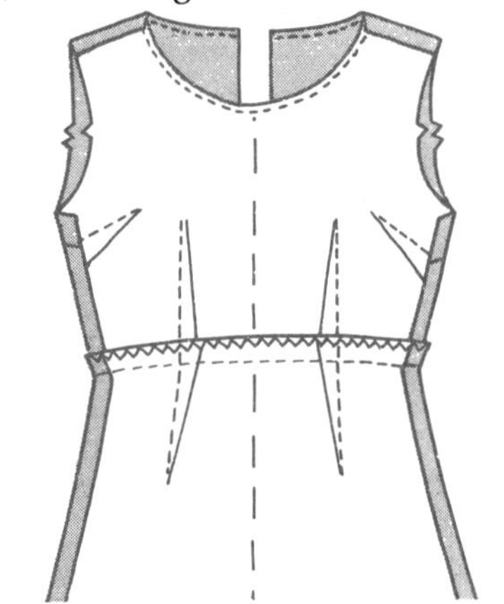

allowances up, then trim and finish edges. Press the right-side.

WAISTLINE REINFORCED WITH RIBBON

Add a firm ribbon inside the waistline of a stretchy garment or to a skirt that is heavily pleated or gathered. Join the bodice and skirt with a plain seam, as described above. Insert the zipper, and make buttonholes as required.

With the garment inside-out, measure around the waist seam line from the edge of one opening to the edge of the other. Cut a piece of 5/8-inch grosgrain ribbon, 1-1/2 inches longer than this measurement. Place a pin at the halfway mark of the ribbon.

Pin the halfway mark of the ribbon at the center front or center back of the garment. Pin the ribbon around the waist seam. Fold the cut ends under. The folded ends must meet exactly.

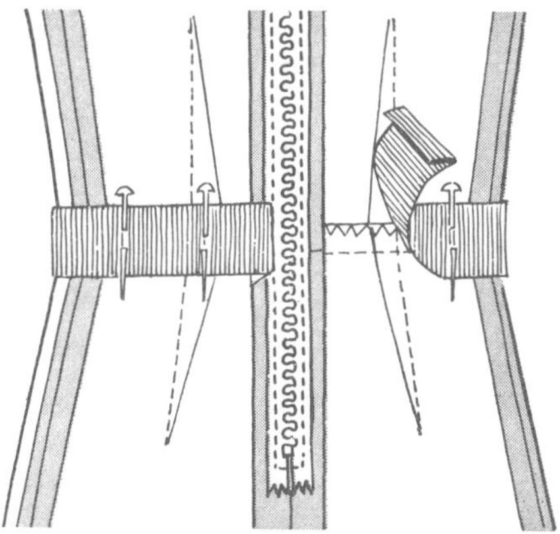

Stitch the ribbon with a few overlapping stitches at seams, darts and ends. Try on and adjust if necessary. Sew hooks and eyes on the folded ends of the ribbon. Edges should meet exactly when fastened.

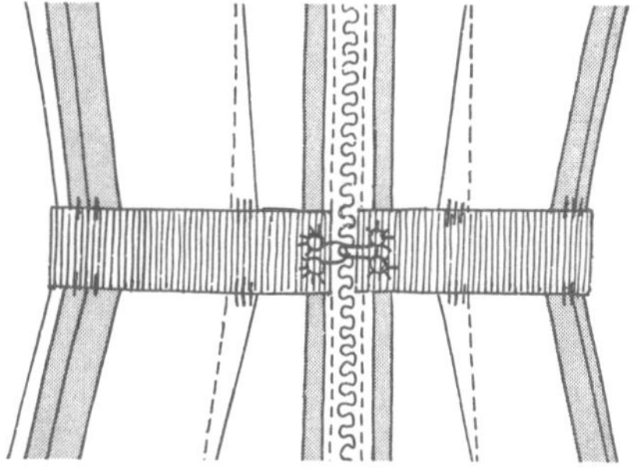

INSET WAISTBAND

An inset waistband fits snugly to the body, emphasizing the design. The bodice, waistband and skirt must fit smoothly. Adjust the fit before stitching together.

Cut a waistband from the garment fabric according to the pattern. Cut a piece of interfacing and a piece of lining from the pattern. Tack or iron interfacing to the wrong-side of the waistband. Match pattern markings, then stay-stitch the bodice edge.

With right-sides together, pin and tack one edge of the waistband to the bodice edge. Match notches.

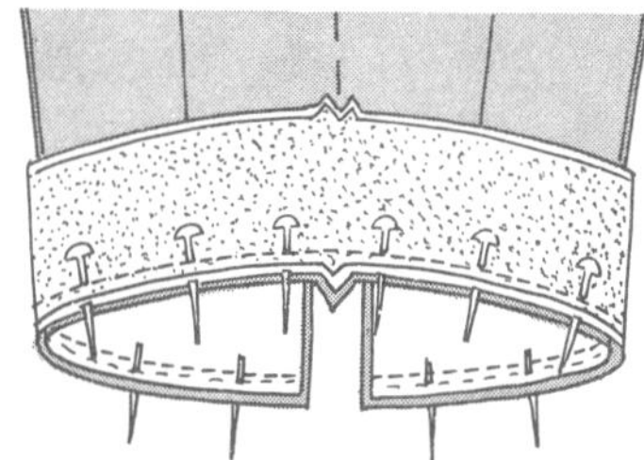

Stay-stitch the waist edge of the skirt.

Put the bodice inside the skirt, with right-sides together. Pin the free edge of the waistband to the skirt waist edge. Match pattern markings.

Tack along the seam edge, and remove pins. Try on the garment to

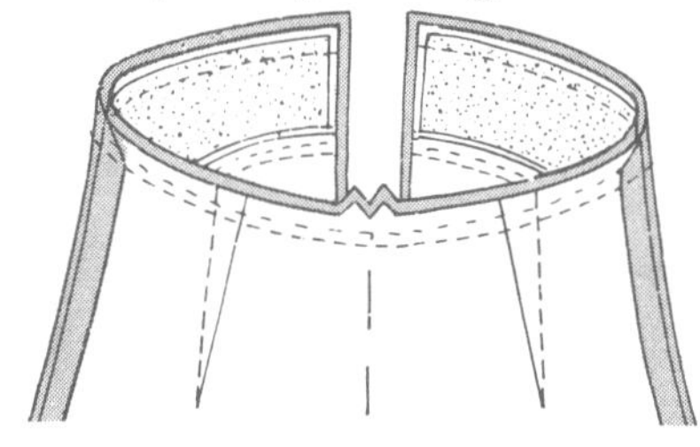

make sure it fits snugly. Stitch the waistband to the skirt edge, then to the bodice edge along seam lines. Remove tacking.

Trim and layer seam allowances on the bodice and skirt allowances to 1/2 inch. Trim the waistband to 1/4 inch and the interfacing to 1/8 inch.

Pull the bodice up, with the wrong-side out. Press the bodice seam allowances down and the skirt seam allowances up. Pin the lining

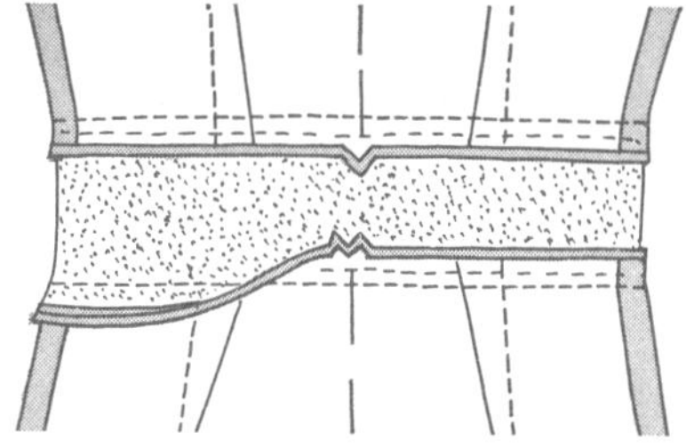

piece over the wrong-side of the waistband. Match seam and pattern markings.

Fold under the top and bottom edges of the lining along seam lines. Slip-stitch in place, catching stitches in the two lines of machine-stitching. Remove all pins and tacking.

Put in the zipper or finish the buttonholes and buttons. Fold under the ends of the lining, and slip-stitch them to the facing or zipper tape.

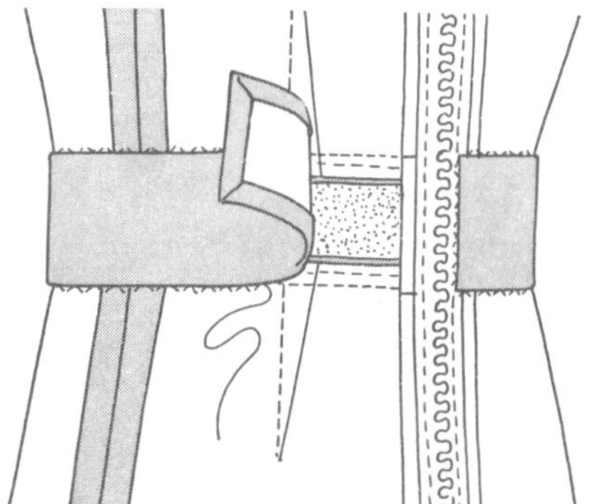

Elastic or Drawstring in Casing

A casing is a tunnel of fabric, often made at the waist of simple garments. The fabric is drawn into gathers or folds by elastic or a drawstring.

CASING FOR ONE PIECE OF ELASTIC

Cut a casing strip of self-fabric. If this is too thick and heavy, use a piece of light fabric or bias tape. Use a pattern piece if given.

Pin, tack and stitch the ends, with right-sides together. Remove tacking. Trim the seam allowances, and press the seam open. Fold under 1/4 inch on each side of the casing, and press in place.

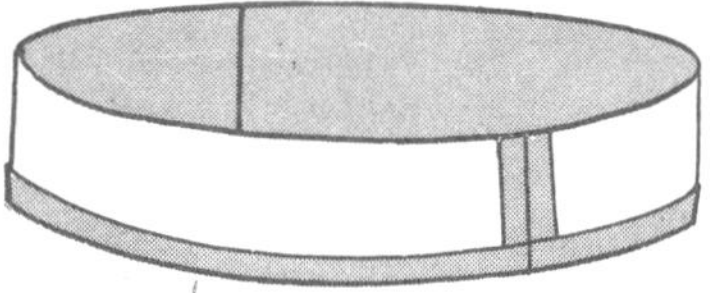

Place the circular casing over the garment, with wrong-sides together. Match pattern markings. Pin and tack the folded edges in place along the pattern markings. Leave a bit open for putting in the elastic.

Machine-stitch the casing along both sides, 1/8 inch from the edges. Leave a small area unstitched.

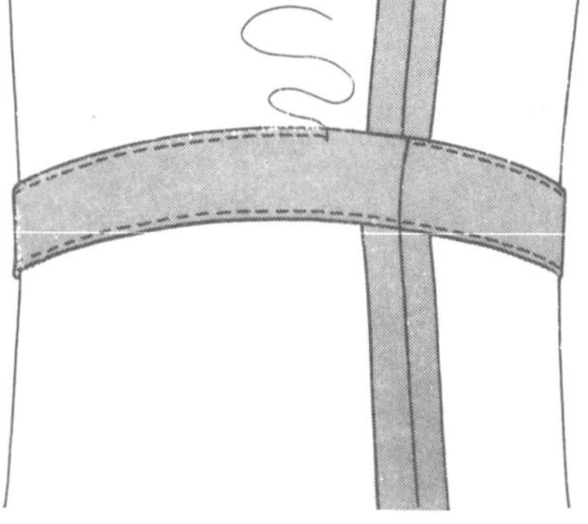

Insert a piece of broad elastic 1 inch longer than the waist measurement. Pull the elastic through, then stitch the two ends together with three rows of stitching.

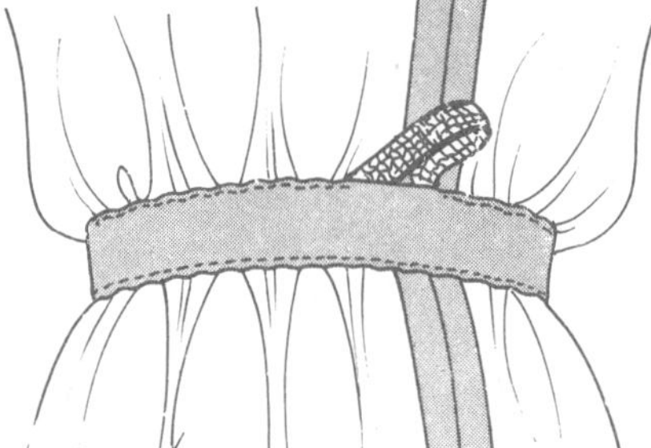

Push elastic back in the casing. Slip-stitch the opening closed. Press and turn right-side out.

CASING FOR DRAWSTRING

A drawstring can be made from self-fabric, like a soft tie belt. You can also use ribbon, cord, tubing or braid in a matching or contrasting color. Use a piece long enough to go around the body and tie in a knot or bow. The opening for pulling the drawstring to the right-side is usually made *before* the casing is attached.

Make two vertical buttonholes in the garment as shown in the pattern.

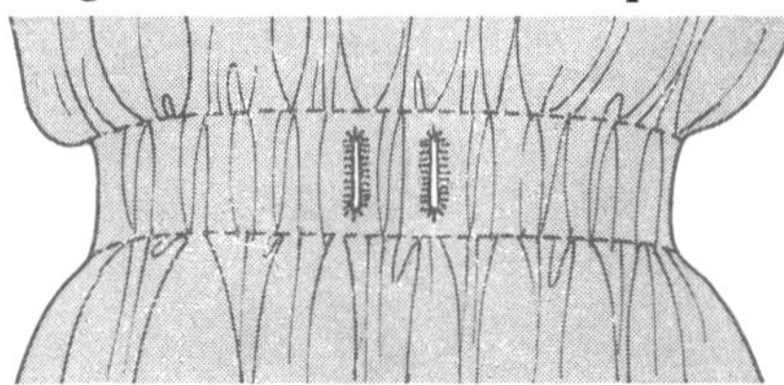

Complete the casing. Thread the drawstring through, and tie the two

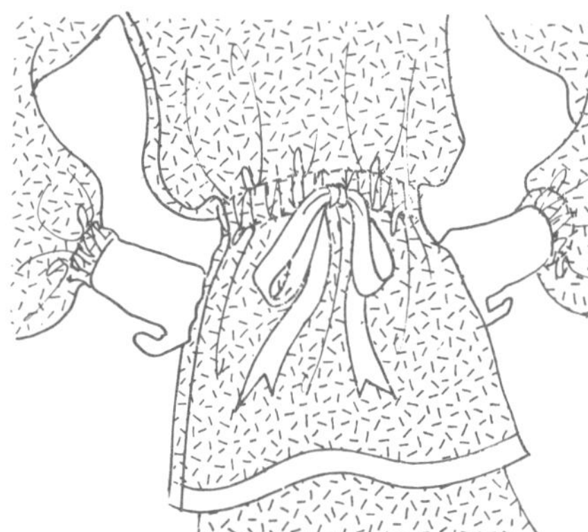

ends. Where there is a suitably placed seam, leave a slot open of the correct size. Reinforce each end.

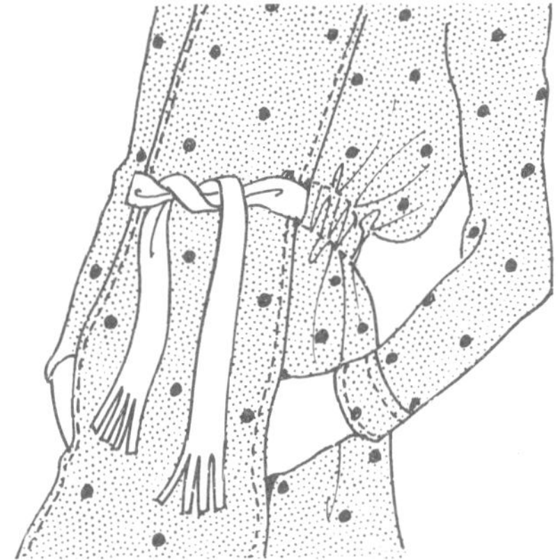

ZIPPERS

Zippers are a strong, secure, quick method of fastening clothes. The newest zippers are light and flexible. They are available in many colors, lengths and styles.

Good-quality zippers have a long life, if cared for and used correctly. They are suitable for jackets, dresses, skirts, pants, sleeves, pockets and soft furnishings. Invisible zippers are available to give a concealed finish to openings. Zippers can also be the focal point of a garment when used with decorative stitching or braid.

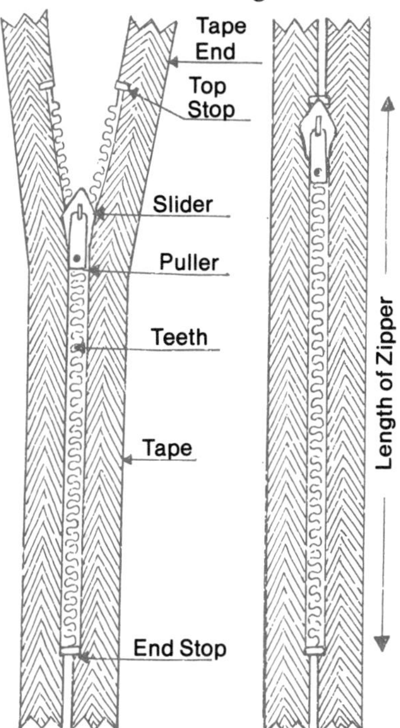

CHOOSING ZIPPERS

Most zippers are available in the following lengths.

4 inch	16 inch
5 inch	18 inch
6 inch	20 inch
7 inch	22 inch
8 inch	24 inch
9 inch	26 inch
10 inch	28 inch
12 inch	30 inch
14 inch	

Your zipper must be long enough for the opening. Do not buy a zipper that is too short. Taking the garment on and off will break the bottom of the zipper.

If your measurements and proportions are the same as the pattern, buy the length of zipper suggested on the pattern package. If not, wait until the fitting stage of the garment to buy a zipper. You may need a longer opening and a longer zipper. On any zipper, the actual opening is about 1/2 inch *less* in length than the zipper size.

TYPES OF ZIPPERS

Choose a zipper suitable for the style and weight of the garment.

Polyester Zipper—This zipper is for man-made and light fabrics. It is machine-washable, drip-dry and resist shrinking.

Dress, Skirt Fastener—This is a light, closed-end zipper with color-metal teeth on cotton tape.

Invisible Zipper—Use this zipper on skirts and dresses. It conceals openings. Teeth are turned in by the runner.

Open-Ended Zipper—Used for jackets and cardigans, the bottom separates, making it easy to remove the garment.

Curved Zipper—Used for trousers and jeans, this zipper comes in many colors.

Fashion Zipper—Found with brass or colored teeth, plain or fancy tape, and normal runners on large ring pulls.

USING ZIPPERS

Be sure the zipper is closed before washing or dry-cleaning. Never open a zipper when it is wet. Preshrink the zipper if necessary by washing and drying it before stitching in a washable garment.

Use the guidelines woven in the zipper tape when sewing it in a garment. Stitching should be parallel to the zipper teeth, never closer than 1/8 inch. This allows the slider to move up and down.

Open the zipper to the bottom when putting on or removing a garment. The bottom stop takes any strain. If not completely open, teeth bear the strain and may be damaged.

Be careful that thread and lining do not get caught in the zipper teeth when closing and opening it. Stitch tape and lining securely out of the way. Fasten all threads. Preserve the life of the zipper by placing a hook and eye at the top to take strain.

When ironing a garment, do not bang the iron against the zipper slider or teeth. It may cause damage. Use a pressing cloth when ironing a zipper on man-made fabric. Use the appropriate heat setting.

Never cut any part of the zipper tape. It is there to support the zipper in use. If cut, fraying can occur and prevent the zipper from working efficiently.

If the slider of the zipper is difficult to move after the garment is dry-cleaned, put beeswax, candlewax or soap on the teeth. It helps lubricate the zipper teeth and allows the slider to move freely.

If wringing is necessary after washing a garment, protect the closed zipper with folds of the fabric. Be sure the zipper is not twisted. Keep the puller tab flat.

ZIPPER INSERTION

Zippers may be put in by machine or by hand. For casual wear, sportswear, children's clothes and garments that receive a lot of washing and wearing, machine-stitch the zipper in place. This method gives long-wear.

Stitching can become part of the fashion detail. To give a couture finish to a well-made garment, hand-sewing is recommended. When fabric is slippery or hard to handle, hand-sewing makes the finish inconspicuous and flexible. The stitch used is a type of back-stitch also called a *stab-stitch.* Stitches are smaller than a usual back-stitch and do not meet one another. Use quarter back-stitches.

Attach the thread securely on the wrong-side of the fabric. Bring it through to the right-side. Take a stitch back about a thread or two. Bring the needle out about 1/4 inch in front of the stitch made. Do not pull the thread too tight or the fabric will pucker. Stitches should lie on the surface of the fabric.

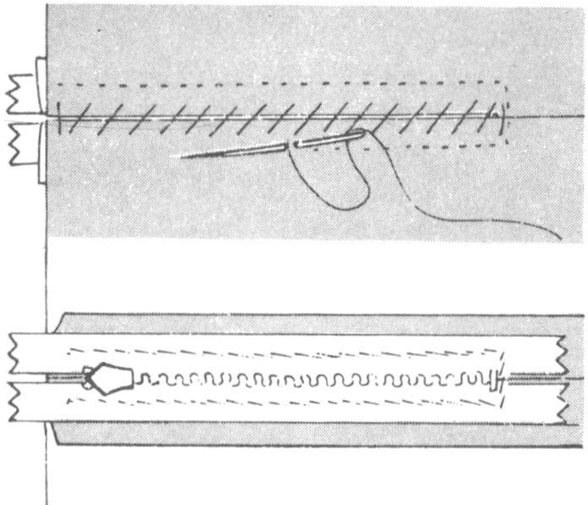

Use the same sewing thread as for the rest of the garment. Use natural or man-made thread, according to the type of fabric. Sew with a single strand of thread when possible. It gives a finer finish and more even-looking stitches. On heavy fabrics, use two rows of stab-stitches. The second row of stitches is spaced between those of the first row. Lubricate thread with beeswax. Also see the sections on *Stitches and Threads,* page 67.

It is easier if the zipper is inserted before other seams are joined, and before waistbands and facings are attached. Press the zipper to remove creases, if necessary.

If machine-sewing, use a zipper foot. This is an essential aid for a crisp, professional-looking finish. A

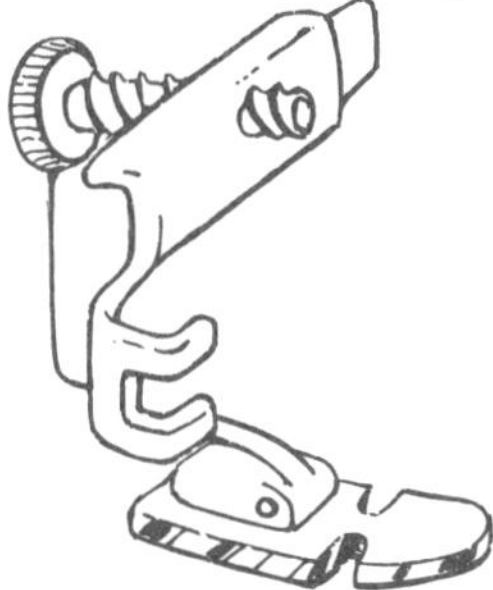

sewing machine has one in its accessory kit.

When inserting a zipper in stretchy fabric or a garment cut on the cross grain, stay-stitch the edges of the zipper opening inside the stitching line. Use matching thread because this stitching is not removed.

If the slider obstructs sewing while machine-stitching, snip and remove tacking on the part already stitched. Replace the foot and continue sewing.

When there is no band in which the zipper tapes may be inserted, miter the tape tops as shown in the diagram.

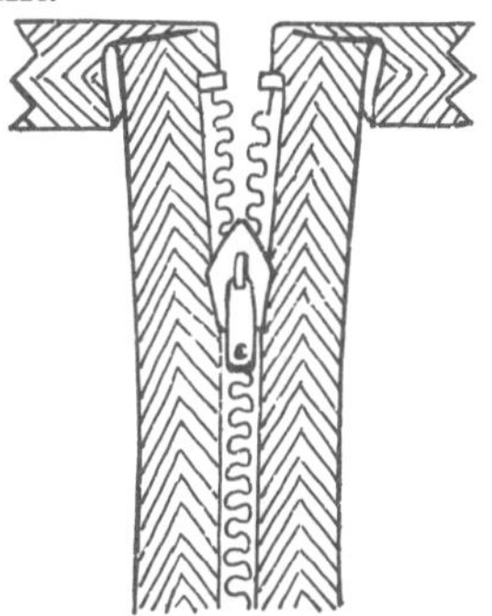

Zipper Shield—When using a zipper with metal teeth, a zipper shield or underlap keeps fine undergarments from being caught or snagged by the zipper. Cut the waistband 2 inches longer than shown in the pattern, then sew the top of the shield in place.

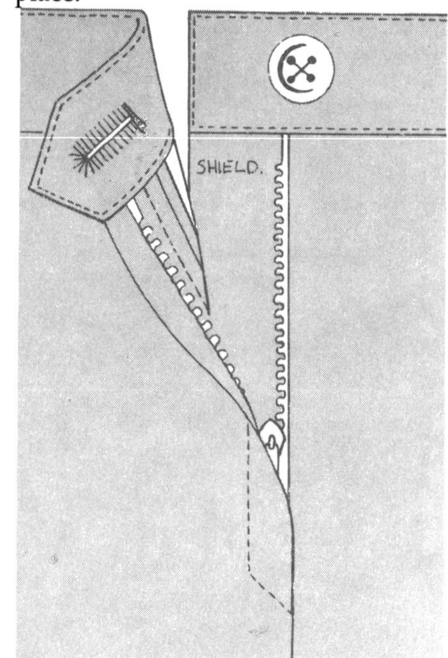

To make a shield, cut a piece of fabric on the straight grain. It should be a little longer than the zipper tape and three times as wide as the zipper. Fold in half lengthwise, and overcast the three raw-edge sides together. Stitch the right-side tape of the zipper to the shield on the side opposite the fold, 1/4 inch from the edge.

When inserting a zipper, fold the shield back to keep it from being caught in the left-side row of stitching. Include it when stitching across the bottom of the zipper.

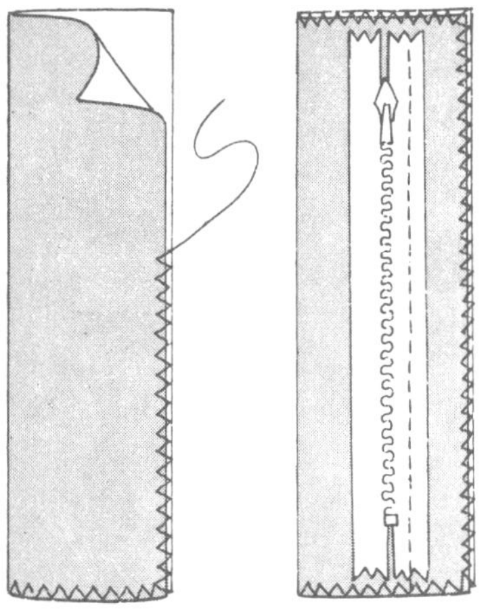

METHODS OF INSERTING ZIPPERS

There are two ways to insert a zipper. There are no rules about when to use either method. Before any application, mark the closure lines with a line of tacking.

Edge-to-Edge or Slot Method—Use this method at the side or back seam of a garment. It is symmetrical in appearance and suitable for a center-front opening. It presents less bulk than the lapped method and is suitable for heavy fabrics.

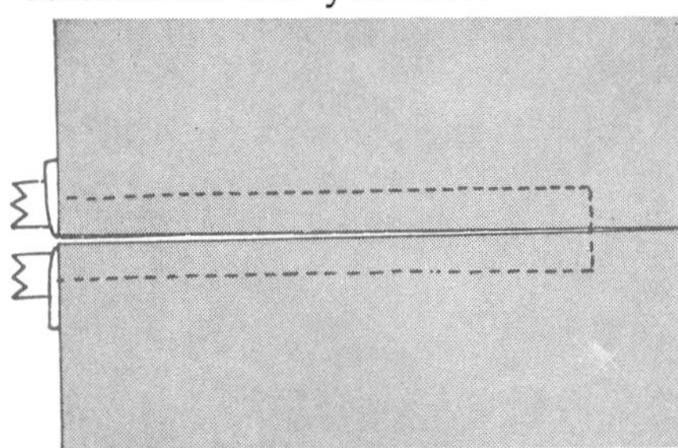

Stitch the seam to the end of opening where the zipper is to be inserted. Back-stitch for security. Tack the opening together along the closure line, using the longest machine-stitch. Press the seam open.

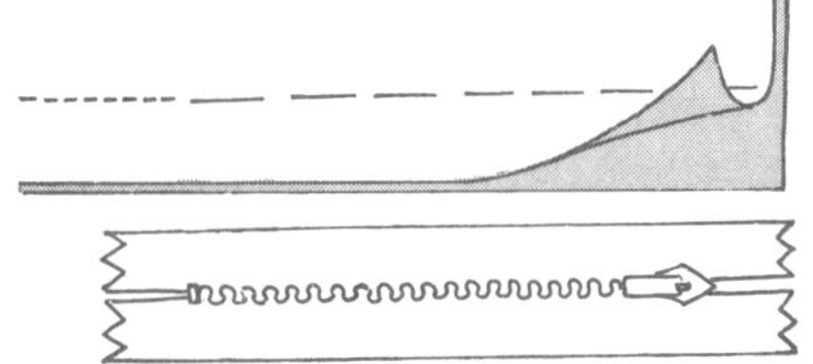

Turn the garment to the wrong-side. With the right-side down, place the zipper along the length of the opening. The slider of the closed zipper should be 1 inch from the top of the opening. The bottom stop should reach the end. Teeth are centered on the seam. Working from the top of the zipper, center 7/8 or 1 inch of the zipper at a time. Put pins at right angles on the tape at 1-inch intervals.

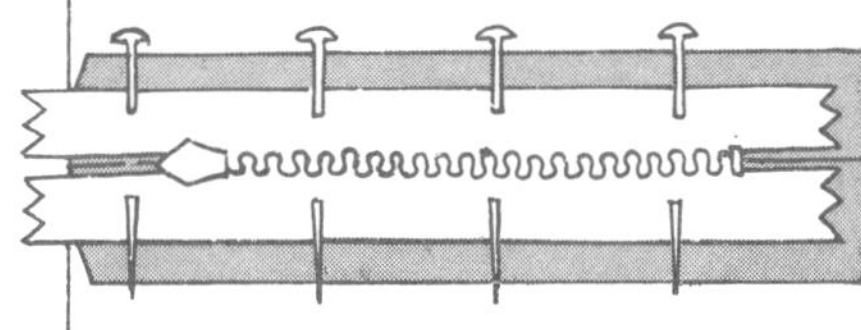

Turn back to the right-side, and tack along both sides of the tape as a guideline for stitching. Keep tacking lines parallel to the teeth, using the line woven in the tape as a guide.

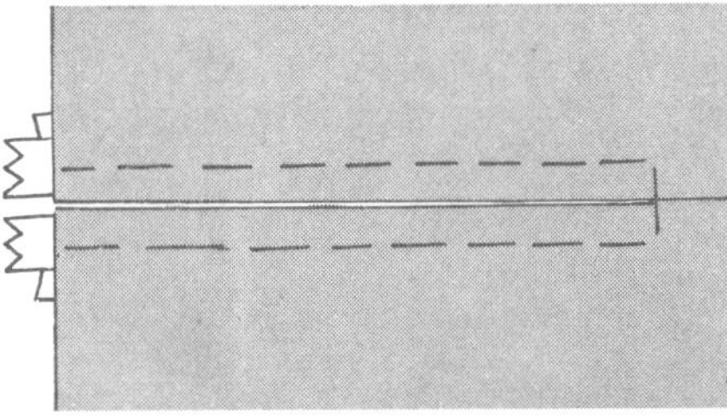

Stitch the zipper in place. Start at the top if stitching by machine, and if the fabric is firm and closely woven. Stitch down one side, pivot the work and stitch across the bottom. Count the number of stitches to the seam line. Stitch the same number on the other side. This row of stitching may be stitched straight or to a point.

Pivot the work on the needle, and stitch up the other side. Depending on the width and weight of the zipper tape, stitching should be 1/8 inch to 3/8 inch from the center line.

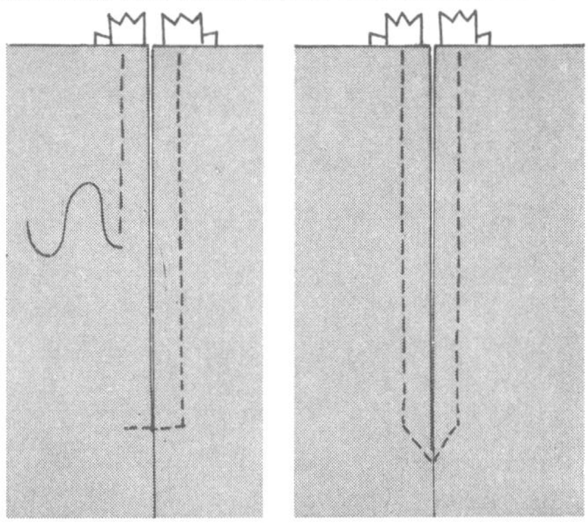

If the fabric slides or gives, sew from the bottom end of the zipper to the top on both sides. When one side has been sewn, stitch across the bottom and up the other side. Remove tacking. Overcast-stitch the tapes to the edges and press.

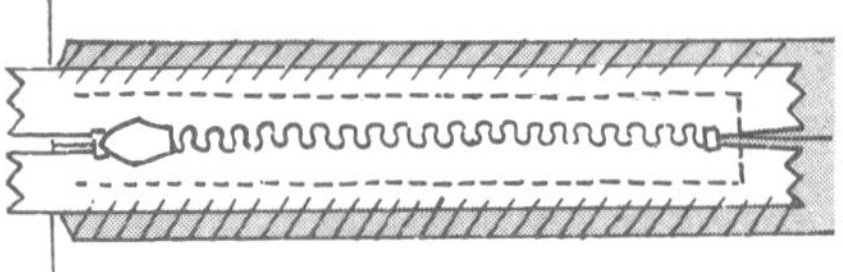

Lapped Method—The most common use of this method is for side and back openings on medium and light fabrics. It covers the zipper completely. It is ideal for snug, closely fitting garments.

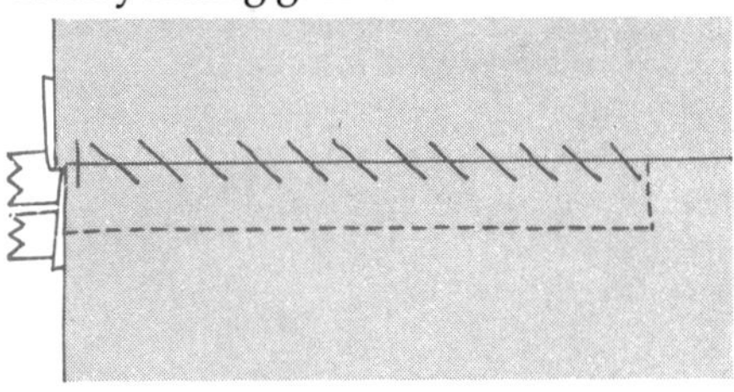

Stitch the seam to the end of the opening where the zipper is to be inserted. Back-stitch at this point for security. Tack the opening together along the closure line, using long machine-stitches. Press the seam open.

Place the zipper face-down on the right seam allowance. Center teeth on the seam line, 5/8 inch from the edge of fabric. Pin and tack in line with the guideline parallel to the teeth all along the side of tape. Stitch 1/8 to 1/4 inch from the zipper teeth, depending on fabric thickness. Stitch from the bottom stop to the end of the tape at the top.

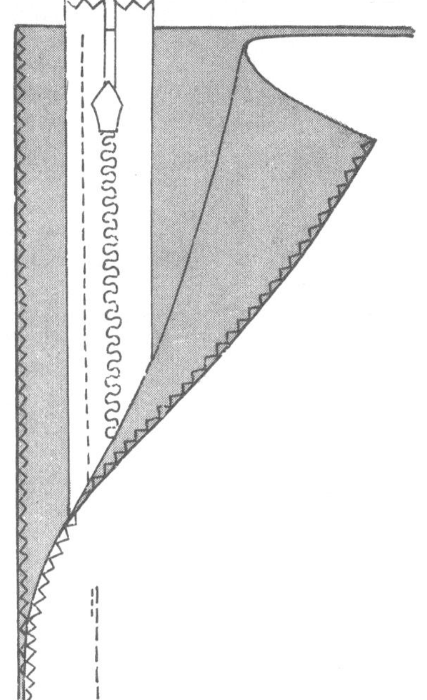

Turn the zipper to the inside. Tack to hold the edge ready for pressing. Cover the closed zipper with a pressing cloth, and press lightly. Machine-stitching is not visible on the right-side of the opening.

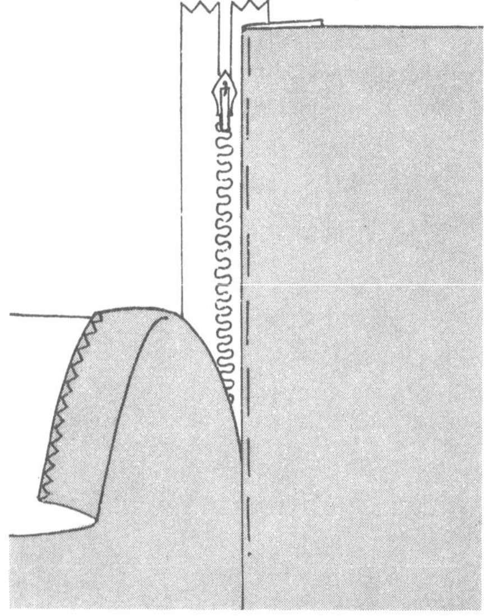

Turn the seam allowance on the left to the wrong-side and tack. Press lightly to flatten the edge, using a pressing cloth. Do not move the iron back and forth because it wrinkles the fold.

Lap the fold over the zipper and extend it 1/8 inch over the seam line on the other side. Start at the top of the opening and work down to the bottom. Pin the flap at 1-inch intervals. This keeps the overlap even all the way down. Working up from the bottom causes an excess of overlap at the top of the zipper. Zipper teeth are recessed under the flap by 1/8 inch tapering away at the bottom to avoid a pucker.

Cross-tack the flap in position as shown in the diagram. Do not remove pins until tacking is complete, or the flap may gape in places.

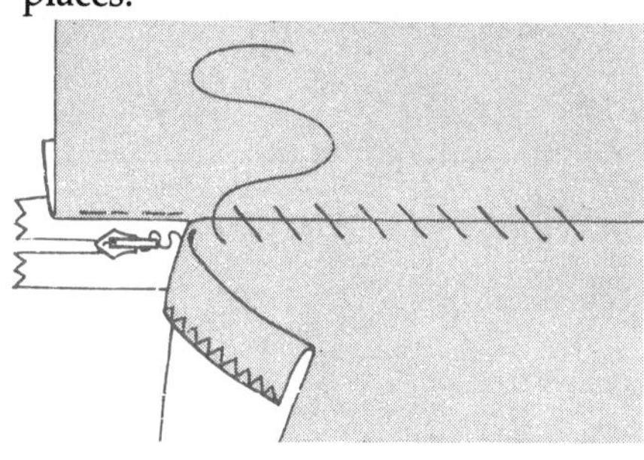

Tack a guideline for stitching on the other side of the zipper teeth. Make it parallel to the woven guide on the tape. Stitch in place by working across the bottom and up the left side of the opening. On light zippers, stitching needs to be 3/8 inch from the folded edge. On heavier zippers, stitch 3/8 to 1/2 inch. Stitching closer than this keeps the fold from covering the slider.

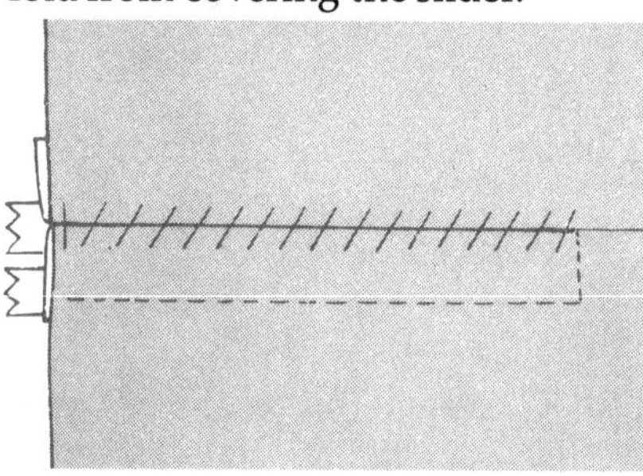

Remove tacking, and overcast tapes to the raw edges. Press carefully, using a pressing cloth.

SPECIAL METHODS

Directions for putting in invisible zippers and putting zippers in a fly opening can be found on the zipper package. When applying an open-end zipper in a blouse, jacket or dress, use the instruction for the edge-to-edge method. Have the end of the tapes level at the bottom.

When putting an open-end zipper in knit fabric, it should be 1-inch less in length than the opening. Ease the fabric so it will not be distorted in any way.

Treat the open-end fitting on a zipper carefully. When inserting one side in the other, tapes must be level before pulling the slider.

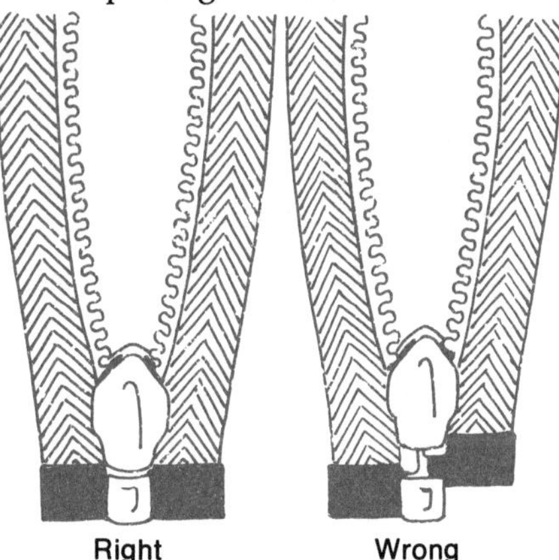

ZIPPERS AS DECORATION

A zipper can be the focal point of a garment. Decorated with braid or tape, it can transform a plain garment into a fancy one. There are many attractive braids on the market. It is possible to create an original effect. The method below is only suitable for a center-front opening.

Sew the center-front seam to the end of the opening. Back-stitch to secure it. Slash in the seam allowance horizontally. Slash 1/8 inch to 1/4 inch into the garment fabric, depending on the weight of zipper

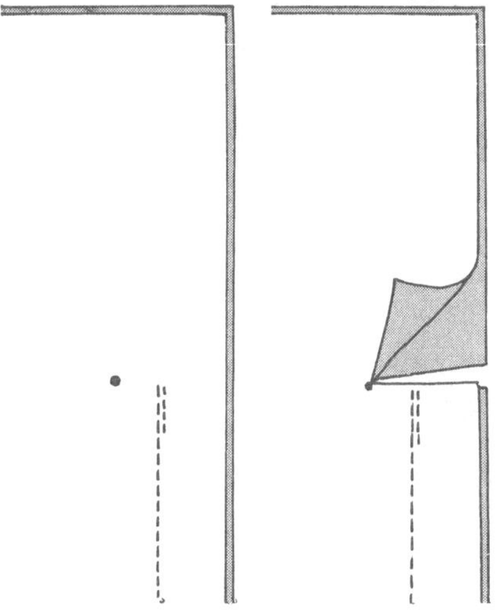

used. On the wrong-side, press the back seam allowance on the seam and overcast.

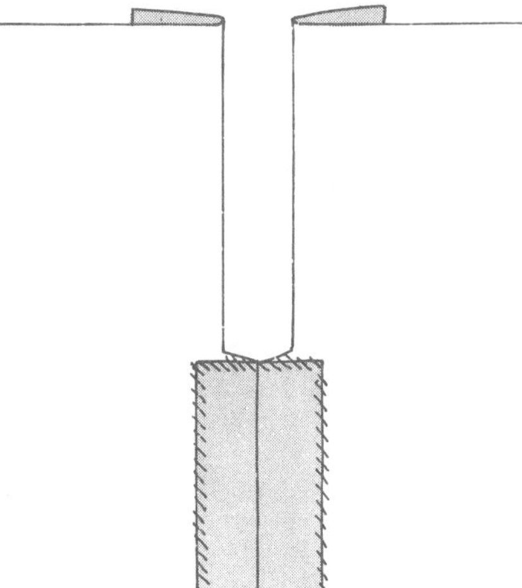

On the right-side, fold the seam allowance on the opening from the end of the slash. Tack in place and press. Stitch braid to the zipper 1/8

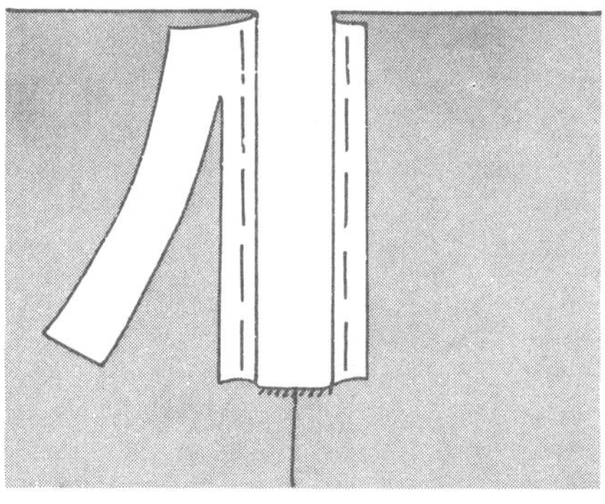

inch from teeth. Make a miter with the tape at the bottom. Pin and tack before final stitching.

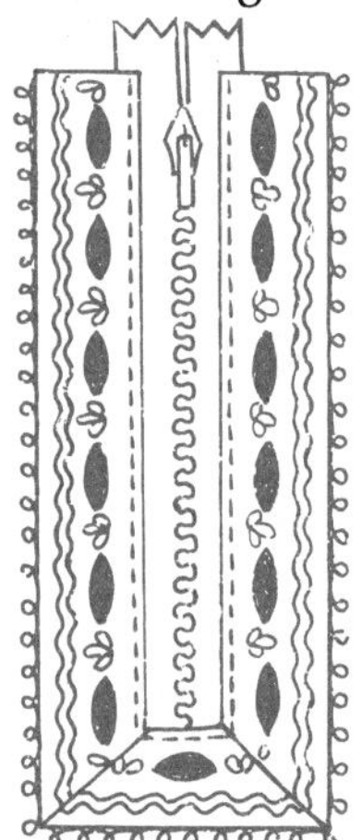

Center the braided zipper unit over the opening. Pin and tack it in position around the edge of the

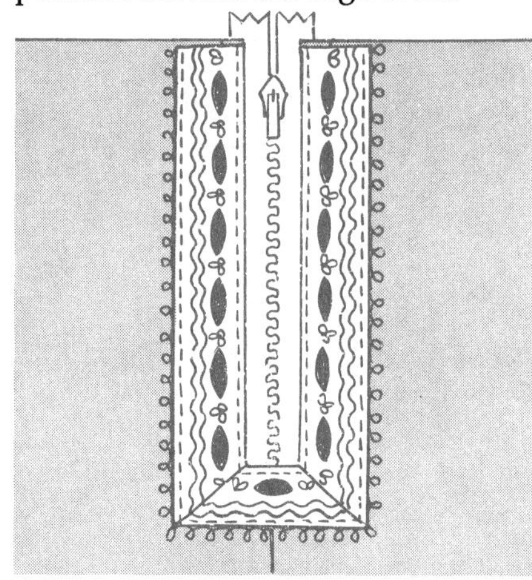

braid. Machine-stitch the zipper unit to the garment around the outside edge of braid, then turn to the wrong-side. Slip-stitch the folded edges to the back of the zipper tapes.

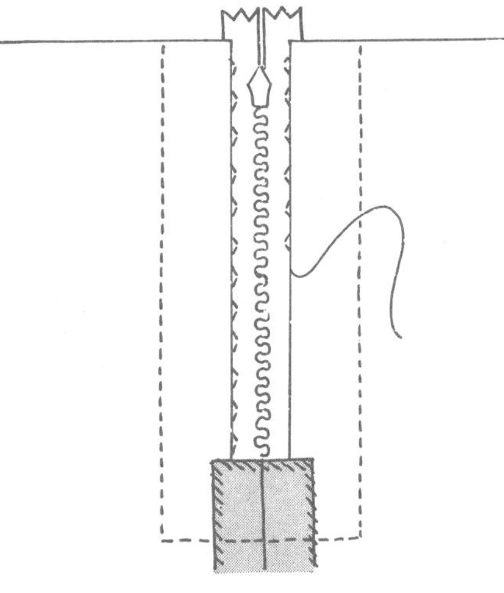

Press carefully using a pressing cloth. Decorate the slider with beads or a fob.

INDEX